The Spirituality of Shiʿi Islam

The Spirituality of Shiʿi Islam

Beliefs and Practices

by
MOHAMMAD ALI AMIR-MOEZZI

I.B.Tauris *Publishers*
LONDON • NEW YORK
in association with
The Institute of Ismaili Studies
London, 2011

Published in 2011 by I.B.Tauris & Co. Ltd
6 Salem Road, London W2 4BU
175 Fifth Avenue, New York, NY 10010
www.ibtauris.com

in association with The Institute of Ismaili Studies
210 Euston Road, London NW1 2DA
www.iis.ac.uk

Distributed in the United States and Canada Exclusively by Palgrave Macmillan,
175 Fifth Avenue, New York, NY 10010

Published in French by J. Vrin (Paris, 2006) as *La religion discrète: Croyances et pratiques spirituelles dans L'islam shi'ite.*

ISBN: 978 1 84511 738 2

A full CIP record for this book is available from the British Library
A full CIP record for this book is available from the Library of Congress

Library of Congress catalog card: available

Typeset in Minion Tra for The Institute of Ismaili Studies
Printed and bound in Great Britain by TJ International, Padstow, Cornwall

FSC
www.fsc.org
MIX
Paper from responsible sources
FSC® C013056

To my mother, *in memoriam*

The Institute of Ismaili Studies

The Institute of Ismaili Studies was established in 1977 with the object of promoting scholarship and learning on Islam, in the historical as well as contemporary contexts, and a better understanding of its relationship with other societies and faiths.

The Institute's programmes encourage a perspective which is not confined to the theological and religious heritage of Islam, but seeks to explore the relationship of religious ideas to broader dimensions of society and culture. The programmes thus encourage an interdisciplinary approach to the materials of Islamic history and thought. Particular attention is also given to issues of modernity that arise as Muslims seek to relate their heritage to the contemporary situation.

Within the Islamic tradition, the Institute's programmes promote research on those areas which have, to date, received relatively little attention from scholars. These include the intellectual and literary expressions of Shiʿism in general, and Ismailism in particular.

In the context of Islamic societies, the Institute's programmes are informed by the full range and diversity of cultures in which Islam is practised today, from the Middle East, South and Central Asia, and Africa to the industrialised societies of the West, thus taking into consideration the variety of contexts which shape the ideals, beliefs and practices of the faith.

These objectives are realised through concrete programmes and activities organised and implemented by various departments of the Institute. The Institute also collaborates periodically, on a programme-specific basis, with other institutions of learning in the United Kingdom and abroad.

The Institute's academic publications fall into a number of inter-related categories:

1. Occasional papers or essays addressing broad themes of the relationship between religion and society, with special reference to Islam.
2. Monographs exploring specific aspects of Islamic faith and culture, or the contributions of individual Muslim thinkers or writers.
3. Editions or translations of significant primary or secondary texts.
4. Translations of poetic or literary texts which illustrate the rich heritage of spiritual, devotional and symbolic expressions in Muslim history.
5. Works on Ismaili history and thought, and the relationship of the Ismailis to other traditions, communities and schools of thought in Islam.
6. Proceedings of conferences and seminars sponsored by the Institute.
7. Bibliographical works and catalogues which document manuscripts, printed texts and other source materials.

This book falls into category two listed above.

In facilitating these and other publications, the Institute's sole aim is to encourage original research and analysis of relevant issues. While every effort is made to ensure that the publications are of a high academic standard, there is naturally bound to be a diversity of views, ideas and interpretations. As such, the opinions expressed in these publications must be understood as belonging to their authors alone.

Contents

Preface and Acknowledgements

It is only since the 1970s, if not as recently as the 1980s, that critical studies on Shiʿi Islam have increased in scope, with a substantial number of scholars making it their primary field of research.[1] Numerous statistics published in the media indicate that, in the West, public interest in Shiʿism and the Shiʿis goes back no more than a few years. It would seem that it took events as dramatic as the civil war in Lebanon, the Islamic revolution in Iran and more recently the war in Iraq (and the related daily atrocities) in order for sustained attention to be given to the specifics of the faith of this minority community of Islam which nonetheless comprises more than 200 million believers.[2]

To this day, Shiʿi beliefs and practices remain relatively unknown and poorly understood. The wider public is often only witness to dramatic demonstrations of exacerbated fanaticism: heavily veiled women, totalitarian mullahs, indoctrinated crowds, public displays of corporal punishment and bloody mourning rituals. These complex forms of the politico-social instrumentalisation of religious belief, notably in its popular component, almost completely obscure the fact that Shiʿism, with its numerous branches, has also one of the richest intellectual and spiritual traditions in Islam; that

1. By Shiʿi Islam I refer to the main branch of Shiʿism, namely Imami or Twelver Shiʿism.

2. See M. A. Amir-Moezzi and C. Jambet, *Qu'est-ce que le shīʿisme?* (Paris, 2004), pp. 11–22 and 75–76.

its history is made up of the lives and work of thousands of brilliant theologians, exegetes, philosophers, artists, scholars, jurists, mystics and men of letters; and that the corpus of Shiʿi texts – one of the richest in the world – is made up of literally thousands of works.[3]

Why such ignorance? First, as just mentioned, academic studies specifically devoted to Shiʿism are for the most part very recent; moreover, Western specialists in this field make up no more than some thirty scholars, to whom one ought to add those rare Shiʿi learned men who apply historico-critical methodology and publish only in the Islamic languages. This is a very limited number when compared with the hundreds of scholars specialising in Sunni Islam who, for more than a century and a half, have been studying a wide range of disciplines in the relevant areas of Arabic and Islamic studies.[4] What is more, most of the Shiʿis themselves have little knowledge or a poor understanding of their own religion. Many, as is so often the case with all religions, do not read the basic texts of their faith, and often rely on the received knowledge of religious authorities. The latter, whether theologians, religious leaders, political theoreticians or leaders of mystical orders, again as is so often the case universally, offer no more than a tendentious, often unilateral, vision of matters related to the faith. There are also the vagaries of history to be considered and the resulting ideological rivalries; consequences in Shiʿism itself include, and this since the Middle Ages, not only the ostracism that thinkers who were considered to be 'deviant' were subjected to but also to the censorship of texts that were judged to be problematic.[5]

---

3. The bibliographical encyclopaedia of Shiʿi works, *al-Dharīʿa ilā taṣānīf al-shīʿa* (Tehran and Najaf, 1353–1398/1934–1978) by Āghā Bozorg al-Ṭihrānī consists of twenty-five large volumes and is still far from exhaustive.

4. See M. A. Amir-Moezzi and S. Schmidtke, 'Twelver-Shiʿite Resources in Europe', *JA*, 285/1 (1997), pp. 74–78.

5. This concerns the treatment meted out by 'rationalist' Doctors of Law, ever since the Middle Ages, to Shiʿis accused of 'extremism' (*ghuluww*) and to a great many mystics and philosophers (see M. A. Amir-Moezzi, *Le Guide divin dans le Shiʿisme original* [Paris and Lagrasse, 1992], pp. 15–58, tr. as *The Divine Guide in Early Shiʿism* [New York, 1994]). For cases of censorship in the early

Finally, Shiʿism defines itself in its foundational sources as an essentially esoteric and initiatory doctrine and does not reveal itself easily. Indeed, the faithful are divided into three categories: the masses (*al-ʿāmma*), the elite (*al-khāṣṣa*) and the elite of the elite (*khāṣṣa al-khāṣṣa* or *akhaṣṣ al-khāṣṣa*). Admittedly, this classification is often applied to Muslims in general, where the 'masses' refer to the Sunni majority, the 'elite' to Shiʿis and the 'elite of the elite' to initiated Shiʿis. However, it is also applied within Shiʿism and in this case the ordinary Shiʿi believers are the 'masses'; the exoteric scholars well versed in exoteric Shiʿi teaching constitute the 'elite'; and the esotericist masters, initiated into the mysteries of hidden teachings exemplify the 'elite of the elite'. The doctrinal and initiatory nature of the secret is even more pertinent if we acknowledge that this tripartite vision of humanity

period, see Amir-Moezzi and Schmidtke, 'Twelver-Shiʿite Resources', 'Appendix', pp. 120–121. Regarding the censorship before the Islamic revolution of modern editions of ancient sources, see the case of the *Tafsīr* by ʿAlī b. Ibrāhīm al-Qummī, a censored version of the edition prepared by al-Sayyid Ṭayyib al-Mūsawī al-Jazāʾirī in Najaf, 1386–1387/1966–1967 (see M. M. Bar-Asher, *Scripture and Exegesis in Early Imāmī Shiism* [Leiden, 1999], pp. 39–45). After the triumph of the Islamic revolution in Iran, some texts that clearly disturbed the 'ultra-rationalist' authorities were censored; for example, in the 1980s, the numerous traditions that make up volumes 7 to 9 of the older edition in thirty-five volumes of *Biḥār al-anwār* by al-Majlisī, regarding Shiʿi hostility towards the first three caliphs, were deleted from the new edition undertaken in Tehran and Qumm (undoubtedly in order not to shock the Sunnis whom the new regime wanted to mobilise for a widespread Islamic revolution); the 'revised' version of *Tuḥfat al-mulūk* by Jaʿfar al-Kashfī (Tehran, n.d. [ca. 1982], with no mention of the editor's name) where half the text especially regarding the divine aspect of the imams in general and ʿAlī in particular is missing (to be compared with older lithographed editions published in Iran, at the end of the nineteenth century); the *Taqrīb al-maʿārif* by al-Ḥalabī in the R. Ustādhī edition (Qumm, 1404/1984) in which the chapter on the first three caliphs was removed (this section was restored in the edition by F. Ḥassūn, Qumm, 1417/1996–1997; an easing of restrictions undoubtedly due to a certain flexibility in the political regime); the section regarding *wilāyat al-faqīh* – differing from the theory of the same name advanced by Khomeynism – in 'Kitāb al-bayʿ', *al-Makāsib al-muḥarrama* of Ayatollah Muḥammad ʿAlī Arākī (Qumm, 1415/1994–1995) (to be compared with the edition published in 1313/1895–1896, pp. 94ff.).

veils yet another truth according to which men can only be of three kinds: the 'master initiator', the 'initiated disciple' and the 'ignorant adversary'.[6]

In a tradition that is traced back to many of the Shiʿi imams, it is stated: 'Our teaching is secret, it is a secret about a secret. It includes an exoteric (*ẓāhir*), esoteric (*bāṭin*) and esoteric of the esoteric (*bāṭin al-bāṭin*) dimension.' It is to be expected then that, in these conditions, parts of the religious teachings, undoubtedly those judged the most essential, are protected by the rules that govern all esoteric doctrines. Hence the use of certain tactics in Shiʿism that illustrate different forms of the discipline of mystery: the 'preservation of secrets' (*taqiyya*, *kitmān*), referring to the believer's strategic dissimulation of his religious affinity when it places him at risk. This practice also has a hidden meaning, namely the protection of those doctrinal teachings considered secret from 'those who are not worthy'. There is also the literary process adopted by certain writers of 'scattering knowledge' (*tabdīd al-ʿilm*) which consists of 'shredding' the exposition of a secret doctrine and dispersing bits of information throughout the various parts of a vast corpus of miscellaneous teachings, with the result that only an especially persevering scholar familiar with the subject is able to discover these disparate elements and reconstitute a coherent whole.[7] For all these various reasons, some intrinsic and others extrinsic to Shiʿism, the religion remains veiled and relatively unknown.

The studies that make up the present work examine some of the less explored aspects of Shiʿi history and spirituality. These studies have appeared in various specialised journals or academic publications between 1992 and 2005. Together they constitute the

---

6. Refer to Chapter 8, this volume.

7. On *taqiyya*, now consult E. Kohlberg, 'Taqiyya in Shīʿī Theology and Religion', in H. G. Kippenberg and G. G. Stroumsa (eds), *Secrecy and Concealment: Studies in the History of Mediterranean and Near Eastern Religions* (Leiden, 1995), pp. 345–380. On *tabdīd al-ʿilm*, see Amir-Moezzi, *Le Guide divin*, index.

series 'Aspects of Twelver Imamology' (see bibliography) supplemented here by four other articles. Updated and placed in an order justifiably their own, these essays seek to restore a certain coherence to what is a priori difficult to reconstruct regarding Shiʿi doctrines and devotional practices.[8] The first two chapters concern the emergence and early developments of Shiʿism.

Chapter 1 analyses 'the religion of 'Alī', which combines ancient Arab beliefs with Jewish, Christian and Qurʾānic concepts of the cult of kinship and the sacred family, representing the early core of what was to progressively and substantially develop to became the Shiʿi religion.[9] Chapter 2 examines the history of the Sasanian princess Shahrbānū – one of those legends that at times carry more historical significance than real events – which would have been, among other things, an early means of bringing together Shiʿis and Iranian converts, thus probably facilitating Shiʿism's acceptance of doctrinal elements deriving from the ancient Iranian religions, notably Mazdaism and Manichaeism.[10]

Chapters 3 to 8 are devoted to the twofold dimension of the figure of the imam,[11] namely the divine (*lāhūt*) and the human (*nāsūt*) elements and the correspondences between them; the theological ideas linked to his nature and ontological status as the Ally of God (*walī Allāh*); the central role of the initiation and the initiates as well as the ontological and anthropological duality in Shiʿism.

8. For editorial considerations, the transcriptions of Arabic and Persian, abbreviations and bibliographical references have been standardised. The original pagination is not provided.

9. 'Considérations sur l'expression *dīn 'Alī*. Aux origines de la foi shiʿite', *ZDMG*, 150/1 (2000), pp. 29–68 (also published with a translation in Turkish in A. Y. Ocak [ed.], *From History to Theology: Ali in Islamic Beliefs* [Ankara, 2005], pp. 27–58).

10. 'Shahrbānū, Dame du Pays d'Iran et Mère des Imams: entre l'Iran préislamique et le shiisme imamite', *JSAI*, 27 (volume dedicated to Shaul Shaked) (2002), pp. 497–549.

11. 'Imam' is written with the 'i' upper case when it relates to the ontological, cosmic, archetypal Imam, and lower case when it relates to the historical imam, the manifestation of the first, or the perceptible level. Also, 'Imami' and 'Twelver' are used interchangeably.

In Chapter 3, the divinity of the metaphysical Imam is analysed through the prism of the 'paradoxical utterances' attributed to the historical imams,[12] whereas the next two chapters follow the course of the gradual immanence of the Imam in man and his cosmogonic and cosmological significance in the economy of the sacred. Thus his role emerges, as both the dispenser of divine knowledge (the historical imam) in the here and now and, ultimately, the very content of this gnosis (the metaphysical Imam).[13] By studying the figure of the Guide as a thaumaturgic sage,[14] the supreme temporal and spiritual authority as well as a theophanic being,[15] Chapters 6 and 7 examine the theological, spiritual and political implications of this Imamology. Finally, Chapter 8 analyses mystical anthropology as the basis for the Shiʿi theory of opposites.[16]

Different aspects of hermeneutics and the way they have spread through Shiʿi spiritual practices form the content of Chapters 9 to 11: the imam as initiator, transmitter and at the same time the

12. 'Aspects de l'imamologie duodécimaine I. Remarques sur la divinité de l'Imam', *Studia Iranica*, 25/2 (1996), pp. 193–216.

13. Chapter 4, 'The Preexistence of the Imam', is taken from sub-chapters II-1 and II-2 in my *Guide divin*, pp. 73–112 (*Divine Guide*, pp. 29–59). Chapter 5 originally appeared as 'L'Imam dans le ciel. Ascension et initiation (Aspects de l'imamologie duodécimaine III)', in M. A. Amir-Moezzi (ed.), *Le Voyage initiatique en terre d'islam. Ascensions célestes et itinéraires spirituels*. Bibliothèque de l'Ecole des Hautes Etudes, vol. 53 (Louvain and Paris, 1997), pp. 99–116.

14. The original in French, 'Savoir c'est pouvoir. Exégèses et implications du miracle dans l'imamisme ancien (Aspects de l'imamologie duodécimaine V)', in D. Aigle (ed.), *Les Miracles des saints dans l'hagiographie chrétienne et islamique médiévale*. Bibliothèque de l'Ecole des Hautes Etudes, vol. 106 (Turnhout, 2000), pp. 241–275.

15. 'Notes à propos de la *walāya* imamite (Aspects de l'imamologie duodécimaine X)', *JAOS*, 122/4 (2002), pp. 722–741 (also published in G. Gobillot [ed.], *Mystique musulmane. Parcours en compagnie d'un chercheur: Roger Deladrière* [Paris, 2002], pp. 21–58 and in G. Filoramo [ed.], *Carisma Profetico. Fattore di innovazione religiosa* [Brescia, 2003], pp. 207–241).

16. 'Seul l'homme de Dieu est humain. Théologie et anthropologie mystique à travers l'exégèse imamite ancienne (Aspects de l'imamologie duodécimaine IV)', *Arabica*, 45 (1998), pp. 193–214 (English trans. in E. Kohlberg (ed.), *Shīʿism* [Aldershot, 2003], article II, pp. 17–39).

object of the hermeneutical method applied to the sacred texts;[17] the internalisation of the imam as an aid in the practices of concentration and visualisation;[18] and, finally, the position of this figure as the actual focal point for acts of devotion or prayer.[19]

Eschatology, the figure of the messianic Saviour – the 'present and hidden' imam of our time – the implications of his Occultation and other hermeneutical practices linked to these issues are dealt with in the last three chapters. The 'organic' correspondences between the disciplines of cosmogony, cosmology and eschatology, both in terms of the individual and in the collective dimension, leading to the appearance in Shiʿism of this triptych which is characteristic of dualist doctrines of an initiatory nature, constitute the theme of Chapter 12.[20] The next chapter is devoted to reports of encounters with the hidden imam, accounts that for over a thousand years have sustained the faith and hopes of the believers.[21] Finally, Chapter 14 is devoted to an examination of the eschatological hermeneutics of the theologico-mystical Shaykhiyya School of Kirman, particularly their central doctrine of the

17. '"Le combattant du *ta'wīl*": un poème de Mollā Sadrā sur 'Alī (Aspects de l'imamologie duodécimaine IX)', *JA*, 292/1-2 (2004), pp. 331–359 (also published in T. Lawson [ed.], *Reason and Inspiration in Islam: Essays in Honour of Hermann Landolt* [London, 2005], pp. 432–454).

18. 'Visions d'imams en mystique duodécimaine moderne et contemporaine (Aspects de l'imamologie duodécimaine VIII)', in E. Chaumont et al. (eds), *Autour du regard: Mélanges islamologiques offerts à Daniel Gimaret* (Louvain and Paris, 2003), pp. 97–124.

19. 'Notes sur la prière dans le shīʿisme imamite', in M. A. Amir-Moezzi, C. Jambet and P. Lory (eds), *Henry Corbin: philosophies et sagesses des religions du Livre*, Bibliothèque de l'Ecole des Hautes Etudes, vol. 126 (Turnhout, 2005), pp. 65–80.

20. 'Fin du Temps et Retour à l'Origine (Aspects de l'imamologie duodécimaine VI)', *RMMM*, special issue, 'Millénarisme et messianisme en Islam', ed. M. Garcia Arenal, 91–94 (2000), pp. 53–72.

21. 'Contribution à la typologie des rencontres avec l'imam caché (Aspects de l'imamologie duodécimaine II)', *JA*, 284/1 (1996), pp. 109–135.

'Fourth Pillar' where initiates have as significant an influence on the spiritual economy as the prophets and imams.[22]

Shiʿi spirituality thus proves to be rather complex. In the diversity of its manifestations, beliefs and practices one finds consistence and coherence in the determining role of knowledge and initiation; in ontological and anthropological dualism and especially in the ambivalence of the figure of the Imam, the alpha and omega of Shiʿism. A veritable soteriological horizon, the presence of the Divine Guide fills the devotional universe to the brim. Just as Christianity is the religion of Christ, Shiʿism may above all be considered that of the imam.

The 'mass of believers', the people of the *ẓāhir*, assuage their thirst for the divine in this world and put their faith in the Hereafter through the Divine Guide. In quest of the *bāṭin*, the 'elite' find salvation in knowledge and the imam's teachings, in the contemplation of doctrines that bear upon his nature and authority, in the hermeneutic of his exegesis of sacred texts. Finally, the 'elite of the elite', seekers of the *bāṭin al-bāṭin*, bearing in mind this absolute exemplar, seek to follow the mysterious path that can lead to the divinisation of man, this 'secret of secrets' of Shiʿi doctrine that the sages have designated by the elegant term *taʾalluh*.[23]

* * *

It gives me great pleasure to express my gratitude here to all those individuals and institutions that have made this publication possible. First of all, Philippe Hoffmann, President of the

22. 'Une absence remplie de présences: herméneutiques de l'Occultation chez les Shaykhiyya (Aspects de l'imamologie duodécimaine VII)', *BSOAS*, 64/1 (2001), pp. 1–18 (English trans. in R. Brunner and W. Ende [eds], *The Twelver Shia in Modern Times: Religious Culture and Political History* [Leiden, 2001], pp. 38–57).

23. Active noun of the fifth form of the root ʾL-H, that gives us *al-ʾiLāH* = *Allāh*. This definition, as incisive as it is grammatically exact, was provided by the Ismaili thinker Nāṣir-i Khusraw: '*mutaʾallih*' (active participle of the same fifth form) meaning 'he who becomes God' ('*mutaʾallih yaʿnī khodā shavandeh*') Nāṣir-i Khusraw, *Kitāb jāmiʿ al-ḥikmatayn*, ed. H. Corbin and M. Moʿīn (Tehran and Paris, 1953), p. 99; English translation, *Twin Wisdoms Reconciled*, IIS, forthcoming.

Section des Sciences Religieuses at the Ecole Pratique des Hautes Etudes (Sorbonne) and Director of the Centre d'Etudes des Religions du Livre (recently renamed Laboratoire d'Etudes sur les Monothéismes) as well as members of this research team (Centre National de la Recherche Scientifique-Ecole Pratique des Hautes Etudes) for their generous support. I am also grateful to those responsible for collective works as well as their directors and editors/writers – then and now – of journals in which the studies that make up this book were first published: Rainer Brunner, Werner Ende, Denise Aigle, Eric Chaumont, Todd Lawson, Geneviève Gobillot, Giovanni Filoramo, Christian Jambet, Pierre Lory; as well as Florian C. Reiter (*Zeitschrift der Deutschen Morgenländischen Gesellschaft*), Yohanan Friedmann (*Jerusalem Studies in Arabic and Islam*), Marcel Bazin and Philippe Gignoux (*Studia Iranica*), Paul Walker (*Journal of the American Oriental Society*), Mohammed Arkoun (*Arabica*), Daniel Gimaret, Denis Matringe and Cristina Scherrer-Schaub (*Journal Asiatique*), Sylvie Denoix (*Revue des Mondes Musulmans et de la Méditerranée*), Gerald Hawting (*Bulletin of the School of Oriental and African Studies*), and also the publishing houses Verdier (Lagrasse and Paris), Peeters (Louvain), Ashgate (Aldershot), Brill (Leiden), State University of New York Press (New York) and Brepols (Turnhout). I extend my gratitude to Richard Goulet, Marie-Odile Goulet-Cazé and once again Philippe Hoffmann as well as those at Editions Vrin for agreeing to publish the original French version of this book in 'Textes et Traditions', a renowned series at this prestigious publishing house. I would also like to thank Farhad Daftary and those in charge at the Institute of Ismaili Studies (London), for having the kindness to publish this book in English, and special thanks to Isabel Miller who edited the English translation. I would also like to express my gratitude to those who translated this work: David Streight (translator of Chapter 4), David Bachrach (Chapter 8), Amy Jacobs (Chapter 14) and especially Hafiz Karmali for his patience and perseverance in translating the rest of the book. I express my sincere gratitude to my wife, Fata, who helped prepare the manuscript. Finally, I wish to acknowledge Etan Kohlberg, my long-standing friend and source of inspiration who first had the idea of publishing this collection.

Abbreviations

AI(U)ON	*Annali dell'Istituto (Universitario) Orientale di Napoli*
BEO	*Bulletin d'Etudes Orientales*
BIFAO	*Bulletin de l'Institut Français d'Archéologie Orientale*
BSL	*Bulletin de Société de Linguistique*
BSOAS	*Bulletin of the School of Oriental and African Studies*
EI2	*The Encyclopedia of Islam*, ed. H. A. R. Gibb et al. (new edn, Leiden, 1960–2004)
EIR	*Encyclopaedia Iranica*, ed. E. Yarshater (London and New York, 1982–)
EJ	*Eranos Jahrbuch*
EPHE	Ecole Pratique des Hautes Etudes (Sorbonne).
GAL	C. Brockelmann, *Geschichte der arabischen Literatur* (Weimar, 1898)
GAS	F. Sezgin, *Geschichte des arabischen Schrifttums* (Leiden, 1967–1986)
IC	*Islamic Culture*
IJMES	*International Journal of Middle East Studies*
IOS	*Israel Oriental Studies*
JA	*Journal Asiatique*
JAOS	*Journal of the American Oriental Society*
JESHO	*Journal of the Economic and Social History of the Orient*

JNES	*Journal of Near Eastern Studies*
JRAS	*Journal of the Royal Asiatic Society of Great Britain and Ireland*
JSAI	*Jerusalem Studies in Arabic and Islam*
JSS	*Journal of Semitic Studies*
MIDEO	*Mélanges de l'Institut Dominicain d'Etudes Orientales du Caire*
MW	*Muslim World*
REI	*Revue des Etudes Islamiques*
RHR	*Revue de l'Histoire des Religions*
RSO	*Rivista degli Studi Orientali*
SI	*Studia Islamica*
WZKM	*Wiener Zeitschrift für die Kunde des Morgenlandes*
ZA	*Zeitschrift für Assyriologie*
ZDMG	*Zeitschrift der Deutschen Morgenländischen Gesellschaft*

Part I: Early Emergence and Ancient Convergence

1

Reflections on the Expression *dīn ʿAlī*: The Origins of the Shiʿi Faith*

In Shiʿi lands generally, and in Iran more particularly, there are a number of compound first names ending in ʿAlī. Many are very common: for instance, *Ḥusayn-ʿAlī, Muḥammad-ʿAlī, Jaʿfar-ʿAlī*; others have a more literary even poetic resonance: *Sayf-ʿAlī* ('Sword of ʿAlī'), *Nūr-ʿAlī* ('Light of ʿAlī'), *Maḥabbat-ʿAlī* or *Mehr-ʿAlī* ('Love of ʿAlī'), *Īmān-ʿAlī* ('Faith of ʿAlī'); still others are quite unusual if not very rare: *Shīr-ʿAlī* ('Lion-ʿAlī'), *Gurg-ʿAlī* ('Wolf ʿAlī'), *Chirāg-ʿAlī* ('Lamp of ʿAlī') and *Dīn-ʿAlī* ('Religion of ʿAlī').

This last appellation has always intrigued me: "ʿAlī's religion'. Is this not the same as Islam, as Muḥammad's religion? How might one explain this term, especially given that *Islām* and *dīn Muḥammad* are used as first names as well? Imagine my surprise when, a few years ago, I encountered the expression *dīn ʿAlī* in certain passages from early historiographical works. What does this term stand for? How can it be interpreted? Although the context is obviously not the same, this chapter is thus an attempt to answer a long-standing question. The chapter consists of five parts: (1) *Dīn ʿAlī* in the works of the historiographers; (2) The uniqueness of ʿAlī; (3) Themes concerning ʿAlī and the ʿAlids; (4) The basis for the religion of ʿAlī (The

* I extend my gratitude to Professors Wilferd Madelung and Etan Kohlberg for their pertinent comments during the process of writing this chapter. Any imperfections that still remain are the responsibility solely of the author.

Qur'ānic bases; and The pre-Islamic bases); (5) Reactions and repercussions.

1. *Dīn ʿAlī* in the works of the historiographers

In certain passages of his monumental work *Ta'rīkh al-rusul wa'l-mulūk*, al-Ṭabarī (d. 310 AH/923 AD) reproduces some reports in which the expression *dīn ʿAlī* appears. The first is found in a long account reported by ʿAṭiyya b. Bilāl about the battle of the Camel in 36/656.[1] At one point during the battle, ʿAmr b. Yathribī al-Ḍabbī *al-rājiz*, a poet-warrior in the camp of the confederates allied against ʿAlī, kills three of his men, ʿIlbā' b. al-Haytham al-Sadūsī, Hind b. ʿAmr al-Jamalī and Zayd b. Ṣūḥān, before being laid low by ʿAmmār b. Yāsir, one of ʿAlī' s oldest supporters. After he had been brought down, he is said to have recited this *rajaz*:

> Let he who knows me not, learn that I am Ibn Yathribī, killer of ʿIlbā' and Hind al-Jamalī. As well as of the son of Ṣūḥān, all (adepts) of ʿAlī's religion.[2]

He is then led to ʿAlī who does not accept his request for *amān*, and orders his execution. According to the author of this account, Ibn Yathribī was the only captive to whom ʿAlī denied a pardon. Al-Ṭabarī does not provide any clarification of his intransigence.

---

1. Al-Ṭabarī, *Ta'rīkh*, ed. M. J. de Goeje et al. (Leiden, 1879–1901), series 1, pp. 3196ff.; ed. M. A. F. Ibrāhīm (Cairo, 1960), vol. 4, pp. 514ff.

2. *Anā li-man yunkirunī ibnu yathribī qātilu ʿilbā'i wa hindi'l-jamalī wa ibnin li-ṣūḥāna ʿalā dīni ʿAlī*; al-Ṭabarī, ed. de Goeje, series 1, p. 3199; ed. Ibrāhīm, vol. 4, p. 517, varies slightly: *ʿIn taqtulūnī* [if you plan to kill me, know that etc.] *fa anā ibnu yathribī qātilu ʿilbā'i wa hindi'l-jamalī thumma bni ṣūḥāna ʿalā dīni ʿAlī.*' See also al-Mufīd, *Kitāb al-Jamal aw al-nuṣra fī ḥarb al-Baṣra* (Najaf, 1963), p. 146; Ibn Shahrāshūb, *Manāqib āl Abī Ṭālib*, ed. M. Burūjerdi (lithograph, Tehran, 1316–1317/1898–1899; Najaf, 1956), vol. 3, p. 156; al-Majlisī, *Biḥār al-anwār*, ed. based on the edition by Kumpānī, 90 vols, in 110 tomes (Tehran and Qumm, 1376–1392/1956–1972), vol. 32, p. 176, in which ʿAmmār b. Yāsir shouts at Ibn Yathribī: 'It is as a follower of ʿAlī's religion that I fight you (*uqātiluka ʿalā dīni ʿAlī*)'.

The reader can reasonably conclude that the *rājiz* (poet-warrior) was executed for rather haughtily boasting about killing three of the most loyal of ʿAlī's companions. During the same period, another erudite scholar, Ibn Durayd Muḥammad b. al-Ḥasan al-Azdī (d. 321/933), reproduces the poem in his *Kitāb al-ishtiqāq*, adding that in order to justify this unique execution, ʿAlī is supposed to have said:

> He [i.e Ibn Yathribī] claimed to have killed [my three companions] because they followed the religion of ʿAlī; well, the religion of ʿAlī is the religion of Muḥammad (*zaʿama annahu qatalahum ʿalā dīn ʿAlī wa dīn ʿAlī dīn Muḥammad*).[3]

According to Ibn Durayd's account, the reason for putting Ibn Yathribī to death was the distinction made by him between the religion of ʿAlī and that of Muḥammad, thus implicitly accusing ʿAlī of professing a deviant religion compared with Islam.[4] Other passages in al-Ṭabarī call into question the explanation provided by *Kitāb al-ishtiqāq*, since in this case the expression is uttered by ʿAlī's supporters. One of these passages appears in a report by the

3. Ibn Durayd, *Kitāb al-ishtiqāq*, ed. ʿA. M. Hārūn (Baghdad, 1399/1979), p. 413; the version of the poem by Ibn Durayd is slightly different: '*Qataltu ʿilbāʾa wa hinda'l-jamalī wa ibnan li-ṣūḥāna ʿalā dīni ʿAlī.*' In the margins of the *unicum* dated the seventh/thirteenth century, used by ʿAbd al-Salām Muḥammad Hārūn, are found earlier notes that often provide different understandings (see the editor's introduction, ibid., pp. 36–37). For the passage cited, the notes in the margin follow the version by al-Ṭabarī in the edition prepared under the guidance of de Goeje; ibid., p. 413, note 2, *in fine*.

4. L. Caetani makes an error of interpretation by comparing this punishment of Ibn Yathribī to that of ʿAbd Allāh b. Sabaʾ, inflicted, according to tradition, by ʿAlī himself, *Annali dell'Islam* (Milan, 1905–1926), vol. 9, p. 142; re: ʿAbd Allāh b. Sabaʾ, see M. G. S. Hodgson, *EI2*). To accuse ʿAlī of professing a deviant religion is entirely different to claiming to defend ʿAlī's cause while professing an 'extremist' doctrine; this error is pointed out by W. Madelung in *The Succession to Muḥammad* (Cambridge, 1997), p. 178, n. 183. Another historiographical source, *Kitāb al-futūḥ* by Ibn Aʿtham al-Kūfī (d. 314/926) gives as the sole reason for the execution of Ibn Yathribī, his violent animosity towards ʿAlī; see Ibn Aʿtham, *al-Futūḥ*, Persian trans. Harawī (sixth/twelfth century), ed. G. Ṭabāṭabāʾī Majd (Tehran, 1374 Sh./1995), pp. 432–433.

famous Abū Mikhnaf (based on ʿUbayd Allāh b. al-Ḥurr al-Juʿfī) regarding Muʿāwiya's order to arrest and execute a large number of ʿAlid rebels led by Ḥujr b. ʿAdī. During an interrogation, one of ʿAlī's partisans, Karīm b. ʿAfīf al-Khathʿamī, is supposed to have had the following conversation with Muʿāwiya:

> Al-Khathʿamī: 'Fear God, Muʿāwiya [literally: God! God! O Muʿāwiya] for you will be led [inevitably] from this transitory place to the final and eternal resting place; there you will be questioned about the reasons for my execution and you will be asked to explain why you shed my blood.'
>
> Muʿāwiya: 'What say you regarding ʿAlī?'
>
> Al-Khathʿamī: '[I say] The same as you: I dissociate myself from the religion of ʿAlī, by which he submits to God (*atabarraʾu min dīni ʿAlī alladhī kāna yadīnu llāha bihi*).' At this [declaration], having difficulty in devising a reply, Muʿāwiya remained silent.[5]

5. Al-Ṭabarī, ed. de Goeje, series 2, p. 143; ed. Ibrāhīm, vol. 5, p. 276. In speaking of these ʿAlids, Muʿāwiya calls them 'rebels among the Turābiyya Sabaʾiyya', a reference to the *kunya* Abū Turāb for ʿAlī (see E. Kohlberg, 'Abū Turāb', *BSOAS*, 41 [1978], pp. 347–352; rpr. in *Belief and Law in Imāmī Shīʿism* [Aldershot, 1991] article VI) and to ʿAbd Allāh b. Sabaʾ. See also the abridged version of this account in al-Balādhurī, *Ansāb al-ashrāf*, vol. 4/a, ed. M. Schloessinger and M. J. Kister (Jerusalem, 1972), p. 225. Admittedly, al-Khathʿamī's response is ambiguous, hence Muʿāwiya's embarrasment. His 'dissociation' from ʿAlī's religion is surely based on the obligation of *taqiyya*, but one wonders if the expression *dīn ʿAlī* does not in fact stem from Muʿāwiya or more generally from ʿAlī's adversaries. The expression does indeed seem to have posed a problem for at least some of ʿAlī's supporters, since it could establish a distinction between 'the religion of ʿAlī' and Islam. According to a report by al-Ṭabarī, during the battle of the Camel, when in order to spare their lives the Azd of Baṣra, declared themselves followers of ʿAlī's religion (*naḥnu ʿalā dīni ʿAlī*), a man from the Banī Layth of Kūfa (no doubt an ʿAlid) mocks them for what they have just said (al-Ṭabarī, ed. de Goeje, series 1, pp. 3,189–3,190; ed. Ibrāhīm, vol. 4, p. 512). However, as we shall see, the expression is sometimes unambiguously attributed to supporters of ʿAlī. Cf. also verses by ʿAlī's Companion al-Nuʿmān b. al-ʿAjlān al-Anṣārī, praising 'the religion of ʿAlī' after the battle of Ṣiffīn, according to al-Minqarī, *Waqʿat Ṣiffīn*, ed. A. M. Hārūn (Cairo, 1382/1962), p. 380 and Ibn Abiʾl-Ḥadīd, *Sharḥ Nahj al-balāgha*, ed. M. A. Ibrāhīm (Cairo, 1965), vol. 1, p. 149.

Still according to al-Ṭabarī, during al-Mukhtār's revolt, Rufāʿa b. Shaddād al-Hamdānī, the former's supporter, recites the following verse while in the heat of battle:

> I am the son of Shaddād, adept of ʿAlī's religion /I am not an ally of ʿUthmān, offspring of a goat.[6]

Finally, according to a tradition reported by Ibn Abī Shayba (d. 235/849) in *al-Muṣannaf*, during the battle of the Camel, Muḥammad b. al-Ḥanafiyya, the son of ʿAlī, spares the life of an adversary when the latter claims to have adopted ʿAlī's religion.[7]

Some elements of this account seem to indicate that the expression is authentic. First is the rarity of such occurrences and their somewhat fortuitous nature. In addition to the care taken in highlighting an expression, one of the features of the apocryphal is its repetitous and frequent usage.[8] I certainly do not claim to have thoroughly examined al-Ṭabarī's monumental *History* in its entirety, but I have read it attentively, and with these few passages, I believe we have a fairly accurate picture. What is more, the expression is alloted to the fiercest adversaries as well as to the loyal and devout supporters of ʿAlī, which tends to indicate that it was a current expression known by all and that its usage by

---

6. *Anā bnu shaddāda ʿalā dīni ʿAlī/lastu li-ʿUthmāna bni arwā bi-walī* (al-Ṭabarī, ed. Ibrāhīm, vol. 6, p. 50). Usage of *arwā* (lit. 'mountain goat') is a play on words with *ʿaffān* (the name of ʿUthmān's father, one meaning of which is 'animal with malodorous skin or hair'). Al-Majlisī reports this account based on al-Ṭabarī's *History*, but his version presents significant differences with the *Taʾrīkh*: for example, the individual is named al-Aḥraṣ b. Shaddād and his verse is a response to a verse by his adversary Ibn Dhabʿān al-Kalbī: 'I am Ibn Dhabʿān al-Karīm al-Mufaḍḍal / One of the leaders among those who dissociate themselves from the religion of ʿAlī (*anā bnu Dhabʿāna'l-karīmi'l-mufaḍḍali/ min ʿaṣabatin yabraʾūna min dīni ʿAlī*)', *Biḥār al-anwār*, vol. 45, p. 381.

7. Ibn Abī Shayba, *al-Muṣannaf*, ed. S. M. al-Laḥḥām, 9 vols (Beirut, 1409/1989), vol. 8, p. 711.

8. See e.g. J. Schacht, 'A Revaluation of Islamic Traditions', *JRAS* (1949), pp. 140–152; G. H. A. Juynboll, *The Authenticity of the Tradition Literature: Discussions in Modern Egypt* (Leiden, 1969), pp. 30ff.

reporters in historiographical traditions was not dictated by partisanship; this moreover would explain the somewhat fortuitous occurrences, with no particular motive for the context in which they appeared. During the course of the following study, we will consider other indications that the expression could have existed at the dawn of Islam.

2. The uniqueness of 'Alī

To my knowledge, 'Alī is the only personality from early Islam – apart from the Prophet of course – with whom the term *dīn* is associated. Thanks to analyses by R. B. Serjeant and, especially, due to the pioneering study by M. M. Bravmann, we know that just as in the earliest days of the new religion of the Arabs, *dīn* in pre-Islamic times designated a set of both secular and sacred laws.[9] By extension, *dīn* also referred to submission to a law or a leader, thus contrasting with the anarchy and wild behaviour associated with *jahl* or ignorance. Gradually becoming more exclusive in the Islamic period, the interpretation of 'religion' would have been derived from this original secular and/or religious sense of the term.[10] The use of the expression *dīn 'Alī* is all the more remarkable since when speaking of his most notable contemporaries, namely the three other *rāshidūn* (rightly guided) caliphs, the sources employ the term *sunna*, almost never *dīn*. Here too, studies by M. M. Bravmann (correcting J. Schacht's analyses), followed

9. R. B. Serjeant, '*Ḥaram* and *ḥawṭah*, the Sacred Enclave in Arabia', in A. R. Badawi (ed.), *Mélanges Taha Husain* (Cairo, 1962), pp. 41–50, esp. p. 42 and p. 50, and 'The "Constitution" of Medina', *The Islamic Quarterly*, 8 (1964), pp. 3–16, esp. 13 (rpr. in *Studies in Arabian History and Civilisation*, London, 1981, articles III and V); M. M. Bravmann, *The Spiritual Background of Early Islam* (Leiden, 1972), see index under '*dāna (dyn)*', '*dīn*', and pp. 4–7 '*Murūwah* and *dīn*'.

10. Bravmann, *The Spiritual Background*, p. 34 and note 1 in which the author argues that the theories advanced by Nöldeke and Horovitz on the Iranian origin of the term are superfluous; see also U. Rubin, *The Eye of the Beholder: The Life of Muḥammad as Viewed by the Early Muslims* (Princeton, 1995), see index under '*dīn*'.

by those of G. H. A. Juynboll demonstrate that *sunna* was initially a clearly marked path on the ground from which one could only waver wilfully, and by extension the path of the elders or sages in a tribe that one ought to follow scrupulously. Although the Qurʾān defines this term as 'path of God', at the dawn of the nascent religion, *sunna* designates a whole set of secular or religious forms of behaviour, attitudes and sayings of sages and role models par excellence, in this instance the Prophet himself and the first caliphs.[11] Both historiographical and purely religious sources allude to the *sunnas* of the first caliphs. Al-Balādhurī (d. ca. 302/892) refers to the *sunna* of Abū Bakr and ʿUmar, as well as that of the Khārijīs, during the arbitration at Ṣiffīn, as also does al-Ṭabarī.[12] The expression '*sunna* of the Two ʿUmars', that is, Abū Bakr and ʿUmar, is found again in poetry by Farazdaq (ca. 109/728)[13] and Ibn Abī Yaʿlā (d. 526/1133), who while citing the *Kitāb al-sunna* by al-Barbahārī (d. 329/941), refers to the *sunna* of Abū Bakr, ʿUmar and ʿUthmān.[14] In my research to date, I have encountered

11. Bravmann, *The Spiritual Background*, see index under '*sanna*', '*sunnah*'; G. H. A. Juynboll, 'Some New Ideas on the Development of *Sunna* as a Technical Term in Early Islam', *JSAI*, 10 (1987), pp. 97–118, esp. pp. 97f. (rpr. in *Studies on the Origins and Uses of Islamic Ḥadīth* [London, 1996], article V); J. Chabbi, *Le Seigneur des tribus. L'Islam de Mahomet* (Paris, 1997), p. 652. For a very rare usage of the expression *dīn ʿUthmān* (forged probably in reaction to the expression *dīn ʿAlī*), see J. van Ess, *Theologie und Gesellschaft im 2. und 3. Jahrhundert Hidschra*, I–VI (Berlin, 1991–1997), see index under '*dīn*' and also vol. 4, pp. 565ff. (on use of the term *dīn*).

12. Al-Balādhurī, *Ansāb al-ashrāf*, vol. 4/b, ed. M. Schloessinger (Jerusalem, 1961), p. 27; al-Ṭabarī, ed. de Goeje, series 1, pp. 3,350–3,351.

13. Cf. *Naqāʾiḍ Jarīr waʾl-Farazdaq*, ed. A. A. Bevan (Leiden, 1905–1909), p. 1013.

14. Ibn Abī Yaʿlā al-Farrāʾ, *Ṭabaqāt al-ḥanābila* (Damascus, 1923; rpr. Beirut, ca. 1980), vol. 2, p. 32. Some reports make a distinction between *sunna* of the Prophet and *sīra* of the caliphs (cf. al-Ṭabarī, ed. de Goeje, series 1, pp. 2786 and p. 2793; al-Yaʿqūbī, *Taʾrīkh*, ed. M. Th. Houtsma [Leiden, 1883], vol. 2, pp. 186–187). Bravmann believes that in this context these two terms are synonymous, *The Spiritual Background*, pp. 124f. For an excellent historical and doctrinal analysis of these passages, see T. Nagel, *Studien zum Minderheitenproblem im Islam*, vol. 1 (Bonn, 1973), pp. 7–44.

the expression *sunnat ʿAlī* only in the anonymous historiographical text from the second–third/eighth–ninth centuries edited as *Akhbār al-dawla al-ʿAbbāsiyya.*[15] The remarkable analysis of this work by M. Sharon shows how this pro-ʿAbbasid source deals with ʿAlī and the ʿAlids,[16] whence the use of the term *sunna* with reference to ʿAlī in order to stress the latter's role as model in the same manner as the other *rāshidūn*. The rarity if not the nonexistence of the expression *sunnat ʿAlī* seems all the more surprising since as far as concerns legal and ritual practice, ʿAlī seems to have taken the same decisions as the first two caliphs. This is no doubt why, much later, marked by their aversion to the Prophet's first three successors, in many cases the Shiʿis would follow the legal teachings of Ibn ʿAbbās rather than those of ʿAlī.[17] Imami literature would itself seek to justify this fact by invoking a form of *taqiyya* practised by ʿAlī, who feared being accused of deviation compared with the path followed by Abū Bakr and ʿUmar.[18] The striking ostracism of the *sunna* concerning ʿAlī is perhaps thus due to the fact that, in speaking of the latter, the term *dīn* was more frequently used, thus emphasising the radical difference of certain positions taken in the area of faith as compared to his predecessors. The traditionalist, Muḥammad b. ʿUbayd b. Abī Umayya (d. 204/819), a fierce opponent of the Kufan Shiʿis, never ceased to vaunt the merits of the first three *rāshidūn*, exhorting his public to follow their *sunna*, no doubt by deliberately deleting ʿAlī from the list of role models

---

15. Ed. Dūrī-Muṭṭalibī (Beirut, 1971), p. 284.

16. Cf. M. Sharon, 'The ʿAbbasid Daʿwa Re-examined on the Basis of a New Source', *Arabic and Islamic Studies* (1973). In this regard, refer also to the important work by M. Q. Zaman, *Religion and Politics under the Early ʿAbbāsids* (Leiden, 1997), see index under '*akhbār*'.

17. Now consult W. Madelung, "Abdallāh b. ʿAbbās and Shiite Law', in U. Vermeulen and J. M. F. van Reeth (eds), *Law, Christianity and Modernism in Islamic Society* (Louvain, 1998), pp. 13–25.

18. According to a tradition going back to imam Muḥammad al-Bāqir reported by Ibn Shabba, *Ta'rīkh al-madīna al-munawwara*, ed. M. F. Shaltūt (Qumm, 1410/1989–1990), p. 217; cited by Madelung, "Abdallāh b. ʿAbbās and Shiite Law', p. 24.

to be followed.[19] It is surely as a reaction against using the expression *dīn ʿAlī*, that, writing at the turn of the fifth and sixth/eleventh and twelfth centuries, Ibn Abī Yaʿlā reports that the *sunna* of the first three caliphs – ʿAlī is thus wilfully excluded – was called 'the original ancient religion', *al-dīn al-ʿaṭīq*.[20] *Dīn ʿAlī* would thus have been much more than a *sunna*, more than a collection of behaviour patterns or decisions relating to daily sacred or secular life. Rather, it seems to designate a whole set of beliefs, professions of faith one might say, touching upon both the sacred and profane, the spiritual as well as the temporal – hence justifying translation of the expression as 'religion of ʿAlī'. Let us attempt to discover the content of this 'religion', at least in its broadest terms.

In his outstanding work *The Succession to Muḥammad*, W. Madelung points out almost all the above-mentioned passages in which our expression appears.[21] An impressive work of erudition and subtle analyses, it treats with numerous fundamental problems in the history of early Islam; this might explain why its eminent author limits himself to a single allusion regarding *dīn ʿAlī*:

---

19. Ibn Ḥajar al-ʿAsqalānī, *Tahdhīb al-tahdhīb*, 12 vols (Hyderabad, 1907–1909; rpr. Beirut, 1968), vol. 9, pp. 328ff. See also a similar opinion held by al-Shāfiʿī, analysed by J. Schacht, *Origins of Muhammadan Jurisprudence* (Oxford, 1950), p. 24. Including ʿAlī among the *rāshidūn* caliphs posed a problem until the ʿAbbasid period. Ibn Ḥanbal would have been the first great non-ʿAlid thinker to have sought to employ the image of ʿAlī to this end; see his *Kitāb al-sunna* (Mecca, 1349/1930), p. 214; Ṣāliḥ b. Aḥmad b. Ḥanbal, *Sīrat al-imām Aḥmad b. Ḥanbal*, ed. F. ʿAbd al-Munʿim Aḥmad (Alexandria, 1981), p. 82. Regarding the rehabilitation of ʿAlī, see also T. Nagel, *Rechtleitung und Kalifat* (Bonn, 1975), pp. 232f.

20. Ibn Abī Yaʿlā al-Farrāʾ, *Ṭabaqāt al-ḥanābila*, vol. 2, p. 32 (or *dīn al-ʿAtīq*, and in this instance it should be translated as 'the religion of ʿAtīq', ʿAtīq being one of the *laqab*s of Abū Bakr); equally the expression *dīn ʿUthmān* replaced at times *raʾy al-ʿUthmāniyya* (al-Ṭabarī, ed. de Goeje, series 2, p. 340) designating those who chose the Banū ʿUmayya over the Banū Hāshim, seems to have been a response to *dīn ʿAlī*.

21. In the course of the very long chapter on ʿAlī's reign, see pp. 178–179, and in the conclusion mainly devoted to Muʿāwiya's rule, p. 338.

> *Dīn ʿAlī* could at this stage have only a limited meaning, most likely the claim that ʿAlī was the best of men after Muḥammad, his legatee (*waṣī*), and as such most entitled to lead the Community.[22]

As we shall see, the above would indeed encapsulate the very fabric of "ʿAlī's religion'; however, each of these facts holds a number of ideas and implicit conceptions – bearing upon both ancestral Arab beliefs as well as the new Islamic faith – that would enable the claim for exclusive legitmacy in the eyes of a number of believers. The meaning of the expression is perhaps limited in scope but nevertheless complex. The aim of this chapter is to attempt to discover the ramifications of this meaning and in modest terms to supplement the masterful study by this renowned Islamic scholar.

3. Themes concerning ʿAlī and the ʿAlids

The sayings of ʿAlī himself offer a most rewarding field of investigation. As is known, authentic or not, they are numerous, filling pages and pages in sources in various literary genres.[23] ʿAlī's life seems to have been especially active: the period of his youth just at the birth of Islam; his relationship with Muḥammad first in Mecca and then Medina; his exploits in war, his spiritual dimension, his family; being overlooked in the matter of the succession to the Prophet; his relationship with the first three caliphs; his short-lived reign – an uninterrupted period of civil war and so on – all constitute a myriad of backdrops reflected in the rich variety of sayings of the most highly placed and colourful character that the Islamic sources present to us.

However, among these many sayings on the most varied of subjects, two themes constitute veritable leitmotifs: the very fact of having been the first man to accept Muḥammad's prophetic message and of having vowed to have absolute faith in and loyalty

22. Madelung, *The Succession*, pp. 178–179.

23. Cf. L. Veccia Vaglieri, 'Sul Nahj al-balāghah e sul suo compilatore ash-Sharīf ar-Raḍī', *AIUON*, special issue (1958), pp. 7ff.

to the new religion (the notion of *sābiqa*); and, especially, the fact of being the Prophet's closest male relative with the strongest blood ties to him (the notion of *qarāba*). As we shall see, the importance of this relationship is so fundamental that it encompasses and even explains the idea of *sābiqa*. In implicit or explicit terms, both from his own perspective and in the eyes of his supporters, these two claims made ʿAlī the only legitimate successor to the Prophet. One need only glance through the historiographical works, for example the sayings of ʿAlī, more specifically those regarding the direction of the community – in which his legitimist claims feature – to pick out the two themes which are omnipresent in the context of the battle of Ṣiffīn,[24] his letters to Muʿāwiya and a letter to his elder brother ʿAqīl b. Abī Ṭālib,[25] or again, his sayings arising from the famous speech by Muḥammad at Ghadīr Khumm.[26]

These are the very themes that enable supporters of ʿAlī to recognise him as the sole legitimate *waṣī* (legatee) to Muḥammad. In the poem reported by al-Balādhurī of the warrior of the Banū ʿAdī who was on the side of ʿĀʾisha, Ṭalḥa and al-Zubayr, and fought against ʿAlī at the battle of the Camel, this title for ʿAlī is an object of ridicule (a point which goes to prove the fact of its existence), since for the Banū ʿAdī, the only true 'legatee' of the Prophet is Abū Bakr, whose daughter is now in battle against the ʿAlids:

---

24. Al-Minqarī, *Waqʿat Ṣiffīn*, ed. ʿA. M. Hārūn (Cairo 1382/1962), pp. 470f.; al-Thaqafī, *Kitāb al-ghārāt*, ed. J. al-Muḥaddith al-Urmawī (Tehran, 1395/1975), pp. 303ff.; al-Masʿūdī, *Murūj al-dhahab*, ed. Barbier de Meynard, rev. C. Pellat (Beirut, 1968–1979), vol. 3, p. 201ff.; (Pseudo-) Ibn Qutayba, *al-Imāma wa'l-siyāsa*, ed. M. M. al-Rāfiʿī (Cairo, 1322/1904), vol. 1, pp. 191f. Also, Madelung, *The Succession*, pp. 240–241 and pp. 270–271.

25. Al-Thaqafī, *K. al-Ghārāt*, pp. 434–435; al-Balādhurī, *Ansāb al-ashrāf*, vol. 2, ed. M. B. al-Maḥmūdī (Beirut, 1974), pp. 74–75. Also, H. Lammens, *Etudes sur le règne du Calife Omaiyade Muʿāwia 1er* (Paris, 1908), p. 175; Madelung, *The Succession*, pp. 263–264.

26. E.g. al-Ṭabarī, de Goeje, series 1, pp. 3350ff.; on *ḥadīth*s concerning Ghadīr Khumm, see e.g. A. J. Wensinck, *Concordance et indices de la tradition musulmane* (Leiden, 1936), see under *wālī*. Also, L. Veccia Vaglieri, *EI2*, under *Ghadīr Khumm*.

> We are 'Adī and we are looking for 'Alī (to kill him) … we will kill all those who oppose the *waṣī* [i.e. Abū Bakr].[27]

Al-Ṭabarī reports that after the assassination of the third caliph, 'Uthmān, poets competed to commemorate the event. Among them, al-Faḍl b. al-'Abbās b. 'Utba b. Abī Lahab took this opportunity to sing the praises of 'Alī:

> Truly, among those who recall (*'inda dhī al-dhikri*), the best among men after Muḥammad is indeed the legatee of the Chosen Prophet/He who, as the first, the closest (*ṣinw* or *ṣunw*) to the Prophet recited the Prayer and who, as the first, defeated the misguided of Badr.[28]

In a letter probably written just before Ṣiffīn and which was reported by some of the historiographers and censored by others, Muḥammad, son of the first caliph, Abū Bakr, violently opposed Mu'āwiya. Referring to 'Alī, he describes him as the first man to have responded positively to Muḥammad's Message, to whom he was related as brother and cousin, of whom he was the legatee, who was the leader of the faithful and the father of his (Muḥammad's) descendants.[29]

---

27. Al-Balādhurī, *Ansāb al-ashrāf*, vol. 2, pp. 245–246.

28. Al-Ṭabarī, ed. Ibrāhīm, vol. 4, p. 426; the term *ṣinw/ṣunw*, that I have translated as 'the closest', literally means 'similar, same' and designates the brother, cousin or son. W. Madelung cites the poem using the edition by de Goeje, series 1, p. 3065, and attributes it instead to the father of al-Faḍl, al-'Abbās b. 'Utba who seems to have been the poet and spokesperson for the Banū Hāshim; *The Succession*, p. 186. Ibn Ḥanbal uses the term to define al-'Abbās's relationship to 'Abd Allāh, Muḥammad's father; see his *Musnad*, ed. Muḥammad al-Zuhrī al-Ghamrāwī (Cairo, 1313/1896), vol. 1, p. 207 and vol. 2, p. 322.

29. Al-Balādhurī, *Ansāb al-ashrāf*, vol. 2, pp. 393ff.; al-Minqarī, *Waq'at Ṣiffīn*, pp. 118ff.; al-Mas'ūdī, *Murūj*, vol. 3, pp. 197ff. Al-Ṭabarī expressly admits to having censored the letter because the masses (*'āmma*) would not have tolerated it; ed. de Goeje, series 1, p. 3248. By this he surely means the Ḥanbalī activists of Baghdad whose hostility towards the great scholar was known to all; cf. al-Iṣfahānī, *Annalium Libri*, ed. Gottwald (Petropoli, 1884), vol. 2, p. 155; Ibn al-Jawzī, *al-Muntaẓam* (Hyderabad, 1357/1938), vol. 6, p. 172.

In one of his *ṭawīls*, the 'Alid poet of Baṣra, Abu'l-Aswad al-Du'alī (d. 69/688), citing his favorite personalities among the immediate blood relations of the Prophet, limits himself to naming 'Alī by the single term *waṣī*.[30] The same leitmotifs are found in sermons by al-Ḥasan, 'Alī's eldest son, made at the mosque in Kūfa after 'Alī's assassination; a sermon also reported by the Sunni al-Balādhurī and the pro-Shi'i Abu'l-Faraj al-Iṣfahānī (d. 356/966).[31] Shi'i sources, and more specifically works of *ḥadīth*, later took up the same themes to the full and embellished themes regarding the *sābiqa* and, even more so, the *qarāba* of 'Alī.

4. The basis of the religion of 'Alī

In what way do these ideas justify being given the appellation 'religion of 'Alī '? How and why might they constitute articles of faith? If 'Alī and his followers laid claim to them in such an obsessive manner and if among both those for and those against the 'Alids the habit had been formed of designating them by the expression *dīn 'Alī*, it is because they were based upon doctrinal and ideological justifications that seemed legitimate from a religious point of view and credible to those who professed them. It appears to me that two categories of 'legitimising proofs' supported these ideas and justified them by giving them the term *dīn 'Alī*: proofs of an Islamic nature based on the text of the Qur'ān and even more so, proofs based on ancestral beliefs.

30. *Dīwān Abu'l-Aswad al-Du'alī*, ed. M. Ḥ. Āl Yāsīn (Beirut, 1974), pp. 119–120; Abu'l-Faraj al-Iṣfahānī, *Kitāb al-Aghānī*, 20 vols (Būlāq, 1285/1868), vol. 12, p. 321 (a shorter version of the poem).

31. *Ansāb al-ashrāf*, vol. 3, ed. M. B. al-Maḥmudī (Beirut, 1974), p. 28; Abu'l-Faraj al-Iṣfahānī, *Maqātil al-Ṭālibiyyīn*, ed. S. A. Ṣaqr (Cairo 1949; rpr., Qumm, 1416/1995), p. 62.

The Qurʾānic bases

Famous for his legendary knowledge of and scrupulous faithfulness to the text of the Qurʾān,[32] ʿAlī could not have failed to present elements of the revealed text in order to legitimise his claims. Here too, Madelung's scholarship will guide us. In a subsection of his dense and pertinent introduction to *The Succession to Muḥammad*, he assiduously examines all the Qurʾānic instances that might serve to justify the ʿAlid claim to lead the Community after the Prophet's death. To my knowledge, this is the first time the evidence has been brought forward with such erudition and precision; it even serves as a focus and fundamental argument for the discourse underlying the entire work.[33] In summarising this work we will thus limit ourselves to concentrating in the main on the Qurʾānic proofs.

Genealogical Table of Muḥammad and ʿAlī

		Quṣayy		
		ʿAbd Manāf		
ʿAbd Shams	Nawfal		Hāshim	al-Muṭṭalib
Umayya				
Ḥarb	Abu'l-ʿĀṣ		ʿAbd al-Muṭṭalib	
Abū Sufyān	ʿAffān	ʿAbbās	ʿAbd Allāh	Abū Ṭālib
Muʿāwiya	ʿUthmān		Muḥammad	ʿAlī
			Fāṭima	
				al-Ḥasan
				al-Ḥusayn

32. See e.g. Ibn Saʿd, *al-Ṭabaqāt al-kubrā*, ed. Iḥsān ʿAbbās, 9 vols (Beirut, 1380/1960), vol. 2, p. 338; Ibn Ḥajar, *Tahdhīb*, vol. 7, p. 338; Ibn al-Athīr, *al-Nihāya fī gharīb al-ḥadīth wa'l-athar*, ed. al-Zāwī and al-Tināḥī, 4 vols (Cairo, 1963–1966; rpr. Beirut, n.d.), vol. 3, p. 102.

33. Madelung, *The Succession*, 'The obligation of the kinship and the families of the prophets in the Qurʾān', pp. 6–18; whence the reaction of certain critics of the book who perceive it as a kind of pro-Shiʿi apologia. This is certainly a flagrant misunderstanding; but further analysis is beyond the scope of the present chapter.

The Qurʾān places great emphasis on respect for family and blood ties:[34]

> Surely God bids to justice and good-doing and giving to kinsmen (*dhi'l-qurbā*); and He forbids indecency, dishonour, and insolence, admonishing you, so that haply you will remember (Q 16:90)
>
> And give the kinsman his right (Q 17:26)
>
> They will question thee concerning what they should expend. Say: 'Whatsover good you expend is for parents (*wālidayn*) and kinsmen (*aqrabīn*), orphans, the needy, and the traveller.' (Q 2:215)

Generosity to close relatives and providing them with material support is a religious duty but on condition that the latter are converts to Islam; though even if they are not, the Muslim is called upon to be just and impartial to those of his relatives who may have maintained their pagan beliefs (Q 4:135; 6:152; 9:23–24 and 113–114).[35] However, in spite of these limitations, the Qurʾān clearly establishes the superiority and pre-eminence of blood ties over all other kinds of bonds or alliances.

> Those who are bound by blood (*ūlu'l-arḥām*) are nearer to one another in the Book of God than the believers and the emigrants. (Q 33:6)

Singing the praises of past converts, the Emigrants and the Helpers, verses 72 to 74 of Sura 8 are followed by the following verse (probably added later on):

> And those who have believed afterwards and emigrated, and struggled with you – they belong to you; but those related by blood are nearer to one another in the Book of God.[36]

---

34. The translation of the Qurʾān used in this work is A. J. Arberry, *The Koran* (Oxford, 1964).

35. Madelung, *The Succession*, pp. 6–7.

36. Ibid., pp. 7–8.

There is yet another important contributing factor for our subject: in the Qur'ānic 'History of Prophets', close relatives of the prophets play a vital role: they are the protectors of the Messengers of God against their adversaries and after the Messengers die, they become their inheritors in both temporal and spiritual matters. The prophets of the Banū Isrā'īl are in fact descendants of one and the same family going back to Noah and Adam; the line of this same family continues up to Jesus (Q 3:33–34 and 19:58). The chain of prophets and the importance of their inheritors in the economy of the sacred, as chosen from among their immediate family, are stressed by verses 84 to 89 of Sura 6:

> And we gave to him [i.e. Abraham] Isaac and Jacob – each one We guided, And Noah We guided before; and of his seed David and Solomon, Job and Joseph, Moses and Aaron – even so We recompense the good-doers – Zachariah and John, Jesus and Elias; each was of the righteous; Ishmael and Elisha, Jonah and Lot – each one We preferred above all beings; and of their fathers, and of their seed, and of their brethren; and We elected them, and We guided them to a straight path.
>
> That is God's guidance; He guides by it whom He will of His servants; had they been idolaters, it would have failed them, the things they did. Those are they to whom We gave the Book, the Judgement, the Prophethood.

All Noah's people are annihilated by the Flood, except for his family (*ahl*), apart from one son and the wife who had betrayed him (Q 11:40 and 45–46; 21:76–77; 23:27; 37:76–77). Similarly, Lot's relatives, except for his traitor-wife, were the only ones spared the catastrophe visited upon the people (Q 54:33–35; 56:10) since his family was composed of those who had ' purified themselves' (*yataṭahharūn*) (Q 27:56). Abraham, a central figure in the Qur'ān, is the patriarch of the prophets of the Banū Isrā'īl. All the prophets and transmitters of Scriptures after him are in fact his direct descendants via Isaac and his grandson Jacob, thus forming an uninterrupted chain of Messengers and Guides (*imāms*)

(Q 2:124; 19:49–50; 29:27; 57:26). Addressing Sarah and speaking about Abraham's family, the angels say:

> What, dost thou marvel at God's command? The mercy of God and His blessings be upon you, O *Ahl al-Bayt*. (Q 11:76)[37]

Moreover:

> Yet We gave the people of Abraham the Book and the Wisdom, and We gave them a mighty kingdom (*mulkan ʿaẓīman*). (Q 4:54)

Moses is assisted in his prophetic mission by his brother Aaron who partakes with him in an intimate relationship with God (Q 20:29–32 and 36; 21:48–49; 25:35). The enigmatic *baqiyya*, a relic containing the divine *sakīna* and signs of divine investiture and royalty of the Banū Isrāʾīl, belongs to the family of the chosen brothers (Q 2:248). Similarly, David has Solomon, his son, inheritor and successor, as his assistant (Q 21:78; 27:16; 38:30). Zachariah, John's father, asks God for a divine son who would inherit the status of prophethood possessed by Jacob's family (Q 19:5–6). As for non-Israelite prophets, in this instance Shuʿayb from the

37. Regarding this phrase, 'Family of the Home' seems to me to be a more precise translation than the more conventional 'People of the House'. *Ahl* in Arabic, both in South Arabian as well as in Ugaritic, corresponds to the Accadian origin *ālu* (W. von Soden, *Akkadisches Handwörterbuch*, Wiesbaden, 1965) and to the Hebrew *ohêl*. The latter designates the nomad's tent (e.g. Genesis 13:5; 18:1; Isaiah 38:12) or the tent as sanctuary (Exodus 33:7; Numbers 11:24) and as Residence/Home (*mishkan*) of God (Psalms 15:1; 27:5) (cf. Gesenius-Buhl, *Hebräisches und aramäisches Handwörterbuch* [17th edn, Leiden, 1951], p. 95, col. 2). *Ahl*, place of residence, home, eventually came to designate those who live in this place, thus the family; it is the same term that according to the *Tāj al-ʿarūs*, gave us the term *āl* (family, descendants), with the letter *h* eliminated: *āl wa aṣluhu ahl ubdilat al-hāʾ hamza fa ṣārat a-a-l-tawālat hamzatān fa ubdilat al-thāniya alifan fa ṣāra āl* (al-Zabīdī, *Tāj al-ʿarūs*, under *āl*). As for the term *bayt*, whether it means a constructed building, a tent or a natural site, it designates a place of residence; 'home' evokes the latter meaning. I shall return to other semantic levels related to *bayt*.

people of Midian and Ṣāliḥ from the Thamūd, their families also play a vital role as protectors and disciples (Q 11:91 and 27:49).[38]

This eminent place accorded close relatives of preceding prophets could not have been left without any parallel with Muḥammad's immediate family. Some Qur'ānic passages are vague and indirect (Q 26:214, "*ashīrataka al-aqrabīn*'; Q42:23, '*al-mawadda fi'l-qurbā*'). Others certainly do refer to the family and blood relatives of the Prophet. These are verses relating to the distribution of a fifth of the spoils (*khums*) and a part of *fay'* – property of the infidels acquired without battle – to close relatives (*dhu'l-qurbā*) of the Prophet (Q 8:41 and 59:7). In the matter of the 'close relatives', practically all the exegetical and historiographical sources are in agreement in recognising the descendants of the brothers Hāshim and al-Muṭṭalib, the sons of Muḥammad's great grandfather, ʿAbd Manāf, to the exclusion of another two of his sons, namely ʿAbd Shams and Nawfal. According to many reports, these allocations compensated somewhat for the fact that Muḥammad's immediate relatives could not benefit from alms or charity (*ṣadaqa, zakāt*). The reason given for this interdiction is that the charity came from the people's 'impurities', whence the purifying function of giving charity. The status of purity associated with the Prophet's family was thus considered incompatible with receiving charity. As in the case of the purity of Lot's family, examined above, the Qur'ān also refers to the purity of Muḥammad's family:

> *O Ahl al-Bayt*, God only desires to put away from you abomination and to cleanse you. (Q 33:33)

38. Madelung, *The Succession*, pp. 8–12. For discussions regarding the term *baqiyya*, cf. R. Paret, 'Die Bedeutung des Wortes *baqīya* im Koran', in *Alttestamentliche Studien Friedrich Nötscher zum 60. Geburtstag* (Bonn, 1950), pp. 168–171; A. Spitaler, 'Was bedeutet *baqīja* im Koran?', in *Westöstliche Abhandlungen Rudolf Tschudi zum 70. Geburtstag* (Wiesbaden, 1954), pp. 137–146.

The spiritual and religious importance of Muḥammad's family is equally noted in the famous verse of the Ordeal, *āyat al-mubāhala* (Q 3:61). Just as the Qur'ān constantly establishes parallels between Muḥammad and previous prophets, in terms of his prophetic mission, the fierce resistance of his people and, finally, his victory thanks to God's support, so the similar status of Muḥammad's family and families of past prophets regarding spiritual and temporal heritage seems obvious. Admittedly, according to the dogma of the 'seal of prophecy' Muḥammad's inheritor could not lay claim to prophethood, however, it is just as true that among elements of the prophetic heritage bequeathed by the Envoys of God to their close relatives, the Qur'ān includes sovereignty (*mulk*), authority (*ḥukm*), wisdom (*ḥikma*), Scriptures (*kitāb*) and the imamate. Given this Qur'ānic evidence, it seems to me that W. Madelung is right to conclude that the Qur'ān advises consultation (*shūrā*) in certain cases but never for what bears upon the succession of prophets.[39]

I will be returning to many of these points. Here I would like to note that, given his privileged relationship with the Prophet, ʿAlī would surely not have missed the opportunity to point to this Qur'ānic evidence in order to legitimise his declarations. In his *Ṭabaqāt*, Ibn Saʿd (d. 230/845) – an author who could hardly be suspected of pro-ʿAlid sympathies – recounts a report that seems especially telling in this regard. In a chapter devoted to 'the heritage of the Messenger of God and what he leaves behind' (*dhikr mīrāth rasūli'llāh wa mā taraka*), as derived from ʿAbbās b. ʿAbd Allāh b. Maʿbad, grandson of al-ʿAbbās b. ʿAbd al-Muṭṭalib, Ibn Saʿd reports that Fāṭima and al-ʿAbbās in the company of ʿAlī approached the elected caliph, Abū Bakr, to ask him for their rightful share of Muḥammad's heritage. Abū Bakr is said to have replied:

39. Madelung, *The Succession*, pp. 12–18.

'The Messenger of God said: "We [the prophets] do not leave behind an inheritance; all that we leave behind is charity." And I am now in charge of all that the Messenger of God left behind.'

Citing the Qur'ān, ʿAlī is said to have replied:

'"Solomon inherited from David" (Q 27:16) and [invoking God when asking Him for a son] Zachariah says: "So give me, from Thee, a kinsman who shall be my inheritor of the House of Jacob" (Q 19:6).'

Abū Bakr: 'By God, surely you know what I know.'

ʿAlī: 'It is the Book of God that speaks here.' After this there was silence and then they parted.[40]

This legitimation by the Qur'ān was certainly a factor in the support that (according to the historiographers) the majority of the Qur'ān reciters (*qurrā'*) gave to ʿAlī at the time of his conflict with Muʿāwiya, especially before the start of the battle of Ṣiffīn and the ensuing arbitration.[41] However, in this early period of Islam, legitimation by the Qur'ān could definitely not guarantee unanimous agreement. The new religion would require several generations of assimilation to profoundly affect people's outlook and to establish itself in their hearts before it could become the kind of social phenomenon capable of shaping minds. To be credible during this early period, a speech or event had to be rooted in ancient, ancestral beliefs and to be supported by the tribal culture of Arab paganism if it were to resonate among recently converted Muslims.

The pre-Islamic basis

For more than a century, a number of eminent Orientalists and specialists in Arabic and Islamic studies have brought to light

40. Ibn Saʿd, *Ṭabaqāt*, vol. 2, p. 315. I. Hrbek, stressing among other things the incompatability of the *ḥadīth* cited by Abū Bakr with the spirit and letter of the Qur'ān, considers it apocryphal, 'Muḥammads Nachlass und die Aliden', *Archiv Orientální*, 18 (1950), pp. 143–149; Madelung, *The Succession*, pp. 360–361.

41. Cf. Minqarī, *Waqʿat Ṣiffīn*, pp. 88ff.; al-Ṭabarī, ed. de Goeje, series 1, pp. 3385–3386.

and examined the remarkable continuity between the pre-Islamic period and the earliest days of Islam with regard to institutions, beliefs and rituals. These scholars include J. Wellhausen and I. Goldziher and the circle responsible for 'From Jāhiliyya to Islam' gathered around M. J. Kister and his colleagues and students, M. Lecker, U. Rubin, H. Busse and others, not to mention J. Henninger, R. B. Serjeant, T. Fahd, A. F. L. Beeston and J. Chelhod, and more recently E. Conte and J. Chabbi. Many of these have been led to study the system of family relations be it in its secular and sacred dimensions or its natural and supernatural aspects.

The outdated thesis presented by H. Lammens in *Le berceau de l'Islam*, according to which hereditary power and dynastic rulers were completely unknown if not utterly detested by the Arabs does not seem tenable any more.[42] Ever since the monumental study by E. Tyan, *Institutions du droit public Musulman*, it has been established that though tribal secular leadership was not actually always hereditary religious leadership and theocratic functions depended directly on the importance of a noble lineage, *nasab*, and that this concept was particularly upheld in the tribe of Quraysh.[43] Even W. M. Watt, who in his biography of Muḥammad at times seem to concur closely with the opinion held by Lammens,[44] concedes in his *Islamic Political Thought*, that the Arabs regularly elected their leaders from specific families.[45] In this regard, the studies by R. B. Serjeant seem decisive. Over the course of a number of publications, the author establishes most convincingly that Muḥammad's rapid success and the ultimate ease he experienced in rallying of a large number of tribes to his cause, were essentially due to the fact that he belonged to a Meccan and Qurashī family; an aristocratic and theocratic family

42. H. Lammens, *Le berceau de l'Islam: l'Arabie occidentale à la veille de l'Hégire* (Rome, 1914), p. 314 et passim.

43. E. Tyan, *Institutions du droit public Musulman* (Paris, 1954–1956), vol. 1, pp. 97ff., 114ff.

44. W. M. Watt, *Muhammad: Prophet and Statesman* (Oxford, 1961), esp. pp. 35–36.

45. W. M. Watt, *Islamic Political Thought* (Edinburgh, 1968), p. 31.

in which religious functions, as was the case throughout Arabia, were hereditary. Were he not part of this lineage, which the English scholar terms 'The Holy Family', Muḥammad would have had no credibility with other tribes.[46]

Well before Muḥammad's time, the Quraysh were held to be a tribe that benefitted from divine protection due to its sacred status as *ahl al-ḥaram*, the People of the Meccan Sanctuary and the area surrounding it. According to U. Rubin, early Muslim exegesis even maintained traces of this ancient belief.[47] Muḥammad's ancestor Quṣayy seems to have been the guardian and leader of the sanctuary; from then on, the different clans of his direct descendants inherited various responsibilities for the ritual functions relating to the pilgrimage: guarding the Kaʿba (*ḥijāba*), providing potable water (*siqāya*), food (*rifāda*) and banners (*liwāʾ*) as well as the privilege of *nadwa*, a term vaguely designating either the council of tribal leadership or the meeting place for the resolution of inter-tribal differences.[48] One finds traces of the hereditary sacred functions of Muḥammad's ancestors in poems by the Prophet's bard, Ḥassān b. Thābit (d. 54/674).[49] Muḥammad himself is said to have designated the 'Holy Family' of the Quraysh as consisting of the descendants of al-Muṭṭalib and those of his brother, Hāshim, the great grandfather of the Prophet (see the

---

46. R. B. Serjeant, 'The Saiyids of Ḥaḍramawt', *An Inaugural Lecture at the School of Oriental and African Studies*, 1956 (London, 1957), pp. 3–29; R. B. Serjeant, '*Ḥaram* and *ḥawṭah*, the Sacred Enclave in Arabia', pp. 41–58; R. B. Serjeant, 'The "Constitution" of Medina', pp. 3–16; R. B. Sergeant, 'The *Sunnah Jāmiʿah*, Pacts with the Yathrib Jews, and the *taḥrīm* of Yathrib: Analysis and Translation of the Documents Comprised in the So-called "Constitution of Medina"', *BSOAS*, 41 (1978), pp. 1–42 (rpr. in *Studies in Arabian History and Civilisation*, articles VIII, III, V and VI).

47. U. Rubin, 'The *īlāf* of Quraysh. A Study of Sūra CVI', *Arabica*, 31–32 (1984), pp. 165–188.

48. R. B. Serjeant, '*Ḥaram* and *ḥawṭah*', pp. 53ff. U. Rubin, 'The Kaʿba: Aspects of Its Ritual Functions and Position in Pre-Islamic and Early Islamic times', *JSAI*, 8 (1986), pp. 97–131.

49. Ḥassān ibn Thābit, *Diwan*, ed. W. N. ʿArafat (London, 1971), vol. 1, p. 109.

genealogical tree above). The canonical works of *ḥadīth* leave no doubt about this by identifying the 'near kin' (*dhu'l-qurbā*) mentioned by the Qur'ān as those that receive the *khums* and *fay'*; the receipt of alms is forbidden to them as descendants of al-Muṭṭalib and even more often of Hāshim.[50] Moreover, we know that ever since pre-Islamic times the Banū'l-Muṭṭalib and the Banū Hāshim were strongly bound to each other by the *ḥilf al-fuḍūl*.[51]

In this connection, the tradition reported by Abū Dāwūd and al-Maqrīzī, on the authority of al-Zuhrī, Saʿīd b. al-Musayyib and Jubayr b. Muṭʿim, is the most significant: after the victory at Khaybar, the Prophet divided the share of the close relatives (*sahm dhi'l-qurbā*) between the Banū Hāshim and the Banū'l-Muṭṭalib, thus excluding the Banū Nawfal and the Banū ʿAbd Shams (Nawfal and ʿAbd Shams are two other brothers of Muṭṭalib and Hāshim). So, the reporter Jubayr b. Muṭʿim (a descendant of Nawfal), and ʿUthmān b. ʿAffān (the future third caliph, descendant of ʿAbd Shams) protest to Muḥammad saying:

> Messenger of God, because of the place God has accorded you amongst them, we do not deny the excellence of the Banū Hāshim. But what of our brothers, the Banū'l-Muṭṭalib? You have given them a share and you have excluded us while our relationship to you is the same as theirs.

---

50. Cf. A. J. Wensinck, *Handbook of Early Muhammadan Tradition* (Leiden, 1927), p. 266. On the part reserved for the Banū Hāshim in the *dīwān* by ʿUmar see Ibn Saʿd, *Ṭabaqāt*, vol. 3, pp. 294ff., completed in al-Balādhurī, *Futūḥ al-buldān*, ed. M. J. de Goeje (Leiden, 1866), series 1, pp. 448ff. On *ʿaṭā'* reserved for the Banū Hāshim see al-Zubayr b. Bakkār, *Jamharat nasab Quraysh*, ed. M. M. Shākir (Cairo, 1381/1961), p. 111. For an exclusively ʿAbbasid appropriation of these facts, refer to Abū Yūsuf, *Kitāb al-kharāj*, ed. I. ʿAbbās (Beirut and London, 1985), pp. 102–104, 142ff.

51. W. M. Watt, *Muḥammad at Mecca* (Oxford, 1953), pp. 6–7; C. Pellat, 'Ḥilf al-fuḍūl', *EI2*.

Muḥammad replies:

> We [the Banū Hāshim] and the Banū'l-Muṭṭalib have never been separated, neither during the *Jāhiliyya* nor in Islam. We and they are one and the same.[52]

The saintliness of the Banū Hāshim becomes evident from the subtle analyses of the *Hāshimiyyāt*, a collection of poems by al-Kumayt b. Zayd al-Asadī al-Kūfī (d. 126/743),[53] undertaken by T. Nagel, M. Sharon and especially by W. Madelung in his monograph dedicated to this work.[54] It seems that among the descendants of Hāshim, Muḥammad recognised his own family as *the* 'Holy Family' par excellence.[55] Muḥammad would have designated this 'Holy Family' by the expression *ahl baytī*, surely having in mind the Qur'ānic occurrences of the expression *ahl al-bayt* that we have examined above. Apart from the purity that the Qur'ān ascribes to Muḥammad's *ahl al-bayt* (Q 33:33), the sacred dimension linked to the term *bayt* must certainly have played a role as well. Indeed, the

52. Abū Dāwūd, *Sunan*, ed. M. M. ʿAbd al-Ḥamīd, 4 vols (Cairo, n.d.), ch. 19, no. 51; al-Maqrīzī, *al-Nizāʿ wa'l-takhāṣum fī mā bayna banī Umayya wa banī Hāshim*, ed. Ḥ. Mu'nis (Cairo, 1984), p. 60 (slightly different and shorter version).

53. Ed. J. Horovitz, *Die Hāšimijjāt des Kumait* (Leiden, 1904; Arabic text reprinted in Qumm, n.d. [ca. 1970]).

54. T. Nagel, *Untersuchungen zur Entstehung des Abbasidischen Kalifats* (Bonn, 1972), pp. 70ff. and pp. 79ff.; M. Sharon, *Black Banners from the East* (Leiden and Jerusalem, 1983), pp. 76ff.; W. Madelung, 'The Hāshimiyyāt of al-Kumayt and Hāshimi Shiʿism', *SI*, 70 (1990), pp. 5–26.

55. In this context, in terms of methodology, traditions concerning 'monotheism', signs of election and the saintliness of the ancestors and close relatives of the Prophet, specifically his grandfather ʿAbd al-Muṭṭalib, his father ʿAbd Allāh and his paternal uncle Abū Ṭālib (ʿAlī's father who adopted and raised Muḥammad after the death of ʿAbd Allāh) cannot be exploited here due to their strong Islamic connotations that in turn prove their later date. Regarding these traditions and the historical problems they pose, see e.g. T. Fahd, *La divination arabe* (Strasbourg, 1971; 2nd edn, Paris, 1987), pp. 82ff. and pp. 260ff.; U. Rubin, 'Prophets and Progenitors in Early Shīʿa Tradition', *JSAI*, 1 (1979); C. Gilliot, 'Muqātil, grand exégète, traditionniste et théologien maudit', *JA*, 279/1–2 (1991), pp. 68–70; M. A. Amir-Moezzi, *Le Guide divin*, pp. 103–104 and note 204 (*Divine Guide*, p. 40); Chabbi, *Le Seigneur des tribus*, pp. 166ff.

religious nature of the vocable, originating from the antique heritage of Semitic languages in which it means temple, sanctuary or a supernatural being's place of residence, is again clearly evident in the ways that the Qurʾān employs the term; for example, in the manner that it designates the Kaʿba or in *al-bayt al-maʿmūr* and in the expression *rabb al-bayt* in the early suras, 105, *al-Fīl* and 106, *Quraysh*.[56]

It is not a matter of determining here the full meaning that Muḥammad attributed to the expression *ahl al-bayt*, at one and the same time of religious, sacred and political import.[57] A great many studies have been dedicated to this, analysing both the diverse classical exegeses of the expression and the material which is of a historical and philological nature: from H. Lammens and R. Strothmann who see in it only an allusion to the Prophet's wives[58] and R. Paret, for whom the *ahl al-bayt* designates adherents of the

56. In Accadian, the term *bīt* designates the temple as a whole, or rooms of which it is made up (W. von Soden, *AHW*); the same evolution is encountered in Hebrew, as well as in Syriac and Arabic. In parallel with its profane, or secular, meaning of 'residence', the religious nature of the term is more specifically emphasised when it is preceded by an article such as *ha-b-baït* in Hebrew (Micah 3:12; Haggai 1:8) (Gesenius-Buhl, *Hebräisches*, pp. 95–98) or *al-bayt* in Arabic (e.g. Q 2:125, 127 etc.). Apparently, during the stage of nomadism, among the Arabs as well as the Hebrews, *bayt* was often followed by the word *il/el* (divinity, supernatural entity or protector), which gives us *batīl/Bêt-El* (whence 'Betyl'). This composite form originally designated the mobile sanctuary in which the symbols and objects required for worship were held, eventually itself becoming the symbol and/or object of worship. Cf. H. Lammens, 'Le culte des Bétyles et les processions religieuses chez les Arabes préislamites', *BIFAO*, 17 (1919–1920), pp. 39–101; T. Fahd, *Le Panthéon de l'Arabie Centrale à la veille de l'Hégire* (Paris, 1968), ch. 1; J. Chabbi, *Le Seigneur des tribus*, see index under '*bayt*', '*beth*', '*bétyle*'. Regarding the meaning of the word in south-Arabia see A. F. L. Beeston, 'The So-called Harlots of Ḥaḍramawt', *Oriens*, 5 (1952), pp. 21ff., 'Kingship in Ancient South-Arabia', *JESHO*, 15 (1972), pp. 251ff.

57. M. Sharon interprets the expression, in a pre-Islamic context, as 'the leading noble families' among tribes, and more exclusively the tribe of the Quraysh; see his '*Ahl al-Bayt* – People of the House', *JSAI*, 8 (1986), pp. 169–184, respectively pp. 183 and 179.

58. Especially in Q 33:33; H. Lammens, *Fāṭima et les filles de Mahomet* (Rome, 1912), p. 97 et passim; R. Strothmann, *Das Staatsrecht der Zaiditen* (Strasbourg, 1912), pp. 19ff.

cult of the Kaʿba,[59] to the meticulously prepared monographs by M. Sharon on the various connotations depending on changing times as well as religious and political trends;[60] studies which seem to me to be decisive regarding certain points and to which I will have the opportunity to return and also considering W. Madelung, according to whom the expression essentially designates the descendants of Hāshim in general.[61] Still, it is useful to recall, as I. Goldziher so aptly demonstrated, that, in spite of the benefit that the ʿAlids were to gain from it, the majority opinion had very early on identified Muḥammad's *ahl al-bayt* with the *ahl al-kisāʾ*, namely Fāṭima, ʿAlī, al-Ḥasan and al-Ḥusayn.[62] As an especially telling example, almost all of the numerous early exegeses of verse 33:33, regarding the purity of Muḥammad's *ahl al-bayt*, as reported by al-Ṭabarī in his monumental Qurʾānic commentary, lean in this direction.[63] Whatever the case may be, in the context of the problem which now preoccupies us, frankly it seems unthinkable that ʿAlī would not have claimed to belong to the Prophet's *ahl al-bayt*. He would have also laid claim exclusively for himself and his progeny to those things in the prophetic heritage concerned with spiritual and temporal matters, thus making of them a veritable collection of articles of faith called *dīn ʿAlī*.[64]

---

59. Especially in Q 11:73 and 33:33; cf. his article 'Der Plan einer neuen, leicht kommentierten Koranübersetzung', in Paret (ed.), *Orientalistische Studien Enno Littmann zu seinem 60. Geburtstag* (Leiden 1935), pp. 121–130, esp. pp. 127f.

60. '*Ahl al-Bayt* – People of the House'; 'The Umayyads as *ahl al-bayt*', *JSAI*, 14 (1991), pp. 115–152; see also his article, 'The Development of the Debate around the Legitimacy of Authority in Early Islam', *JSAI*, 5 (1984), pp. 121–142.

61. 'The *Hāshimiyyāt* of al-Kumayt', esp. pp. 15, 21, 24–25.

62. I. Goldziher, *Muslim Studies*, ed. S. M. Stern, vol. 2 (London, 1971), pp. 103ff.; see also sources noted by M. Sharon, '*Ahl al-Bayt* – People of the House', pp. 172–173.

63. Al-Ṭabarī, *Jāmiʿ al-bayān*, ed. M. M. Shākir and A. M. Shākir (Cairo, 1373–1388/1955–1969), vol. 22, pp. 5–7.

64. In his long letter to Muʿāwiya, reported by several historiographers (Minqarī, al-Balādhurī, al-Ṭabarī) and analysed by Madelung (*The Succession*, pp. 212ff.), ʿAlī seems to have identified the *ahl al-bayt* with the Banū Hāshim

ʿAlī is actually related to Muḥammad by the two principal aspects of Arab familial ties (*qarāba*), namely *nasab* and *muṣāhara*. Terms difficult to render in translation, the first conveys the sense of genealogy, provenance or paternal lineage, ties by blood or by alliance, noble birth and affinity. The second, as rich in meaning as the first, evokes in its original sense the idea of fusing and thus affinity, relationship through women, an alliance by marriage. Thus, in general, *nasab* refers to a relationship by blood and *muṣāhara* to a link or alliance by marriage.[65] ʿAlī was Muḥammad's cousin, the son of his paternal uncle, one of the noblest relationships characterising *nasab* according to the tribal conception.[66] Once he became the Prophet's son-in-law, he was also related by *muṣāhara*, thus fulfilling with regard to the latter, the condition of *wālī*, that is, relative by blood and/or by alliance;[67] the significance this term was to acquire later in Shiʿism is well known.

Other facts pertaining to ancestral beliefs about the supranatural aspects of relationships also seem to have played a role in the establishment of 'the religion of ʿAlī'. In the context of our

---

and Banū'l-Muṭṭalib; however, concerning succession to the Prophet, he would most certainly have thought of himself and his sons, al-Ḥasan and al-Ḥusayn.

65. See P. Bonte, E. Conte, C. Hames and A. W. Ould Cheikh, *Al-Ansāb. La quēte des origines* (Paris, 1991), pp. 65ff. The third aspect of the *qarāba* is the *riḍāʿa* (adoption by milk); see ibid., pp. 73ff. For a more detailed analysis, see J. Cuisenier and A. Miquel, 'La terminologie arabe de la parenté. Analyse sémantique et analyse componentielle', *L'Homme*, 5/3–4 (1965), pp. 15–79. In the Qur'ān, these two terms are inseparably linked in verse 25:54: 'And it is He who created of water a mortal, and made him kindred of *blood* and *marriage* (*fa jaʿalahu nasaban wa ṣihran*)'. E. Conte proposes 'relatives (by blood ties) and allies (by virtue of marriage or women)', see *Al-Ansāb. La quête des origines*, p. 66.

66. At the moment when the tribe is defined as an organic group of relatives descended from the same lineage – *awlād al-ʿamm*; on this important notion, studies by the earliest major Arabic and Islamic scholars are still the most reliable reference works; see for example I. Goldziher, 'Polyandry and Exogamy among the Arabs', *The Academy*, 13/26 (1880); J. Wellhausen, 'Die Ehe bei den Arabern', *Nachrichten von der Königlichen Gesellschaft und der Georg-Augustus-Universität zu Göttingen*, 11 (1893); O. Proksch, *Über die Blutrache bei den vorislamischen Arabern und Mohammeds Stellung zu ihr* (Leipzig, 1899), esp. pp. 33ff.

67. Cf. Chabbi, *Le Seigneur des tribus*, p. 654.

subject, these beliefs seem inextricably linked to certain aspects of Muḥammad's personality as perceived by certain of his contemporaries.[68] Muḥammad could have truly possessed a supranatural aura in their eyes. T. Fahd has shown the continuity of ancient magic-related personas such as the 'soothsayer' (*kāhin*), the 'poet' (*shāʿir*), the clairvoyant (*ʿarrāf*), and so forth alongside the prophetic figure of Muḥammad: one finds here and there, obviously with different combinations and justifications, communication with supernatural beings, different kinds of divination, inspirations and oracles, healing powers, use of a particular language, knowledge of hidden things, power over objects and so forth. By means of in-depth analyses, this great scholar has, in my view, demonstrated to what extent ancient Arab beliefs and prophethood encountered one another and influenced each other.[69] According to numerous passages in the Qur'ān, Muḥammad was compared by his adversaries to *kāhin*s, *sāḥir*s and *shāʿir*s (Q 37:36; 52:29; 59:42). He was often accused of being possessed or inspired by *jinn*s (expressions *majnūn* or *mā bihi … min jinna*). J. Chabbi argues that this was a means by which the Prophet's adversaries sought to trivialise his actions, that is to say to portray him as a kind of magical character, not in a relationship with God but with different kinds of 'genies', characters familiar to Arabia from time immemorial.[70]

Linked to the famous question of Muḥammad's human 'informants', relentlessly upheld by his adversaries, Hūd b.

68. On this point of view, now consult U. Rubin, *The Eye of the Beholder. The Life of Muḥammad as Viewed by the Early Muslims* (Princeton, 1995).

69. Fahd, *La divination arabe*, pp. 63ff. ('Divination et prophétie'), pp. 88ff. ('Prophète et divin') and p. 263, passim; see also T. Fahd, 'Le monde du sorcier en Islam', in *Le monde du sorcier* (Paris, 1966), pp. 155–204. On the difficulty in translating the term *kāhin* (priest – soothsayer – oracle – doctor), see *La divination arabe*, pp. 94f. Regarding *shāʿir* ('poet'), etymologically 'he who knows' and has theurgic knowledge, see also F. Rosenthal, *Knowledge Triumphant: The Concept of Knowledge in Medieval Islam* (Leiden, 1971), pp. 12–13.

70. *Le Seigneur des tribus*, pp. 182–183 and pp. 527–529.

Muḥkim/Muḥakkam (second half of third/ninth century) reports a saying by al-Ḥasan al-Baṣrī (d. 110/728), according to which one of these presumed informants was a servant of Ibn al-Ḥaḍramī, the famous soothsayer of the age of the *jāhiliyya*.[71] In another report, reproduced by al-Baghawī (d. 516/1122), the same al-Ḥasan speaks of ʿUbayd b. al-Khaḍir, an Ethiopian soothsayer.[72] According to Ibn al-Athīr, before his conversion to Islam, ʿUmar b. al-Khaṭṭāb regarded the Prophet as a *kāhin* and a *shāʿir*.[73] Finally, according to a report by Ibn Saʿd, not a supporter of the ʿAlid cause, at the beginning, Muḥammad himself was concerned about being a soothsayer.[74]

We know that in a number of ancient belief systems, body fluids such as blood, sperm, saliva, milk and sweat, are considered to be agents for thaumaturgic transmission; they can bear and transmit beneficial or harmful elements, faculties, virtues or spiritual influences from the bearer to another, more specifically, by heredity, to their descendants.[75] The Arabs, too, held these kinds of beliefs. The *kāhin* was believed to have the power to master and direct consciously and wilfully what he transmitted by his bodily fluids.[76] Muḥammad appears to have been

---

71. Hūd b. Muḥkim/Muḥakkam al-Ḥawwārī, *Tafsīr*, ed. B. Sharīfī (Beirut, 1990), vol. 2, p. 389.

72. Abū Muḥammad al-Baghawī, *Tafsīr al-Baghawī al-musammā bi-Maʿālim al-tanzīl*, Ḥ. ʿA. al-ʿAkk and M. Sawār (Beirut, 1992), vol. 3, p. 361. Regarding the Prophet's 'informants', now consult C. Gilliot, 'Les "informateurs" juifs et chrétiens de Muḥammad', *JSAI*, 22 (1998), pp. 84–126, a study which revisits and very usefully supplements the preceding works by A. Sprenger and T. Nöldeke (respectively: *Das Leben und die Lehre des Moḥammad*, 2 vols, [Berlin, 1861–1862], and 'Hatte Muḥammad christliche Lehrer?', *ZDMG*, 12, [1858], pp. 699–708).

73. *Usd al-ghāba*, ed. M. Fāyiḍ et al. (Cairo, 1963–1972), vol. 4, p. 74.

74. Ibn Saʿd, *Ṭabaqāt*, 1/1, p. 129.

75. Cf. e.g. A. van Gennep, *Les rites de passage* (Paris, 1909), pp. 41ff.

76. T. Witton Davies, *Magic, Divination and Demonology* (London, 1933; rpr. Baghdad, n.d. [ca. 1960]), pp. 70ff.; E. O. James, *The Nature and Function of Priesthood* (London, 1955), pp. 87ff.; J. Henninger, *La société bédouine ancienne* (Rome, 1959), index; J. Chelhod, *Les structures du sacré chez les arabes* (Paris, 1986), pp. 189f.

associated with this conception in a number of reports regarding him, both directly and allusively, in which the subject of different organic fluids is discussed.

The exchange of blood made two men brothers or allied relatives.[77] J. Wellhausen is right to compare the result of Arab blood pacts with *Verbrüderung* and *adoptio in fratres*.[78] In spite of the great discretion of the Islamic sources, it seems certain that rituals of 'the pact of chosen brotherhood' (*muʾākhāt*), practised twice by the Prophet upon his arrival in Medina, were accompanied by the exchange of blood. A practice, originating according to L. Caetani, from the ancient Arabic *ḥilf*,[79] and already a subject of the pre-Islamic poetry of al-Aʿshā Maymūn,[80] it carried infinitely more weight than Qurʾānic and/or Islamic arguments in winning over the Anṣār in Medina. According to a report given by Ibn Hishām, on the occasion of the second meeting in ʿAqaba, faced with the reluctance of the Medinans to conclude a pact with him, Muḥammad declares:

> Your blood is mine. I am one of you and you are mine. Your enemies are my enemies; your friends, my friends. Choose twelve leaders among you in order to represent you in the ritual of the oath (*ḥilf*).[81]

---

77. W. Robertson Smith, *Kinship and Marriage in Early Arabia* (2nd edn, Cambridge, 1903), pp. 50f. and his *Lectures on the Religion of the Semites* (2nd edn, Edinburgh, 1914), pp. 314ff., 479ff.

78. *Reste arabischen Heidentums* (Berlin and Leipzig, 1884), pp. 124, 127–128.

79. *Annali dell'Islam*, vol. 1, p. 408.

80. 'They swear by darkly intense black blood: we never wish to separate,' cited by J. Wellhausen, *Reste arabischen Heidentums* p. 128, and reported by E. Conte, 'Entrer dans le sang. Perceptions arabes des origines', in *Al-Ansāb. La quête des origines*, p. 92.

81. Ibn Hishām, *al-Sīra al-nabawiyya*, ed. M. Saqqā, I. Abyārī and ʿA. Shalabī (2nd edn, Cairo, 1955), vol. 1, pp. 446 and 454; al-Ṭabarī, de Goeje, series 1, pp. 1,220–1,221.

During the battle of Ḥunayn in the year 8/630, in the midst of the general disarray of Muslim victims when ambushed by the Hawāzin, the Prophet asks his uncle ʿAbbās b. ʿAbd al-Muṭṭalib to use his booming voice to remind the troops of bonds sealed by blood.[82] The different episodes narrated in Ibn Hishām's account demonstrate that this kind of speech, rooted in ancient culture, was more favourably received by the Arabs than the prophetic statements made by Muḥammad.[83] The second pact of brotherhood is of even more interest to us. This, of course, is the ritual of the *muʾākhāt*, promoted by Muḥammad (according to Ibn Ḥabīb)[84] among the Muslims of Mecca, from the Meccan period onwards; or (according to Ibn Hishām)[85] upon his arrival in Medina among both the Meccans and Medinans.

During the 'twinning' ritual, Muḥammad chose ʿAlī as his brother. What is remarkable is that according to Ibn Ḥabīb the *muʾākhāt*, made on 'the basis of law (?) and sharing' (*ʿalāʾl-ḥaqq waʾl-muʾāsāt*) implied that upon the death of either individual, the other, his 'brother', had priority as inheritor,[86] which seems authentic, since in verses 4:33, 8:75 and especially 33:6, the Qurʾān seems to call this institution into question vigorously by stressing the priority of a relationship over the pact of brotherhood.[87] On the basis of, among others, Roman legal sources concerning the governing of the Bedouin population in Syria during the fifth century AD and studied by Bruns and Sachau (once more proving this to be an age-old practice), E. Conte concludes that the *muʾākhāt*, sealed by blood, made 'twin brothers' of close relatives

82. Ibn Hishām, *Sīra*, vol. 2, pp. 442–443.

83. Cf. on this subject, W. Atallah, 'Les survivances préislamiques chez le Prophète et ses Compagnons', *Arabica*, 24/3 (1977), pp. 299–310.

84. *Kitāb al-muḥabbar*, ed. I. Lichtenstaedter (Hyderabad, 1942), pp. 70ff.

85. Ibn Hishām, *Sīra*, vol. 1, pp. 344–346; also, Serjeant, 'The "Constitution" of Medina', p. 6.

86. Ibn Ḥabīb, *Kitāb al-muḥabbar*, p. 71.

87. See also W. M. Watt, 'Muʾākhāt', *EI2*; Conte, 'Entrer dans le sang. Perceptions arabes des origines', pp. 93–99.

(*qarāʾib*), who were classified as first cousins (*ibnāʾl-ʿamm*) and as a consequence inheritors of the male lineage (*ʿaṣaba*); by establishing a relationship, the 'twinning' pact created a common filiation between 'brothers';[88] which is to say that the *muʾākhāt* itself enabled ʿAlī to claim the prophetic heritage; this may explain the almost complete silence of non-Shiʿi sources on this episode in the life of Muḥammad, a rather curious silence about one of the founding acts of the Muslim community in Medina.[89]

There is more. For the Arabs, just like nobility, *kahāna* is hereditary. The qualities of the *kāhin* or nobles are transmitted by various means, including the sperm of the father.[90] In pre-Islamic Arabia, in order to bear children of distinguished pedigree, the Bedouins went so far as to 'lend' their wives to nobles whose sperm was highly praised.[91] In terms of the qualities of saintliness, Islamic sources speak repeatedly about the power of transmission of the seminal substance from Muḥammad's ancestors, manifested by the 'Light' and symbolised by the *ṣulb* (kidney, loins), an organ regarded as the repository of the semen.[92] Passing via the uterus (*raḥim*) of the woman, the repository for her 'seed', the man's semen forms the milk in the mother's breast, which in turn enables the transmission of the father's qualities to his child; whence the inseparable link between sperm and milk that one finds in expressions such as 'milk is from man'

88. Conte, 'Entrer dans le sang. Perceptions arabes des origines', p. 94.

89. Regarding the total silence of the sources, see D. Santillana, *Istituzioni di diritto musulmano malichita con riguardo anche al sistema sciafiita* (Rome, 1938), vol. 1, p. 196, note 8; consult also the 'skeletal' bibliography of the article 'Muʾākhāt' by W. M. Watt.

90. For example Fahd, *La divination arabe*, pp. 23ff.

91. On this practice called *iktisāb*, i.e. 'obtaining' (of the seminal substance and thus noble race), see al-Alūsī, *Bulūgh al-arab fī maʿrifat aḥwāl al-ʿarab* (Cairo, 1928), vol. 2, p. 4. The custom still designated by the terms *iktisāb* or *kasb*, is to this day practised among some Yemeni tribes, cf. J. Chelhod, 'Du nouveau à propos du "matriarcat" arabe', *Arabica*, 28/1 (1981), p. 82.

92. For sources and studies on this subject see Amir-Moezzi, *Guide divin*, see index under '*ṣulb*', '*aṣlāb*' and '*nūr*'.

(*al-laban min al-marʾ*), 'the reproductive milk' (*laban al-faḥl*) or 'the unique sperm' (*liqāḥ wāḥid*) that designate both the man's seminal fluid as well as the woman's milk.[93] The father's sperm provides the child's flesh and blood (*dam wa laḥm*); the mother gives form to this matter and completes the formation of the child by her milk, which is compared to the father's sperm.[94] Issuing from the same Hāshimid seed as the Prophet and married to Fāṭima, ʿAlī also became the father of the male descendants of Muḥammad. And Fāṭima, whose most common title among the Shiʿis is 'the Confluence of two Lights' (*majmaʿ al-nūrayn*),[95] being born from Muḥammad's seed and the recipient of ʿAlī's, becomes the other factor in the transmission of prophetic virtues. ʿAlī seems to have been fully convinced of these laws.

According to a report by al-Ṭabarī, during his conflict with Muʿāwiya, just before the arbitration of Ṣiffīn, at the moment in Kūfa when part of his army had dispersed, ʿAlī at one point decided to engage in battle and to fight to the death if necessary. However, upon seeing al-Ḥasan and al-Ḥusayn he realised that if they were to perish, the Muslims would be entirely deprived of descendants of the Prophet. The conclusion one draws from al-Ṭabarī's account is that this was the main reason that led ʿAlī put a halt to the campaign.[96] As reported by al-Maqrīzī, some Muslims held the opinion that if ʿAlī had directly succeeded the Prophet, as the father of al-Ḥasan and al-Ḥusayn, people would have concluded that the caliphate was a hereditary sovereignty (*mulk mutawārath*). This seems historically plausible.[97]

---

93. J. Schacht, *The Origins of Muhammadan Jurisprudence* (Oxford, 1950), p. 194 and n. 4; S. Altorki, 'Milk-Kinship in Arab Society: An Unexplored Problem in the Ethnography of Marriage', *Ethnology*, 19 (1980), pp. 233–244, esp. 234ff.

94. P. Bonte, 'Egalité et hiérarchie dans une tribu maure', in *Al-Ansāb. La quête des origines*, p. 158 et passim.

95. See al-Ṭurayḥī, Fakhr al-Dīn, *Majmaʿ al-baḥrayn wa maṭlaʿ al-nayyirayn* (Tehran, 1321/1903), index under '*majmaʿ al-nūrayn*'.

96. Al-Ṭabarī, ed. de Goeje, series 1, pp. 3,346–3,347.

97. *Al-Nizāʿ wa'l-takhāṣum*, p. 92.

Saliva is also considered a factor in thaumaturgic transmission. The giving of saliva is the famous practice known as *taḥnīk*, termed 'sputation' by C. Gilliot.[98] However, according to Arab lexicographers, Ibn Manẓūr or al-Zabīdī for example, the verbal form means 'to rub the roof of the mouth' when accompanied with a complementary noun (*ḥannaka bi-* e.g. *ḥannakahu bi-tamratin*, rub the roof of another's mouth with a [crushed] date, *ḥannakahu bi'l-iṣbiʿ*, with a finger). Employed without a complement, it means to put one's saliva in someone's mouth (*ḥannaka Zaydun ʿAmran*, lit.: with his saliva, Zayd rubs the roof of ʿAmr's mouth); in the latter instance, the meaning may be clarified by the addition of the word, 'saliva' (*ḥannakahu bi-rīqihi*).[99] Saliva can protect, heal, transmit virtues or skills, but also destroy or humiliate. Depending on the intention of one who uses it, it may be an initiation, a blessing, a medicament or a malign act.[100] Both *ḥadīth* and *sīra* literature as well as historiographical works report many examples of *taḥnīk* by the Prophet. The aim is either therapeutic: Muḥammad in this mannner cured the ailing hand of Umm Jalīl bint al-Mujallal's son[101] and epilepsy in a seven-year-old child;[102] or initiatory: Muḥammad transmitted knowledge to Ibn ʿAbbās;[103] or especially the transmission

98. In his fundamental article 'Portrait "mythique" d'Ibn ʿAbbās', *Arabica*, 32 (1985), pp. 127–184; pp. 143–144.

99. *Lisān al-ʿarab, Tāj al-ʿarūs.*

100. Van Gennep, *Les rites de passage*, pp. 138–139 (*taḥnīk* as initiatory ritual); J. Desparmet, *Le mal magique* (Algiers and Paris, 1932), pp. 98ff.

101. Ibn Ḥanbal, *Musnad*, ed. Muḥammad al-Zuhrī al-Ghamrāwī (Cairo, 1313/1896), vol. 3, p. 107.

102. Ibn Isḥāq, *Sīra Ibn Isḥāq al-musammāt bi-kitāb al-mubtada' wa'l-mabʿath wa'l-maghāzī*, ed. M. Ḥamidullāh (Rabat, 1976), p. 103; al-Bukhārī, *Ṣaḥīḥ*, 3 vols (Cairo, 1378/1958), 'ṭibb', 21.

103. Ibn Kathīr, *al-Bidāya wa'l-nihāya* (Beirut, 1977), vol. 8, p. 295. See Gilliot, 'Portrait "mythique" d'Ibn ʿAbbās', p. 143; cf. also Van Gennep, *Les rites de passage*, p. 138. In 1973, I witnessed ritual of *taḥnīk* among the Qādirī dervishes of Iranian Baluchistan; according to them, the master transmits *ʿilm* and *ʿamal* to the disciple, which to the dervishes mean initiatory knowledge and supernatural powers.

of blessings and moral virtues: there are many accounts of parents taking their children to the Prophet in order that he may practise *taḥnīk*;[104] other accounts speak of new converts who ask the Prophet to perform *taḥnīk*.[105] It is useful here to note the direct link between *taḥnīk* and *baraka/tabarruk*. In a number of *ḥadīth*s, both roots are used (*fa-yubarriku 'alayhim wa yuḥannikuhum*; *ḥannakahu fa-barraka 'alayhi*, etc.).[106]

Baraka, a word in Muslim hagiography which eventually comes to mean a kind of mysterious and beneficial flow, an energy or spiritual influx transmitted by contact, affecting living things and objects, originally meant abundant rain or the camping of a camel nearby a source of water; or yet again what the camel does during this stay, that is, chewing on its food and (once mixed in saliva) feeding its little ones with it. In his excellent article on this point, J. Chelhod demonstrates how this latter meaning led to the interpretation of *baraka* as the spiritual energy that the father transmits to his newly born child by placing him upon his knees and putting saliva in his mouth, blessing him and in this way

104. Al-Bukhārī, *Ṣaḥīḥ*, ''*aqīqa*', 1; '*adab*', 109; Muslim, *al-Jāmiʿ al-ṣaḥīḥ*, 2 vols (rpr. Istanbul, 1383/1963), '*adab*', vol. 1, pp. 23–28, '*ṭahāra*', 101; Ibn Ḥanbal, *Musnad*, vol. 3, pp. 105–106, 171, 175, 181, 188, 254 and 288; vol. 4, p. 399; vol. 6, pp. 93, 212, 347. Abū Dāwūd, *Sunan*, '*adab*', 107. On this aspect of the practice, now consult A. Giladi, 'Some Notes on *taḥnīk* in Medieval Islam', *JNES*, 3 (1988), pp. 175–179.

105. Al-Bukhārī, *Ṣaḥīḥ*, '*manāqib al-Anṣār*', 45; '*zakāt*', 69, '*dhabā'iḥ*', 35; al-Tirmidhī, *al-Jāmiʿ al-ṣaḥīḥ/Sunan*, ed. A. M. Shākir, 5 vols (Cairo, 1356/1937), '*manāqib*', 44; Abū Dāwūd, Sunan, 'jihād', 52. In their translation of the *Ṣaḥīḥ* by al-Bukhārī, O. Houdas and W. Marçais seem to wish to ignore the meaning of *taḥnīk* employed without a complementary noun; indeed the term is regularly translated with the complement (in this instance, 'a date'), even when the original text does not mention it; see El-Bokhâri, *Les traditions islamiques*, 4 vols (Paris, 1903–1914, rpr. 1977), see vol. 2, pp. 681ff. and n. 2. In the 5th volume (intro. and amends by M. Hamidullah, Paris, 1981), the error has not been corrected.

106. Refer to the preceding two footnotes.

according him his protection.[107] The common element between *taḥnīk* and *baraka* is the idea of a nourishing and invigorating liquid (rain, saliva and even a source of water) for both the body and the soul, which constitutes a true blessing.

Here too, as in the case of *muʾākhāt* examined above, ʿAlī and his sons al-Ḥasan and al-Ḥusayn seem to have been ostracised by non-Shiʿi authors. There is no mention of them in the numerous *ḥadīths* or accounts concerning *taḥnīks* by the Prophet. Ibn Kathīr (d. 774/1373), a pro-ʿAbbasid author, goes so far as to say that as far as he knew, except for Ibn ʿAbbās, no one had received saliva from the Prophet;[108] it is unthinkable that he would not have been aware of at least some of the numerous traditions reported in the canonical works of *ḥadīth* noted above. How can one imagine that Muḥammad had thus 'blessed' a large number of his companions and followers, overlooking his own 'brother', cousin, future son-in-law who was also undoubtedly one of his closest companions? Yet still, is it conceivable that the Prophet would have 'blessed' a large number of children only to neglect, forget or deliberately deprive his very own grandchildren, his own male descendants, of this blessing? To my knowledge, only Shiʿi literature reports *taḥnīks* that the Prophet practised upon ʿAlī and the sons born

107. J. Chelhod, 'La *baraka* chez les Arabes', *RHR*, 148/1 (1955), pp. 68–88; see also by him, *Les structures du sacré chez les arabes*, index and esp. pp. 58–62.

108. Ibn Kathīr, *al-Bidāya wa'l-nihāya*, vol. 8, p. 295; elsewhere, he recognises that 'prophetic heritage' returns to the immediate family of the prophets, Ibn Kathīr, *al-Bidāya*, vol. 5, p. 290; also his *Tafsīr*, ed. Beirut, 1966, vol. 5, pp. 452f., but seems to maintain that this family consists of ʿAbbās and his descendants (*Tafsīr*, vol. 5, pp. 456–457, a pro-ʿAbbasid version of the *ḥadīth ahl al-kisāʾ*, in which these are identified as ʿAbbās and his sons).

to Fāṭima – a practice that, according to the same sources, the imams were to continue.[109]

Adopted at very young age by his paternal uncle Abū Ṭālib, before the advent of Islam Muḥammad was 'the adopted brother' of his cousin ʿAlī. This *qarāba*, as well as the spiritual links between them were such that ʿAlī did not hesitate to embrace the religion proclaimed by Muḥammad. Friend and no doubt blessed confidant of the latter, his constant companion, 'twinned' with him by virtue of the *mu'ākhāt* ritual, during which there may have been an exchange of blood, an intrepid warrior fighting for his Cause, ʿAlī married Fāṭima, Muḥammad's daughter and became the father of the only male descendants of the Prophet, al-Ḥasan and al-Ḥusayn. Some Companions had the privilege of one or many of these kinds of relations with Muḥammad, but none of them apart from ʿAlī had all these kinds of relationship with him. What is more, he had the exclusive privilege of two fundamental *qarāba*s: 'twinning' and fathering male descendants. Thus, ʿAlī had cogent reasons, confirmed in his opinion by the Qur'ān and even more so by ancient beliefs, for believing in his own divine election and that of his progeny by Fāṭima later on. Surely it is this 'election' that constituted the essential core of what his contemporaries would have called *dīn ʿAlī*.

109. For examples and sources see Amir-Moezzi, *Guide divin*, pp. 193–195 (*Divine Guide*, pp. 76–77). Here the Prophet not only introduces his saliva into the mouth but also into the eyes of the recipient. Moreover, he does the same with his sweat. See also Sulaym b. Qays (Ps.), *Kitāb Sulaym b. Qays al-Hilālī*, ed. M. B. al-Anṣāri, 3 vols (Qumm, 1416/1995), vol. 2, p. 779, no. 26. Yūsuf al-Baḥrānī, *al-Durar al-najafiyya* (Qumm, n.d.), pp. 281 and 287.

5. Reactions and consequences

Whatever the expression *ahl bayt al-nabī*, which rapidly became synonymous with *āl Muḥammad, āl al-nabī, āl al-rasūl* and so on, was originally meant to communicate, ʿAlī would surely not have failed to claim it for himself and his household. Certain Hāshimids, especially the ʿAlids, seem to have made this claim from the first/seventh century; this seems to be apparent, for example, in a few verses of ancient poets such as Abu'l-Aswad al-Du'alī (d. 69/688), Kuthayyir ʿAzza (d. 105/723) or al-Kumayt b. Zayd (d. 126/743).[110] From the extensive and pertinent analyses of the expression and its religious and political implications conducted by M. Sharon in many of his publications, it transpires that popular opinion during this period identified the *ahl bayt al-nabī* with the Hāshimids in general and more specifically with the household of ʿAlī (this is also what emerges from a large number of *ḥadīth*s on the *ahl al-kisā'*, analysed by I. Goldziher; see above) – without, however, this popular respect actually translating into a recognition of the right to govern the community.[111] Of those who partook of this respect, some ʿAlids seem to have been the first to claim political legitimacy, in other words, that the caliphate was exclusively reserved for ʿAlī. One can reasonably assume that they were followers of '*dīn ʿAlī*'. M. Sharon examines the probable influence of the Jewish conception of the House of David, as strongly felt in Iraq, on the population in Kūfa, homeland and bastion of the ʿAlids. According to this conception, leadership of the community remains exclusively reserved for the descendants of the House of David.[112] Elsewhere, the same scholar seems to include the influence of the Christian concept of the 'Holy Family' (equally

110. For the first and third, see above. For the second, see al-Iṣfahānī, *Kitāb al-aghānī*, vol. 9, p. 14; al-Nāshi' al-Akbar, *Masā'il al-imāma*, ed. J. van Ess (Beirut, 1971), p. 26.

111. M. Sharon, 'The Umayyads as *ahl al-bayt*', addendum in response to the article *'Hāshimiyyāt'* by W. Madelung, pp. 151–152.

112. Ibid., p. 126; Jewish Exilarchate (in Arabic *ra's al-jālūt*, from the Aramaic *rêsh galūtha*, lit. 'Leader of the Diaspora') resided in Iraq and represented, in himself, the divine election of descendants of the House of

highly present in Iraq during the early centuries of Islam), by underscoring the constant comparisons that Shiʿi literature establishes between the figures of Mary and Fāṭima.[113]

He considers entirely plausible, the historical existence of a recension of the Qurʾān from Kūfa in which ʿAlī and members of his family would have been mentioned numerous times,[114] just as Imami *ḥadīth*s, repeatedly and openly declared until the mid-fourth/tenth century.[115]

Quite apart from certain violent reactions against the importance accorded to a relationship with the Prophet or against the legitimacy of the Prophet's family, for example by the Khārijīs,[116] the anti-caliph ʿAbd Allāh b. al-Zubayr,[117] and some *ahl al-ḥadīth*,[118] non-ʿAlid members of the Prophet's family and their descendants, in this instance the Umayyads and subsequently the ʿAbbāsids,

---

David. Also, M. Gil, 'The Exilarchate', in D. Frank (ed.), *The Jews of Medieval Islam* (Leiden, 1995), pp. 33–65.

113. Sharon, '*Ahl al-Bayt* – People of the House', p. 173. For sources and studies regarding these comparisons, now consult M. A. Amir-Moezzi, 'Fāṭema', section 1, *EIr*, vol. 9, pp. 400–402.

114. 'The Umayyads as *ahl al-bayt*', p. 127.

115. On this version of the Qurʾān, see e.g. E. Kohlberg, 'Some Notes on the Imāmite Attitude to the Qur'an', in S. M. Stern, A. Hourani and V. Brown (eds), *Islamic Philosophy and the Classical Tradition* (Oxford, 1972), pp. 209–224; Amir-Moezzi, *Guide divin*, pp. 200–227 (*Divine Guide*, pp. 79–91); M. M. Bar-Asher, 'Variant Readings and Additions of the Imāmī-Shīʿa to the Quran', *IOS*, 13 (1993), pp. 39–74. And now consult M. A. Amir-Moezzi and E. Kohlberg, 'Révélation et falsification: introduction à l'édition du *Kitāb al-Qirāʾāt* d'al-Sayyārī', *JA*, 293/2 (2005), pp. 663–722.

116. Cf. e.g. al-Ṭabarī, ed. de Goeje, series 1, p. 3350.

117. According to an account by al-Zuhrī, reported by al-Balādhurī, Ibn Zubayr considered the Prophet's family to be 'petty and bad' (*uhayla sūʾ/saw*', *Ansāb al-ashrāf*) vol. 5, ed. S. Goetein (Jerusalem, 1936), p. 372.

118. Those, for example, that transmitted traditions regarding the *kufr* of Muḥammad's father and ancestors; cf. Muslim, vol. 1, pp. 132–133; al-Ḥalabī, *al-Sīrat al-ḥalabiyya* (Beirut, n.d.), vol. 1, p. 29; al-Ṭabarī, *Jāmiʿ al-bayān*, vol. 11, pp. 30–31. For the anti-ʿAlid twist given to these traditions, see al-Zurqānī, *Sharḥ ʿalāʾl-Mawāhib al-laduniyya liʾl-Qasṭallānī* (Cairo, 1329/1911), vol. 1, p. 179, according to which 'the infidel father' of the *ḥadīth* in fact designates Abū Ṭālib, since in Arabic 'one who raises a child is also called father'.

would also have responded by trying to appropriate the title of *ahl al-bayt*. Although his prudent approach prevents M. Sharon from explicitly declaring his stance on the matter, on many occasions he seems to suggest that Umayyad and ʿAbbasid attempts to identify with the *ahl bayt al-nabī* would have been in reaction to ʿAlid claims that were much older.[119] At one point, their common position against the Umayyads drew the ʿAlids and ʿAbbāsids[120] closer together. However, once in power, the ʿAbbāsids distanced themselves from the ʿAlids by describing themselves as the only 'Holy Family', as witnessed by, among other things, the attempt to undermine the status of Fāṭima and the presentation of ʿAbbās b. ʿAbd al-Muṭṭalib and his sons as the *ahl al-kisāʾ*.[121]

Moreover, the study of *dīn ʿAlī* seems to corroborate allusions made by G. H. Sadighi and E. Kohlberg that the process of ʿAlī's glorification, transforming his historical character into a semi-legendary figure of heroic and even sacred dimensions, can be traced back to very early times, namely the period of his caliphate or even that immediately after the death of the Prophet.[122] A certain

---

119. '*Ahl al-Bayt* – People of the House', p. 183; 'The Umayyads as *ahl al-bayt*', pp. 127, 151.

120. Gilliot, 'Portrait "mythique" d'Ibn ʿAbbās', pp. 159ff., esp. p. 161; Madelung, "Abd Allāh b. ʿAbbās and Shiʿite Law'.

121. Sharon, '*Ahl al-Bayt*', pp. 174, 176–179, esp. p. 177. Although not having especially examined the issue, it seems to me that many of the accounts regarding Ibn ʿAbbās's privileged relationship with the Prophet including the transmission of prophetic knowledge (reports presented and analysed in detail by Gilliot in 'Portrait "mythique"', esp. pp. 134, 140, 142–143, 151–152, 156) are modelled on the abundant reports about ʿAlī in early Shiʿi works. This issue merits further attention, see Sharon, *Black Banners from the East*, pp. 126–140 and more especially pp. 93–99 and J. van Ess, 'Les Qadarites et les Ghailānīya de Yazīd III', *SI*, 31 (1970), p. 285.

122. Gh. Ḥ. Ṣadīqī, *Jonbesh hā-ye dīnī-ye Īrānī dar qarn hā-ye dovvom va sevvom-e hejrī* (Tehran, 1372 Sh./1993), pp. 225–226 (this publication is a completed and updated version of the author's thesis, *Les mouvements religieux iraniens aux II et IIIe siècles de l'hégire* [Paris, 1938]); E. Kohlberg, 'Some Imāmī Shīʿī Views on the *ṣaḥāba*', *JSAI*, 5 (1984) (rpr. in *Belief and Law*, article IX), pp. 145–146. See also F. Daftary, "Alī in Classical Ismaili Theology', in A. Y. Ocak (ed.), *From History to Theology: Ali in Islamic Beliefs* (Ankara, 2005), pp. 59–82.

reaction against the violent and repressive policies of the first Umayyads, especially Muʿāwiya and his son Yazīd, equally seems to have been a catalyst for this process.[123] "ʿAlī's religion' seems thus to have been the early nucleus of what was later to become Shiʿism. Imami sources have retained some reports, admittedly rare, in which one finds the expressions *dīn ʿAlī, dīn Ḥasan* and *dīn Ḥusayn,* the latter two apparently variants of ʿAlī's religion under the imamates of these two sons.[124]

With the doctrinal implications that ensued, Shiʿism – in its different forms and in relative terms, of course – seems to have been the development of components found in the religion of

---

123. Madelung, *The Succession*, pp. 309–310.

124. We have already examined two reports by al-Majlisī (d. 1111/1699–1700) in his *Biḥār al-anwār* (notes 2 and 6 above). See also *Biḥār*, vol. 44, p. 125 (a letter from Ziyād b. Abīhi to Muʿāwiya in which he writes that the Ḥaḍramīs are followers of ʿAlī's religion – based on *Kitāb Sulaym b. Qays*, a work of uncertain attribution but cited by authors of the fourth/tenth century); vol. 4, p. 213 (a letter from al-Ḥusayn to Muʿāwiya in which he refers to the same letter from Ziyād – based on the *Rijāl* by al-Kashshī, d. fourth/tenth century); vol. 45, p. 136 (Yazīd b. Muʿāwiya says to Zaynab bint ʿAlī: 'Your father [ʿAlī] and your brother [al-Ḥusayn] excluded themselves from the religion.' Zaynab: 'If your grandfather [Abū Sufyān], your father [Muʿāwiya] and you had been Muslims, you would have returned to the grace and religion of God, the religion of my father and brother.' Based on the *Manāqib* by Ibn Shahrāshūb, d. 588/1192); also al-Mufīd (d. 413/1022): *al-Irshād*, ed. H. Rasūlī Maḥallātī (Tehran, 1346 Sh./1968), vol. 2, pp. 106–107 (during the battle of Karbalāʾ, Nāfiʿ b. Hilāl al-Bajalī, a supporter of al-Ḥusayn, recites the following verse: 'I am Ibn Hilāl al-Bajalī / I am a follower of the religion of ʿAlī / And the religion of the latter is the religion of the Prophet.' His adversary replies: 'I am the follower of the religion of Uthmān'; it remains for Nāfiʿ to retort: 'You are [in fact] a follower of the religion of Satan'; also *Biḥār al-anwār*, vol. 45, p. 19 and n.1 by the editor on the faulty metre of the poem; in the version reported by Ibn Shahrāshūb in *Manāqib āl Abī Ṭālib*, 3 vols [Najaf, 1956], vol. 3, p. 252, other verses are attributed to Nāfiʿ: 'I am the young Yemeni man of the Bajalīs / My religion is that of Ḥusayn and ʿAlī'; *Biḥār*, vol. 45, p. 27); Ibn Shahrāshūb, *Manāqib*, vol. 3, p. 251 (also during the battle of Karbalāʾ, verses by ʿAbd al-Raḥmān b. ʿAbd Allāh al-Yazanī: 'I am the son of ʿAbd Allāh of the Āl Yazan / My religion is that of Ḥusayn and Ḥasan'; *Biḥār*, vol. 45, p. 22). In addition, apart from written sources, Shiʿism has also retained *'Dīn ʿAlī'* as a personal name, as seen at the beginning of this chapter.

ʿAlī:[125] the cult·of *qarāba*, the notion of prophetic heritage, the divine election of ʿAlī and his descendants, the ancestral and natural, but also supra-natural, aspects, thaumaturgic and initiatory elements linked to the prophetic 'Holy Family'.

---

125. It is useful to note here a remarkable and probably ancient evolution in which the aspects which are specifically Arab and ancestral and which underlie a large part of *dīn ʿAlī*, progressively experienced a transmutation of an initiatory and esoteric nature in Shiʿism. This evolution seems to date especially from the period of the imamates of Muḥammad al-Bāqir (d. 115 or 119/732 or 737) and Jaʿfar al-Ṣādiq (d. 148/765) (cf. J. Ruska, *Arabische Alchemisten*. II. *Jaʿfar al-Ṣādiq, der sechste Imām* [Heidelberg, 1924]; M. E. G. Hodgson, 'How Did the Early Shīʿa Become Sectarian?', *JAOS*, 75, 1955). To illustrate this evolution, allow me to limit myself to examples drawn from early Imami *ḥadīths*: the replacement of the tribal concept of *ḥilm* by *ʿaql* (which I have, in this particular context, translated as 'intelligence of the sacred' or 'hiero-intelligence') which, in terms of wisdom, is equivalent to *ʿilm* (in the sense of 'initiatory knowledge') (cf. *Guide divin*, esp. pp. 15–28 and 174–199 [*Divine Guide*, pp. 6–11 and 69–79]). The content of the Prophet's saliva (or sweat) is said to be 'initiatory knowledge' ('Alī often begins his sermons with these words: 'O people! Question me before you lose me! I am the Bearer of initiatory knowledge; I carry in me the Prophet's saliva that he made me drink drop by drop. Question me for I hold the knowledge of Beginnings and Ends', for example, Ibn Bābūya al-Ṣadūq, *Amālī/Majālis*, ed. M. B. Kamareʾī [Tehran, 1404/1984], p. 341). After receiving Muḥammad's saliva in his eyes, 'Alī acquired the power 'to see' and to know the true nature of people; see for example, al-Ṣaffār al-Qummī, *Baṣāʾir al-darajāt*, ed. M. Kuchebāghī (2nd edn, Tabriz, n.d. [ca. 1960]), p. 390. When Muḥammad taught ʿAlī the 'thousand chapters' of knowledge, both men perspired and the sweat of each ran upon the body of the other (*Baṣāʾir*, p. 313; see also *Guide divin*, pp. 193–194 [*Divine Guide*, pp. 176–177]). In the series of traditions regarding the 'tripatriate division of humanity', some, surely the earliest, employ tribal terminology ('We [i.e. the imams] are the descendants of Hāshim, our Shiʿis are Arabs of noble stock [*al-ʿarab*] and the others, Bedouins of inferior descent [*al-aʿrāb*]'; 'We are noble Arabs [*ʿarabī*], our believers are protected allies [*mawālī*] and those that do not possess the same doctrine as us are vile [*ʿilj*]'). Others, clearly later, take up the same division by introducing the initiatory dimension ('Men are divided into three categories: the wise initiator [*ʿālim*, i.e. the imam], the initiated disciple [*mutaʿallim* 'the imam's faithful'] and the foam carried by the wave [*ghuththāʾ* i.e. the non-believers]'; 'The [true] men are only of two kinds: the wise initiator and the initiated disciple. The others are but vile beings [*hamaj*]'). Regarding these traditions and their analysis, see M. A. Amir-Moezzi, 'Seul l'homme de Dieu est humain. Théologie et anthropologie mystique à travers l'exégèse imamite ancienne (Aspects de l'imamologie duodécimaine IV)', *Arabica*, 45 (1998), pp. 193–214 (Chapter 8, this volume).

2

Shahrbānū, Lady of the Land of Iran and Mother of the Imams: Between Pre-Islamic Iran and Imami Shiʿism*

For Twelver Shiʿis, as well as a large number of Sunnis, it is a fact that the third imam, al-Ḥusayn b. ʿAlī b. Abī Ṭālib (killed at Karbalāʾ in 61/680), married the daughter of Yazdgird III, the last Sasanian emperor. Known more popularly as Shahrbānū, she gave birth, still according to tradition, to ʿAlī b. al-Ḥusayn Zayn al-ʿĀbidīn (d. 92/711 or 95/714), the fourth Shiʿi imam. Consequently, the line of imams, from the fourth to the twelfth and last, is said to be her progeny. The figure of Shahrbānū, Sasanian princess and mother of the imams, seems particularly important in the connections that link Imami Shiʿism to pre-Islamic Iran. The present chapter seeks to examine the origin, development and implications of traditions centred on this figure.

1

Ibn Saʿd (d. 230/844–845), is undoubtedly one of the earliest authors to mention the mother of imam Zayn al-ʿĀbidīn. However, he makes no mention of the fact that she belonged to the royal family of Iran:

* I cordially thank Professors Shaul Shaked, Yohanan Friedmann and Frantz Grenet for their attentive reading of the first draft of this chapter and for their pertinent comments.

> Her mother was a slave (of her father; *umm walad*) named Ghazāla who, after (the death) of al-Ḥusayn married Zuyayd *mawlā* of the latter and bore 'Abd Allāh b. Zuyayd, who is thus the uterine brother of 'Alī b. al-Ḥusayn.[1]

Some years later, Ibn Qutayba (d. 276/889) in his *Ma'ārif*, takes up the same information and adds to it somewhat:

> As for 'Alī b. al-Ḥusayn [known as] al-Aṣghar, al-Ḥusayn has no descendants except through him. It is reported that his mother was originally from Sind [*Sindiyya*; thus probably a slave from this region] named Sulāfa or Ghazāla who after [the death] of al-Ḥusayn became the wife of Zubayd [and not Zuyayd, as noted in Ibn Sa'd], *mawlā* of the latter, and bore 'Abd Allāh b. Zubayd, who is thus the uterine brother of 'Alī b. al-Ḥusayn.[2]

There is still no mention of the Sasanian royal family. Similarly, almost all the authors of the histories and earlier or later historiographical studies that chronicled the invasion of Iran and the fate of the last Sasanian sovereign and his family, usually with remarkable attention to detail, on this point are silent. They do however, with many variants, provide a list of the children, including the daughters, of Yazdgird III, but do not give the least indication about the eventual capture of one these daughters by Muslim soldiers or any relationship between her and the Shi'i imams.[3] However, a report supplied by

---

1. Ibn Sa'd, *al-Ṭabaqāt al-kubrā*, ed. I. 'Abbās (Beirut, 1377–1380/1957–1960), vol. 5, p. 211.

2. Ibn Qutayba, *al-Ma'ārif*, ed. Th. 'Ukāsha (4th edn, Cairo, 1995), pp. 214–215.

3. See e.g. al-Balādhurī (d. 279/892), *Futūḥ al-buldān*, ed. M. de Goeje (Leiden, 1866; rpr. 1968), pp. 262–313; elsewhere, in his *Ansāb al-ashrāf*, 3 vols, ed. M. B. al-Maḥmūdī (Beirut, 1974), vol. 3, pp. 102–103 and 146, al-Balādhurī writes that the mother of 'Alī b. al-Ḥusayn was a slave named Sulāfa originally from Sijistān; Ibn 'Abd Rabbih (d. 328/940), *al-'Iqd al-farīd* (Cairo, 1316/1898), vol. 3, pp. 103ff.; al-Mas'ūdī (d. 345–346/956–957), *Murūj al-dhahab*, ed. and Fr. trans. by Barbier de Meynard (Paris, 1861–1877), vol. 4, pp. 190ff.; in addition, al-Mas'ūdī devotes long passages to 'Alī b. al-Ḥusayn (see index, vol. 9, p. 112), but says nothing about his mother; Miskawayh (d. 421/1038), *Tajārib al-umam*,

ʿAlī b. Muḥammad al-Madāʾinī, al-Ṭabarī's (d. 310/923) well-informed Iranian source, says that around the year 31/650–651, during the conquest of Nīsābūr, ʿAbd Allāh b. ʿĀmir b. Kurayz, captured two daughters of the Kisrā family (*āl*), named Bābūnaj (= Bābūna/Bānūya?) and ṬHMĪJ or ṬMHĪJ (= Ṭahmīnaj > Tahmīna?).

According to another version, the event occurred during the siege of Sarakhs and the famous Arab conqueror offered one of two daughters to a certain al-Nūshajān (I shall return to this name), but the other died.[4] Nowhere does the great historiographer say that these are the daughters of the Iranian king, or that there was any connection to the ʿAlid imams. The same is true of sources as varied and historically far apart as the *Kitāb al-kharāj* by the Ḥanafī judge Abū Yūsuf (d. 182/798) and the *Shāh-nāma* of the pro-Shiʿi poet Firdawsī (d. 410/1019) both of whom, though surely for different reasons, took an interest in the fate of the last Sasanian sovereign of Iran and his descendants.[5]

One of the very first texts to suggest a connection between a daughter of the last Sasanian emperor and the imams seems to be *Kitāb al-akhbār al-ṭiwāl* by Abū Ḥanīfa al-Dīnawarī (d. ca. 282/894–895). According to this text, under the caliphate of ʿAlī during the

ed. H. F. Amedroz and D. S. Margoliouth (*The Eclipse of the Abbasid Califate*) (London, 1920–1921), vol. 1, pp. 145–220; Ibn al-Athīr (d. 630/1233), *Akhbār-e Īrān az* al-Kāmil-e *Ibn Athīr* (excerpt from *al-Kāmil fi'l-ta'rīkh* [rpr. Beirut, 1385–1386/1965–1966] and Persian trans. by M. I. Bāstānī Pārīzī [Tehran, 1349 Sh./1971], pp. 209–335. The daughters of Yazdgird III, in varying number and diverse appelations according to the sources, are for example said to be named 'DRK (var. 'WZD, ARDK, ĀDhRK), ShHĪN (var. Shāhīn, SHZ), MRDĀWAND (var. MRDĀWZNDĀ, MRDĀWĀR), Tahmīna, Bānūya (var. Bābūna).

4. Al-Ṭabarī, *Ta'rīkh al-rusul wa'l-mulūk*, ed. M. de Goeje, series 1, p. 2887; ed. M. A. F. Ibrāhīm, vol. 4, p. 302; on al-Ṭabarī and the conquest of Iran see the introduction by T. Nöldeke, *Geschichte der Perser und Araber zu Zeit der Sasaniden aus der arabischen Chronik des Tabari* (Leiden, 1879; rpr. 1973) and G. Rex Smith to *The History of al-Ṭabarī*, vol. 15: *The Conquest of Iran* (Albany, NY, 1994).

5. Abū Yūsuf Yaʿqūb b. Ibrāhīm, *Kitāb al-kharāj*, ed. I. ʿAbbās (Beirut and London, 1985), p. 30; Abu'l-Qāsim Firdawsī, *Shāh-nāma* (Moscow edn, rpr. Tehran, 1350 Sh./1972), 9, pp. 358ff.

conquest of Nīsābūr, Khulayd b. Ka's, the newly appointed governor of Khurāsān,[6] realises that one of the daughters of Kisrā who had just arrived from Kābul was leading a revolt against the Muslims. He fights the insurgents, captures the princess and sends her to ʿAlī, who asks her if she wishes to marry his son al-Ḥasan. The young lady proudly replies that she will not marry one who takes orders from another (i.e. the son who obeys the father) but that she is ready to marry the caliph himself. ʿAlī replies that he is too old, and lists the virtues of his eldest son; but the princess is not convinced. At this point, an Iranian noble, a *dihqān* from ʿIrāq named Narsī, presents himself as a candidate for marriage; but ʿAlī frees her, gives her liberty to go where she wants and allows her to make her own choice of husband.[7] As we shall soon see, the complicity between ʿAlī and the princess, as well her pride (a mark of nobility) and her freedom, are elements that play a key role in Shiʿi versions of the account.

It was really after the third century AH, or perhaps from the second half of it onwards, that reports about the Sasanian wife of imam al-Ḥusayn increased in number. A contemporary of al-Dīnawarī, the philologist Muḥammad b. Yazīd al-Mubarrad (d. 286/900) is perhaps the earliest, and undoubtedly the only non-Shiʿi author of this period to report a tradition implying as much, in his *al-Kāmil fiʾl-lugha*, by strongly emphasising the woman's nobility:

> The mother of ʿAlī b. al-Ḥusayn was Sulāfa, daughter of Yazdgird [the King], of noble stock (*maʿrūfat al-nasab*), one of the chosen women [due to the nobility of her race, *wa kānat min khiyarāt al-nisāʾ*]. [Regarding this] it is said that ʿAlī b. al-Ḥusayn was asked: 'You are one of the finest men [as regards treatment of parents,

6. Al-Ṭabarī, we have seen, believes this conqueror was ʿAbd Allāh b. ʿĀmir b. Kurayz. As for Khulayd, ʿAlī's general, al-Ṭabarī identifies him as Khulayd b. Ṭarīf.

7. Abū Ḥanīfa al-Dīnawarī, *al-Akhbār al-ṭiwāl*, ed. V. Guirgass (Leiden, 1888), chapter on the battle of the Camel *in fine*, p. 163; Persian trans. by Ṣ. Nash'at (Tehran, 1346 Sh./1968), p. 169, tr. M. Mahdavī Dāmghānī (Tehran, 1366 Sh./1988), p. 191.

> *abarr al-nās*] and yet you never eat from the same plate as your mother?' He replied, 'I do not wish my hand to reach for something that her eyes have already chosen, for fear of thwarting her desires.'
>
> It is said about ʿAlī b. al-Ḥusayn that he is the son of the two chosen ones (*ibn al-khiyaratayn*), for according to the Prophet's saying '[a]mong his servants God has two chosen ones; His chosen ones among the Arabs are Quraysh and among the non-Arabs (*al-ʿajam*) are the Persians.'[8]

Several Shiʿi authors who are exact contemporaries of al-Mubarrad repeat the same story. The chronicler Aḥmad b. Abī Yaʿqūb al-Yaʿqūbī (d. 292/904) as well as the heresiographers Saʿd b. ʿAbd Allāh al-Ashʿarī and al-Ḥasan b. Mūsā al-Nawbakhtī (both d. ca. 300/912–913) limit themselves to a brief allusion to the fact that the woman in question was the daughter of the last Sasanian ruler.[9]

From this period onwards, it is above all the Imami authors who take up the theme. First, in his *Baṣāʾir al-darajāt*, al-Ṣaffār al-Qummī (d. 290/902–903) reports, perhaps for the first time, an amplified version of the account that should be cited in its

8. Al-Mubarrad, *al-Kāmil*, ed. M. A. al-Dālī (3rd edn in 4 vols, Beirut, 1418/1997), vol 2, pp. 645–646; on the *ḥadīth* mentioned and its sources see p. 646, note 2 by the editor.

9. Al-Yaʿqūbī, *Taʾrīkh*, ed. M. Th. Houtsma (Leiden, 1883, rpr. Qumm, 1414/1994), vol. 2, pp. 246–247 and 303 ('Among the sons of al-Ḥusayn, ʿAlī al-Akbar who had no descendants as he was killed [at a young age] at al-Ṭaff [Karbalāʾ], and his mother was Laylā bint Abī Murra b. ʿUrwa b. Masʿūd al-Thaqafī; then ʿAlī al-Aṣghar [i.e. Zayn al-ʿĀbidīn] whose mother was ḤRĀR daughter of Yazdgird whom [her husband] al-Ḥusayn called Ghazāla'); al-Ashʿarī, Saʿd b. ʿAbd Allāh, *al-Maqālāt waʾl-firaq*, ed. M. J. Mashkūr (Tehran, 1963), p. 70; al-Nawbakhtī, *Firaq al-shīʿa*, ed. H. Ritter (Istanbul, 1931), p. 53 (her name before captivity: Jahān Shāh 'sovereign of the world' bint Yazdgird b. Shahriyār; after captivity: Sulāfa). On the relationship between these two earliest heresiographical Shiʿi texts, see W. Madelung, 'Bemerkungen zur imamitischen Firaq-Literatur', *Der Islam*, 43 (1967), pp. 37–52 (rpr. in *Religious Schools and Sects in Medieval Islam* [London, 1985], article XV).

entirety. This is a *ḥadīth* going back to the fifth imam, Abū Jaʿfar Muḥammad al-Bāqir (d. ca. 119/737):

> When they sought to take the daughter of Yazdgird to [the caliph] ʿUmar [b. al-Khaṭṭāb], she came to Medina; young girls climbed higher [to see her] and the mosque [where ʿUmar presided] was illuminated by her radiant face. Once she caught sight of ʿUmar inside the mosque, she covered her face and sighed: *ʿAh bīrūz bādā hurmuz*ʾ [in Persian: *Ah pīrūz bādhā hormoz*; May Hormoz, i.e. Ahura Mazda, be victorious = may God be victorious?]. ʿUmar became angry and said: ʿShe is insulting me.ʾ At this point, the Commander of the Faithful [ʿAlī] intervened and said to ʿUmar: ʿDo not meddle, leave her alone! Let her choose a man among the Muslims and he will pay her price [to her as she is a slave] from the spoils he earned.ʾ ʿUmar then said to the girl: ʿChoose!ʾ She stepped forward and placed her hand on al-Ḥusayn's head. The Commander of the Faithful asked: ʿWhat is your name?ʾ ʿJahān Shāh [in Persian: sovereign of the world]ʾ, she answered. And ʿAlī added: ʿShahr Bānūya also [in Persian: Lady of the Land + the typically Iranian suffix *ūya*].ʾ He then turned to al-Ḥusayn and said to him: ʿAbū ʿAbd Allāh [al-Ḥusayn's *kunya*]! She will be the mother of your son who shall be the best of those living in the world [i.e. an imam in the person of ʿAlī b. al-Ḥusayn Zayn al-ʿĀbidīn].ʾ[10]

At this point, the evolution of the tradition seems well under way, and as we shall see later, there will be other developments. Many elements in al-Ṣaffār's account are noteworthy; just as in al-Mubarrad, and perhaps even more so, ʿIranian-nessʾ and royalty are pronounced. For the first time, it would appear, Persian is used in the text. Although the sentence in Persian is much too short, the prose style seems older, modelled after expressions employed by Iranian

10. Al-Ṣaffār al-Qummī, *Baṣāʾir al-darajāt*, ed. M. Kūchebāghī (2nd edn, Tabrīz, ca. 1960), ch. 7, section 11 (ʿthe imams speak all languagesʾ), no. 8, p. 335. Regarding the author and his work, see M. A. Amir-Moezzi, ʿAl-Ṣaffâr al-Qummî (d. 290/902–903) and his *Kitâb baṣâʾir al-darajât*ʾ, *JA*, 280/3–4 (1992), pp. 221–250. A. J. Newman, *The Formative Period of Twelver Shīʿism* (Richmond, 2000), chs 5 and 7.

prisoners-of-war.[11] If my understanding of the sentence is correct, its purpose is to insist upon the piety (read monotheism) of the princess and certainly not her Mazdean faith (later ver sions of the tradition present a princess converted to Islam). 'Alī's intervention is obviously what is of most importance. Thanks to his knowledge of what is hidden and in the future, he recognises the princess and knows the fate that awaits her. Protection of the princess and perfect complicity with her, the fact that he speaks her language (hence the presence of this *ḥadīth* in this particular chapter) and that he insists upon her noble status (it is up to her to choose a husband), his vehement reaction to 'Umar, clearly explaining that he cannot rise to the occasion and that this event is beyond him, the prediction of the birth of a future imam, all fully justify the mention of the Light of royal Glory transmitted by the princess and the fact that this Light can even illuminate the Prophet's mosque in Medina, where the caliph of the Muslims presides.[12]

This information takes on great significance when we consider the importance of the notion of Light in Imamism, in which, briefly stated, the *nūr al-walāya* transmitted by seminal fluid and bearing initiatic knowledge and charisma is transmitted from

---

11. M. T. Bahār, *Sabk shenāsī. Tārīkh-e taṭawwor-e nathr-e fārsī*, 3 vols (2nd edn, Tehran, 1337 Sh./1959), vol. 1, ch. 5, pp. 208ff., on usage of the volitive *bādhā/bādh/bād* in Persian of the first three centuries of Islam, ch. 10, pp. 356–358; also S. Nafīsī, *Tārīkh-e naẓm va nathr dar Īrān va dar zabān-e fārsī tā pāyān-e qarn-e dahom-e hejrī* (Tehran, 1344 Sh./1966), vol. 1, p. 83.

12. On the Light of Glory *xvarenah/xwarr(ah)/farnah/farra* and its central role in the spiritual dimension of royalty in ancient Iran, see e.g. H. W. Bailey, *Zoroastrian Problems in the Ninth-Century Books* (Oxford, 1943), chs 1 and 2, pp. 1–77; also, Gh. Gnoli, 'Un particolare aspetto del simbolismo della luce nel Mazdeismo e nel Manicheismo', *AION*, N.S., 12 (1962), pp. 95–128, '*Axvaretem Xvareno*', *AION*, 13 (1963), pp. 295–298 and 'Un cas possible de différenciation lexicale entre *dari* et *fârsi*', in C. H. de Fouchécour and Ph. Gignoux (eds), *Etudes irano-aryennes offertes à Gilbert Lazard* (Paris, 1989), pp. 151–164; Duchesne-Guillemin, '*Le xvarenah*', *AION*, s. linguistica, 5 (1963), pp. 19–31, 'La royauté iranienne et le xvarenah', in Gh. Gnoli and A. V. Rossi (eds), *Iranica* (Naples, 1979), pp. 375–386 and 'Encore le *xvarenah*', *Studia Iranica*, 20 (1991), pp. 193–195; P. O. Skjaervø, '*Farnah*: mot mède en vieux-perse?', *Bulletin de Société de Linguistique,* 78 (1983), pp. 241–259.

imam to imam.[13] Thus, from ʿAlī Zayn al-ʿĀbidīn onwards, the imams are the bearers of a twofold Light: the Light of *walāya* inherited from ʿAlī and Fāṭima (and thus Muḥammad) and the Light of Glory from the ancient kings of Iran, transmitted by Shahrbānū. Finally, to my knowledge, the text by al-Ṣaffār is the first in which the Sasanian princess is called by this specific name (in the form of Shahrbānūya). The enigmatic turn of phrases exchanged between the princess and ʿAlī is such that one is hard pressed to tell whether this name is indeed one of the names of the princess that ʿAlī reveals, or whether it is he that confers the name on his future daughter-in-law.[14] In either case, the acknowledgement and complicitity between the parties is undeniable.

In his *Kāfī*, Muḥammad b. Yaʿqūb al-Kulaynī (d. 329/940) calls the princess Salāma (surely a *taṣḥīf* of Sulāfa) and reports the same tradition as al-Ṣaffār with some minor variants.[15] He

---

13. For more details refer to U. Rubin, 'Pre-existence and light. Aspects of the concept of Nūr Muḥammad', *IOS*, 5 (1975), pp. 62–119, and 'Prophets and Progenitors in the Early Shīʿa Tradition', *JSAI*, 1 (1979), pp. 41–65; M. A. Amir-Moezzi, *Guide divin*, sections II-1 and II-2, pp. 75–112 (*Divine Guide*, pp. 29–59), 'Twelver Shiʿism: Cosmogony and Cosmology', *EIr*, vol. 6, pp. 317–322, and 'Considérations sur l'expression *dīn ʿAlī*. Aux origines de la foi shiʿite', *ZDMG*, 150, 1 (2000), pp. 29–68 (Chapter 1, this volume).

14. Shahrbānū ('Lady of the Land', i.e. of Iran) seems to be a title for a queen or princess from the Parthian period, and not a first name. According to Firdawsī, *Shāh-nāma*, vol. 2, p. 909, Rostam's wife, Gīv's sister, carries this title; and according to Th. Nöldeke, *Das iranische Nationalepos* (2nd edn, Berlin and Leipzig, 1920), p. 7, Gīv was a Parthian ruler. Elsewhere, in the Parthian romance *Vīs o Rāmīn*, the queen mother Shahrū, mother of Vīs, is also called Shahrbānū; Fakhr al-Dīn Gorgānī, *Vīs o Rāmīn*, ed. M. Mīnovī (and M. J. Maḥjūb) (Tehran, 1337 Sh./1959), see index under *'Shahrū'*. On calling into question the Parthian origin of *Vīs o Rāmīn*, a theory maintained by among others V. Minorsky and M. Boyce, see A. Ḥ. Zarrīnkūb, review of the Maḥjūb edition in *Sokhan*, IX/10 (1337 Sh./1960), pp. 1,015–1,018.

15. Al-Kulaynī, *al-Uṣūl min al-Kāfī*, ed. J. Muṣṭafawī with Persian trans. in 4 vols (vols 1–3, Tehran, n.d.; vol. 4, Tehran, 1386/1966), Kitāb al-ḥujja, 'Bāb mawlid ʿAlī b. al-Ḥusayn', vol. 2, no 1. pp. 368–369. Main differences with the version by al-Ṣaffār: 1. The princess's sentence: *uf bīrūj bādā hurmuz* (S. J. Muṣṭafawī renders it, without any explanation, in a curious Persian translation that is as unjustified as it is incomprehensible: 'Heavens! The

then adds: 'It was said of ʿAlī b. al-Ḥusayn that he is the son of the two chosen ones, for the chosen of God among the Arabs are the (Banū) Hāshim and among the non-Arabs, the Persians.'[16] Finally, al-Kulaynī ends his report with a verse that he attributes to the famous ʿAlid poet from Baṣra, Abu al-Aswad al-Du'alī (d. 69/688), and which he says is about ʿAlī b. al-Ḥusayn:

> The son who links [i.e. who descends the same time as] Kisrā and Hāshim is the most noble among those who wear the amulet [against the evil eye]
>
> (*wa inna ghulāman bayna Kisrā wa Hāshimin la-akramu man nīṭat ʿalayhi al-tamā'imu*).[17]

---

existence of Hormoz is shrouded in darkness' (i.e. Hormoz is now unfortunate; *vāy rūzgār-e hormoz siyāh shod*). Perhaps he considered *rūj* to be synonymous with *rūz* (day, light) and so *bī-rūj* = *bī-rūz* = without light, obscure/dark; still, what does this sentence mean? Who might Hormoz be? The father of the princess is called Yazdgird b. Shahriyār b. Shīrūya b. Kisrā Abarwīz. 2. Here, upon ʿAlī's injunction it is nevertheless ʿUmar who authorises the young woman to choose a husband. Did the version reported by al-Ṣaffār seem too audacious and thus improbable?

16. Cf. here above, the version by Mubarrad. Hāshim replaces Quraysh and the sentence is no longer presented as a Prophetic *ḥadīth*.

17. Al-Kulaynī, *al-Uṣūl*, vol. 2, p. 369. The poem does not appear in the *Dīwān* by Abu'l-Aswad al-Du'alī, ed. M. Ḥ. Āl-Yāsīn (Beirut, 1974) and with good reason, the verse is modelled after that by Ibn Mayyāda, a poet from the Umayyad period, an Iranian (on his maternal side):

I am the son of Abī Salmā and my grandfather is Ẓālim / And my mother is Ḥasān, noble descendant of Persians

A boy linking Kisrā and Ẓālim / Is he not nobler among those who wear the amulet (against the evil eye)?

anā ibnu Abī Salmā wa jaddī Ẓālimū/wa ummī Ḥasān akhlaṣat-hā l'aʿājimu/a laysa ghulāmun bayna Kisrā wa Ẓālimi/bi-akrami man nīṭat ʿalayhi al-tamā'imu

Abu'l-Faraj al-Iṣfahānī, *Kitāb al-aghānī* (Būlāq, 1285/1868), vol. 2, pp. 262, 294, 330 and vol. 14, p. 104. As one might have realised, 'Kisrā' does not necessarily refer to an Iranian king but is perhaps a title of the nobility; see M. Morony, 'Kisrā' *EI2*; Ibn Abi'l-Thalj al-Baghdādī (d. 325/936–937) a contemporary of al-Kulaynī provides the following names for the mother of the fourth imam: Khilwa, Shahzanān, Shahrbānūya daughter of Yazdgird and daughter of al-Nūshaḥān (sic) (instead of Nūshajān; see *infra*); *Ta'rīkh al-a'imma* (Qumm, 1396/1976), p. 24.

Another contemporary source, *Ithbāt al-waṣiyya*, attributed to al-Masʿūdī (d. 345–346/956–957), reports an account which includes some new elements. According to this, two daughters of Yazdgird are captured and reduced to slavery under ʿUmar. The latter is ready to sell them. ʿAlī then intervenes, declares that the daughters of a king are not sold in the marketplace and asks a woman from the *Anṣār* to present both girls for marriage to noble men from the *Muhājirūn* and *Anṣār*. The first men to lay eyes upon them are ʿAlī's two sons, al-Ḥasan, who marries Shahrbānū and al-Ḥusayn, who marries Jahānshāh. ʿAlī then tells al-Ḥusayn to take special care of his wife, for she will give birth to an imam.[18] Although this report attempts to establish parity between the sons of ʿAlī, thus reinforcing links between descendants of the Kings of Iran and the Shiʿi imams, nevertheless, the last sentence underscores the fact that the imamate well and truly continues in the Ḥusaynid lineage. The report then adds that the mother of ʿAlī b. al-Ḥusayn died in Medina while giving birth.[19] The child was entrusted to a nurse who nursed and educated him. He called the latter 'Mother', and once an adult, he gave her hand in marriage to his *mawlā*. The Umayyads (i.e. his adversaries) said that he was thus disgraced and dishonoured. Ibn Qutayba had already written that ʿAlī b. al-Ḥusayn had given his mother (and not his nurse called 'mother') in marriage to the *mawlā* of his father al-Ḥusayn and that he himself had married a slave whom he liberated on that occasion. He was subsequently mocked by the Umayyad ʿAbd al-Malik.[20]

18. Al-Masʿūdī (attrib.), *Ithbāt al-waṣiyya* (Qumm, 1417/1996), p. 170. C. Pellat opts instead for the authenticity of attribution of the book to the author of *Murūj al-dhahab*; see his article 'Masʿūdī et l'imāmisme', in *Le shīʿisme imāmite*, Actes du Colloque de Strasbourg (6–9 May 1968) (Paris, 1970), pp. 69–90; however, also refer to the very sceptical and often pertinent remarks by T. Khalidi, *Islamic Historiography: The Histories of Masʿūdī* (Albany, 1975), pp. 138, note 2 and pp. 163–164.

19. *Ithbāt al-waṣiyya*, pp. 170–171.

20. Ibn Qutayba, *al-Maʿārif*, p. 215. Reproached by ʿAbd al-Malik, ʿAlī b. al-Ḥusayn would thus have opposed the example of the Prophet who had

With the next author, the renowned Ibn Bābūya al-Ṣadūq (d. 381/991), this episode takes an enigmatic turn that perhaps has special significance. In his *ʿUyūn akhbār al-Riḍā*,[21] al-Shaykh al-Ṣadūq reports a tradition going back to the eighth imam, ʿAlī b. Mūsā al-Riḍā (d. 203/818), in which the latter, finding himself in Khurāsān as heir to al-Maʾmūn, says to the Iranian Sahl b. al-Qāsim al-Nūshajānī: 'Between you [the Iranians, the Nūshajānī family?] and us [the imams] there is a relationship (*inna baynanā wa baynakum nasaban*).' Faced with the surprised reaction and curiosity of his interlocutor, al-Riḍā replies that the conqueror of Khurāsān, ʿAbd Allāh b. ʿĀmir b. Kurayz, captured two of Yazdgird's daughters and sent them to the caliph ʿUthmān b. ʿAffān (the story, in keeping with historical accuracy, does not take place during the siege of al-Madāʾin and ʿUmar's caliphate but during ʿUthmān's rule and the conquest of Khurāsān where the last Sasanian emperor and his family had sought refuge). The two daughters were given to al-Ḥasan and al-Ḥusayn. Both died during labour, al-Ḥusayn's wife while giving birth to ʿAlī b. al-Ḥusayn. The account continues with the episode of the nurse. She was al-Ḥusayn's slave and the young ʿAlī knew no other mother but her; she was known by people as the 'mother' of ʿAlī b. al-Ḥusayn. As we shall shortly see, 'the people' here are synonymous with the adversaries of the imam, that is, the Umayyads from accounts by Ibn Qutayba and the (Pseudo-?) al-Masʿūdī. This point in the account is interrupted by an enigmatic sentence that may be interpreted in two ways according to whether we read the verb *zawwaja* in the active or passive form:

- And people claimed that he (i.e. ʿAlī b. al-Ḥusayn) gave his 'mother's' hand in marriage (*zawwaja ummahu*).

---

married the freed slave Ṣafiyya bint Ḥuyayy and who gave the hand of his cousin – the daughter of his paternal aunt – Zaynab bint Jaḥsh, in marriage to his liberated *mawlā*, Zayd b. Ḥāritha.

21. Ed. M. al-Ḥusaynī al-Lājevardī (Tehran, 1378/1958), vol. 2, ch. 35, no. 6, p. 128; Persian trans. by Riḍāʾī and Ṣāʿidī, based on the edition by M. B. Bihbūdī (Tehran, 1396/1976), vol. 2, p. 487.

- And people claimed that he married his 'mother' (*zuwwija ummahu*).

Admittedly the first reading in the active form is more plausible and more in keeping with versions already cited by Ibn Qutayba and the (Pseudo-?) al-Masʿūdī. However, one may wonder why the complement of the verb is not given: to whom did ʿAlī b. al-Ḥusayn give his 'mother' in marriage? The verb *zawwaja* in the active form, in the sense of to 'marry a woman', is almost always employed with the direct accusative of the female and with *min* or *bi-* of the male.[22] Here we have only *zawwaja ummahu*, which enables a reading in the passive (*zuwwija* in the passive is synonymous with the fifth form *tazawwaja*), so much so that the text immediately adds *maʿādh Allāh*, 'it displeases God', as if to highlight the ignominy of the assertion, namely marrying one's own mother (as if the first interpretation were not as scandalous!).[23] The question may justifiably be asked: while the traditions reported by Ibn Qutayba and (Pseudo-?) al-Masʿūdī are clear, even syntactically, why does the tradition reported by Ibn Bābūya maintain (deliberately no doubt) an ambiguity that creates confusion?

I will be advancing a hypothesis that may seem audacious but is plausible in the context of this tradition. Since the account seeks to link the descendants of pre-Islamic Iranian kings to the Shiʿi imams, one can reasonably believe that the listeners and/or

22. Ibn Qutayba: *zawwaja ʿAlī b. al-Ḥusayn ummahu min mawlāh*; al-Masʿūdī (attrib.): *zawwajahā bi-mawlāh*.

23. In the next part of the account, we encounter the same issue twice: *fa-zawwaja-hā/fa-zuwwija-hā* and *zawwaja/zuwwija ʿAlī b. al-Ḥusayn ummahu*. The Persian translators of *ʿUyūn akhbār al-Riḍā* opt for the first interpretation; however, S. J. Shahīdī, in his excellent article on the popular beliefs regarding Shahrbānū (an article that I will revisit further below), prefers the second interpretation, pointing out the fact that from ancient times, according to popular belief, the despicable Umayyads had arranged to circulate a rumour that the fourth imam had married his own mother; Sayyid Jaʿfar Shahīdī, 'Baḥthī dar bāre-ye Shahrbānū', in *Cherāgh-e rowshan dar donyā-ye tārīk* (Tehran, 1333 Sh./1954–1955), pp. 175–176.

readers sensitive to this fact saw in the episode of the marriage of the 'mother' a similarity to the notion of *xwētōdas/xwēdōdah*, the incestuous marriage of the kings, priests and nobility of ancient Iran.[24] The Muslims had heard – admittedly only rather superficially – of this practice and the educated folk, especially the supporters of 'Arab-ness' did not miss an opportunity to recall this episode in order to point out the decadence and corruption of pre-Islamic Iranian culture.[25] In this context, our tradition seems to have two objectives in mind: first, in the eyes of Muslims in general, and more specifically the Shiʿis, to clear the Iranians of early times of this accusation which ultimately stems from misinformation and slander from malicious adversaries (not unlike the rumours spread by the Umayyads regarding the fourth imam). The 'incestuous marriage' is only a metaphor and symbol, just as the appellation 'mother' for the nurse is a metaphor. Then, in the eyes of the Iranian converts – or those about to adopt Imami Shiʿism – the fourth imam is described as one who perpetuates a highly respected symbolic practice (since according to ancient Iranian belief, a son issued from *xwētōdas/xwēdōdah* is the most

24. Ever since the publication of the fundamental text by E. W. West, 'The Meaning of the *Khvêtûk-das* or *Khvêtûtâd*', in *The Sacred Books of the East*, ed. M. Müller, vol. XVIII, *Pahlavi Texts*, Part II: *The Dâdistân-i Dinik and the Epistles of Manuchikar* (Oxford, 1882), Appendix 3; see J. S. Slotkin, 'On a Possible Lack of Incest Regulations in Old Iran', *American Anthropologist*, 49 (1947), pp. 612–617; on the same point, W. H. Goodenough, 'Comments on the Question of Incestuous Marriages in Old Iran', *American Anthropologist*, 51 (1949), pp. 326–328; B. Spooner, 'Iranian Kinship and Marriage', *Iran*, 4 (1966), pp. 51–59 and esp. C. Herrenschmidt, 'Note sur la parenté chez les Perses au début de l'empire achéménide', in H. Sancisi-Weerdenburg and A. Kuhrt (eds), *Achaemenid History*, vol. II : *The Greek Sources* (Leiden, 1987), pp. 53–67, and 'Le *xwētōdas* ou mariage "incestueux" en Iran ancien', in P. Bonte (ed.), *Epouser au plus proche. Inceste, prohibitions et stratégies matrimoniales autour de la Méditerranée* (Paris, 1994), pp. 113–125.

25. See e.g., al-Jāḥiẓ, *al-Bayān wa'l-tabyīn*, ed. 'A. M. Hārūn, 4 vols (rpr. Cairo, n.d.), vol. 2, p. 260, and *al-Ḥayawān*, ed. 'A. M. Hārūn, 7 vols (Cairo, n.d.), vol. 5, p. 324; Abu'l-ʿAlā al-Maʿarrī, *al-Luzūmiyyāt*, ed. Khānjī (Cairo, 1924), vol. 1, p. 172. For other sources see esp. G. Monnot, *Penseurs musulmans et religions iraniennes. 'Abdal-Jabbār et ses devanciers* (Paris, 1974), index under 'inceste'.

worthy to become either a priest or a king, in other words, the most capable of holding spiritual and temporal powers), is in Shiʿi terms, an imam par excellence. I will have much more to say regarding the tradition reported by al-Ṣadūq, and it seems to me that what remains to be said about it in due course will corroborate even more so what has just been observed.

The disciple of Ibn Bābūya al-Ṣadūq, al-Shaykh al-Mufīd (d. 413/1022), introduces yet more variants to the texture of the story. In his *Irshād*, he very briefly mentions that ʿAlī b. al-Ḥusayn al-Akbar's (and no longer al-Aṣghar) mother was Shāh-i Zanān,[26] daughter of Kisrā Yazdgird (and further Yazdgird b. Shahriyār b. Kisrā). The story here apparently takes place during ʿAlī's caliphate, when ʿAlī, through his agent Ḥurayth b. Jābir al-Ḥanafī,[27] who was sent to the East (*al-mashriq*, often synonymous with Khurāsān), received the two daughters of the Iranian emperor. ʿAlī offers the first, Shāh-i Zanān, to his son al-Ḥusayn and by her he fathers Zayn al-ʿĀbidīn; he offers the second (she is not named) to his supporter Muḥammad b. Abī Bakr (son of the first caliph), who fathers a son by her, al-Qāsim.[28] To my knowledge, the brief version by al-Mufīd, that introduces Muḥammad b. Abī Bakr into the story is without precedent. When one considers the nature of his work as a whole (apart perhaps from his *Kitāb al-ikhtiṣāṣ*) and his position in Buyid Baghdad,[29] one can

---

26. Most probably instead of the Shāh-i Jahān/Jahān-Shāh that we have already encountered; in any case, it is a more appropriate variant as it means 'Sovereign (lit. King) of women'. According to al-Ṭabarī the title of Shāh-i Zanān was held by the Sasanian queen Būrān/Pūrān (Dokht) who ruled briefly in her own name, in 9–10/630–631; see Nöldeke, *Geschichte der Perser*, p. 399 and note.

27. On him see e.g. al-Ṭūsī, *Rijāl* (Najaf, 1380/1961), p. 39, no. 26.

28. Muḥammad b. Muḥammad b. al-Nuʿmān al-Mufīd, *al-Irshād*, text and Persian translation with commentary by H. Rasūlī Maḥallātī (Tehran, 1346 Sh./1968), vol. 2, ch. 5, p. 137 and ch. 6, p. 138.

29. See M. J. MacDermott, *The Theology of al-Shaikh al-Mufīd (d. 413/1022)* (Beirut, 1978); A. A. Faqīhī, *Āl-e Būye va owḍāʿ-e zamān-e īshān* (2nd edn, Tehran, 1365 Sh./1986), index, under 'Mufīd'; see *Guide divin*, index, under 'Mufīd'.

perhaps suggest that he sought through this to bring the Shiʿis and Sunnis closer. But this version seems not to have had any future either.

On the other hand, his Iranian contemporary, Abū Jaʿfar al-Ṭabarī al-Ṣaghīr, known as Ibn Rustam (fifth/eleventh century), reports one of the longest and most interesting versions of the Shahrbānū tradition in his *Dalāʾil al-imāma*.[30] To summarise: when the Persian captives arrived in Medina, ʿUmar wanted to sell them as slaves. ʿAlī vigorously defended the Iranians and, referring to the sayings of the Prophet, insisted on their nobility and pure intentions, all the while declaring that it was foretold that he would have descendants by them (*lā budda min an yakūna lī minhum dhurriyya*). Upon this, he liberated the slaves belonging to him. The Banū Hāshim, *Muhājirūn* and *Anṣār*, in other words, those considered the noblest among Muslim Arabs, followed suit by offering their shares to ʿAlī. Thwarted, ʿUmar was obliged to do the same.

ʿAlī then declared that the Persian women now freed were to choose their husbands for themselves, if they so wished. It is thus that Shahrbānūya bint Kisrā was able to chose al-Ḥusayn as her husband and ʿAlī as 'godfather' (*wālī*). One of the 'pillars' (*arkān*) of Imamism, Ḥudhayfa b. al-Yamān al-ʿAbsī,[31] ʿAlī's famous Companion, read the marriage sermon (*khuṭba*). It is also reported that Shahrbānūya had a sister, Morvārīd ('Pearl'), who chose al-Ḥasan for her husband. An important section of the account concerns the dialogue in Persian interspersed with Arabic between ʿAlī and the princess:

ʿAlī: '*Mā ismuki?*' [Arabic] What is your name?
Princess: '*Shāh-i Zanān*'. [Persian] Sovereign [lit. King] of Women.

---

30. Ibn Rustam al-Ṭabarī al-Ṣaghīr, *Dalāʾil al-imāma* (Qumm, 1413/1992), pp. 194–196; an abridged version of this tradition is also reported in the early anonymous text, *Alqāb al-rasūl wa ʿitratihi* in *Majmūʿa nafīsa fī taʾrīkh al-aʾimma* (Qumm, 1406/1985), p. 253.

31. For more information and further sources concerning him, now consult M. Lecker, 'Ḥudhayfa b. al-Yamān and ʿAmmār b. Yāsir. Jewish converts to Islam', *Quaderni di Studi Arabi*, 11 (1993), pp. 149–162.

ʿAlī: ʻ*Na Shāh-i Zanān nīst magar dukhtar-i Muḥammad wa hiya sayyidat nisā*ʾ [*sic, nisā*ʾ without the article] *anti Shahrbānūya wa ukhtuki Murwārīd bint Kisrā*.ʼ [Persian] No! No one is the ʻSovereign of Womenʼ except for Muḥammadʼs daughter [i.e. Fāṭima] [Arabic] who is Sayyidat [al-]Nisāʾ [which may also be translated as ʻSovereign of Womenʼ]. You are Shahrbānūya and your sister is Morvārīd, daughter[s] of Kisrā.

Princess: ʻ*Āriya*.ʼ [Persian] Yes.[32]

The Persian of the text is from the fourth and fifth/tenth and eleventh centuries:[33] the Pārsī *magar* as a particle of exception has replaced the Sasanian Darī *judh* (or *judhāk*) or *bēyēk*.[34] The same is true for the Pārsī negative *na* that replaces *nai*. The verbal form *nīst (na/nê + ast)* seems to date from the third and fourth/ninth and tenth centuries.[35] And it is noteworthy that, for the first time, a parallel is established between Shahrbānū and Fāṭima. This point is all the more striking because even the name of Shāh-i Zanān (see note 26 above) seems to correspond to some famous titles given to Fāṭima: ʻSayyidat al-Nisāʾʼ, ʻSayyidat Nisāʾ al-ʿĀlamīnʼ, ʻSayyidat al-Niswānʼ, ʻSayyidat Nisāʾ al-Dunyā

32. Ibn Rustam al-Ṭabarī al-Ṣaghīr, *Dalāʾil al-imāma*, p. 196. On the theory of the ancient Iranian origin of the term *morvārīd* (pearl) and the refutation of its supposed late Greek etymology, see B. Sarkārātī, ʻMorvārīd pīsh-e khūk afshāndanʼ, reprinted in his *Sāye hā-ye shekār shodeh* (Tehran, 1378 Sh./1999), pp. 51–70, esp. pp. 64–70. On the Mithraic symbolism of the pearl, see M. Moqaddam, *Jostār dar bāre-ye Mehr va Nāhīd* (Tehran, 1978), pp. 32ff. Cf. also I. Gershevitch, ʻMargarites the pearlʼ, in Fouchécour and Gignoux (eds), *Etudes irano-aryennes offertes à Gilbert Lazard* (Paris, 1989), pp. 113–136.

33. M. T. Bahār, *Sabk-shenāsī*, vol. 1, ch. 9, p. 283ff.

34. Ibid., vol. 1, p. 336; S. Nafīsī, *Tārīkh-e naẓm va nathr*, vol. 1, p. 94. On these various Iranian languages refer also to G. Lazard, ʻ*Pahlavi, pârsi, dari*: les langues de l'Iran d'après Ibn al-Muqaffaʿʼ, in C. E. Bosworth (ed.), *Iran and Islam: In Memory of the late Vladimir Minorsky* (Edinburgh, 1971), pp. 361–391, and ʻ*Pârsi* et *dari*: nouvelles remarquesʼ, in C. Altman et al. (eds), *Aspects of Iranian Culture: In Honour of Richard Nelson Frye. Bulletin of the Asian Institute*, N.S. 4 (1990), pp. 141–148; both articles have now been published in G. Lazard, *La formation de la langue persane* (Paris, 1995), sections 3 and 9.

35. M. T. Bahār, *Sabk-shenāsī*, vol. 1, ch. 10, pp. 343–344 and 349ff.

wa al-Ākhira', etc.[36] Although the parallel obviously flatters Shahrbānū, it simultaneously underscores Fāṭima's superiority.

During this same fifth/eleventh century, the Ziyārid prince 'Unṣur al-Maʿālī Kay Kāwūs b. Iskandar, probably a Sunni, also reports a beautiful version of the story in his *Qābūs-nāma*, one of the masterpieces of medieval Persian prose. The captive princess, here called Shahrbānū, is on the verge of being sold by the caliph 'Umar. Then 'Alī enters the story and dissuades him by citing a Prophetic *ḥadīth*, according to which 'the progeny of kings are not to be bought and sold (*laysa'l-bayʿ ʿalā abnāʾ al-mulūk*)'. Shahrbānū is then respectfully taken to Salmān al-Fārisī, another stalwart hero of Shiʿism. Seated beside him, she declares that it is up to her to choose her husband. She acknowledges 'Umar's nobility but finds him too old.[37] Regarding 'Alī she announces: 'He is truly noble and suits me but I would be ashamed before Fāṭima al-Zahrā in the hereafter; so I do not want him.' Al-Ḥasan b. 'Alī is also deemed worthy but the princess says that he already has many wives. Finally, al-Ḥusayn is chosen, for his nobility surely, but also because he is a virgin as is Shahrbānū, since (as it is said) 'for a virgin bride, she says, only a virgin groom will do (*dokhtar-e dūshīze rā shū-ye dūshīze bāyad*)'.[38]

In the next century, in his *Manāqib*, Ibn Shahrāshūb al-Māzandarānī (d. 588/1192) records the tradition reported by al-Shaykh al-Mufīd and especially that by Ibn Rustam al-Ṭabarī al-Ṣaghīr that he

36. Ibn Shahrāshūb, *Manāqib āl Abī Ṭālib*, 3 vols (Najaf, 1956), 'Bāb manāqib Fāṭima; faṣl fī ḥilyatihā wa tawārīkhihā', vol. 3, p. 133; Ḥusayn b. 'Abd al-Wahhāb, *'Uyūn al-muʿjizāt* (Najaf, 1369/1950), pp. 46–47.

37. The account clearly seeks to rehabilitate the second caliph and to restore his image tarnished by Shiʿi versions.

38. 'Unṣur al-Maʿālī Kay Kāwūs b. Iskandar b. Qābūs b. Voshmgīr, *Qābūs-nāma*, ed. Gh. Ḥ. Yūsufī (8th edn, Tehran, 1375 Sh./1996), ch. 27 and pp. 137–138. Cf. al-Rāzī al-Ṣanʿānī (d. 460/1068), *Ta'rīkh Ṣanʿā'*, ed. Ḥ. b. 'A. al-'Amrī (Beirut–Damascus, 1989), p. 109 (*khiyarat Allāh min Quraysh wa khiyaratuhu min Fāris*). Here, the Arabic name of Shahrbānū is Ḥabbadhā.

reproduces in a version with significant variants.[39] In general, Ibn Shahrāshūb's version summarises the text from *Dalāʾil al-imāma* or its source, which tends to show – if still necessary – that numerous versions of the Shahrbānū story were simultaneously in circulation in Imami milieus. The dialogue in Persian interspersed with Arabic has been deleted. Greater emphasis is placed on the wisdom and nobility of the entire Iranian people ('the Persians are wise and noble', *al-furs ḥukamāʾ kuramāʾ*)[40] as well as on the Light that is al-Ḥusayn ('auroral light and glistening star', *al-nūr al-sāṭiʿ wa al-shihāb al-lāmiʿ*).[41] Elsewhere, Ibn Shahrāshūb provides other information in fragments regarding Shahrbānū: she is the mother of imam ʿAlī al-Aṣghar Zayn al-ʿĀbidīn.[42] She was present at Karbalāʾ, and after the massacre of al-Ḥusayn and his family she drowned herself in the Euphrates to escape the humiliation of captivity by Yazīd.[43] The poem about imam Zayn al-ʿĀbidīn with a reference to the Prophet's *ḥadīth* on the Quraysh and Persians as the 'Two chosen of God' (based on the *Rabīʿ al-abrār* by al-Zamakhsharī) was attributed to Abu'l-Aswad al-Du'alī (see al-Kulaynī's version above).[44] Finally, there is a passage on the different names for the mother of the fourth imam:

> His mother was Shahrbānūya, daughter of Yazdgird b. Shahriyār al-Kisrā; one still called her Shāh-i Zanān, Jahān Bānūya, Sulāfa, Khawla and Shāh-i Zanān bint Shīrūya b. Kisrā Abarwīz and Barra bint al-Nūshajān [I shall comment on this name], but [only?] the first name is correct (*al-ṣaḥīḥ huwa'l-awwal*). The Commander

---

39. Ibn Shahrāshūb, *Manāqib*, 'Bab fī imāmat Abī ʿAbd Allāh al-Ḥusayn, faṣl fi'l-muqaddimāt', vol. 3, pp. 207–208.

40. Ibid. p. 207.

41. Ibid., p. 208, l. 8.

42. Ibid., 'Bāb fī imāmat al-Ḥusayn, faṣl fī tawārīkhihi wa alqābihi', vol. 3, p. 231.

43. Ibid., 'Faṣl fī maqtalihi', vol. 3, p. 259.

44. Ibid., 'Bāb imāmat Abī Muḥammad ʿAlī b. al-Ḥusayn, faṣl fī siyādatihi', vol. 3, pp. 304–305.

of the Faithful (ʿAlī) had called her Maryam and, it is said, also Fāṭima. She bore the title of Sayyidat al-Nisā'.[45]

Two brief comments may be made about this list: first, the parallel with Fāṭima becomes more pronounced since Shahrbānū bore the name of Fāṭima (what is more, a name that was given in person by ʿAlī) as well as her title: 'Sovereign of Women'. Then, with 'Barra bint al-Nūshajān', this is the third time the name Nūshajān (see the texts by al-Ṭabarī and Ibn Bābūya above) is encountered. I shall address this more extensively below.

During the same period, Quṭb al-Dīn al-Rāwandī (d. 573/1177–1178) reports in his *al-Kharā'ij* what appears to be the last noteworthy version so far known of the Shahrbānū tradition.[46] The Iranian scholar seems to have endeavoured to report a version that would be a synthesis of many others (al-Ṣaffār, al-Kulaynī, Ibn Rustam al-Ṭabarī al-Ṣaghīr), even including some additional information. According to this tradition, which goes back to the fifth imam, the story took place during ʿUmar's caliphate. The princess arrived in Medina, bathed in light (al-Ṣaffār's version is slightly less dramatic at this point for it is no longer the mosque [*masjid*] where the caliph presides that is illuminated by the face of the young girl, but the place where the caliph sits [*majlis*]). In this account there is the princess's exclamation (here *a fīrūzān*), the caliph's anger, ʿAlī's intervention, the freeing of the princess and her choice of al-Ḥusayn as husband. At this point, al-Rāwandī reports a new dialogue in Persian interspersed with Arabic between ʿAlī and the young woman:

ʿAlī [Persian]: '*Che nāmī dārī ay kanīzak*. Young lady, what is your name?' (Arabic): '*Ay aysh ismuki yā ṣabiyya*. What is your name, young lady?'

Princess [Persian]: '*Jahān Shāh bār khudhāh*; Jahān Shāh, O Lord!'

45. Ibid., 'Faṣl fī aḥwālihi wa ta'rīkhihi', vol. 3, p. 311.

46. Al-Rāwandī, *al-Kharā'ij wa'l-jara'iḥ* (Qumm, 1409/1988–1989), vol. 2, ch. 15, no. 67, pp. 750–751.

ʿAlī [as if a question]: ʿ*Shahrbānūya*?'

Princess [Persian]: '*Kh(w)āharam Shahrbānūya.* My sister [is called] Shahrbānūya.' [Arabic]: '*Ay tilka ukhtī.*' That's my sister.

ʿAlī [Persian]: '*Rāst gofti.*' You have spoken the truth. [Arabic]: '*Ay ṣadaqti.*' You are right.

Then ʿAlī speaks to al-Ḥusayn and tells him that his new wife is 'the Mother of the Legatees [i.e. the imams], those of pure descent' (*umm al-awṣiyā' al-dhurriyya al-ṭayyiba. sic*).

Once again the Persian is of a later period, that is, at the earliest dating from the fourth/tenth century. The interrogative particle *che* (those), vocatives (*ay* and *bār*) as well as the diminuitive *ak* (in *kanīz-ak*) are evidence of this.[47] Al-Rāwandī then reports that the princess died giving birth to ʿAlī b. al-Ḥusayn and finally gives the 'extraordinary account' (*qiṣṣa ʿajība*) of her conversion to Islam. According to this account, before the arrival of the Muslim army, the princess experienced two dreams. In the first, she sees the Prophet Muḥammad accompanied by al-Ḥusayn arriving at her father's palace. He gives her in marriage to al-Ḥusayn, after a sermon delivered by the Prophet. In the second dream, she sees Fāṭima, who converts her to Islam and predicts the arrival of Muslim troops, adding that no harm will come to her as she is promised to her son al-Ḥusayn.

Slightly before the accounts of Ibn Shahrāshūb and al-Rāwandī, the anonymous Iranian author of *Mujmal al-tawārīkh*, a Persian text written in 520/1126, calls the wife of imam al-Ḥusayn 'Shahrnāz' (Bounty of the Land; a *taṣḥīf* for Shahrbānū?), daughter of Yazdgird the King or Subḥān (a *taṣḥīf* for Nūshajān?), King of Persia (*malek-e Pārs*).[48] Other authors – whether Imami or

47. M. T. Bahār, *Sabk-shenāsī*, respectively 1:406, 408 and 413–416; P. Nātel Khānlarī, *Zabān shenāsī-ye fārsī* (2nd edn, Tehran, 1344 Sh./1966), pp. 70–71.

48. Anonymous, *Mujmal al-tawārīkh wa'l-qiṣaṣ*, ed. M. T. Bahār (Tehran, 1318 Sh./1940), p. 456.

not – such as al-Faḍl b. al-Ḥasan al-Ṭabrisī (d. 548/1153), ʿAlī b. ʿĪsā al-Irbilī (d. 693/1293) and Ibn Khallikān (d. 681/1282) to the relatively modern al-Nūrī al-Ṭabrisī (d. 1320/1902), including Muḥammad Bāqir al-Majlisī (d. 1111/1699–1700) and his disciple ʿAbd Allāh al-Baḥrānī al-Iṣfahānī, do no more than reproduce one or more of the reports just described.[49] Between the third/ninth and the sixth/twelfth century, the Shahrbānū story would have reached full evolution, at least in its literary written form. As we shall see, the oral version spread via by popular beliefs underwent a different process.

2

According to the earliest sources, the mother of ʿAlī b. al-Ḥusayn Zayn al-ʿĀbidīn, known as ʿAlī al-Aṣghar, was an oriental slave, originally from Sind or Sijistān, thus perhaps actually Iranian, since both regions were provinces of the former Sasanian empire. Al-Ḥusayn b. ʿAlī, her master and then spouse, called her Sulāfa

49. See e.g. al-Faḍl al-Ṭabrisī/Ṭabarsī, *Iʿlām al-warā* (Najaf, 1390/1970), p. 256; al-Irbilī, *Kashf al-ghumma*, ed. H. Rasūlī Maḥallātī (Qumm, 1381/1961), vol. 2, p. 107; Sibṭ Ibn al-Jawzī, *Tadhkirat khawāṣṣ al-umma* (rpr. Tehran, n.d.), p. 183; Ibn Khallikān, *Wafayāt al-aʿyān* (lithography, n.p., 1284/1867), p. 374 (based on *Rabīʿ al-abrār* by al-Zamakhsharī). In this case, three daughters of Yazdgird are given in marriage by ʿAlī to Muḥammad son of ʿAbū Bakr, ʿAbd Allāh, son of ʿUmar and al-Ḥusayn, his own son respectively. ʿUthmān, although one of the four 'rightly-guided' caliphs, is excluded from the list. The tradition is most likely anti-Umayyad); Ḥasan b. ʿAlī al-Qummī, *Tārīkh-e Qumm*, ed. S. J. Tihrānī (Tehran, rpr. 1361 Sh./1982), p. 195; Ibn ʿInaba, *ʿUmdat al-ṭālib fī ansāb āl Abī Ṭālib* (Qumm, 1417/1996), pp. 172–173; Qāḍī Aḥmad b. Muḥammad Ghaffārī, *Tārīkh-e Jahān ārā* (Tehran, 1343/1924), p. 25; al-Ḥurr al-ʿĀmilī, *Ithbāt al-hudāt* (3rd edn, Tehran, 1364 Sh./1985), vol. 4, p. 441; Hāshim al-Baḥrānī, *Ḥilyat al-abrār* (Qumm, 1397/1976), vol. 2, pp. 7f., and *Madīnat al-maʿājiz* (Tehran, n.d.), p. 129; al-Majlisī, *Biḥār al-anwār* (Tehran-Qumm, 1376–1392/1956–1972), vol. 46, pp. 7ff.; al-Baḥrānī al-Iṣfahānī, *ʿAwālim al-ʿulūm* (Qumm, 1409/1988), vol. 18, pp. 6ff.; Muḥammad Bāqir al-Māzandarānī, *Jannat al-naʿīm* (lithograph, n.p., 1296/1878), pp. 205–206; Ḥusayn al-Nūrī al-Ṭabrisī/Ṭabarsī, *Mustadrak al-wasāʾil* (Qumm, 1407/1986), vol. 13, pp. 375ff. The list is obviously not exhaustive.

and/or Ghazāla. Once an adult, ʿAlī al-Aṣghar freed her and gave her in marriage to a 'client' of his father. Here we have almost all the likely historic elements that can be gleaned from Ibn Saʿd, Ibn Qutayba and other third/ninth century chroniclers. For reasons we shall try to clarify, numerous accounts were circulated, especially in Iranian Imami milieus, insisting that the mother of imam Zayn al-ʿĀbidīn was the daughter of Yazdgird III, the last Sasanian king of Iran.

Just before the Arab invasion, many Iranian nobles escaped from the capital, al-Madā'in-Ctesiphon, taking their women (free or enslaved), their wealth and valuables.[50] However, many other Iranians belonging to the noble class were not so fortunate; they were captured and reduced to slavery by the Muslim conquerors.[51]

It is nevertheless certain that none among them belonged to the king's immediate family. In his monograph devoted to the Sasanians, M. J. Mashkūr reviews the opinions of a number of specialists in Iranian studies and historians of Sasanian Iran regarding the family of Yazdgird III. J. Darmesteter, T. Nöldeke, B. Spuler and A. Christensen all allude to the Shiʿi story of Shahrbānū, all the while stressing its legendary and biased nature.[52] According to these scholars, who base their work specifically on non-Shiʿi

50. Abū Yūsuf, *Kitāb al-kharāj*, p. 30; al-Dīnawarī, *al-Akhbār al-ṭiwāl*, p. 129; Miskawayh, *Tajārib al-umam*, vol. 1, p. 219; Ibn al-Athīr, *Akhbār-e Īrān az* al-Kāmil, pp. 209–210.

51. Al-Balādhurī, *Futūḥ al-buldān*, pp. 262ff.; al-Masʿūdī, *Murūj*, vol. 1, pp. 309ff.

52. M. J. Mashkūr, *Sāsāniyān* (revised edn, Tehran, ca. 1339 Sh./1960), vol. 2, pp. 1284ff. As a whole, these scholars of Iranian studies only accord cursory importance to the story; which is perfectly understandable in the context of the issues that preoccupy them; see also Mashkūr, *Īrān dar ʿahd-e bāstān. Dar tārīkh-e aqvām va pādshāhān-e pīsh az Islām* (2nd edn, Tehran, 1347 Sh./1968), pp. 488ff. The numerous names given to the Iranian princess and her father are perfectly in keeping with the legendary nature of the character (the daughter: Barra, Fāṭima, Ghazāla, ḤRĀR, Jahān Bānūya, Jahān Shāh, Khawla, Khilwa, Maryam, Salāma, Sayyidat al-Nisā', Shāh-e Zanān, Shahrbān, Shahrbānū, Shahrbānūya, Shahrnāz, Sulāfa, Umm Salama; the father: Malik Harā, Malik Qāshān, Nūshajān, Shīrūya b. Kisrā, Subḥān Malik Pārs, Yazdgird); see also Ḥ. Karīmān, *Ray-e bāstan* (Tehran, 1345–1349 Sh./1966–1970), vol. 1, p. 409.

historiographical sources, the woman or women and children of the emperor were simply evacuated from the capital well before the invasion and were not captured.[53] In addition, sources from T'ang China concerning the Arab conquest of Iran, the last Sasanian emperor and his descendants also remain silent about the eventual captivity of one of Yazdgird III's relatives.[54]

Some elements that appear sporadically in recurring versions of the Shahrbānū legend seem to have come to light in reaction to certain historical facts. It is not entirely impossible, for example, that the association of a noblewoman named Ghazāla, captured in al-Madā'in and given in marriage to a noble Arab, was inspired by the fact that ʿUthmān, one of the sons of the wealthy Companion ʿAbd al-Raḥmān b. ʿAwf, had as mother a certain Ghazāl bint Kisrā, who was captured during the siege of the Sasanian capital by Saʿd b. Abī Waqqāṣ.[55]

---

53. Mashkūr, *Sāsāniyān*, vol. 2, pp. 1288–1290 and 1344–1347; see also S. Nafīsī, *Tārīkh-e ejtemāʿī-ye Īrān az enqerāḍ-e Sāsāniyān tā enqerāḍ-e Omaviyān* (Tehran, 1342 Sh./1964), pp. 13ff. On Yazdgird's death at the age of 35 in 32/652, he had seven sons and five daughters. According to M. J. Mashkūr and S. Nafīsī they included Ādharak, Shahīn, Mardāwand, Bābūna (Bānūya) and Tahmīna (see note 3 above). According to A. Christensen, *L'Iran sous les Sassanides* (rpr. Osnabrück, 1971), ch. 10, pp. 508–509, the name Shahrbānū seems to have been made popular by al-Masʿūdī's *Murūj al-dhahab* although the manuscipts are corrupted at this very point. Now also consult the monograph devoted to Yazdgird III by A. Hassuri (ʿA. Ḥaṣūrī), *Ākherīn Shāh* (Tehran, 1371 Sh./1992), where there is no mention of Shahrbānū.

54. J. Marquart, *Irānshahr nach der Geographie des Ps. Moses Xorenac'i* (Berlin, 1901), pp. 68–69; E. Chavannes, *Documents sur les Tou-kiue (Turcs) occidentaux* (St Petersburg, 1903), pp. 171–173; J. Harmatta, 'The Middle Persian-Chinese Bilingual Inscription from Hsian and the Chinese-Sāsānian Relations', in *La Persia nel medioevo* (Accademia Nazionale dei Lincei, Rome, 1971), pp. 363–376, esp. 373–375; M. G. Morony, *Irak after the Muslim Conquest* (Princeton, 1984), index, under 'Yazdgird III'; R. G. Hoyland, *Seeing Islam as Others Saw it* (Princeton, 1997), pp. 243ff. The study by C. ʿA. Aʿẓamī Sangesarī, 'Bāzmāndegan-e Yazdgerd-e sevvom', *Īrān Shenākht*, 10 (1377 Sh./1998), pp. 183–191, is rather perfunctory, based on very few sources, hardly drawing upon any previous studies, and not of use to scholars.

55. Ibn Saʿd, *Ṭabaqāt*, vol. 3, p. 128. Ghazāl would have been the name given to the female slave by her master. Her father's name seems to indicate that she was of noble stock.

Moreover, some reports recorded by historiographers describe the capture and enslavement of a descendant of Yazdgird III under the caliphate of al-Walīd b. ʿAbd al-Malik (86–97/705–715). Captured in northern Khurāsān, the young lady would have been sent to the governor of Iraq al-Ḥajjāj b. Yūsuf al-Thaqafī who offered her to the caliph. She gave birth to Yazīd b. al-Walīd known as ʿal-Nāqiṣʾ, that is Yazīd III, and perhaps Ibrāhīm b. al-Walīd.[56] The somewhat forced insistence on the liberation of the princess to the extent of freely choosing her spouse, in this case al-Ḥusayn b. ʿAlī, is surely, as we shall see, done in order to attract the sympathy of Iranians, but also perhaps arises from the claim of the ʿAbbasids, at least up to al-Manṣūr (caliph from 137/754 to 159/775), of being descendants of an uninterrupted line of free mothers and fathers. In this regard, the long letter from al-Manṣūr to the Ḥasanid Muḥammad al-Nafs al-Zakiyya takes on great significance. The latter's uprising (aggravated by that led by his brother Ibrāhīm) lasted from 132/749 to 145/762. In this letter, al-Manṣūr takes pride in the fact that the ʿAbbasids are of pure and free descent, paternal and maternal. At the same time he mocks the Ḥasanid and Ḥusaynid ʿAlids who count among their mothers a large number of female slaves. It is interesting to note in

56. Al-Ṭabarī, ed. M. de Goeje, series 1, p. 2873 series 2, pp. 1247 and 1874. According to al-Ṭabarī, Yazīd III's mother was Yazdgird's grandaughter. In series 2, p. 1874, this mother is known as Shāh-i Āfarīd (pehlevi: Shāhāfrid) and a rather interesting distich is attributed to Yazīd III:

I am the son of Kisrā and Marwān / One of my grandfathers is a *qayṣar*, another a *khāqān*.

It is therefore possible that Yazīd III al-Nāqiṣ was a model for subsequent genealogical speculations regarding ʿAlī Zayn al-ʿĀbidīn. See also, Ibn ʿAbd Rabbih, *al-ʿIqd al-farīd*, vol. 3, p. 103; Ibn al-ʿIbrī, *Mukhtaṣar al-duwal* (Tehran, n.d.), pp. 118–119; Ibn al-Athīr, *Akhbār-e Īrān az* al-Kāmil, vol. 2, pp. 334–335; refer also to A. Amīn, *Ḍuḥā'l-Islām* (Cairo, 1933), vol. 1, p. 11. Al-Mubarrad, one of the first to report the tradition linking Sulāfa, ʿAlī b. al-Ḥusayn Zayn al-ʿĀbidīn's mother, to the last of the Sasanians, attempts to reconcile both reports and writes that Sulāfa was Yazīd al-Nāqiṣ's paternal or maternal aunt; *al-Kāmil fi'l-lugha*, ed. al-Dālī, vol. 2, p. 646.

passing that the letter makes no mention of ʿAlī b. al-Ḥusayn Zayn al-ʿĀbidīn's mother.[57]

Having considered the formal details, let us now focus on what constitutes the core of the legend as it appears in the most recurrent versions. A Sasanian princess, bearer of the Light of Glory of the Iranian kings, arrives in Medina. Defying the caliph ʿUmar, supported by ʿAlī and speaking in Persian to him, she chooses al-Ḥusayn b. ʿAlī as her husband, eventually giving birth to ʿAlī Zayn al-ʿĀbidīn, who in turn will succeed al-Ḥusayn as imam, thus becoming 'the Mother of Legatees'. The story is obviously highly charged in doctrinal, ethnic and political terms. It is at once pro-Shiʿi and pro-Iranian and both elements are presented in such a manner as to be inseparable. This is a fundamental aspect of the account that one must always bear in mind. More precisely, one can add that in its Shiʿism, the story undeniably stems from the Ḥusaynid current and in its 'Iranianism' seems to emerge from radical circles. Considered together, these elements conspire to challenge a certain Sunni Arabo-centrist 'orthodoxy'.

Let us examine matters more closely. The Shahrbānū tradition is clearly of Ḥusaynid confession. It is true that, concerned about a kind of balance and stronger rapprochement between Shiʿis and Iranians, a good many versions depict two Iranian princesses who each marry al-Ḥasan and al-Ḥusayn respectively, but at the same time, with a stubborn insistance, al-Ḥusayn's wife is presented as the mother of future imams.[58] Ibn Shahrāshūb precedes the Shahrbānū story with a rather long development arguing for the legitimacy of the Ḥusaynid lineage of imams and consequently

57. Al-Mubarrad, *al-Kāmil*, ed. M. Z. Mubārak (Cairo, 1356/1937), vol. 2, pp. 1275–1278 (refer to the sources cited in notes from the editor); al-Ṭabarī, *Ta'rīkh*, ed. de Goeje, series 3(1), pp. 211–215.

58. Al-Masʿūdī (attrib.), *Ithbāt al-waṣiyya*, p. 170; Ibn Bābūya, *'Uyūn akhbār al-Riḍā*, vol. 2, p. 128; Ibn Rustam al-Ṭabarī al-Ṣaghīr, *Dalā'il al-imāma*, p. 196. The version reported by al-Mufīd, *Irshād*, vol. 2, p. 138, in which Imam al-Ḥasan is replaced by Muḥammad b. Abī Bakr is an isolated case.

the illegitimacy of al-Ḥasan's descendants.[59] Let us recall that in its different variants the tradition would have started circulating from the third/ninth century onwards, only a few decades after the revolt of the Zaydi Ḥasanid brothers, Muḥammad b. 'Abd Allāh al-Nafs al-Zakiyya and Ibrāhīm, a revolt that very quickly seems to have aroused great sympathy, even among the non-'Alid scholars, both in the Ḥijāz as well as in Iraq.[60] Some decades later, just after the execution of al-Amīn in 198/813, another Ḥasanid Zaydi rebel, Ibn Ṭabāṭabā, who was supported by the famous Abu'l-Sarāyā, was declared *al-Riḍā min āl Muḥammad* on Jumādā II 199/January 815 in Baghdad itself, only to be killed a month later.[61] Among other things, was the Shahrbānū story intended to counteract the popularity of the Zaydis and/or the Ḥasanids, especially in Shi'i milieu, both Iranian and assimilated?

Then, ever since the version reported by al-Ṣaffār al-Qummī in the third/ninth century until Ibn Rustam al-Ṭabarī al-Ṣaghīr in the fifth/eleventh and al-Rāwandī in the sixth/twelfth centuries, the tradition clearly highlights two elements: the magnificence of Persian royalty (Light emanating from the princess, her noble status, the freedom to choose her husband) and the importance of the Persian language (the dialogue with 'Alī, imam par excellence, in a language that he speaks well, in contrast with 'Umar, adversary par excellence of Shi'ism, who does not speak the language at all).

---

59. Ibn Shahrāshūb, *Manāqib*, vol. 3, pp. 206–207.

60. See al-Ṭabarī, ed. M. de Goeje, series 3, pp. 189–265; Abu'l-Faraj al-Iṣfahānī, *Maqātil al-Ṭālibiyyin*, ed. A. Ṣaqr (Cairo, 1949), pp. 260–299 and 354ff.; C. von Arendonk, *Les débuts de l'imamat zaydite du Yémen*, tr. J. Ryckmans (Leiden, 1960), pp. 44ff.; T. Nagel, 'Ein früher Bericht über den Aufstand des Muḥammad b. 'Abdallāh im Jahre 145h', *Der Islam*, 46 (1970), pp. 227–262; M. Q. Zaman, *Religion and Politics under the Early 'Abbasids. The Emergence of the Proto-Sunnī Elite* (Leiden, 1997), pp. 44–45 and 73–76.

61. See H. A. R. Gibb, 'Abu'l-Sarāyā al-Shaybānī', *EI2*, vol. 1, pp. 153–154 and B. Scarcia Amoretti, 'Ibn Ṭabāṭabā', *EI2*, vol. 3, pp. 975–976. On 'Alid rebellions at the beginning of the 'Abbasid caliphate see F. Omar, *The 'Abbāsid Califate 750/132–786/179* (Baghdad, 1969), ch. 4; J. Lassner, *The Shaping of 'Abbāsid Rule* (Princeton, 1982), pp. 69–87; H. Kennedy, *The Early 'Abbāsid Caliphate* (London, 1986), pp. 198–213.

Now in the eyes of some Iranian men of letters in early Islamic centuries, these two notions are the most important elements of Iranian identity. It would perhaps be anachronistic to speak of the 'nationalism' of these educated individuals but it would be just as naive to deny that there was among them a heightened sensitivity, even a kind of historical consciousness of their cultural identity crystalised around a certain perception of royalty and the Persian language. To explain his admiration for the history of the Iranian nation and its continuity, al-Ṭabarī invokes the uninterrupted succession of royal dynasties, from the origins of time up to the advent of Islam.[62]

In his *al-Āthār al-bāqiya*, Abū Rayḥān al-Bīrūnī (d. 440/1048) discusses the case of those Iranians who hoped that the Buyids would be agents of change or effect the restoration of the sovereignty of the Iranian monarchs and the religion of the Magi. At the same time, he is surprised that sensible folk should place their hopes in the Daylamīs – those who do not even speak adequate Persian – instead of having faith (as is apparently the case with al-Bīrūnī himself) in the ʿAbbasid dynasty, a dynasty that emerged from Khurāsān and that was brought to power by true Persians (*ʿajam*).[63] In its presentation and justification, Miskawayh's

62. Al-Ṭabarī, ed. M. de Goeje, series 1(1), p. 353; See also J. Chabbi, 'La représentation du passé aux premiers âges de l'historiographie califale', in *Itinéraires d'Orient. Hommages à Claude Cahen*, Res Orientales VI (Paris, 1995), pp. 21–46. For the importance of 'the History of Kings' in the ancient perception of Iranian culture see also Th. Nöldeke, *Geschichte der Perser und Araber*, pp. xix–xxiii and *Das iranische Nationalepos*, pp. 14–16; W. Barthold, *Mussulman Culture*, tr. Sh. Suhrawardy (Calcutta, 1934, rpr. Philadelphia, 1977), pp. 49–50; G. Widengren, 'The Sacral Kingship of Iran', in *La regalità sacra* (Leiden, 1959), pp. 242–257; M. G. S. Hodgson, *The Venture of Islam: Conscience and History in a World Civilization* (Chicago, 1961–1974), vol. I, *The Classical Age of Islam*, pp. 454ff.; E. Yarshater, 'Iranian National History', in E. Yarshater (ed.), *Cambridge History of Iran*, vol. 3(1) (Cambridge, 1983), pp. 359–477. For al-Masʿūdī's pro-Iranian stance, see T. Khalidi, *Islamic Historiography: The Histories of Masʿūdī*, pp. 90–91.

63. Al-Bīrūnī, *al-Āthār al-bāqiya ʿan al-qurūn al-khāliya*, ed. C. E. Sachau (Leipzig, 1878), p. 213; tr. Sachau, *The Chronology of Ancient Nations* (London, 1897, rpr. Frankfurt, 1969), p. 197. Cf. al-Jāḥiẓ, *al-Bayān wa al-tabyīn*, vol 3,

oeuvre, particularly his *Tajārib al-umam*, is from beginning to end filled with admiration for these two characteristics of Iranian culture; one readily understands why F. Rosenthal termed him 'the Persian nationalist philosopher'.[64] The same is also true for Firdawsī of Ṭūs in his monumental *Shāh-nāmā*. The role played by these kinds of thinkers is certainly not negligible in the sense that even the non-Iranian dynasties such as the Ghaznavids, Saljūqs and Ilkhāns rapidly adopted Persian and traced their origins to the ancient kings of Iran instead of to Muslim saints or Turko-Mongolian heroes.[65]

For almost a century now, many scholars have sought to show how these Iranian thinkers had, since the formation of Muslim culture, perceived of themselves as inheritors of a glorious cultural past and so constituting the vital last link in the chain of 'the History of Salvation', that is, of Islam.[66] M. Grignaschi, and more recently

---

p. 366, where it states that the Umayyad state is regarded as Arab and the ʿAbbasid state as Persian Khurāsānian. For differing opinions on the nature of the ʿAbbasid revolution (esp. those of M. A. Shaban, M. Sharon and J. Lassner) and for criticism of these opinions see E. Daniel, 'Arabs, Persians and the Advent of the Abbasids Reconsidered', *JAOS*, 117/3 (1997), pp. 542–548 as well as the extensively researched and much documented work by E. Yarshater, 'The Persian Presence in the Islamic World', in R. G. Hovannisian and G. Sabagh (eds), *The Persian Presence in the Islamic World* (Cambridge, 1998), pp. 4–125, particularly pp. 59–74. For the importance of Persian in the ancient perception of Iranian culture, see F. Gabrieli, 'Literary Tendencies', in G. E. von Grunebaum (ed.), *Unity and Variety in Muslim Civilization* (Chicago, 1955), pp. 87–106.

64. F. Rosenthal, *A History of Muslim Historiography* (Leiden, 1952), p. 122.

65. See R. Levy, 'Persia and the Arabs', in A. J. Arberry (ed.), *The Legacy of Persia* (Oxford, 1953), pp. 56–73, esp. pp. 66ff.; B. Spuler, 'Iran: the Persistent Heritage', in G. E. von Grunebaum (ed.), *Unity and Variety in Muslim Civilization*, pp. 167–182, particularly 176–177; see also W. Madelung, 'The Assumption of the Title Shahanshah by the Buyids and the Reign of the Daylam (*Dawlat al-Daylam*)', *JNES*, 28 (1969), pp. 84–108 and 168–183, rpr. in *Religious and Ethnic Movements in Medieval Islam* (London, 1992), article 8.

66. Among many other examples, see I. Goldziher, 'Islamisme et parsisme', *RHR*, 43 (1901), pp. 1–29, and *Muslim Studies*, tr. S. M. Stern and C. R. Barber (London, 1967–1971), vol. 1, pp. 135f.; G. E. von Grunebaum, 'Firdausī's Concept of History', in his *Islam: Essays in the Nature and Growth of a Cultural Tradition* (London, 1955), pp. 175f.; M. G. Morony, 'The Effects

C. H. de Fouchécour, Sh. Shaked and A. Tafazzoli have brilliantly demonstrated how what Gustav von Grunebaum calls 'the Persian Humanities' crystalise around the figure of the 'king' and royal ethics as transmitted to Islamic culture by the literary genre of the Mirrors for Princes (possibly an equivalent to *naṣīḥat al-mulūk*).[67] All that, according to learned Iranian 'nationalists', constitutes the sophistication of Persian culture and is designated by terms such as *honar* or *adab*, namely ethics, good manners, courtesy, refinement of the mind and humanism; it is transmitted essentially by

---

of the Muslim Conquest on the Persian Population of Irak', *Iran*, 14 (1976), pp. 41–55, and 'Conquerors and Conquered: Iran', in G. H. A. Juynboll, *Studies on the First Century of Islamic Society* (Carbondale and Edwardsville, IL, 1982), pp. 73–87; E. Yarshater, *Iranian National History*, in *The Cambridge History of Iran*, vol. 3 (Cambridge, 1983), esp. pp. 360ff., and 'The Persian Presence in the Islamic World', in R. G. Hovannisian and G. Sabagh (ed.), *The Persian Presence in the Islamic World* (Cambridge, 1998), pp. 4–125; C. E. Bosworth, 'The Persian Contribution to Islamic Historiography in the Pre-Mongol Period', in *The Persian Presence in the Islamic World*, pp. 218–236; M. Moḥammadī Malāyerī, *Farhang-e Īrānī-ye pīsh az eslām wa āthār-e ān dar tamaddon-e eslāmī va adabiyyāt-e 'arab* (Tehran, 1374 Sh./1995).

67. Among the many publications by M. Grignaschi on the subject, see e.g. 'Quelques spécimens de la littérature sassanide conservés dans les bibliothèques d'Istanbul', *JA*, 240 (1967), pp. 33–59; 'La *Nihâyatu-l-arab fî akhbâri-l-Furs wa-l-'Arab* (first section)', *Bulletin d'Etudes Orientales*, 22 (1969), pp. 15–67, 'La *Nihâyatu-l-arab fî akhbâri-l-Furs wa-l-'Arab* et les *Siyaru Mulûki-l-'Ajam* du Ps. Ibn al-Muqaffa'', Ibid., 26 (1973), pp. 83–184, and 'La *Siyâsatu-l-'âmmiyya* et l'influence iranienne sur la pensée politique islamique', in *Hommage et Opera Minora*, vol. 3, *Monumentum H.S. Nyberg*, *Acta Iranica* (Leiden, 1975), pp. 124–141; C. H. de Fouchécour, *Moralia. Les notions morales dans la littérature persane du 3e/9e au 7e/13e siècle* (Paris, 1986); Sh. Shaked, 'Andarz in Pre-Islamic Persia', *EIr*, vol. 2, pp. 11–16. In general, Sh. Shaked is one of the foremost specialists on the subject of the transmission of Iranian themes to Islamic culture. His numerous publications on the subject have now been gathered in one volume: *From Zoroastrian Iran to Islam* (Aldershot, 1995); A. Tafazzoli (Tafaḍḍolī), *Tārīkh-e adabiyyāt-e Īrān pīsh az eslām*, ed. Ž Āmūzegār (Tehran, 1376 Sh./1997), pp. 180–250; see also T. Qāderī, 'Matn hā-ye akhlāqī-andarzī dar zabān hā-ye Īrānī-ye miyāne-ye gharbī va sharqī', in A. Kāwūs Bālā Zādeh (ed.), *Mehr o dād o bahār. Memorial Volume of Dr Mehrdād Bahār* (Tehran, 1377 Sh./1998), pp. 221–232.

the Persian language and this literature.[68] Well before translating the Qurʾān into Persian received authorisation from the inner circle of scholars in Sāmānid Transoxiana,[69] the respectability, even the sacred nature, of the Persian language was stressed, at the very least since the *fatwā* by Abū Ḥanīfa (d. 150/767), as reported in *al-Fiqh al-akbar*, according to which the Names, Attributes and Organs of God may be uttered in Persian as well as in the original Arabic.[70]

---

68. F. Rosenthal, *A History of Muslim Historiography*, pp. 141–142; M. Moḥammadī Malāyerī, *Tārīkh va farhang-e Īrān dar dowrān-e enteqāl az ʿaṣr-e Sāsānī be ʿaṣr-e islāmī* (Tehran, 1372 Sh./1993), vol. 1, *Del-e Īrān-shahr* (Tehran, 1375 Sh./1996) vol. 2; N. Pourjavady (Pūrjavādī), '*Mā be majles-e mehtarān sokhan nagūyīm.* Fārsī gūyī-ye 'Abd Allāh-i Mubārak va adab-e Īrānī', *Nashr-e Dânesh*, N.S., 16/4 (1378 Sh./1999) vol. 2, pp. 21–25. In this latter article, it is significant that the only two citations of the Khurāsānian ascetic from Marw, 'Abd Allāh b. al-Mubārak (d. 181/797), reproduced in Persian in Arabic sources (namely, *al-Ansāb* by al-Samʿānī from Marw and *Siyar al-salaf* by Abu'l-Qāsim al-Taymī from Iṣfahān), relate to good manners: 1) *khord pīsh-e Ḥafṣ pāy derāz nemīkonad*, 'In the presence of Ḥafṣ, the younger (i.e. 'Abd Allāh b. al-Mubārak himself), do not stretch out one's legs', and 2) *mā be majles-e mehtarān sokhan nagūyīm*, 'Where great men are gathered, it is out of turn for me to speak'. In the account of the famous meeting between the mystics, Abū Ḥafṣ al-Ḥaddād of Nīsābūr and Junayd al-Baghdādī, originally from Nihāwand, taken aback by the politeness of the former's disciples, the latter tells him that they have been initiated into the good manners of kings. See e.g. al-Qushayrī, *al-Risāla*, ed. 'A. H. Maḥmūd and M. b. al-Sharīf (Cairo, 1974), vol. 2, p. 563; 'Aṭṭār, *Tadhkira al-awliyā'*, ed. M. Esteʿlāmī (2nd edn, Tehran, 1355 Sh./1977), p. 395; both authors are from Nīsābūr; cf. the expression *adab al-mulūk*. One will have noticed that the protagonists as well as the authors are all Iranians, mainly Khurāsānī.

69. M. Moḥammadī Malāyerī, *Tārīkh va farhang-e Īrān*, pp. 127ff.

70. Al-Imām Abū Ḥanīfa, *al-Fiqh al-akbar* (2nd edn, Hyderabad, 1399/1979), p. 7 (curiously, the only exception is the Persian term *dast* ['hand'], which Abū Ḥanīfa does not authorise the use of for *yad* in the expression *yad Allāh*); the namesake of the Ḥanafi legal school is said to have allowed those who spoke Persian to say *khodāy bozorg ast* ('God is Great') instead of *Allāhu akbar*; see 'A. A. Ṣādeqī, *Takvīn-e zabān-e fārsī* (Tehran, 1357 Sh./1978), p. 64; M. Moḥammadī Malāyerī, *Tārīkh va farhang-e Īrān*, p. 130. On the sacred nature of Persian and its ability to transmit wisdom and religious concepts, see W. Barthold, *Mussulman Culture*, pp. 50ff. and much more recently N. Pourjavady (Pūrjavādī), 'Ḥekmat-e dīnī va taqaddos-e zabān-e fārsī', in his

The staunchest defenders of this Iranian cultural identity, as is well known, were the scribes or secretaries of state of Iranian origin of the ʿAbbasid era, the famous *kuttāb* of whom Ibn al-Muqaffaʿ (executed ca. 140/757), is the emblematic figure. In the context of our subject, the *Kitāb dhamm akhlāq al-kuttāb* by al-Jāḥiẓ (d. 255/869), who saw himself as defender and champion of religious orthodoxy and Arab culture, is especially telling.[71] In a strongly sardonic passage, al-Jāḥiẓ denounced the pro-Iranian stance taken by official secretaries of state and their disdain for Arab and Islamic traditions: they know the maxims of Buzurjmihr, the Testament of Ardashīr, the epistles of ʿAbd al-Ḥamīd and the *Adab* by Ibn al-Muqaffaʿ by heart. Their bedside reading includes the Book of Mazdak and *Kalīla va Dimna*. They praise only the policies of Ardashīr Bābakān, the administration of Anūshiruwān and admire Sasanian methods of government. Thus they consider themselves more expert than ʿUmar in administrative affairs, than Ibn ʿAbbās in Qurʾānic exegesis, than Muʿādh b. Jabal in knowledge of the licit and the illicit, than ʿAlī in his judgements and arbitration. They do not read the Qurʾān regularly and do not consider exegesis, law or the study of traditions to be basic sciences.[72]

By evoking the milieu of the Iranian *kuttāb* one is inevitably reminded of the pro-Iranian Shuʿūbiyya, the people that al-Jāḥiẓ

Būy-e jān (Tehran, 1372 Sh./1993), pp. 1–37 where many studies have been cited and examined usefully.

71. ʿAmr b. Baḥr al-Jāḥiẓ, *K. Dhamm akhlāq al-kuttāb* in *Rasāʾil* al-Jāḥiẓ, ed. ʿA. M. Hārūn (Cairo, 1965), vol. 2, pp. 185–199, ed. ʿA. Muhannā (Beirut, 1988), vol. 2, pp. 199–134. Also edited in J. Finkel, *Three Essays of Abū ʿOthmān ibn Baḥr al-Jāḥiẓ* (Cairo, 1926), under the title *Dhamm al-kuttāb*, pp. 40–52.

72. Ed. Hārūn, pp. 191ff.; ed. Muhannā, pp. 126ff.; ed. Finkel, pp. 46ff.; passage cited by E. Yarshater, 'The Persian Presence in the Islamic World', pp. 70–71, based on the edition by Hārūn. French translation in Ch. Pellat, 'Une charge contre les secrétaires d'Etat attribuée à Jāḥiẓ', *Hespéris*, 43 (1956), pp. 29–50. On al-Jāḥiẓ's stance, refer also to *Kitāb al-ḥayawān*, vol. 7, pp. 68ff., and *al-Bayān wa'l-tabyīn*, vol. 3, pp. 6–7.

wanted to fight.[73] Might one conclude that the Shahrbānū tradition was born in the milieu of pro-Shuʿūbī Iranian scribes? This is quite likely considering that it was in the third/ninth century, just when the tradition began to circulate widely, that the Shuʿūbiyya movement reached its peak.

For the historian of early Islam, Ḥusaynid Shiʿism, opposition to Zaydi Shiʿism, sustained Iranianism, Iranian intellectualism and the challenging of pro-Arab Sunni orthodoxy, all unmistakably evoke the ambiance of the court presided over by al-Ma'mūn 'son of the Persian' in Marw, one of the great cities of Khurāsān, just at the time when in the year 200/815 he designated the Shiʿi imam of the Ḥusaynid line, ʿAlī b. Mūsā al-Riḍā, as his successor. Indeed, al-Ma'mūn seems to have sought this moment to re-establish the alliance between the ʿAbbasids, ʿAlids and Persians,

---

73. On the connection between scribes and the Shuʿūbiyya see e.g. H. A. R. Gibb, 'The Social Significance of the Shuʿūbiyya', in *Studia Orientalia Ioanni Pedersen Dicata* (Copenhagen, 1953), pp. 105–114, rpr. in *Studies on the Civilization of Islam*, ed. by S. J. Shaw and W. R. Polk (Boston, MA, 1962), pp. 62–73; M. B. Sharīf, *al-Ṣirāʿ bayn al-mawālī wa'l-ʿarab* (Cairo, 1954), passim; ʿA. ʿA. Dūrī, *al-Judhūr al-ta'rīkhiyya li'l-shuʿūbiyya* (Beirut, 1962), passim; W. M. Watt, *Islamic Political Thought* (Edinburgh, 1968), see index under 'Ibn al-Muqaffaʿ' (French translation, *La pensée politique de l'Islam* [Paris, 1995], pp. 94–99 and 129f.); M. Carter, 'The Kātib in Fact and Fiction', *Abr Nahrain*, 11 (1971), pp. 42–55; R. Mottahedeh, 'The Shuʿûbîyah Controversy and the Social History of Early Islamic Iran', *IJMES*, 7 (1976), pp. 161–182; P. Crone and M. Cook, *Hagarism: the Making of the Islamic World* (Cambridge, 1977), pp. 108–112; C. E. Bosworth, 'The Persian Impact on Arabic Literature', in E. Beeston et al., *Cambridge History of Arabic Literature: Arabic Literature to the End of the Umayyad Period* (Cambridge, 1983), pp. 155–167; M. Chokr, *Zandaqa et zindîqs en Islam au second siècle de l'hégire* (Damascus, 1993), ch. 5. For other sources on the Shuʿūbiyya, see S. Enderwitz, *EI2*, vol. 9, pp. 533–536. On al-Jāḥiẓ's anti-Shuʿūbism and anti-Shiʿism, now consult Enderwitz, *Gesellschaftlicher Rang und ethnische Legitimation. Der arabische Schriftseller Abū 'Uthmān al-Ǧāḥiẓ über die Afrikaner, Perser und Araber in der islamischen Gesellschaft* (Freiburg, 1979), see index under 'Shuʿūbīya'; also Ch. Pellat, 'Ǧāḥiẓ à Bagdad et à Sāmarrā', *RSO*, 27 (1952), pp. 63ff., rpr. in *Etudes sur l'histoire socio-culturelle de l'Islam (VIIe-XVe s.)* (London, 1976), article 1, and 'Jāḥiẓ', *EI2*, vol. 2, pp. 395–398, esp. pp. 396b–397a; see also his *The Life and Works of Jāḥiẓ: Translations of Selected Texts* (London, 1969), pp. 272–275.

an alliance that in the past had led to the victory of the *daʿwa hāshimiyya*, and fell apart after the assassination of Abū Muslim when the ʿAbbasids seized power.[74]

In my view, the tradition reported by Ibn Bābūya in his *ʿUyūn* implicitly contains some valuable information in this regard.[75] First, it is possible that the great traditionalist from Rayy had collected this report, like many others in this same work, on his journey to Khurāsān; this is all the more credible since he reports it from a Khurāsānī, apparently unknown except for his name, Abū ʿAlī al-Ḥusayn b. Aḥmad al-Bayhaqī.[76] Then, in the body of the *ḥadīth* it is said that imam al-Riḍā held court when he was in Khurāsān, being already designated crown prince by al-Ma'mūn. The eighth imam's interlocutor, as we have seen, is a certain Sahl b. al-Qāsim al-Nūshajānī, who to my knowledge is not mentioned in Imami

74. See M. Rekaya, 'al-Ma'mūn', *EI2*, vol. 6, pp. 315–323. On the relations between the ʿAbbasid caliph and Shiʿi movements in general and imam al-Riḍā in particular, see e.g. the now classic study by F. Gabrieli, *al-Ma'mūn e gli ʿAlidi* (Leipzig, 1929); D. Sourdel, 'La politique religieuse du calife ʿabbāsside al-Ma'mūn', *REI*, 30/1 (1962), pp. 26–48; E. L. Daniel, *The Political and Social History of Khurasan under Abbassid Rule (747–820)* (Minneapolis and Chicago, IL, 1979), see index under 'al-Ma'mūn'; W. Madelung, 'New Documents Concerning al-Ma'mūn, al-Faḍl b. Sahl and ʿAlī al-Riḍā', in W. al-Qāḍī (ed.), *Studia Arabica et Islamica. Festschrift for Iḥsān ʿAbbās* (Beirut, 1981), pp. 333–346; D. G. Tor, 'An Historiographical Re-examination of the Appointment and Death of ʿAlī al-Riḍā', *Der Islam*, 78/1 (2001), pp. 103–128. On al-Ma'mūn and the challenge to Sunni orthodoxy, obviously reaching its peak in the *miḥna*, see the classic study by W. M. Patton, *Aḥmad ibn Ḥanbal and the Miḥna* (Leiden, 1897); M. Hinds, 'Miḥna', *EI2*; J. van Ess, 'Ibn Kullāb et la *Miḥna*', *Arabica*, 37 (1990), pp. 173–233, and *Theologie und Gesellschaft* (1994), vol. 3, pp. 446–80; J. A. Nawas, 'A Reexamination of Three Current Explanations for al-Ma'mūn's Introduction of the *Miḥna*', *IJMES*, 26 (1994), pp. 615–629; M. Q. Zaman, *Religion and Politics under the Early ʿAbbāsids*, index under '*Miḥna*' and 'Ma'mūn'. Also, M. Cooperson, *Classical Arabic Biography: The Heirs of the Prophets in the Age of al-Ma'mūn* (Cambridge, 2000).

75. Refer to note 21 above; *ʿUyūn akhbār al-Riḍā*, vol. 2, ch. 35, *ḥadīth* no. 6, p. 128.

76. In the present state of knowledge, the chain(s) of transmitters for different versions of the Shahrbānū story – when such exist of course – do not contribute much of any great import to the issue here.

prosopographic works. However, some fragmentary information is provided by other sources regarding the Nūshajānī family. The name is clearly a patronymic — 'agān', very likely based on Anôsh 'immortal', itself abridged from a composite name typical of Pahlavi onomastics; Nūshajānī would thus be the Arabicised form of Anôshagān. According to the geographer Ibn al-Faqīh (third/ninth century), Nūshajān or Nūshanjān was the last Transoxanian Iranian province before China, in the extreme north-east of Greater Khurāsān, in the border region between al-Shāsh and the Chinese territories. The province, divided into greater and lesser Nūsha(n)jān, consisted of several large and small towns and was populated 'by Turks, Zoroastrians (*majūs*) worshippers of fire and *zindīqs*', Manicheans (*mānawiyya*). The family name is thus derived from this region; however Ibn al-Faqīh's assumption is perhaps mistaken.[77] The Nūshajānī family seems to have regularly received Sasanian kings and courtiers. Their ancestor would have been Nūshajān, son of Wahraz, the first Iranian governor of

77. Ibn al-Faqīh al-Hamadhānī, *Kitāb al-buldān*, ed. Y. al-Hādī (Beirut, 1416/1996), p. 635; information taken up by Yāqūt al-Ḥamawī (d. 626/1228), *Mu'jam al-buldān*, ed. F. Wüstenfeld (Leipzig, 1866; rpr. Tehran, 1965), vol. 4, p. 833, Beirut edn (1376/1957), vol. 5, p. 311. Yāqūt refers to Ibn al-Faqīh via al-Sam'ānī (d. 562/1166), but the latter, in his *Ansāb*, speaks only of a Nūshajānī Sufi living in the convent of the famous mystic from Kāzarūn, namely Abū Isḥāq al-Kāzarūnī; see al-Sam'ānī, *al-Ansāb*, facsimile reproduction of the manuscript by D. S. Margoliouth (London and Leiden, 1912), p. 571b, held at the British Museum; unless it is another Sam'ānī or from a work other than the *Ansāb*. See also G. Le Strange, *The Lands of the Eastern Caliphate* (2nd edn, Cambridge, 1930; rpr. London, 1966), index under *Ansāb*. The author wonders if one ought to identify Greater Nūsha(n)jān with the Khotan region. The region described by Ibn al-Faqīh corresponds to Barskhān (or Barsghān) as noted by other geographers such as Qudāma, Ibn Khurdādhbih and al-Kāshgharī: these are lands around Lake Issyk-kul in current-day Kirghizistan; see *Ḥudūd al-'Ālam, The Regions of the World*, tr. V. Minorsky (Oxford–London, 1937), pp. 292ff. and p. 292, n. 3. It appears that the Sasanians never exercised any authority over these distant lands. 'Nūshajān' would thus be a dummy name due to an erroneous reading of the term Barskhān/Barsghān. The notoriety of the Nūshajānī family, having nothing to do with the region mentioned by Ibn al-Faqīh and most likely of Sasanian nobility, would thus have been a factor in establishing this corrupt manuscript tradition.

Yemen, special envoy of the king, Anūshiruwān.[78] Ibn Hishām and al-Jāḥiẓ allude to the strong ties that bound the family to the Sasanian court, links that afforded the Nūshajānī great political influence.[79]

We have seen that, according to the *Taʾrīkh* by al-Ṭabarī,[80] ʿAbd Allāh b. ʿĀmir b. Kurayz offered one of the girls from the Kisrā family captured at Sarakhs to a certain al-Nūshajān (see above). If we are to trust several reports recorded by Abu'l-Faraj al-Iṣfahānī in his *Aghānī*, the family seems to have maintained its power even after the advent of Islam. During both the Umayyad and ʿAbbasid caliphates, the Nūshajānī would have retained a large part of their vast lands, fortune and influence. However, some of their palaces must have been ruined, as we can infer from the compositions by Muḥammad b. Bashīr (ʿAbbasid period), who declaimed nostalgic poetry about the ruined palaces of the family's glorious ancestors to their descendants in their superb mansion in Jaʿfariyya, the capital's aristocratic suburb.[81]

Aḥmad b. Sahl al-Nūshajānī, who could be the son of imam al-Riḍā's mysterious interlocutor in our *ḥadīth*, aroused the jealousy of the caliph al-Muʿtaḍid (r. 279–290/892–902) because of his lavish lifestyle and considerable social and political influence. Al-Iṣfahānī writes that the Baghdadi house of the Nūshajānī family was not only constantly frequented by poets, musicians and

78. Al-Masʿūdī, *Murūj al-dhahab*, vol. 3, pp. 166ff., in particular pp. 176–177.

79. Ibn Hishām, *al-Sīra al-nabawiyya*, ed. M. Saqqā, I. Abyārī and ʿA. Shalabī (2nd edn, Cairo, 1955), vol. 1, pp. 43–44; al-Jāḥiẓ, *Rasāʾil al-Jāḥiẓ*, vol. 1, p. 201 and vol. 2, p. 290. In his entry on 'Nahr al-marʾa', Yāqūt al-Ḥamawī writes that the name of the location ('Lady's River'), in Baṣra, is named after a woman, Kāmwar/Kāmūr-Zād bint Narsī whose palace was offered to the conqueror Khālid b. al-Walīd by her first cousin (and husband most probably) al-Nūshajān b. JSNSMĀH (?); see Yāqūt, *Muʿjam al-buldān*, ed. Wüstenfeld, vol. 4, p. 844, Beirut edn, vol. 5, p. 323.

80. Ed. de Goeje, series 1, p. 2,887; ed. Ibrāhīm, vol. 4, p. 302.

81. Al-Iṣfahānī, *Kitāb al-aghānī*, vol. 3, p. 130 and vol. 12, p. 136.

singers but also by men of letters, thinkers and scribes (*kuttāb*).[82] The mention of *kuttāb* and the sustained good relations between the Nūshjānī family and the Sasanian royal house leads one to believe that their home could very well have been a meeting place for the pro-Iranian Shuʿūbiyya.

In this context, the note by Ibn Shahrāshūb informing us that Shahrbānū was sometimes called Barra bint al-Nūshajān (*wa yuqāl hiya Barra*; cf. the report by al-Ṭabarī) is seen in an unexpected light.[83] Similarly, it is noteworthy that in his *Aghānī*, Abu'l-Faraj al-Iṣfahānī often gives Abu'l-Aswad al-Duʾalī the name Ẓālim b. ʿAmr al-Nūshajānī.[84] It should be recalled that in al-Kulaynī and Ibn Shahrāshūb, to cite only two sources, it is to Abu'l-Aswad that the verse praising the fourth imam (descendant of Hāshim and Kisrā) is attributed.[85] Thus numerous connections link different members of the Nūshajānī family (originally or de facto Mazdaean?): on the one hand, to the Sasanian court and nobility, and on the other, to the Ḥusaynid Shiʿis. One may thus reasonably believe that it was not impossible for the Shahrbānū story to have originated in their entourage.

---

82. Ibid., vol. 3, p. 131 and vol. 8, p. 88. According to information provided by L. Massignon, referring to *Maktūbāt* by ʿAyn al-Quḍāt al-Hamadhānī, the eminent chamberlain Naṣr al-Qushūrī at some time after 288/899–900 had bought a property in Baghdad from a certain Nūshajānī, director of the *barīd*, see L. Massignon, *La Passion de Hallâj* (rpr. Paris, 1975), vol. 1, p. 474, which once again brings us to the highly placed Iranian bureaucrats or civil servants of the ʿAbbasid state.

83. Ibn Shahrāshūb, *Manāqib āl Abī Ṭālib*, vol. 3, p. 311. See above.

84. Al-Iṣfahānī, *Kitāb al-aghānī*, vol. 1, p. 49; vol. 11, p. 105; vol. 15, p. 97; vol. 18, p. 132. Elsewhere, the ʿAlid poet is called Ẓālim b. ʿAmr b. Sufyān (or ʿUthmān); clearly the grandfather's name and its orthographic representation poses a problem. See e.g. al-Marzubānī, *Akhbār shuʿarāʾ al-shīʿa*, ed. M. Ḥ. al-Amīnī (Najaf, 1388/1968), p. 27; al-Ṭūsī, *Rijāl*, ed. M. Ḥ. Āl-Baḥr al-ʿUlūm (Najaf, 1380/1961), p. 95, note from the editor; Ḍiyāʾ al-Dīn Yūsuf al-Ṣanʿānī, *Nasmat al-saḥar bi-dhikr man tashayyaʿa wa shaʿar*, ed. K. S. al-Jabbūrī (Beirut, 1420/1999), vol. 2, p. 276 and the editor's note on sources.

85. Al-Kulaynī, *al-Uṣūl*, vol. 2, p. 369; Ibn Shahrāshūb, *Manāqib*, vol. 3, p. 305. See above.

In the *ḥadīth* reported by Ibn Bābūya, one finds a member of the Nūshajānī family in the entourage of al-Maʾmūn and ʿAlī b. Mūsā al-Riḍā in Marw. What we have just noted above makes this historically plausible. And given the family's past as well as its position during the Sasanian era, it would not be illogical to read into these ambiguous lines of the *ḥadīth* (which, as we have seen, reminds us of the Iranian notion of *xwētōdas/xwēdōdah*) a pro-Iranian Shuʿūbism more radical than in other toned-down versions.[86]

Thus the Shahrbānū story would have emerged in the pro-Iranian Shuʿūbī entourage of the Nūshajānī family at al-Maʾmūn's court in Khurāsān. The last sentence of the *ḥadīth* reported by Ibn Bābūya is a telling sign: 'Sahl b. al-Qāsim (al-Nūshajānī) says, 'There was not a single Ṭālibid [Ḥusaynid Alid?] amongst us who did not copy my version of this *ḥadīth* from al-Riḍā (*mā baqiya Ṭālibī ʿindanā illā kataba ʿannī hādhāʾl-ḥadīth ʿan al-Riḍā*).'[87]

It may be possible to be more precise regarding the dating of this tradition. Immediately after the failure of the revolt by the Ḥasanid, Ibn Ṭabāṭabā, in 199/815, two Ḥusaynids, both sons of Mūsā al-Kāẓim and half-brothers of ʿAlī al-Riḍā, initiated insurrections against the ʿAbbasid regime in Baghdad: Zayd known as

---

86. See above. Through these historical elements and the figure of Shahrbānū one senses a conflict between a radical Iranism that seeks, for example, to establish equal status between the Iranian princess and Fāṭima (see e.g. Ibn Shahrāshūb, *Manāqib*, vol. 3, p. 311: Shahrbānū has the same title as Fāṭima, i.e. Sayyidat al-Nisāʾ. ʿAlī gave this name to two of the most sacred women, according to the Shiʿis, namely Fāṭima and Maryam/Mary) and a more moderate Iranianism that attempts to maintain the superiority of Fāṭima (e.g. in the version reported by Ibn Rustam al-Ṭabarī al-Ṣaghīr, *Dalāʾil al-imāma*, p. 196 in which it is explicitly stated that Sayyidat al-Nisāʾ refers only to Fāṭima and as such the princess could not be named Shāh-e Zanān which is almost the Persian equivalent of the title granted to the Prophet's daughter).

87. Ibn Bābūya, *ʿUyūn*, vol. 2, p. 128. On the intellectual influence of the Iranians in al-Maʾmūn's state and their convergence with the ʿAlids see also the intriguing report by al-Jahshiyārī, *Kitāb al-wuzarāʾ waʾl-kuttāb*, ed. ʿA. I. al-Ṣāwī (Cairo, 1357/1938), pp. 256ff.

'al-Nār' (literally 'the Fire', that is, the incendiary one) in Baṣra and Ibrāhīm known as 'al-Jazzār' (the Butcher) in Yemen. It was at this point, in 200/815–816, in Khurāsān that al-Ma'mūn initiated his great effort at reconciliation between the ʿAlids and ʿAbbasids, a movement widely supported by a large number of Iranians. As the Ḥasanid Zaydīs consistently proved to be too aggressive, he opted for reconciliation with the Ḥusaynids in an especially spectacular style: not only did he save the two sons of Mūsā al-Kāẓim who had just been proclaimed anti-caliphs at Baṣra and in Yemen, but on 2 Ramaḍān 201/24 March 817 he designated their brother ʿAlī – wise enough to remain above the fray – as his successor, conferring him the title *al-Riḍā min āl Muḥammad*.[88]

It did not take long for the ʿAbbasids in Baghdad, supported by a large section of the *ahl al-sunna wa al-jamāʿa*, to react. The sons of al-Mahdī led the opposition against al-Ma'mūn: when al-Manṣūr b. al-Mahdī refused to be proclaimed caliph, his step-brother Ibrāhīm b. al-Mahdī accepted the title on 28 Dhu'l-Ḥijja 201/17 July 817.[89] Now, al-Manṣūr was born of al-Buḥturiyya, daughter of Khorshīd the last Dābūyid *isfahbadh* (high-ranking military official) from Ṭabaristān, and his step-brother Ibrāhīm was born of Shakla, daughter of the last *maṣmughān* (great Zoroastrian priest) from the district of Damāwand. Both opponents of al-Ma'mūn were therefore descendants of high-ranking Iranian nobility on the maternal side. The Arab nobility of their father's side was not in question either. One may thus reasonably believe that in al-Ma'mūn's entourage it was envisaged that they should do even better with regard to his successor: ʿAlī al-Riḍā, a descendant of Hāshim (on the paternal side), would have as his grandmother a woman not simply belonging to the nobility, but to no less than the Iranian royal family.

Some months later, al-Ma'mūn initiated his policy of rapprochement with the ʿAbbasid aristocracy in Iraq. His first concession was

88. M. Rekaya, 'al-Ma'mūn', *EI2*, pp. 318–319.

89. Ibid., p. 319.

the announcement of his return to Baghdad and his departure from Marw on 10 Rajab 202/22 January 818. It was during this journey that both major obstacles to this rapprochement were eliminated: the Iranian al-Faḍl b. Sahl on 2 Shaʿbān 202/13 February 818 in Sarakhs and the Ḥusaynid imam ʿAlī al-Riḍā on 29 Ṣafar 203/5 September 818.[90] Thus, the Shahrbānū story – at least in its core form – emerged among the Iranian-Shuʿūbī Nūshajānī family in al-Maʾmūn's entourage in Marw, the Khurāsānian capital, between March 817 (the proclamation of ʿAlī al-Riḍā as heir) or the month of July of the same year (proclamation of Ibrāhīm b. al-Mahdī's caliphate in Baghdad) and January 818 (when al-Maʾmūn abandoned his pro-ʿAlid policy).

3

'One never knows what the past will hold tomorrow.'[91] This proverb perfectly illustrates the posthumous fate of the figure of Shahrbānū both in popular Shiʿism and throughout Iran, the lands of which she is said to be the Lady. In literary traditions, as we have seen, the Sasanian princess dies either upon the birth of her son Zayn al-ʿĀbidīn, or drowns in the Euphrates after witnessing the massacre of her family at Karbalā. Popular belief decided otherwise. It is as if such a death did not satisfy Iranian

90. Ibid., pp. 319–320. Let us also point out that the Jewish Exilarch, the *Rosh Golah* (Aramaic: *rēsh galūtha*, 'leader of the diaspora'; Arabic: *raʾs jālūt/raʾs al-jālūt*) Bustanai, contemporary of imam al-Ḥusayn, is also said to have married an Iranian princess; see M. Gil, *A History of Palestine 634–1099* (Cambridge, 1992), see index under 'Bustanai, exilarch'. On the convergence between Jews and Shiʿis, now consult S. M. Wasserstrom, 'The Shīʿīs are the Jews of our Community: An Interreligious Comparison within Sunnī Thought', *IOS*, 14 (1994), pp. 297–324, on Bustanai and al-Ḥusayn, p. 316; now in Wasserstrom, *Between Muslim and Jew: the Problem of Symbiosis under Early Islam* (Princeton, 1995), ch. 3.

91. Proverb cited by the anthropologist F. Aubin, 'La Mongolie des premières années de l'après-communisme: la popularisation du passé national dans les mass média mongols (1990–1995)', *Etudes Mongoles et Sibériennes*, 27 (1996), p. 323.

tradition, which sought to find a more useful and glorious end for its princess.

In a pioneering study devoted to popular beliefs about Shahrbānū, Sayyid Jaʿfar Shahīdī relates the most frequently told version of the oral legend of the daughter of Yazdgird III, here called Bībī (Lady; also grandmother) Shahrbānū: after the day of ʿĀshūrā, Bībī Shahrbānū was able to escape, as her husband had predicted, on his horse Dhu'l-janāḥ. Pursued by her terrible enemies, she reaches mount Ṭabarak in Rayy, central Iran. Exhausted and alone, she invokes God to deliver her from her assailants; but, as a Persian, instead of saying *yā hū* ('O God!' lit. 'O He') she mistakenly cries out *yā kūh* ('O Mountain!'). The rock miraculously opens and offers her refuge. However, a corner of her dress gets caught in the opening when the mountain closes behind her. A short while later her pursuers notice the trapped fabric and realise that a miracle has taken place – Shahrbānū's saintliness becomes apparent. The site becomes the sanctuary of the princess, a place of pilgrimage, and remains so to this day.[92]

An almost identical story explains the Zoroastrian sanctuary of Bānū Pārs (the Lady of Persia), in the north-western plain of Yazd, south of the town of ʿAghdā. Here one encounters the daughter of Yazdgird III (in this instance called Khātūn Bānū), the escape and chase given by the Arabs, the distress of the princess and the appeal for help, the miracle of the mountain – opening and closing behind the young woman, ending with the piece of fabric (here it is the princess's scarf that is caught between the rocks).[93]

92. S. J. Shahīdī, 'Baḥthī dar bāre-ye Shahrbānū', in *Cherāgh-e rowshan dar donyā-ye tārīk*, pp. 186ff. This study, focused mainly on the popular beliefs regarding Shahrbānū as well as the sanctuary found in Rayy, hardly deals with the literary tradition of the princess's story.

93. Jamshīd Sorūsh Sorūshiyān, *Farhang-e beh-dīnān*, ed. M. Sotūdeh (Tehran, 1334 Sh./1956), p. 204. No connection is established between the Sasanian princess and the Shiʿi imams. In a fiercely anti-Muslim Zoroastrian account dating from the ninth/fifteenth century, Shahrbānū and Bānū Pārs are presented as sisters, the daughters of Yazdgird III. The first, married to

More generally, themes such as the escape of the Iranian nobility (male and female), or often members of the royal family, in the face of Arab invaders and their miraculous rescue by God acting through the natural world, are frequently seen in the foundation legends of Zoroastrian sanctuaries in central and southern Iran.[94] According to the study by S. J. Shahīdī, mention of the sanctuary in Rayy becomes more frequent in sources from the Safawid period on. Apparently, it was shortly before this period that what was once a pilgrimage site (*mazār*) became the tomb (*maqbara, marqad*) of Shahrbānū.[95] Indeed, not only Shahīdī but also Ḥosayn Karīmān in his classic monograph devoted to the old city of Rayy, citing the archeological works of Sayyid Moḥammad Taqī Moṣṭafavī, dates the oldest section of the sanctuary to the

Muḥammad by force, died without bearing any children. The second, also coveted by the 'Prophet of the Arabs', fled and was saved by the mountain; for the purposes of discretion, this manuscript is written in a mixture of Persian and Avestan (see the untitled manuscript R VIII/1B at the K. R. Cama Oriental Institute in Bombay, fols. 430a–433a).

94. *Farhang-e beh-dīnān*, p. 204 (sanctuary of Pīrī Sabz also known as Pīrī Chakchakū, pilgrimage site of Princess Nāzbānū, hidden here); pp. 205–206 (sanctuary of Pīrī Hrisht, north-east of Ardakān: a travelling companion of Yazdgird's daughter or the daughter herself chased by Arabs and saved by the mountain); p. 206 (Shozdī Fozel = Shāhzāde Fāḍil, 'Prince Fāḍil'), sanctuary of a Sasanian princess in Yazd, p. 207 (Norakī, in southern Yazd: sanctuary of Zarbānū, princess of Yazd married to the king of Fārs, fled pursued by the Arabs and hidden in the mountains near Norakī), p. 211 (Shāh-e Harāt, north-east of Kirmān, governor of Yazdgird, pursued by the Arabs, hidden near a source henceforth called Pāy-e Shāh). Cf. also E. Strack, *Six Months in Persia* (London, 1882), vol. 1, p. 119 (cave of the Lady - *ghār-e Bībī* - and sanctuary for the Damsel in distress — *Bībī darmānda* — in Fārs province) and vol. 1, p. 227–228 (sanctuary of the Lady of Life — *Ḥayāt Bībī* — between Bāfq and Kirmān). On these pilgrimage sites refer also to R. Shahmardān, *Parastesh gāh-hā ye zartoshtiyān* (Bombay, 1345 Sh./1967).

95. S. J. Shahīdī, 'Baḥthī dar bāre-ye shahrbānū', pp. 186–187. According to some popular beliefs, the princess did not die here but was hidden or rendered invisible by the mountain; cf. also E. G. Browne, *A Literary History of Persia* in 4 vols (Cambridge, 1928), vol. 1, p. 131 where belief in Shahrbānū's occultation — *ghā'ib shodan* — is alluded to.

ninth/fifteenth century, shortly before the Safawid period.[96] Neither Abū Dulaf, in his description dated 330/940 of the Ṭabarak Mountain in Rayy nor al-Qazwīnī (sixth/twelfth century), in his *Kitāb al-naqḍ*, which includes a detailed listing of sacred sites located in Rayy, say anything about Shahrbānū's sanctuary,[97] which shows that, almost independently of the development of the literary tradition, the oral tradition develops and reaches maturity around the ninth and tenth/fifteenth and sixteenth centuries. Although it is apparently impossible to date precisely the Zoroastrian legends just cited, it nonetheless seems they go back to an earlier period.[98] It is therefore likely that they were at the source of the foundational legend regarding the Bībī Shahrbānū sanctuary in Rayy. Moreover, the presence of an ancient Zoroastrian 'tower of silence' (*dakhma*) on the same Ṭabarak mountain, further north, would also corroborate the existence of links between the sanctuary of Shahrbānū and Iranian Zoroastrianism.

In a certain fashion, the figure of Shahrbānū and her sanctuary seem to reflect the continuation of ancient Mazdean beliefs. A few years after the works of S. J. Shahīdī, Moḥammad Ebrāhīm Bāstānī Pārīzī, another Iranian scholar, once again took an interest in Bībī Shahrbānū in the context of his studies on Iranian toponyms, including the terms meaning woman, lady, princess and so on

96. S. J. Shahīdī, 'Baḥthī dar bāre-ye shahrbānū', pp. 187ff.; Ḥ. Karīmān, *Ray-e bāstān* (Tehran, 1345–1349 Sh./1966–1970), vol. 1, pp. 403–416 citing at length S. M. T. Moṣṭafavī, 'Boqʿe-ye Bībī Shahrbānū dar Rayy', *Eṭṭelāʿāt*, 5/2 (1331 Sh./1952), pp. 15–24 as well as the article of the same title in *Gozāresh hā-ye bāstān-shenāsī*, 3 (1334 Sh./1956), pp. 3–40, in which results of the archeological excavations previously published in earlier works are now revisited and supplemented. The most ancient item of the sanctuary seems to be the cenotaph dated 888/1483–1484.

97. Abū Dulaf, *Safar-Nāmeh-e Abū Dulaf dar Īrān*, ed. V. Minorsky, tr. A. F. Ṭabāṭabā'ī (Tehran, 1342 Sh./1964), 'al-Risāla al-thāniya', p. 31. 'Abd al-Jalīl al-Qazwīnī, *Kitāb al-naqḍ*, ed. al-Muḥaddith al-Urmawī (Tehran, 1979), p. 643.

98. Information from *Dārāb Hormazyār's Rivāyat*, ed. M. R. Unvala (Bombay, 1922), vol. 2, pp. 158–159, indicates that the Bānū Pārs sanctuary was already a place of frequent visitation in the tenth/sixteenth century.

(*Bānū, Khātūn, Bībī, Dokhtar* etc.).[99] Through extensive research into both the archeological evidence and written sources as well as folkloric legends and popular beliefs, Bāstānī Pārīzī convincingly establishes that in most cases, the sites bearing these kinds of names, at one time in the near or distant past, were locations for a temple and/or a cult of Ānāhītā/Anāhīd/Āb Nāhīd/Nāhīd, the very popular goddess of water and fertility: Ardvīsūr Anāhīd of the Zoroastrian pantheon. It is interesting to note that Anāhīd seems to have been the patron goddess of the Sasanians.[100]

Some years after Bāstānī Pārīzī's study, and drawing extensively on studies by S. J. Shahīdī and M. E. Bāstānī Pārīzī, Mary Boyce came to the same conclusions, by means of a well-documented comparison between the foundational legends for sanctuaries of Shahrbānū and Bānū Pārs.[101] The title 'Bānū' (the Lady) is the ancient title for Anāhīd. From the Avesta onwards, the goddess is called *Aredvī sūrā bānū*.[102]

In Pahlavi documents as well, the titles of *Bānū* or *ābān Bānū* (the Lady of the Waters) are associated with Anāhīd, Ardvīsūr or Ardvīsūr Amshāsfand.[103] Citing and using all these references,

99. M. E. Bāstānī Pārīzī, 'Benā hā-ye dokhtar dar Īrān', *Majalla-ye bāstān shenāsī*, 1–2 (1338 Sh./1959), pp. 105–137, and esp. the voluminous collection on the subject: *Khātūn-e haft qalʿe* (Tehran, 1344 Sh./1966; 3rd. edn, Tehran, 1363 Sh./1984), pp. 150–368; the Bībī Shahrbānū sanctuary is referred to in passing on p. 246.

100. R. Ghirshman, *Iran, Parthes et Sassanides* (Paris, 1962), p. 149 and *Bîchâpour* (Paris, 1971), vol. 1, p. 65; however, refer also to the nuances introduced by M. L. Chaumont, 'Anāhīd, iii. The Cult and its Diffusion', *EIr*, vol. 1, p. 1,008a.

101. M. Boyce, 'Bībī Shahrbānū and the Lady of Pārs', *BSOAS*, 30/1 (1967), pp. 30–44. The renowned English Iranologist had already presented a paper on this topic at the Royal Asiatic Society in May 1965 (ibid., p. 36, n. 19).

102. Y 68.13, see J. Darmesteter, *Le Zend-Avesta* (Paris, 1892–1893), vol. 1, p. 419, n. 25.

103. *Saddar Nasr* and *Saddar Bundehesh*, ed. B. N. Dhabhar (Bombay, 1909), pp. 116–118 and 149, English trans. by Dhabhar, *The Persian Rivāyats of Hormazyar Framarz* (Bombay, 1932), pp. 537–538 and 559; *Dārāb Hormazyār's Rivāyat*, ed. M. R. Unvala (Bombay, 1922), vol. 1, pp. 93 and 219–220 (tr. Dhabhar, pp. 96 and 221).

Boyce also alludes to the inscriptions of Iṣṭakhr and Paikuli in which Anāhīd is called 'Lady'.[104] Although no trace of a pre-Islamic monument was found at Bībī Shahrbānū's mount, citing the *History* of Herodotus to support her claims, Boyce believes that a simple rock near a natural source of water (which is the case at Bībī Shahrbānū) could have served as a temple for the worship of Anāhīd.[105] She even believes that the titles held by the Sasanian princess in Shiʿi texts such as Lady of the Land (i.e. Iran) (Shahrbānū), Sovereign of Women (Shāh-e zanān) and Lady of the Universe (Jahān bānū) could very well have been held by Anāhīd well before Islamicisation of the site.[106]

What further corroborates a hypothesis of continuity between Anāhīd, goddess of water/fertility and Shahrbānū, mother of the imams, is that in a large number of popular versions of the

104. M. Boyce, '*Bībī* Shahrbānū', pp. 36–37; also M. L. Chaumont, 'Anāhīd', *EIr*, vol. 3, p. 1008. On the widespread cult of Anāhīd in pre-Islamic Iran, see M. L. Chaumont, 'Le culte de Anâhitâ à Stakhr et les premiers Sassanides', *RHR*, 153 (1958), pp. 154–175, and 'Le culte de la déesse Anâhitâ (Anahit) dans la religion des monarques d'Iran et d'Arménie au 1er siècle de notre ère', *JA*, 253 (1965), pp. 167–181.

105. Ibid., p. 43. In her article, 'Anāhīd, i, Ardwīsūr Anāhīd and ii, Anaitis', *EIr*, vol. 1, pp. 1003–1006, M. Boyce traces the cult of the goddess back to Rayy during the Parthian period, p. 1004.

106. 'Shahrbānū and the Lady of Pārs', p. 38; the author gleans these titles from the prayer book — *ziyārat-nāma* — distributed at the entrance to the sanctuary in Rayy. We have seen that these titles are already noted in the various written versions of the Shahrbānū story. See also Boyce, 'Anāhīd', p. 1005b. On the analogy between titles given to Bībī Shahrbānū and Anāhitā (alias Nana), see also the Sogdian title *panchī Nana dhvambana*, 'Nana, Lady of Panch,' i.e. the Pendjikent region, on coins issued by this town; see W. B. Henning, 'A Sogdian God', in *Selected Papers II = Acta Iranica* 15 (2nd series-VI) (Leiden-Tehran, Liège, 1977), pp. 617–630; esp. p. 627, n. 68. No doubt in symmetry with *Khshathra pati*, 'Lord of the Lands', a title sometimes given to Mithra; see M. Boyce, *A History of Zoroastrianism*, vol. 2, pp. 266–268. On the links – as close as they are complex – between Anāhitā and Nana, now consult F. Grenet and B. Marshak, 'Le mythe de Nana dans l'art de la Sogdiane', *Arts Asiatiques*, 53 (1998), pp. 5–18.

princess story she is also called Ḥayāt Bānū, the Lady of Life;[107] the relationship between life, water and fertility is obvious. In Mithraism, as well as in popular Mazdeism, (A)Nāhīd, mother of Mithra/Mehr, is a virgin; now, according to some popular Imami beliefs, Shahrbānū, although a mother, remains a virgin.[108] Moreover, visits to the sanctuary in Rayy are exclusively reserved for women (and on rare occasions for *sayyids*, men, thus to the actual or presumed descendants of imams considered the 'sons' of Shahrbānū); but most of all, infertile women visit the site to seek

---

107. M. E. Bāstānī Pārīzī, *Khātūn-e haft qalʿe*, p. 246 who also cites the name Nīk Bānū, 'the Good Lady'; cf. above Ḥayāt Bībī and her sanctuary mentioned by E. Strack, *Six Months in Persia*, vol. 1, pp. 227–228. In a Zoroastrian poem of an unknown period, the princess at the Pīrī Chakchakū sanctuary (note 94 above) is called Ḥayāt Bānū; see Ardashīr b. Shāhī (or Bonshāhī), *Ganjīne-ye adab* (Bombay, 1373/1952), p. 84.

108. On the virginity of (A)Nāhīd, Mithra/Mehr's mother, see M. Moqaddam, *Jostār dar bāre-ye Mehr va Nāhīd* (Tehran, 1978), vol. 1, pp. 29ff. Regarding Shahrbānū's virginity, Ṣ. Hedāyat, *Neyrangestān* (Tehran, rpr. 1344 Sh./1966), p. 118. One may advance two other hypotheses on the parallel features between Anāhīd as Mithra's mother and the figure of Shahrbānū: 1) Mithra, 'the Petrogenous', born of a rock; on this legend originating probably in Asia Minor or the Caucasus, see F. Cumont, *Les mystères de Mithra*, (rpr. Paris, 1985, from the 3rd edn, Brussels, 1913), pp. 132ff.; On the many monuments representing Mithra born from a rock, see F. Cumont, *Textes et monuments relatifs aux mystères de Mithra* (Bruxelles, 1896–1899), vol. 1, pp. 161ff.; M. J. Vermaseren, *Corpus Inscriptionum et Monumentorum Religionis Mithriacae* (La Haye, 1956–1960), vol. 1, pp. 158ff.; there is thus an analogy between the rock, a symbol of incorruptibility that gives birth to an Iranian god and Anāhīd, the deity's mother, eternally young and virgin. Shahrbānū, received by the rock at the mountain in Rayy, literally identifies with her. One finds the same analogy, even identity with the Lady of the Rock. 2) Identification of the trinity Ahura Mazdā/(marrying his daughter:) Spenta Aramati/(to give birth to his son:) Vohu Manah with the trinity Ahura Mazdā/Anāhīd/Mithra resuscitates the 'incestuous marriage' archetypal par excellence by placing the Iranian goddess at the centre of the trinity, see e.g. G. Widengren, *Les religions de l'Iran* (Paris, 1968), pp. 256ff., which obviously evokes *xwētōdas/xwēdōdah* regarding the mother of the fourth imam as we have already seen.

healing and fertility from the Lady of the Land; and this has been the case ever since ancient times.[109]

Apart from these reasons indicated by Bāstānī Pārīzī and Boyce, namely the prior existence of a sanctuary for Anāhīd,[110] the choice of Rayy may also be explained by the fact that it was from this city in 20/641 that Yazdgird III launched a last appeal to his people to put up strong resistance against Muslim troops before escaping to Khurāsān. Moreover, the city of Rayy, although almost entirely Iranian in population (with a minimal Arab presence), had always been one of the most important bastions of all forms of Shiʿism (Zaydism, Ismailism, Qarmatism and of course Imamism) and remained so until the sixth/twelfth century.[111] Finally, during al-Maʾmūn's reign, pre-Islamic Iranian religious traditions would

---

109. Bāstānī Pārīzī, *Khātūn-e haft qalʿe*, p. 246. Apart from Shahrbānū, in Persian literature, the goddess Anāhīd also seems to have been transformed into another Sasanian princess, namely Shīrīn; see P. P. Soucek, 'Farhād and Ṭāq-i Bustān: the Growth of a Legend', in *Studies in Art and Literature of the Near East in Honour of Richard Ettinghausen* (Washington, 1974), pp. 27–52. Moreover, the chapter devoted to Shahrbānū in M. R. Eftekhār-Zādeh, *Īslām dar Īrān. Shuʿūbiyye nehḍat-e moqāvamat-e mellī-ye Īrān ʿalayh-e Omaviyān va ʿAbbāsiyān* (Tehran, 1371 Sh./1992), pp. 98ff., though well documented, is nonetheless much too tainted by its ideological and polemical stance to be appropriately used in a scholarly study. Similarly, the treatment reserved for Shahrbānū in D. Pinault, 'Zaynab bint ʿAlī and the Place of the Women of the Households of the First Imāms in Shīʿite Devotional Literature', in G. R. G. Hambly (ed.), *Women in the Medieval Islamic World* (New York, 1998), pp. 80–81 (the entire article pp. 69–98) is rather a shallow summary to be useful here.

110. Though advanced prudently, Ḥ. Karīmān's hypothesis according to which the Shahrbānū sanctuary would actually have been a Zoroastrian *dakhma* where lie the bodies of Hormoz (son of Yazdgird II) and his family, all assassinated by Pērōz, the other son of the Sasanian king, seems hard to support (*Ray-e bāstān*, vol. 1, p. 379 and pp. 414–415). Indeed according to the Iranian scholar, the transfer of the site to Shiʿism enabled it to be protected from the destructive rage of recent converts; now, another ancient Zoroastrian cemetry, visited in the early fourth/tenth century by Abū Dulaf (*Safar-Nāmeh*, 'al-risāla al-thāniyya', p. 31), is located on the same mountatin. It was neither destroyed nor Islamicised. Why reserve such different treatment to locations of the same kind found on the same site? On the contrary, a 'pagan' temple is usually more in need of protection from the zeal of believers of a new religion than a cemetry.

111. V. Minorsky-C. E. Bosworth, 'al-Rayy', *EI2*, vol. 8, pp. 487–489.

have survived in Rayy since the city seems to have sheltered a still active Manichean community.[112]

Unlike epic religious accounts, in which Shahrbānū seems to have only a minor role,[113] *taʿziya*, Shiʿi Persian theatre, shows strong evidence of her popularity. In the catalogue of *taʿziya* plays in the Cerulli collection held at the Vatican Library, Ettore Rossi and Alessio Bombaci have classified more than thirty plays in which Shahrbānū, sometimes called Shāh-e zanān, features. Usually, the scene takes place on the day of Karbalāʾ and the play describes the mourning and courage of the martyred imam's wife. Some plays (nos 30–424–429–461–579–948 and 1,000) also portray the princess of Iran being captured, her dialogue with ʿAlī and her marriage to al-Ḥusayn. Finally, Shahrbānū's escape to Rayy and the mountain miracle are the scenarios in two plays (no. 466 - on the hidden princess - and no. 945).[114] In almost all

112. Gh. Ḥ. Ṣadīqī, *Jonbesh hā-ye dīnī-ye īrānī dar qarn hā-ye dovvom va sevvom-e hejrī* (Tehran, 1372 Sh./1993) a supplemented and updated version of the author's doctorate thesis, *Les mouvements religieux iraniens au IIe et IIIe siècles de l'hégire* (Paris, 1938), see index under 'Yazdānbakht' drawing on Ibn al-Nadīm and al-Bīrūnī.

113. For example, she only appears once and in a cursory manner at the beginning of the voluminous *Abū Muslim-nāma*, though curiously as the daughter of Zayd the Jew (*Abū Muslim-nāma*, the version reported by Abū Ṭāhir al-Ṭarṭūsī, ed. H. Esmaïli, 4 vols [Tehran, 1380 Sh./2001], vol. 1, p. 92.) However, the Sasanian princess seems to have been emulated in this literature; see e.g. Princess Dhī Funūn Pākdāman, daughter of the King of Irām, who marries the son of ʿAlī, Muḥammad b. al-Ḥanafiyya in *Ḥikāyat-e Muḥammad-e Ḥanafiyye*, cited by J. Calmard, 'Moḥammad b. al-Ḥanafiyya dans la religion populaire, le folklore, les légendes dans le monde turco-persan et indo-persan', *Cahiers d'Asie Centrale*, 5–6 (1998), pp. 201–220, particularly pp. 214–215. Moreover, in the beliefs of some villages in Simnān, Shahrbānū is the sister of a (Mazdean?) prophet named Sīnelūm whose sanctuary on 'the Mountain of Prophets' *(Kūh-e peyghambarān)*, has remained a very popular pilgrimage site; see C. A. Azami, 'Payghambarān Mountain Temple', *Journal of the K.R. Cama Oriental Institute*, 73 (1987), pp. 45–55, and 'Parmgar Fire Temple', *Journal of the K.R. Cama Oriental Institute*, 74 (1988), pp. 200–206.

114. E. Rossi and A. Bombaci, *Elenco di drami religiosi persiani (fondo mss. Vaticani Cerulli)* (Vatican City, 1961), index, p. 386, under 'Šahrbānū'; also C. Virolleaud, *Le théâtre persan* (Paris, 1950), pp. 7–8.

these works, sympathy for Iran and its pre-Islamic past are readily apparent.

The convergence between pre-Islamic Iran and Imami Shiʿism by virtue of Shahrbānū is just as emphatic in some popular rituals dedicated to the wife of the third imam. Sacrifices offered to Bībī Shahrbānū – horses, lambs and cattle – are the same as those offered to Bānū Pārs/Anāhīd of ʿAghdā in Yazd.[115] The main ritual offering in the sanctuary at Rayy is a bowl of water[116] – an element of nature of which Anāhīd is the goddess. In some regions of Iranian Khurāsān, among the mourning rituals that mark the first ten days of the month of Muḥarram in commemoration of the death of the martyrs at Karbalā', elegies (Persian: *mātam* = Arabic: *marthiya, nawḥa*) dedicated to Shahrbānū and often called 'the Farewell of (or: to) Shahrbānū' (*wadāʿ-i Shahrbānū*) occupy an important place. Processions reciting these elegies almost invariably pass by a Zoroastrian cemetery; if the ritual is not carried out, people believe that the villages will be victim to drought or floods, that is to say, in either case natural disasters related to water.[117]

---

115. M. Boyce, 'Bībī Shahrbānū and the Lady of Pārs', pp. 42–43. However, the author is right to stress the difference between the respective moods of the sanctuaries: while the Shiʿis make their pilgrimage in sadness, mourning and with lamentations, the Zoroastrians, for whom joy is a form of energy that derives from Ahura Mazda, render worship in a lighthearted manner, with laughter, music and song, p. 44.

116. S. J. Shahīdī, 'Baḥthī dar bāre-ye shahrbānū', p. 189.

117. Ibid., p. 180–181; also M. R. Eftekhār-Zādeh, *Islām dar Īrān* (Tehran, 1371 Sh./1992), pp. 130–132: the elegy given as: '*Ey shahrbānū al-wadāʿ, ey shahrbānū al-wadāʿ*', copied from the notebook of an official in the village, comes from the region of Bīrjand, in southern Khurāsān. The Sogdian Manichean text on the Nana cult, published by Henning in 'The Murder of the Magi', in *Selected Papers II* = *Acta Iranica*, 15, pp. 139–150, though quite fragmentary, offers striking parallels with this cult of Bībī Shahrbānū: one finds the same intermingling of the funerary cult, lamentations and 'the drought curse'; see also F. Grenet and B. Marshak, 'Le mythe de Nana dans l'art de la Sogdiane', pp. 7–9 and F. Grenet in *L'Annuaire de l'École Pratique des Hautes Etudes, Sciences Religieuses*, 105 (1996–1997), pp. 213–217, particularly p. 216.

I am personally acquainted with some Zoroastrian women from the Kirmān region who regularly make a pilgrimage to the Shahrbānū sanctuary in Rayy. This is not an isolated case. It is true that they would only need to veil themselves in order to disguise themselves among the masses of visiting Muslim women. Although they have not explicitly said so, it seems perfectly plausible that they visit the site to worship the popular Lady Anāhīd.[118] As J. Chabbi has so aptly observed, 'In order to survive in a present that denies it, the past must advance masked.'[119]

4

The figure of Shahrbānū may be situated within the complex network of relations between Iranians and Shiʿis. These relations naturally belong to the wider framework of the attitude of Iranians towards Islam and the authorities that represented it during the first centuries of the Hijra. This framework was extensively studied in its myriad forms.[120] One could say that this attitude exhibited itself in three ways, each influenced by a number of currents: first, a violent, radical attitude, at times leading to rejection, plain and simple – whether one thinks of the political convergence that linked the Kaysānī ʿAlids and Iranian nobility from the Mukhtār revolt in 66/685,[121] or the Khurramī revolts, particularly

118. Jamshīd Sorūsh Sorūshiyān lists a certain number of sacred sites visited by Zoroastrians and Shiʿis alike: Setī Pīr in Maryam-Ābād of Yazd (*Farhang-e behdīnān*, p. 206), Āb-e Morād, west of Kirmān (pp. 207–208), Shāh Mehr-īzad, north of Kirmān (p. 209), Shāh Varahrām-īzad in Kirmān itself which the Shiʿis call 'Master Murtaḍā ʿAlī of the Zoroastrians', *Pīr Morteḍā ʿAlī-ye gabrān* (p. 210) and Kūh Borīda in Zerīsf, east of Kirmān (p. 211).

119. J. Chabbi, *Le Seigneur des tribus. L'Islam de Mahomet* (Paris, 1997), p. 402.

120. Now consult an analysis by E. Yarshater, 'The Persian Presence in the Islamic World'; refer also to his excellent bibliography, pp. 100–125.

121. According to historiographical sources, only Persian was spoken in Mukhtār's army; see al-Dīnawarī, *al-Akhbār al-ṭiwāl*, p. 302; al-Ṭabarī, *Taʾrīkh*, ed. de Goeje series 2, p. 647. Although the assertion seems exaggerated, the reactions of the Umayyad authorities led by the caliph ʿAbd al-Malik b. Marwān, as reported

of the Zoroastrian Sunbādh in Rayy (around 138/756) whose army seems to have consisted of Neo-Mazdakites, Zoroastrians and Shiʿis, or of Bābak in Ādharbāyjān (from 201 to 223/816–838) undoubtedly seeking to overcome Islam with a view to restoring the Magian religion of the Persian royal house,[122] or the Qarmaṭī Shiʿis led by Abū Ṭāhir al-Jannābī/Ganāvehī when in 319/931 he transferred power to a young Persian from Isfahan, who according to prophecies attributed to Zoroaster and Jāmāsp, was meant to be the *Mahdī* or agent for the restoration of Magian rule;[123] and to free-thinkers, among them some of Iranian origin, who, according to the heresiographers, often hid their Manicheism and sometimes radical 'Iranism' in the guise of Shiʿi *rafḍ*.[124]

---

by other categories of sources appear to corroborate this kind of information; see e.g., Abu'l-Ḥajjāj Yūsuf b. Muḥammad, *Kitāb alif bā'* (Cairo, 1287/1870), vol. 1, p. 24; al-Damīrī, *Ḥayāt al-ḥayawān al-kubrā* (Cairo, 1306/1888), vol. 2, pp. 78. See also Ḥ. Taqī-Zādeh, *Az Parvīz tā Changīz* (2nd edn, Tehran, 1330 Sh./1952), p. 70; Gh. Ḥ. Ṣadīqī, *Jonbesh hā-ye dīnī-ye īrānī*, p. 42.

122. S. Nafīsī, *Bābak-e Khurramdīn, delāvar-e Ādharbāyjān* (Tehran, 1342 Sh./1963), see index under 'Zoroastrian' etc.; W. Madelung, 'Khurramiyya ou Khurramdīniyya', *EI2*, vol. 5, pp. 65–67, in particular p. 65b; E. Yarshater, 'Mazdakism' in E. Yarshater (ed.), *The Cambridge History of Iran*, vol. 3(2) (Cambridge, 1983), pp. 1,001ff. 'A. Mīr Feṭrūs, 'Jonbesh-e sorkh jāmegān. Bar rasī-ye manābe'', *Iran Nameh*, 9/1 (1991), pp. 57–89.

123. W. Madelung, 'Ḳarmaṭī', *EI2*, vol. 4, pp. 687–692, particularly pp. 688b–689a; now consult S. J. Ḥamīdī, *Nehḍat-e Abū Saʿīd Ganāvehī* (3rd edn, Tehran, 1372 Sh./1993), ch. 5. Let us not forget the Pārsiyān neo-Mazdakis who in 536/1141–1142 joined the Nizārī Ismailis, loyal supporters of Ḥasan-i Ṣabbāḥ, see W. Madelung, 'Mazdakism and the Khurramiyya', in his *Religious Trends in Early Islamic Iran* (Albany, NY, 1988), pp. 1–12.

124. For example, Bashshār b. Burd, Ibn Abi'l-ʿAwjā', Abū Shākir, Abū 'Īsā al-Warrāq, Ibn Ṭālūt, Ibn al-Rāwandī; see Gh. Ḥ. Ṣadīqī, *Jonbesh hāye dīnī-ye īrānī*, pp. 130–135; also G. Vajda, 'Les zindīqs en pays d'Islam au début de la période abbasside', *RSO*, 17 (1937), pp. 173–229; M. Chokr, *Zandaqa et Zindîqs en Islam au second siècle de l'hégire* (Damascus, 1993), see index under the names above. S. Stroumsa, *Freethinkers of Medieval Islam: Ibn al-Rāwandī, Abū Bakr al-Rāzī and Their Impact on Islamic Thought* (Leiden, 1999), index. See also Ibn Ḥazm, *al-Fiṣal*, vol. 2, pp. 115–116; Baghdādī, *al-Farq*, p. 173; Niẓām al-Mulk, *Siyāsat-nāma*, ed. J. Shaʿār (Tehran, 1364 Sh./1986), pp. 25, 249, 279, 285f.

A second category of Iranians, consisting mostly of intellectuals, the educated and thinkers, seem to have made an unconditional commitment to the new religion and even its language, to the extent of becoming its most important advocates. Indeed, until proven otherwise, no discernible Iranian trait is perceptible in the works of such figures as al-Bukhārī, Muslim, Ibn Mājja, al-Tirmidhī, al-Nasā'ī, or even Sībawayh, al-Ḥasan al-Baṣrī or Ibn Qutayba.[125]

Finally, in a third category, mainly of intellectuals and politicians, men of letters and activists, and in which many tendencies co-exist or at times confront each other, from the most moderate to the most radical, with a range between the two, the protagonists seem to be ardent Muslims, though still holding on to their sense of Iranian identity, that is, the sentiment, even historical consciousness, of belonging to a great culture and an ancient civilisation. In a general way, the twofold conviction found in this third category would have led the Iranians to filter elements belonging to ancient Iranian culture into the new religion; in other words, to 'Islamicise' some traits of pre-Islamic Iranian civilisation and religious sentiment.[126] Thus, they seem to have been convinced of the need for preventing the loss of some traits considered essential, not

---

125. See e.g. E. Yarshater, 'The Persian Presence in the Islamic World', pp. 93ff. With regard to Ibn Qutayba, although in his *'Uyūn al-akhbār* and *Ma'ārif*, he reproduces the essential works of Ibn al-Muqaffa', this seems to be more of a literary exercise than a deeply felt pro-Iranian sentiment. In any case, his anti-Shu'ūbi sentiments, admittedly moderate, are evident in his *Kitāb al-'arab*, ed. M. Kurd 'Alī, *Rasā'il al-bulaghā'* (2nd edn, Cairo, 1365/1946), pp. 344–377.

126. For the denunciation of this 'infiltration' of Islam by the Iranians, see e.g. al-Baghdādī, *al-Farq* (Cairo, 1328/1910), pp. 269–271; al-Maqdisī, *al-Bad' wa'l-ta'rīkh*, ed. and tr. Cl. Huart (Paris, 1901–1903), vol. 5, pp. 133ff.; Ibn al-Nadīm, *Fihrist*, ed. M. R. Tajaddod (Tehran, 1350 Sh./1971), p. 188; al-Bīrūnī, *al-Āthār al-bāqiya*, p. 213; al-Mas'ūdī, *al-Tanbīh wa'l-ishrāf*, ed. M. de Goeje (Leiden, 1893–1894), p. 395; Ibn Ḥazm, *al-Fiṣal*, vol. 1, p. 36 and vol. 2, p. 91; al-Balkhī, Abu'l-Ma'ālī Muḥammad b. Ni'mat, *Bayān al-adyān*, ed. M. T. Dānesh Pazhūh (Tehran, 1376 Sh./1997), ch. 5, pp. 106ff.; al-Maqrīzī, *al-Khiṭaṭ* (Būlāq, 1853), vol. 2, p. 462; Ibn al-Jawzī, *Naqd al-'ilm wa'l-'ulamā' aw talbīs Iblīs* (Cairo, 1340/1921), p. 212.

only for Iranian culture but also for Islam since they could provide it with fundamental elements that would render it a universal religion and a veritable civilisation. This would have been the position of a large majority of the pro-Iranian Shuʿūbiyya. In this case, it is no longer a case of threatening the permanence of the Islamic empire, but rather fighting for its future orientation. It is not the destruction of the state that is envisaged but the refashioning of its institutions, its political and social values, its structures of thought, in a word, all that would contribute to the development of its culture.[127] It was due to numerous obvious points of convergence in the opinion of various eminent specialists, that Shiʿism in its different forms constituted one of the most favourable terrains for this category of Iranian.[128] Apparently, the Shuʿūbī Irano-Shiʿi milieu in which the Shahrbānū tradition was nurtured belonged to this third category.[129]

---

127. H. A. R. Gibb, 'The Social Significance of the Shuʿūbiyya', pp. 62ff.; S. Enderwitz, *Gesellschaftlicher Rang und ethnische Legitimation*, pp. 50ff. and 141ff.; the author supplements theories advanced by Hamilton Gibb by essentially demonstrating that in addition to one culture triumphing over another, it is also a matter of the status, social and political privileges of the new civil servants.

128. See among others, I. Goldziher, *Muhammedanische Studien*, 'Arab und ʿAjam' (Halle, 1888), vol. 1, pp. 101–146; *Die Shuʿūbijja*, pp. 147–176, esp. 168ff.; ibid., pp. 177–218, esp. 201ff.; E. Blochet, 'Etudes sur l'histoire religieuse de l'Iran, I. De l'influence de la religion mazdéenne sur les croyances des peuples turcs', *RHR*, 38 (1898), pp. 26–63, particularly pp. 37ff. and 54ff.; B. Spuler, 'Iran: the Persistant Heritage', pp. 171–172; J. K. Choksy, *Conflict and Cooperation: Zoroastrian Subalterns and Muslim Elites in Medieval Muslim Society* (New York, 1997), see index under 'Shi'ism', as well as the great many pages in three important Persian works: ʿA. Eqbāl, *Khāndān-e Nawbakhtī* (Tehran, 1311 Sh./1932); M. Moḥammadī Malāyerī, *Tārīkh va farhang-e Īrān*, and Gh. Ḥ. Ṣadīqī, *Jonbesh hā-ye dīnī-ye īrānī*. At times, the attitude of certain authors (Muḥammad Ghazālī, Suhrawardī Shaykh al-Ishrāq) seems rather 'tactical': in order to save some Iranian cultural elements, it seems necessary to severely criticise others. This issue merits a separate study.

129. Generally speaking, this seems to be the case in the milieu of the first great Imami traditionalists from the Schools of Rayy and Qumm (see *Guide divin*, pp. 48–54 [*Divine Guide*, pp. 19–21]) and this in spite of some fiercely anti-Arab traditions, perhaps stemming from the first category, also found in the compilations of these traditionalists (e.g. certain eschatological *ḥadīths*

The relationship between pre-Islamic Iranian culture and Islam in general, as well as the convergences, even political connivance, between Shiʿis and Iranians, as we have seen, have been widely studied; on the other hand, links of a doctrinal and religious nature between ancient Iranian religions and Imami Shiʿism constitute a field of research that is still almost completely unexplored. In this dense assemblage of material, the Shahrbānū tradition forms a part of those elements that link Imamism to ancient Iran and by the same means serve to rehabilitate pre-Islamic Iranian culture.

Let us limit ourselves to some noteworthy examples: the tradition according to which the celestial Book of Zoroaster consisted of 12,000 volumes containing all Knowledge and in which ʿAlī is depicted as the ultimate connaisseur of this Book;[130] a tradition praising the justice of Iranian royalty, particularly of King Anūshiruwān, during whose reign the Prophet was born;[131] the emblematic figure of Salmān the Persian as the Iranian sage, the

regarding the return of the *qā'im*; see *Guide divin*, pp. 294–295 [*Divine Guide*, pp. 115–123], and 'Eschatology, iii. In Imami Shiʿism', *EIr*, vol. 8, p. 578).

130. Al-Kulaynī, *al-Furūʿ min al-Kāfī*, 4 vols (Tehran, 1334 Sh./1956), vol. 1, p. 161; Ibn Bābūya, *Amālī/al-Majālis*, Arabic text and Persian trans. by M. B. Kamare'ī (Tehran, 1404/1984), p. 206, *Kitāb al-tawḥīd*, ed. al-Ḥusaynī al-Ṭihrānī (Tehran, 1398/1978), p. 7, and *Kitāb man lā yaḥḍuruhu'l-faqīh*, ed. al-Mūsawī al-Kharsān (5th edn, n. p., 1390/1970), vol. 1, p. 17; al-Ṭūsī, *Tahdhīb al-aḥkām*, ed. al-Mūsawī al-Kharsān (Najaf, 1958–1962), vol. 1, p. 381. ʿAlī as an expert on Zoroastrianism is also found in Sunni sources, e.g. Abū Yūsuf, *Kitāb al-kharāj*, p. 129; al-Ṣanʿānī, *al-Muṣannaf*, ed. Ḥ. al-R. al-Aʿẓamī (Beirut, 1972), vol. 6, pp. 70–71; for other Sunni sources see also Y. Friedmann, 'Classification of Unbelievers in Sunnī Muslim Law and Tradition', *JSAI*, 22 (1998), p. 180 n. 78. On recourse to the figure of ʿAlī for the preservation of certain Iranian traditions from the Sasanian period, see Sh. Shaked, 'From Iran to Islam: On Some Symbols of Royalty', *JSAI*, 7 (1986), pp. 85–87 (rpr. in *From Zoroastrian Iran to Islam*, article VII), and 'A Facetious Recipe and the Two Wisdoms: Iranian Themes in Muslim Garb', *JSAI*, 9 (1987), pp. 31–33 (now in *From Zoroastrian Iran to Islam*, article IX); For other Shiʿi *ḥadīth*s see also M. Moʿīn, *Mazdayasnā va ta'thīr-e ān dar adabiyyāt-e fārsī* (Tehran, 1326 Sh./1948), with an introduction by H. Corbin.

131. Al-Majlisī, *Biḥār al-anwār*, vol. 15, pp. 250, 254, 279ff.

ideal Muslim and archetype of the Shiʿi initiate;[132] the glorification of two of the greatest Iranian festivals, Nawrūz and Mihrigān in *ḥadīths* going back to the Shiʿi imams and texts by Imami thinkers;[133] mourning rituals for al-Ḥusayn as a continuation of funerary rituals not unlike ancient practices for the Iranian hero Siyāvash.[134]

In this context, and when we consider the fundamental importance of filiation and the cult of kinship in Shiʿism since earliest times,[135] the figure of Shahrbānū takes on special meaning. In the ninth/fifteenth century, Jamal al-Dīn Aḥmad b. ʿAlī, known as Ibn ʿInaba (d. 828/1424) wrote that a number of Ḥusaynid

---

132. L. Massignon, 'Salmân Pâk et les prémices spirituelles de l'Islam iranien', in his *Opera Minora* (Beirut, 1963), vol. 1, pp. 443–483; H. Corbin, *En Islam iranien* (Paris, 1971–1972), see index under 'Salmân'; ʿA. Mohājerānī, *Barrasī-ye seyr-e zendegī va ḥekmat va ḥokūmat-e Salmān-e fārsī* (Tehran, 1378 Sh./1999).

133. For the *ḥadīths* see J. Walbridge, 'A Persian Gulf in the Sea of Lights: the Chapter on Naw-Rūz in the *Biḥār al-Anwār*', *Iran*, 35 (1997), pp. 83–92; among thinkers, see e.g. praises of ʿAlī regarding Iranian festivals in poems by al-Sharīf al-Raḍī (d. 406/1016), *Dīwān* (rpr. Qumm, n.d.), pp. 134ff. and his brother al-Sharīf al-Murtaḍā (d. 436/1044), *Dīwān* (Tehran, 1365 Sh./1986), pp. 56ff. as well as in the poems of the former's disciple, newly converted from Zoroastrianism: Mahyār al-Daylamī (d. 428/1036), cited by M. Moḥammadī Malāyerī, *Tārīkh va farhang-e Īrān*, pp. 188–190. On Nawrūz being considered ʿAlī's birthday by the Bektashis, see F. De Jong, 'The Iconography of Bektashism. A Survey of Themes and Symbolism in Clerical Costume, Liturgical Objects and Pictorial Art', *The Manuscripts of the Middle East*, 4 (1989), note 56.

134. See Sh. Meskūb, *Sūg-e Siyāvash* (Tehran, 1971), pp. 82ff.; E. Yarshater, 'Taʿzieh and Pre-Islamic Mourning Rituals in Iran', in P. J. Chelkowski (ed.), *Taʿzieh: Ritual and Drama in Iran* (New York, 1979), pp. 80–95; ʿA. Bolūkbāshī, 'Tābūt gardānī, namāyeshī tamthīlī az qodrat-e qodsī-ye khodāvandī', *Nashr-e Dânesh*, 16/4 (1378 Sh./2000), pp. 32–38, particularly pp. 33–34. On the identification, made in popular Persian literature, between the Iranian hero Rustam and ʿAlī, see S. Soroudi, 'Islamization of the Iranian National Hero Rustam in Persian Folktales', *JSAI*, 2 (1980), pp. 365–383. The article by A. B. Agaeff, 'Les croyances mazdéennes dans la religion chiite', *Transactions of the Ninth International Congress of Orientalists* (London, 1893), pp. 505–514 is now quite outdated.

135. See M. A. Amir-Moezzi, 'Considérations sur l'expression *dīn ʿAlī*', *ZDMG*, 150/1 (2000), pp. 29–68 (Chapter 1, this volume).

Shi'is and even some Sunnis (? *al-'awāmm*) take pride in the fact that 'Alī b. al-Ḥusayn, in his very being, combined prophethood (*al-nubuwwa*, by virtue of his descent from Muḥammad) and royalty (*al-mulk*, due to his Sasanian descent).[136] Here, the genealogist seems to have in mind mainly Iranians, mostly Ḥusaynid Shi'is, but apparently also non-Shi'is. It seems quite telling that for many centuries, almost without exception, the writers who have reported the main versions of the Shahrbānū story have been Iranians or Iranianised Imamis: Ṣaffār, Nawbakhtī, Ash'arī Qummī, Kulaynī, Ibn Bābūya, Kay Kāwūs b. Iskandar b. Qābūs, Ibn Rustam Ṭabarī, the unknown author of *Mujmal al-tawārīkh wa'l-qiṣaṣ*, Rāwandī, Ibn Shahrāshūb.[137]

Adding the Light of Royal Glory to that of *walāya* stemming from Muḥammad and 'Alī, Shahrbānū gives a double legitimacy, Shi'i and Iranian, to her sons, the imams of Ḥusaynid lineage, as well as a dual nobility, Qurashī, and Sasanian. Thus she becomes the main link between the relationship which unites pre-Islamic Iran and Imamism. Much later, an analogous effort was made with regard to the mother of the twelfth imam, the Imami Mahdī, described in some versions as the granddaughter of the Byzantine

---

136. Ibn 'Inaba, *'Umdat al-ṭālib fī ansāb āl Abī Ṭālib*, p. 173. The author, himself an Arab of Ḥijāzī origin and Ḥasanid descent, criticises this attitude, arguing that the nobility of the fourth imam is solely due to the fact that he is a descendant of the Prophet. This kind of polemic lives on today; see e.g. comments made by 'A. Ḥ. al-Amīnī in response to an Egyptian scholar in *al-Ghadīr fi'l-kitāb wa'l-sunna wa'l-adab* (Beirut, 1397/1977), vol. 33, pp. 317–318. On polemics of a political nature regarding this subject see e.g. M. Fischer, *Iran: from Religious Dispute to Revolution* (Cambridge, 1980), pp. 260–261; Y. Richard, *L'Islam Chi'ite. Croyances et idéologies* (Paris, 1991), p. 115.

137. Note that the presence of al-Mubarrad, one of the first authors to describe 'Alī b. al-Ḥusayn's mother as belonging to the Sasanian royal house, is quite mysterious (cf. above); is this sympathy for the 'Alid cause? (see R. Sellheim, 'al-Mubarrad', *EI2*, vol. 7, pp. 281–284, particularly p. 281b). Or rather, is this a form of teasing aimed at his friend al-Jāḥiẓ whose anti-Shi'i, anti-Iranian and anti-Shu'ūbī sentiments were hardly secret. Such is probably the case given that this kind of jocular behaviour was common among the intellectual circles of the large cities.

emperor, himself a descendant of the apostle Simon.[138] Thus the Imami Messiah would in his person bring together on the one hand Lights of Islam, Mazdaeism and Christianity and on the other Arab, Persian and Byzantine nobility. This attempt was unsuccessful and the tradition did not increase in popularity, undoubtedly because, in the eyes of Imami Shiʿis, Byzantium was less important than Iran.

---

138. Ibn Bābūya, *Kamāl al-Dīn*, ed. ʿA. A. Ghaffārī (Qumm, 1405/1985), vol. 2, ch. 41, pp. 417–423; al-Ṭūsī, *Kitāb al-ghayba* (Tabrīz, 1322/1905), pp. 134–139; Ibn Rustam al-Ṭabarī al-Ṣaghīr, *Dalāʾil al-imāma*, pp. 489ff.; see *Guide divin*, p. 265 (*Divine Guide*, p. 108).

Part II: On the Nature of the Imam: Initiation and Dualism

3

Some Remarks on the Divinity of the Imam*

In some – it must be said – rather discrete texts, diluted in the mass of traditions that early Twelver compilations contain, the Imam is not only presented as the man of God par excellence but as participating fully in the Names, Attributes and Acts that theology usually reserves for God alone. This 'figure' of the Imam presents a number of fundamental similarities with the variously named Cosmic Man of the Near and Middle Eastern spiritual and religious traditions. In many respects, it seems also to lie behind the reiteration of this ancient notion in Muslim spirituality.[1] It is

---

* 'Imam' is written with the 'i' upper case when it relates to the ontological, cosmic, archetypal Imam, and lower case when it relates to the historical imam, manifestation of the first or the perceptible level. Also, 'Imami' and 'Twelver' are used interchangeably.

1. In the present state of our knowledge, it still appears daring to wish to establish links among the diverse pre-Islamic religious traditions and the numerous schools of thought derived from them; even more so because a substantial number of doctrines claim, more or less explicitly, to have emerged from several among them. We can only limit ourselves to a few bibliographical references; for discussions on 'Man in the image of God' in Jewish, Christian and Judeo-Christian traditions, consult the extensive bibliography in L. Scheffczyk (ed.), *Der Mensch als Bild Gottes* (Darmstadt, 1969), pp. 526–538; also T. H. Tobin, *The Creation of Man: Philo and the History of Interpretation* (Washington, DC, 1983). On the recurring motif of *Imago Dei* in Hellenistic and Gnostic thought, see U. Bianchi (ed.), *La 'doppia' creazione dell'uomo negli Alessandrini, nei Cappadoci nella gnosis* (Rome, 1978). On the concept of Primordial Man in Iranian religions, see the bibliographical study by C. Colpe, 'Der "Iranische

equally true that obvious similarities exist between the Imam-God of Shiʿi texts and the Perfect Man (*al-insān al-kāmil*) of Muslim theosophy, an ontologically necessary intermediary between God and the world, the mysterious ultimate goal and 'Secret of secrets' for the theosopher.[2]

In this regard, the most representative and outspoken Shiʿi texts are undoubtedly certain sermons attributed to ʿAlī (assassinated in 40/661), the imam par excellence and the 'father' of all the historic imams of all Shiʿi branches. So often does the identity of the speaker

---

Hintergrund" der islamischen Lehre vom Vollkommenen Menschen', in Ph. Gignoux (ed.), *Recurrent Patterns in Iranian Religions. From Mazdaism to Sufism, Studia Iranica*, 11 (1992). On the Perfect Man in Mazdaeism, see M. Molé, *Culte, mythe et cosmologie dans l'Iran ancien* (Paris, 1963), Book III, ch. 3. On the Primordial Man in Manichaeism, see H. C. Puech, *Le manichéisme, son fondateur, sa doctrine* (Paris, 1949) (Bibliography to be supplemented by H C. Puech, 'le Manichéisme', in *l'Histoire des Religions, Encyclopédie de la Pléiade*, vol. 2, pp. 523–645). For Assyro-Babylonian religions, one will find valuable information in S. Parpola, 'The Assyrian Tree of Life: Tracing the Origins of Jewish Monotheism and Greek Philosophy', *Journal of Near Eastern Studies*, 52/3 (1993), pp. 161–208.

2. Apart from the now classic works on Muslim mysticism that include more or less full discussions on the Perfect Man (e.g. works by Nicholson, Asin Palacios, Massignon, Arberry, Anawati-Gardet, Ritter, Schimmel, Corbin, Izutsu), there are cited below some monographs containing particularly interesting elements: H. H. Schaeder, 'Die islamische Lehre vom Vollkommenen Menschen', *ZDMG*, 79 (1925), pp. 192–268 (partially translated into Arabic by 'A. R. Badawī, see below); L. Massignon, 'L'Homme Parfait en Islam et son originalité eschatologique', *Eranos Jahrbuch*, 15 (1948), pp. 287–314 (now in *Opera Minora* [Paris, 1969], vol. 1, pp. 107–25); partially translated into Arabic by 'A. R. Badawī in *al-Insān al-kāmil fi'l-Islām* (Cairo, 1950); R. Arnaldez, 'al-Insān al-Kāmil', *EI2*, vol. 3, pp. 1271–1273; W. M. Watt, 'Created in His Image: A Study of Islamic Theology', *Transactions of Glasgow University Oriental Society*, 18 (1959–1960), pp. 36–49; G. C. Anawati, 'Le nom suprême de Dieu *(Ism Allāh al-Aʿẓam)*', *Atti del Terzo Congresso di Studi Arabi e Islamici* (Naples, 1967); M. Takeshita, *Ibn Arabi's Theory of the Perfect Man and its Place in the History of Islamic Thought* (Tokyo, 1987); Ph. Gignoux, '*Imago Dei*: de la théologie nestorienne à Ibn al-ʿArabi', in Ph. Gignoux (ed.), *Recurrent Patterns in Iranian Religions: From Mazdaism to Sufism, Studia Iranica*, Cahier 11 (Paris, 1992), pp. 13–27; the work by B. Radtke, *The Concept of wilāya in Early Sufism* (London, 1993), includes valuable information on the earliest developments of the notion in mystical milieus.

shift, from one sentence to another, between God and the Imam that one could describe these sermons as 'theo-imamosophical'. In a long succession of affirmations, whose repeated hammering in assonant prose, resulted, it is said, in a collective trance on the part of his auditors, the first imam boldly declares his identification with the cosmic *Anthropos*, the Perfect Man, who, in the words of Massignon, is not divinity humanised but humanity rendered divine.[3] To convey an idea of the import of these texts, I point out only some of these affirmations, to return to them in greater detail in the second part: 'I am the Secret of secrets, I am the Guide of the Heavens, I am the *First* and the *Last*, I am the *Apparent* and the *Hidden*, I am the *Compassionate*, I am the Face of God, I am the Hand of God, I am the Archetype of the Book, I am the Cause of causes . . . [the terms in italics are Qur'ānic names of God].' Some specialists have denounced the late date for the redaction of these sermons.[4] In addition, since the sixth/twelfth century, a large number of Imami scholars considered these sermons to belong to 'extremist' Shi'ism (the *ghuluww* movement)[5]

3. L. Massignon, 'L'Homme Parfait en Islam', *Opera Minora*, vol. 1, pp. 109–110.

4. 'A. Ḥ. Zarrīnkūb, *Arzesh-e mīrāth-e ṣūfiyye* (Tehran, 1343 Sh./1965), pp. 281–282; K. M. al-Shaybī, *al-Fikr al-shī'ī wa'l-naza'āt al-ṣūfiyya* (2nd edn, Baghdad, 1395/1975), pp. 253–254; among traditionalist scholars, Sayyid Muṣṭafā Āl Ḥaydar, *Bishārat al-Muṣṭafā* (Tehran, n.d.), pp. 75f., 214f.; Ja'far al-'Āmilī, *Dirāsa fī 'alāmāt al-ẓuhūr* (Qumm, 1411/1990), pp. 110f. The arguments advanced by F. Sezgin, who tends to consider the entire text of one of these sermons (the *khuṭbat al-bayān*) as historically authentic, are not supported by the texts and are far from convincing, F. Sezgin, *Geschichte des arabischen Schrifttums*, vol. 4 (Leiden, 1971), p. 22. Let us recall that from al-Ma'mūn's time (198–218/813–833), nearly two hundred sermons attributed to 'Alī were in circulation and this number rapidly doubled, see L. Veccia Vaglieri, 'Sul *Nahğ al-balāghah* e sul suo compilatore ash-Sharīf ar-Raḍī', *AIUON*, special issue (1958), pp. 7f.

5. Based on the introduction by Sayyid Kāẓim Rashtī (d. 1259/1843) to his *Sharḥ al-khuṭbat al-taṭanjiyya* (Tabriz, 1270/1853). It is true that since the earliest heresiographical treatises, the divinisation of the imam becomes one of the regular accusations levelled against 'extremist' Shi'is (see M. G. Hodgson 'Ghulāt', *EI2*, vol. 2, pp. 1,119–1,121; also W. al-Qāḍī, 'The Development of the Term *Ghulāt* in Muslim Literature with Special Reference to the Kaysāniyya', in

and excluded them from Twelver doctrine, recognised as 'moderate' Shiʿism. The apocryphal nature of these sermons, in their developed form, does indeed seem undeniable; just the philosophical and astronomy-related vocabulary in most of the versions is proof of the late date for their definitive versions.

In this first section therefore, I by no means seek to establish their authenticity but simply to show that, on the one hand, similar speeches existed from an early period in Shiʿi–ʿAlid milieu and, on the other hand, Twelver imamological doctrine as it has been reported by early compilations of *ḥadīth*s enables such a conception of the Imam and also consists of texts that could be considered the first steps of the sermons at issue. If it is true, as Corbin stresses: 'Even if the sermon was not in reality pronounced by the 1st imam . . . it was, at a given moment [pronounced] by an eternal Imam, in the Shiʿi consciousness, and it is this that matters from a phenomenological point of view,'[6] it remains no less true that the origin and development of the notion of the Imam-God in Imami Shiʿism has a history that deserves consideration. As a result, according to Watt,[7] for the early period of Shiʿism, namely

A. Dietrich (ed.), *Akten des VII. Kongresses für Arabistik und Islamwissenschaft* (Göttingen, 1976), pp. 295–319, esp. pp. 299f. and 306f.). Neither the *Nahj al-balāgha*, compiled by al-Sharīf al-Raḍī (d. 406/1016), nor the *Biḥār al-anwār* by Majlisī II (d. 1111/1699), contain theo-imamosophical sermons. The main reason for such silence on the matter, must be the division of the Twelvers, after the major occultation of the twelfth imam (ca. 329/940–941), into two distinct currents both in nature and 'vision of the world': the original 'non-rational esoteric' trend and the much later 'theologico-legal rational' trend. The second, now predominant and in the majority, often accused the first of 'literalism' (*ḥashw*) and 'extremism' (*ghuluww*); regarding this subject see *Guide divin*, pp. 15–58 (*Divine Guide*, pp. 6–22).

6. H. Corbin, *En Islam iranien. Aspects spirituels et philosophiques* (Paris, 1971), vol. 1, p. 96, n. 64.

7. W. Montgomery Watt, *The Formative Period of Islamic Thought* (Edinburgh, 1973), under 'proto-Shiʿism'.

of ‘proto-Shiʿism’, the distinction between extremist and moderate Shiʿism proves to be completely artificial.[8]

The glorification of ʿAlī by his supporters is a process that transformed the historical individual into a semi-legendary figure of tragic and heroic proportions; it harks back to a very early period since the first signs may be traced to the time that immediately followed ʿAlī's assassination if not earlier, to the time just after the latter failed to succeed the Prophet. Early on, this personality acquired cosmic dimensions: the archetypal Imam, manifestation of a primordial Light proceeding from divine Light, a theophanic entity.[9] He transmitted his qualities to other imams of his progeny, even to the imams' initiates. Indeed, according to heresiographic authors, during the course of the first three centuries of Islam, a large number of Shiʿi sects and movements conceived one or another imam or such and such a follower as being the Locus of Manifestation (*maẓhar*) of God.[10] The oldest

8. *Guide divin*, pp. 313–316 (*Divine Guide*, pp. 129–130); also M. A. Amir-Moezzi, ‘Notes sur deux traditions ‘hétérodoxes’ imāmites’, *Arabica*, 41 (1994), pp. 127–133.

9. Cf. E. Kohlberg, ‘Some Imāmī Shīʿī Views on the *ṣaḥāba*’, *Jerusalem Studies in Arabic and Islam*, 5 (1984), pp. 145–146 (rpr. in *Belief and Law in Imāmī Shīʿism* [Aldershot, 1991], article IX); Gh. Ḥ. Ṣadīqī, *Jonbesh-hā-ye dīnī-ye īrānī dar qarn-hā-ye dovvom va sevvom-e hejrī* (completed and updated version of the author's thesis, Gh. H. Sadighi, *Les mouvements religieux iraniens aux IIe et IIIe siècles de l'hégire* [Paris, 1938]), (Tehran, 1372 Sh./1993), pp. 225f.; *Guide divin*, pp. 75f. (*Divine Guide*, pp. 29f.). See also Chapter 1 of this publication.

10. One must point out that, contrary to the accusations levelled by the heresiographers, especially the Sunnis, no Shiʿi sect, even the most ‘extremist’, seems to have claimed that the ‘Locus of Manifestation’ was God in Essence. For all Shiʿis, at the level of Essence, God is absolutely ineffable and unknowable. This forms the very theological foundation of imamology; we shall return to this important matter. There is no question thus of divinisation by incarnation but by theophanic participation, the mode of participation differing according to the ‘Locus of Manifestation’ preferred by the sect. Cf. L. Massignon, ‘Salmân Pâk et les prémices spirituelles de l'Islam iranien’, *Société d'Études Iraniennes*, 7 (1934) (rpr. *Opera Minora*, vol. 1, pp. 443–483, esp. pp. 467–472). For these Shiʿi sects see the list by ʿA. Eqbāl, *Khānedān-e Nawbakhtī* (Tehran, 1311 Sh./1933), pp. 249–267.

among these sects seems to have been the enigmatic Saba'iyya[11] who in a certain number of their doctrinal traits were probably identical to the Kaysāniyya,[12] supporters of the imamate of Muḥammad b. al-Ḥanafiyya and very likely the first Shi'is with gnostic-like ideas. Thus, a Kaysānite proclamation, dating from 278/890–891 and reproduced by al-Ṭabarī (d. 310/923) in his *Ta'rīkh*, appears to be the oldest written attestation of this type of sermon in an 'Alid milieu.[13] Two Nuṣayrī texts that, according to Silvester de Sacy and Massignon, date to the late third century AH, reproduce fragments of these two sermons, the *Bayān* and *Taṭanjiyya* (see section 2 below); the Jābirian corpus (second half of the third to the early fourth century AH) contains a citation from the first.[14] In the early fourth century, these attestations grew

11. Supporters of the enigmatic 'Abd Allāh b. Saba'; see M. G. Hodgson, "Abd Allāh b. Saba", *EI2*.

12. Cf. J. van Ess, 'Das *Kitāb al-irjā'* des Ḥasan b. Muḥammad b. al-Ḥanafiyya', *Arabica*, 21 (1974) and 22 (1975), esp. 1974, pp. 31f.

13. Al-Ṭabarī, *Ta'rīkh al-rusul wa'l-mulūk*, ed. M. A. F. Ibrāhīm (Cairo, 1960), *sub anno* 278, vol. 10, pp. 25–26. According to al-Ṭabarī, the Kaysānī declaration comes from a Qarmaṭī document.

14. A. I. Silvestre de Sacy, *Chrestomathie arabe* (Paris, 1806), vol. 2, p. 83; L. Massignon, 'L'Homme Parfait en Islam', *Opera Minora*, pp. 122–123; the two Nuṣayrī texts are: 1) one that de Sacy calls 'the catechism of the Nuṣayrīs' in MS 5188 (Collection de Sacy), BN Paris, fol. 95f. and 2) *Kitāb al-hidāyat al-kubrā* (Beirut, 1406/1986) by the Nuṣayrī thinker Abū 'Abd Allāh (b.) Ḥusayn b. Ḥamdān al-Khaṣībī (d. 346/957 or 358/969), cited by Massignon in 'L'Homme Parfait', p. 123. The Nuṣayrī *majmū'a* (MS Arabic 1450, BN, Paris) contains a text attributed to al-Mufaḍḍal b. 'Umar al-Ju'fī (famous disciple of the sixth and seventh imams) on 'Alī's divinity; this text is of a later period and dates from the seventh/thirteenth c. See M. M. Bar-Asher and A. Kofsky, 'The Nuṣayrī Doctrine of 'Alī's Divinity and the Nuṣayrī Trinity According to an Unpublished Treatise from the 7th/13th Century', *Der Islam*, 72/2 (1995), pp. 258–292 – now consult their *The Nuṣayrī-'Alawī Religion: An Enquiry into its Theology and Liturgy* (Leiden, 2002); re. this manuscript see also Cl. Huart, 'La poésie religieuse des nosaïris', *JA*, 14 (1879), pp. 241–248; L. Massignon, 'Esquisse d'une bibliographie nuṣayrie', in *Mélanges syriens offerts à Monsieur René Dussaud* (Paris, 1939), pp. 913–922 = *Opera Minora*, vol. 1, pp. 640–649; and now a series of studies by M. M. Bar-Asher and A. Kofsky in 'A Tenth Century Nuṣayrī Treatise on the Duty to Know the Mystery of Divinity', *BSOAS*, 58 (1995), pp. 243–250 – and

in number. Some fragments of the sermons are reported by the Twelver Muḥammad b. ʿUmar al-Kashshī[15] and certain phrases of the 'eschatological prophecies' (*malāḥim*) that feature at the beginning of some versions of the *khuṭbat al-bayān* are cited in a satirical pastiche by the anonymous author of *Abu'l-Qāsim*[16] as well as by al-Maqdisī in his *Bad'*,[17] which at least goes to show that the early nucleus of what would later become these sermons was known before 350/960. The second half of the third to the first half of the fourth century is also the period given for the redaction of all the first major compilations from the Twelver tradition.[18] These bear the mark of what I have elsewhere named the early 'non-rational esoteric tradition',[19] 'salvaging' a good number

---

then published in *The Nuṣayrī-ʿAlawī Religion*; see above. For the corpus of Jābir see *Kitāb al-usṭuqus al-uss al-thānī*, in E. J. Holmyard (ed.), *The Arabic Works of Jābir b. Ḥayyān* (Paris, 1928), pp. 79–96, cited on p. 89. For the dating of this corpus see P. Lory, *Jābir b. Ḥayyān, Dix Traités d'alchimie. Les dix premiers Traités du Livre des Soixante-Dix* (Paris, 1983), pp. 34–51.

15. Al-Kashshī, *Maʿrifat akhbār al-rijāl* (Bombay, 1317/1899), p. 138 (notice on Maʿrūf b. Kharrabūdh who traces the chain of transmission for the sayings of ʿAlī to imam Muḥammad al-Bāqir [d. ca. 119/737]); see also al-Māmaqānī, *Tanqīḥ al-maqāl*, 3 vols (Tehran, 1349/1930), vol. 3, p. 227.

16. Edited by A. Mez, *Die Renaissance des Islams* (Heidelberg, 1922; rpr. Hildesheim, 1968), ch. 5, pp. 57f. On *malḥama,* pl. *malāḥim*, see the article 'Malāḥim' by D. B. MacDonald in *EI2*.

17. Muṭahhar b. Ṭāhir al-Maqdisī, *Kitāb al-bad' wa'l-ta'rīkh (Le Livre de la Création et de l'Histoire)*, ed. and French trans. by Cl. Huart, 6 vols (Paris, 1899–1919), vol. 2, p. 174 and vol. 5, p. 136.

18. Regarding these compilations and their authors see e.g. E. Kohlberg, 'Shīʿī Hadīth', in A. F. L. Beeston et al. (eds), *Arabic Literature to the End of the Umayyad Period* (Cambridge, 1983), pp. 299–307, esp. pp. 303–306; *Guide divin*, pp. 48–58 (*Divine Guide*, pp. 19–22); the authors we will call upon most here include: al-Ṣaffār al-Qummī (290/902–903), Furāt b. Ibrāhīm al-Kūfī (ca. 300/912; an author with obvious Zaydī sympathies but claimed by the Imamis; for more on him see M. M. Bar-Asher, *Scripture and Exegesis in Early Imāmī Shiism* [Leiden and Jerusalem, 1999], pp. 29–32 et passim), ʿAlī b. Ibrāhīm al-Qummī (ca. 307/919), Muḥammad b. Masʿūd al-ʿAyyāshī (ca. 320/932), Muḥammad b. Yaʿqūb al-Kulaynī (329/940–941), Ibn Bābūya al-Ṣadūq (381/991).

19. Cf. above note 5.

of traditions originating from other Shi'i movements (Kaysāni, Ismaili, Wāqifi, etc.) and incorporating them into the Twelver corpus.[20] This monumental corpus does not contain any of the sermons that interest us here, but includes texts that in a fashion clearly predict them. These texts are probably of non-Twelver Shi'i origin but they can be integrated into Twelver imamology if one takes a synoptic view of them. Indeed, at this 'mythical' stage of doctrinal language, when conceptualisation is practically absent and abstract terminology of a philosophical kind is only in its initial stages, when the conceptual distinction between the human nature of the imam (*nāsūt*) and his divine nature (*lāhūt*)[21] is not yet clearly established in Shi'i milieus, an entire process of doctrinal elaboration seemed necessary in order for imamology to reach its peak in the figure of the Imam-God. Therefore it is by adopting a phenomenological perspective that we will attempt to discern the successive phases of this development.

According to Imami theology, the Divine Being, in his Essence, absolutely transcends all imagination, intelligence or thought. In his Essence, which constitutes his Absolute Being, God remains the inconceivable Transcendent that cannot be described or apprehended except in terms by which He describes Himself through His revelations. At this level, the term 'thing' (*shay'*), one of utmost neutrality, can be applied to God. According to sayings attributed to many of the imams, God constitutes the reality of 'thing-ness' (*shay'iyya*), unintelligible and indefinable (*ghayr ma'qūl wa lā maḥdūd*) that places Him beyond the two

20. J. van Ess, *Theologie und Gesellschaft im 2. und 3. Jahrhundert Hidschra* (Berlin and New York, 1990), vol. 1, pp. 306f. (on the eschatological notion of 'return to life' – *raj'a* – see also E. Kohlberg, *EI2*); M. A. Amir-Moezzi, 'Al-Ṣaffâr al-Qummî (d. 290/902–3) and his *Kitâb baṣâ'ir al-darajât*', *JA*, 280, 3–4 (1992), pp. 232f. (on the notion of occultation – *ghayba* –, the number of imams and their identity, as well as other information about the Qā'im, the eschatological Saviour).

21. Cf. R. Arnaldez, 'Lāhūt and Nāsūt', *EI2*.

limits of agnosticism (*ta'ṭīl*) and assimilationism (*tashbīh*).[22] The Essence of God is *the* Thing about which man is only able to hold a negative discourse, denying all that could enable a conceivable representation of Him. Indeed, throughout the theological traditions, a whole series of negations characterise sayings of the imams regarding God: negation of a corporeal or formal conception (*jism/ṣūra*),[23] negation of space (*makān*), time (*zamān*), immobility (*sukūn*) and movement (*ḥaraka*), descent (*nuzūl*) and ascent (*ṣu'ūd*), qualification (*tawṣīf*) and representation (*tamthīl*), and so on.[24]

However, if things had remained thus, God would have been forever absolutely beyond the reach of man and this theology would have been a simple agnosticism. Thus, God in his infinite grace wished to make himself known to his creatures and had Himself described by a certain number of Names and Attributes. Now, revealed to man by the Most Beautiful Names of God (*al-asmā' al-ḥusnā*) these bear the Locus of Manifestation, Vehicles and Organs applicable to all of creation in general and humanity in particular. It is thanks to these theophanic Organs that God 'reaches' men and they in turn gain access to what is knowable

22. Cf. e.g. al-Kulaynī, *al-Uṣūl min al-Kāfī*, ed. J. Muṣṭafawī, with Persian trans., 4 vols (Tehran, n.d. [4th vol., tr. H. Rasūlī Maḥallātī, dates from 1386/1966]), 'Kitāb al-tawḥīd', 'Bāb iṭlāq bi-annahu shay'', vol. 1, pp. 109f.; Ibn Bābūya, *Kitāb al-tawḥīd*, ed. H. al-Ḥusaynī al-Ṭihrānī (Tehran, 1398/1978), ch. 7 'Bāb annahu tabārak wa ta'ālā shay'', pp. 104f. On the application of the term 'thing' to God in Muslim theology in general see D. Gimaret, *Les noms divins en Islam* (Paris, 1988), pp. 142–150.

23. Al-Kulaynī, *al-Uṣūl*, 'Bāb al-nahy 'ani'l-jism wa'l-ṣūra', vol. 1, pp. 140f.; Ibn Bābūya, *Kitāb al-tawḥīd*, ch. 6 ('Bāb annahu 'azza wa jall laysa bi-jism wa lā ṣūra'), pp. 97f.

24. Al-Kulaynī, *al-Uṣūl*, 'Bāb al-ḥaraka wa'l-intiqāl', vol. 1, pp. 169f.; Ibn Bābūya, *Kitāb al-tawḥīd*, ch. 28 ('Bāb nafy al-makān wa'l-zamān wa'l-sukūn wa'l-ḥaraka wa'l-nuzūl'), pp. 173f.; ch. 2 ('Bāb al-tawḥīd wa nafy al-tashbīh'), pp. 31f.; Ibn Bābūya, *'Uyūn akhbār al-Riḍā*, ed. M. Ḥ. Lājevardī (Tehran, 1378/1958), ch. 11 ('Bāb fī … al-tawḥīd'), pp. 114f.; Ibn Bābūya, *Kitāb al-khiṣāl*, ed. 'A. A. Ghaffārī (Qumm, 1403/1984), p. 2.

in Him.[25] Thus one distinguishes two ontological levels of the Divine Being: that of Essence, indescribable, inconceivable; the level of the Unknowable, of God in his vertiginous unmanifested concealment. Secondly, the level of Names and Attributes which is also that of Acts undertaken by the Organs of God; this is the level of the revealed God, of the Unknown wishing to be known.[26] Throughout the corpus of traditions, the imams tirelessly repeat that they are the Vehicles for the Attributes, the Organs of God. Applying their spiritual hermeneutics (*ta'wīl*) to Qur'ānic terminology they constantly say:

> We are the Eye (*'ayn*) of God, we are the Hand (*yad*) of God, we are the Face (*wajh*) of God, we are His Side (*janb*), His Heart (*qalb*), His Tongue (*lisān*), His Ear (*udhn*).[27]

It is in order to support this aspect of God that the imam is also designated by names such as 'the Proof of God' (*ḥujjat Allāh*), 'the Vicar of God' (*khalīfat Allāh*), 'the Path of God' (*ṣirāṭ Allāh*), 'the Threshold of God' (*bāb Allāh*) and is described by Qur'ānic expressions such as 'the Greatest Sign' (*al-āyat al-kubrā*,

---

25. On apophatic theology and the notion of theophany as one of its consequences, esp. in the gnostic milieu, see H. Corbin, *Le paradoxe du monothéisme* (Paris, 1981), esp. the first section; H. Corbin, *En Islam iranien*, vol. 4, index, under '*tanzîh*' and 'theophanies'.

26. On the Names and Attributes in general, see al-Kulaynī, *al-Uṣūl*, vol. 1, pp. 143f.; Ibn Bābūya, *Kitāb al-tawḥīd*, ch. 11, pp. 139ff.

27. Obviously here one has the ontological Imam, the Cosmic Man, Locus of the Manifestation of God, of whom the historical imam is in turn the manifestation on the perceptible level. See e.g. al-Ṣaffār al-Qummī, *Baṣā'ir al-darajāt*, ed. Mīrzā Kūchebāghī (2nd edn, Tabriz, n.d. [editor's introduction is dated 1380/1960]), section 2, ch. 3, pp. 61–64 and ch. 4, pp. 64–66 (commentaries on the term *wajh* in the Qur'ān); al-Kulaynī, *al-Usūl*, 'Kitāb al-tawḥīd', 'Bāb al-nawādir', vol. 1, p. 196; 'Kitāb al-ḥujja', 'Bāb jāmi' fī faḍl al-imām wa ṣifātihi', vol. 1, pp. 283f.; Ibn Bābūya, *Tawḥīd*, ch. 12, pp. 149f. (commentary on 'All things perish, except His Face', Qur'ān, *al-Qiṣaṣ*, 28:88), ch. 22, pp. 164f. (ma'nā janb Allāh), ch. 24, pp. 167f. (ma'nā'l-'ayn wa'l-udhn wa'l-lisān), *'Uyūn*, pp. 114–116 and 149–153 and *Kamāl al-dīn*, ed. 'A. A. Ghaffarī (Qumm, 1405/1985), ch. 22, vol. 1, pp. 231f.

Q 79:20), 'the Exalted Symbol' (*al-mathal al-aʿlā*, Q 16:60), 'the Most Secure Arch' (*al-ʿurwat al-wuthqā*, Q 2:256 or 21:22).[28] Commenting on the Qur'ānic verse 7:180, 'To God belong the Names Most Beautiful; so call Him by them', the sixth imam, Jaʿfar al-Ṣādiq (d. 148/765), is said to have declared:

> By God, we [the imams], are the Most Beautiful Names; no action by a devoted servant is accepted by God, if it is not accompanied by knowledge of us.[29]

In this division between Essence/Names and Organs one discerns a transposition, at the level of the divine, of an omnipresent division in Shiʿi milieu of all reality into two aspects: *bāṭin* (esoteric, hidden) and *ẓāhir* (exoteric, apparent). The esoteric, hidden, unmanifested aspect of God would thus be his Essence, forever inaccessible; His Organs, Vehicle of his Names, would constitute His exoteric or revealed aspect. The Imam, exoteric facet of God, is thus the veritable *Deus Revelatus*; knowledge of his reality is equivalent to the knowledge of what is knowable in God. In a tradition going back to the third imam al-Ḥusayn b. ʿAlī (61/680) one reads: 'O Mankind! God created His servants in order that they may know Him for when they know Him, they worship Him and free themselves from the worship of all else except for Him.' Someone then asks the imam: 'What is knowledge of God?' 'For people of every period, it is knowledge of the imam [of the time] to whom they owe obedience.'[30]

28. For example, al-Ṣaffār, *Baṣā'ir al-darajāt*, section 2, ch. 3, pp. 16–17; Ibn Bābūya, *al-Amālī*, ed. and Persian trans. by M. B. Kamare'ī (Tehran, 1404/1984), 'majlis' 9, no. 9, p. 35, 'majlis' 10, no. 6, pp. 38–39; al-Majlisī, *Biḥār al-anwār*, 35 vols (Tehran, n.d.), vol. 32, pp. 212–213; vol. 34, pp. 109–110.

29. *'Naḥnu wa'llāhi al-asmā al-ḥusnā allatī lā yaqbalu'llāh min al-ʿibād ʿamalan illā bi-maʿrifatinā'*; al-ʿAyyāshī, *Tafsīr*, ed. H. Rasūlī Maḥallātī (Tehran, n.d.), vol. 2, p. 42, no. 119; al-Kulaynī, *al-Usūl*, 'Kitāb al-tawḥīd', 'Bāb al-nawādir', vol. 1, p. 196.

30. *'Ayyuhā'l-nās inna'llāha jalla dhikruhu mā khalaqa'l-ʿibād illā li yaʿrifūhu fa-idhā ʿarafūhu ʿabadūhu fa idhā ʿabadūhu'staghnau bi ʿibādatihi ʿan*

The aim of creation is thus knowledge of the Creator by his creatures; the Imam, theophanic being is the 'Supreme Symbol' of what can be known of God, and therefore constitutes the reason for and aim of creation. 'He who knows us knows God, and he who knows us not, knows not God,' the imams repeat.[31] 'It is thanks to us that God is known', relates a tradition dating back to Jaʿfar al-Ṣādiq, 'and thanks to us that He is worshipped.'[32] 'Without God, we would not be known, and without us, God would not be known,' adds another tradition attributed to the same sixth imam.[33]

Another, similar saying, also attributed to Jaʿfar, introduces another step in the development of the doctrine of the imam's divinity. This step is characterised by the allusive sayings that can easily be compared to the famous 'ecstatic utterances (*shaṭaḥāt*)' of the mystics:[34]

ʿibāda man siwāh faqāla lahu rajul fa mā maʿrifat Allāh qāla marifa ahl kulli zamān imāmahum alladhī yajibu alayhim tāʿatuhu', Ibn Bābūya, *ʿIlal al-sharāʾiʿ* (Najaf, 1385/1966), ch. 9 "illa khalq al-khalq', p. 9, no. 1. One must always bear in mind that according to Twelver doctrine, each prophet-legislator is accompanied in his mission by one or more imams whose mission is to initiate the elite of believers in the esoteric aspect of the prophetic Message (see *Guide divin*, pp. 96–112 [*Divine Guide*, pp. 38–44]).

31. '*Man ʿarafanā faqad ʿarafa'llāh wa man ankaranā faqad ankara'llāh*', e.g. Ṣaffar, *Baṣāʾir al-darajāt*, section 1, ch. 3, p. 6; Ibn Bābūya, *Kamāl al-dīn*, ch. 24, p. 261, no. 7; *Nahj al-balāgha* (note 5 above), ed. and Persian trans. by ʿA. N. Fayḍ al-Islām (4th edn, Tehran, 1351 Sh./1972), p. 470.

32. '*Binā ʿubida'llāh... wa flaw lanā mā ʿubida'llāh*', Ibn Bābūya, *Tawḥīd*, ch. 12, p. 152, no. 9.

33. '*Law lā Allāh mā ʿurifnā wa law lā naḥnu mā ʿurifa'llāh*', Ibn Bābūya, *Tawḥīd*, ch. 41, p. 290, no. 10.

34. These are speeches in which 'God speaks in the first person in the words of a mystic often in a state of ecstasy', such as 'I am the Truth' by Ḥallāj or 'Glory to me' by Basṭāmī; regarding *shaṭḥ*, see e.g. the admirable work by L. Massignon in *Essai sur les origines du lexique technique de la mystique musulmane* (Paris, 1922) and *La Passion de Hallāj, martyr mystique de l'Islam*, 4 vols (rpr. Paris, 1975), see index under '*shaṭḥ*'; H. Corbin's introduction to Rūzbehān Baqlī Shīrāzī, *Sharḥ-e shaṭḥiyyāt*, ed. H. Corbin and M. Moʿīn (Paris and Tehran, 1966; rpr. 2004); also ʿA. R. Badawī, *Shaṭaḥāt al-ṣūfiyya* (3rd edn, Kuwait, 1978); P. Nwiya, *Exégèse coranique et langage mystique* (Beirut, 1970), under '*shaṭḥ*'. As

> God made us His Eye among his worshippers, his Eloquent Tongue among His Creatures, His Hand of benevolence and mercy extended above His servants, His Face thanks to which one is guided towards Him, His Threshold that leads to Him, His Treasure in the heavens and on earth . . . It is by our act of worship that God is worshipped, without us God could not be worshipped.[35]

Now this last sentence can also be read as follows: 'It is due to the fact that we [the imams] are worshipped that God is worshipped; without us, God could not be worshipped (*bi-ʿibādatinā ʿubida'llāh law lā naḥnu mā ʿubida'llāh*).' The rather audacious ambiguity seems deliberate for not only does the identification of God with the physical person of the imam seem the logical, final outcome of previous phases of imamology, but other *shaṭaḥāt* of the same tenor are found in the early corpus.[36] A remarkable fact

we shall see further, some mystics did not hesitate to consider ʿAlī's sermons the quintessential 'paradoxical pronouncements'. It nevertheless seems to me that the similarity between the paradoxical pronouncements of the imams and the *shaṭaḥāt* of the Sufis are only formal, since the premises and conclusions of each of these currents of thought, as well as the theology which underpins them, are different. The subject is much too complex to be treated with here; for analysis on the nature of *shaṭḥ*, see C. Ernst, *Words of Ecstasy in Sufism* (New York, 1985); P. Lory, 'Les paradoxes mystiques (*shatahât*) dans la tradition soufie des premiers siècles', *Annuaire de l'EPHE, Sciences Religieuses*, 102 (1994–1995) and 103 (1995–1996); P. Ballanfat, 'Réflexions sur la nature du paradoxe. La définition de Rûzbehân Baqlî Shîrâzî', *Kâr Nâmeh*, 2–3 (1995), pp. 25–40.

35. '*Wa jaʿalanā ʿaynahu fī ʿibādihi wa lisānahu'l-nāṭiq fī khalqih wa yadahu'l-mabsūṭa ʿalā ʿibādihi bi'l-ra'fa wa'l-raḥma wa wajhahu'lladhī yu'tā minhu wa bābahu'lladhī yadullu ʿalayhi wa khazā'inahu fī samā'ihi wa arḍih... bi ʿibādatinā ʿubida'llāh lā law naḥnu mā ʿubida'llāh*', Ibn Bābūya, *Tawḥīd*, ch. 12, pp. 151–152, no. 8.

36. This process of disseminating particularly delicate doctrinal elements occurs regularly in the early corpus; it constitutes one aspect of the Shiʿi obligation 'to preserve or guard a secret' (*taqiyya, kitmān, khab'*) and for the first time in the works of Jābir, it seems to have been called 'the process of the deliberate dissemination of information' (*tabdīd al-ʿilm*, literally: 'scattering of knowledge'); cf. *Guide divin*, index under '*tabdīd al-ʿilm*'; on its usage in the Jabirian corpus whose Shiʿi allegiance is no longer in question, see P. Kraus, *Jābir b. Ḥayyān. Contribution à l'histoire des idées scientifiques dans l'islam* (Cairo, 1942; rpr. Paris, 1986), vol. 1, pp. xxvii–xxx; P. Lory, *Dix Traités d'alchimie. Les*

is that all these sayings, or at least those that we have been able to find, seem to be attributed to the same imam, Ja'far al-Ṣādiq.[37] Commenting on the Qur'ānic verse 39:69, 'And the earth shall shine with the light of its Lord', Ja'far says: 'The Lord of the earth is the Imam of the earth.'[38] A disciple asks the sixth imam to explain the meaning of the verse, 'and when you threw [the sentence is addressed to the Prophet] it was not yourself that threw, but God that threw' (Q 8:17). Ja'far is said to have replied: 'It is because it was 'Alī who gave the darts to the Messenger of God who threw them.'[39] Finally, a dialogue between the same imam and his disciple Abū Baṣīr is highly significant in this regard:

> The Disciple: 'Tell me if on the Day of Resurrection, the initiates[40] will be able to see God.' Ja'far: 'Yes, but they will have already seen

---

dix premiers Traités du Livre des Soixante-Dix (Paris, 1983), pp. 53 and 242f.; H. Corbin, *Alchimie comme art hiératique* (Paris, 1986), pp. 183–184 and n. 84 (tr. of 'Livre du Glorieux' by 'Jābir'). On Shi'i *taqiyya* in general, now consult E. Kohlberg, 'Taqiyya in Shī'ī Theology and Religion', in H. G. Kippenberg and G. G. Stroumsa (eds), *Secrecy and Concealment. Studies in the History of Mediterranean and Near Eastern Religions* (Leiden, 1995), pp. 345–380, a work which admirably supplements the previous study on the same topic by the Israeli scholar 'Some Imāmi-Shī'i Views on *taqiyya*', *JAOS*, 95 (1975), pp. 395–402 (rpr. in *Belief and Law in Imāmī Shī'ism*, article 3).

37. Which corroborates the status of 'founder' that Muslim gnosis generally (Sufism, theosophy, the occult sciences etc.) reserves for imam Ja'far; regarding this subject, see e.g. J. Ruska, *Arabische Alchemisten*, vol. 2: *Ǧa'far al-Ṣādiq, der Sechste Imam* (Heidelberg, 1924); P. Kraus, *Jābir b. Ḥayyān*; J. B. Taylor, 'Ja'far al-Ṣādiq, Spiritual Forebear of the Sufis', *Islamic Culture* (1966); T. Fahd, 'Ǧa'far al-Ṣādiq et la tradition scientifique arabe', in *Le shī'isme imāmite*, Actes du Colloque de Strasbourg, 6–9 May 1968 (Paris, 1970).

38. '*Rabb al-arḍ ya'nī imām al-arḍ*', 'Alī b. Ibrāhīm al-Qummī, *Tafsīr*, ed. Ṭ. al-Mūsawī al-Jazā'irī (Najaf, 1386–87/1966-68; rpr. Beirut, 1411/1991), vol. 2, p. 256.

39. "*Alī nāwala rasūl Allāh al-qabḍa'llatī ramā bihā*', al-'Ayyāshī, *Tafsīr*, vol. 2, p. 52, nos 32–34.

40. '*al-mu'minūn*' literally 'the believers'; in technical Twelver terminology, the term *mu'min* designates a Shi'i initiated by the imam into the esoteric dimension of the faith and is contrasted with the term *muslim* (literally 'one who submits') which in the same context, designates he who submits to the exoteric aspect

Him well before the advent of this Day.' 'When?' 'When He asked them: "Am I not your Lord and they replied, 'Yes [Q 7:172]'".' Then, reports the disciple, the master remained silent for a long time before declaring: 'The initiates already see Him in this world before the Day of Resurrection. *Do you not see Him at this very moment* [*before you*]?' 'May I serve you as a ransom, can I report this teaching with your approval?' 'No, for a negator unaware of the deeper meaning of these words will use them to accuse us of assimilationism and unbelief.'[41]

In such an imamological context, it is not surprising to encounter traditions – in the early Twelver corpus – that unambiguously proclaim texts of theo-imamosophical sermons attributed to ʿAlī.

From the heights of the pulpit in the mosque at Kūfa, ʿAlī, Commander of the initiates, declared: 'By God, I am the Rewarder (*dayyān*) of men the Day of Rewarding; I am he who assigns the Garden or the Fire, no one enters without my designation; I am the

---

of the faith; see my analysis, 'Etude du lexique technique de l'ésotérisme imāmite', *Annuaire de l'EPHE, section des sciences religieuses*, 102 (1994–1995), p. 215.

41. Abū Baṣīr: *'Akhbirnī ʿani'llāh ʿazza wa jall hal yarāhu'l-mu'minūn yawm al-qiyāma qāla naʿam wa qad ra'awhu qabla yawm al-qiyāma fa-qultu matā qāla ḥīna qāla lahum 'a lastu bi-rabbikum qālū balā thumma sakata sāʿatan thumma qāla wa inna'l-mu'minīn la-yarawnahu fi'l-dunyā qabla yawm al-qiyāma 'a lasta tarāhu fī waqtika hādhā faqultu lahu juʿiltu fidāk fa-'uḥaddithu bihādhā ʿanka fa-qāla lā fa-innaka idhā ḥaddathta bihi fa-ankarahu munkirun jāhil bi maʿnā mā taqūluhu thumma qaddara ʿalaynā anna dhālika tashbīh wa kufr'*, Ibn Bābūya, *Tawḥīd*, ch. 8, p. 117, no. 20. Cf. *Guide divin*, p. 141, note 277 (*Divine Guide*, p. 54); in *A Shiʿite Anthology* (New York, 1981), p. 42, W. Chittick provides a translation of this tradition without pointing out the 'paradoxical words' that it contains. Regarding Jaʿfar's three disciples with the *kunya* Abū Baṣīr, see *Guide divin*, p. 87, note 182 (*Divine Guide*, p. 34). This concern regarding the incomprehension of non-initiates is constantly present in the early corpus; see e.g. al-Kulaynī, *al-Rawḍa min al-Kāfī*, ed. and Persian trans. by H. Rasūlī Maḥallātī (Tehran, 1386/1969), vol. 1, p. 81; Ibn Bābūya, *Kamāl al-dīn*, vol. 23, pp. 254–255 no. 4, *ʿIlal al-sharāʾiʿ*, ch. 7, pp. 5f. and *ʿUyūn*, vol. 26, no. 22, pp. 262f. (*ḥadīth faḍl al-nabī wa'l-ḥujaj ʿalā'l-malāʾika*), where matters are repeatedly stressed in order to avoid confusion between 'the Proofs of God' and God – I have translated excerpts from this extensive tradition in *Guide divin*, pp. 89–91 (*Divine Guide*, pp. 35–36).

> Great Judge [between good and evil; *al-fārūq al-akbar*] . . . I hold the decisive Word (*faṣl al-khiṭāb*); I hold the penetrating Insight into the Path of the Book . . . I have learnt the science of fortune and misfortune; and the science of judgements; by me the Completion of Religion; I am the deed of Kindness enacted by God for His creatures'[42] and elsewhere: 'I am the Queen Bee (*ya'sūb*) of the initiates; I am the First of the first believers; I am the successor to the Messenger of the Lord of the worlds; I am the Judge of the Garden and the Fire.'[43]

In a tradition that goes back to the Prophet Muḥammad, he is said to have praised 'Alī thus:

> Here is the most radiant Imam, tallest lance of God, the greatest Threshold of God; whosoever longs for God, so let him enter through this Threshold . . . Without 'Alī, truth would not be distinguished from falsehood, nor believer from non-believer; without 'Alī, it would not have been possible to worship God . . . no Curtain (*sitr*) hides God from him, no Veil (*ḥijāb*) lies between God and him! For 'Alī himself is the Curtain and Veil.[44]

---

42. *'Wa'llāhi innī la-dayyān al-nās yawm al-dīn wa qasīm al-janna wa'l-nār lā yadkhuluhā'l-dakhīl illā 'alā iḥdā qismī wa innī'l-fārūq al-akbar... lī faṣl al-khiṭāb wa baṣartu sabīl al-kitāb... wa 'alimtu 'ilm al-manāyā wa'l-balāyā wa'l-qaḍāyā wa bī kamāl al-dīn wa anā'l-ni'mat llatī an'ama'llāhu 'alā khalqih'*, Furāt b. Ibrāhīm al-Kūfī, *Tafsīr*, ed. Muḥammad al-Kāẓim (Tehran, 1410/1990), p. 178, no. 230.

43. *'Anā ya'sūb al-mu'minīn wa anā awwal al-sābiqīn wa khalīfa rasūl rabb al-'ālamīn wa anā qasīm al-janna wa'l-nār'*, al-'Ayyāshī, *Tafsīr*, vol. 2, pp. 17–18, no. 42; al-Majlisī, *Biḥār al-anwār*, vol. 3, p. 389. On 'Alī as 'Leader' or 'Commander of the Bees' (*amīr al-naḥl*), see I. Goldziher, 'Schi'itisches', *ZDMG*, 44 (1910), pp. 532–533, re-issued in *Gesammelte Schriften*, ed. J. de Somogyi (Hildesheim, 1967–1970), vol. 5, pp. 213–214.

44. *'Hādhā'l-imām al-aẓhar wa rumḥu'llāh al-aṭwal wa bābu'llāh al-akbar fa-man arāda'llāh falyadkhul min al-bāb... law lā 'Alī mā abāna'l-ḥaqq min al-bāṭil wa lā mu'min min kāfir wa mā 'ubida'llāh... lā yasturuhu min Allāh sitr wa lā yaḥjibuhu 'ani'llāh ḥijāb bal huwa'l-ḥijāb wa'l-sitr'*, Fūrāt b. Ibrāhīm, *Tafsīr*, p. 371, no. 503.

Regarding the verses, 'Of what do they question one another?/ Of the solemn tiding/ whereon they are at variance' (Q 78:1–3), 'Alī is said to have declared to his followers: 'By God, I am the solemn Tiding . . . God has no more solemn Tiding, nor greater Sign, than me.'[45]

45. *'Anā wa'llāh al-naba' al-'aẓīm... wa'llāhi mā li'llāh naba' a'ẓam minnī wa lā li'llāh āya a'ẓam minnī*', ibid., pp. 533–534, nos 685–686. As might be realised, the notion of 'Man (in general) in the image of God' does not exist in Imami Shi'ism. In any case, the radically dualist Shi'i vision that divides all creatures, thus humans as well, into 'beings of Light' and 'beings of Darkness', designated in various ways, renders such a conception impossible (on Twelver dualism, see *Guide divin*, pp. 91f. [*Divine Guide*, p. 36] and Chapter 8 in this publication). The famous tradition 'God created Adam in his image' (*khalaqa 'llahū Ādam 'alā ṣūratih*) carries no special importance in the early corpus and in the words of the imams is interpreted in two ways that are perfectly 'orthodox', in keeping with the view of Sunni theologians:

a) the attribution (*iḍāfa*) of 'image' (*ṣūra*, lit. 'form') to God is interpreted in the same general sense as the attribution of the Ka'ba to Him when He calls it 'My House' (*baytī*) or the attribution of all created things to Him as being His work (cf. Twelver interpretation: al-Kulaynī, *al-Uṣūl min al-Kāfī*, 'Kitāb al-tawḥīd', 'Bāb al-rūḥ', vol. 1, p. 182; Ibn Bābūya, *Tawḥīd*, vol. 6, p. 103, no. 18. cf. Sunni interpretation: Ibn Khuzayma, *K. al-tawḥīd*, ed. M. Kh. Harrās (Cairo, 1388/1968), p. 39; al-Juwaynī, *al-Shāmil fī uṣūl al-dīn*, ed. A. S. al-Nashshār, B. F. 'Awn and S. M. Mukhtār (Alexandria, 1389/1969), p. 561; Ibn Fūrak, *Mushkil al-ḥadīth*, ed. M. M. 'Alī (Cairo, 1979), p. 57 and ed. D. Gimaret (Damascus, 2003), pp. 21f.

b) the possessive adjective 'his' does not refer to God, but to a particular individual mentioned in some versions of the tradition. According to these versions, the Prophet meets a person who slaps another or humiliates him by making an insulting remark about his physical appearance; the Prophet then intervenes and says: 'Do not do that because God created Adam in his (i.e. the humiliated person's) image', meaning that all men are made in the same image as Adam 'the father of humanity'. For the Twelver interpretation see Ibn Bābūya, *Tawḥīd*, ch. 12, p. 152, no. 10. Sunni interpretation: Ibn Khuzayma, *K. al-tawḥīd*, pp. 36–38; al-Juwaynī, *al-Shāmil*, p. 560; al-Juwaynī, *K. al-irshād*, ed. J. D. Luciani (Paris, 1938), p. 93; see also W. M. Watt, 'Created in His Image'. For Sunni sources, see M. Takeshita, *Ibn Arabi's Theory of the Perfect Man*, p. 16, n. 2 and p. 29, n. 58 (information provided by Daniel Gimaret, to whom I am most grateful).

On the other hand, one can say without fear of extrapolation that in Shi'ism the Imam is made in the image of God and that the adept initiated to the esoteric doctrine has been made in the image of the Imam (on the ontological and

Without exception, all these quotations are drawn from the Twelver corpus said to be 'moderate'; as we have noted before, the distinction between moderate and extremist Shiʿism, at least during the early period and especially in the 'esoteric non-rational' tradition, proves to be artificial.[46] This distinction seems to have been made later, mainly by the first heresiographers at the end of the third century and the beginning of the fourth century AH. In 'proto-Shiʿism', the boundaries between different trends seem to have been more easily penetrated and the movement of followers between different sects if not simultaneous adherance to several branches of belief would have been common practice.

* * *

There is great confusion regarding the titles and texts of the sermons as reported by various authors in different periods. A large majority of these writers are Shiʿis, others are Sunni mystics. At times, the same title is given to different sermons, at others,

---

anthropposophical function of initiation see *Guide divin*, pp. 75–95 and 174–199 [*Divine Guide*, pp. 29–38 and 69–79]; also M. A. Amir-Moezzi, 'Réflexions sur une évolution du shiʿisme duodécimain: tradition et idéologisation', in *Les Retours aux Écritures. Fondamentalismes présents et passés*, ed. E. Patlagean and A. Le Boulluec [Louvain and Paris, 1993], pp. 63–81 and esp. pp. 63–69). Thus, the Imam – exoteric dimension of God – as we have seen, is at the same time the esoteric dimension of the initiated faithful.

46. Cf. note 8 above and the related text. One may conclude, as does H. Modarressi, that these kinds of traditions were current in the entourage of the imams, among the Mufawwiḍa or even the 'extremist' Ṭayyāra (cf. H. Modarressi, *Crisis and Consolidation in the Formative Period of Shīʿite Islam: Abū Jaʿfar ibn Qiba al-Rāzī and his Contribution to Imāmite Shīʿite Thought* [Princeton, 1993], esp. pp. 21f.); still, the 'moderate' corpus contains a large number of these traditions and enables the development of a 'supra-rational' imamology. In this regard, comments by the famous contemporary Imami scholar, ʿAbdallāh al-Māmaqānī (d. 1932) in his *Tanqīḥ al-maqāl* (cf. note 15 above) are highly significant: 'We have stated on many occasions that the accusations of extremism levelled by the early [scholars] (*al-qudamāʾ*) do not deserve to be taken into consideration since many aspects that are essential to Imami doctrine (*ḍarūriyyāt al-madhhab*) were held by them to be extremist' (*Tanqīḥ*, vol. 1, p. 349).

almost identical texts are known by different names; sometimes, versions of the same sermon differ greatly, the length of the text varies substantially and in general, the more one advances in time, the more the texts are embellished and interwoven. All occurs as if the authors, in the same assonant prose style and depending on their spiritual or literary concerns, are adding to one or many early kernels of a sermon increasingly numerous affirmations.

Based on the most recurrent material, one could say that at our disposal we have three theo-imamosophical sermons attributed to 'Alī, each closely related to the other: the Sermon of the Clear Declaration (*khuṭbat al-bayān*), the Sermon of Glory (*khuṭbat al-iftikhār*) and the Sermon of the Gulf (*al-khuṭbat al-taṭanjiyya/ṭatanjiyya/ṭaṭanjiyya*, an enigmatic word that one passage of the text explains as being synonymous with *khalīj*, in the sense of 'gulf').[47]

The last appears to be the oldest since, as we have seen, quite a long version was already reported in Nuṣayrī texts dating from the end of the third century AH.[48] The Ismaili thinker and propagandist Mu'ayyad fi'l-Dīn al-Shīrāzī (d. 470/1077) provides a more elaborate version in his *Majālis*.[49] The Twelver theosopher and traditionist, Rajab al-Bursī (d. 814/1411), in his *Mashāriq* reproduces more or less the same text as al-Shīrāzī,

47. Regarding these three sermons, H. Corbin has contributed partial translations, interpretations and additional information (see *En Islam iranien*). There is a *ḥadīth*, and not a sermon attributed to 'Alī on the human and divine nature of the imām; this *ḥadīth* is related to our sermons and is reported by Rajab al-Bursī (cf. below). On this tradition see H. Corbin, 'La gnose islamique dans le recueil de traditions (*Mashāriq al-anwār*) de Rajab Borsi', *Annuaire de l'EPHE, section des sciences religieuses* (1968–1969, 1969–1970), rpr. in *Itinéraire d'un enseignement*, Institut Français de Recherche en Iran (Tehran, 1993), pp. 104f. and 111f.; T. Lawson, 'The Dawning Places of the Lights of Certainty in the Divine Secrets Connected with the Commander of the Faithful by Rajab Bursī', in *The Legacy of Mediaeval Persian Sufism*, ed. L. Lewisohn (London and New York, 1992), pp. 267–269. In general, the *Mashāriq* by al-Bursī contains many sayings of the same nature attributed to 'Alī.

48. Cf. note 14 above and the relevant text.

49. Al-Mu'ayyad fi'l-Dīn al-Shīrāzī, *al-Majālis al-Mu'ayyadiyya*, ed. M. Ghālib, vols 1 and 3 (Beirut, 1974 and 1984), vol. 1, pp. 171–173.

although according to other authors, elements from the Sermon of Clear Declaration are inserted there.[50] Al-Bursī's version served not only Mullā Muḥsin al-Fayḍ al-Kāshānī (d. 1091/1680) in his *Kalimāt maknūna*, but also al-Sayyid Kāẓim al-Rashtī (d. 1259/1843), grand master of the theologico -mystical School of the Shaykhiyya, for his monumental unfinished commentary on the Sermon of the Gulf,[51] as well an Imami scholar who died in the early twentieth century, ʿAlī Yazdī Ḥāʾirī in his *Ilzām al-nāṣib*.[52]

The Sermon of Glory would have been of Twelver origin; in fact it was only reported in its more elaborate version by authors belonging to this branch of Shiʿism. It appears that this sermon was reported for the first time under this title by the great scholar Ibn Shahrāshūb (d. 588/1192) in his *Manāqib*.[53] In his *Jāmiʿ al-asrār*,[54] the mystical thinker Ḥaydar Āmolī/ Āmulī (d. ca. 790/1387–1388) cites excerpts

---

50. Al-Ḥāfiẓ Rajab al-Bursī, *Mashāriq anwār al-yaqīn* (10th edn, Beirut, n.d.), pp. 166–170; see also note 47 above. An English translation of a substantial portion of the Sermon of the Gulf, as it appears in Bursī, is provided by T. Lawson in his article mentioned above (note 47), pp. 269–270. Now also consult a partial French translation of Bursī's work, by H. Corbin entitled *Les Orients des Lumières* (Paris and Lagrasse, 1996) (tr., ed. and finished by P. Lory). According to al-Ṭihrānī, *al-Dharīʿa ilā taṣānīf al-shīʿa*, 25 vols (Tehran and Najaf, 1353–1398/1934–1978), vol. 7, pp. 198–199, this sermon is the same as the Sermon of the Climes (*khuṭbat al-aqālīm*) partially reported by Ibn Shahrāshūb (d. 588/1192) in his *Manāqib*.

51. Muḥsin al-Fayḍ al-Kāshānī, *Kalimāt maknūna*, ed. ʿA. ʿUṭāridī Qūchānī (Tehran, 1383/1963), pp. 167–168 and 196ff. Texts studied by T. Lawson in 'The Hidden Words of Fayḍ Kāshānī', in M. Szuppe (ed.), *Iran: Questions et connaissances*, vol. 2, 'Périodes médiévale et moderne' (Paris, 2002), pp. 427–447, esp. pp. 438–439. Al-Sayyid Kāẓim al-Rashtī, *Sharḥ al-khuṭbat al-taṭanjiyya* (Tabriz, 1270/1853).

52. ʿAlī al-Yazdī al-Ḥāʾirī, *Ilzām al-nāṣib fī ithbāt al-ḥujjat al-ghāʾib* (Isfahan, 1351/1932; rpr. Tehran, n.d.), pp. 212–214.

53. Ibn Shahrāshūb, *Manāqib āl Abī Ṭālib*, ed. M. Burūjerdi (Tehran, 1316–1317/1898–1899), pp. 71–72.

54. Sayyid Ḥaydar Āmolī, *Jāmiʿ al-asrār wa manbaʿ al-anwār*, ed. H. Corbin and O. Yahia (Tehran and Paris, 1969), pp. 10–11.

(which in other authors' works belong to one of the other two sermons that concern us here). Rajab al-Bursī, a contemporary of Āmolī, reproduces a sermon under this same title that is significantly different.[55] The erudite Shaykh Āghā Bozorg Ṭihrānī (d. 1969), unrivalled connoisseur of Twelver texts, postulates that the Sermons of Glory and Clear Declaration belong to the same original text of which yet another part, in this case called the Sermon of Silhouettes (*khuṭbat al-ashbāḥ*) is reported in the *Nahj al-balāgha*.[56]

The Sermon of the Clear Declaration (or more precisely the texts known under this title), itself also originating from an earlier nucleus, is it seems the most reproduced of these three sermons; the most read, meditated and commented on by both Shiʿi theosophers and Sunni mystics.[57] Some texts dating from the second half of the third century and more certainly the early fourth century AH, containing quotations from this sermon have already been mentioned.[58] Of these, one can point out a (lost?) commentary by the great figure of Iranian Ismailism, Ḥasan (b.) al-Ṣabbāḥ (d. 518/1124).[59] Of the Sunni mystics, with however Shiʿi sympathies, one can cite Muḥammad b. Ṭalḥa al-Ḥalabī al-Shāfiʿī (d. 652/1254) and Sayyid Muḥammad Nūrbakhsh (d. 869/1464),

55. Rajab al-Bursī, *Mashāriq anwār*, pp. 164–166.

56. Āghā Bozorg al-Ṭihrānī, *al-Dharīʿa*, vol. 7, pp. 198f.

57. The *khuṭbat al-bayān* is often part of an 'eschatological prophecy' (*malḥama*, pl. *malāḥim*; see the article by D. B. MacDonald cited above in note 16) attributed to ʿAlī. It was analysed and partialy translated by L. Massignon in his article on the Perfect Man (see note 2 above). The text used by Massignon is reproduced, based on MS 2661, BN, Paris, fols. 21b–24a, by ʿA. R. Badawī in *al-Insān al-kāmil*, pp. 139–143. The beginning of the text is almost identical to excerpts from the *khuṭbat al-iftikhār* reported by Ḥaydar Āmolī.

58. Cf. above, notes 14 to 17 and the related texts.

59. Khayrkhāh-i Harātī, *Kalām-i pīr. A Treatise on Ismaili Doctrine*, ed. and tr. W. Ivanow (Bombay, 1935), pp. 79–81 of the Persian text.

who reproduced excerpts from this sermon and considered them to be 'ecstatic utterances par excellence'.[60] Twelver authors who studied the *khuṭbat al-bayān*, that is, cited it, commented on it, translated it into Persian or versified it in Arabic or Persian are far too numerous to be listed here. Let us limit ourselves to a few famous individuals: Ḥaydar Āmolī and Rajab al-Bursī already noted; al-Qāḍī Sa'īd al-Qummī (d. ca. 1103/1691–1692); master of the Ni'matullāhī order, Nūr 'Alī Shāh (d. 1212/1798); Ja'far Kashfī (d. 1267/1850–1851) (we will return to Kashfī); Mīrzā Abu'l-Qāsim Rāz Shīrāzī, master of the Dhahabiyya order (d. 1286/1869) and Yazdī Ḥā'irī, cited earlier, who in his *Ilzām al-nāṣib*, reports three long versions of this sermon.[61]

---

60. Muḥammad b. Ṭalḥa al-Ḥalabī, *al-Durr al-munaẓẓam fi'l-sirr al-a'ẓam* (n.p., 1331/1912), pp. 83–85, also cited by al-Qundūzī, *Yanābī' al-mawadda* (Najaf, 1384/1965), pp. 112–113; Sayyid Muḥammad Nūrbakhsh, *al-Risālat al-i'tiqādiyya*, ed. M. Molé in *Professions de foi de deux kubrâwîs: 'Alî-i Hamadânî et Muḥammad Nûrbakhsh*, *BEO*, 17 (1961–1962), p. 193 of the Arabic text; see also M. Molé, 'Les kubrâwiyya entre sunnisme et shi'isme aux 8e et 9e s. de l'hégire', *REI* (1961), p. 129.

61. Ḥaydar Āmolī, *Jāmi' al-asrār*, pp. 382, 411 and in the same volume *Naqd al-nuqūd fī ma'rifat al-wujūd*, p. 676; Rajab al-Bursī, *Mashāriq anwār al-yaqīn*, pp. 170–172 (the author does not provide the title of the sermon); al-Qāḍī Sa'īd al-Qummī, 'Sharḥ ḥadīth al-ghamāma', in *Kitāb al-arba'īniyyāt*, cited by H. Corbin, *En Islam iranien*, vol. 4, pp. 152f. (see also Corbin, *Itinéraire d'un enseignement*, pp. 96f.); and al-Qāḍī Sa'īd al-Qummī, *al-Arba'īniyyāt li-kashf anwār al-qudsiyyāt*, ed. N. Ḥabībī (Tehran, 1381 Sh./2003), pp. 38ff; Nūr 'Alī Shāh, 'Manẓūm-e khuṭbat al-bayān', in *Divān-e Nūr 'Alī Shāh Iṣfahānī* (Tehran, 1349 Sh./1970) and in *Majmū'e-ye āthār-e N. 'A.sh. Iṣfahānī* (Tehran, 1350 Sh./1971); Ja'far Kashfī, *Tuḥfat al-mulūk*, 2 vols (lithograph, Iran, n.d.), vol. 1, pp. 20–28; Abu'l-Qāsim Rāz Shīrāzī, *Sharḥ kitāb khuṭbat al-bayān* (sic, instead of *Kitāb sharḥ khuṭbat al-bayān*) (Shiraz, n.d.); al-Yazdī al-Ḥā'irī, *Ilzām al-nāṣib*, pp. 193–211. For other authors see al-Ṭihrānī, *al-Dharī'a*, vol. 7, pp. 200–201 and vol. 13, pp. 218–219. For an alchemical hermeneutical reading of the *khuṭbat al-bayān* by Aydamur Jaldakī (d. 750/1349–1350 or 761/1360–1361), see H. Corbin, *Alchimie comme art hiératique*, ed. P. Lory (Paris, 1986), ch. 1.

Of these, the Iranian theosopher Ja'far Kashfī's version is especially interesting.[62] In his major work, *Tuḥfat al-mulūk*, dedicated to the Qājār prince Muḥammad Taqī Mīrzā, a son of Fatḥ 'Alī Shāh (hence the title that literally means 'the Gift offered to Sovereigns'), when commenting upon it, Kashfī reports the Arabic text of a relatively short sermon that he calls *khuṭbat al-bayān*. Indeed, a substantial portion of the text is a kind of medley of previous versions of this sermon but Kashfī also adds a number of elements drawn from two of our other sermons, namely the *khuṭbat al-taṭanjiyya* and the *khuṭbat al-iftikhār*. Moreover, he deletes the theological introduction (*dībāja*), listing some of the Names and Works of God, as well as the 'eschatological prophecy' (*malḥama*) from the beginning of the *khuṭbat al-bayān*, no doubt considering them far from the main thrust of the sermon, which, according to him is imamological. There is a particularly interesting fact here: though a philosopher and very keen student of astronomy, Kashfī nonetheless deletes assertions of an overly philosophical nature or those that relate to astronomy – assertions that had been later added on to an early nucleus. Thus the Iranian thinker achieves a coherent synthesis of the three sermons and introduces a text that stands a chance of being close to one

62. On Sayyid Ja'far b. Abī Isḥāq al-'Alawī al-Mūsawī al-Dārābī al-Burūjirdī called 'al-Kashfī' see Muḥammad 'Alī Mudarris, *Rayḥānat al-adab* (Tabriz, n.d.), vol. 3, p. 366, no. 568; H. Corbin, *Histoire de la philosophie islamique* (Paris, 1986) (a volume containing both sections of the work otherwise published separately in 1964 and 1974), esp. pp. 487–489 and *Face de Dieu, Face de l'Homme* (Paris, 1983), pp. 345–358; S. A. Arjomand, *The Shadow of God and the Hidden Imam* (Chicago, 1984), pp. 225f.; M. Momen, *An Introduction to Shi'i Islam. The History and Doctrine of Twelver Shi'ism* (Oxford, 1985), pp. 194f. On al-Kashfī's work, see also H. Corbin, 'Cosmogonie et herméneutique dans l'œuvre de Sayyed Ja'far Kashfī', *Annuaire EPHE* (1970–1971) (rpr. in *Itinéraire d'un enseignement*, pp. 125–129). Not unlike a number of other theosophers, al-Kashfī's affiliation with the Uṣūliyya is linked to a late development within this movement. This gradual acceptance of an esoteric and theosophical hermeneutics of Imamism seems to have been a development that began in the early seventeenth century; it awaits further study.

of several early theo-imamosophical sermons. For these reasons Jaʿfar Kashfī's version seems to me to be especially representative of this genre of texts attributed to ʿAlī:[63]

> From the top of the pulpit in the mosque at Kūfa, ʿAlī, Commander of the initiates delivered this sermon: 'People! Question me before you lose me![64] For I am the Treasurer of Knowledge;[65] I am the Mountain of magnanimity;[66] I hold the Keys of the Unknown; I am the Mystery of the Unknown; I am the Mystery of Mysteries;[67] I am the Tree of Lights; I am the Guide of the Heavens; I am the One who is intimate with those who praise God; I am the intimate friend of Gabriel; I am the pure Chosen One of Michael; I am the Conductor of

---

63. Jaʿfar Kashfī, *Tuḥfat al-mulūk*, 2 vols (lithograph, Iran, n.d.); this edition offers some variations as compared to the lithograph edition (riddled with errors of all kinds), produced in one volume in-folio (Iran, 1276/1859–1860). The abridged (one ought to say censured) version of the *Tuḥfat al-mulūk* which appeared fairly recently (Tehran, n.d. [ca. 1980s]) does not contain the text of the sermon; it should be noted that more than half the content of the old editions of the work has been left out of this new edition. I have not here translated the author's comments in Persian. The terms in italics are Qur'ānic Names of God. The Arabic text of this sermon is provided at the end of the present study.

64. 'The pulpit in the mosque at Kufa' and this first sentence are *topoï* attributed to ʿAlī; the *minbar* in the mosque at Kūfa, his capital, is the favoured site for sermons by the first imam. The sentence is a direct allusion to the fact that ʿAlī is held to be the wise, initiated one and thus the source par excellence of knowledge.

65. 'Treasurer of Knowledge' is a recurring title often given to the imams; see *Guide divin*, index, under '*khâzin, khuzzân, khazana*'.

66. *Ḥilm*, crucial virtue of tribal ethics, is practically impossible to render in translation by one word, according to Ch. Pellat it ranges from 'serene justice to balance, forbearance and lenience encompassing self-control and the dignity of good order', cf. *EI2*, vol. 3, p. 403.

67. The identity of the speaker shifts, from one affirmation to another, between, on the one hand, the historical imam, manifestation on the perceptible level of the ontological Imam and guardian of the divine Mystery, and on the other hand, the ontological Imam, the Revealed God and thus the content of this Mystery.

Thunder; I am the Witness of the Pact;[68] I am the Face of God; I am the Eye of God; I am the Hand of God; I am the Tongue of God;[69] I am the Light of God;[70] I am the Treasure of God in the heavens and on the earth;[71] I am the Power; I am the Manifestation of [or He who manifests] the Power; I am the Rewarder (*dayyān*)[72] on the Day of Rewards; I am Judge of the Garden and Fire; I am the Garden and the Fire; I am the Two-horned One [*Dhu'l-qarnayn*; cf. Q 18:83, 86 and 94] mentioned in the earlier scripture; I am the First Adam; I am the First Noah; I am Noah's Companion and Saviour; I am the Companion of Job the tested, and his Healer; I am the Companion of Abraham and his Secret;[73] I am the Commander of the Initiates; I am the Source of Certitude; I am the Thunder; I am the Cry for Truth [Q 23:41 and 50:42]; I am the Hour for the negators [a recurring Qur'ānic expression]; I am the Call that brings forth those entombed; I am the Lord of the Day of Resurrection; I am the one who has raised up the Heavens; I am the Proof of

68. Reference either to what is traditionally called 'the primordial Covenant' (*mīthāq*; cf. Q 7:172), or to the Pact (*'ahd*) concluded between God and Adam (Q 20:115). On the Imami conception of the *mīthāq*, see *Guide divin,* index under '*mithâq, mawâthîq*', and M. A. Amir-Moezzi, 'Cosmogony and Cosmology in Twelver Shi'ism', *EIr*, vol. 6, pp. 317–322; on the Imami version of Q 20:115, see *Guide divin*, p. 212 (*Divine Guide*, p. 85) and M. M. Bar-Asher, 'Variant Readings and Additions of the Imāmī-Šī'a to the Qur'ān', *Israel Oriental Studies*, 13 (1993), p. 64. On this verse see the monograph by R. Gramlich, 'Der Urvertrag in der Koranauslegung (zu Sura 7, 172–173)', *Der Islam*, 60 (1983), pp. 205–230.

69. On these assertions refer to note 27.

70. On the Imam as Light of God, see *Guide divin*, under '*nûr*' and 'Cosmogony and Cosmology', *EIr*, vol. 6, as well as the excellent article by U. Rubin, 'Pre-existence and Light. Aspects of the Concept of Nūr Muḥammad', *Israel Oriental Studies*, 5 (1975).

71. Compare with the assertion, 'I am the Treasurer'; the historical imam is the Treasurer par excellence of the divine Treasure whereas the ontological cosmic Imam is its actual content (cf. note 67 above).

72. Although it does not appear in the Qur'ān, this Name is generally considered one of the Divine Names; see D. Gimaret, *Les noms divins*, esp. pp. 350–351.

73. I believe this is an allusion to the Imami belief according to which the Imam, as Light, physically and spiritually accompanies the prophets and imams through the sacred history of humanity; cf. *Guide divin*, pp. 96–112 (Adamic Humanity: the 'voyage' of Light) (*Divine Guide*, pp. 38–44).

God on earth and in the heavens; I am the Light of guidance; I am the Most Beautiful Names by which one invokes Him; I am the Overseer of the deeds of all creatures; Among them, I am the Vicegerent of God the Creator; I am the Lord of the First Creation;[74] I am the Lord who released the first Flood; I am the Lord of the second Flood; I am with the Calamus and I was before the Calamus [Q 68:1 and 96:4] ; I am with the [Well-Preserved] Tablet and I was before the [Well-Preserved] Tablet [Q 85:22]; I am the Lord of primordial pre-eternity; I was the Steward (*mudabbir*)[75] of the primordial Universe when neither your heaven nor earth had come into being; I am He who in pre-existence, concluded the Pact with the spirits and He who declared to them, by the commandment of the Eternal: "Am I not your Lord ?" [Q 7:172]; I am the Leader of the initiates, I am the Standard of the well-guided; I am the Guide of the Pious; I am the Certitude; I am the one who speaks by divine revelation;[76] I am the Governor of the stars and their Steward by the commandment of my Lord and through the science He reserved for me; I am he who will spread justice and equality on earth just as before it overflows with oppression and injustice [or 'darkness'];[77] I am the one Concealed, the Awaited for the Spectacular Affair; I am the Sinai, the inscribed Book, the inhabited Dwelling; the Elevated Firmament; the swarming Sea [Q 52:1–6]; I am the Master of Hermeneutics [of the Sacred Book]; I am the Commentator of the Gospels; I am the Scholar of the Torah; I am the Archetype of the Book [Q 3:7; 13:39; 43:41]; I am the Decisive Word [Q 38:20]; I am the *First*, I am the *Last*, I am the *Hidden*, I am the

74. On the many creations, see *Guide divin*, p. 101, note 201 (*Divine Guide*, p. 40).

75. cf. D. Gimaret, *Les noms divins*, esp. p. 326.

76. On the imam receiving inspiration (*ilhām*) and divine revelation (*waḥy*) and the modalities of the latter, see *Guide divin*, pp. 176f. (*Divine Guide*, pp. 70ff.).

77. Time-honoured expression for the advent of the Qā'im/Mahdī, the eschatological Saviour, at the End of Time. In this case, as in the following affirmation, there is identification with the Shiʿi Mahdi, the hidden imam (refer to Chapters 12 to 14, this volume).

Manifest; I am the Light of the prophets;[78] I am the Friendship of the Friends [of God]; I am Adam and Seth; I am Moses and Joshua; I am Jesus and Simon [Peter];[79] I am Ḥanbathā' (?) of the Blacks; I am Bashīr (?) of the Turks; I am Jirjīs (?) of the Franks;[80] I am the one who Illuminates the sun, the moon and the stars; I am the Recorder of the Resurrection; I am the Riser of the Hour; I am *The Creator*, I am the Created; I am the Contemplator; I am the Contemplated; I am the Lord of the Ka'ba, I am the month of Ramaḍān; I am the Night of Destiny [Q 97:1–3] I am *He who gives (mu'ṭī)*; I am *He who takes (qābiḍ)*; I am the Interior of the Sacred Space; I am the Pillar of the People; I am the Light of lights; I am the Bearer of the [divine] Throne with the Devoted [angels?];[81] I am the Pearl of the Oysters; I am the Mountain of Qāf;[82] I am the Key of Invisible; I am the Lamp of Hearts;[83] I am the Splendour of all Beauty [or 'intelligence' or 'metallic vessel, *ẓurūf*';[84] I am the Secret of the Letters; I am the meaning of the *ṭawāsīn*;[85] I am the esoteric of the *ḥawāmīm*; I am the Lord of the *alif-lām-mīm*; I am the *nūn* of the Calamus

78. Here, as in the following assertions, an allusion is made to the ontological Imam as Light transmitted from prophet to prophet and imam to imam; regarding this complex notion consult the studies mentioned above in notes 70 and 73; see also U. Rubin, 'Prophets and Progenitors in Early Shi'a Tradition', *Jerusalem Studies in Arabic and Islam*, 5 (1984).

79. On the initiatory lineage of the prophets and their imams, see *Guide divin*, pp. 102f., esp. p. 107 ('spiritual genealogy') (*Divine Guide*, p. 40, esp. 41).

80. These names apparently designate the prophets of 'the peoples' mentioned. Let us simply point out that *beshir* means 'prophet' in Turkish (from the Arabic *bashīr*, 'herald of good news') and that Jirjīs generally designates Saint George, cf. Carra de Vaux, 'Djirdjīs', *EI2*.

81. On the imams as 'Bearers of the Divine Throne' (*ḥamalat al-'arsh*), see *Guide divin*, index under '*'arsh*'.

82. On the 'psycho-cosmical' Mountain of Qāf, see the analyses by H. Corbin in *Corps spirituel et Terre céleste. De l'Iran mazdéen à l'Iran shi'ite* (Paris, 1979), under 'Qāf'.

83. On the Imam as 'Light of the heart', see *Guide divin*, pp. 112f. (*Divine Guide*, pp. 44f.).

84. Kashfī interprets the term as 'beauty in all that is beautiful' *(jamāl-e har jamīl), Tuḥfat al-mulūk*, vol. 1, p. 26.

85. An allusion, as in the following two allusions to the separated letters that feature at the head of certain suras of the Qur'ān.

[Q 68:1]; I am the Lamp [in] Darkness; I am He who makes firm the lofty mountains; I am He who makes the sources of water rise; I am He who makes the rain fall; I am He who enables the leaves to grow; I am He who makes the colours burst forth and fruit ripen; I am the Bestower of nourishment; I am the Resurrector of the dead; I am he for whom the sun returned twice on its trajectory and he whom the sun saluted twice;[86] And I am He who prayed with the Messenger of God towards the *Qiblatayn*;[87] I am the Hero [of the Battles] of Badr and Ḥunayn;[88] I am He who enabled Moses to cross the sea; I am He who drowned the Pharaoh and his armies; I am He who spoke from the lips of Jesus while he was still in the cradle; I am He who speaks all languages;[89] I am He who traverses the seven heavens and the seven earths in the blink of an eye;[90] I am the *Mahdī* of all moments; I am the Jesus of the Time; I am the Master of the Balance;[91] I am the *Compassionate*, I am the *Merciful*; I am the *High*; I am the *Most High*; I am the Queen Bee of the initiates;[92]

---

86. An allusion to a miracle by ʿAlī, famous in the tradition; see e.g. *Guide divin*, p. 231 (*Divine Guide*, p. 92), and esp. the monograph by L. Capezzone, 'Un miracolo di ʿAlī ibn Abī Ṭālib: i versi attribuiti ad al-Sayyid al-Ḥimyarī e il modello storiografico delle fonti relative al *radd al-šams*', in *In memoria di Francesco Gabrieli (1904–1996)*, *RSO*, 71, supp. 2 (1997), pp. 99–112.

87. According to the tradition, Jerusalem (original direction for prayer at the beginning of Muḥammad's mission) and Mecca.

88. See e.g. H. Laoust, 'Le rôle de ʿAlî dans la *Sîra* chiite', *REI*, 30/1 (1962), pp. 7–26.

89. See e.g. al-Ṣaffār, *Baṣāʾir al-darajāt*, section 7, chs 11–16, pp. 333–354 (knowledge of all languages, the language of the various holy books, the language of the birds, of wild beasts and the 'metamorphosed' – *al-musūkh*).

90. For example, al-Ṣaffār, *Baṣāʾir al-darajāt*, section 8, chs 12–15, pp. 397–409.

91. On the identification of the cosmic Balance with the Imam in general and ʿAlī in particular, see e.g. ʿAlī b. Ibrāhīm al-Qummī, *Tafsīr*, ed. al-Mūsawī al-Jazāʾirī (Najaf, 1386–1387/1966–1968), vol. 2, p. 354 (commentary by al-Riḍā on Q 55:7–9).

92. On the symbolism of the bees and honey as representative of Shiʿi initiates and the initiatory teaching of the imams respectively, see e.g. al-Majlisī, *Mirʾāt al-ʿuqūl* (Tehran, 1404/1984), vol. 9, p. 170; for other references, see E. Kohlberg, 'Taqiyya in Shīʿī Theology and Religion', pp. 358–59, n. 74; see also note 43 above.

I am the Certitude of those who know with certitude; I am the Lion of the sons of Banū Ghālib; I am ʿAlī b. Abī Ṭālib.'[93]

93. Text of *khuṭbat al-bayān* (version by Jaʿfar Kashfī):
Ayyuhā'l-nās as'alūnī qabla an tafqidūnī innī khāzin al-ʿilm wa anā ṭūr al-ḥilm/ ʿindī mafātīḥ al-ghayb wa anā sirr al-ghayb/anā sirr al-asrār/anā shajarat al-anwār/ anā dalīl al-samāwāt/anā anīs al-musabbiḥāt/anā khalīl Jabra'īl/anā ṣafī Mīkā'īl/ anā sā'iq al-raʿd/anā shāhid al-ʿahd/ana wajh Allāh/anā ʿayn Allāh/anā yad Allāh/ anā lisān Allāh/anā nūr Allāh/anā kanz Allāh fi'l-samāwāt wa fi'l-arḍ/anā'l-qudra/ anā maẓhar [*muẓhir*] *al-qudra fi'l-arḍ/anā dayyān yawm al-dīn/anā qasīm al-janna wa'l-nār/anā'l-janna wa'l-nār/anā Dhu'l-Qarnayn al-madhkūr fi'l-ṣuḥuf al-ūlā/anā Ādam al-awwal/anā Nūḥ al-awwal/anā ṣāḥib Nūḥ wa munjīhi/anā ṣāḥib Ayyūb wa shāfīhi/anā ṣāḥib Ibrāhīm wa sirruh/anā amīr al-mu'minīn/anā ʿayn al-yaqīn/anā'l-raʿd/anā'l-ṣayḥa bi'l-ḥaqq/anā'l-sāʿa li'l-mukadhdhibīn/anā'l-nidā' al-mukhrij man fi'l-qubūr/anā ṣāḥib yawm al-nushūr/anā aqimtu'l-samāwāt/anā ḥujjat Allāh fi'l-arḍ wa'l-samāwāt/anā nūr al-hudā/anā'l-asmā' al-ḥusnā allatī yudʿa bihā/anā'l-nāẓir ʿalā aʿmāl al-khalā'iq/anā fi'l-khalā'iq khalīfat al-ilāh al-khāliq/anā ṣāḥib al-khalq al-awwal/anā ṣāḥib al-ṭūfān al-awwal/anā ṣāḥib al-ṭūfān al-thānī/anā maʿa'l-qalam qabl al-qalam/anā maʿa'l-lawḥ qabla'l-lawḥ/anā ṣāḥib al-azaliyyat al-awwaliyya/anā mudabbir al-ʿālam ḥīna lā samā'ukum hādhihi wa lā ghabrā'ukum/anā ākhidh al-ʿahd ʿalā'l-arwāḥ fi'l-azal/wa anā'l-munādī lahum 'alastu bi-rabbikum bi-amri qayyūmi lam yazal/anā sayyid al-mu'minīn/anā ʿalam al-muhtadīn/anā imām al-muttaqīn/ anā'l-yaqīn/anā'l-mutakallim bi'l-waḥy/anā ṣāḥib al-nujūm wa mudabbiruhā bi amri rabbī wa ʿilmī lladhī khaṣṣanī bihi/anā lladhī amla'a'l-arḍ ʿadlan wa qisṭan kamā muli'at jawran wa ẓulman* [*ẓuluman*]*/anā'l-ghā'ib'l-muntaẓar li'l-amr al-ʿaẓīm/anā'l-ṭūr wa kitāb masṭūr wa'l-bayt al-maʿmūr wa'l-saqf al-marfūʿ wa'l-baḥr al-masjūr/anā mu'awwil al-ta'wīl/anā mufassir al-injīl/anā ʿālim al-tawrā/anā umm al-kitāb/anā faṣl al-khiṭāb/anā al-awwal/anā al-ākhir/anā'l-bāṭin/anā'l-ẓāhir/anā nūr al-anbiyā'/anā walāyat al-awliyā'/anā Ādam wa Shīth/anā Mūsā wa Yūshaʿ/anā ʿIsā wa Shamʿūn/ anā Ḥanbathā'* [?] *al-Zanj/anā Bashīr* [?] *al-Turk/anā Jirjīs al-Faranj/anā munawwir al-shams wa'l-qamar wa'l-nujūm/anā qayyim al-qiyāma/anā qayyim al-sāʿa/anā'l-khāliq/anā'l-makhlūq/anā'l-shāhid/anā'l-mashhūd/anā ṣāḥib al-Kaʿba/anā shahr Ramaḍān/anā Laylat al-Qadr/anā'l-muʿṭī/anā'l-qābiḍ/anā bāṭin al-ḥaram/anā ʿimād al-umam/anā nūr al-anwār/anā ḥāmil al-ʿarsh maʿa'l-abrār/anā lu'lu' al-aṣdāf/anā jabal Qāf/anā miftāḥ al-ghuyūb/anā sirāj al-qulūb/anā nūr al-ẓurūf/anā sirr al-ḥurūf/ anā maʿnā'l-ṭawāsin/anā bāṭin al-ḥawāmīm/anā ṣāḥib alif-lām-mīm/anā'l-nūn wa'l-qalam/anā miṣbāḥ al-ẓulam/anā rāsi'l-jibāl al-shāmikhāt/anā fājir al-ʿuyūn al-jāriyāt/ anā munzil al-maṭar/anā mūriq al-shajar/anā mukhrij al-lawn wa'l-thamar/anā muqaddir al-aqwāt/anā nāshir al-amwāt/anā lladhī raddat lī al-shams marratayn wa sallamat ʿalayya karratayn/wa sallaytu maʿa rasūl Allāh al-qiblatayn/anā ṣāḥib Badr wa Ḥunayn/anā jāwaztu bi-Mūsā fi'l-baḥr/wa aghraqtu Firʿawn wa junūdahu/ anā'l-mutakallim ʿalā lisān ʿĪsā fi'l-mahd/anā'l-mutakallim bi kulli lisān/anā lladhi ajūzu'l-samāwāt al-sabʿwa'l-arḍīn al-sabʿ fī ṭurfati ʿayn/anā mahdī'l-awān/anā ʿĪsā'l-zamān/anā ṣāḥib al-mīzān/anā'l-raḥmān/anā'l-raḥīm/anā'l-ʿalī/anā'l-aʿlā/anā yaʿsūb al-mu'minīn/anā yaqīn al-mūqinīn/anā layth Banī Ghālib/anā ʿAlī ibn Abī Ṭālib.*

4

The Pre-Existence of the Imam

This chapter might best begin by briefly recalling a few basic facts covered in almost all studies on Imamism. First, Imami doctrine is entirely dominated by the holy group consisting of the Prophet Muḥammad, his daughter Fāṭima and the twelve imams, referred to as the 'Fourteen Impeccables' (*maʿṣum*), or the 'Fourteen Proofs' (*ḥujja*). These individuals form a whole that alone faithfully reflects the two ways in which, according to Shiʿism, Divine Truth (*al-ḥaqq*) is manifested to humanity. One of these is obvious, apparent, exoteric (*ẓāhir*), and enclosed within it is the other, which is secret, hidden, esoteric (*bāṭin*). The exoteric side of the Truth is manifested through lawgiving prophecy (*nubuwwa*), bringing to the mass of humanity (*ʿāmma*) a Sacred Book that 'descended from Heaven' (*tanzīl*); Muḥammad is both the prototype and the culmination of this first aspect. The esoteric side of the Truth is revealed through the mission of the imams (*walāya*),[1] accompanying each prophetic mission, bringing to the elite of the believers (*khāṣṣa*) the only true interpretation (*taʾwīl*) of the Holy Book; together, the twelve imams, but in particular ʿAlī, who is considered the father of the eleven others, are the plenary manifestation of this second aspect. Fāṭima, called the 'Confluence of the Two Lights' (*majmaʿ al-nūrayn*), reflects the 'place' where the two aspects

1. On the earlier Imami definition of *walāya* see Chapter 7, this volume.

intersect.[2] Of course, the prophet (*nabī*) also has knowledge of the esoteric side of religion; he is thus also *wālī*, but he reserves his esoteric teaching for his imam(s) exclusively; on the other hand, the imam is never considered the *nabī*. This is a crucial point, since in Imami texts the terms *wālī*, *ḥujja*, *ūlu'l-amr* and so forth, generally reserved for the imams, sometimes also apply to the prophets.[3]

The worlds before the world: the Guide-Light

The event took place a few thousand years before the creation of the world,[4] in an immaterial 'place' called the Mother of the Book

---

2. Doctrinal information concerning the person of Fāṭima is rare in early Imami texts. A mystical doctrine of sorts developed around her, either in Ismaili circles or in the works of later Imami authors. For the first of these, see especially L. Massignon's studies, 'Der Gnostische Kult der Fāṭima im Shiitischen Islam', 'La Mubāhala de Médine et l'hyperdulie de Fāṭima', 'La notion du voeu et la dévotion musulmane à Fāṭima', in his *Opera Minora*, vol. 1, pp. 514–522, 550–572, 573–591, respectively; H. Corbin, *Corps spirituel et Terre céleste* (Paris, 1979), pp. 82–99. For the second case, see T. Sabri's thesis, based exclusively on later Imami sources and in particular on the *Biḥār al-Anwār*: 'L'hagiographie de Fāṭima d'après *le Bihār al-Anwār* de Muḥammad Bāqir Majlisī (d. 1111/1699)' (University of Paris, III, 1969). Finally, note the virtual non-existence of an early Imami bibliography of Fāṭima in H. Lammens's work, *Fāṭima et les filles de Mahomet* (Rome, 1912), and in the otherwise well researched article by L. Veccia Vaglieri in *EI2*, vol. 2, pp. 861–870. In the course of the present discussion there will be occasion to examine some early material on Fāṭima (now see M. A. Amir-Moezzi and J. Calmard, 'Fāṭema', *EIr*).

3. There is no need to delve deeply into this basic material here, as it is found in almost all studies devoted to Imamism; the best presentation, despite being somewhat ahistorical in parts, is that of H. Corbin; see, e.g., *En Islam iranien*, vol. 1, Book One, 'Aspects du shīʿisme duodécimain', in toto and *Histoire de la philosophie islamique*, First Part, II, A, 3 and 4, pp. 69–85.

4. The figures given most frequently are 2,000, 7,000 and 14,000 years before the creation (*al-khalq*) of Adam or before the world (*al-dunyā*); for 2,000 years, see, e.g., Ibn Bābūya, *ʿIlal*, ch. 116, p. 134, ch. 139, p. 174; *Amālī*, 'majlis' 18, p. 75; al-Nuʿmānī, *Kitāb al-ghayba*, ed. ʿA. A. Ghaffārī (Tehran, 1397/1977), p. 131; Ibn Shahrāshūb, *Manāqib*, vol. 1, p. 183. For 7,000 years, see e.g. Ibn Bābūya, *ʿIlal*, ch. 156, pp. 208f. For 14,000 years, see, e.g., Ibn Bābūya, *Kamāl al-dīn*, pp. 275 and 335–336; Ibn al-Biṭrīq al-Ḥillī, *al-ʿUmda fī ʿuyūn ṣiḥāḥ*

(*umm al-kitāb*).[5] From his own light, God made a luminous ray spring forth, and from this ray he made a second ray proceed; the first was the light of Muḥammad, that of Prophecy (*nubuwwa*), that of the exoteric (*ẓāhir*); the second, of identical nature but subordinate to the first, was the light of ʿAlī, that of the Imamate or of *walāya*, of the esoteric (*bāṭin*):

> Two thousand years before creation, Muḥammad and ʿAlī were one light before God … light formed from one main trunk from which sprang a shining ray…. And God said: 'Here is a light [drawn] from my Light; its trunk is prophecy and its branch is the Imamate; prophecy belongs to Muḥammad, my servant and messenger, and the Imamate belongs to ʿAlī, my Proof and my Friend. Without them I would have created none of my creation.' This is why ʿAlī always said, 'I proceed from Muḥammad [or from Aḥmad] as one clarity proceeds from another.'[6]

Throughout the traditions of the imams, the Prophet himself frequently says that he was created with ʿAlī, before the creation of the world, out of one and the same light.[7] The very names of

---

al-akhbār (n.p., n.d.), p. 75 (referring to Aḥmad b. Ḥanbal: '*Kuntu anā wa ʿAlī nūran bayna yadayyi'llāh ʿazza wa jalla qabla an yakhluqa Ādam bi arbaʿa ʿashara alfa ʿāmin*'; this tradition does not appear in the *Musnad*).

5. A Qur'ānic expression (Q 3:7, 13:39 and 43:4). See Ibn Bābūya, *ʿIlal*, ch. 70, pp. 79f. Of the Sunni sources, see al-Suyūṭī, *al-Khaṣā'iṣ al-kubrā*, ed. M. Kh. Harrās (Cairo, 1967), vol. 1, p. 10 (referring to Aḥmad b. Ḥanbal: '*Innī ʿinda'llāh fī ummī'l-kitāb la-khātamu'l-nabiyyīn wa inna Ādam la-munjadil fī ṭīnatihi*'; cf. *Musnad*, vol. 4, pp. 127–128 where only *ʿinda* is read as *ʿabd*).

6. '*Inna Muḥammadan wa ʿAliyyan kānā nūran bayna yadayy Allāh qabla khalq al-khalq bi-alfay ʿām … dhālika'l-nūr … lahu aṣlan qad tashʿʿaba minhu shuʿāʿ lāmiʿ … hādhā nūrun min nūrī aṣluhu nubuwwa wa farʿuhu imāma ammā'l-nubuwwa fa li Muḥammad ʿabdī wa rasūlī wa ammā'l-imāma fa li ʿAlī ḥujjatī wa waliyyī wa law lā humā lama khalaqtu khalqī … qāla ʿAlī anā min Muḥammad/Aḥmad ka'l-ḍaw' min al-ḍaw*', a tradition attributed to Jaʿfar, Ibn Bābūya, *ʿIlal*, ch. 139, p. 174; for the traditions of the other imams, see ibid., ch. 111, pp. 131f.

7. '*Khuliqtu anā wa ʿAlī min nūr wāḥid qabla an tukhlaqa'l-dunyā*', Ibn Bābūya, *Amālī*, 'majlis' 41, no. 10, p. 236; Ibn al-Biṭrīq, *al-ʿUmda*, pp. 44–45 and *Khaṣā'iṣ waḥy al-mubīn fī manāqib amīr al-mu'minīn* (n.p., n.d.); ed. M. B.

these two archtypes of prophecy and the imamate are forged from the Names of God. In a prophetic tradition, Muḥammad states: 'In me God placed prophecy and benediction (*al-nubuwwa wa'l-baraka*), and in ʿAlī He placed the imamate [var. eloquence] and a chivalrous spirit (*al-imāma/al-faṣāḥa wa al-furūsiyya*); then He gave us names, having our names derive from His: from His name "The Praised Lord of the Throne" (*Dhu'l-ʿarsh maḥmūd*), He formed my name, Muḥammad, and from His name "The Supreme" (*al-aʿlā*), He formed the name of ʿAlī.'[8] In a series of *ḥadīth qudsī* reported by either the Prophet or the imams, God proclaims that the name of Muḥammad is taken from His own name *al-Maḥmūd* (the Praised) and that of ʿAlī from His name *al-ʿAlī al-Aʿlā* (the Supreme Superior).[9]

---

al-Maḥmūdī (Tehran, 1406/1986), pp. 37–38 and 109–110. On the light of ʿAlī, often called 'the shimmering light' (*nūr shaʿshaʿānī*), see Ibn Bābūya, *'Ilal*, vol. 1, ch. 120, p. 144 and vol. 2, ch. 1, p. 313; Ibn Bābūya, *Amālī*, 'majlis' 55, pp. 347–348, no. 6.

8. Ibn Bābūya, *'Ilal*, ch. 116, pp. 134–135.

9. Ibn Bābūya, *Kamāl al-dīn*, vol. 1, ch. 23, p. 252, no. 2; Ibn Bābūya, *'Uyūn*, vol. 1, ch. 6, no. 27, p. 58; al-Nuʿmānī, *Kitāb al-ghayba*, p. 137; al-Khazzāz al-Rāzī, *Kifāyat al-athar*, ed. A. Kūhkamare'ī (Qumm, 1401/1980), pp. 152–153; Ibn ʿAyyāsh al-Jawharī, *Muqtaḍab al-athar*, ed. H. Rasūlī Maḥallātī (Qumm, n.d.), p. 23; al-Ṭūsī, *Kitāb al-ghayba*, p. 95. It is not necessary to re-examine the concept of *nūr muḥammadī* as dealt with by other Sunnis; on this subject, see, e.g., I. Goldziher, 'Neuplatonische und Gnostische Elemente im Hadīt', *ZA* (1908), pp. 324f.; T. Andrae, *Die Person Muhammeds in Lehre und Glauben seiner Gemeinde* (Stockholm, 1918), pp. 313f.; F. Rosenthal, *Knowledge Triumphant*, pp. 157f.; L. Massignon, 'Nūr Mūḥammadī', *EI*; U. Rubin, 'Pre-existence and Light. Aspects of the Concept of Nūr Muḥammad', *IOS*, pp. 62–119; for the traditions concerning Muḥammad as the first creation and his light in non-Sufi works, see, e.g., Ibn Hishām, *al-Sīrat al-nabawiyya*, vol. 1, pp. 164–166; Ibn Saʿd, *Ṭabaqāt*, vol. 1, pp. 1–60; al-Ṭabarī, *Ta'rīkh*, series 2, pp. 243f.; al-Bayhaqī, *Dalā'il al-nubuwwa*, ed. M. ʿUthmān (Cairo, 1969), vol. 1, pp. 64–86. The concept found its broadest developments among the mystics, e.g. Ibn Sabʿīn describes more than thirty-three forms of Muḥammadan light; see *Rasā'il Ibn Sabʿn*, ed. ʿA. R. Badawī, 'Risāla fī anwār al-nabī' (Misr, n.d.), pp. 201–211, and for a bibliography see the Western studies cited previously. For the Sunni reactions to Shiʿi traditions about the primordial lights of the Prophet and the imams, see T. Andrae, *Die Person Muhammeds*, pp. 319f.; Rubin, 'Pre-Existence and Light', pp. 113–114.

Other traditions relate that the primordial light that was drawn from the Divine Light was that of the *ahl al-bayt,* the 'five of the cloak' (*ahl al-kisā'*: Muḥammad, 'Alī, Fāṭima, al-Ḥasan and al-Ḥusayn), or even that of the Fourteen Impeccables (the Prophet, his daughter and the twelve imams); in this case, the light of *walāya* is represented by all the imams, that of Fāṭima being placed at the junction of the two lights of prophecy and the imamate; sometimes, Fāṭima and her light are passed over in silence in favour of the light of the Prophet and the twelve imams.[10] Likewise, it is said that the names of the 'five of the cloak' were derived from the Names of God and inscribed on the Divine Throne (*al-'arsh*). According to one *ḥadīth*, when Adam was brought to life by the breath of God, he lifted his eyes towards the Throne and saw five inscriptions; asking God about this, he received the following reply: 'First there is Muḥammad, for I am *al-maḥmūd* (the Praised One); second, there is 'Alī, for I am *al-'ālī* (the Most High); third, there is Fāṭima, for I am *al-fāṭir* (the Creator); fourth, there is al-Ḥasan, for I am *al-muḥsin* (the Benefactor): and fifth, there is al-Ḥusayn, for I am *dhu'l-iḥsān* (the Lord of Kindness).'[11]

In his *Tafsīr*, commenting on verse 37 ('And Adam received words from his Lord') of the second Sura of the Qur'ān, *Sūrat al-Baqara*, Ja'far al-Ṣādiq said:

> God was, and nothing of His creation existed; then He created five creatures from the light of His glory (*nūr 'aẓamatihi*) and He gave each of them a name derived from His own Names. Being the Praised One, He called His prophet Muḥammad; being the Most High, He called the prince of the believers 'Alī; being the creator of the heavens and the earth, He created the name of Fāṭima; possessing the most beautiful names (*al-asmā' al-ḥusnā*), He forged the

10. See, e.g., Ibn Bābūya, *'Ilal*, ch. 116, pp. 135f.; Ibn Bābūya, *Kamāl al-dīn*, ch. 31, p. 319; Ibn Bābūya, *Khiṣāl*, vol. 2, pp. 307–310; al-Khazzāz al-Rāzī, *Kifāyat al-athar*, pp. 110–111 and 169–170.

11. Ibn Bābūya, *'Ilal*, ch. 116, p. 135; Ibn al-Biṭrīq, *al-'Umda*, p. 120 and *Khaṣā'iṣ*, p. 145; al-Ḥurr al-'Āmilī, *al-Jawāhir al-saniyya fī al-aḥādith al-qudsiyya* (Baghdad, 1964), pp. 233, 278, 304–305, 307.

> names of al-Ḥasan and al-Ḥusayn; then He placed these names to the right side of His throne.... these were the five names that Adam received from his Lord.[12]

It might be useful here, parenthetically, to add some of the definitions given by the imams of the 'Throne'. According to these, *al-ʿarsh* appears to be the name given to the Knowledge and the Power of God. As the Divine Seat (*al-kursī*) is the hermeneutic reference (*ta'wīl*) to the visible side, the exoteric part of the Invisible World (*ẓāhir min al-ghayb*), the Throne is, in the same way, its hidden esoteric face (*bāṭin min al-ghayb*); the Seat is the source of the created world, the visible manifestation of the Invisible, while the Throne, marked by the essence of prophecy and of the imamate, is Religion; it contains the esoteric mysteries of the Invisible and the explanations of the mysteries of the world:

'The Throne is not God Himself,' says the eighth imam, 'The Throne is a name that denotes Knowledge and Power, and it contains everything.'[13]

---

12. See the fragments from al-Nuʿmānī's recension of Jaʿfar al-Ṣādiq's *Tafsīr*, which appeared under al-Murtaḍā's name, under the title *al-Muḥkam wa'l-mutashābih* (lithograph, Iran, n.d.), p. 72; this passage does not appear in either of the two editions of the *Tafsīr*, ed. P. Nwyia and 'A. Zayʿūr; it is true that these were edited using the recension of the mystic al-Sulamī in his *Ḥaqā'iq al-tafsīr*, where the author expurgated any typically Shiʿi allusion from the original text of the *Tafsīr*. The only manuscript of the *Ḥaqā'iq* where this passage appears is curiously MS 43, Yenı Camı, Istanbul (cf. P. Nwyia, *Exégèse coranique et langage mystique* [Beirut, 1970], p. 159, note 3). It must be added that the Imami interpretation of the *āyat al-nūr* (Q 24:35) sees, in the different forms and instruments of light cited in this verse, allusions to the lights of the different individuals that make up the Fourteen Impeccables; see, e.g., al-Kulaynī, *al-Uṣūl*, 'Kitāb al-ḥujja', 'Bāb inna'l-a'imma ... nūr Allāh', vol. 1, p. 278, no. 5; Ibn al-Biṭrīq, *al-ʿUmda*, pp. 186, 219–220; Ibn Shahrāshūb, *Manāqib*, vol. 1, pp. 240f.; al-Majlisī, *Biḥār al-anwār*, vol. 23, pp. 304f.

13. '*Al-ʿarsh laysa huwa Allāh wa'l-ʿarsh ism ʿilm wa qudra wa ʿarsh fīhi kullu shay*", al-Kulaynī, *al-Uṣūl*, 'Kitāb al-tawḥīd', 'Bāb al-ʿarsh wa'l-kursī', vol. 1, p. 177, no. 2; see also vol. 1, p. 179, no. 6, Jaʿfar al-Ṣādiq's words where the Throne is associated with Knowledge.

According to a tradition of al-Bāqir reported by his son Jaʿfar al-Ṣādiq, 'The Throne is the Religion of Truth'.[14] 'These two [the Seat and the Throne] are two of the greatest thresholds of the invisible worlds,' says Jaʿfar al-Ṣādiq. 'They are themselves invisible, and intimately connected in the Invisible, for the Seat is the exoteric Threshold [var. hermeneutic; *taʾwīl*] of the Invisible; it is the place where those created beings from which all things proceed appear; the Throne is the esoteric Threshold that contains the Knowledge of how, of existence, of quantity, of limit, of where, of Volition, and of the attribute of Will; it contains also the Knowledge of words, of movements and of immobility (?), as well as the Knowledge of the Return and of the Origin.'[15]

As will be seen, initiatory Knowledge (*al-ʿilm*) and to a certain extent the consequence of *ʿilm*, miraculous powers (*al-qudra, al-aʿājīb*), constitute the two principles characteristic of the existence of the imams. The imams say that their doctrine, which they often refer to as 'the True Religion', contains all the esoteric mysteries of the universe as well as the answers to all questions about the domain of the Sacred. We know that each religion, according to the imams, has two indissoluble aspects, the exoteric, manifested by revelation and the teachings of the prophet of the religion, and the esoteric, manifested by the teachings of each prophet's imam. We also know that, according to an early idea, one which belongs as much to the domain of the religious as it does to the domain of the supra-natural, a

14. *'Al-ʿarsh dīn al-ḥaqq'*, Ibn ʿAyyāsh al-Jawhārī, *Muqtaḍab al-athar*, p. 75.

15. *'Liʾannahumā bābān min akbar abwāb al-ghuyūb wa humā jamīʿān ghaybān wa humā fiʾl-ghayb maqrūnān liʾannaʾl-kursī huwaʾl-bāb [huwaʾl-taʾwīl] al-ẓāhir min al-ghayb alladhī minhu maṭlaʿ al-badʿ wa minhuʾl-ashyāʾ kulluhā waʾl-ʿarsh huwaʾl-bāb al-bāṭin alladhī yūjad fīhi ʿilm al-kayf waʾl-kawn waʾl-qadr waʾl-ḥadd waʾl-ʿayn waʾl-mashīʿa wa ṣifat al-irāda wa ʿilm al-alfāẓ waʾl-ḥarakāt waʾl-tark wa ʿilm al-ʿawd waʾl-bad"*, Ibn Bābūya, *Kitāb al-tawḥīd*, ch. 50 'Bāb al-ʿarsh wa ṣifātih', pp. 321–322, no. 1; the text is difficult: why this irregular enumeration? Does the '*mashīʿa wa ṣifat al-irāda*' group always depend on *ʿilm*? Is this not rather a case of the Divine Will being placed on the same plane as Knowledge? Does *al-tark* (lit. 'abandonment', 'desertion', 'tranquility') really mean 'immobility' in this case? (The Persian translator of the work, Muḥammad ʿAlī b. Muḥammad Ḥasan Ardakānī, renders it thus: *Asrār-e towḥīd* [Tehran, n.d.], p. 369.)

'name' is not a simple appellation, but is the sonorous representation of the essential reality of the named; the Throne, marked by the names of the Prophet and the imams, carries in it the primordial essence of prophecy and the imamate, that is, the essence of Religion, in this case that of the imams. This parallel between the Throne and Imami doctrine is underscored by two successive traditions reported by al-Kulaynī. In the first, the *ḥujja*s are the 'bearers of the Throne';[16] in the second, God calls them 'the bearers of my Knowledge and my Religion'.[17] When it is realised to what extent the content of Imami doctrine is dominated by those individuals known as the Impeccables, the fact that the Throne can carry their names at the same time as it is being carried by them is easier to understand. Thus, one can ask whether *al-ʿarsh* does not, when used purely in reference to the imams, refer to the archetype or the celestial counterpart of the Cause (*amr*) of the imams, a cause intimately linked to the Imam in the usual ontological understanding of the word, as will be seen throughout this present work.

As for the ontological modalities of the lights of the Impeccables, a number of traditions describe them as being 'silhouettes of light' (*ashbāḥ nūr*). In reply to the question, 'What were you before the creation of Adam?' the third imam, al-Ḥusayn b. ʿAlī replied, 'We were silhouettes of light revolving around the Throne of the All-Merciful.'[18] In other traditions we see expressions like 'spirits made of light' (*arwāḥ min nūr*),[19] or 'shadows of light' (*aẓilla*

16. Al-Kulaynī, *al-Uṣūl*, 'Kitāb al-tawḥīd', 'Bāb al-ʿarsh wa'l-kursī', vol. 1, p. 179, no. 6: '*ḥamalat al-ʿarsh*'.

17. Ibid., no. 7, '*Ḥamalat dīnī wa ʿilmī*'.

18. Ibn Bābūya, *ʿIlal*, ch. 18, p. 23; also ch. 156, p. 208; see also, e.g., al-Majlisī, *Biḥār*, vol. 11, pp. 150f. and 192f. (citing al-Ḥasan al-ʿAskarī's *Tafsīr*); in Sunni literature, the expression *ashbāḥ nūr*, or simply *ashbāḥ*, probably borrowed from the Shiʿis, refers in general to the form of the angels, described as being 'luminous subtle bodies' (*ajsām laṭīfa nūrāniyya*); cf. al-Zurqānī, *Sharḥ ʿalā al-Mawāhib*, vol. 1, pp. 9f.

19. Ibn Bābūya, *ʿIlal*, ch. 130, p. 162 and *Kamāl al-dīn*, vol. 2, ch. 33, pp. 335–336, no. 7.

nūr).[20] One might think of luminous entities of an extremely subtle substance: 'Before his [material] creation, the imam … was a shadow made from breath, on the right side of the Divine Throne.'[21] It must be emphasised that, according to certain (imprecise and allusive) details, this cosmogonic stage did not come about in the primordial 'world' of the Mother of the Book, characterised by that original dart of light (the unique and also double light of prophecy and *walāya*), but in a later world. Names like 'the first world of the shadows' (*'ālam al-aẓillat al-awwal*), or 'the first world of the particles' (*'ālam al-dharr al-awwal),* used with caution in cosmogonic contexts, appear to have been applied to this second 'world'.[22] Passing from the Mother of the Book to the First World of the Shadows might thus mark the transformation of formless light into light with a human shape. In a *ḥadīth* reported by al-Ḥusayn b. 'Alī, the Prophet relates a story about the angel Gabriel. Having seen Muḥammad's name written on the material covering the Throne, Gabriel asked God to show him what the name contained, since it was certainly the most glorious of creatures. God led his angel into the First World of Particles, showed him twelve corporal silhouettes, and said: 'Here is the light of 'Alī b. Abī Ṭālib, here is the light of al-Ḥasan and that of al-Ḥusayn … [and so on, up to the light of the twelfth imam, the

---

20. Al-Nu'mānī, *Kitāb al-ghayba*, p. 328; Ibn 'Ayyāsh, *Muqtaḍab*, p. 15; al-Majlisī, *Biḥār*, vol. 15, p. 25 (citing al-Kulaynī); sometimes these shadows of light are described as being green, cf. ibid., vol. 15, pp. 23 and 24. 'We [the imams] were near our Lord, and other than us there was no one; we were enveloped in green shadows': *'kunā 'inda rabbinā laysa 'indahu ghayrunā fī ẓillatin khaḍrā'*; 'the first of God's creations was Muḥammad and us, the *ahl al-bayt*, out of the Light of His Majesty (*min nūr 'aẓamatihi*); then from us He made the same number of green shadows (*fa awqafanā aẓilla khaḍrā'*), set before Him; and at that time the sky and the earth, the day and the night, the sun and the moon had not yet come into being.'

21. *'Fa'l-imām … ẓillan qabla khalqihi nasamatan 'an yamīn 'arshihi'*, al-Nu'mānī, *Kitāb al-ghayba*, p. 328; al-Khazzāz al-Rāzī, *Kifāyat al-athar*, p. 112.

22. See, e.g., al-Nu'mānī, *Kitāb al-ghayba*, pp. 274 and 309; Ibn Bābūya, *Amālī*, 'majlis' 89, p. 612, no. 9.

Qā'im].'[23] In a number of his ascensions into heaven, the Prophet reached the pre-existential World of the Shadows or Particles, and there looked upon the lights of the twelve Imams (or those of the Fourteen Impeccables).[24]

What do these subtle entities of light do? They float suspended before the Throne of God,[25] or float around it in an archetypal circumambulation, bearing witness to the Unicity of God and praising His Glory. Several different words are used to describe these activities, but it would appear that they can be divided into two principal categories: the first is Unification, witnessing the Unicity (*tahlīl, tawḥīd*); and the second is Glorification or Sanctification (*taḥmīd, tamjīd, tasbīḥ, taqdīs*). 'Twelve silhouettes of light [suspended] between heaven and earth ... attesting to the Unicity of God and exalting His Glory.'[26] 'God created the light of His majesty, Muḥammad, 'Alī and the eleven other imams; He created them [like] spirits enveloped in the clarity of His light [so that] they might worship Him even before creation, glorifying and sanctifying Him.'[27]

---

23. *''An al-Ḥusayn b. 'Alī 'an al-nabī ... qāla akhbaranī Jabra'īl ... yā rabb hadhā'l-ism al-maktūb fī surādiq al-'arsh 'arinī a'azza khalqika 'alayka* (sic) *qāla fa-'arāhu'llāhu 'azza wa jall ithnay 'ashara ashbāḥan abdānan ... hādhā nūr 'Alī*', al-Khazzāz, *Kifāya*, pp. 169–170. It is noteworthy that here the lights of the imams are contained in the name of Muḥammad, and constitute the reality of this name.

24. See, e.g., al-Khazzāz, *Kifāya*, pp. 110–111; Ibn Bābūya, *Khiṣāl*, vol. 1, p. 156; according to the Imami tradition, the Prophet had a number of ascensions, the most frequently tendered number being 120; see al-Majlisī, *Biḥār*, vol. 18, pp. 387f. (citing esp. al-Ṣaffār al-Qummī and Ibn Bābūya). See also ch. 5.

25. '*Mu'allaqa*' (lit. 'suspended') or '*bayn al-samā' wa'l-arḍ*' (lit. 'between the heaven and the earth', but thus must be understood in the sense of 'floating', since neither the heaven nor the earth was yet created).

26. *'Ithnay 'ashara ashbāḥan min nūr bayn al-samā' wa'l-arḍ ... yuwaḥḥidūna'llāh 'azza wa jall wa yumajjidūnahu*', a prophetic *ḥadīth*, see al-Khazzāz, *Kifāya*, p. 170; Ibn 'Ayyāsh, *Muqtaḍab*, p. 23.

27. A tradition that goes back to the fourth imam, 'Alī b. al-Ḥusayn: '*inna'l-lāha tabārak wa ta'ālā khalaqa Muḥammadan wa 'Aliyyan wa'l-a'immat al-aḥad 'ashar min nūr 'aẓamatih arwāḥan fī ḍiyā' nūrih ya'budūnahu qabla khalqi'l-khalq yusabbiḥūna'llāh 'azza wa jall yuqaddisūnahu*', Ibn Bābūya, *Kamāl al-dīn*, ch. 31, no. 1, pp. 318–319; on this subject see also Ibn Bābūya,

Then other shadows or particles surge forth from this same pre-existential world; there is no information about just 'when' this new creation took place or 'how much' time separated it from the formation of the luminous entities of the Imams; but these luminous bodies, as has been seen, were created and dedicated themselves to the worship of their creator at a time when nothing had yet been brought into being. The creation of new shadows thus constitutes a later stage. The shadows constitute the pre-existential entities of what might be called 'pure beings'. In fact, several kinds of shadows are presented in a great number of traditions from different compilations, with no regard for order or clarity. They can be divided into three categories:

1. The shadows of future spiritual and non-human inhabitants of heaven and earth (*al-rūḥāniyyūn min ahl al-samāwāt wa'l-arḍ*), that is, the different categories of angels and the supernatural entities of the earth (including, perhaps, the *jinn*).[28]
2. The shadows of prophets, numbering 124,000, with particular emphasis on those prophets 'endowed with firm resolution' (*ūlu'l-ʿazm*); there are five of the latter for Imamis: Noah, Abraham,

---

ʿIlal, ch. 18, p. 23; ch. 97, p. 118, and ch. 157, pp. 208–209; Ibn Bābūya, *ʿUyūn*, vol. 1, ch. 26, pp. 262f.; al-Khazzāz, *Kifāya*, p. 171; Ibn ʿAyyāsh, *Muqtaḍab*, p. 25; al-Majlisī, *Biḥār*, vol. 15, p. 26.

28. See,- e.g.,- al-Ṣaffār, *Baṣā'ir*, pp. 67 and 69; al-Nuʿmānī, *Kitāb al-ghayba*, p. 137; Ibn ʿAyyāsh, *Muqtaḍab*, p. 58; Ja'far b. Muḥammad al-Qummī, *Kāmil al-ziyārāt*, pp. 26–27; in Imami tradition, the *jinn*, although classified as being among the *rūḥāniyyūn*, are nevertheless generally considered to be obedient to the imams, and thus beneficent. In this point of view, they are opposed to the *nasnās* (or *nisnās*), maleficent supernatural monsters that live on earth and are compared to the faithful of the adversaries of the imams. Regarding belief in *jinn* among Muslim scholars in general, interesting information may be found in Shihāb al-Dīn b. Ḥajar (d. 973/1565), *al-Fatāwā al-ḥadīthiyya* (Cairo, 1325/1907), pp. 166f.; for the early literature on this subject, see Ibn al-Nadīm, *al-Fihrist*, ed. Flügel, p. 308.

Moses, Jesus and Muḥammad; in this particular case it is of course the shadows of the first four that are being referred to.[29]

3. The shadows of the believers (*muʾminūn*) among the descendants of Adam, that is, the faithful of the imams of all times, those initiated into the esoteric dimension of all religions, as distinguished from simple practisers (*muslimūn*, lit. 'the Muslims'), who are submissive to exoteric religion without understanding its deep meaning.[30]

Then came the time of the sacred pre-temporal Pact (*al-mīthāq*); the term is used more than twenty times in the Qur'ān, where it has most frequently the technical meaning of an Alliance between God and humanity, and with the prophets in particular (*mīthāq al-nabiyyīn*; cf. Q 3:81 and 33:7). Almost all Muslim commentators apply the term to the contract of faith between God and men, in a pre-existential 'time' before their birth. The scriptural proof of this episode would seem to be found initially in verse 172 in Sura 7, *al-Aʿrāf*, although the term *mīthāq* itself is not there present: 'When your Lord brought forth descendants from the loins of the sons of Adam, He had them bear witness against one another: "Am I not your Lord?" They answered, "Verily, we bearwitness."

29. See e.g. al-Ṣaffār, *Baṣāʾir*, pp. 70, 74–75; Ibn Bābūya, *ʿIlal*, ch. 101, p. 122; Ibn ʿAyyāsh, *Muqtaḍab*, p. 41; al-Majlisī, *Biḥār*, vol. 51, pp. 149f.; for the list of *ūluʾl-ʿazm* prophets (cf. Q 46:35) and the reasons why Adam cannot be counted among them, see e.g. Ibn Bābūya, *ʿIlal*, ch. 101, passim.

30. See, e.g., al-Ṣaffār, *Baṣaʾir*, pp. 79–80; al-Kulaynī, *al-Uṣūl*, 'Kitāb al-imān wa'l-kufr', vol. 3, ch. 3, pp. 12f.; Ibn Bābūya, *Faḍāʾil al-shīʿa*, ed. Ḥ. Fashāhī (Tehran, 1342 Sh./1963–1964), pp. 11–12. On the opposition of *muʾmin* and *muslim*, see ch. 3, note 40; on the plane of the perceptible world and during the time of the historical imams of Islam, these two terms referred, respectively, to 'the true Shiʿis', those initiated by the imams, and the mass of Muslims, meaning the Sunnis or those who were only nominally Shiʿis: those who had not been initiated into the esoteric side of Islam.

He did this lest, on the Day of the Resurrection, they say, "We were caught not expecting this." '[31]

In Imami traditions of a cosmogonic character, other developments were elaborated around this central concept. The Pact takes place in the world of shadows or particles that, for this reason, is also called the World of the Pact (*'ālam al-mīthāq*). It is with the 'pure beings' in the form of particles or shadows made 'conscious' that God draws up the sacred pact.[32] In the Imami tradition this primordial Covenant entails a quadruple oath, although all four parts of the oath are rarely mentioned together in a single *ḥadīth*: an oath of worship (*'ubūdiyya*) of God, oaths of love and fidelity to (*walāya*) Muḥammad and his prophetic mission, to the imams and their sacred Cause, and also to the Mahdī as the universal saviour who appears at the End of Time:[33]

---

31. On the idea of *mīthāq* and its later developments, especially in mystical literature, see L. Massignon, 'Le Jour du covenant', *Oriens*, 15 (1962), pp. 14–24; L. Massignon, *La passion de Hallāj*, under '*mīthāq*'; L. Gardet, 'Les Noms et les statuts', *SI*, 5 (1956); L. Gardet, 'Fins dernières selon la théologie musulmane', *Revue Thomiste*, 2 (1957); R. Gramlich, 'Der Urvertrag in der Koranauslegung (zu Sura 7, 172–173)'.

32. In reply to the question 'How then did they [the pure beings] respond if they were only particles?' (*kayfa ajābū wa hum dharr*), Abū 'Abd Allāh Ja'far al-Ṣādiq said: 'In the world of the Pact, [God] instilled in them that which they needed to answer his questions' (*ja'ala fihim mā idhā sa'alahum ajābū ya'nī fi'l-mīthāq*); al-Kulaynī, *al-Uṣūl*, 'Kitāb al-īmān wa'l-kufr', vol. 3, ch. 4, p. 19. Although the statement of the sixth imam remains vague, the commentators did not hesitate to see in it an allusion to conscience (*shu'ūr*), to the faculty of perception-comprehension (*idrāk*), or the faculty of emitting sounds (*nuṭq*) (cf. al-Majlisī, *Mir'āt al-'uqūl*, vol. 2, pp. 12–13, citing particularly al-Mufīd and al-Murtaḍā). The disciple who asked Ja'far al-Sadiq the question was Abū Baṣīr; the sixth imam had three disciples with this *kunya*: Layth b. al-Bukhturī al-Murādī, 'Abd Allāh b. Muḥammad al-Asadī al-Kūfī and Yaḥyā b. Abi'l-Qāsim al-Asadī al-Makfūf (cf. Mudarris, *Rayḥānat al-adab*, vol. 7, pp. 34–37); the first appears to have been the closest of the three since he was known as being one of the 'apostles' (*ḥawārī*) of the sixth imam (al-Kashshī, *Ma'rifa akhbār al-rijāl* [Bombay, 1317/1899], pp. 7 and 113).

33. This is why, in Imami tradition, the plural *mawāthīq* is often used; see, e.g., al-Ṣaffār, *Baṣā'ir*, pp. 70–71 and 80–81; al-Kulaynī, *al-Uṣūl*, vol. 3, pp. 12–13; al-Nu'mānī, *Kitāb al-ghayba*, p. 274; Ibn Bābūya, *'Ilal*, vol. 1, ch. 97, p. 117 and ch. 104, p. 124; vol. 2, ch. 1, pp. 312f.; al-Ḥurr al-'Āmilī, *al-Jawāhir al-saniyya*, p. 215; al-Majlisī, *Biḥār*, vol. 26, pp. 279–280.

> Then God made the prophets take an oath, saying to them: 'Am I not your Lord? Is not Muḥammad here My messenger, and is 'Alī not the prince of the believers?' The prophets answered 'Yes', and prophetic status was firmly established for them (*fa-thabatat lahum al-nubuwwa*); and God made 'the resolute prophets' take an oath, saying: 'I am your Lord, Muḥammad is My messenger, 'Alī is the prince of the believers, his heirs (*awṣiyā'uhu*, i.e., the other imams) are, after him, the rulers accountable for my My Order (*wulāt amrī*) and the guardians of the treasures of My Knowledge (*khuzzān 'ilmī*), and the Mahdī is he through whom I will bring My religion to victory, through whom I will show My power, through whom I will take vengeance on My enemies, and through whom I will be worshipped whether they will so or not.' [The resolute prophets] answered: 'We so affirm, Lord, and bear witness.'[34]

Although the *ḥadīth*s offer no details on the matter, it would seem logical to place the 'Primordial Initiation' after this Pact of the fourfold oath. In fact, it is said that in the world of shadows, the pre-existential entities of the Impeccables taught the sacred sciences to the shadows of 'pure beings'. These sciences being secret, the future initiate could receive them only after taking a solemn oath, according to a universal rule of all esoteric or initiatory doctrines. Ja'far al-Ṣādiq said: 'We were spirits of light, and we taught the secrets of the Science of the Unity and the Glory to the shadows.'[35] 'We were silhouettes of light revolving around the Throne of the All-Merciful,' said Ḥusayn b. 'Alī, 'and we taught

---

34. Al-Ṣaffār, *Baṣā'ir*, section 2, ch. 7, no. 2; see also al-Kulaynī, *al-Uṣūl*, 'Kitāb al-īmān wa'l-kufr', vol. 3, ch. 1, p. 12, no. 1451; al-Majlisī, *Biḥār*, vol. 26, p. 279, no. 22. As it is reported in what follows in this tradition, Adam, who is also a prophet, remains indecisive and lacks the resolve to take the oaths of *walāya*; he thus does not deserve to be counted among the *ūlu'l-'azm*; the Qur'ānic verse, 'We had already made a Pact with Adam, but he forgot it: We have found no firm resolve in him' (*wa laqad 'ahidnā ilā Ādam min qablu fa-nasiya wa lam najid lahu 'azman*, Q 20:115) is understood in this sense. In other traditions, we are told that only later, after being materially created, does he recognise the sacred supremacy of the Impeccables, repents and takes the fourfold oath of fidelity and is redeemed (see, e.g., al-Majlisī, *Biḥār*, vol. 21, pp. 311–312, citing al-Kulaynī and Ibn Bābūya).

35. '*Kunnā arwāḥ nūr fa-nu'allimu'l-aẓilla asrār 'ilm al-tawḥīd wa'l-taḥmīd*'', Ibn 'Ayyāsh, *Muqtaḍab al-athar*, p. 23.

Praise, the formula for Unicity, and Glorification, to the angels.'[36] The luminous entities of the Prophet and the Imams, being the first created by God and the first to have recognised divine Unicity and Majesty, initiate the other shadows of the World of the Pact into what they have known and to what they have spent their time doing since the origin of this World, namely Unification and Glorification of the Lord. In a long *ḥadīth* reported by the eighth imam, ʿAlī b. Mūsā al-Riḍā, and the chain of transmission for which goes back from imam to imam as far as the Prophet, further details are brought of this Primordial Initiation; this is the tradition sometimes known by the title 'the superiority of the Prophet and the Proofs [i.e. the imams] over the angels' (*ḥadīth faḍl al-nabī wa'l-ḥujaj ʿalā'l-malā'ika*);[37] the Prophet said:

> ʿAlī, how could we not be superior to the angels when we preceded them (*sabaqnāhum*) in the knowledge of the Lord as well as in praising Him, in witnessing His Unicity, and in glorifying Him. Certainly our spirits were the first of God's creations, and

---

36. *'Kunnā ashbāḥ nūr nadūru ḥawla ʿarsh al-Raḥmān fa-nuʿallimu'l-malā'ika al-tasbīḥ wa'l-tahlīl wa'l-taḥmīd'*, Ibn Bābūya, *ʿIlal*, ch. 18, p. 23.

37. With some slight variation, Ibn Bābūya reports this tradition a number of times, in several of his works: *ʿIlal*, ch. 7, pp. 5f.; *Kamāl al-dīn*, ch. 23, pp. 254–55, no. 4; *ʿUyūn*, vol. 1, ch. 25, pp. 262f., no. 22. My translation is of the version from *ʿIlal*, which seems to be the most complete. The author most probably took the tradition from one of his no longer extant reference books: the *Kitāb tafḍīl al-anbiyā' wa'l-a'imma ʿalā'l-malā'ika* (cf. *ʿIlal*, pp. 20–27 and 211f.), a work by Muḥammad b. Baḥr al-Ruhnī (from Ruhn, not far from Kirmān, in Persia), the Imami author of at least three known works; apparently, all three have been lost, but fragments have survived thanks to later authors. They are, *al-Furūq bayna'l-abāṭīl wa'l-ḥuqūq* (cf. Ibn Bābūya, *ʿIlal*, pp. 211–220) and *al-Ḥujja fī ibṭā' al-qā'im* (cf. *Kamāl al-dīn*, vol. 2, pp. 352–357 and 417–423, and al-Ṭūsī, *Kitāb al-ghayba*, pp. 104–108 and 124–128). (We are greatly indebted to Professor Etan Kohlberg who, since the original French publication of this work, has pointed out a fourth title of al-Ruhnī's, *Muqaddimāt ʿilm al-Qur'ān*, cited by Ibn Ṭāwūs in his *Saʿd al-suʿūd* [Najaf, 1369/1950], pp. 227–228 and 279–281.) Al-Ruhnī lived from the middle of the third to the beginning of the fourth century AH; he is considered as an 'extremist' (*ghālī*) by some authors of Imami *Ṭabaqāt*. On Ruhnī, see e.g. al-Kashshī, *Ikhtiyār maʿrifat al-rijāl*, p. 147; al-Najāshī, *Rijāl*, pp. 189, 219, 271; al-Ṭūsī, *al-Fihrist* (ed. Najaf, 1356/1937), p. 132; Ibn Dāwūd al-Ḥillī, *Rijāl* (Najaf, 1972), pp. 270 and 277.

immediately thereafter He had us praise him and profess His Unicity. Then He created the angels, and when they contemplated our spirits in the form of a unique light, they recognised the grandeur of our Cause (*amr*); we began to praise [God] in order to teach the angels that we are created beings and that God is absolutely transcendent for us (*innahu munazzah ʿan ṣifātinā*). The angels, as they witnessed the divine transcendence, began to praise us. And when the angels saw the majesty of our rank (*sha'n*), we began to profess divine Unicity so that they might learn that there is no god but God (*lā ilāha illā llāh*) and that we are not gods, but only worshippers.... And when the angels saw the elevation of our position (*maḥall*), we began to bear witness to the grandeur of God, so that they might know that God is the greatest (*Allāhu akbar*).... And when the angels were witness to the noble force and power (*al-ʿizza wa'l-quwwa*) that God had placed in us, we began to recite: 'There is no force nor power but through God (*lā ḥawl wa lā quwwa illā bi'llāh*) so that the angels would know that we ourselves have no force or power but through God (*lā ḥawl lanā wa lā quwwa illā bi'illāh*).'[38] And when they saw that which God had so generously granted to us (*mā anʿama'llāh bihi ʿalaynā*) and how He had made obedience obligatory in our case, we said, 'Praise be to God' (*al-ḥamdu li'llāh*), so that the angels might learn our gratitude to God for this gift. And they repeated, 'Praise be to God.' It is thus thanks to us that the angels were guided towards knowledge of the Unicity of God and [knowledge of the words] of Unification and Glorification.[39]

---

38. The noun *ḥawl* had two principal meanings in early Arabic. The first is force, and the second is change, upheaval, transformation. Although in the holy words *lā ḥawl wa lā quwwa illā bi'llāh* only the first of these meanings can be applied, in the words of the Prophet *lā ḥawl lanā wa lā quwwa illā bi'llāh* (where just the word *lanā* is inserted into the sacred phrase), the ambiguity appears to have been kept on purpose, and applying the second meaning to the phrase gives, 'We are not subject to change and we have our Power only through God'; this latter is found in the versions of *ʿIlal al-sharā'iʿ* (p. 6) and *ʿUyūn akhbār al-Riḍā* (vol. 1, p. 263), but in *Kamāl al-dīn* (p. 255), the word *lanā* is taken out of the Prophet's speech, and one finds the sacred phrase as such.

39 Note that in what is taught during this Primoridal Initiation are found four phrases commonly used by all Muslims, as well as four phrases from the mystics' *dhikr: lā ilāha illā'llāh, Allāhu akbar, lā ḥawl wa lā quwwa illā bi'llāh,* and *al-ḥamdu li'llāh*; in the very first phase of initiation, although the phrase taught is not specified, it might be supposed that it is *subḥāna'llāh* ('We began to praise God', *fa-sabbaḥnā*), another phrase of *dhikr*. According to the mystics,

Another event is said to have taken place in the World of the shadows: the creation of Adam's descendants, in the form of particles, out of Earth and Water. The term 'Second World of Particles' might be fitting for this stage, since, on the one hand, it would explain the name attributed to the First World of Particles, and on the other hand it would correspond to this progressive creation of less and less subtle, more and more material worlds. In a commentary on Qur'ān 7:172 (cf. above), the fifth imam, Muḥammad al-Bāqir, relates words that his father, the fourth imam, 'Alī Zayn al-'Ābidīn, spoke in his presence:

> God took a handful of earth (*turāb*) from which he created Adam, and poured sweet, pleasant water into it, and left it for forty days; then he poured salty, brackish water[40] into it, and left it for another forty days; once the clay was ready to knead, he rubbed it vigorously, and out of it sprang the descendants of Adam, in the form of particles, from the right and left sides of this clay; God then ordered them into the fire. 'The People of the Right' (*aṣḥāb al-yamīn*) obeyed and the Fire became cold and harmless for them; 'The People of the Left' (*aṣḥāb al-shimāl*) disobeyed and refused to go into it.[41]

There is a whole series of cosmogonic traditions, both parallel and complementary, concerning the division of creatures into two opposite groups: there are the beings of light and knowledge on the

---

these phrases are extremely powerful and contain numerous spiritual secrets. Cf. also the words of Ja'far al-Ṣādiq: 'We taught the secrets of the Science of Unification and Glorification to the shadows.'

40. As will be seen (ch. 12) dark Ignorance (*al-jahl*) was created from the 'briny ocean' (*al-baḥr al-ujāj*), while Hiero-Intelligence (*al-'aql*), in the same way as the Impeccables, was that which was first created by God, proceeding from the divine light and taken from the right side of the Throne.

41. Al-Ṣaffār, *Baṣā'ir*, section 2, ch. 7, pp. 70 and 71, nos 2 and 6.; cf. also the same tradition with slight variations in al-Kulaynī, *al-Uṣūl*, 'Kitāb al-īmān wa'l-kufr', ch. 1, no. 1449, vol. 3, p. 10, no. 2. In tradition no. 1,448 from this same work, it is said that 'the People of the Right' are the people of obedience (*ṭā'a*) and Paradise, while 'the People of the Left' are those of disobedience (*ma'ṣiya*) and Hell; on the *aṣḥāb al-yamīn* and the *aṣḥāb al-shimāl*, see also Ibn 'Ayyāsh al-Jawharī, *Muqtaḍab al-athar*, pp. 9–10. These last expressions are from the Qur'ān (56:27 and 41).

one hand, and the beings of darkness and ignorance on the other: we have already seen the *ḥadīth* concerning the Armies of Hiero-Intelligence and those of Ignorance, the 'People of the Right' and those 'of the Left', and we will soon have occasion to see the case of the 'People of *ʿIlliyyīn*' and those of '*Sijjīn*'. These terms refer of course to the Imams and their initiated faithful in the former case, and to the enemies of the Imams and their partisans on the other.

Adam's offspring likewise took an oath before God, but this oath covers only one point: the Unicity of the Creator. Two important details accompany this fact. First, it is said that after this oath the original human nature (*fiṭra*) was marked by recognition of Divine Unicity, a recognition called '*islām*'; it is known that in Imami terminology this term, the opposite of '*īmān*', technically refers to exoteric submission to religion. The second is that all the descendants of Adam, the believers (*mu'min*) as well as the infidels (*kāfir*), took this oath. The 'believers' or the 'People of the Right' are at this stage the subtle materialisation of the human 'pure beings' of the First World of the Shadows; thus, they have already taken oaths of *walāya*, the oaths of the esoteric part of religion. The 'People of the Left', on the other hand, although monotheistic in their original nature, can only fall into 'infidelity', forget their oath and disobey God, since they have failed to recognise *walāya*.[42]

---

42. See al-Kulaynī, *al-Uṣūl*, vol. 3, ch. 5 ('Bāb fiṭrat al-khalq ʿalā'l-tawḥīd'), pp. 19–21; there are five traditions here, four of which date to Jaʿfar al-Ṣādiq, and the other to Muḥammad al-Bāqir. The five give commentaries on the following verses: Q 7:172 (cited above); 30:30 'according to the original nature that God gave to men' (*fiṭrat Allāh allatī faṭara'l-nās ʿalayhā*); 31:25 'And if you ask them who created the heavens and the earth, they answer: God' (*wa la'in sa'altahum man khalaqa'l-samāwāt wa'l-arḍ la-yaqūlunna Allāh*'), as well as in commentary on the Prophetic tradition: 'Each newborn child has the original nature' (*kullu mawlūd yūlad ʿalā'l-fiṭra*). The aim of these elements seems evident: first, to give an ontological and archetypal dimension to the opposition *mu'min/muslim*, and then to denounce the implicit infidelity of the 'Sunni'/exoteric Muslims who fail to recognise *walāya*. The choice of the terms *islām* and *muslim* to denote submission to the exoteric part of religion to the exclusion of the esoteric is evidently not gratuitous. On this concept, in a general sense, see G. Gobillot,

What characterises the Impeccables in this World of particles, besides their role as initiating masters of the 'pure beings', is what might be called the faculty of 'divine foresight'. What this means is that they 'see' in the particles (*al-dharr*) or in the 'clay' (*al-ṭīna*) of Adam's offspring (both the 'pure' and the 'impure') all his offspring's natures and their future destinies, down to the least of their thoughts, words and deeds. The miraculous powers of the imams, relative to the reading of thoughts and to physiognomy during their existence in the sensible world, are sometimes presented as resulting from a remembrance of what they had 'seen' in 'the clay' of men in the World of particles.[43] We thus see a kind of archetype of the two main traits of the existence of the imams in these two characteristics of the Impeccables, that is,

---

La conception originelle (fiṭra), ses interprétations et fonctions chez les penseurs musulmans (Cairo, 2000).

43. There are both traditions that allude to, and traditions that deal directly with, this gift of pre-existential 'seeing' of the Impeccables (called *ru'ya*, vision, or *'ilm al-ṭīna*, the science of the Clay, by the texts). 'The Day of Alliance with the Particles, God received the oaths of our faithful regarding the recognition of our mission as imams, recognition of his own lordship, and recognition of the prophetic mission of Muḥammad. Then he showed Adam's descendants to Muḥammad while they were still in the Clay, in the form of shadows; then he created them from the Clay with which he had created Adam, and the Messenger of God knew them and he made them known to 'Alī, and we [the other imams] also knew them' (the words of Abū Ja'far Muḥammad al-Bāqir, *'Inna'llāh akhadha mīthāq shī'atinā bi'l-walāya lanā wa hum dharr yawma akhdh al-mīthāq 'alā al-dharr wa'l-iqrār lahu bi'l-rubūbiyya wa li-Muḥammad bi'l-nubuwwa wa 'araḍa'llāh 'alā Muḥammad banī Ādam fi'l-ṭīn wa hum aẓilla wa-khalaqahum min al-ṭīnat allati khalaqa minhā Ādam wa 'arafahum rasūl Allāh wa 'arrafahum 'Alīyyan wa naḥnu na'rifuhum'*), al-Ṣaffar, *Baṣā'ir*, p. 89. 'The imam knows the characteristics and the names of his faithful as well as those of his enemies, thanks to his knowledge of the Clay from which they were created' (the words of Ja'far al-Ṣādiq, *'Inna'l-imām ya'rifu shi'atahu wa a'dā'ahu bi-wujūhihim wa asmā'ihim bi 'ilm al-ṭīnat allati khuliqū minhā'*) Ibn 'Ayyāsh, *Muqtaḍab*, p. 41; also, *Baṣā'ir*, p. 390; see also in this latter source, section 2, chs 14–16 (*bāb fī rasūl Allāh annahu 'arafa mā ra'a fi'l-aẓilla wa'l-dharr; bāb fī amīr al-mu'minīn annahu 'arafa mā ra'a fi'l-mīthāq; bāb fi'l-a'imma annahum ya'rifūna mā ra'aū fi'l-mīthāq*), pp. 83–90; for allusions to this subject, see, e.g., Ibn Bābūya, *'Ilal*, ch. 139, p. 173; *'Uyūn*, vol. 2, p. 227 and *Faḍā'il al-shī'a*, p. 31, no. 27.

Initiation and Divine Foresight, the traits being their initiatory knowledge and their ability to perform miracles. We shall return to both of these later.

The table here is an attempt to sum up the cosmogony and anthropogony of Twelver Shiʿism as covered so far in our discussion.

WORLDS	**INHABITANTS AND THEIR FUNCTIONS**
THE LIGHT OF GOD	
The Mother of the Book	The formless lights of the 'impeccables' *('aql)*
The First World of Particles or the World of Shadows or the World of the Pact	Lights formed from the Impeccables (Unification and Glorification) Initiation after the four oaths of recognition of the esoteric and the exoteric) Shadows of pure beings (angels, prophets, believers = the Armies of *'aql*) (the four oaths on the esoteric and the exoteric, followed by learning the secrets of Unification and the Glorification)
The Second World of Particles	Particles of Adam's descendants made out of Clay (the People of the Right = the Armies of *'aql* = the believers) (the People of the Left = the Armies of *jahl* = the adversaries) (the oath of recognition of the exoteric Unicity that characterises original nature)
Towards the creation of the material, sensible world	

Adamic humanity: the 'voyage' of the Light

It is after this event that the creation of the material world takes place, and it is within this world that the major event of the creation of spirits (*arwāḥ*), of hearts (*qulūb*), and of bodies (*abdān*) must be placed. Here again we are faced with the radical and omnipresent division of all beings into two opposing groups that have been in conflict with each other since the time of the creation. On one side are the Guides and their faithful, and on the other are the Enemies and their partisans. A substantial number of traditions supply the following material on the subject of these powerful parallels: the spirit and the heart (which is where the spirit is believed to reside) of the Impeccables were created out of a Clay located above the *'Illiyyin*, while their bodies were formed from the Clay of the *'Illiyyin* itself. The spirit and the heart of the faithful of the Imam, as well as the spirit and the heart of the prophets, were formed from the Clay of the body of the Imam, and the bodies of the faithful and of the prophet were formed from a Clay located beneath the *'Illiyyin*. On the other hand, the spirits, hearts and bodies of the Enemies of the Imam were formed from the Clay of the *Sijjīn*; the spirits and hearts of their partisans were formed from this same Clay, while their bodies were formed from a clay located below the *Sijjīn*.[44]

44. See, e.g., al-Ṣaffār, *Baṣā'ir*, section 1, chs 9 and 10, pp. 14–25; al-Kulaynī, *al-Uṣūl*, 'Kitāb al-ḥujja', 'Bāb khalq abdān al-a'imma wa arwāḥihim wa qulūbihim', vol. 2, pp. 232–234, and 'Kitāb al-imān wa'l-kufr', 'Bāb ṭīnat al-mu'min wa'l-kāfir', vol. 3, pp. 2–16. These traditions are not always clear, and in the work of al-Kulaynī, in particular, the confusion between the entities created on the one hand and the provenance of the Clay from which they were formed on the other, destroys the balance and the correspondence of the system. Al-Ṣaffār al-Qummī appears to be more methodical than his disciple in this regard; one of the traditions he reports seems to constitute a kind of systhesis of details on the subject, namely *Baṣā'ir al-darajāt*, section 1, ch. 9, p. 14, no. 2: 'The fifth imam said, "God created [the bodies of] Muḥammad and his family [i.e. Fāṭima and the imams] from the Clay of *'Illiyyin*, and he created their spirits and their hearts from a Clay located above the *'Illiyyin*, He created

[above the *ʿIlliyyin*] the spirits and hearts of the Impeccables	
[*ʿIlliyyin*] the bodies of the Impeccables	[*Sijjīn*] spirits, hearts, and bodies of the Enemies
Spirits and hearts of their faithful, and of the prophets	Spirits and hearts of their partisans
[below the *ʿIlliyyin*] bodies of the faithful of the Impeccables, and those of the prophets	[below the *Sijjīn*] bodies of the partisans of the Enemies

The terms *ʿIlliyyūn* (*ʿIlliyyin* in the accusative) and *Sijjīn* are from the Qurʾān, and are seen, respectively, in verses 18–21 and 7–9 of Sura 83 (*Surat al-Muṭaffifīn*):

[the bodies] of our faithful as well as [those] of the prophets from a Clay found beneath the *ʿIlliyyin*, while he created their spirits and their hearts from the Clay of the *ʿIlliyyin* itself. This is why the hearts of our faithful come from the bodies of the Family of Muḥammad. Likewise, God created the enemy of the Family of the Prophet [his spirit, his heart and his body] as well as the spirits and the hearts of his partisans, from the Clay of the *Sijjīn*, and [the bodies of] the latter from a clay located below the *Sijjīn*; this explains how the hearts of the partisans come from the bodies of the others [i.e. their leaders, the enemies of the imams], and why all hearts long for their bodies." ' This material constitutes the theoretical bases of an ancient spiritual practice, perhaps the most important, the 'vision with the heart', see *Guide divin*, pp. 112–145 and, in this book, Chapters 10 and 11. On this subject, see also Ibn Bābūya, *ʿIlal*, ch. 96, p. 117, nos. 12–15. A kind of dualism can be seen here. The Qurʾān speaks of a number of creatures made of different substances (the angels of light, the *jinn* of fire and human beings of clay), but in no case are creatures made of two different substances. This concerns a kind of dualism, of course not the principal kind, but consisting of a division of nature. The pre-existential 'worlds' are reminiscent of various Iranian speculations about the creation in the *mênôg* state; the cosmic battle from the origin of creation has shades of the Iranian myth of the Primordial War (cf. Chapter 12). Nonetheless, this radical dualism is sometimes nuanced by rare traditions; see, e.g., *Baṣāʾir*, section 1, ch. 9, pp. 15–17, nos 5, 7, 8, 10 (the 'mixture of Clays').

> Surely, the Book of the Pure is in the *'Illiyyin*
> And what will have you know what the *'Illiyyūn* is?
> It is a Book covered with characters
> Those who are admitted into the Proximity of God will see it.[45]
> Surely, the Book of the impious is in the *Sijjīn*
> And what will have you know what the *Sijjīn* is?
> It is a Book covered with characters.[46]

Commentators have identified *'Illiyyin* and *Sijjīn* respectively as one of the highest levels of Paradise and one of the lowest levels of Hell; the root *'-l-w* or *'-l-y* evokes the idea of elevation, of height, of domination, and the root *s-j-n* that of imprisonment, detention and burying in the ground. Similarly, some authors have also seen, as the Qur'ānic text appears to suggest, that the 'names' of the elect and the damned are given in the two divine books. In this sense, *'Illiyyūn* (the term also exists in Hebrew and in Chaldean, where it refers to something placed highly, or at a high elevation) may be compared to the 'Book of Life' of Judeo-Christian tradition (cf. Exodus 32:32–33; Daniel 12:1; Psalms 69:29; Luke 10:20; Revelation 20:15, etc.). In Imami tradition, the Qur'ānic texts cited previously are almost always accompanied by the *ḥadīth* concerning creation that derives from the*'Illiyyin* and *Sijjīn*, and even though there is a lack of detail from the imams on the subject,[47] it would appear as though the two concepts (the

---

45. *Kallā inna kitāb al-abrār la-fī 'Illiyyin/wa mā adrāka mā 'Illiyyūn/kitābun marqūm/yashhaduhu'l-muqarrabūn.*

46. *Kallā inna kitāb al-fujjār la-fī Sijjīn/wa mā adrāka mā Sijjīn/kitābun marqūm.*

47. According to a tradition going back to al-Bāqir, *'Illiyyin* and *Sijjīn* denote, respectively, the 'seventh heaven' and the 'seventh earth' (al-Qummī, *Tafsīr*, under Q 83:7–9, 18–21); in a tradition that the same author attributes to Ja'far, 'the impious' of the Qur'ānic verse are identified as Abū Bakr and 'Umar, just as 'the pure' are identified as the Fourteen Impeccables (ibid.). In Ja'far al-Ṣādiq's *Tafsīr* there are interesting details about 'the pure ones' (*abrār*) and 'the impious' (*fujjār*) that the Qur'ānic text directly relates to *'Illiyyin* and *Sijjīn*, respectively. Commenting on Q 82:12–13: 'Yes, the pure ones [will be plunged] into felicity and the impious into a furnace' (*inna'l-abrāra la-fī na'īm wa inna'l-fujjāra la-fī jaḥīm*), he says, 'Felicity is knowledge and contemplation

name of the place and the name of the Book) are equally present. It should be added that in early Imamism a cosmic book could denote a metaphysical world, such as we saw in the case of the Original World of *umm al-kitāb*.[48] In one of Jaʿfar al-Ṣādiq's traditions, *ʿIlliyyin* is replaced by the Throne:

> God created us [i.e. our entities of light or our spirits] from the light of His Majesty, then He gave form to our creation (*ṣawwara khalqanā*) from a well-guarded secret Clay taken from under the Throne, and He had our light inhabit our form; we are thus luminous human creatures (*naḥnu khalqan wa basharan nūrāniyyīn*), endowed with that which God has not bestowed upon any other. And He created the spirits of our faithful from our Clay, and their bodies from another, well guarded and secret, but lower than ours.

(*al-naʿīm al-maʿrifa wa'l-mushāhada*) and the furnace is ignorance and obscurity' (*al-jaḥīm al-jahl wa'l-ḥijāb*, lit. 'being hidden behind a veil'); another 'reading': 'the furnace is those [carnal] souls for whom the fires of Hell have been lit' (*al-jaḥīm al-nufūs fa-inna lahā nayrān tattaqid*), ed. P. Nwyia, p. 228 [501]). Although in al-Sulamī's recension the technical terms used take on a connotation of orthodox 'mysticism', it must be pointed out that in an early Imami context, these terms are charged with doctrinal meanings; 'knowledge' is divine knowledge, of course, but this is not possible except through knowledge of the Imam, who by his ontological status and because of his cosmic role is that aspect of God that can be known; 'contemplation' is vision of the luminous entity of the Imam in the subtle centre of the heart, thus constituting the vision of the 'Face of God' (see Chapter 3 here); the terms 'ignorance' and 'obscurity' are likewise to be understood in this context. For the different interpretations of *ʿIlliyyin* in the Imami tradition, see al-Majlisī, *Biḥār*, vol. 3, p. 65; for a general view, see R. Paret in *EI2* under *ʿIlliyyin*.

48. In Imamism, the 'Book' (*kitāb*), as a concept, is of particular doctrinal importance; the 'Book' is the container, the vehicle of essential knowledge, of the science of realities in a general as well as a particular sense; a certain correspondence can be detected between the 'Superior Books' (*umm al-kitāb, ʿIlliyyin*) that contain 'information' of a divine order and 'the speaking book' that the imam is, the vehicle for all the sacred sciences (cf. the expression *kitāb nāṭiq/Qur'ān nāṭiq*, referring to the IMAM; see, e.g., the 'index' to the *Biḥār*, entitled *Safīnat al-Biḥār*, by ʿAbbās al-Qummī, ed. 1355/1936, and also M. Ayoub, 'The Speaking Qur'ān and the Silent Qur'ān', in A. Rippin [ed.], *Approaches to the History of the Interpretation of the Qur'ān* [Oxford, 1988], pp. 177, 198); this correspondence might similarly be considered as between *Sijjīn*'s 'Inferior Book' and the Enemies of the Imams, the Guides of Darkness (*a'immat al-ẓalām*).

> Other than our faithful and the prophets, God endowed no other creatures in this way. It is for this reason that only we and they [i.e., our initiated disciples, the pure human beings, the prophets, and the faithful of the imams] deserve to be called men, while the others are no more than gnats destined for the fires of Hell [lit. 'this is why we and they have become men and the other men, gnats destined for the fires of Hell' (*wa li-dhālik ṣirnā naḥnu wa hum al-nās wa ṣāra sā'iru'l-nās hamajan li'l-nār wa ilā'l-nār*)].[49]

Two points from this series of traditions should be borne in mind. First of all, there is the fact of finding this equality of 'level of being' between the faithful of the imams (that is, the 'believers' who have been initiated into the esoteric dimension of religion) on the one hand, and the prophets on the other. This implies the same spiritual status for both. These two groups of humans, like the angels (as we have seen), created simultaneously in the form of shadows in the First World of Particles, together took the four oaths of fidelity and were initiated by the Impeccables into the secrets of the Sacred Sciences. According to Imami tradition, those initiated into the esoteric dimension of religion have the same spiritual 'weight' as the prophets in the universal economy of the Sacred and in the battle against the Armies of Ignorance. The second point that should be taken into consideration is the consubstantiality of the heart of the faithful believer and the body of the imam. This fact constitutes the cosmogonic and propositional basis for

49. Al-Kulaynī, *al-Uṣūl*, 'Kitāb al-ḥujja', 'Bāb khalq abdān al-a'imma', vol. 2, no. 2, pp. 232–233; for the replacement of *'Illiyyin* by *'arsh*, see also al-Ṣaffār, *Baṣā'ir*, section 1, ch. 9, no. 12, p. 17. It would be interesting to show how in Sunni tradition, Mecca (and sometimes Medina) constitutes the terrestrial counterpart to the celestial Abode with the Clay from which the Prophet was created; cf. e.g. al-Zurqānī, *Sharḥ*, vol. 1, p. 43; al-Ḥalabī, *al-Sīra al-ḥalabiyya*, vol. 1, p. 147; for other sources, see M. J. Kister, 'You Shall Only Set Out for Three Mosques', *Muséon*, 82 (1969), p. 187, n. 63. The mention of Medina is undoubtedly due to the belief that the clay of each individual comes from the place where he will be buried (*turbatu'l-shakhṣ madfanuhu*), see, e.g., al-Zurqānī, *Sharḥ*, vol. 1, pp. 42–43. On this subject, see also H. Corbin, *Temple et contemplation* (Paris, 1980), index under 'Ka'ba' and 'Mekke'.

the most important spiritual practice in early Imamism, that of the practice of vision with (or in) the heart (*al-ruʾya biʾl-qalb*).[50]

At the time of the creation of the human race, the single and dual Light of prophecy/imamate, also called the Light of Muḥammad and ʿAlī, was placed in Adam by God;[51] it was because of this light that the angels were commanded to prostrate themselves before Adam, which they all did with the exception of Iblīs, who was forever damned by God because of his haughty disobedience:[52] 'Then

50. Amir-Moezzi, *Guide divin*, Part II-3 (excursus) (*Divine Guide*, Part II-3 [excursus]), and here below, Chapters 10 and 11.

51. This probably refers to Adam in the present cycle of humanity; actually, the belief in cyclical creations and successive humanities exists in early Imamism, although no specific details or developments are furnished on the subject by the imams; the tradition upon which this belief is based can be found in a commentary by Muḥammad al-Bāqir on Q 50:15: 'Are We [God is speaking] then fatigued from the first creation, such that they are in doubt about a new creation?' (*ʾa fa-ʿayīnā biʾl-khalq al-awwal bal hum fī labsin min khalqin jadīd*); Muḥammad al-Bāqir: 'When these creatures and this world are annihilated by God (*inna llāha ʿazza wa jall idhā afnā hādhāʾl-khalq wa hādhāʾl-ʿālam*) and the people of Paradise and Hell inhabit the Abodes that they deserve, God will create a new world different from this one, with other creatures, not divided into male and female (*min ghayr fuḥūla wa lā unāth*), who will worship Him and will bear witness to His Unicity; and He will create a new earth to support them, and to give them refuge He will create a new sky. Do you think that this is the only world God created? That he did not create races of humanity other than you (*basharan ghayrakum*)? Certainly not, for He has created thousands upon thousands of worlds with thousands upon thousands of Adams, and you dwell upon only the last of these worlds, in the midst of the last of these Adamic humanities (*laqad khalaqa Allāh alfa alf ʿālamin wa alfa alf Ādama anta fī ākhir tilkaʾl-ʿawālim wa ulāʾika al-ādamiyyin*). Cf. Ibn Bābūya, *Kitāb al-tawḥīd*, ch. 38, p. 277, no. 2; the speaker for the fifth imam is here Abū ʿAbd Allāh Jābir b. Yazīd al-Juʿfī (d. 128/745 or 132/749), the famous disciple of the fifth and sixth imams to whom we owe the transmission of a great number of traditions of a theosophical nature; on him, see, e.g., al-Kashshī, *Rijāl*, p. 126; al-Najāshī, *Rijāl*, see index; al-Ṭūsī, *Rijāl*, p. 111, no. 6, and p. 163, no. 30; al-Ardabīlī, *Jāmiʿ al-ruwāt* (Qumm, 1331 Sh./1953), vol. 1, p. 144. The doctrinal developments of the theme of successive creations can, in particular, be attributed to Ismaili authors; on this subject, see esp. H. Corbin, *Temps cyclique et gnose ismaélienne* (Paris, 1982).

52. Cf. also Q 7:11f.; 15:26f.; 17:61f.; 18:50; 38:74f. Iblīs is regarded in Imami traditions as the archetypal personification of the 'guides of darkness', the 'enemies of the imams and of the Shiʿi' (the *nawāṣib* in general); he is the first

God created Adam and deposited us in his loins and commanded the angels to prostrate themselves before him so that we might be glorified (through Adam); their prostration was the proof of their adoration of God and their respect and obedience towards Adam because of our presence in his loins.'[53]

Starting from Adam, this Light begins its 'voyage' through the generations of humanity, traversing the manifestations of time and space of the sacred history of (the present?) humanity, to reach its ultimate predestined vehicles, the historical Muḥammad and the historical 'Alī, and to be transmitted through them to the other imams. The Prophet said:

> We were silhouettes of light until God wanted to create our form; He transformed us into a column of light (*ṣayyaranā 'amūda nūrin*) and hurled us into Adam's loins; then He caused us to be transmitted through the loins of fathers and the wombs of mothers without our being touched by the filth of associationism or any adultery due to unbelief (*akhrajanā ilā aṣlāb al-ābā' wa arḥām al-ummahāt wa lā yuṣībunā najas al-shirk wa lā sifāḥ al-kufr*); and when He had us reach the loins of 'Abd al-Muṭṭalib [the grandfather of both the Prophet and 'Alī], He divided the light in two and placed half in the loins of 'Abd Allāh [the Prophet's father] and the other half in the loins of Abū Ṭālib [the Prophet's uncle and the father of 'Alī]; Āmina [the Prophet's mother] received in her breast the half that was for me, and she brought me into the world; likewise, Fāṭima the daughter of Asad [the mother of 'Alī] received in her breast the half that was for 'Alī, and brought him into the world. Then God had the column [of light] come to me and I begat Fāṭima; likewise, He made it go to 'Alī and he begat al-Ḥasan and

---

to have failed to recognise the light of prophecy/imamate; from this perspective, he may be identified with *jahl*, the universal counter-power of Ignorance and Darkness (*Divine Guide*, part I.1, and, in this book, Chapter 12).

53. The prophetic *ḥadīth* of 'the superiority of the Prophet and the Proofs over the angels', Ibn Bābūya, *'Ilal*, p. 6, *Kamāl al-dīn*, p. 255: '*thumma inna llāha tabārak wa ta'ālā khalaqa Ādam fa-awda'anā ṣulbahu wa amara'l-malā'ika bi'l-sujūd lahu ta'ẓīman lanā wa ikrāman wa kāna sujūduhum li'llāh 'azza wa jall 'ubūdiyyatan wa li-Ādam ikrāman wa ṭā'atan li-kawninā fī ṣulbih.*'

al-Ḥusayn.... Thus, this light will be transmitted from imam to imam until the Day of Resurrection.[54]

---

54. Ibn Bābūya, *'Ilal*, vol. 1, ch. 156, p. 209; the phrase about 'the loins of the fathers and the wombs of the mothers' being free from any impiety or infidelity refers to the religious status of the genealogical ancestors of the Prophet, a problem dealt with at length in the literature of the *sīra* and the *Ḥadīth*; from the Imami point of view, all the ancestors of the Prophet, and consequently of the imams, were 'Muslims' in the sense of being 'monotheists', and practised the religion of Abraham, that of the *ḥanīfs*; this fact implies, among other things, that their children were not illegal, and thus the allusion to 'adultery due to infidelity' (cf., e.g., Ibn Bābūya, *Amālī*, 'majlis' 89, p. 614, no. 11; Ibn Shahrāshūb, *Manāqib āl Abī Ṭālib*, vol. 1, pp. 37f. and 132f.; al-Majlisī, *Biḥār*, vol. 11, pp. 10f., and vol. 15, pp. 117–127 and 172f.: *'Ittafaqati'l-imāmiyya 'alā anna wālidayi'l-rasūl wa kulla ajdādih ilā Ādam kānū muslimīn bal kānū min al-ṣiddīqīn wa'l-ḥunafā'*"). A great number of Sunni authors are of the same opinion, emphasising especially the monotheism of 'Abd al-Muṭṭalib and his sons, 'Abd Allāh and Abū Ṭālib (see, e.g., Ibn Sa'd, *Ṭabaqāt*, vol. 1 (1), pp. 1, 2, 5, 31: the Prophet: *'innamā kharajtu min nikāḥ wa lam akhruj min sifāḥ min ladun Ādam lam yuṣibnī min sifāḥ ahl al-jāhiliyya shay'un*'; al-Bayhaqī, *Dalā'il al-nubuwwa*, vol. 1, pp. 131f.; al-Suyūṭī, *al-Khaṣā'iṣ al-kubrā*, vol. 1, pp. 93–96; Ibn al-Jawzī, *al-Wafā bī aḥwāl al-Muṣṭafā fi'l-ta'rīkh* [Hyderabad, 1357/1938], vol. 1, pp. 35f. and 77–78; al-Qasṭallānī, *Irshād al-sārī li sharḥ Ṣaḥīḥ al-Bukhārī* [Beirut, 1323/1905], vol. 6, pp. 31f.; al-Ḥalabī, *al-Ṣīrat al-ḥalabiyya*, vol. 1, pp. 42f.; al-Zurqānī, *Sharḥ*, vol. 1, pp. 66f., 174f.). It seems to have been above all the Hashimid tradition, pro-Shi'i but especially pro-'Abbasid, that glorified the religious excellence of the Prophet's ancestors in general, and that of 'Abd al-Muṭṭalib in particular, in its propaganda against the Umayyads; let it be remembered that 'Abd al-Muṭṭalib is the common ancestor of 'Abd Allāh, Abū Ṭālib and al-'Abbās; as their ancestor, he is presented as a monotheist, as pious and emanating the light of prophecy that he carried within him; Umayya, the ancestor of the Umayyads, is presented as his exact opposite (cf., e.g., Ibn Hishām — the Hashimid sympathies of his teacher, Ibn Isḥāq, are well known — *al-Sīrat al-nabawiyya*, vol. 1, p. 180; al-Balādhurī, *Ansāb al-ashrāf*, vol. 4b, p. 18 — the words of 'Abd Allāh b. Abbās against the Umayyad caliph Yazīd b. Mu'āwiya and reported by 'Awāna b. al-Ḥakam [d. 147/764]; on him and his pro-'Abbasid sympathies, see *GAS*, vol. 1, p. 307, and esp. A. A. Dūrī, *Nash'at al-'ilm al-ta'rīkh' inda'l-'arab* [Beirut, 1960], pp. 36f.; for the opposition of 'Abd al-Muṭṭalib and Umayya, see also al-Iṣfahānī, *Kitāb al-aghānī*, vol. 1, pp. 8–9). Fakhr al-Dīn Rāzī, while deductively demonstrating the truth of this detail concerning 'genealogical purity', implicitly recognises its Shi'i origin (*al-Tafsīr al-kabīr* [Beirut, 1981–1983], vol. 24, pp. 173–174); actually, a certain number of Sunni scholars, beginning with the famous Muslim, reacted rather quickly to the assertion that the immediate forebears of the Prophet were 'Muslims'. Muslim

This tradition and others – especially the terms used therein, particularly 'loins' (*aṣlāb*) and 'wombs' (*arḥām*) – suggest that the transmission of the legacy of light takes place physically, via the seminal substance. This substance, containing the light of prophecy/imamate (and for the majority of Sunni authors, the light of prophecy only), adorns the body, and particularly the forehead, of the individual that conveys it with a supernatural brilliance;[55] but according to another series of traditions, this transmission also takes place, this time by a spiritual route, along the initiatory chain of the prophets and their heirs (*waṣī*, pl. *awṣiyā'*), that is, their imams. In contrast to the Sunni tradition, here all the ancestors of the Prophet, be they spiritual or physical, were illumined by the single light of Muḥammad and 'Alī, a light that is divided, as we have seen, only when it reaches 'Abd al-Muṭṭalib. The Prophet says, "Alī and I were created from the same light…. When Adam reached Paradise, we were in him [lit. in his loins]…. When Noah boarded the Ark, we were in him; when Abraham was thrown into the fire, we were in him…. God never ceased transmitting us from pure loins to pure wombs (*wa lam yazal yanqulunā'llāhu 'azza wa jall min aṣlāb ṭāhira ilā arḥām ṭāhira*) until the moment we reached 'Abd al-Muṭṭalib; there, he divided our light in two.'[56]

---

relates the *ḥadīth* where the Prophet says to a convert: 'My father and yours are now in hell' (Muslim, *Ṣaḥīḥ*, vol. 1, pp. 132–133; see also al-Zurqānī, *Sharḥ*, vol. 1, p. 79, where he refers to Muslim, adding that by his father the Prophet actually meant Abū Ṭālib, who had brought him up: '*Wa arāda bi-abīhi annahu Abū Ṭālib wa li-annahu rabbāhu wa al-'arab tussamī'l-murabbī aban*'; see also al-Ḥalabī, *al-Ṣīrat al-ḥalabiyya*, vol. 1, p. 29; al-Ṭabarī, *Jāmi' al-bayān*, vol. 11, pp. 30–31). For other Sunni sources, see C. Gilliot, 'Muqātil', *JA*, 279 (1991), pp. 68–70.

55. On this subject and the sources, both Shi'i and Sunni, see Rubin, 'Pre-Existence and Light', pp. 62–119; for the Light of 'Abd al-Muṭṭalib, pp. 94–96; for that of 'Abd Allāh and Āmina, pp. 84–89; for that of Abū Ṭālib, pp. 75–76.

56. Ibn Bābūya, *'Ilal*, ch. 116, pp. 134–135; see also Ibn Bābūya, *Kamāl al-dīn*, vol. 1, ch. 24, p. 275, no. 25. For the presence of the light of *nubuwwa/walāya* in Adam, see also Ibn 'Ayyāsh, *Muqtaḍab*, p. 32; al-Majlisī, *Biḥār*, vol. 21, pp. 311–312; in Abraham, see Ibn 'Ayyāsh, *Muqtaḍab*, p. 33; al-Majlisī, *Biḥār*, vol. 21, p. 315; in Moses, see Ibn 'Ayyāsh, *Muqtaḍab*, p. 41; and al-Majlisī,

In fact, Imami tradition recognises two distinct genealogies for the Prophet and the imams; the first, which might be called 'natural descent', corresponds basically, although there have been the inevitable alterations in certain names, to one or other of the classical genealogies of the Prophet in Sunni literature. The second, 'spiritual descent', which is composed of the uninterrupted chain of the prophets and their imams since the time of Adam, is typically Imami.[57] The classical sources have been used in constructing these two lists (Ibn Bābūya and Ibn ʿAyyāsh al-Jawharī in particular); they have been completed and checked, on the one hand using the details available in the *Ithbāt al-waṣiyya*, an Imami work attributed to al-Masʿūdī (d. 345/956) and dedicated entirely to the idea of Imami *waṣiyya*,[58] and on the other hand with the biblical names; some names, nevertheless, remain unidentifiable.

Biḥār, vol. 51, p. 149. The idea of Muḥammad's prophetic descent is also admitted in the Sunni tradition, but despite the opinion of Goldziher, who sees a Neoplatonic kind of spiritual transmission ('Neuplatonische und Gnostische Elemente im Hadīt', p. 340), for Sunni authors it appears to be more a case of a physical transmission via seminal fluid; cf. Ibn Saʿd, *Ṭabaqāt*, vol. 1/1, p. 5 ('*wa min nabiyyin ilā nabiyyin wa min nabiyyin ilā nayiyyin ḥattā akhrajaka nabiyyan*'), also Ibn Kathīr, *Tafsīr* (Beirut, 1966), vol. 5, p. 215 ('*yaʿnī taqallubahu min ṣulbi nabiyyin ilā ṣulbi nabiyyin ḥattā akhrajahu nabiyyan*'); al-Suyūṭī, *al-Khaṣāʾiṣ*, vol. 1, p. 94 ('*Mā zālaʾl-nabiyyu yataqallabu fī aṣlāb al-anbiyāʾ ḥattā waladathu ummuhu*'); cf. also al-Zurqānī, *Sharḥ*, vol. 1, p. 67 and al-Ḥalabī, *al-Ṣīrat al-ḥalabiyya*, vol. 1, p. 29. For some authors it was the 'seal' marked on the body of the Prophet by the prophetic light that made him the 'Seal of the prophets'; on this subject and on theological discussions on this theme, which ended up being an Islamic article of faith, see H. Birkland, *The Legend of Opening of Muḥammad's Breast* (Oslo, 1955); Y. Friedmann, 'Finality of Prophethood in Sunni Islam', *JSAI*, 7 (1986), pp. 177–215.

57. This double genealogy is reminiscent of the double 'natural' and 'royal' descent of Jesus (in Luke 3:23–38 and Matthew 1:1–17, respectively); as will be seen, there is considerable overlap in the ancestors who appear on the two lists.

58. *Ithbāt al-waṣiyya liʾl-imām ʿAlī b. Abī Ṭālib ʿalayhiʾl-salām*, attributed to al-Masʿūdī (Najaf, n.d.); on this work and the problems of its attribution, see Ch. Pellat, 'Masʿūdī et l'imāmisme', in *Le Shīʿisme imāmite*, pp. 69–90.

1) Natural genealogy, in ascending order: Muḥammad – ʿAbd Allāh (or Abū Ṭālib) – ʿAbd al-Muṭṭalib – Hāshim – ʿAbd Manāf – Quṣayy (or Fihr) – Kilāb – Murra – Kaʿb – Luʾayy – Ghālib – (Fihr) – Mālik-al-Naḍr (or Quraysh) – Kināna – Khuzayma–Mudrika – Ilyās – Muḍar – Nizār – Maʿadd – ʿAdnān–Ūdd – Udad–al-Yasaʿ – al-Hamyasaʿ – Salāmān – Nabt – Ḥaml – Qaydār – Ismail/Ishmael (the father of the Arabs), and from there, we pass on the the non-Arabs: Abraham, Terah (Tāriḥ) – Nahor (Nāḥūr) – Serug (Sarūgh) – Reu (Arʿū) – Peleg (Fālij) – Eber (Hābir) – Shelah (Shāliḥ) – Arpachshad (Arfahshad) – Shem – Noah – Lamech (Lāmak) – Methuselah (Mattūshalaḥ) – Enoch (Ukhnūkh)/Idris – Jared (Yārad) – Mahalaleel (Mahlāʾīl) – Cainan (Qaynān) – Enos (Anūsh) – Seth (Shīth) – Adam.[59]

2) Spiritual genealogy, in descending order: Adam, Seth (Shīth/Hibatu'llāh) – Cainan – MkhLT (alteration of Mahlāʾīl/Mahalaleel) – Maḥūq (?) – Ghathmīshā (or Ghanmīshā, or Ghathmīthā?) – Enoch/Idrīs – Noah – Shem – Ghāthās (or ʿAthāmir?) – Barghīshāsā (or Barʿīthāshā?) – Japhet (Yāfith) – BRH (alteration of Tārih/Terah?) – JFNH (or JFSH or JFĪSH?) – ʿImrān – Abraham – Ishmael – Isaac – Jacob/Israel – Joseph – Bithriyā (?) – Shuʿayb – Moses – Joshua (Yūshaʿ) – David – Solomon – Āṣaf b. Barakhiyā – Zachariah – Jesus – Simeon (Shamʿūn) – John (Yaḥyā) – Mundhir b. Shamʿūn – Salama (or Salīma) – Barda (or Barza or Bāliṭ or Abī, this last name referring perhaps to a 'father' of the church?) – Muḥammad –ʿAlī – the eleven imams.[60]

A few of the biblical prophets (especially the *ūlu'l-ʿazm*) and their imams are common to the two lists; what gives them this high

59. Cf., e.g., Ibn ʿAyyāsh, *Muqtaḍab*, pp. 51–52; *Ithbāt al-waṣiyya*, pp. 75–90; compare with al-Masʿūdī, *Murūj al-dhahab*, ed. Barbier de Meynard, vol. 1, pp. 80–83, and vol. 4, p. 115.

60. Cf., e.g., Ibn Bābūya, *Kamāl al-dīn*, vol. 1, ch. 22, pp. 211–213, no. 1, ch. 58, nos 4 and 5, and vol. 2, p. 644; Ibn Bābūya, *Kitāb al-faqīh*, vol. 4, ch. 72, pp. 129–130; this spiritual filiation takes up nearly seventy pages of the *Ithbāt al-waṣiyya* (pp. 8–74), where the list is more than twice as long (seventy-six names instead of thirty-five); the author attempts to place the prophets and their heirs 'historically' by giving the names of biblical prophets and the kings contemporary with them, those of Persia and of Greece; compare with the *Murūj al-dhahab*, vol. 1, pp. 72–73. See also the excellent article by E. Kohlberg, 'Some Shiʿi Views on the Antediluvian World', *SI*, 52 (1980), pp. 41–66.

religious rank is the presence in them of the light of Muḥammad and ʿAlī (and thus, of the eleven other imams, since ʿAlī represents all of them). This is why, throughout the Imami tradition, the imams are constantly compared to the prophets and saints of Israel, although they are superior to them, since it is through the light of the imams that they have acquired their sacred status. Muḥammad said:

> I am the master of the prophets; my heir [ʿAlī] is the master of the *waṣiyyūn,* and his *awṣiyāʾ* [the other imams] the masters of the other *awṣiyāʾ* '[*waṣiyyūn* and *awsiyā*, lit. 'heirs'; is there a difference between these terms? Why use two different terms?]; the sages [we will see that in early Imami terminology *ʿālim*, pl. *ʿulamāʾ*, refers to the imam as spiritual initiator] are the heirs of the prophets; the sages of my Community are like the prophets of the people of Israel.[61]

61. *ʿAnā sayyid al-anbiyāʾ wa waṣiyyī sayyid al-waṣiyyin wa awṣiyāʾuhu sāda'l-awṣiyāʾ ... al-ʿulamāʾ warathat al-anbiyāʾ ...ʿulamāʾ ummatī ka-anbiyāʾ Banī Isrāʾīl*', cf., e.g., al-Ṣaffār, *Baṣāʾir*, section 1, ch. 2; Ibn Bābūya, *Kamāl al-dīn*, pp. 211–212. For comparisons between the Impeccables and the prophets and saints of the Bible, see, e.g., Ibn Bābūya, *Kamāl al-dīn*, pp. 25–26 ('Alī has the qualities of the earlier prophets); Ibn Shahrāshūb, *Manāqib*, vol. 3, p. 46 (the relationship between the Prophet and ʿAlī is compared to that of Moses and Joshua; al-Shahrastānī takes the origin of this idea back to the mysterious partisan of ʿAlī, ʿAbd Allāh b. Saba', cf. *al-Milal wa'l-niḥal*, ed. Kaylānī [Cairo, 1967], vol. 1, p. 174; M. G. S. Hodgson, 'Abd Allāh b. Saba', *EI2*), vol. 2, p. 219 ('Alī compared with Aaron), vol. 3, p. 166 (al-Ḥasan and al-Ḥusayn compared with the two sons of Aaron, Shabar and Shubayr), vol. 2, p. 164 ('Alī compared with Shem), vol. 1, p. 258 (the twelve imams and the twelve chiefs, *naqībs*, of the Tribes of Israel); al-Masʿūdī, *Ithbāt al-waṣiyya*, p. 259 (the twelve imams and the twelve apostles of Jesus); al-Khawārizmī, *al-Manāqib*, Najaf, 1965, p. 85 (al-Ḥasan and Abraham, al-Ḥusayn and Moses, ʿAlī b. al-Ḥusayn and Aaron); in certain traditions the imams are considered prophets, even by their adversaries (al-Kulaynī, *al-Rawḍa*, vol. 1, p. 173, the words of the Umayyad Hishām b. ʿAbd al-Malik; Ibn Bābūya, *Amālī*, 'majlis' 47, p. 278, no. 4, the words of the Khawārij). On this theme, see also A. J. Wensinck, 'Muḥammad und die Propheten', *Acta Orientalia*, 2 (1924); R. Selheim, 'Prophet, Chalif und Geschichte', *Oriens*, 18–19 (1965–1966); M. J. Kister, 'Ḥaddithū 'an Banī Isrā'īl', *IOS*, 2 (1972).

The transmission of light constitutes perhaps the most important element of the key idea of *waṣiyya*.[62] In the texts, this transmission is referred to as *naql* (transport, transferal), *taqallub* (return, an allusion to the 'return trip' that the Light takes back to Muḥammad and 'Alī, its first source; or derived from the term *qālab*, the 'cernal envelope' here inhabited by the Light), or *tanāsukh*, which in the context of certain transmigrationist trends in Islam is usually translated as 'metempsychosis',[63] but which here must be translated rather as 'metemphotosis' (lit. 'the displacement of light'). In one of his sermons, 'Alī states: 'God deposited them [i.e. the light of the Impeccables carried by the seminal substance] in the most noble places they could be placed, and had them rest in the best of resting places; the glorious loins assured their transmission to the purified wombs.'[64] The Shi'i

---

62. The 'Sacred Legacy' is composed of a certain number of material objects also: the Sacred Books of the earlier prophets, the Secret Books (*Jafr*, *Jāmi'a* etc.), and certain objects with supernatural powers that belonged to the prophets (Adam's cloak, the Ark of the Covenant for Moses, and the weapon of Muḥammad). Here again, we find the two ideas of Knowledge and Power that characterised the pre-existence of the Imams and that will continue to characterise their existence. 'The written investiture' (*al-naṣṣ*) is merely the evidence of the transmission of the 'Legacy' designed to prove to the faithful the authenticity of the heir (on the *naṣṣ* of the imams, see, e.g., al-Kulaynī, *al-Uṣūl*, 'Kitāb al-ḥujja', vol. 2, pp. 40–120; al-Mufīd, *al-Irshād*, the section dedicated to the *naṣṣ* of each imam within each relevant chapter). According to a tradition attributed to Ja'far al-Ṣādiq, *al-waṣiyya* is also the name of a Sealed Book (*kitāb makhtūm*) that descended from heaven to the Prophet; this book contained twelve sealed letters containing the missions reserved for each imam (al-Nu'manī, *Kitāb al-ghayba*, pp. 82–83).

63. On this subject, see Rainer Freitag, *Seelenwanderung in der islamischen Häresie* (Berlin, 1985); Guy Monnot, 'La transmigration et l'immortalité', in *Islam et religions* (Paris, 1986), pp. 279–295.

64. '*Fa-stawda'ahum fī afḍal mustawda'in wa aqarrahum fī khayr mustaqarr tanāsakhat-hum karā'im al-aṣlāb ilā muṭahharāt al-arḥām*', *Nahj al-balāgha*, p. 279, no. 93; the seeds of a belief in certain forms of reincarnation are found in the early writings of the imams; the word *maskh* in the sense of a debasing reincarnation in an animal form is seen a number of times (cf., e.g., al-Ṣaffār, *Baṣā'ir*, section 7, ch. 16, pp. 353–354; al-Kulaynī, *al-Rawḍa*, vol. 1, p. 285; vol. 2, p. 37; Ibn Bābūya, *'Uyūn*, vol. 1, ch. 17, p. 271; al-Nu'mānī, *Kitāb al-ghayba*,

poet Kumayt b. Zayd al-Asadī (d. 125/742), singing of the light of glory of the prophet, uses the same term: 'The long branches of your tree run through your lineage from Eve to Āmina, /From generation to generation you were sent through the brilliance of silver and gold.'[65]

It would appear that the term, in the technical sense of 'metemphotosis', is of Imami origin, and that from there was gradually passed on, probably via 'extremist' (*ghulāt*) circles with greater or lesser connections to Shiʿism, to transmigrationist milieus, taking on the meaning of 'metempsychosis'.

There have been a number of previous studies dedicated to the concept of *waṣiyya* in Islam in general and in Shiʿism in particular;[66] the majority of them (Hodgson, Watt, Sharon, Momen) have reduced *waṣiyya* to nothing more than its political aspect. The double 'natural' and 'spiritual' descent has been considered the proof of the 'Arabo-Persian conflict' (Goldziher)

---

p. 387). This theme is more fully developed in the literature of Bāṭinī Shiʿis and especially in the corpus associated with Jābir b. Ḥayyān, where we see the appearance, perhaps for the first time, of a whole series of terms used for referring to different kinds of reincarnation: *naskh* (reincarnation in another human form), *maskh* (reincarnation in an animal form), *faskh* (in a vegetable form), *raskh* (in a mineral form) cf. *The Arabic Works of Jābir b. Ḥayyān*, ed. E. J. Holmyard [Paris, 1928], 'Kitāb al-bayān', p. 11; *Mukhtār rasā'il Jābir b. Ḥayyān*, ed. P. Kraus [Paris and Cairo, 1935], 'Kitāb al-ishtimāl', pp. 549–550; *Zeitschrift für Geschichte des arabischen-islamischen Wissenchaften*, Arabic texts, ed. M. 'A. Abū Rīda, 1 (1984), 'Kitāb al-maʿrifa', p. 57; Sharhrastānī, *Livre des religions*, tr. Gimaret-Monnot, p. 512, notes.

65. *'Mā bayna Ḥawwā'a in nusibta ilā/Āminata 'tamma nabtuka'l-hadabū. Qarnan fa-qarnan tanāsukhuka laka/'l-fiḍḍatu minhā bayḍā'a wa'l-dhahabū'*, al-Kumayt b. Zayd, *Ḥāshimiyyāt* (Qumm, n.d.), p. 69.

66. I. Goldziher, *Muslim Studies*, ed. S. M. Stern (London, 1971), vol. 1, pp. 45f. and 135f.; Goldziher, *Vorlesungen über den Islam* (Heidelberg, 1910), pp. 217f.; M. G. S. Hodgson, 'How Did the Early Shīʿa Become Sectarian?', *JAOS*, 75 (1955), pp. 1–13; W. Montgomery Watt, 'Shīʿism Under the Umayyads', *JRAS* (1960), pp. 158–172; U. Rubin, 'Prophets and Progenitors in Early Shīʿa Tradition', *JSAI*, 1 (1979), pp. 41–64; M. Sharon, 'The Development of the Debate Around the Legitimacy of Authority in Early Islam', *JSAI*, 5 (1984), pp. 121–142, esp. pp. 139–141; M. Momen, *An Introduction to Shīʿi Islam*, ch. 2.

or that of an opposion between the 'Arab Shī'ites of the North and the Arab Shī'ites of the South' (Rubin). Great erudition and rigour of argumentation have not prevented, on occasion, the adherence to an extremely reductionist point of view or the arrival at conclusions that are incomplete; the question of ethnic and cultural mixing at the dawn of Islam is far from being clearly defined, a similarity of ideas does not necessarily prove cultural influence, especially since similar forms may have different content and different forms may have analogous content; one word is not tantamount to a demonstration, and we cannot conclude that there is influence because there is analogy. Within the framework of the history of ideas, the question of the vitality of an early belief possibly influencing the form or content of a new belief remains an open one; neither tribal affiliation nor geographical proximity can necessarily demonstrate the adoption or the assimilation of complex ideas. It is evident that this complex network of problems cannot be solved in the space of a chapter or an article. In the present work we shall be more prudent and remain faithful to the limits that we imposed upon ourselves at the beginning; we shall examine the problem only from within Imamism and within the framework of Imamism's own worldview. It is clear that the idea of the 'Sacred Legacy', giving legitimacy to unquestionable 'inheritors', has political implications, but the idea appears more than anything to be an illustration and an application of two important doctrinal 'axioms' of Imamism: first, the dogma according to which the earth can never be without living Proof of God, otherwise it would be annihilated (*'inna'l-arḍ lā takhlū min al-ḥujja', 'law baqiyat al-arḍ bi-ghayr imām la-sākhat', 'law lam yabqā fi'l-arḍ illā'thnān la-kāna aḥaduhumā al-ḥujja'*, etc.); the Shi'i imams constitute the continuation of an uninterrupted chain of imams from the origin of our form of humanity onwards, a chain that guarantees universal Salvation, and whose last link is the twelfth imam, the Mahdī, who is present but hidden until the end of this cycle of humanity. The second 'axiom' is that all reality is composed of a *ẓāhir* (an apparent, exoteric aspect) and a *bāṭin* (a hidden, esoteric aspect); from this point of view, the 'natural descent' would be the *ẓāhir* of the transmission of prophetic/'imami' light, which is brought about through the seminal substance, while the 'spiritual descent' constitutes the *bāṭin*, the transmission that occurs through initiation.

5

The Imam in Heaven: Ascension and Initiation

> One who does not believe in the following three things does not belong among our faithful: the ascension to heaven (*al-mi'rāj*); interrogation at the tomb (*al-musā'ala fi'l-qabr*); and intercession (*al-shafā'a*).[1]

According to this tradition and others of the same kind reported by Ibn Bābūya al-Ṣadūq, belief in the celestial ascension is clearly one of the Imami articles of faith. But whose ascension? These traditions remain silent on this subject, as they do about intercession. And with reason, for during the period when Ibn Bābūya was writing it was firmly established in Shi'i milieus that, like the Prophet, the imam is capable of heavenly ascent (as well as intercession) and this – as we shall see – in spite of attempts to reserve the term *mi'rāj* for the heavenly journey made by the Prophet Muḥammad. The silence of the tradition regarding this point

1. A tradition going back to imam Ja'far al-Ṣādiq; cf. Ibn Bābūya (d. 381/991), *Amālī* (= *Majālis*), ed. M. B. Kamare'ī (Tehran, 1404/1984), 'majlis' 49, no. 5, pp. 294–295. Elsewhere, Ibn Bābūya reports a tradition with the same *isnād*, in which belief in the existence of Paradise and Hell is added to the list; see Ibn Bābūya, *Ṣifāt al-shī'a*, ed. Ḥ. Fashāhī (with the text from *Faḍā'il al-shī'a*) (Tehran, 1342 Sh./1963–1964), p. 28. Another tradition going back to imam al-Riḍā extends the list (in addition to the four objects of faith listed in the main text and this note): the Basin, *al-ḥawḍ*, the Bridge *ṣirāṭ*, the Scales, *mīzān*, Resurrection of the Dead, Reward and Punishment), cf., ibid., p. 30.

seems to be deliberate because the subject would have been especially delicate during this period.[2]

Imami traditionists were among the earliest authors of *kutub al-miʿrāj*, which were probably no more than compilations of *ḥadīths* attributed to the imams. The same al-Ṣadūq wrote a *Kitāb ithbāt al-miʿrāj*[3] in which he undoubtedly had recourse to the material used in *Kitāb al-miʿrāj* by his father, ʿAlī b. al-Ḥusayn b. Bābūya (d. 329/940–941).[4] Well before them, in the second century AH, Hishām b. Sālim al-Jawālīqī, a famous disciple of the sixth and seventh imams, seems to have written the first *Kitāb al-miʿrāj*.[5] In addition to accounts of the Prophet's ascension without any specifically Shiʿi element,[6] the oldest compilations of

2. This is the period when the early 'non-rational esoteric' tradition was ever more marginalised, progressively giving way to domination by the 'rational theologico-legal trend'. See M. A. Amir-Moezzi, *Guide Divin*, pp. 33–48 (*Divine Guide*, pp. 13–19). Ibn Bābūya seems to have been the last great compiler of the early tradition, while at the same time attempting to manage the rationalist movement; in his 'profession of faith' (*Risālat al-iʿtiqādāt al-imāmiyya* [Tehran, n.d.], English tr. A. A. A. Fyzee as *A Shiʿite Creed*, Oxford, 1942), an especially moderate text with a rational argument, he lists all the objects of faith cited above (note 1) except *miʿrāj*, which was undoubtedly considered much too delicate an issue. This moderate approach in no way prevented his disciple, Shaykh al-Mufīd (d. 413/1022), an eminent personality of the theologico-legal tradition from criticising him, mainly for a lack of clarity in his reasoning, cf. al-Mufīd, *Kitāb sharḥ ʿaqāʾid al-Ṣadūq aw taṣḥīḥ al-iʿtiqād*, ed. A. Charandābī (Tabriz, 1371/1951).

3. Also called *Kitāb al-miʿrāj*, cited by the author in his *Khiṣāl*, ed. ʿA. A. Ghaffārī (Qumm, 1403/1983), pp. 85 and 293; see also al-Ṭūsī (d. 460/1067), *Fihrist kutub al-shīʿa*, ed. Sprenger and ʿAbd al-Ḥaqq (rpr. Mashhad, 1972); although a work that has apparently been lost, we still find long excerpts in later Imami authors, particularly in al-Ḥasan b. Sulaymān al-Ḥillī (d. early nineth/fifteenth century), *Mukhtaṣar baṣāʾir al-darajāt* (Qumm, n.d.); for other authors who cite from this work, see al-Ṭihrānī, *al-Dharīʿa ilā taṣānīf al-shīʿa* (Tehran and Najaf, 1353–1398/1934–1978), vol. 21, pp. 226–227, no. 4737.

4. Cf. e.g. al-Najāshī (d. 450/1058), *Rijāl* (Bombay, 1317/1899; rpr. Qumm, n.d.), p. 199.

5. Ibid., p. 339; J. van Ess, *Theologie und Gesellschaft im 2. und 3. Jahrhundert Hidschra* (Berlin, 1991–1997), vol. 1, p. 345 and vol. 5, p. 69.

6. For example, the extensive *miʿrāj* account going back to Jaʿfar in ʿAlī b. Ibrāhīm al-Qummī (d. ca. 307/919), *Tafsīr* (lithograph, Iran, 1313/1895),

Twelver traditions (from the late third and throughout the fourth century AH) and almost all closely connected to the early 'esoteric non-rational tradition', report numerous traditions that list various modes of the imam's presence in heaven.

The celestial ascent of the Prophet and the *walāya* of ʿAlī

In Twelver versions of the *miʿrāj* story, at every important step of his night journey and celestial ascent, Muḥammad, in some manner or other, is depicted in the presence of ʿAlī. In accordance with the divine decision, the main aim is the revelation, to Muhammad, of ʿAlī as his successor.

This revelation is first engraved in the lofty sacred places that the Prophet visits during his experience.

> 'During my night journey to heaven', Muḥammad tells his daughter Fāṭima, 'inscribed on the Rock of Jerusalem (*ṣakhra bayt al-maqdis*) I saw "There is no god except God, Muḥammad is the messenger of God; I assist him with his lieutenant and I protect him with his lieutenant (*ayyadathu bi-wazīrihi wa naṣartuhu bi-wazīrih*)"; I then asked [the angel] Gabriel who my lieutenant was. He replied: "ʿAlī b. Abī Ṭālib." And once I reached the Lotus of the Limit (*sidrat al-muntahā*), I saw incribed: "I am God, there is no god save I alone, Muḥammad is My chosen one among My creatures (*ṣafwatī min khalqī*). I assist him with my lieutenant and I protect him with my lieutenant." Once again I asked Gabriel the same question and he replied as before. Once I went beyond the Lotus and arrived at the Throne (*ʿarsh*) of the Lord of the worlds, I saw inscribed on each of the supports (*kull qāʾima min qawāʾim*)

---

pp. 375–376 that constitutes a parallel version of the Sunni version by Abū Saʿīd al-Khudrī, cf. e.g. Ibn Hishām, *al-Sīrat al-nabawiyya*, ed. Saqqāʾ et al. (rpr. Beirut, n.d.), vol. 2, pp. 44–50, and the lengthy descriptions by al-Burāq of the inhabitants of each heaven, the torments of those condemned to Hell or the delights of Paradise; in general terms, see al-Majlisī (d. 1111/1699), *Biḥār al-anwār* (Tehran and Qumm, 1376–1392/1956–1972), vol. 18/2, pp. 282–409, who reports several of these traditions.

> of the Throne: "I am God, there is no god save I, Muḥammad is My dear friend (*ḥabībī*). I assist him with his lieutenant and I protect him with his lieutenant.'"[7]

According to a tradition going back to Jaʿfar al-Ṣādiq, which relates the story of Muḥammad's initiation during the *miʿrāj* into the forms of the *adhān*, the ablution ritual and the canonical prayer, ʿAlī's name as *khalīfa* of the Prophet is inscribed on the fine white sheet (*raqq abyaḍ*) that envelops the Inhabited Dwelling (*al-bayt al-maʿmūr*), the celestial prototype of the Kaʿba.[8] According to a prophetic tradition reported by the Companion Jābir al-Anṣārī,[9] during his visit to the seventh heaven, above each of the gates (*bāb*) to this heaven, on each of the veils of light (*hujub al-nūr*) and upon each of the pillars (*rukn*) of the divine Throne, Muḥammad saw the following inscription: 'There is no god except God, Muḥammad is the messenger of God, ʿAlī is the Commander of the Believers.'[10]

---

7. Al-Qummī, *Tafsīr*, p. 653; Ibn Bābūya, *Khiṣāl*, p. 207 (where it is added: 'Then I raised my head and saw inscribed in the depths (*buṭnān*) of the Throne: "I am God ... Muḥammad is my servant and messenger, I assist etc" '). Regarding the inscription on the Throne, see also Ibn Bābūya, *Amālī*, 'majlis' 38, no. 3, pp. 215–216; Ibn Bābūya, *ʿIlal al-sharāʾiʿ* (Najaf, 1385/1966), p. 5 (inscription on the base of the Throne, *sāq* instead of *qāʾima*); al-Khazzāz al-Rāzī (d. second half fourth/end tenth century), *Kifāyat al-athar*, ed. A. Kūhkamareʾī (Qumm, 1401/1980), pp. 105, 118, 156, 217, 245 (in which Gabriel is not present and the term *wazīr* is replaced by the name ʿAlī; further, the names of the other imams also feature in the inscription; I shall return to this).

8. Ibn Bābūya, *ʿIlal al-sharāʾiʿ*, pp. 312–316, in particular p. 314; to be compared with Muḥammad b. Masʿūd al-ʿAyyāshī (d. ca. 320/932), *Tafsīr*, ed. H. Rasūlī Maḥallātī (Qumm, 1380/1960), vol. 1, pp. 157–159, who reports an exactly parallel version of this tradition in which there is no reference to ʿAlī.

9. On the role of this Companion in the Shiʿi *isnād*s, see E. Kohlberg, 'An Unusual Shiʿi *isnād*', *IOS*, 5 (1975) , pp. 142–149 (rpr. in *Belief and Law in Imāmī Shīʿism*, Aldershot, 1991, article VIII).

10. Al-Ḥasan b. Sulaymān al-Ḥillī, *Mukhtaṣar baṣāʾir al-darajāt*, p. 142 (citation based on the *Kitāb al-miʿrāj* by Ibn Bābūya); see also Ibn Bābūya, *Amālī*, 'majlis' 27, no. 8, pp. 131–132 (in which the Prophet says that ʿAlī's *walāya* is a divine decree and refers to the latter using formulaic statements such

As we know, during the course of his ascension, Muḥammad encounters many prophets and angels; according to the different traditions, these holy figures also variously reiterate the sacred nature of ʿAlī's *walāya*. As cited above, in the extensive tradition regarding the Prophet's initiation into the *adhān*, ablution and canonical prayer, the angels of each heaven ask Muḥammad to convey their greetings to ʿAlī, adding that they have pledged allegiance on the occasion of the pre-eternal Pact (*mīthāq*) with God, to remain loyal to ʿAlī and his cause until the Day of Resurrection.[11] In a parallel tradition dating back to Muḥammad al-Bāqir, the angels of the various different heavens as well as Jesus, Moses and Abraham, encountered in the seventh heaven, sing the praises of ʿAlī and call him the legatee (*waṣī*) and vicegerent (*khalīfa*) of Muḥammad.[12] Elsewhere, all the previous prophets declare that the ultimate aim of their missions was the preparation and proclamation of Muḥammad's *nubuwwa* and ʿAlī's *walāya*; further, to make the Prophet aware of their very own *shahāda*:

> We bear witness that there is no god except God, He is Alone and has no associate, Muḥammad is the Messenger of God and ʿAlī, the legatee of Muḥammad is the Commander of the Faithful.[13]

---

as 'Vicegerent of God' – *khalīfat Allāh*, 'Proof of God' – *ḥujjat Allāh*, 'Guide of Muslims' – *imām al-muslimīn*, etc.).

11. Ibn Bābūya, *ʿIlal al-sharāʾiʿ*, pp. 312–316 (cf. note 8 above).

12. Al-Ḥillī, *Mukhtaṣar baṣāʾir al-darajāt*, pp. 139–140 (based on *Kitāb al-miʿrāj* by Ibn Bābūya). For speeches by Jesus, Moses and Abraham referring to ʿAlī with statements such as 'Commander of the Faithful' (*amīr al-muʾminīn*), 'Leader of Muslims' (*sayyid al-muslimīn*) and 'Best among the Best' (lit. 'a horse leading a troop of horses that have a white mark on their foreheads and four white hooves', *qāʾid al-ghurr al-muḥajjalīn*), cf. Ibn Ṭāwūs (d. 664/1266), *al-Yaqīn fī imrat amīr al-muʾminīn* (Najaf, 1369/1950), pp. 83–87 (for the Shiʿis, all these formulaic statements refer exclusively to ʿAlī).

13. Furāt al-Kūfī (d. ca. 300/912), *Tafsīr*, ed. M. al-Kāẓim (Tehran, 1410/1990), p. 182; (Pseudo-?) al-Masʿūdī (d. 345/956), *Ithbāt al-waṣiyya* (Najaf, n.d.), p. 99; Muḥammad b. ʿAlī al-Karājakī (d. 449/1057), *Kanz al-fawāʾid* (Tabriz, n.d.), pp. 256–260; Ibn Ṭāwūs, *al-Yaqīn fī imrat amīr al-muʾminīn*, pp. 87–88.

Finally, in the last phase of the *miʿrāj*, when the Prophet is in the divine Presence, God himself speaks of ʿAlī's noble status. According to an entire series of traditions, God describes ʿAlī with a succession of formulae rendered in assonant prose such as 'Commander of the Faithful, leader of Muslims, Best among the best,[14] Guide of the devout (*imām al-muttaqīn*), Queen-Bee of the faithful (*yaʿsūb al-muʾminīn*),[15] First Vicegerent to the Seal of the prophets (*awwalu khalīfa khātim al-nabiyyin*), etc.'[16] Elsewhere, God praises ʿAlī using other formulaic statements:

> The standard of guidance (*ʿalam al-hudā*), the guide of My Friends (*imām awliyāʾī*), the light of those that obey Me (*nūr man aṭāʿanī*), your [God is obviously addressing the Prophet] legatee and inheritor (*waṣiyyuka wa wārithuka*), defender of the faith, etc.[17]

---

14. Cf. note 12 above.

15. On this title for ʿAlī, namely 'Commander of the Bees' (*amīr al-naḥl*), and regarding the Shiʿis called Bees, see I. Goldziher, *Gesammelte Schriften*, ed. J. Desomogyi (Hildesheim, 1967–1970), vol. 5, pp. 210–214.

16. Al-Qummī, *Tafsīr*, p. 561; al-ʿAyyāshī, *Tafsīr*, vol. 1, p. 160; al-Kulaynī (d. 329/940–941), *al-Uṣūl min al-Kāfī*, ed. J. Muṣṭafawī, 4 vols with Persian trans. (Tehran, n.d. [vol. 4 tr. H. Rasūlī Maḥallātī is dated 1386/1966]), 'Kitāb al-ḥujja', vol. 2, p. 166; (Jaʿfar al-Ṣādiq, to whom this tradition goes back, concludes: 'By God, ʿAlī's *walāya* does not depend on anyone except God who declared it out loud, *mushāfahatan*, to Muḥammad'); Ibn Bābūya, *Khiṣāl*, p. 116 and *Amālī*, 'majlis' 49, no. 16, p. 300, 'majlis' 56, no. 7, p. 352, and 'majlis' 92, no. 4, p. 631. We encounter these formulaic statements rendered in assonant prose in a number of sermons attributed to ʿAlī, particularly in those I have termed elsewhere 'theo-imamosophical sermons', M. A. Amir-Moezzi, 'Aspects de l'imāmologie duodécimaine I. Remarques sur la divinité de l'Imām', *Studia Iranica*, 25/2 (1996), pp. 193–216 (Chapter 3 in this publication).

17. Al-Qummī, *Tafsīr*, pp. 572–573; al-Karājakī, *Kanz al-fawāʾid*, p. 314; Ibn Ṭāwūs, *al-Yaqīn*, pp. 89–91. It is interesting to note that these traditions at once report the Shiʿi version of a well-known episode of the *miʿrāj* concerning 'the dispute of the Supreme Assembly' (*ikhtiṣām al-malaʾ al-aʿlā*), especially with regard to the definition of 'expiations' (*kaffārāt*) or 'degrees' (*darajāt*). The Sunni versions report that the 'expiations (or degrees) require the following actions: ablution on cold mornings (or when it is unpleasant), travelling on foot to attend collective prayers and waiting for one prayer after another' (*isbāgh al-wuḍūʾ fiʾl-sabarāt* [or *fiʾl-makrūhāt*] *waʾl-mashy ilāʾl-jamāʿāt/jumuʿāt waʾntiẓār al-ṣalāt baʿd al-ṣalāt*); cf. e.g. Ibn Ḥanbal, *Musnad* (Cairo, 1313/1896),

In a rather long account of the Prophet's *mi'rāj*, having designated 'Alī as Muḥammad's successor, God declares that He derived the name Muḥammad from His own name, al-Maḥmūd, and that of 'Alī from his name al-'Alī (or al-A'lā), and that both proceed from His own Light.[18] This is why God demands from the angels and all the inhabitants of the heavens (*sukkān al-samāwāt*) a threefold testimony of faith: His own unicity, the mission of Muḥammad and the *walāya* of 'Alī.[19]

However, the *walāya* of 'Alī is not limited to the spiritual and temporal role of the terrestrial 'Alī. *Walāya* is the most important cosmic and ontological status in the universal economy of the sacred – we shall return to this in greater detail – and its ultimate symbol, the cosmic 'Alī, tends to fuse with God. Some traditions, in which the deliberate ambiguity is barely veiled by more nuanced expressions, actually report this.

> 'My Lord had me travel by night', says the Prophet, 'and He revealed to me from behind the Veil what He revealed and among other things said to me: "Muḥammad! 'Alī is *The First*, 'Alī is *The Last*, and *He knows absolutely everything* [*'Alī al-awwal wa 'Alī al-ākhir wa huwa bi-kulli shay'in 'alīm*; the terms in italics are divine names and attibutes in the Qur'ān]." I then said: "Lord! Aren't you Yourself all these things?" He replied: "Muḥammad!… I am God and there is no God save I; I am The First for there is none before Me. I am The Last for there is none after Me. I am *The Manifest* (*al-ẓāhir*) for there is none above Me. I am *The Hidden* (*al-bāṭin*) for there is none below Me. I am God; there is no god

vol. 5, p. 43; Ibn Khuzayma, *Kitāb al-tawḥīd* (Cairo, 1388/1968), p. 218. After 'collective prayers' Shi'i sources read: 'Led by you [God is addressing the Prophet] or by the imams descended from you'; a fourth degree (*kaffāra/daraja*) is also given: 'Remain loyal to me [Muḥammad is speaking] and to the people of my Family until death' (*walāyatī wa walāya ahl baytī ḥattā'l-mamāt*); cf. also Ibn Bābūya, *Khiṣāl*, p. 85.

18. Furāt, *Tafsīr*, pp. 73–74; Ibn Bābūya, *Kamāl al-dīn*, ed. 'A. A. Ghaffārī (Qumm, 1405/1985), vol. 1, p. 252; al-Khazzāz al-Rāzī, *Kifāyat al-athar*, pp. 72, 110, 152; Ibn 'Ayyāsh al-Jawharī (d. 401/1011), *Muqtaḍab al-athar*, ed. H. Rasūlī Maḥallātī (Qumm, n.d.), pp. 11, 24, 26–27, 38; al-Ḥillī, *Mukhtaṣar*, p. 160.

19. Furāt, *Tafsīr*, pp. 342–343 and 452–453.

> except Me who knows all things. O Muḥammad! ʿAlī is the first for he is the first among the imams to have pledged allegiance to Me; he is the last for he is the last imam whose soul I shall take and because 'the Important Being who will speak to them' is he;[20] he is the apparent for I make everything that I confide in you apparent to him, thus you need not hide anything from him; he is the hidden for I hide in him the secret I tell you. Between you and Me there is no secret that I would hide from him. ʿAlī knows absolutely everything that I have created, lawful or unlawful."'[21]

According to another tradition attributed to the Prophet, God addresses him sounding just like ʿAlī:

> The Messenger of God was asked: 'In which language (*lugha*) did your Lord speak to you during the night of *miʿrāj*?' He replied: 'He spoke to me in ʿAlī's language so much so that I asked Him: "Lord! Is it You or ʿAlī who speaks to me?" And he replied: "Aḥmad! I am a Thing (*shayʾ*) different from other things. I cannot be compared to other people nor described by things. I created you from My Light and created ʿAlī from yours; I have sounded the depths of your heart and found nothing more dear to you than ʿAlī b. Abī Ṭālib. Well, I speak to you as ʿAlī does so your heart may be at ease."'[22]

---

20. An allusion to the eschatological verse, 'And when the word is fulfilled concerning them We shall bring forth an important being (lit. great beast) of the earth to speak unto them because mankind had not faith in Our revelations', Q 17:82.

21. Al-Ṣaffār al-Qummī, *Baṣāʾir al-darajāt*, section 10, ch. 18, no. 36, pp. 514–515 (a tradition of the Prophet reported by Jaʿfar al-Ṣādiq). On identification of the Revealed God with the ontological imam as symbolised by the cosmic ʿAlī, refer to my study, 'Remarques sur la divinité de l'Imām' (Chapter 3 in this publication). See also Sulaym b. Qays (Ps.), *Kitāb Sulaym b. Qays al-Hilālī*, ed. Anṣārī, vol. 2, no. 72, pp. 933–934; al-Ḥusayn b. ʿAbd al-Wahhāb, *ʿUyūn al-muʿjizāt* (Najaf, n.d.), p. 4; al-Daylamī, *Irshād al-qulūb*, vol. 2, p. 64; al-Juwaynī, *Farāʾid al-simṭayn*, ch. 38.

22. Al-Muwaffaq b. Aḥmad al-Khwārazmī (d. 586/1190), *Manāqib* (Qumm, n.d.), p. 87; al-Majlisī, *Biḥār al-anwār*, vol. 18/2, pp. 386–387, *Irshād al-qulūb* (Tehran, 1334 Sh./1956), vol. 2, p. 28 and *Ḥayāt al-qulūb* (Tehran, n.d.), vol. 2, p. 297.

ʿAlī in heaven

The presence of ʿAlī, the imam par excellence, in heaven is not confined to his *walāya*. For example, he has a mansion in each heaven that the Prophet visits during his celestial ascension.[23] In the highest of the sacred realms, God has created an angel that is identical to ʿAlī, thus responding to a longing of the angels for a constant vision of ʿAlī. In an elaborate account of the *miʿrāj* reported by Abū Dharr al-Ghifārī, it is said that after hearing the praises of ʿAlī sung by the inhabitants of the respective heavens, Muḥammad's journey ends in the seventh heaven where the angels conclude:

> We made our desire to see ʿAlī known to God and He created an angel identical to him for us [lit. 'in his form', *fī ṣūratihi*] and seated him on the right side of the Throne.... Now whenever we long to see the terrestrial ʿAlī (*ʿAlī fi'l-arḍ*) we look upon his celestial image (*mithālihi fi'l-samā'*).[24]

In some, admittedly rare, traditions, ʿAlī accompanies the Prophet on his heavenly journeys:

> 'O ʿAlī', says Muḥammad, 'God made you appear before me in seven places (*mawāṭin*)... The second place was when Gabriel introduced himself to me and I was raised to heaven. Then Gabriel

23. Al-Ḥillī, *Mukhtaṣar*, pp. 152–155 (based on *Kitāb al-miʿrāj* by Ibn Bābūya); here the angels call ʿAlī 'the young man of the Banū Hāshim' (*fatā min Banī Hāshim*).

24. Furāt, *Tafsīr*, p. 374; see also Ibn Bābūya, *ʿUyūn akhbār al-Riḍā*, pp. 110–111 (in the depths of the Throne, the Prophet sees an angel playing with a sword of light, just as ʿAlī does with Dhu'l-Faqār); al-Karājakī, *Kanz al-fawā'id*, p. 258 (immediately below the Throne, Muḥammad meets the angel and asks him: "Alī! Have you arrived in heaven before me?' Gabriel explains that this is an angel identical to ʿAlī); al-Ḥillī, *Mukhtaṣar*, p. 132 (still according to *Kitāb al-miʿrāj* by Ibn Bābūya; the angel – ʿAlī in this case – is in the fifth heaven); al-Majlisī, *Irshād al-qulūb*, vol. 2, pp. 28–29 (according to *Kifāyat al-ṭālib* by al-Ḥāfiẓ al-Shāfiʿī = *Biḥār al-anwār*, vol. 18/2, pp. 386–387; the angel – ʿAlī – is in the fourth heaven).

asked me: "Where is your brother [i.e. 'Alī]?" I said: "I left him where I was." Then Gabriel asked me to pray to God to bring you near me. I prayed and straight away you were with me. Then were revealed to me the seven heavens and seven earths with all their inhabitants, all that is found therein as well as the angel placed between them; and all that I saw you saw as well . . . The fourth place was when, on Friday night, the kingdom (*malakūt*) of the heavens and the earth and all that it contains were shown to me; there, missing you, I prayed to God and straight away you were with me. You saw all that I saw.'[25]

Indeed, although the terms *isrā'* and *mi'rāj* seem to have been reserved for the Prophet, according to other *ḥadīth*s, it is clearly recognised that 'Alī is capable of celestial travel:

Ibn 'Abbās reports: 'I heard the Messenger of God say: "God gave me five things and gave five things to 'Alī; He gave me the sum total of speech [*jawāmi' al-kilam*, i.e. traditionally the Qur'ān] and gave him the sum total of initiatory Knowledge (*jawāmi' al-'ilm*).[26] He made me a prophet, and him, successor to a prophet

---

25. Al-Ṣaffār, *Baṣā'ir al-darajāt*, section 2, ch. 20, no. 3, p. 107 and no. 10, p. 108. In later works, such as the *Tafsīr* of al-Qummī, the impact of the tradition is lessened, though only slightly, since it is no longer 'Alī in person who accompanies the Prophet but his *mithāl*, his 'image' or 'imaginal being' (according to Henry Corbin's masterly translation of the term). These texts are undoubtedly among the earliest to mention the term *mithāl* in the sense of 'imaginal entity' (refer to Furāt cited above in note 24 and the relevant text that employs the term); al-Qummī, *Tafsīr*, p. 111 (*fa idhā anta ma'ī*, 'and at once you were with me' replaced by *wa idhā mithāluka ma'ī*, 'and at once your imaginal entity was with me'); see also al-Mufīd, *Amālī* (= *Majālis*) (Iran, 1345/1926), pp. 50–51; Ibn Ṭāwūs, *al-Yaqīn*, pp. 83–87 (*mithl* instead of *mithāl*). In a tradition reported by the same Ibn Ṭāwūs in his *Sa'd al-su'ūd* (Najaf, 1369/1950), pp. 100–101, when Muḥammad leads the prophets in prayer, Abraham (his spiritual father) is on his right and 'Alī (his spiritual son) on his left. On 'Alī's presence in heaven on the occasion of the *mi'rāj* according to the Bektashis, see F. De Jong, 'The Iconography of Bektashism. A Survey of Themes and Symbolism in Clerical Costume, Liturgical Objects and Pictorial Art', *The Manuscripts of the Middle East*, 4 (1989), pp. 8ff.

26. In other words, the Prophet is the messenger of the exoteric aspect of the divine Word whereas the imam holds its hidden, esoteric meaning; on Imami *'ilm* that, depending on the context, I translate as 'secret science'

> [lit. 'a legatee', *waṣī*].[27] He offered me [the paradisiacal fountain of] al-Kawthar and offered him [the heavenly fountain of] al-Salsabīl. He graced me with revelation (*waḥy*) and him with inspiration (*ilhām*). He had me travel by night to Him and He opened the gates of heaven for 'Alī and unveiled the [celestial] veil such that he saw what I saw." '[28]

Moreover, it is said that 'Alī has the power to ride the clouds and scale the heavens (*rukūb al-saḥāb wa'l-taraqqī fi'l-asbāb wa'l-aflāk*), a power that he shares with the last imam, the Qā'im.[29] According to the tradition, two kinds of clouds may be mounted, enabling ascension to the heavens: *al-dhalūl* ('the manageable') a white cloud, and *al-ṣa'b* ('the unruly'), a dark cloud swollen with rain, thunder and lightning. Riding the first was reserved for Dhu'l-Qarnayn, the ancient double-horned hero;[30] the second for

---

or 'initiatic science', see *Guide divin*, pp. 174–199 (*Divine Guide*, pp. 69–79); also M. A. Amir-Moezzi, 'Réflexions sur une évolution du shi'isme duodécimain. Tradition et idéologisation', in É. Patlagean and A. Le Boulluec (ed.), *Les retours aux Écritures. Fondamentalismes présents et passés* (Louvain and Paris, 1993) and E. Kohlberg, 'Imam and Community in the Pre-Ghayba Period', in S. A. Arjomand (ed.), *Authority and Political Culture in Shi'ism* (New York, 1988) (rpr. in *Belief and Law*, article XIII), pp. 25–26.

27. On the identity of the *waṣī* and imam, see *Guide divin*, index under '*waṣī, awṣiyā', waṣiyya*'.

28. Ibn Bābūya, *Khiṣāl*, p. 293; al-Mufīd, *Amālī*, p. 64 (where the term *mi'rāj* is added after *isrā'*: 'He offered me the night journey and celestial ascension and offered him the opening of the heavenly gates and veils such that etc.,')

29. Al-Ṣaffār, *Baṣā'ir al-darajāt*, section 8, ch. 15, pp. 408–409. The imams themselves are supposed to have declared that, with regard to supernatural powers, they are not all equal; e.g. al-Riḍā: 'We [the imams] are equal in knowledge and courage; however, in terms of supernatural [gifts], that depends on the orders that we have received.' (section 10, ch. 8, no. 3, p. 480); and Ja'far: 'Some imams have greater thaumaturgical Science than others' (ibid., no. 2, p. 479). For another reading of this latter tradition, see E. Kohlberg, 'Imam and Community', p. 30.

30. Dhu'l-Qarnayn (Q 8:83–98) was especially known among the Semitic peoples as a symbol of Power, both in temporal and spiritual terms. Identified in legend with Alexander the Great, in some ways he becomes the archetypal hero of initiatic journeys; cf. A. W. Budge, *The History of Alexander the Great being the Syrian Version of the Pseudo-Callisthenes* (Cambridge, 1989); M. S. Southgate, 'Alexander in the Works of Persian and Arab Historians of the Islamic

ʿAlī and the Qāʾim.[31] It is thus that ʿAlī was able to visit the seven heavens and seven earths, five of which are inhabited and two uninhabited.[32]

The reference to the last imam sharing with ʿAlī the ability to ascend the heavens leads us to the next step in examining this issue.

The Imams in Heaven

Though less frequently than ʿAlī, and evoked more discretely or allusively, the other imams and their *walāya* are also present in accounts of Muḥammad's *miʿrāj*. In the final phase of his ascension, where even Gabriel must abandon his flight lest 'his wings burn', left alone with God Muḥammad asks:

> 'Lord! Who are my legatees?' – 'Your legatees are engraved on the feet of my Throne (*awṣiyāʾuka'l-maktūbūn ʿalā sāq ʿarshī*).' And while facing my Lord [Muḥammad is speaking], I glanced at the feet of the Throne, and I saw twelve lights each containing an inscription in green indicating the names of my legatees, from the first, ʿAlī b. Abī Ṭālib to the last, the Mahdī of my community.[33]

Other traditions speak of the names of the twelve imams engraved on the Throne without mentioning their light(s),[34] and others still to the individuals, without referring to lights or names:

Era', in *Iskandarnama: A Persian Medieval Alexander Romance*, tr. M. S. Southgate (New York, 1978).

31. Beliefs shared in other forms, by 'extremist' Shiʿis, the Sabaʾiyya and Bayāniyya; cf. Shahrastānī, *Livre des religions et des sectes*, vol. I, Fr. trans. by D. Gimaret and G. Monnot (Paris and Louvain, 1986), p. 510 and n. 18 (by D. Gimaret).

32. Cf. also *Guide divin*, pp. 237–238 (*Divine Guide*, p. 95).

33. This tradition is part of an extensive tradition entitled *faḍl al-nabī wa'l-ḥujaj ʿalā'l-malāʾika*, often cited by Ibn Bābūya, e.g. *ʿIlal al-sharāʾiʿ*, pp. 5f., *Kamāl al-dīn*, pp. 254f., *ʿUyūn akhbār al-Riḍā*, pp. 262f. Regarding the probable origin of this *ḥadīth* and for the translation of some parts of it, see *Guide divin*, pp. 89–91 (in this publication, refer to Chapter 4, note 37 and the corresponding text).

34. For example, al-Khazzāz, *Kifāyat al-athar*, pp. 74, 105, 118, 217 and 245.

> Muḥammad: 'I directed my attention towards the right of the Throne and I saw 'Alī, Fāṭima, al-Ḥasan, al-Ḥusayn, 'Alī b. al-Ḥusayn… and the Mahdī.'[35]

The kingdom of the heavens and the earth is open to the imams. They are the guardians of the celestial and terrestrial treasures of God[36] and may visit the *malakūt* just like Abraham (Q 6:74) and Muḥammad. Commentating on verse Q 6:74, 'So We were showing Abraham the kingdom of the heavens and earth, that he might be of those having sure faith', Jaʿfar al-Ṣādiq is said to have declared:

> God made Abraham discover the seven heavens such that he saw beyond the Throne and He made him discover the earth such that he saw what is in the Air [that supports the earth];[37] He did the same for Muḥammad as well as for your master [i.e. Jaʿfar al-Ṣādiq] and will do the same for the imams that succeed him.[38]

Traversing the heavens is even part of the miraculous powers (*qudra, aʿājīb*) of the imams.[39] The same imam asks a visiting Yemeni:

35. Ibn 'Ayyāsh al-Jawharī, *Muqtaḍab al-athar*, pp. 11 and 38; al-Karājakī, *Kanz al-fawā'id*, p. 258. Fāṭima's presence in *miʿrāj* accounts is rare and discreet. Apart from a reference to her in the tradition just cited, she is sometimes present during the dialogue between Muḥammad and God when the Prophet receives an order to give her hand in marriage to 'Alī; cf. al-Karājakī, *Kanz al-fawā'id*, p. 314. Moreover, it is during a *miʿrāj* that the Prophet eats a fruit in Paradise that in 'his loins', becomes the seed of Fāṭima; cf. Furāt, *Tafsīr*, pp. 75–76 and 211; al-Qummī, *Tafsīr*, pp. 341–342; Ibn Bābūya, *'Ilal al-sharā'iʿ*, pp. 183–184; see also M. A. Amir-Moezzi (with J. Calmard), 'Fāṭima Daughter of Muḥammad', *EIr*, vol. 9, pp. 400–404.

36. For example, al-Ṣaffār, *Baṣā'ir al-darajāt*, section 2, ch. 19, pp. 103–106.

37. According to one version of traditional cosmology; see M. A. Amir-Moezzi, 'Cosmogony and Cosmology in Twelver Shiʿism', *EIr*, vol. 6, pp. 317–322, especially the first section.

38. Al-Ṣaffār, *Baṣā'ir al-darajāt*, section 2, ch. 20, no. 2, p. 107.

39. Regarding these powers see *Guide divin*, section III. 4., pp. 228–242 (*Divine Guide*, pp. 91–99). See also Chapter 6, this volume.

> ʻAmong you, are there any initiated sages (*ʿulamāʾ*)?ʼ[40] ʻYes,ʼ replied the visitor. ʻHow far does their knowledge extend?ʼ ʻIn one night they are able to travel a distance that takes two months, they practice divination based on the behaviour of birds and omens marked upon the earth (*yazjurū al-ṭayr wa yaqīfūʾl-āthār*).ʼ[41] Jaʿfar al-Ṣādiq then declares: ʻThe initiate from Medina [i.e. the imam himself] is even more knowledgeable than your initiates, for in an hour of the day he travels the distance the sun covers in one year . . . and he visits twelve suns and twelve moons, twelve Sunrises and twelve Sunsets, twelve Earths, twelve Seas and twelve Worlds.ʼ[42]

Other traditions reveal the highly initiatic dimension of the power to journey (*qudrat al-sayr*), all the while underscoring the imam's spiritual capacity for celestial ascent. Three sayings attributed to the sixth imam regarding the knowledge acquired every Friday night (*al-ʿilm al-mustafād fī laylatiʾl-jumuʿa*) – one aspect of the imam's initiatic science – gives a good illustration of these dimensions:

> By God, every Friday night, our spirits [i.e. of the imams], accompanied by those of the prophets, make the pilgrimage to the divine Throne and return to our bodies only when satiated with the sum of knowledge (*jamm al-ghafīr min al-ʿilm*).[43]
>
> On Friday nights, it is permitted for the spirits of deceased prophets and legatees [i.e. past imams] as well as the legatee who is amongst you [i.e. the present imam] to make the heavenly journey (*yaʿruju ... ilāʾl-samāʾ*) to the Throne of their Lord. There, they circle seven times around the Throne, and at each of its supports recite a prayer of two *rakʿas*. Then the spirits return to their bodies. That is why the prophets and the legatees awake in the morning

40. In the context of the ʻesoteric supra-rationalʼ tradition, this *ḥadīth* by itself justifies my translation of the term *ʿilm*, as ʻsecret initiatic scienceʼ and the term *ʿālim* as ʻinitiated sageʼ; see the references provided above in note 26.

41. Types of ornithomancy and geomancy; cf. T. Fahd, *La divination arabe* (2nd edn, Paris, 1987), respectively pp. 403 f. and 432 f.

42. Al-Ṣaffār, *Baṣāʾir al-darajāt*, section 8, ch. 12, nos 14 and 15, p. 401.

43. Ibid., section 3, ch. 8, no. 6, p. 132.

[on Fridays] filled with joy and the legatee among you awakes with his knowledge abundantly multiplied (*zīda fī 'ilmihi mithl jammi'l-ghafīr*).[44]

On Friday night, the Prophet, messenger of God [i.e. Muḥammad] and the imams make the pilgrimage to the divine Throne, and I, too, make the journey in their company, returning only after acquiring [new] knowledge; without this, the knowledge that I possess already would disappear.[45]

The initiate's ascension and the relationship between *nubuwwa* and *walāya*

In the Twelver conception, the initiatory nature of the heavenly journey is infinitely more pronounced than its visionary aspect. As for the apocalyptical, eschatological dimension, it is conspicuous by its absence. Ascension to heaven is one means, among others, of receiving revelations and elements of sacred Knowledge (*'ilm*); moreover, the visions that are presented to the initiate during his experience serve to increase his knowledge of the mysteries concerned with God and the universe. It is this initiation that sanctifies the one who ascends to heaven.[46] Early Shi'i literature thus appears

44. Al-Kulaynī, *Uṣūl min al-Kāfī*, 'Kitāb al-ḥujja', 'Bāb anna'l-a'imma yazdādūn fī laylati'l-jumu'a 'ilman', vol. 1, no. 1, pp. 372–373.

45. Ibid., vol. 1, no. 3, pp. 373–374. Indeed it is said that the imam's knowledge must inexorably increase or disappear; initiation must also continue all life long (cf. al-Ṣaffār, *Baṣā'ir*, section 3, ch. 8, nos 1 and 5, pp. 130–131; section 8, chs 9 and 10, pp. 392–396; al-Kulaynī, *Uṣūl*, 'Bāb law lā anna'l-a'imma yazdādūn la nafida mā 'indahum', vol. 1, pp. 374–375). Regarding the knowledge acquired on Friday night see also Furāt, *Tafsīr*, p. 381.

46. For the initiatic dimensions of the *mi'rāj*, see B. Schrieke, 'Die Himmelsreise Muhammeds', *Der Islam*, 6 (1916); J. Horovitz, 'Muhammeds Himmelfahrt', *Der Islam*, 9 (1919). On the initiatory and sanctifying aspects of the *mi'rāj*, see A. M. Piemontese, 'Le voyage de Mahomet au Paradis et en Enfer: une version persane du *mi'rāj*', in C. Kappler (ed.), *Apocalypses et voyages dans l'au-delà* (Paris, 1987), esp. p. 298. Now consult M. A. Amir-Moezzi, 'Me'rāj', *EIr* and C. Gruber and F. Colby (eds), *The Prophet's Ascension: Cross Cultural Encounters with the Islamic Mi'rāj Tales* (Bloomington, IN, 2010).

as one of the main elements in the preservation of an ancient theme in spirituality and, more specifically, Muslim initiation.[47]

Initiate par excellence, the imam is able to traverse the sky and the heavens; initiator par excellence, he can also enable his initiate to travel to the same places. Al-Ṣaffār al-Qummī (d. 290/902–903), whose *Baṣā'ir al-darajāt* is undoubtedly one of the earliest compilations of an esoteric nature to have come down to us,[48] devotes an entire chapter to accounts of the supra-natural journeys of the disciples led by the imams.[49] In one of these accounts, Jābir b. Yazīd al-Juʿfī (d. 128/745 or 132/749), an especially intimate disciple of the fifth and sixth imams,[50] asks Muḥammad al-Bāqir to explain how Abraham had seen the kingdom of the heavens and the earth. The imam then changes his clothing and lifts his arm; the ceiling of the house instantly splits open and the master guides the disciple on a journey that leads them successively to the Land of Darkness (*ẓulumāt*), where Dhu'l-Qarnayn had been before, to the Fountain of Life (*ʿayn al-ḥayāt*), from which Khaḍir had imbibed, to the kingdom of the heavens and the earth and,

---

47. On the subject of initiatic heavenly journeys in pre-Islamic religious cultures, see e.g. B. Schrieke, 'Die Himmelsreise', esp. pp. 5–6; F. Raphaël et al. (eds), *L'apocalyptique*, Actes du Colloque du Centre de Recherches d'Histoire des Religions de l'Université de Strasbourg, 1974 (Paris, 1987), esp. J. Schwartz, 'Le voyage au ciel dans la littérature apocalyptique', pp. 91–126; M. Dean-Otting, *Heavenly Journeys: A Study of the Motif in Hellenistic Jewish Literature* (Frankfurt, Bern and New York, 1984); *La Bible. Ecrits intertestamentaires*, ed. A. Duppont-Sommer and M. Philonenko (Paris, 1987), pp. 549–552; H. Busse, 'Jerusalem in the Story of Muḥammad's Night Journey and Ascension', *Jerusalem Studies in Arabic and Islam*, 14, 'Third Colloquium From Jāhiliyya to Islam', vol. 2 (1991), esp. p. 6, notes 17 to 25, and pp. 21–25.

48. See my article 'Al-Ṣaffār al-Qummī (d. 290/902–3) and his *Kitāb baṣā'ir al-darajāt*', *JA*, 280/3–4 (1992), pp. 221–250.

49. Al-Ṣaffār, *Baṣā'ir al-darajāt*, section 8, ch. 13, pp. 402–407.

50. Several traditions of an initiatic and esoteric nature are reported in his name; regarding this figure, refer to al-Kashshī (mid fourth/tenth century), *Rijāl* (Bombay, 1317/1899), p. 126; al-Najāshī, *Rijāl*, under al-Juʿfī; al-Ṭūsī, *Rijāl* (Najaf, 1380/1961), p. 111, no. 6 and p. 163, no. 30; al-Ardabīlī, *Jāmiʿ al-ruwāt* (Qumm, 1331 Sh./1953), vol. I, p. 144.

finally, to the celestial worlds, where the deceased imams are to be found.[51]

In another account, Abū Baṣīr, also a close disciple of the sixth imam,[52] tells how, embarking on a silver vessel (*safīna min fiḍḍa*) that appeared through the miraculous powers of his master, he was led to the celestial world where tents of silver (*khiyām min fiḍḍa*) housing the deceased of the *ahl al-bayt* were pitched.[53] In the eschatological corpus, among the prodigious powers attributed to the initiated companions of the Qā'im, some *ḥadīth*s refer to the power to travel as clouds or to walk upon them; it is thus that during the final Rising (*qiyām*) against the forces of Evil, they will speedily join forces with their master in Mecca.[54]

It is but a minor leap from being led upon a heavenly journey by a master initiator to being initiated into the art of celestial ascent; and this task seems to have been accomplished by some adepts. To my knowledge, compilations of Twelver traditions make no mention of the disciple's ability to traverse the heavens, but heresiographical literature has maintained traces of sayings related to at least two adepts (accused of extremism, *ghuluww*) describing their personal heavenly journeys.[55] First, Abū Manṣūr al-'Ijlī, who was a disciple of the fifth imam, Muḥammad al-Bāqir, and was executed on the orders of Yūsuf al-Thaqafī, the governor of

51. Al-Ṣaffār, *Baṣā'ir al-darajāt*, section 8, ch. 13, no. 4, pp. 404–405.

52. Regarding these three disciples of Ja'far bearing the *kunya* Abū Baṣīr, see *Guide divin*, pp. 86–87, n. 182 (*Divine Guide*, p. 34); (this volume, Chapter 4, note 32).

53. Al-Ṣaffār, *Baṣā'ir al-darajāt*, no. 5, pp. 405–406.

54. See e.g. al-Kulaynī, *al-Rawḍa min al-Kāfī*, text with Persian trans. by H. Rasūlī Maḥallātī (Tehran, 1389/1969), vol. 2, p. 145; al-Nu'mānī (d. 345 or 360/956 or 971), *Kitāb al-ghayba*, ed. 'A. A. Ghaffārī (Tehran, 1397/1977), ch. 20, pp. 445f.; Ibn Bābūya, *Kamāl al-dīn*, vol. 2, pp. 654 and 672; see also M. A. Amir-Moezzi 'Eschatology in Twelver Shi'ism', *EIr*, vol. 8, pp. 575–581.

55. The distinction between 'moderate' and 'extremist' Imamism seems to have been a later development. In any case, it seems rather artificial and *a posteriori* with regard to the early 'non-rational esoteric' tradition; see *Guide divin*, pp. 312–16 (*Divine Guide*, pp. 129–130) and 'Remarques sur la divinité de l'Imam' (Chapter 3, this volume).

Iraq between 120/738 and 126/744. According to the heresiographers, speaking in clearly Christological terms, he claimed to have been raised to heaven and seen God who caressed his head with His Hand – thus appointing him His *masīḥ* – supposedly stating: 'O my son! Descend and deliver [My Message to others].'[56] Next, the famous Abu'l-Khaṭṭāb, a disciple of the sixth imam, Ja'far al-Ṣādiq, who shortly after Abū Manṣūr, claimed to have made a 'celestial night journey' from his own city of Kūfa to the seat of his master in Medina.[57]

Celestial journeys and aerial travel are thus possible for the initiate, whether an imam or his initiated disciple. This is one of the ideas that may be deduced from the early Imami corpus regarding celestial ascent. Though linked to the first, a second, subtler concept concerns the superiority of *walāya* to *nubuwwa*. This especially delicate notion is implicitly present throughout the Imami corpus, in suggestive tones and by allusion; traditions bearing upon celestial ascent seem to constitute fertile ground for clarifying the relationship between *walāya* and *nubuwwa* in early Imamism.[58]

Generally speaking, we know that *nubuwwa* is concerned with the exoteric aspect (*ẓāhir*) of Truth, revealed by Muḥammad, whereas the imam/*wālī*, often symbolised by 'Alī, imam par excellence, reveals the *walāya* or esoteric, hidden aspect (*bāṭin*) of this same Truth. Often there is even identification on the one hand between Muḥammad and the *ẓāhir* and on the other between 'Alī

56. Al-Nawbakhtī, *Firaq al-Shī'a*, ed. H. Ritter (Istanbul, 1931), p. 34; Sa'd b. 'Abd Allāh al-Qummī, *al-Maqālāt wa'l-firaq*, ed. M. J. Mashkūr (Tehran, 1963), p. 46; al-Ash'arī, *Maqālāt al-Islāmiyyīn*, ed. H. Ritter (rpr. Wiesbaden, 1963), p. 9; al-Kashshī, *Rijāl*, p. 196; Shahrastānī, *Livre des religions*, p. 520 (and note 88 in which D. Gimaret corrects the reading by Ritter in Nawbakhtī, *Firaq*); H. Halm, *Die islamische Gnosis. Die extreme Schia und die 'Alawiten* (Zurich and Munich, 1982), pp. 86f.; J. van Ess, *Theologie und Gesellschaft*, vol. 1, p. 377 and vol. 5, p. 71.

57. For sources, refer to J. van Ess, *Theologie*, vol. 1, p. 277.

58. I have already briefly discussed this subject in my article, 'Notes sur deux traditions "heterodoxies" imamites', *Arabica*, 41 (1994), esp. pp. 128–131.

and the *bāṭin*. These two emblematic Figures each in turn contain two levels: there is the cosmic, universal, archetypal, esoteric Muḥammad of whom the historic, exoteric Muḥammad is the manifestation par excellence. Similarly, the historical ʿAlī constitutes the *ẓāhir* and the manifestation par excellence of a cosmic, universal, archetypal ʿAlī. In the early corpus, where the language is still in its 'mythic' state and conceptualisation almost entirely absent, one never speaks of *nubuwwa* or *walāya* be it particular or universal, but on the one hand simply of Muḥammad and ʿAlī or, as we have seen, of Muḥammad and ʿAlī 'on earth' and, on the other hand, Muḥammad and ʿAlī 'in heaven' or of their Lights;[59] and still, the lines of demarcation are not always clear. Now, one must at the same time bear in mind some axiomatic information: the pre-eminence of *bāṭin* over *ẓāhir* and thus of the cosmic-archetypal over the perceptible-historical. Admittedly, the exoteric forms the basis and foundation for the esoteric, but without the esoteric, the exoteric loses its very reason for being.

The concrete expression of *walāya*, the imam, is the alpha and omega of Shiʿi teaching, and the knowledge of his secret reality is presented throughout as equivalent to the recognition of God and as the ultimate goal of creation.[60] *Walāya* constitutes the very essence of *nubuwwa*, without which it loses its significance and sense of direction. In a tradition reported by imam al-Ḥusayn b. ʿAlī it is said that the angel Gabriel asked God to reveal the content of Muḥammad's name to him. God then showed the angel the Light of the twelve imams.[61] Cosmic *walāya* – here symbolised by the Light of all the imams – forms the content of Muḥammad's essential reality, symbolised by his name. Imamology, in the etymological

---

59. On these notions that concur with those of the primordial Lights of Muḥammad and the imams, see U. Rubin, 'Pre-existence and Light. Aspects of the Concept of Nūr Muḥammad', *IOS*, 5 (1975), pp. 62–119; *Guide divin*, pp. 73–112 (*Divine Guide*, pp. 29–38) and 'Cosmogony and Cosmology in Twelver Shiʿism', *EIr*, section 2.

60. See e.g. Chapters 3 and 7 in this volume.

61. Al-Khazzāz al-Rāzī, *Kifāyat al-athar*, p. 170.

sense of the term, that is, the knowledge of the imam, forms the secret content, the *bāṭin* of the prophetic message. According to a *ḥadīth* going back to Muḥammad al-Bāqir and taken up by Jaʿfar al-Ṣādiq:

> ʿAlī is a divine Sign (*āya* – just like a verse of the Qurʾān) for Muḥammad. The latter summons [the people] to ʿAlī's *walāya*.[62]
>
> While commenting on Q 91:1, 'Did we not expand thy breast for thee [O Muḥammad]?' Jaʿfar al-Ṣādiq is supposed to have said that '(God expanded his breast) for the *walāya* of ʿAlī.'[63] And the Prophet himself supposedly said:
>
> 'The Angel Gabriel came to me and said: "Muḥammad ! Your Lord has designated for you the love and *walāya* of ʿAlī."'[64]

---

62. Al-Ṣaffār, *Baṣāʾir al-darajāt*, section 2, ch. 7, nos 5 and 8, pp. 71–72 (al-Bāqir) and ch. 9, no. 5, p. 77 (al-Ṣādiq).

63. *Baṣāʾir al-darajāt*, section 2, ch. 8, no. 3, p. 73.

64. *Baṣāʾir al-darajāt*, no. 9, p. 74 (a tradition going back to imam al-Bāqir). The pre-eminence of the *walī*'s Cause over the exoteric message of the *nabī* is also evident in the dialectic of *īmān/islām*; in Imami technical terminology, the first term designates faith in the initiatory teachings of the imams, whereas the second denotes submission only to the exoteric religion. Replying to the question: 'What is the difference between Islam and faith (*īmān*)?', Jaʿfar answers: 'Islam is the exoteric dimension to which people adhere [*al-islām huwa'l-ẓāhir alladhī ʿalayhi'l-nās* – this latter term is one of the names by which the imams refer to non-Shiʿi Muslims]: both professions of faith relate to the unicity of God and to Muḥammad's mission of prophethood, canonical prayer, alms giving, the pilgrimage to Mecca and the fast during the month of Ramaḍān. Now, in addition to all this, faith is knowledge of our teaching. He who professes and practices [these rituals] without knowing this, although a Muslim, has gone astray (*kāna musliman wa kāna ḍāllan*)'; al-Kulaynī, *Uṣūl*, 'kitāb al-īmān wa'l-kufr', vol. 3, p. 39. The same sixth imam reiterates: 'Islam is the profession of divine unicity and acceptance of our Prophet's mission; it is by Islam that the blood wit is exacted, that conditions for marriage and inheritance are regulated. It is [a collection of] exoteric laws obeyed by the majority of people [*akthar al-nās*, another expression designating the 'Sunnis', non-initiated Muslims as opposed to the 'minority', *aqall al-nās*, i.e. initiated believers of the imams]. As for faith, it is a guidance that manifests itself in the heart. Exoterically, faith is joined with Islam, whereas esoterically, Islam is not joined with faith (*inna'l-īmān yushāriku'l-islām fi'l-ẓāhir wa'l-islām la yushāriku'l-īmān fi'l-bāṭin*). Faith is thus superior (*arfaʿ*) to Islam'; al-Kulaynī, *Uṣūl*, vol. 3, pp. 41–42; for the equivalence established between *īmān* and the doctrine of the imams, see also e.g.

If *walāya* consitutes the hidden essence of the historical Muḥammad's message, and if he is the master initiator of the historical ʿAlī, as the imams regularly say, it is so because he was initiated, during his numerous celestial ascensions, not only in to the secrets of the cosmic *walāya* but also into those of the historical *walāya*, that is, to his own essential reality and the ultimate content of his message.

In almost all the Imami accounts of the *miʿrāj*, as has been seen above, Muḥammad is confronted at one point or another in his heavenly journey with the *walāya* of ʿAlī (both cosmic and terrestrial) and the magnitude of the latter's ontological status.

> The prophet was raised up to heaven one hundred and twenty times; not a single journey went without God entrusting the Prophet with the *walāya* of ʿAlī and the imams [that come] after him, to a greater extent than that by which He recommended to him canonical obligations.[65]

The successive *miʿrāj*s mark the different steps of Muḥammad's initiation because it is due to them that he progressively learns his own reality, the meaning of his prophetic message and his duties

---

al-Nuʿmānī, *Kitāb al-ghayba*, pp. 131 and 188; Ibn Bābūya, *Amālī*, 'majlis' 93, pp. 639f.

65. Al-Ṣaffār, *Baṣāʾir*, section 2, ch. 10, no. 10, p. 79 (tradition attributed to Jaʿfar); Ibn Bābūya, *Khiṣāl*, pp. 600–601 (the canonical obligations, *farāʾiḍ*, are often said to be determined and established in relation to *walāya*; cf. e.g. Ibn Bābūya, *ʿIlal al-sharāʾiʿ*, pp. 312f.). On the number of *miʿrāj* undertaken by the Prophet, refer to the remarks made by al-Majlisī in *Biḥār al-anwār*, vol. 18/2, pp. 306–307 outlining the doubts that must have existed among Imami scholars, not only on the number of *miʿrāj*s, but also with regard to the locations where they took place (Mecca or Medina), as well as their exact nature (corporeal or spiritual). To my knowledge, the early corpus remains largely indifferent to these preoccupations. It seems to me that according to the early conception, apart from the celestial ascension on Friday nights whose spiritual nature is explicitly stated, the other 'supernatural travels' occurred physically; in this regard, refer to the learned introduction by N. Mayel-Heravi to his *Meʿrāj-Nāma-ya Abū ʿAlī Sīna be enḍemām-e taḥrīr-e ān az Shams al-Dīn Ebrāhīm Abarqūhī* (Mashhad, 1365 Sh./1986), pp. 11–67.

as the messenger of God. One tradition is especially significant in this regard. This is a commentary on Q 10:94–95, attributed to Ja'far al-Sadiq:[66]

> When the messenger of God was elevated to heaven by night, God revealed to him what He wished to reveal about the grandeur and glory of 'Alī. He [i.e. Muḥammad] was then introduced to the Inhabited Abode where the prophets were gathered to follow him in prayer. [At this moment] – [a sense of doubt or hesitation][67] crossed the mind of God's messenger regarding the immensity of what was revealed to him about 'Alī (*'urida fī nafs rasūli'llāh min 'iẓam mā ūḥiya ilayhi fī 'Alī*). God then had this message revealed:
>
> So, if thou art in doubt (*shakk*) regarding what We have sent down to thee, ask those who recite the Book before thee [Q 10:94, that is to say the prophets] regarding his supreme character (*faḍlihi*; i.e. 'Alī's) We have sent down in their sacred Books what We have sent down in your Book.
>
> The truth has come to thee from thy Lord; so be not of the doubters, nor be of those who cry lies to God's signs so as to be of the losers [Q 10:95].[68]

Surprising at first glance, this tradition takes on its full significance when one considers that the historical prophet is here placed before the archetypal Imam who is not only superior to him but also to all of creation, since the Imam, the cosmic *wālī*, is the plenary mani-

---

66. Regarding this tradition, see M. M. Bar-Asher, 'Deux traditions hétérodoxes dans les anciens commentaires imamites du Coran', *Arabica*, 37 (1990), pp. 291–314 and M. A. Amir-Moezzi, 'Notes' (note 58 above).

67. The next part of the account and the use of the term *shakk* in the verse justifies this interpolation.

68. Al-Qummī, *Tafsīr*, p. 212; note that in this context, 'the Truth' and 'Signs of God' from verse 10:95 are to be understood as allusions to the *walāya* of 'Alī. For other commentaries on this verse, refer to the sources provided by M. M. Bar-Asher in 'Deux traditions hétérodoxes dans les anciens commentaires imamites du Coran'.

festation of the divine Names and Attributes, the culmination of all that is knowable in God, the veritable *Deus Revelatus*.[69]

It is hardly surprising, then, that the terrestrial Muḥammad (still in the midst of his apprenticeship, since this was one *miʿrāj* among others) was astonished and fearstruck before the highest manifested Truth. Even the superiority of the terrestrial Muḥammad over the terrestrial ʿAlī is presented in quite a nuanced manner. It is true that the former is the master initiator of the latter, but as we have seen, only after being initiated himself in the secrets of the archetypal Imam whose absolute manifestation is the terrestrial ʿAlī. The historical prophet can fulfill this responsibility as the master initiator of the imam because in his very being is combined both *walāya* and *nubuwwa*, the first constituting the foundation and essence of the second.[70]

Cosmic *walāya* is the source for *nubuwwa*, just as terrestrial *walāya* is its necessary extension. The universal *wālī* constitutes the ultimate content of Revelation communicated to the *nabī*, just as the historical *wālī* is the initiator of its hidden meanings. Apart from the power of being the messenger of the literal Revelation, in other words, apart from legislating prophethood (*risāla*), the *wālī*, master of the *bāṭin* and plenary manifestation of the cosmic Imam, enjoys all the prerogatives of the *nabī*. He is capable of all that the latter is capable, including, naturally, celestial ascent.

---

69. Cf. Chapter 3 here; also *Guide divin*, pp. 114–118 (*Divine Guide*, pp. 44–46).

70. Ultimately, the Prophet is but 'the warner' (*al-mundhir*) whereas the IMAM is 'the guide' (*al-hādī*), cf. Furāt, *Tafsīr*, p. 206; ʿAlī b. al-Ḥusayn b. Bābūya (d. 329/940), *al-Imāma wa'l-tabṣira min al-ḥayra* (Qumm, 1404/1984), p. 132, commentary on Q 13:7: 'Thou art only a warner, and a guide to every people.' It is noteworthy that apart from the cosmo-anthropogonic traditions and those concerning the 'History of the Prophets' which in some ways constitute an extension of the first (see the references provided above in note 59 and E. Kohlberg, 'Some Shīʿī Views on the Antediluvian World', *SI*, 52 [1980], pp. 41-66 [rpr. in *Belief and Law*, article 16], the early corpus is unaware of the archetypal Muḥammad. Both in heaven and on earth, all takes place as though the *nabī* only constituted the initial impulse of a dynamic that has an enduring meaning solely due to the *wālī*.

6

Knowledge is Power: Interpretations and Implications of the Miracle in Early Imamism

Twelver *Hadīth* is infused with the miraculous and the marvellous.[1] One of the most remarkable qualities of the imams is their capacity to accomplish miracles and to master mysterious forces; there is no distinction here between the marvellous in religion on the one hand and thaumaturgy on the other.[2] Early Shiʿism, as it emerges from its oldest sources, and also in heresiographical literature, presents an undeniable thaumaturgic-spiritual dimension. Miracles even constitute an essential aspect of the Shiʿi concept of the prophet's continuity through *walāya*. I will attempt to present here a two-part account of the economy of the phenomenon of the miracle and its development during the course of the formative

1. On Imami *ḥadīth* literature and its principal sources, see G. Lecomte, 'Aspects de la littérature du *ḥadīth* chez les imāmites', in *Le shīʿisme imāmite*, Actes du colloque de Strasbourg, 6–9 mai 1968) (Paris, 1970), pp. 91–101; H. Löschner, *Die dogmatischen Grundlagen des schiʿitischen Rechts* (Cologne, 1971), especially the introduction; Modīr Shānetchī, 'Kotob-e arbaʿe-ya ḥadīth-e shīʿe', *Nāme-ya Āstān-e Qods*, 18 / 1–2, new series (1975), pp. 22–71; E. Kohlberg, 'Shīʿī Ḥadīth', in A. F. L. Beeston et al., *The Cambridge History of Arabic Literature*, vol. I: *Arabic Literature to the End of Umayyad Period* (Cambridge, 1983), pp. 299–307; M. ʿA. Mahdavī Rād, A. ʿĀbedī, ʿA. Rafīʿī, 'Ḥadīth', in *Tashayyoʿ. Seyrī dar farhang va tārīkh-e tashayyoʿ* (Tehran, 1373 Sh./1994). For the earliest sources see also M. A. Amir-Moezzi, *Guide divin*, pp. 51–56 (*Divine Guide*, pp. 20–22); refer also to Chapter 3, this volume.

2. See Amir-Moezzi, *Guide divin*, pp. 182–185 and the entire section III.4, 'Sacred Power', pp. 228–242 (*Divine Guide*, pp. 72–73 and 91–99).

period of Twelver Shiʿism: 1) miracles among the imams; 2) miracles in the entourages of the imams and in Shiʿi milieus.

Elsewhere, I have described certain miraculous powers attributed to the imams.[3] In what follows I will attempt to supplement this information and demonstrate its connection to other doctrinal chapters as well as its implications for Imami religious history since the early centuries of the Hijra.

Belief in the miraculous powers of the imams and the plethora of texts about the subject are truly ancient phenomena in Shiʿism. Such interest seems to have begun with the process of the glorification of ʿAlī (d. 40/661), whereby his supporters transformed an individual from a historical personage into a semi-legendary figure of tragic and heroic proportions. The first indications of this process appear to date back to the period that immediately followed his assassination, if not earlier, to when he was bypassed for the succession after the Prophet's death.[4] Shortly thereafter, his character acquired a cosmic and superhuman dimension: the archetypal Perfect Man, theophanic Being – the manifestation of a primordial Light drawn from the divine Light. He transmitted these qualities to other imams descended from him, even to their initiates.[5] According to heresiographers, during the first three centuries of Islam, a relatively large number of movements and Shiʿi sects regarded one or other of the imams, or one of their followers, as the locus of manifestation (*maẓhar/majlā*) of God (*maẓhariyya* even becomes an article of faith in early Imami

3. Ibid., pp. 233ff.

4. Gh. Ḥ. Ṣadīqī, *Jonbesh-hāye dīnī-ye īrānī dar qarn-hāye dovvom va sevvom-e hejrī* (Tehran, 1372 Sh./1993), pp. 225ff.; E. Kohlberg, 'Some Imāmī Shīʿī Views on the *ṣaḥāba*', *JSAI*, 5 (1984) pp. 145-146, (rpr. in *Belief*, article IX); see also the dense text by van Ess, *Theologie und Gesellschaft im 2. und 3. Jahrhundert Hidschra*, vol. I (Berlin and New York, 1990), pp. 233ff., and 397–403 (on the influence of the Stoics via Iranian dualism, and the Jews, on early Shiʿi theology). Refer also to Chapter 1 in this volume.

5. Amir-Moezzi, *Guide divin*, pp. 75ff. (*Divine Guide*, p. 29); Chapters 3 and 8 in this volume.

tradition).[6] The oldest of these sects seems to have been the enigmatic Saba'iyya who, at least in some doctrinal elements, were probably identical to the Kaysāniyya, the supporters of the imamate of Muḥammad b. al-Ḥanafiyya, who was one of 'Alī's sons, and most likely the first Shi'is with truly esoteric ideas.[7] Being a locus of manifestation is in itself a miracle; it is therefore quite natural for such a person to be a thaumaturge.

According to Imami and other bio-bibliographical works, since the second century AH, the Shi'is began to compose 'books' on the various miraculous powers of the imams. These were, most likely, more or less extensive collections of *ḥadīth*s on the subject. It appears that none of this literature has come down to us; however, their titles in the recensions provided in bio-bibliographies speak volumes. Indeed, it is very common to find titles such as *Kitāb al-mu'jizāt* (Book of Miracles), *Kitāb mu'jizāt al-nabī wa'l-a'imma* (Book of the Miracles of the Prophet and the imams), *Kitāb mu'jizāt al-a'imma* (Book of the Miracles of the imams), *Kitāb al-a'ājīb* (Book of supra-natural powers), *Kitāb a'ājīb al-a'imma* (Book of the supra-natural powers of the imams) and so forth, and also less obviously telling titles taken up by later authors for their books, or the devoted almost always to the miracles of the imams: *Kitāb dalā'il al-imāma* (Book of Proofs of imamate) (miracles constituting the most striking proofs), *Kitāb al-malāḥim* (Book of eschatological prophecies) (proving

6. See e.g. L. Massignon, 'Salmān Pāk et les prémices spirituelles de l'Islam iranien', *Cahiers de la Société d'Etudes Iraniennes*, 7 (1934) (= *Opera Minora*, Paris, 1969, vol. I, pp. 443–483); M. G. S. Hodgson, 'How did the Early Shī'a Become Sectarian?', *JAOS*, 75 (1955), pp. 5–97; Hodgson, 'Ghulāt', *EI2*, vol. 2, pp. 1,119–1,112. For these kinds of Shi'i sects, see the list made by 'A. Eqbāl, *Khānedān-e Nawbakhtī* (Tehran, 1311 Sh./1933), pp. 249–267.

7. For the relationship between the Saba'iyya and Kaysāniyya see J. van Ess, 'Das *Kitāb al-irjā'* des Ḥasan b. Muḥammad b. al-Ḥanafiyya', *Arabica*, 21 (1974) and 22 (1975), esp. 21, pp. 31ff.; regarding these two sects, refer to Shahrastani, *Livre des religions et des sectes*, vol. I, Fr. trans. with intro. and notes by D. Gimaret and G. Monnot (Louvain and Paris, 1986), index, see the corresponding notes by D. Gimaret.

the imam's Knowledge of the future) and *Kitāb al-nawādir* (Rare and unusual traditions) (which, among much later authors very often contain *ḥadīth*s on the miracles or supra-natural powers of the imams).[8] The earliest compilations of Imami traditions that have come down to us, almost all written roughly between 235 and 390/850 and 1000, devote much importance to the miracles and thaumaturgic powers of the imams: *al-Maḥāsin* by al-Barqī (274 or 280/887 or 893), *Baṣā'ir al-darajāt* by al-Ṣaffār (290/902–903)[9], *al-Imāma* by 'Alī b. al-Ḥusayn b. Bābūya (329/940), *Uṣūl min al-Kāfī* by al-Kulaynī (329/940–941), *Kitāb al-ghayba* by al-Nu'mānī (345 or 360/956 or 971), *Kāmil al-ziyārāt* by Ibn Qūlūya (369/979), the oeuvre of Ibn Bābūya al-Ṣadūq (381/991),[10] *Kifāyat al-athar* by al-Khazzāz (second half of the fourth/end of the tenth century) and even the exegetical works by Furāt b. Furāt al-Kūfī (ca. 300/912), by 'Alī b. Ibrāhīm al-Qummī (ca. 307/919) and al-'Ayyāshī (ca. 320/932), etc.[11] The oldest monograph that has come down to us would be the work by Abū Ja'far Muḥammad b. Jarīr al-Ṭabarī 'al-Ṣaghīr' (who was born in the second half of

---

8. To come across these titles, one need only leaf through works such as al-Najāshī (d. 405/1014), *Kitāb al-rijāl* (Bombay, 1317/1899), or (Tehran, n.d. [ca. 1970]); al-Tūsī (d. 460/1067), *Fihrist kutub al-shī'a*, ed. Sprenger and 'Abd al-Ḥaqq (rpr. Mashhad, 1972) or Ibn al-Nadīm (d. 380/990 – for this date see R. Sellheim, 'Das Todesdatum des Ibn al-Nadīm', *IOS*, 2, 1972, pp. 428–432), *al-Fihrist*, ed. M. R. Tajaddod (Tehran, 1971). See also Āghā Bozorg al-Ṭihrānī, *al-Dharī'a ilā taṣānīf al-shī'a*, 25 vols (Tehran–Najaf, 1353–1398/1934–1978), see under the titles cited above. This material and that which follows makes one wonder about the categorical assertions made by H. Modarressi, *Crisis and Consolidation in the Formative Period of Shī'ite Islam* (Princeton, 1993), pp. 44–45, who maintains that belief in the miracles of the imams was only professed by a minority of 'extremist' Shi'i.

9. Regarding this compiler and his work, see Amir-Moezzi, 'Al-Ṣaffār al-Qummī (d. 290/902–903) et son *Kitāb baṣā'ir al-darajāt*', *JA*, 280/3–4 (1992), pp. 221–250.

10. Al-Najāshī, *Rijāl*, p. 305, even cites a monograph by al-Ṣadūq, *Kitāb dalā'il al-a'imma wa mu'jizātihim,* which seems to have been lost.

11. On these works and their authors, see Amir-Moezzi, *Guide divin*, pp. 51–57 (*Divine Guide*, pp. 20–22); Bar-Asher, *Scripture and Exegesis*; Newman, *The Formative Period.*

the fourth century AH and died in the first half of the fifth century AH), *Nawādir al-muʿjizāt fī manāqib al-aʾimmat al-hudāt.*[12] This marks the beginning of an immense body of literature of which only a few of the major titles of particular importance are given here, for instance *al-Kharāʾij waʾl-jarāʾiḥ* by Quṭb al-Dīn Saʿīd al-Rāwandī (d. 573/1177–1178),[13] *Ithbāt al-hudāt biʾl-nuṣūṣ waʾl-muʿjizāt* by al-Ḥurr al-ʿĀmilī (1104/1693),[14] *Madīnat al-maʿājiz fī dalāʾil al-aʾimmat al-aṭhār wa maʿājizihim* by al-Sayyid Hāshim b.

12. Latest edition: Qumm, 1410/1990. In *Dalāʾil al-imāma*, al-Tabarī 'al-Saghīr' also devotes much space to the miracles of each imam. On this author, see F. Sezgin, *Geschichte der arabischen Schrifttums*, vol. I (Leiden, 1967), p. 540. On the authenticity of *Dalāʾil al-imāma* and its other appellations, see the detailed discussion in Ṭihrānī, *Dharīʿa*, vol. 8, pp. 241–247; on citations from the first two missing chapters of this work of Ibn Ṭāwūs, see E. Kohlberg, *A Medieval Muslim Scholar at Work. Ibn Ṭāwūs and his Library* (Leiden, 1992), pp. 140–141.

13. Latest edition: Qumm, 1409/1990 in 3 vols. Although the title does not indicate it at first glance, this work is entirely devoted to the miracles of the Prophet and the twelve imams. The author himself explains the title: 'And I have entitled [the work] *al-Kharāʾij waʾl-jarāʾiḥ* because the miracles that they [the Prophet and the imams] have revealed [lit.: the or their miracles (that have) emerged — *kharajat*, same root as *kharāʾij* — upon their hands (i.e. by them)] authenticate their claims, and because [the miracles] vindicate [*tuksibu* = one of the meanings of *jaraḥa* and *ijtaraḥa*, same root as *jarāʾiḥ*] the truthfulness of the claimant who did indeed perform them' (*wa sammaytuhu bi kitāb al-kharāʾij waʾl-jarāʾiḥ li-anna muʿjizātihim allatī kharajat ʿalā aydīhim muṣaḥḥiha li-daʿāwīhim li-annahā tuksibuʾl-muddaʿī wa man ẓaharat ʿalā yadihi ṣidq qawlih*) (al-Rāwandī, *Kharāʾij*, vol. 1, p. 19). Al-Rāwandī added five of his treatises on the same topic at the end of this work: *Kitāb nawādir al-muʿjizāt, al-Muwāzāt bayn muʿjizāt nabiyyinā (ṣ) wa muʿjizāt awṣiyāʾihi wa muʿjizāt al-anbiyāʾ, Kitāb umm al-muʿjizāt* (=Qurʾān), *al-Farq bayn al-ḥiyal waʾl-muʿjizāt, Kitāb ʿalāmāt wa marātib nabiyyinā (ṣ) wa awṣiyāʾihi.* On al-Rāwandī see e.g., al-Kh(w)ānsārī, *Rawḍāt al-jannāt*, ed. A. Ismāʿīliyān (Qumm, 1390–1392/1970–1972), vol. 4, pp. 5–9; al-ʿĀmilī, *Aʿyān al-shīʿa* (Damascus and Beirut, 1354–1382/1935–1963), vol. 35, pp. 16–24.

14. Al-Ḥurr al-ʿĀmilī, *Ithbāt al-hudāt biʾl-nuṣūṣ waʾl-muʿjizāt* (Tehran, 1364 Sh./1985). Regarding the author, see e.g. M. ʿA. Mudarris, *Rayḥānat al-adab*, 8 vols (Tabriz, n.d.), vol. 2, pp. 31–33; al-Māmaqānī, *Tanqīḥ al-maqāl* (Tehran, 1349/1930), vol. 3, p. 106.

Sulaymān al-Baḥrānī (1107 or 1109/1695–1696 or 1697–1698),[15] chapters in the numerous works belonging to the genre known as the *manāqib*, beginning with *al-Irshād fī maʿrifat ḥujaj Allāh ʿalāʾl-ʿibād* by Shaykh al-Mufīd (413/1022),[16] and *Manāqib āl Abī Ṭālib* by Ibn Shahrāshūb (588/1192),[17] not to mention countless pages devoted to the subject by such notable authors as Yaḥyā b. al-Ḥasan Ibn al-Biṭrīq (600/1203), Raḍī al-Dīn Ibn Ṭāwūs (664/1266), ʿAlī b. ʿĪsā al-Irbilī (696/1296), Rajab al-Bursī (eighth/fourteenth century), Muḥammad Bāqir al-Majlisī (1111/1699), Ḥusayn al-Ṭabarsī/Ṭabrisī al-Nūrī (1320/1902) and so on.

The prodigious powers and miracles of the imams, that the sources most often designate by terms such as *muʿjiza*, pl. *muʿjizāt/maʿājiz* ('miracle'), *uʿjūba*, pl. *aʿājīb* (lit. 'that which surprises', 'that which amazes' hence amazing powers) or quite simply *qudra* ('power'),[18] may be considered the results either of their ontological or initiatory rank if not both combined, so inseparable are these two aspects of the imams. The terrestrial imam, Friend or Ally (*wālī*) of God is, on the perceptible level, a manifestation of the celestial, archetypal, cosmic Imam. As Light produced from the divine Light, the imam is the Organ of God, that is, the medium of the Names and Attributes of God. He is the *Deus revelatus*, the

15. Hāshim b. Sulaymān al-Baḥrānī, *Madīnat al-maʿājiz fī dalāʾil al-aʾimmat al-aṭhār wa maʿājizihim* (Tehran, n.d. [ca. 1960]). Regarding the author, now consult W. Madelung, 'Baḥrānī, Hāshem', *EIr*, vol. 3, pp. 528–529.

16. Al-Mufīd, *al-Irshād fī maʿrifa ḥujaj Allāh ʿalāʾl-ʿibād*, ed. and Persian trans. by H. Rasūlī Maḥallātī (Tehran, 1346Sh./1968; rpr. Qumm, n.d. [ca. 1985]). Regarding the author see M. J. Mc Dermott, *The Theology of al-Shaikh al-Mufīd (d. 413/1022)* (Beirut, 1978), and the introduction by I. K. A. Howard, *The Book of Guidance*, English trans. of the *Irshād* by al-Mufīd (London, 1981).

17. Ibn Shahrāshūb, *Manāqib āl Abī Ṭālib* (Beirut, 1405/1985), 4 vols: based on the Najaf ed. (1375–1376/1956), 3 vols. Regarding the author, consult Amir-Moezzi, 'Ebn Shahrāshūb', *EIr*, vol. 8, pp. 53–54.

18. For the last two terms, less frequent than the first, see e.g., al-Ṣaffār al-Qummī, *Baṣāʾir al-darajāt*, ed. M. Kūchebāghī (2nd edn, Tabriz, n.d. [ca. 1960]), section 10, ch. 18 ('Bāb al-nawādir fī'l-a'imma wa aʿājībihim'); section 8, chs 12–15 (mā uʿṭiya al-a'imma min al-qudra…al-qudra allatī aʿṭāhum Allāh… fī qudrat al-a'imma…).

ineffable Essence of God being the unknowable – *Deus Absconditus*.[19] This privileged ontological status explains why the terrestrial imam's life – even before his birth – is marked by miracles. The entire process of his birth, from conception, pregnancy to delivery, is accompanied by a series of wondrous phenomena. At birth he is radiant, clean and already circumcised; the umbilical cord is already severed. He speaks from the cradle and grows at an extraordinary rate. Whilst in the mother's womb he communicated with angels and other celestial beings; at his birth a column of light (*'amūd min nūr*) appears before him, linking him to heaven and providing him with all kinds of knowledge, and so on.[20] Moreover, the cosmo-anthropogonic traditions relate that the first thing that marks the existence of the Imam, from the original world of the *umm al-kitāb* – well before the creation of the perceptible world – is his initiation by God into the sacred and secret Sciences of Unification and Glorification.[21]

Initiated by God, the imam is in turn the wise initiator par excellence. *'Ilm*, secret initiatory science is part of the very being of the imam and one of its direct consequences is his supernatural power and ability to perform miracles.[22] Essential to the thaumaturgical powers of the imam is a body of sacred and/or occult knowledge. To this end, even elements linked to his ontological status are presented as sources of his knowledge and thus of

19. On theology of the Twelver imamate, see Amir-Moezzi, *Guide divin*, pp. 75–81 (*Divine Guide*, pp. 29–32) and 'Cosmogony', in particular pp. 319–320; see also Chapters 3 and 8, this volume.

20. For all this information and early sources that provide it, see *Guide divin*, II.4 pp. 145–154 (*Divine Guide*, 'Conception and Birth', pp. 56–61).

21. *Guide divin*, pp. 82ff. (*Divine Guide*, p. 32); Chapter 4, this volume.

22. On *'ilm* in early Imamism, see *Guide divin*, III.2, pp. 174–199 (*Divine Guide*, 'The Sacred Science', pp. 69–79); on the evolution of this term's meaning see M. A. Amir-Moezzi, 'Réflexions sur une évolution du shi'isme duodécimain: tradition et idéologisation', in E. Patlagean and A. Le Boulluec (eds), *Les retours aux Écritures. Fondamentalismes présents et passés* (Louvain and Paris, 1993), pp. 63–82, esp. pp. 64–69; see also E. Kohlberg, 'Imam and Community in the Pre-Ghayba Period', in S. A. Arjomand (ed.), *Authority and Political Culture in Shi'ism* (Albany, NY, 1988), pp. 25–53 (rpr. in *Belief*, article 13), esp. pp. 25–27.

his power. For example, the 'column of light' that the imam can visualise at will and throughout his life, contains answers to his questions and knowledge of hidden things.[23] Two other sources of inspiration, both supra-natural powers, one of which 'marks his heart' and the other 'pierces his eardrum' provide him with knowledge of the future.[24] Endowed with a sacred spirit (*rūḥ al-quds*) he is able to communicate with celestial beings that procure for him extraordinary inspired knowledge; he is himself able to make the celestial ascension mainly for initiatory purposes.[25]

Transmission of initiatory knowledge takes place mostly in an occult fashion. The Light of imamate is already itself partially hereditary and can be transmitted by semen; other bodily fluids (saliva, sweat) introduced into pores of the skin and into the mouth and eyes of the disciple, as well as on his body or

---

23. Al-Ṣaffār, *Baṣā'ir*, pp. 431–443; al-Kulaynī, *al-Uṣūl min al-Kāfī*, ed. J. Muṣṭafawī, 4 vols (Tehran, n.d.) vol. 2, pp. 225–231; al-Kulaynī, *al-Rawḍa min al-Kāfī*, ed. H. Rasūlī Maḥallātī (Tehran, 1389/1969), vol. 1, pp. 182–183; al-Ṭurayḥī, *Majma' al-baḥrayn wa maṭla' al-nayyirayn* (Tehran, 1321/1903), see under '*'amūd*' and '*nūr*'. Regarding the visionary power of the imams, see E. Kohlberg, 'Vision and the Imams', *Mélanges Gimaret*, pp. 125–157.

24. For the 'marking of the heart' (*nakt/qadhf/qar' [fī] al-qalb*) and 'the piercing of the eardrum' (*naqr/nakt fī al-udhn/al-sam'/al-asmā'*) see e.g. al-Ṣaffār, *Baṣā'ir*, pp. 316–319; al-Kulaynī, *al-Uṣūl*, vol. 1, pp. 394ff.; al-Kulaynī, *Rawḍa*, vol. 1, p. 182; al-Ṭurayḥī, *Majma'*, index. With regard to these two powers, the traditions often employ the terms *waḥy* and *ilhām*.

25. On the presence of the Holy Spirit in the imam, see al-Ṣaffār, *Baṣā'ir*, pp. 445–450; al-Kulaynī, *al-Uṣūl*, vol. 2, pp. 15–17; on communication with celestial beings, mainly the angels and the Holy Spirit, see e.g. al-Ṣaffār, *Baṣā'ir*, pp. 319–326 and 368–374; al-Kulaynī, *al-Uṣūl*, vol. 2, pp. 13–15; al-Nu'mānī, *Kitāb al-ghayba*, ed. 'A. A. Ghaffārī and Persian trans. by M. J. Ghaffārī (Tehran, 1363 Sh./1985), pp. 95 and 126; Ibn Bābūya, *'Ilal al-sharā'i' wa'l-aḥkām* (Najaf, 1385/1966), ch. 146, pp. 182ff.; al-Ṭabarī, *Dalā'il al-imāma* (Qumm, 1413/1994), pp. 270–271; al-Baḥrānī, *Madīna*, p. 394. It is for this reason that the imam is called *al-muḥaddath* ('the one to whom celestial beings speak') and *al-mufahham* ('the one to whom is given understanding from the Most High'), see E. Kohlberg, 'The Term "Muḥaddath" in Twelver Shī'ism', in *Studia Orientalia memoriæ D.H. Baneth dedicata* (Jerusalem, 1979), pp. 39–47 (rpr. in *Belief*, article V). On the celestial ascension of the imam see Chapter 5, this volume.

by placing the hand upon his chest enables the transmission of secret knowledge.[26]

A portion of the prodigious knowledge of the imams stems from certain secret texts: the white *Jafr* that contains a section on revelations of previous prophets, writings of the imams and sages of the past, the Knowledge of Fortune and Misfortune (*ʿilm al-manāyā wa'l-balāyā*), the science of the past and future; the Book of Fāṭima which, among other things, contains an account of the various states of Muḥammad after death; the Book of ʿAlī containing an account of 'all that will occur in the world until the Day of Resurrection'; the Book of Rulers of the World (enabling knowledge of who will, or will not, be successful in attaining power); the Book of the People of Paradise and those of Hell (enabling the recognition and distinguishing of good souls from evil ones).[27]

The imams know the Supreme or Greatest Name of God (*al-ism al-aʿẓam* or *al-ism al-akbar*) with its almost limitless supra-natural powers and they are in possession of 'icons of power' carrying the miraculous forces of the prophets: Adam's Tunic; Solomon's Seal, Joseph's Tunic; the Staff, Ark and Tablets of Moses; Muhammad's weapon was (perhaps the same as the terrifying red *Jafr*), an invincible weapon of the Qā'im at the

---

26. On transmission by seminal fluid, see *Guide divin*, II-2, pp. 96–112 (*Divine Guide*, pp. 38–44); see also U. Rubin, 'Pre-existence and Light. Aspects of the Concept of Nūr Muḥammad', *IOS*, 5 (1975), pp. 62–119; Rubin, 'Prophets and Progenitors in the Early Shīʿa Tradition', *JSAI*, 1 (1979), pp. 64–98. On transmission by other means, see e.g. al-Ṣaffār, *Baṣā'ir*, pp. 313 and 390; al-Nuʿmānī, *Ghayba*, p. 204; Ibn Bābūya, *al-Amālī* (= *al-Majālis*), ed. M. B. Kamare'ī (rpr. Tehran, 1404/1984), 'majlis' 28, no. 5, p. 136 and 'majlis' 55, no. 1, p. 341; Ibn Bābūya, *Kamāl al-dīn wa tamām al-niʿma*, ed. ʿA. A. Ghaffārī (rpr. Qumm, 1405/1985), vol. 2, ch. 42, p. 425.

27. On these sacred Texts and the secrets of the imams, see Amir-Moezzi, *Guide divin*, pp. 185–189 (*Divine Guide*, pp. 73–75) and especially the monograph by E. Kohlberg, 'Authoritative Scriptures in Early Imami Shiʿism', in E. Patlagean and A. LeBoulluec (eds), *Les retours aux Écritures. Fondamentalismes présents et passés* (Louvain and Paris, 1993), pp. 295–312.

End of Time.[28] The esoteric sciences and their miraculous effects are also part of the resources of the imams: divination, transmutation of objects, communicating with the dead (especially with the spirits of prophets and saints), astrology or, more specifically, precise knowledge of the stars and their influence over life on earth.[29] Further still, there is the knowledge of consciences and souls (*ʿilm al-aḍmār wa'l-anfus*), knowledge of the Clay (*ʿilm al-ṭīna*; i.e. knowledge about man's original nature), knowledge of the faculty of vision and physiognomy (*firāsa/tafarrus/tawassum*), knowledge of all languages, including those of the animals

---

28. On the Greatest Name, see e.g., al-Ṣaffār, *Baṣā'ir*, pp. 208–219; (Pseudo-?) al-Masʿūdī, *Ithbāt al-waṣiyya* (Najaf, n.d.), p. 202; Ibn Bābūya, *Amālī*, 'majlis' 71, no. 10, pp. 467f.; al-Ṭabarī, *Dalā'il*, pp. 251f., pp. 414, 420; al-Ṭabarī 'al-Ṣaghīr', *Nawādir al-muʿjizāt fī manāqib al-a'immat al-hudāt* (Qumm, 1410/1990), p. 188; Ibn Shahrāshūb, *Manāqib*, vol. 4, pp. 230f.; al-Irbilī, *Kashf al-ghumma fī maʿrifat al-a'imma*, ed. H. Rasūlī Maḥallātī (Tabriz; rpr. Qumm, 1381/1962), vol. 2, p. 385; al-Baḥrānī, *Madīna*, pp. 358 and 544; al-Majlisī, *Biḥār al-anwār*, 110 tomes in 90 vols (Tehran and Qumm, 1376–1392/1956–1972), vol. 27, pp. 25–28. On the 'icons of power' see e.g. al-Ṣaffār, *Baṣā'ir*, pp. 174–190; al-Kulaynī, *al-Uṣūl*, vol. 1, pp. 335ff.; Ibn ʿAyyāsh al-Jawharī, *Muqtaḍab al-athar* (Tehran, 1346/1927), pp. 56–57.

29. On divination: al-Ṣaffār, *Baṣā'ir*, pp. 389f.; Ibn Bābūya, *Amālī*, 'majlis' 64, no. 16 *in fine*, p. 416; a tradition by ʿAlī narrated by al-Sharīf al-Raḍī, *Nahj al-balāgha*, ed. and Persian trans. by ʿA. N. Fayḍ al-Islām (Tehran, 1351 Sh./1972), p. 177, that censors the reference to divination. On the transmutation of objects: Ibn Bābūya, *Amālī*, 'majlis' 29, no. 19, pp. 148–149; Ibn Bābūya,*ʿUyūn akhbār al-Riḍā*, ed. M. H. Lājevardī (Tehran, 1378/1958), vol. 1, pp. 95–96; al-Ṭabarī, *Dalā'il*, pp. 169f., 198ff., 397ff.; al-Ṭabarī, *Nawādir*, pp. 103f., 113f., 179ff.; Ḥurr al-ʿĀmilī, *Ithbāt*, vol. 5, pp. 158ff., 254ff.; al-Baḥrānī, *Madīna*, pp. 204ff., 293ff., 523ff. On communication with the dead: al-Ṣaffār, *Baṣā'ir*, pp. 274–284 (where the most audacious and interesting traditions are grouped together); on astrology: al-Kulaynī, *Rawḍa*, vol. 2, pp. 166, 196–197, 279–280 and as a general reference, Ibn Ṭāwūs, *Faraj al-mahmūm fī ta'rīkh ʿulamā' al-nujūm* (Qumm, 1363 Sh./1985), devoted to astrology and riddled with *ḥadīth*s (plus those that also contain, among other passages, the first two chapters previously lost of the *Dalā'il* by al-Ṭabarī on the astrological science possessed by ʿAlī [pp. 202–207]). See also the thesis by Z. Matar, 'The *Faraj al-mahmūm* of Ibn Ṭāwūs: A Thirteenth Century Work on Astrology and Astrologers' (New York University, 1986) and especially E. Kohlberg, *A Medieval Muslim Scholar at Work: Ibn Ṭāwūs and his Library* (Leiden, 1992), index.

and the 'transformed' (*al-musūkh*); power to revive the dead, to cure disease and heal the sick, to walk on water, to travel and transport others (their disciples in this case) through the air, to other 'worlds', to different regions of the world, to ride the clouds,[30] and this list is far from exhaustive.

In principle, all the Impeccable Ones are able to perform the full range of miracles;[31] however, in terms of the twelve imams, it appears that each one of them has a preference for a certain number of specific miracles. Indeed, our hagio-biographical sources do not uniformly attribute all miraculous deeds to all the imams.[32] In this form of casting, the principal role is reserved

30. On these powers and the earliest sources that report them, see Amir-Moezzi, *Guide divin*, pp. 233-239 (*Divine Guide*, pp. 93–95); (on p. 237 [p. 94], I note that the earliest sources, the *Baṣā'ir* by al-Ṣaffār in this case, attribute the power to ride clouds to the first and last imams; one should add that in later sources, this miracle seems to have been extended to other imams; cf. e.g., the fourth imam in Ṭabarī, *Nawādir*, p. 113; Ṭabarī, *Dalā'il*, p. 199; al-ʿĀmilī, *Ithbāt*, vol. 5, p. 254; al-Baḥrānī, *Madīna*, p. 293; and the sixth imam in al-Ṭabarī, *Nawādir*, p. 137; *Dalā'il*, p. 249; al-ʿĀmilī, *Ithbāt*, vol. 5, p. 453; al-Baḥrānī, *Madīna*, p. 357).

31. Our sources often (but not always) begin with the miracles of the Prophet; however, in most cases these are much fewer and less spectacular than those of the imams. This procedure seems to have two aims: first to stress the fact that the imams are only continuing the work of the Prophet; and secondly, to hint at the superiority of the *bāṭin* – represented by the imam – over the *ẓāhir* – represented by the Prophet, an idea that is a recurring motif in Imamism, especially early on. Moreover, there seem to be very few ancient sources that relate the miracles performed by Fāṭima; regarding this, see e.g. al-Rāwandī, *Kharā'ij*, vol. 2, pp. 524–540; Ibn Shahrāshūb, *Manāqib*, vol. 4, pp. 115–119; T. Sabri, 'L'hagiographie de Fātima d'après le *Bihār al-anwār* de Muhammad Bāqir al-Majlisī (d. 1111/1699)' (PhD thesis, University of Paris, III, 1969), see under 'Miracles', and my article (with J. Calmard), 'Fāṭema', *EIr*.

32. Indeed a tradition has ʿAlī al-Riḍā (al-Ṣaffār, *Baṣā'ir*, p. 480) saying: 'We [the imams] are equal in knowledge and bravery; and as for our [supra-natural] gifts, that depends on what we have received as commandments' (*naḥnu fi'l-ʿilm wa'l-shajāʿa sawā' wa fi'l-ʿaṭāyā ʿalā qadri mā nu'maru bihi*), and another traditon dating back to Ja'far al-Ṣādiq (al-Ṣaffār, *Baṣā'ir*, p. 479): 'Some imams have greater thaumaturgical knowledge than others' (*al-a'imma baʿḍuhum aʿlam min baʿḍ*). See also the comments by E. Kohlberg, 'Imam and Community in the Pre-Ghayba Period', in S. A. Arjomand (ed.), *Authority and*

for 'Alī, imam par excellence and father of all the others, then, to a lesser extent, to the sixth imam, Ja'far al-Ṣādiq, the veritable 'developer' of Imami doctrine. Let us briefly review the various types of miracle that the sources attribute most frequently to the different imams:

1. 'Alī b. Abī Ṭālib (d. 40/661): practically all the types of miracle mentioned above. The chapter devoted to 'Alī's miraculous powers is almost always the most extensive one in our sources,[33] perhaps with more emphasis placed on his knowledge of the invisible world (*al-ghayb*),[34] his ability to intervene in cosmic matters,[35] his command over the divinatory sciences and his prophecies.[36]

Political Culture in Shi'ism (Albany, NY, 1988), pp. 25–53 (rpr. in *Belief*, article XIII), p. 30.

33. For example, al-Ṭabarī, *Nawādir*, pp. 56–172; al-Rāwandī, *Kharā'ij*, vol. 1, pp. 171–235; Ibn Shahrāshūb, *Manāqib*, vol. 2, pp. 83–175; al-Baḥrānī, *Madīna*, pp. 78–190; al-Majlisī, *Biḥār*, see index (in 30 vols, Qumm, 1991–1992), see index under '*mu'jizāt 'Alī*'. One should add the vast literature of the *manāqib* of 'Alī.

34. Al-Rāwandī, *Kharā'ij*, vol. 1, pp. 177ff.; Ibn Shahrāshūb, *Manāqib*, vol. 2, pp. 94–112; 'Alī b. 'Īsā al-Irbilī, *Kashf al-ghumma fī ma'rifat al-a'imma*, ed. H. Rasūlī Mahallātī (Tabriz; rpr. Qumm, 1381/1962), vol. 1, pp. 273–286.

35. (Pseudo) Sulaym b. Qays, *Kitāb al-saqīfa* (Qumm, n.d.), p. 234; al-Ṣaffār, *Baṣā'ir*, pp. 217–2119; Shādhān b. Jabra'īl, *al-Faḍā'il* (Najaf, 1381/1962), p. 69; Ibn Bābūya, *Amālī*, 'majlis' 71, no. 10, pp. 467f.; Ibn Shahrāshūb, *Manāqib*, vol. 1, pp. 120–128; al-Irbilī, *Kashf*, vol. 1, pp. 274ff.; al-Ḥusayn b. 'Abd al-Wahhāb, *'Uyūn al-mu'jizāt* (Najaf, n.d.), p. 4. See also L. Capezzone, 'Un miracolo di 'Alī b. Abī Ṭālib: i versi attribuiti ad al-Sayyid al-Ḥimyarī e il modello storiografico delle fonti relative al *radd al-šams*', in *In memoria di Francesco Gabrieli (1904–1996)*, *RSO*, 71, suppl. 2 (1997), pp. 99–112.

36. Al-Ṣaffār, *Baṣā'ir*, pp. 389f.; Ibn Ṭāwūs, *Faraj al-mahmūm fī ta'rīkh 'ulamā' al-nujūm* (Qumm, 1363 Sh./1985), pp. 102ff.; another work by Ibn Ṭāwūs, *al-Malāḥim wa'l-fitan* (e.g. Qumm, 1398/1989, entitled *al-Malāḥim wa'l-fitan fī ẓuhūr al-ghā'ib al-muntaẓar*), contains many eschatological prophecies by 'Alī; al-Majlisī, *Biḥār*, vol. 58, pp. 229ff.

2. Al-Ḥasan b. ʿAlī (d. 49/669): levitation[37] and power over objects.[38]
3. Al-Ḥusayn b. ʿAlī (d. 61/680): knowledge of the future, especially foreknowledge of his own violent death at Karbalāʾ.[39]
4. ʿAlī Zayn al-ʿĀbidīn (d. 92 or 95/711 or 714): celestial ascension,[40] power over objects (particularly the episode in which, after Muḥammad b. al-Ḥanafiyya laid claim to the imamate, in his presence, the Black Stone of the Kaʿba was made to speak in favour of Zayn al-ʿĀbidīn's imamate; which, according to our sources, convinced Ibn al-Ḥanafiyya).[41]

37. Al-Ṭabarī, *Nawādir*, pp. 100ff.; al-Ṭabarī, *Dalāʾil*, pp. 166–169; al-ʿĀmilī, *Ithbāt*, vol. 5, pp. 158f.; al-Baḥrānī, *Madīna*, pp. 203ff.

38. Al-Ṭabarī, *Nawādir*, pp. 104f.; al-Rāwandī, *Kharāʾij*, vol. 1, pp. 238ff.; al-ʿĀmilī, *Ithbāt*, vol. 5, pp. 160f.; al-Majlisī, *Biḥār*, vol. 43, pp. 323ff.

39. Al-Ṭabarī, *Nawādir*, pp. 107ff.; al-Ṭabarī, *Dalāʾil*, pp. 182ff.; al-Rāwandī, *Kharāʾij*, vol. 1, pp. 245ff.; Ibn Shahrāshūb, *Manāqib*, vol. 3, p. 211 f.; Ibn Ṭāwūs, *al-Luhūf fī qatlā al-ṭufūf* (Qumm, 1364 Sh./1985), pp. 26ff.; al-ʿĀmilī, *Ithbāt*, vol. 5, pp. 206ff.; al-Majlisī, *Biḥār*, vol. 44, pp. 180ff.; al-Baḥrānī, *Madīna*, pp. 238ff.

40. Al-Ṭabarī, *Nawādir*, pp. 113ff.; al-Ṭabarī, *Dalāʾil*, pp. 199ff.; al-ʿĀmilī, *Ithbāt*, vol. 5, pp. 254ff.; al-Baḥrānī, *Madīna*, pp. 293ff.

41. Al-Ṣaffār, [*Baṣāʾir*], pp. 522–523; al-Kulaynī, *al-Uṣūl*, vol. 1, pp. 282–283; ʿAlī b. al-Ḥusayn Ibn Bābūya, *al-Imāma waʾl-tabṣira min al-ḥayra* (Qumm, 1404/1984), pp. 60–62; al-Ṭabarī, *Dalāʾil*, pp. 206–208; al-Rāwandī, *Kharāʾij*, vol. 1, pp. 257–258; Abuʾl-Faḍl al-Ṭabarsī/Ṭabrisī, *Iʿlām al-warā bi-aʿlām al-hudā*, ed. M. al-Kharsān (3rd edn, Qumm, 1970), p. 258; Ibn Shahrāshūb, *Manāqib*, vol. 3, p. 288; al-Ḥasan b. Sulaymān al-Ḥillī, *Mukhtaṣar baṣāʾir al-darajāt* (Najaf, 1370/1950), pp. 14 and 170; al-ʿĀmilī, *Ithbāt*, vol. 3, p. 292 and vol. 5, p. 123; al-Majlisī, *Biḥār*, vol. 45, p. 347 and vol. 46, pp. 22 and 111–113; al-Baḥrānī, *Madīna*, p. 297 (clearly this is an anti-Kaysānī tradition, so much so that in several versions, the reporter is none other than Abū Khālid Kankar al-Kābulī, a Kaysānī deserter who accepted the imamate of ʿAlī b. al-Ḥusayn; now consult L. Capezzone, 'Abiura dalla Kaysāniyya e conversione all'Imāmiyya: il caso di Abū Khālid al-Kābulī', *RSO*, 66/1–2 (1992), pp. 1–14.

5. Muḥammad al-Bāqir (d. ca. 119/737): power over objects,[42] power of supra-natural travel.[43]
6. Ja'far al-Ṣādiq (d. 148/765): as stated above, a great many miracles are attributed to this imam, with particular emphasis on: thaumaturgical use of the Greatest Divine Name,[44] the power of supra-natural travel (*qudrat al-sayr*, i.e. travel for himself as well as transporting others, in this case, his closest disciples),[45] prediction of the deaths of others (especially his followers).[46]
7. Mūsā al-Kāẓim (d. 183/799): miraculous powers ever since his early childhood,[47] power to become invisible (especially when

---

42. Al-Ṭabarī, *Nawādir*, pp. 133f.; al-Ṭabarī, *Dalā'il*, pp. 219f.; al-Rāwandī, *Kharā'ij*, vol. 1, pp. 272ff.; al-Irbilī, *Kashf*, vol. 2, pp. 141ff.; al-'Āmilī, *Ithbāt*, vol. 5, pp. 292f. and 315f.; al-Baḥrānī, *Madīna*, pp. 322f.

43. Al-Ṭabarī, *Nawādir*, pp. 135f.; al-Rāwandī, *Kharā'ij*, vol. 1, pp. 285f.; al-Ḥillī, *Mukhtaṣar*, p. 15; al-'Āmilī, *Ithbāt*, vol. 5, p. 317; al-Majlisī, *Biḥār*, vol. 46, pp. 252f.; al-Baḥrānī, *Madīna*, pp. 323f.

44. Al-Ṣaffār, *Baṣā'ir*, pp. 237–238; al-Ṭabarī, *Dalā'il*, pp. 251–252; al-Rāwandī, *Kharā'ij*, vol. 1, p. 296; al-Irbilī, *Kashf*, vol. 2, p. 199; Ibn Shahrāshūb, *Manāqib*, vol. 3, pp. 357ff.; al-Baḥrānī, *Madīna*, p. 358.

45. Al-Ṣaffār, *Baṣā'ir*, pp. 397–407; al-Ṭabarī, *Nawādir*, pp. 138ff.; al-Ṭabarī, *Dalā'il*, p. 249; al-'Āmilī, *Ithbāt*, vol. 5, pp. 453ff.; al-Baḥrānī, *Madīna*, pp. 357ff.

46. Al-Ṣaffār, *Baṣā'ir*, p. 283; al-Ṭabarī, *Dalā'il*, pp. 256ff. and 286; al-Mufīd, *al-Ikhtiṣāṣ*, ed. 'A. A. Ghaffārī (Qumm, n.d.), pp. 84f.; al-Rāwandī, *Kharā'ij*, vol. 2, pp. 647f.; Ibn Ṭāwūs, *Faraj*, p. 229 (predicted the deaths of Sawra b. Kulayb, al-Mu'allā b. Khunays, Abū Ḥamza al-Thumālī). See also J. Loebenstein, 'Miracles in Šī'ī Thought. A Case Study of the Miracles Attributed to Imām Ǧa'far al-Ṣādiq', *Arabica*, 50/2 (2003), pp. 199–244.

47. Al-Kulaynī, *al-Uṣūl*, vol. 1, p. 247 and vol. 3, p. 16; al-Mas'ūdī, *Ithbāt*, p. 162; Ibn Shu'ba, *Tuḥaf al-'uqūl 'an āl al-rasūl*, ed. 'A. A. Ghaffārī with Persian trans. by M. B. Kamare'ī (rpr. Qumm, 1404/1984), p. 411; al-Ṭabarī, *Dalā'il*, p. 326; al-Mufīd, *al-Irshād fī ma'rifa ḥujaj Allāh 'alā'l-'ibād*, ed. and Persian trans. by H. Rasūlī Maḥallātī (Tehran, 1346 Sh./1968; rpr. Qumm, n.d., [ca. 1985]), p. 290; Ibn Ḥamza, *al-Thāqib fī al-manāqib*, ed. N. R. 'Ulwān (Beirut, 1411/1992), p. 433; al-Irbilī, *Kashf*, vol. 2, p. 221; Abū Muḥammad al-'Āmilī al-Nubāṭī, *al-Ṣirāṭ al-mustaqīm ilā mustaḥaqqī'l-taqdīm* (Najaf, 1338/1919), vol. 2, pp. 163f.

imprisoned by the caliph Hārūn al-Rashīd)[48] and miracles in the presence of this caliph.[49]

8. ʿAlī al-Riḍā (d. 203/818): resurrection of the dead[50] and miracles in the presence of the caliph al-Maʾmūn.[51]
9. to 11. The three imams, Muḥammad al-Jawād (d. 220/835), ʿAlī al-Naqī (d. 254/868) and al-Ḥasan al-ʿAskarī (d. 260/874): power over objects.[52]
12. Muḥammad b. al-Ḥasan al-Mahdī (the hidden imam, the eschatological Saviour): before his minor occultation (which, according to tradition, occurred in 260/874 on the death of his

48. Al-Ṭabarī, *Dalāʾil*, pp. 320f.; al-ʿĀmilī, *Ithbāt*, vol. 5, p. 566; al-Majlisī, *Biḥār*, vol. 44, p. 66; al-Baḥrānī, *Madīna*, pp. 427f.

49. Ibn Bābūya, *ʿUyūn akhbār al-Riḍā*, ed. M. H. Lājevardī (Tehran, 1378/1958), vol. 1, pp. 95–96, vol. 2, pp. 95f. and 100f.; Ibn Bābūya, *Amālī*, 'majlis' 29, no. 19, pp. 148f.; al-Mufīd, *Irshād*, pp. 293ff.; al-Ṭabarī, *Dalāʾil*, pp. 315ff.; al-Ṭabarī, *Nawādir*, pp. 163ff.; al-Rāwandī, *Kharāʾij*, vol. 1, p. 334; Ibn Shahrāshūb, *Manāqib*, vol. 4, pp. 303ff.; Ṭabrisī, *Iʿlām*, pp. 302f.; al-Nubāṭi, *al-Ṣirāṭ al-mustaqīm*, vol. 2, pp. 192ff. The fact that, in these kinds of traditions, the ʿAbbasid caliph was accused by the Shiʿis of having poisoned the seventh imam clearly had a polemical aim: Hārūn is all the more injust because he was well aware of the imam's miracles and thus his saintliness and legitimacy.

50. Ibn Bābūya, *ʿUyūn*, vol. 2, pp. 167ff.; al-Ṭabarī, *Nawādir*, pp. 168f.; al-Ṭabarī, *Dalāʾil*, p. 363; Ibn Ṭāwūs, *Faraj*, p. 231.

51. Ibn Bābūya, *ʿUyūn*, vol. 2, pp. 184ff. and 214ff.; al-Ṭabarī, *Dalāʾil*, pp. 360 and 376–382; al-Rāwandī, *Kharāʾij*, vol. 1, pp. 350ff.; Ibn Shahrāshūb, *Manāqib*, vol. 4, pp. 370ff.; Ibn Ḥamza, *Thāqib*, pp. 467ff.; Ibrāhīm b. Muḥammad al-Juwaynī, *Farāʾid al-simṭayn*, ed. M. B. al-Maḥmūdī (Beirut, 1398/1979), vol. 2, p. 212; al-Nubāṭī, *Ṣirāṭ*, vol. 2, pp. 197ff.; al-Majlisī, *Biḥār*, vol. 49, p. 300 and vol. 82, p. 46; al-Baḥrānī, *Madīna*, p. 498. Same comment as note 49.

52. On Muḥammad al-Jawād being gifted with miraculous powers since his childhood: see e.g. al-Ṭabarī, *Nawādir*, pp. 179ff.; al-Ṭabarī, *Dalāʾil*, pp. 397ff.; al-Rāwandī, *Kharāʾij*, vol. 1, p. 373ff.; al-Irbilī, *Kashf*, vol. 2, p. 365ff.; al-ʿĀmilī, *Ithbāt*, vol. 6, pp. 184ff.; al-Baḥrānī, *Madīna*, pp. 523ff. On ʿAlī al-Naqī: al-Ṭabarī, *Nawādir*, pp. 184ff.; al-Ṭabarī, *Dalāʾil*, pp. 412ff.; al-Rāwandī, *Kharāʾij*, vol. 1, pp. 396ff.; al-Majlisī, *Biḥār*, vol. 50, p. 144; al-Baḥrānī, *Madīna*, pp. 547ff. On al-Ḥasan al-ʿAskarī: al-Kulaynī, *al-Uṣūl*, vol. 1, pp. 507f.; al-Ṭabarī, *Nawādir*, pp. 190ff.; al-Ṭabarī, *Dalāʾil*, pp. 426ff.; al-Rāwandī, *Kharāʾij*, vol. 1, pp. 421f.; al-ʿĀmilī, *Ithbāt*, vol. 6, pp. 344ff.; al-Baḥrānī, *Ḥilyat al-abrār fī faḍāʾil Muḥammad wa ālihiʾl-aṭhār* (Qumm, 1397/1978), vol. 2, pp. 491f.

> father): miraculous powers of the child imam;[53] and after his major occultation (which according to the tradition occurred in 329/940): ability to help those in difficulties with miraculous powers and to initiate the loyal faithful by supra-natural means.[54]

The imam is capable of performing miracles because he is a divine initiate and, further, because he is part of the divine being and his knowledge is of divine origin.[55] Thus, the theological, anthropological and initiatory content of *walāya* is put into effect to provide a veritable exegesis of the miracle. Certain especially audacious *ḥadīth*s clearly illustrate this conception. After causing light to burst from the sky (which just about made Medina explode) imam al-Ḥasan b. ʿAlī is said to have declared:

> We [the imams] are the First and the Last; we are the Commanders; we are the Light. The Light of spiritual beings [i.e. non-material celestial beings] comes from us. We illuminate by the Light of God. We render joyful by its/His joy [or 'we spiritualise by its/His spirit'; the pronoun can refer either to the light or to God; the ambiguity

---

53. See Amir-Moezzi, *Guide divin*, section IV. 2 ('L'imām et son occultation: aspects ésotériques'), pp. 264–270 (*Divine Guide*, ch. 4, section 2); also e.g., al-Rāwandī, *Kharāʾij*, vol. 1, pp. 455ff.; al-Irbilī, *Kashf*, vol. 2, pp. 498ff.; al-Majlisī, *Biḥār*, vol. 51, pp. 4ff.; al-Baḥrānī, *Madīna*, pp. 590ff.; *Ḥilya*, vol. 2, pp. 536ff.

54. For these miracles and others performed by the hidden imam during the Occultation, refer to Chapter 13 in this volume. Once departed from the perceptible world the other imams also continued to perform miracles. According to a tradition dating back to ʿAlī: 'Among us, he who dies is not dead' (*yamūt man māta minnā wa laysa bi-mayyit*) (al-Ṣaffār, *Baṣāʾir*, p. 275); on the *post-mortem* condition of the imams, see also *Baṣāʾir*, pp. 405–406 and 424–428; al-Ṭabarī, *Nawādir*, pp. 146–148; al-Ṭabarī, *Dalāʾil*, pp. 294–296; al-Baḥrānī, *Madīna*, pp. 373–376 and Amir-Moezzi, *Guide divin*, p. 243 (*Divine Guide*, p. 99). Practically all the hagio-biographical sources contain a sub-chapter on the miracles of an imam after death ('Bāb fī muʿjizātihi baʿd wafātih', or other similar titles). An entire form of literature reports miracles that have taken pilgrims by surprise at the imams' tombs (see Ḥ al-Najafī, *al-Durra al-bahiyya fī faḍl Karbalāʾ wa turbatihā al-zakiyya* [Najaf, 1970]; ʿA. Ḥ. Balāghī, *Tārīkh-e Najaf-e ashraf va Ḥīra* [Tehran, 1328 Sh./1949–1950] – modern sources that provide valuable early pieces of information on the subject).

55. Chapters 3 and 8, this volume.

> is clearly deliberate]. Within us, its resting-place; towards us, its source. Our last is like unto our first and our first like unto our last.[56]

Once, the fourth imam, ʿAlī Zayn al-ʿĀbidīn, transformed himself into a winged creature and disappeared into the heavens. Upon his return, he explained that he had reached the highest heaven (*aʿlā ʿilliyyin*). Then to an amazed disciple, he continued:

> We [the imams] are the ones who created it [i.e. the highest heaven], so how could we be unable to ascend to it? We are the Bearers of the [divine] Throne and we are seated upon the Throne; the Throne (*ʿarsh*) and the Pedestal (*kursī*) belong to us.[57]

After performing several miracles, Jaʿfar al-Ṣādiq declares:

> We bring forth light in darkness; we are the oft-frequented House (*al-bayt al-maʿmūr*; Q 52:4); whoever enters there is safe; we are the Magnificence of God and His Greatness . . . We are beyond all description. . . . it is because of us eyes light up, ears listen, hearts are filled with faith.[58]

The imams initiate their closest disciples into secret knowledge and even, according to certain rare and allusive *ḥadīths*, the most profound mysteries of this knowledge. ʿAlī had taught the archetypal initiated follower, Salmān al-Fārisi, the Greatest Name of God, which

56. *ʿNaḥnu al-awwalūn wa'l-ākhirūn wa naḥnu al-āmirūn wa naḥnu al-nūr nunawwiru al-rūḥāniyyin nunawwiru bi-nūri'llāh wa nurawwiḥu bi-rawḥih* [or *bi-rūḥih*] *fīnā maskanuhu wa ilaynā maʿdinuhu al-ākhir minnā ka'l-awwal wa'l-awwal minnā ka'l-ākhir'*, al-Ṭabarī, *Nawādir*, p. 103; al-Ṭabarī, *Dalā'il*, pp. 168–169; al-ʿĀmilī, *Ithbāt*, vol. 5, p. 157; al-Baḥrānī, *Madīna*, pp. 204–205.

57. Al-Ṭabarī, *Nawādir*, p. 116; al-Ṭabarī, *Dalā'il*, p. 201; al-ʿĀmilī, *Ithbāt*, vol. 5, p. 256; al-Baḥrānī, *Madīna*, p. 294.

58. Al-Ṭabarī, *Dalā'il*, pp. 270–271; al-Baḥrānī, *Madīna*, pp. 394–395. On other sayings of the imams that may be compared with the ecstatic utterances (*shaṭaḥāt*) of the mystics, refer to Chapter 3, this volume.

is an enigmatic key to the most prodigious of miracles.[59] Rushayd al-Hajarī, another of 'Alī's disciples, had been initiated into the secret Science of Fortune and Misfortune (*'ilm al-manāyā wa'l-balāyā*).[60] The astonishing descriptions of God provided by the 'two Hishāms', Ibn al-Hakam and Ibn Sālim al-Jawālīqī (companions of the fifth, sixth and seventh imams) seem to bear witness more to their visionary experiences than to purely theological speculations; do they not relate, by their 'anthropomorphist' descriptions of what they perceived during miraculous visions of God, what the imams had initiated them into?[61] A *ḥadīth* going back to 'Alī al-Riḍā alludes to the fact that every initiated follower has the potential to become a fount of inspiration (*muḥaddath*).[62]

At the same time, many *ḥadīths* stress the relationship, the ontological affinity, between the imam and his adept. For example, a series of anthropogonical traditions on the creation of spirits (*arwāḥ*), hearts (*qulūb*, i.e. the seat of the soul) and bodies (*abdān*): the heart and soul of an imam is created from a Clay found above the celestial Dwelling, *'Illiyyin*, and the body, from Clay of the same *'Illiyin*. The hearts and souls of their initiated followers are also created from this Clay of *'Illiyin* and their bodies

---

59. Al-Kashshī, *al-Rijāl* (Bombay, 1317/1899) (summary by Abū Ja'far al-Ṭūsī, *Ikhtiyār ma'rifat al-rijāl,*), p. 8; Mufīd, *Ikhtiṣāṣ*, p. 11; al-Nūrī al-Ṭabarsī/Ṭabrisī, *Nafas al-Raḥmān fī faḍā'il Salmān* (Tehran, 1285/1868), pp. 31 and 59 (pagination by hand).

60. Al-Kashshī, *Rijāl* p. 52; al-Mufīd, *Ikhtiṣāṣ*, p. 77; al-Ṭabarī, *Nawādir*, p. 98; al-Ṭabarī, *Dalā'il*, p. 325; al-Rāwandī, *Kharā'ij*, vol. 1, p. 310; Ibn Ḥamza *Thāqib*, p. 434; al-'Āmilī, *Ithbāt*, vol. 5, p. 504; al-Baḥrānī, *Madīna*, p. 459; al-Ardabīlī, *Jāmi' al-ruwāt* (Qumm, 1331 Sh./1953), vol. 1, p. 319.

61. Cf. al-Shahrastānī, *Livre des religions et des sectes*, Fr. trans. with intro. and notes by D. Gimaret and G. Monnot (Louvain and Paris, 1986), vol. 1, pp. 531–538 (especially notes by D. Gimaret, pp. 531–532 and 535); J. van Ess, *Theologie und Gesellschaft im 2. und 3. Jahrhundert Hidschra* (Berlin and New York, 1990), vol. 1, pp. 342–379 (to be compared with what the author says about Muqātil b. Sulaymān, vol. 2, p. 530); Amir-Moezzi, *Guide divin*, pp. 139–141 (*Divine Guide*, pp. 54–55).

62. Ibn Bābūya, *Ma'ānī al-akhbār*, ed. 'A. A. Ghaffārī (Tehran, 1379/1959), p. 172.

from a Clay found below the same *'Illiyin*. The adept's heart is thus consubstantial with the imam's body, his master initiator.[63] According to other *ḥadīths* of the same kind, the cosmic Intelligence (*'aql*) and its Armies (the cosmogonical archetype of the Imam and his followers) all originate from an Ocean of sweet and pleasant waters[64] and the People of the Right (*aṣḥāb al-yamīn*, i.e. the imam and his people) are created from one and the same petrified Clay with the same sweet Water.[65] In the symbol of the 'Tree of *walāya*', God is said to be its roots, Muḥammad the trunk, the imams its branches, initiatory knowledge the fruit, and the initiated faithful the leaves.[66] There is thus an 'organic' link between the imam and his initiate. By means of the imam who is from the revealed Being of God, the initiate also participates in the divine Being. Like the imam, the adept thus also possesses the ontological and initiatory qualities required for performing miracles.

---

63. Imami dualism similarly requires that the imam's Enemy (*'aduww al-imām*) and his supporters be created from the infernal ' Residence', *Sijjīn*; cf. e.g. al-Barqī, *Kitāb al-maḥāsin*, ed. J. Muḥaddith Urmawī (Tehran, 1370/1950), vol. 1, pp. 31f.; al-Ṣaffār, *Baṣā'ir*, pp. 14–19; al-Kulaynī, *al-Uṣūl*, vol. 2, pp. 232–234; Ibn Bābūya, *'Ilal*, pp. 117–118; Amir-Moezzi, *Guide divin*, pp. 96–100 (*Divine Guide*, pp. 38–39); Chapters 3 and, especially, 8, this volume.

64. Just as cosmic Ignorance (*jahl*) and its Armies (archetypal Enemies of the imam and his supporters) originate in an Ocean of bitter and salty Water; on these traditions see e.g. al-Barqī, *Maḥāsin*, vol. 1, pp. 196–198; al-Kulaynī, *al-Uṣūl*, vol. 1, pp. 24–27; al-Mas'ūdī, *Ithbāt*, pp. 15–17; Ibn Shu'ba, *Tuḥaf*, pp. 423–425; Amir-Moezzi, *Guide divin*, pp. 18–21 (*Divine Guide*, pp. 7–8) and Amir-Moezzi, 'Cosmogony and Cosmology in 'Twelver Shi'ism', *EIr*, vol. 4, pp. 317–322, esp. p. 320. Also, Chapter 12, this volume.

65. Just as People of the Left (*aṣḥāb al-shimāl*, i.e. adversaries of the imams, forces of injustice and counter-initiation) are created from Clay hardened with bitter Water; see e.g. al-Ṣaffār, *Baṣā'ir*, pp. 70–71; Muḥammad b. Mas'ūd al-'Ayyāshī, *Tafsīr*, ed. H. Rasūlī Maḥallātī (Tehran, 1380/1960), vol. 2, pp. 39–40; Kulaynī, *al-Uṣūl*, vol. 3, p. 10.

66. For variants of this tradition see al-Ṣaffār, *Baṣā'ir*, pp. 58–60; 'Alī b. Ibrāhīm al-Qummī, *Tafsīr*, ed. Ṭ. al-Mūsawī al-Jazā'irī (Najaf, 1386–1387/1966–1968), vol. 1, pp. 398–399; Furāt b. Furāt al-Kūfī, *Tafsīr*, ed. M. al-Kāẓim (Tehran, 1410/1990), pp. 219–220; al-'Ayyāshī, *Tafsīr*, vol. 2 p. 224; al-Baḥrānī, *al-Burhān fī tafsīr al-Qur'ān* (Tehran, n.d.), vol. 2, p. 311; as well as Chapter 8 below *in fine*.

Indeed, the heresiographical sources repeatedly tell us that from a very early period onwards, many adepts in the entourage of the imams claimed to possess thaumaturgical powers by frequently vaunting their initiatory knowledge and the immanence in them of the imam's divine particle (*juzʾ ilāhī*).[67] The effect of the penchant for esoterism in Shiʿi circles, along with widespread social dissatisfaction, meant that many of the adepts who advertised their theurgic powers attracted a considerable number of people. The adepts thus led a double life, both initiatory and political. Many went so far as to rebel against the authority of the Umayyad and ʿAbbasid regimes, or were openly hostile to other groups; thus many of them met with a violent death.[68] Moreover, miracles conferred religious authority on those who performed

---

67. In the present state of research, the exact date of the traditions just mentioned is not known. The oldest sources that report them date from the third/ninth century; however, simply their apologetic and proselytising nature leads one to believe that at least the early 'kernel' texts circulated in ʿAlid milieus from a very early period onwards. The theory of the creation of Shiʿis from an Ocean of sweet and luminous Water and of their adversaries from an Ocean of bitter and murky Water is, for example, attributed by the heresiographers to al-Mughīra b. Saʿīd al-ʿIjlī, the esoterist who was familiar with the teachings of the fifth imam, at the end of the first or in the early second century AH. See, e.g., al-Nawbakhtī, *Firaq al-shīʿa*, ed. H. Ritter (Istanbul, 1931), pp. 52ff.; al-Ashʿarī, *Maqālāt al-Islāmiyyīn*, ed. H. Ritter (2nd edn, Wiesbaden, 1963), pp. 6 and 23; al-Baghdādī, *al-Farq bayn al-firaq*, ed. M. ʿAbd al-Ḥamīd (Cairo, n.d.), pp. 57 and 238; al-Baghdādī, *Uṣūl al-dīn* (Istanbul, 1928), pp. 74 and 331; al-Kashshī, *Rijāl*, pp. 145, 148, 196–197; Ibn Ḥazm, *al-Fiṣal fī al-milal* (Baghdad, n.d.), vol. 4, p. 18; al-Maqrīzī, *Kitāb al-mawāʿiẓ wa'l-iʿtibār fi-dhikr al-khiṭaṭ wa'l-āthār* (Būlāq, Cairo, 1256/1840), vol. 4, p. 176; Ibn Abi'l-Ḥadīd, *Sharḥ Nahj al-balāgha*, 4 vols (Cairo, 1330/1911), vol. 2, p. 309; al-Shahrastānī, *Livre des religions*, pp. 515ff.

68. The variety of individuals and the increase in number of groups clearly demonstrates that the term 'Shiʿism' suggests a unity that in fact never existed. In order to reflect reality more closely, during the medieval period, not unlike today, one might speak of 'Shiʿisms'; J. van Ess demonstrates this convincingly in *Theologie*, vol. 1, pp. 233–403; more generally, on the esoterico-political Shiʿi sects see A. S. al-Sāmarrāʾī, *al-Ghuluww wa'l-firaq al-ghāliya fi'l-ḥaḍāra al-islāmiyya* (Baghdad 1392/1972); H. Halm, *Die islamische Gnosis: die extreme Schia und die ʿAlawiten* (Zurich and Munich, 1982) and M. Moosa, *Extremist Shiites. The Ghulat Sects* (New York, 1987) (focusing more on the modern and contemporary periods).

them, as well as undeniable political influence. The corpus of Twelver *ḥadīth*s itself repeatedly refers to a miracle as a 'sign' (*'alāma*) or 'proof' (*dalīl*) of imamate, just as he is the prophet's proof of prophethood.[69] Let us study the examples of some key figures in early Shi'ism.

According to the Kaysāniyya, 'Alī's son Muḥammad b. al-Ḥanafiyya possessed initiatory knowledge and had received from al-Ḥasan and al-Ḥusayn all the wisdom required for the esoteric interpretation of the Qur'ān as well as knowedge of 'the horizons and souls' (*'ilm al-āfāq wa'll-anfus*; cf. Q 41:53; i.e. the external and internal worlds). He is said to have miraculously entered into occultation in order to return later to save the world from injustice.[70] One of his supporters, the Medinan Ḥamza b. 'Umāra al-Barbarī, professed his divinity and declared himself his messenger.[71] Another Kaysānī save the world, the famous Mukhtār b. Abī 'Ubayd al-Thaqafī (whom certain traditions identify with Kaysān, 'Alī's emancipated slave and the sect's namesake), appears to have claimed to own a Pedestal (*kursī*) containing, not unlike the Israelite's Ark of the Covenant, the divine Presence (*sakīna*) and Relics with the thaumaturgical powers of previous prophets (*baqiyya*). On the battlefield, he placed this seat at the head of his army to render it invincible and attract the support of angels who are said to have flown in to his troops in the form of white pigeons.[72]

---

69. See e.g. al-Ṭabarī, *Nawādir*, pp. 104 and 140; al-Ṭabarī, *Dalā'il*, pp. 169, 250–251, 263; al-Rāwandī, *Kharā'ij*, vol. 2, p. 636; al-Irbilī, *Kashf*, vol. 2, p. 19; al-'Āmilī, *Ithbāt*, vol. 5, pp. 158, 451, 454; al-Baḥrānī, *Madīna*, pp. 204, 357, 393.

70. Al-Nawbakhtī, *Firaq*, pp. 20–21; al-Ash'arī, *Maqālāt*, pp. 18ff.; al-Baghdādī, *Farq*, pp. 27ff.; al-Shahrastānī, *Livre des religions*, pp. 437–438; al-Maqrīzī, *Khiṭaṭ*, vol. 4, p. 174; al-Murtaḍā b. Dā'ī al-Ḥusaynī, *Tabṣirat al-'awāmm fī maqālāt al-anām* (Tehran, 1327/1909), p. 421; W. Madelung, 'al-Khaṭṭābiyya', *EI2*, vol. 4, pp. 1,163–1,164.

71. Al-Baghdādī, *Farq*, p. 25; Ṣadīqī, *Jonbesh*, p. 225.

72. Al-Nawbakhtī, *Firaq*, pp. 24–25; al-Baghdādī, *Farq*, pp. 31–37; al-Shahrastānī, *Livre des religions*, pp. 439–443; H. Laoust, *Les schismes dans l'Islam* (Paris, 1977), pp. 27ff. On *sakīna* and *baqiyya* in the Ark of the Israelites see Q 2:248; also A. Spitaler, 'Was bedeutet *baqīja* im Koran?', in *Westöstliche*

Coming from the Kaysāniyya, ʿAbd Allāh b. Muʿāwiya declared that the Spirit of God (*rūḥ Allāh*), or the Holy Spirit (*rūḥ al-quds*), transmigrated from one human form (*shakhṣ*) to another and then entered him after having been with Muḥammad b. al-Ḥanafiyya and his son Abū Hāshim. Such a person is thus obviously invested with thaumaturgical powers.[73]

Another supporter of Abū Hāshim, Bayān b. Samʿān al-Nahdī, seems to have made a synthesis of those ideas attributed to the Saba'iyya and the Kaysāniyya. According to the heresiographers, he professed the divinity of ʿAlī, who is said to have transmitted his 'divine particle' to his son Muḥammad and grandson Abū Hāshim. Although he did not belong to the *ahl al-bayt*, he claimed to have received the divine particle of the imams by means of the phenomenon of transmigration. He thus considered himself an imam invested with miraculous powers such as knowledge of the Invisible and future events.[74]

Al-Mughīra b. Saʿīd al-ʿIjlī was very probably a disciple of imam Muḥammad al-Bāqir. After the latter's death, he supported the Ḥasanid Muḥammad b. ʿAbd Allāh al-Nafs al-Zakiyya. Shortly thereafter he declared that he himself was an imam (or prophet, according

---

Abhandlungen Rudolf Tschudi zum Siebzigsten Geburtstag (Wiesbaden, 1954) and R. Paret, *Der Koran. Kommentar und Konkordanz* (Stuttgart et al., 1978), vol. 2, pp. 52–53.

73. Al-Nawbakhtī, *Firaq*, pp. 246f.; al-Ashʿarī, *Maqālāt*, pp. 6f.; al-Shahrastānī, *Livre des religions*, pp. 448–449. (Pseudo-) al-Nāshi' al-Akbar, *Uṣūl al-niḥal*, ed. J. van Ess as *Frühe muʿtazilische Häresiographie* (Beirut and Wiesbaden, 1971). W. Madelung convincingly attributes the work to Jaʿfar b. Ḥarb in 'Frühe muʿtazilische Häresiographie: das *Kitāb al-uṣūl* des Ǧaʿfar b. Ḥarb?', *Der Islam*, 57 (1980) (rpr. in *Religious Schools and Sects*, article VI), p. 37 and al-Baghdādī, *Farq*, p. 29 attributes these theories not to ʿAbd Allāh b. Muʿāwiya but ʿAbd Allāh b. Ḥarb (or b. al-Ḥārith). See also Laoust, *Les schismes*, pp. 35–36; W. F. Tucker, "Abd Allāh b. Muʿāwiya and the Janāḥiyya: Rebels and Ideologues of the late Umayyad Period', *SI*, 51 (1980), pp. 39–57.

74. Al-Nāshi', *Uṣūl*, § 60; al-Nawbakhtī, *Firaq*, pp. 25f.; al-Ashʿarī, *Maqālāt*, pp. 5 and 23; al-Baghdādī, *Farq*, p. 236; al-Shahrastānī, *Le livre des religions*, pp. 450–451; also M. G. S. Hodgson 'Bayān b. Samʿān', *EI2*, vol. 1, p. 1150 and especially W. F. Tucker, 'Bayān b. Samʿān and the Bayāniyya: Shīʿite Extremists of Umayyad Iraq', *Muslim World*, 65 (1975), pp. 86–109.

to other traditions), having received a 'spirit' from al-Nafs al-Zakiyya due to which he could revive the dead, heal the sick and know hidden things. He also claimed to have had luminous visions of God and to know the Greatest Name.[75]

Abū Manṣūr al-ʿIjlī would also have belonged to the entourage of imam al-Bāqir. Upon the death of the latter, he first declared himself an imam and then, probably later on, a prophet. Advancing the theory of a continuous cycle of prophethood until the end of the world, he claimed, that like Muḥammad, he had undertaken a celestial journey (*miʿrāj*) during which God made him His *masīḥ*, that is, one upon whom God has placed his hand or God's Anointed.[76]

Similarly, the famous supporter of imam Jaʿfar, Ab'l-Khaṭṭāb al-Asadī al-Ajdaʿ, claimed to have been able to make a celestial journey and to transport himself as if by magic.[77] His disciple

75. See note 67 above. On the 'Sabaʿism' of al-Mughīra see also Ibn Qutayba, *'Uyūn al-akhbār* (Cairo, 1383/1963), vol. 2, p. 149; Ibn Qutayba, *al-Maʿārif*, ed. Th. 'Ukāsha (Cairo, 1960), p. 623; al-Ṭabarī, *Ta'rīkh al-rusul wa'l-mulūk*, ed. de Goeje, series 2, p. 1619; now refer to W. F. Tucker, 'Rebels and Gnostics: al-Mughīra b. Saʿīd and the Mughīriyya', *Arabica*, 22 (1975), pp. 42–61; Halm, *Gnosis*, pp. 89ff. and S. Wasserstrom, 'The Moving Finger Writes: Mughīra b. Saʿīd's Islamic Gnosis and the Myths of its Rejection', *History of Religions*, 25/1 (1985), pp. 62–90.

76. Al-Nāshi', *Uṣūl*, p. 40; al-Nawbakhtī, *Firaq*, pp. 34f.; Saʿd b. 'Abd Allāh al-Qummī, *al-Maqālāt wa'l-firaq*, ed. M. J. Mashkūr (Tehran, 1963), p. 46; al-Ashʿarī, *Maqālāt*, pp. 9 and 24; al-Baghdādī, *Farq*, pp. 243f.; al-Baghdādī, *Uṣūl*, p. 331; al-Kashshī, *Rijāl*, p. 196; Ibn Ḥazm, *Fiṣal*, vol. 4, p. 185; al-Shahrastānī, *Livre des religions*, pp. 519–521; Maqrīzī, *Khiṭaṭ*, vol. 4, p. 176; Ḥusaynī, *Tabṣira*, p. 419; now consult W. F. Tucker, 'Abū Manṣūr al-ʿIjlī and the Manṣūriyya: A Study in Medieval Terrorism', *Der Islam*, 54 (1977), pp. 39–57, 'terrorism' because, according to the heresiographers, the supporters of Abū Manṣūr ambush their adversaries and killed them by strangulation; on these *khannāqūn* ('stranglers'), see also C. Pellat, *Le milieu baṣrien et la formation de Ǧāḥiẓ* (Paris, 1953), pp. 199–201. Also Halm, *Gnosis*, pp. 86ff.

77. Al-Nāshi', *Uṣūl*, § 63 and 75; al-Nawbakhtī, *Firaq*, pp. 37 and 58; al-Ashʿarī, *Maqālāt*, pp. 10ff.; al-Baghdādī, *Farq*, pp. 247ff.; al-Kashshī, *Rijāl*, pp. 187ff.; Ibn Ḥazm, *Fiṣal*, vol. 4, pp. 186–187; al-Maqrīzī, *Khiṭaṭ*, vol. 4, p. 174; al-Shahrastānī, *Le livre des religions*, pp. 522ff.; B. Lewis, 'Abū al-Khaṭṭāb', *EI2*, vol. 1, pp. 137–138; W. Madelung, 'al-Khaṭṭābiyya', *EI2*, vol. 4, pp. 1,163–1,164;

Bazīgh/Buzaygh b. Mūsā (or b. Yūnus) professed the imam Jaʿfar's divinity and claimed that every initiate could receive divine revelation. Followers of the latter spoke of themselves as immortal and as able to communicate with the dead.[78]

Heresiographers and prosopographers call these figures Shiʿi 'exaggerators' or 'extremists' (*ghālī*, pl. *ghulāt/ghālūn*).[79] Imami *ḥadīths* do the same, and there are many traditions in which one or another imam disavows or publicly curses such and such a follower for drifting away into what our texts consider an extremist deviation. As a result, from the early period on, authors made a clear distinction in Imamism between a 'moderate' version (that of the imams) and an 'extremist' variety (that of the *ghulāt*), rejected by the imams. But to what extent are these disavowals and curses convincing? Is the opposition between teachings dating back to the historical imams and those attributed to the 'extremists' as clear as the sources would have us believe? There are indications that a more nuanced view is called for. Putting aside the inevitable distortions on the part of the heresiographers, which are hard to confirm, there are indications that justify questioning, in this early phase of Shiʿism, any clear distinction between a 'moderate' and 'extremist' trend. Among the most representative doctrines and conceptions held by the 'extremists', we point out: an allegorical and esoteric interpretation of the Qur'ān (*ta'wīl*); reincarnation – particularly those of their adversaries into animals (*maskh*); belief in the superhuman, read divine, nature of the initiated Sage (the notion of *juz' ilāhī*); inherence of the divine in the human (*ḥulūl*), the transmigrationist doctrine (*tanāsukh*) which, for early Shiʿism

---

A. A. Sachedina, 'Abū al-Khaṭṭāb', *EIr*, vol. 1, pp. 329f; Halm, *Gnosis*, pp. 199ff. Also H. Corbin, *L'Iran et la philosophie* (Paris, 1990), pp. 190–217.

78. Al-Ashʿarī, *Maqālāt*, p. 12; al-Baghdādī, *Farq*, pp. 39–40; al-Kashshī, *Rijāl*, p. 197; Ibn Ḥazm, *Fiṣal*, vol. 4, p. 186; al-Shahrastānī, *Le livre des religions*, p. 524; al-Maqrīzī, *Khiṭaṭ*, vol. 4, p. 174. Another sub-sect of the Khaṭṭābiyya, the Maʿmariyya, believed its leader Maʿmar b. Khaytham, to be a prophet capable of performing miracles (al-Ashʿarī, *Maqālāt*, p. 11; al-Baghdādī, *Farq*, p. 39; al-Maqrīzī, *Khiṭaṭ*, vol. 4, p. 175).

79. Cf. e.g. M. G. S. Hodgson, 'Ghulāt', *EI2*, vol. 2, pp. 1119–1121.

should not, it seems be rendered as metempsychosis but rather as metemphotosis (i.e. the 'organic' transmission of prophet-imamic Light);[80] belief in the occultation (*ghayba*) of the eschatological Saviour and of course the ability of those other than the prophets to perform miracles.[81] Now, all these ideas are present, in one form or another, in the early corpus of the sayings of the imams.[82] The most notable difference pertains to antinomianism (*ibāḥa*) that one does not find at all in the Imami corpus and that constitutes a constant accusation levelled against the 'extremists'; however, in some cases is this not 'exaggeration' on the part of the heresiographers?[83]

In addition, the earliest Twelver *kutub al-rijāl* that have come down to us, those by al-Kashshī, al-Najāshī or al-Ṭūsī (fourth and

---

80. Cf. Amir-Moezzi, *Guide divin*, p. 109 (*Divine Guide*, p. 42) et passim; Chapter 4, this volume.

81. Apart from the works on the subject already cited (van Ess, Halm, Hodgson, Moosa, Tucker etc.) see also e.g. I. Friedländer, ''Abdallāh b. Saba', der Begründer der Shī'a und sein Jüdischer Ursprung', *Zeitschrift für Assyriologie*, 23 (1909), pp. 32–63; R. Strothmann, 'History of Islamic Heresiography', *Islamic Culture*, 17 (1938), pp. 95–110; S. Moscati, 'Per una storia dell'antica shi'a', *RSO*, 30 (1955), pp. 56–70; P. J. Vatikiotis, 'The Rise of Extremist Sects and the Dissolution of the Fatimid Empire in Egypt', *Islamic Culture*, 46 (1957), pp. 121–142; W. al-Qāḍī, 'The Development of the Term *ghulāt* in Muslim Literature with Special Reference to the Kaysāniyya', in *Akten des VII Kongresses für Arabistik und Islamwissenschaft* (Göttingen, 1976), pp. 86–99; G. Monnot, 'La transmigration et l'immortalité', *MIDEO*, 14 (1980), pp. 149–166, (rpr. in *Islam et religions* [Paris, 1986], article XII); R. Freitag, *Seelenwanderung in der islamischer Häresie* (Berlin, 1985), esp. pp. 1–112; A. Straface, 'Il concetto di estremismo nell' eresiografia islamica', *AION*, 56 (1996), pp. 471–487; A. Straface, '*Ḥulul* and *Tağassud*: Islamic Accounts of the Concept of Incarnation', in U. Vermeulen and J. M. F. Van Reeth (ed.), *Law, Christianity and Modernism in Islamic Society* (Leuven, 1998), pp. 125–132; M. A. Amir-Moezzi, 'Heresy', *Encyclopaedia of the Qor'ān*.

82. Cf. Amir-Moezzi, *Guide divin*, see index.

83. It is interesting to see that in the *Baṣā'ir* by al-Ṣaffār, one of the oldest compilations of Imami traditions that has come down to us, it is only the antinomians who are described as extremists, since the absolute superiority of the *bāṭin* over the *ẓāhir* among them leads to the simple elimination of the latter (al-Ṣaffār, *Baṣā'ir*, pp. 526–537, especially the long letter from imam Ja'far to al-Mufaḍḍal al-Ju'fī, pp. 526–536).

fifth/tenth and eleventh centuries) for example, describe many 'extremist' disciples of the imams. Al-Ṭūsī (460/1067) in particular, seems to be the first to systematically present the doctrinal beliefs of individuals in the entourage of the imams in order to distinguish, according to the proper criteria, true believers from those gone astray by belief in errant doctrines.[84] In his *Rijāl*, he has arranged the chapters in the order of the companions (*aṣḥāb*) of the imams from 'Alī to al-'Askarī.[85] Now, many of the notices end with formulaic statements such as *fa-yurmā bi'l-ghuluww* ('and he was accused of extremism') and *ghālin mal'ūn* ('cursed extremist', i.e. cursed by the imam). What is especially interesting to note is that, in a number of cases, an 'extremist' follower, cursed and banished by an imam is found among the followers of one or more of the subsequent imams, which shows that in spite of the 'public condemnation', he continued to frequent the imams and to benefit from their teachings. Examples of this include: Muḥammad b. Sulaymān al-Baṣrī al-Daylamī (the 'cursed' disciple of the seventh but then a disciple of the eighth imam);[86] Muḥammad b. al-Fuḍayl al-Azdī al-Ṣayrafī (an 'extremist' who was familiar with the teachings of the sixth, seventh and eighth imams);[87] al-Ḥasan b. 'Alī b. Abī 'Uthmān (disciple of the ninth and tenth imams),[88] just as Muḥammad b. 'Abd Allāh b. Mihrān al-Karkhī;[89] Aḥmad b. Hilāl al-Baghdādī (disciple of the tenth and eleventh imams);[90]

84. See M. A. Amir-Moezzi, 'Remarques sur les critères d'authenticité du ḥadīth et l'autorité du juriste dans le shī'isme imāmite', *SI*, 85 (1997), pp. 5–39, esp. pp. 22–25; on al-Ṭūsī, see M. A. Amir-Moezzi, 'al-Ṭūsī', *EI2*.

85. Abū Ja'far al-Ṭūsī, *Kitāb al-rijāl* (Najaf, 1380/1961).

86. Ibid., pp. 359 and 386.

87. Ibid., pp. 297, 360 and 389, cf. also al-Ṭūsī, *Fihrist kutub al-shī'a*, ed. Sprenger and 'Abd al-Ḥaqq (rpr. Mashhad, 1972), p. 174.

88. Al-Ṭūsī, *Rijāl*, pp. 400 and 413 (also al-Najāshī, *Rijāl*, pp. 48–49; al-Ṭūsī, *Fihrist*, p. 73); author of *Kitāb al-nawādir* probably on miracles.

89. Al-Ṭūsī, *Rijāl*, pp. 406 and 423 (also al-Najāshī, *Rijāl*, p. 270; al-Ṭūsī, *Fihrist*, p. 181); author of a number of texts, among them *Kitāb al-nawādir, Kitāb al-malāḥim* ('eschatological prophecies') and *Manāqib Abi'l-Khaṭṭāb*.

90. Al-Ṭūsī, *Rijāl*, pp. 410 and 428, also al-Ṭūsī, *Fihrist*, p. 6.

and Isḥāq b. Muḥammad al-Baṣrī[91] or al-Ḥasan b. Muḥammad b. Bābā al-Qummī[92] and Muḥammad b. al-Ḥasan al-Baṣrī (disciple of the ninth, tenth and eleventh imams).[93]

The curse alone, therefore, does not prove a divergence in doctrine. One might even be led to believe that the imam's curse, when sincere and not a strategic manoeuvre, was not due to *what* the followers said but *because* they said it, in other words, because they betrayed the rule, standard for all esoteric traditions of an initiatory nature, namely to dissimulate or keep a secret (*taqiyya, kitmān, khab'*).[94] A *ḥadīth* dating back to imam Ja'far al-Ṣādiq is especially significant in this regard:

> It happens that I confer a teaching to someone; then he leaves me and reports it exactly as he heard it from me. Because of this, I declare that it is lawful to curse him and to dissociate oneself from him.[95]

---

91. Al-Ṭūsī, *Rijāl*, pp. 411 and 428.

92. Ibid., pp. 414 and 430.

93. Ibid., pp. 407, 424 and 436, also al-Ṭūsī, *Fihrist*, p. 182.

94. On this very important practice for Shi'ism, see I. Goldziher, 'Das Prinzip der *takijja* im Islam', *ZDMG*, 60 (1906), pp. 201–204 (rpr. in *Gesammelte Schriften*, ed. J. de Somogyi [Hildesheim, 1967–1970], vol. 5, pp. 59–72); K. M. al-Shaybī, 'al-Taqiyya uṣūluhā wa taṭawwuruhā', *Revue de la Faculté des Lettres de l'Université d'Alexandrie*, 16 (1962–1963), pp. 14–40; E. Meyer, 'Anlass und Anwendungsbereich der *taqiyya*', *Der Islam*, 57 (1980), pp. 246–280; E. Kohlberg, 'Some Imāmī-Shī'ī Views on *taqiyya*', *JAOS*, 95 (1975), pp. 395–402 (rpr. *Belief and Law*, III); E. Kohlberg, 'Taqiyya in Shī'ī Theology and Religion' in H. G. Kippenberg and G. G. Stroumsa (eds), *Secrecy and Concealment: Studies in the History of Mediterranean and Near Eastern Religions* (Leiden, etc., 1995), pp. 345–380; van Ess, *Theologie*, vol. 1, pp. 312–315; Amir-Moezzi, *Guide divin*, index under '*taqiyya*'.

95. Al-Nu'mānī, *Kitāb al-ghayba*, ed. 'A. A. Ghaffārī and Persian trans. by M. J. Ghaffārī (Tehran, 1363 Sh./1985), ch. 1, p. 57, no. 7. Elsewhere, it is reported from Muḥammad al-Bāqir that keeping initiatory Knowledge secret (*kitmān al-'ilm*) is a tradition that dates back to the time of Noah; see al-Kulaynī, *al-Uṣūl*, vol. 1, pp. 64–65. See also imam Ja'far who allows his disciples to express their compassion for Abu'l-Khaṭṭāb, although he himself had cursed him (al-Kashshī, *Rijāl*, p. 189).

The distinction between 'moderate' and 'extremist' Shiʿism appears to be artificial in terms of the early period unless one considers the imams themselves to be 'extremist', which would be at odds with the entire corpus and their sayings.[96] With regard to all that has been observed above, in addition to the confirmed cases of Salmān al-Fārisī and Rushayd al-Hajarī, possessing thaumaturgical knowledge leads one to believe that the imams would have conceived it possible for an initiated follower to perform miracles without being a prophet or imam, or even necessarily belonging to the *ahl al-bayt*. This seems even theoretically legitimate since such a believer is ontologically of the imam and possesses initiatory knowledge or, in other words, he has the fundamental elements of *walāya*.[97] In this area, the only obliga-

96. I have devoted many studies to demonstrate the artificial nature and lateness of this distinction; indeed it is the thesis that underlies much of *Le Guide divin*; as well as Chapters 3 to 5, this volume; see also 'Al-Ṣaffār al-Qummī (d. 290/902–903) et son *Kitāb baṣā'ir al-darajāt*', *JA*, 280/3–4 (1992), pp. 221–250; 'Notes sur deux traditions "heterodoxes" imāmites', *Arabica*, 41 (1994), pp. 127–133, esp. pp. 128–131. Even if one believes as does Hodgson, see his 'Ghulāt', or H. Modarressi, see *Crisis and Consolidation in the Formative Period of Shīʿite Islam* (Princeton, 1993), esp. pp. 21ff., that 'extremist' ideas were first professed by the *ghulāt* and not the imams (which from an historical perspective is practically impossible to verify; nor have either of these authors claimed it is), it is nevertheless the case that the 'orthodox' (thus reputedly 'moderate') Imami corpus contains almost all of them in one form or another.

97. This concurs with an influential current in early mysticism in which, in contrast to the ascetic current, miracles and the miraculous played a fundamental hagiographical role. Cf. now B. Radtke, 'The Concept of *Wilāya* in Early Sufism', in L. Lewisohn (ed.), *Classical Persian Sufism: From its Origins to Rumi* (London and New York, 1993), pp. 483–496; the classification of miracles suggested by R. Gramlich, *Die Wunder der Freunde Gottes. Theologien und Erscheinungsformen des islamischen Heiligewunders* (Freiburger Islamstudien, 11) (Wiesbaden, 1987), in the second section, does not sufficiently take into account certain Shiʿi material. Much later, when the dogma of the *muʿjiza* reserved exclusively for the prophets is established, classical Sufism, at least in its speculative and scholarly dimension, diminishes the importance of the miracle (henceforth called *karāma*) as proof of saintliness; cf. D. Gril, 'Le miracle en islam, critère de la sainteté?', in D Agile (ed.), *Saints orientaux, Hagiographies médiévales comparées* (Paris, 1995), vol. 1, pp. 69–81. Unlike the ascetico-mystical currents, early Shiʿism does not conceive the miracle as a possible result of piety and moral rectitude; rather

tion the imams seem to have required of them was discretion, absolute respect for *taqiyya*. The initiate was obliged to keep his supra-natural Powers secret.

The requirement for discretion had its own reasons, of an esoteric, but also political and socio-communal nature. The miracle, as we have seen – a sign and proof of imamate – conferred on the thaumaturge an undeniable authority. The 'gnostic revolutionaries'[98] not only jeopardised the safety of the Shiʿis by exposing them to the wrath of those in power, but also defied the supreme authority of the imams. The many *ḥadīth*s of the imams against 'the desire to rule' (*ṭalab al-ri'āsa*) are obviously a call to a quietist and apolitical stance;[99] but they are also most likely a denunciation of all other authority except their own, including that of the 'gnostic revolutionaries', all the more so since most of the *ḥadīth*s date back to the imams al-Bāqir and, especially, Jaʿfar, who counted the largest number of 'extremists' among their disciples:[100]

> Forsaken is he who seeks to command;[101] Distrust those who command and consider themselves leaders. By God, the man behind whom is heard the sound of sandals [belonging to his supporters] will only perish and cause to perish;[102] Cursed is the one who believes himself leader, cursed is he who attempts to become one,

the miracle is described as an almost certain consequence of an ontological disposition and of secret knowledge, itself acquired due to piety, purity and especially *walāya* or alliance with the imams.

98. According to Wasserstrom's expression, 'The Moving Finger', p. 27.

99. Cf. *Guide divin*, pp. 155–173, esp. pp. 170–171 (*Divine Guide*, pp. 61ff., esp. p. 68).

100. See al-Kulaynī, *al-Uṣūl*, vol. 3, pp. 405–407 ('Kitāb al-īmān wa'l-kufr', 'Bāb ṭalab al-ri'āsa'); on 'those who claim to be leaders' (*mutara''asūn*), see al-Kashshī, *Rijāl*, pp. 148, 151–152 and 207–208; al-Majlisī, *Biḥār*, vol. 15, tome 3, pp. 102–104. The term *ri'āsa* designates both religious and political leadership; a *ra'īs* can at once be a political leader, a leader of men, a theologian or jurist 'head of a School'.

101. Al-Kulaynī, *al-Uṣūl*, ibid., nos 2 and 7.

102. Ibid., no. 3.

> cursed is one who declares himself thus;[103] Avoid leading [people] and avoid following them leaders.[104]

The authority of the imams was not threatened solely by their miracle-working followers and activists. It was also undermined by certain theologians and jurists in their community. Indeed, from the imamates of al-Bāqir and especially al-Ṣādiq onwards, certain individuals in the entourage of the imams seemed to profess theological doctrines that were independent of those of their masters: Zurāra b. Aʿyan (d. 150/767) of Byzantine Christian origin, Hishām b. Sālim al-Jawālīqī and Muḥammad b. al-Nuʿmān 'Muʾmin' (or according to his adversaries 'Shayṭān') al-Ṭāq, both with Murjiʾī Jahmī tendencies, Hishām b. al-Ḥakam (d. ca. 179/795–796) in whom Dayṣāni influences are evident, and two of the companions of Zurāra, Muḥammad b. Muslim and Burayd b. Muʿāwiya.[105] In the *Rijāl* by al-Kashshī the latter three are justifiably called *al-mutaraʾʾisūn fī adyānihim* ('those who call themselves leaders in [i.e. because of] their religious beliefs').[106] The imams seem to have been obliged to maintain a paradoxical attitude towards these kinds of 'disciples': on the one hand they criticised them most harshly, if not dissociating themselves from them and cursing them for their independence vis-à-vis the authority of the imams; and, on the other hand, they tolerated them because the Imami cause needed their theological acumen for polemical debates with followers of other religious groups.[107] From the ima-

---

103. Ibid., no. 4.

104. Ibid., no. 5. On *riʾāsa* see also E. Kohlberg, '*Barāʾa* in Shīʿī doctrine', *JSAI*, 7 (1986), pp. 139–175, esp. 158–161 and, 'Imam and Community in the Pre-Ghayba Period', in S. A. Arjomand (ed.), *Authority and Political Culture in Shiʿism* (Albany, NY, 1988), pp. 25–53 (rpr. in *Belief and Law*, XIII), pp. 35–37.

105. On these individuals and their ideas, now consult van Ess, *Theologie*, vols 1 and 2, see index.

106. Al-Kashshī, *Rijāl*, pp. 151, 174 and 208; Kohlberg, '*Barāʾa*', p. 158; Kohlberg, 'Imam', p. 36.

107. Al-Kashshī, *Rijāl*, p. 168; Kohlberg '*Barāʾa*', pp. 158–160; Kohlberg, 'Imam', pp. 36–37.

mate of al-Riḍā (183 to 203/799 to 818) onwards, the independence of regional scholars with regard to the authority of the imams increased. The historical reasons for this are obvious: the expansion of Imamism and the ever-growing communities establishing themselves in the most remote regions far away from the imams (especially in central and north-eastern Iran and as far as Central Asia);[108] and also the fact that the imams were very closely observed by the 'Abbasid authorities; the ninth, tenth and eleventh imams in particular spent practically their entire lives under surveillance. Jurists in the old Imami centre of Qumm seem to have benefitted the most from this situation in which direct communication with the imam became increasingly problematic. The following two examples are revealing: imam al-Riḍā himself gave full authority to Zakarīyā b. Ādam in Qumm to settle any legal issues faced by the Shi'is in Iran, by comparing his importance in this city with that of imam al-Kāẓim in Baghdad.[109] Aḥmad b. Muḥammad al-Ash'arī al-Qummī, a disciple of the eighth, ninth and tenth imams and a powerful leader of the community in Qumm, without any authorisation from the imam accused three important individuals in the community of *waqf* or *ghuluww* and excommunicated them: Abū Sumayna al-Ṣayrafī, scholar and esoterist; Sahl b. Ziyād al-Ādamī, himself a disciple of the ninth, tenth and eleventh imams; and finally, Aḥmad b. Muḥammad al-Barqī, author of the famous *Kitāb al-maḥāsin*.[110]

---

108. On the history of the conversion of the Iranian peoples to Imami Shi'ism see A. Mishkāt Kermānī, *Tārīkh-e tashayyu' dar Īrān* (Tehran, 1358 Sh./1980); R. Ja'fariyān, *Tārīkh-e tashayyu' dar Īrān: az āghāz tā qarn-e dahom-e hejrī* (Qumm, 1375 Sh./1996).

109. Al-Mufīd, *Ikhtiṣāṣ*, pp. 83f.; al-Kashshī, *Rijāl*, p. 496; Kohlberg, '*Barā'a*', p. 160; Kohlberg, 'Imam' pp. 37–38. See also the important letter by al-Riḍā to his disciple 'Abd Allāh b. Jundab, reported by al-Kashshī, *Rijāl*, p. 489, cited and analysed by M. M. Bar-Asher, *Scripture and Exegesis in Early Imāmī Shiism* (Leiden, 1999), pp. 98–99.

110. Al-Najāshī, *Rijāl*, p. 234; 'Alī al-Quhpā'ī, *Majma' al-rijāl* (Isfahan, 1384–1387/1964–1967), vol. 3, p. 179 and vol. 5, pp. 264–265; Muḥammad Taqī al-Tustarī, *Qāmūs al-rijāl* (Tehran, 1379/1958), vol. 1, pp. 189, 390 and 420; Kohlberg, '*Barā'a*', pp. 160–161; Kohlberg, 'Imam', p. 39.

According to the tradition, the minor Occultation of the twelfth and last imam began in 260/874, leading, seventy lunar years later in 329/941, to his definitive or major Occultation.[111] The imam is no longer present, or according to the Imami belief that gradually imposed itself and equates Imamism with Twelverism,[112] he is and will remain hidden until the End of Time. Even the institution of the hidden imam's delegation held by a single person (*niyāba/sifāra/wikāla*) seems to be a later conceptual development;[113] it is no less true that the four individuals later recognised as having been successively the 'representatives' of the imam during the minor Occultation, were particularly important spiritual and financial authorities. The first two, 'Uthmān b. Saʿīd al-ʿAmrī/al-ʿUmarī and his son Muḥammad b. 'Uthmān (d. ca. 305/917) were already financial agents, that is, collectors of religious taxes for the tenth and eleventh imams. They remained so after the Occultation, on behalf of the hidden imam, as did both their 'successors', al-Ḥusayn b. Rawḥ al-Nawbakhtī (d. 326/937) and ʿAlī b. Muḥammad al-Simmarī (d. 329/941).[114] These four 'delegates' would have belonged to

111. On this period see Javad Ali, 'Die beiden ersten Safire des Zwölften Imams', *Der Islam*, 25 (1939), pp. 197–227; M. al-Ṣadr, *Ta'rīkh al-ghayba al-ṣughra* (Beirut, 1972); A. A. Sachedina, *Islamic Messianism: the Idea of the Mahdī in Twelver Shiʿism* (Albany, NY, 1981), pp. 41ff.; J. M. Hussain, *The Occultation of the Twelfth Imam: A Historical Background* (London, 1982); V. Klemm, 'Die vier *Sufarā'* des Zwölften Imams. Zur formativen Periode der Zwölferschia', *Die Welt des Orients*, 15 (1984), pp. 126–143; Modarressi, *Crisis*, passim; S. A. Arjomand, 'The Crisis of the Imamate and the Institution of Occultation in Twelver Shiʿism', *IJMES*, 28 (1996), pp. 491–515.

112. E. Kohlberg, 'From Imāmiyya to Ithnā-ʿashariyya', *BSOAS*, 39 (1976), pp. 521–534 (rpr. in *Belief and Law*, XIV) and 'Early Attestations of the Term *ithnāʿashariyya*', *JSAI*, 24 (2000), pp. 343–357; Amir-Moezzi, *Guide divin*, pp. 245–264 (*Divine Guide*, pp. 99–108) and 'Al-Ṣaffār', pp. 236–242; Chapter 13, this volume.

113. This is a central thesis of the very well researched and convincing work by Klemm, 'Die vier *Sufarā'*'.

114. Refer to the studies given in note 111.

the category of jurist-theologians,[115] the majority of whom took a very sceptical view of miracles performed by anyone other than the imam. However, once the institution of the 'delegation' was elevated to the status of an article of faith, different miracles were attributed to the four delegates:[116] powers of divination, clairvoyance, knowledge of languages, reading thoughts, writing from a distance, power over objects, knowledge of the science of letters and of course supra sense-perceptible communication with the hidden imam.[117] According to Imami belief, the miracle-working powers the four delegates were due to their privileged relationship with the hidden imam and the initiation they received from him. Indeed these miracles were proof of their legitimacy and lent credibility to their claims.

Shortly thereafter, things were to change radically for the majority of the Twelvers. From the second half of the fourth/tenth century, the 'theologico-legal-rational' movement, which continues to this day, began to dominate, thus marginalising the original 'esoteric non-rational' current.[118] After the Occultation

---

115. The Imami scholar from Basra, Ibn Nūḥ al-Sīrāfī (early fifth/eleventh century) had compiled a legal compenduim called *Akhbār al-wukalā' al-arbaʿa* (al-Najāshī, *Rijāl*, p. 63) or *Kitāb akhbār al-abwāb* (al-Ṭūsī, *Fihrist*, p. 62).

116. Their canonisation was owed especially to Ibn Bābūya (d. 381/991) and his work *Kamāl al-dīn wa tamām al-niʿma*, ed. ʿA. A. Ghaffārī (rpr. Qumm, 1405/1985); see e.g. Chapter 12, this volume.

117. Ibn Bābūya, *Kamāl*, vol. 2, pp. 486, 501–504, 507–510, 516–522; Amir-Moezzi, *Guide divin*, pp. 273–275 (*Divine Guide*, pp. 112–113).

118. I have devoted several studies to this process: *Guide divin*, pp. 15–48 (*Divine Guide*, pp. 6–19); 'Ṣaffār', pp. 223–242; 'Réflexions sur une évolution du shiʿisme duodécimain: tradition et idéologisation', in E. Patlagean and A. Le Boulluec (eds), *Les retours aux Écritures. Fondamentalismes présents et passés* (Louvain and Paris, 1993), pp. 63–82; 'Remarques sur les critères d'authenticité du ḥadīth et l'autorité du juriste dans le shīʿisme imāmite', *SI*, 85 (1997), esp. pp. 17–28. Belief in the miraculous powers of the imams is discussed by al-Mufīd who accuses thinkers belonging to al-Nawbakhtī's family, mainly influenced by Muʿtazilism, of rejecting them. Al-Mufīd, *Awāʾil al-maqālāt*, ed. F. Zanjānī (Tabriz, 1371/1951–1952), French tr. D. Sourdel, *L'imamisme vu par le cheikh al-Mufīd* (Paris, 1972), pp. 40–41; see also McDermott, *The Theology*, p. 112 and Modarressi, *Crisis*, p. 44.

and the following period of confusion and rapid growth of a number of more or less short-lived schisms,[119] Doctors of Law and scholastic theologians were to become ever more powerful, mercilessly fighting Shiʿi movements led by the 'gnostic' thaumaturges who often cherished revolutionary and messianic ideas.[120] The authority of these threatened that of the Doctors of Law and

---

119. This is the period known as *ḥayra* (confusion, perplexity). A. A. Sachedina lists up to thirteen schisms after the death of al-ʿAskarī (*Messianism*, pp. 42–55). Among the famous defections from imamism, the case of Ibn Ḥawshab Manṣūr al-Yaman is known; he became an Ismaili and an important figure; see H. Halm, 'Die *Sīrat Ibn Ḥaushab*. Die ismailitische *daʿwa* im Jemen und die Fatimiden', *Die Welt des Orients*, 12 (1981), pp. 107–135.

120. See the works by S. A. Arjomand, in particular his introduction to the collective work published under his direction, *Authority and Political Culture in Shīʿism* (Albany, NY, 1988): 'Shiʿism, authority and political culture', pp. 1–24; also his 'The Consolation of Theology: Absence of the Imam and Transition from Chiliasm to Law in Shiʿism', *The Journal of Religion*, 21 (1996), pp. 548–571 and 'The Crisis of the Imamate and the Institution of Occultation in Twelver Shiʿism', *IJMES*, 28 (1996), pp. 491–515. In this regard, the role of the imami jurist-theologians of Baghdad and Qumm, Abū Sahl al-Nawbakhtī at the helm, in the trial and execution of al-Ḥallāj (who was initiated into several 'extremist' Shiʿi sects, the friend of a number of notable personalities of esoteric Shiʿism and the eponym of the esoteric Shiʿi sect al-Ḥallājiyya) seems especially significant. L. Massignon who masterfully discusses the responsibility of the Shiʿis in the tragic fate of the executed mystic, nevertheless gives too monolithic an impression of Shiʿism and fails to stress sufficiently the fact that, with al-Ḥallāj as an example, Shiʿi scholars sought to eliminate their esoterist co-religionists and/or to take their place in key posts in the ʿAbbasid administrative and financial offices. The role played by al-Ḥusayn b. Rawḥ al-Nawbakhtī, third 'representative' of the hidden imam, in the trial and execution of the Shiʿi Ḥallājian esoterist al-Shalmaghānī mirrors that played by Abū Sahl al-Nawbakhtī in the tragedy of al-Ḥallāj and led to the same sorry end. Note that the latter was executed in 309/921, and al-Shalmaghānī in 322/933; one might wonder to what extent the successive victories of Imami jurist-theologians of the rationalist current and their infiltration of the structures of ʿAbbasid power contributed to the Buyid seizure of power (themselves Shiʿis and rationalists) in 334/945. Many esoterist Imamis were to join the Qarmaṭis of Baḥrayn or the Fatimid Ismailis. This subject deserves a separate study; see L. Massignon, *La passion de Hallâj. Martyr mystique de l'Islam* (Paris, 1975), see index: al-Nawbakhtī (A. Sahl Ismāʿīl b. ʿAlī), al-Nawbakhtī (Hy. b. Rawh), al-Shalmaghānī (A. Jaʿfar M. b. ʿAlī Ibn Abu'l-ʿAzāqir).

the theologians, and the spirituality they preached was much too 'unwieldy' to be controlled. For the rationalist trend, the four representatives were to be the last among the initiated faithful able to perform miracles. The term *'ilm*, hitherto meaning initiatory science or knowledge providing access to miraculous powers, was now completely 'disavowed' and henceforth designated only the religious sciences, mainly rational theology and canonic law.[121] Certain later thinkers, admittedly isolated cases, would go so far as to question the superhuman knowledge of the imams,[122] no doubt in order to reduce the distance between the imams and the jurist-theologians (endowed with strictly human knowledge) and by so doing, to increase the latter's charismatic authority. The ancient adage 'knowledge is power' still remained valid, but its content changed; 'knowledge' was no longer initiatory science but that of the theologico-legal disciplines. 'Power' was no longer thaumaturgical ability but temporal authority. In the absence of the imam and except for him, miracles were not proof of saintliness; quite the contrary, they attested to the lies and falsehood of the one who claimed to be capable of performing them since they were now considered to be no more than just 'amazing tricks' (*makhārīq*), 'conjuring' (*sha'badha*) and 'ruses' or crafty stratagem (*ḥīla*).[123]

At the same time, the earliest major compilers of *ḥadīth*s were successful in transmitting an impressive number of esoteric and occult teachings that they traced back to the imams. Over the

121. On the evolution of the term, see Amir-Moezzi, 'Réflexions sur une évolution du shi'isme duodécimain'; also J. Matīnī, "Ilm va 'ulamā' dar zabān-e Qor'ān va aḥādīth', *Iran-Nameh*, II/3 (1363 Sh./1984), pp. 147–162.

122. Al-Mufīd, *Sharḥ 'aqā'id al-Ṣadūq aw Taṣḥīḥ al-i'tiqād* (Tabriz, 1371/1951), pp. 65f. (where the author condemns this 'reductionism' [*taqṣīr*] by certain scholars from Qumm); al-Mufīd, *Awā'il*, p. 41; al-Sharīf al-Murtaḍā, *Tanzīh al-anbiyā'* (Najaf, 1380/1960), pp. 221ff. (in an introduction to the tragedy at Karbalā, the author seriously questions Imam al-Ḥusayn's foreknowledge). Al-Ash'arī had maintained that some groups among the Imamis put stock in the miraculous powers of the imams (al-Ash'arī, *Maqālāt*, pp. 50–51), which tends to indicate that the Imamis of his period differed on this subject.

123. Cf. e.g. al-Rawandī, *Kharā'ij*, vol. 3, pp. 1018ff.

course of centuries, and on the margins of rationalist domination, a number of isolated thinkers would perpetuate and then transmit this original tradition (for example, al-Rāwandī or Ibn al-Biṭrīq in the sixth/twelfth century; Ibn Ṭāwūs, al-Irbilī and thinkers from the School of Baḥrayn; Ibn Saʿāda, ʿAlī b. Sulaymān and Maytham/Mītham al-Baḥrānī in the seventh/thirteenth century; Ḥaydar al-Āmulī and Rajab al-Bursī in the eighth/fourteenth century; Ibn Abī Jumhūr al-Aḥsāʾī in the ninth–tenth/fifteenth–sixteenth centuries, etc.).[124] The persistence of the early tradition, along with

---

124. Studies on some of these thinkers exist; on Ibn Ṭāwūs, see especially E. Kohlberg, *A Medieval Muslim Scholar at Work. Ibn Ṭāwūs and his Library* (Leiden, 1992) and Kohlberg, "ʿAlī b. Mūsā ibn Ṭāwūs and his Polemic against Sunnism', in the Proceedings of the Symposium *Religionsgespräche im Mittelalter* (Berlin, 1992), pp. 325–350; see also Z. Matar, 'The *Faraj al-mahmūm* of Ibn Ṭāwūs: a Thirteenth-Century Work on Astrology and Astrologers' (PhD, New York University, 1986), as well as two of her articles on the same subject, 'Some Additions to the Bibliography of Mediaeval Islamic Astronomy from the *Faraj al-Mahmūm* of Ibn Ṭāwūs', *Archiv Orientalni*, 57 (1989), pp. 319–322 and 'The Chapter on Death-Prediction (*Qaṭʿ/Quṭūʿ*) from the *Kitāb Faraj al-Mahmūm* by Ibn Ṭāwūs', in A. Regourd and P. Lory (eds), *Sciences occultes et Islam*, *BEO*, 44 (1993), pp. 119–125. On the School of Baḥrayn, see A. al-Oraibi, 'Shīʿī Renaissance. A Case Study of the Theosophical School of Bahrain in the 7th/13th Century' (McGill University Montreal, 1992). On Ḥaydar al-Āmulī, see the introduction by H. Corbin to Ḥaydar al-Āmulī, *Jāmiʿ al-asrār wa manbaʿ al-anwār*, ed. H. Corbin and O. Yahia (Tehran and Paris, 1969); H. Corbin, *En Islam iranien*, 4 vols (Paris, 1971–1972), Book IV/1, III, pp. 149–213; P. Antes, *Zur Theologie des Schiʿa. Eine Untersuchung des Jāmiʿ al-asrār wa Manbaʿ al-anwār von Sayyid Ḥaidar Āmolī* (Fribourg, 1971). On Rajab al-Bursī, see H. Corbin, 'La gnose islamique dans le recueil de traditions (*Mashāriq al-anwār*) de Rajab Borsī', *Annuaire de l'EPHE, Sciences Religieuses*, 1968–1969 and 1969–1970 (rpr. in *Itinéraire d'un enseignement* [Tehran and Paris, 1993], pp. 104–114); T. Lawson, 'The Dawning Places of the Lights of Certainty in the Divine Secrets Connected with the Commander of the Faithful by Rajab Bursī', in L. Lewisohn (ed.), *The Legacy of Mediaeval Persian Sufism* (London and New York, 1992), pp. 261–276; P. Lory's introduction to a partial translation of the *Mashāriq* in Rajab al-Bursi, *Les Orients des Lumières*, tr. H. Corbin (Paris, 1996). On Ibn Abī Jumhūr, see W. Madelung, 'Ibn Abī Jumhūr al-Aḥsāʾī's Synthesis of *Kalām*, Philosophy and Sufism', in *La signification du Bas Moyan Âge dans l'histoire et la culture du monde musulman* (Actes du 8e Congrès de l'Union européenne des arabisants et islamisants) (Aix-en-Provence, 1978), pp. 147–156 (rpr. in Madelung, *Religious Schools*, article 13); S. Schmidtke, 'The Influence of Shams al-Dīn Shahrazūrī

the resurgence in Iran of mystical Imami brotherhoods from the tenth/sixteenth century onwards (more than six centuries after the time of the imams), enabled the miraculous powers of the believer, initiated by the imam through supra sense-perceptible means, to once more gain acceptance, and this in spite of persecution, at times violent, by the rationalist jurists.[125] But that is another story.

(7th/13th century) on Ibn Abī Jumhūr al-Aḥsāʿī (d. after 904/1499). A Preliminary Note', in L. Edzard and C. Szyska (eds), *Encounters of Words and Texts: Intercultural Studies in Honor of Stefan Wild on the Occasion of his 60th Birthday. Presented by his Pupils in Bonn* (Hildesheim, 1997), pp. 223–232 and now especially S. Schmidtke, *Theologie, Philosophie und Mystik im zwölfershiʿitischen Islam des 9./14. Jahrhunderts. Die Gedankenwelten des Ibn Abī Jumhūr al-Aḥsāʾī (um 838/1434-35 – nach 906/1501)* (Leiden, 2000).

125. See R. Gramlich, *Die schiitischen Derwischorden Persiens*, vol. 1: *Glaube und Lehre* (Wiesbaden, 1976).

7

Notes on Imami *Walāya*

As is widely known, Shiʿism is centred on the notion of *walāya*. The Shiʿis refer to themselves as 'the people of *walāya*' (*ahl al-walāya*). The charisma of the imam, the very nature of his Person, seems entirely focused on this concept. This chapter attempts to examine the content of *walāya* – and especially ways in which the term is understood – to foster a better appreciation of what may be considered the very substance of the Shiʿi faith in general and Imami beliefs in particular.

Walāya and the Qur'ān

When one considers the evidence of of the earliest Imami sources that have come down to us, that is to say sources mainly from the pre-Buyid period, one realises that for almost all Shiʿis, the so-called ʿUthmānian Qur'ānic vulgate was a censured and falsified version of the original revelation received by Muḥammad. This much more voluminous version, than the one known to all, was recorded in the recension by ʿAlī and remains in the possession of the Imams to be revealed universally by the Qā'im at the End of Time.[1]

1. On this topic see now E. Kohlberg and M. A. Amir-Moezzi, *Revelation and falsification: The* Kitāb al-Qirā'āt *of Aḥmad b. Muḥammad al-Sayyārī* (Leiden, 2009), pp. 24–46; J. Eliash, 'The Shiʿite Qur'ān Reconsideration of Goldziher's Interpretation', *Arabica*, 16 (1969), pp. 15–24; E. Kohlberg, 'Some

This explosive belief was apparently abandoned from the Buyid period onwards by the dominant trend of Imamism, yet to some extent it was still held to secretly and has continued to nourish certain minority branches to the present day.[2] Early sources include quotations from this 'complete' Qurʾān, containing words, expressions or parts of sentences that at times differ significantly from the official recension.[3] Now, among these expressions 'censured'

Notes on the Imāmite Attitude to the Qurʾān', in S. Stern, A. Hourani and V. Brown (eds), *Islamic Philosophy and the Classical Tradition: Essays Presented to Richard Walzer* (Oxford, 1972), pp. 209–224; T. Lawson, 'Notes for the Study of a 'Shīʿī Qurʾān', *Journal of Semitic Studies*, 36 (1991), pp. 279–295; M. A. Amir-Moezzi, *Guide divin*, pp. 200–227 (*Divine Guide*, pp. 79–90); M. M. Bar-Asher, 'Variant Readings and Additions of the Imāmī-Shīʿa to the Quran', *IOS*, 13 (1993), pp. 39–74 and *Scripture and Exegesis in Early Imāmī Shiism* (Leiden, 1999), pp. 88ff. See also A. Falaturi, 'Die Zwölfer-Schia aus der Sicht eines Schiiten: Problem ihrer Untersuchung', in *Festschrift Werner Caskel* (Leiden, 1968), pp. 2–95; H. Modarressi, 'Early Debates on the Integrity of the Qurʾān', *SI*, 77 (1993), pp. 5–39; P. Sander, 'Koran oder Imām? Die Auffassung von Koran im Rahmen der imāmitischen Glaubenslehren', *Arabica*, special no., 'Les usages du Coran, Présupposés et méthodes', 47/3–4 (2000), pp. 420–440; T. Bayhom-Daou, 'The Imam's Knowledge and the Quran According to al-Faḍl b. Shādhān al-Nīsābūrī (d. 260 A.H./874 A.D.)', *BSOAS*, 64/2 (2001), pp. 188–207. Appearing to be more ideogical than scientific, the latter four studies contain problems relating to methodology and employment of sources. The first two studies attempt at all costs to demonstrate the 'orthodox' nature of the Shiʿi attitude towards the Qurʾan at all times and in all places. The next two unconvincingly attribute Imami criticism of the vulgate to Shiʿi *ghulāt* and describe the principal Imami trend (which might that be?) as having always been 'moderate' and 'rationalist', or essentially 'legalist', according to the latest study, to be precise. These points of view do not stand up to the evidence from countless traditions as reported by the earliest sources and employed by the other studies mentioned in this note. Finally, I have not had the time to employ, as it deserves, the excellent and recently published work of Dakake M. Massi, *The Charismatic Community: Shiʿite Identity in Early Islam* (New York, 2007), a monographic study devoted to the concept of *walāya*.

2. Regarding the extension of this question to the modern and contemporary period see R. Brunner, *Die Schia und die Koranfälschung* (Würzburg, Deutsche Morgenländische Gesellschaft, 2001).

3. For these quotations see, for instance, W. St. Clair Tisdall, 'Shiʿah Additions to the Koran', *The Moslem World*, 3/3 (1913), pp. 227–241 (based on a manuscript of the Qurʾan from Bankipore, India, dated sixteenth or seventeenth

by 'enemies' of the Shi'is, those that recur most frequently would have concerned 'Alī, the descendants of the Prophet (i.e. the imams) and their *walāya*.[4] To cite a few examples (expressions in addition to the official vulgate are in italics):

> Q 2:87: ... and whensoever there came to you *Muḥammad* [instead of a messenger] to reveal something *concerning the muwālāt of 'Alī* [here *muwālāt* is synonymous with *walāya,* see below] with that your souls had not desire for, did you become arrogant, and some *among the Family of Muḥammad* cry lies to, and some slay?[5]

---

century AD); Amir-Moezzi, *Guide divin*, pp. 210–214 (*Divine Guide*, pp. 84–85); M. M. Bar-Asher, 'Variant Readings', pp. 39–74, 51–72 and esp. Kohlberg and Amir-Moezzi, *Revelation and Falsification* (Arabic text).

4. The reader will forgive us for not immediately translating this term and others belonging to the same root WLY. This study attempts to show, among other things, the semantic complexity of these terms and thus the difficulty in translating them once and for all. It should be specified straight away that this work deals exclusively with the Shi'i technical meanings and not the entire, especially wide-ranging, semantic field related to this root; to cite just one example, the root WLY takes up almost ten folio pages formatted in two columns in Ibn Manẓūr's, *Lisān al-'arab* (3rd edn, Beirut, 1414/1994), pp. 15, 406–415. Out of numerous relevant studies, these are some important works bearing mainly upon mysticism, M. Chodkiewicz, *Le Sceau des saints. Prophétie et sainteté dans la doctrine d'Ibn 'Arabī* (Paris, 1986), see index under 'WLY'; J. van Ess, *Theologie und Gesellschaft im 2. und 3. Jahrhundert Hidschra, Eine Geschichte des religiösen Denkens im frühen Islam* (Berlin, 1990–1997), vol. 4, index of technical terms, under '*w-l-y*'; H. Landolt, 'Walāyah', *The Encyclopedia of Religion*, vol. 15, pp. 316–323; B. Radtke and J. O'Kane, *The Concept of Sainthood in Early Islamic Mysticism* (London, 1996); G. Elmore, *Islamic Sainthood in the Fullness of Time, Ibn al-'Arabī's Book of the Fabulous Gryphon* (Leiden, 1999), particularly pp. 111–140 (on the influence of Shi'ism upon the eschatological hagiography in Ibn 'Arabī); P. Walker, 'Wilāya', in Shī'ism, *EI2*, vol. 10, pp. 208–209; and now see Dakake, *The Charismatic Community*.

5. Al-Kulaynī, *al-Uṣūl min al-Kāfī fī 'ilm al-dīn*, ed. J. Muṣṭafawī, 4 vols (Tehran, n.d.), 'Kitāb al-ḥujja', 'Bāb fīhi nukat wa nutaf min al-tanzīl fi'l-walāya', vol. 2, p. 285, no. 31; cf. al-Sayyārī, *Kitāb al-Qirā'āt* in E. Kohlberg and M. A. Amir-Moezzi, *Revelation and Falsification*, p. 18, no. 51 (Arabic text) and p. 76 (notes).

Q 4:167–170: Surely the unbelievers who are unjust [instead of those who deny and are unjust], *regarding the rights of the Family of Muḥammad*, God would not forgive them, neither guide them on any road/ but the road to Gehenna, therein dwelling forever and ever; and that for God is an easy matter./ O men, the Messenger has now come to you with the truth *about the walāya of ʿAlī* from your Lord; so believe; better is it for you. And if you deny *the walāya of ʿAlī* know that to God belongs all that is in the heavens and in the earth.[6]

Q 5:67: O Messenger, deliver that which has been sent down to thee from the Lord *regarding ʿAlī*.[7]

Q 7:172: And when thy Lord took from the Children of Adam, from their loins, their seed, and made them testify touching themselves, 'Am I not your Lord?' *Is Muḥammad not the messenger of God, ʿAlī not the Prince of initiates*? They said, 'Yes, we testify.'[8]

---

6. ʿAlī b. Ibrāhīm al-Qummī, *Tafsīr*, ed. al-Mūsawī al-Jazā'irī (Najaf, 1386–1387/1966–1968), vol. 1, p. 159; Muḥammad al-ʿAyyāshī, *Tafsīr* (Qumm, 1380/1960), vol. 1, p. 285; al-Kulaynī, *al-Uṣūl*, vol. 2, p. 295, no. 59; Hāshim b. Sulaymān al-Baḥrānī, *al-Burhān fī tafsīr al-Qur'ān*, 5 vols (Tehran, n.d.), vol. 1, p. 428; al-Fayḍ al-Kāshānī, *al-Ṣāfī fī tafsīr al-Qur'ān*, 2 vols (Tehran, n.d.), vol. 1, p. 414; Muḥammad Bāqir al-Majlisī, *Biḥār al-anwār*, 110 vols (Tehran, 1376–1392/1956–1972), vol. 36, p. 99; cf. al-Sayyārī, *Kitāb al-Qirā'āt* in *Revelation and Falsification*, p. 39, no. 138 (Arabic text) and p. 106 (notes).

7. Al-Sayyārī, *Kitāb al-Qirā'āt* in *Revelation and Falsification*, p. 45, no. 165 (Arabic text) and pp. 155–166 (notes); al-Qummī, *Tafsīr*, vol. 2, p. 201; al-Fayḍ al-Kāshānī, *al-Ṣāfī*, vol. 1, pp. 460, 462– 463; al-Baḥrānī, *al-Burhān*, vol. 1, p. 501 has, instead of *fī ʿAlī*, the expression *anna ʿAliyyan mawlā'l-mu'minīn*.

8. Al-Sayyārī, *Kitāb al-Qirā'āt* in *Revelation and Falsification*, p. 52, no. 195 (arabic text) and pp. 125–126 (notes); al-ʿAyyāshī, *Tafsīr*, vol. 2, p. 41; al-Baḥrānī, *al-Burhān*, vol. 2, p. 50; al-Ḥurr al-ʿĀmilī, *Ithbāt al-hudāt* (rpr. Tehran, 1364 Sh./1985), vol. 3, p. 545; al-Majlisī, *Biḥār al-anwār*, vol. 9, p. 256. For this technical translation of *amīr al-mu'minīn* (i.e. ʿAlī), literally 'Prince of the believers' and the notion of *mu'min* as the loyal-faithful Shiʿi initiated into the teaching of the imams see Amir-Moezzi, *Guide divin*, pp. 174–199 (*Divine Guide*, pp. 69–79) and index under '*īmān*' and '*mu'min*'; as well as Chapter 8, this volume. On this verse see also the article by R. Gramlich, *Der Islam*, 60 (1983), pp. 205–230.

Q 16:24: And when it is said to them, 'What has your Lord sent down *regarding 'Alī*?' they say, 'Fairy-tales of the ancients.'[9]

Q 17:89: We have indeed turned about for men in this Qur'ān every manner of similitude; yet most men refuse all but unbelief in the *walāya of 'Alī*.[10]

Q 33:71: Whoesover obeys God and His Messenger concerning the *walāya of 'Alī* and *the walāya of the imams after him*, has won a mighty triumph.[11]

Q 40:13: because when God was called to alone, *as well as that [the unicity] of the People of walāya* you disbelieved.[12]

Q 41:27: So We shall let the unbelievers *who have fosaken the walāya of the Prince of the initiates* taste a terrible chastisement *in this world*, and shall recompense them with the worst of what they were working.[13]

Q 42:13: He has laid down for you *O Family of Muḥammad* as religion that He charged Noah with, and that We have revealed to thee, *O Muḥammad*, and that We charged Abraham with, Moses

---

9. Ibrāhīm al-Kūfī, *Tafsīr*, ed. M. al-Kāẓim (Tehran, 1410/1990), p. 234; al-Qummī, *Tafsīr*, vol. 1, p. 383; al-'Ayyāshī, *Tafsīr*, vol. 2, p. 257; al-Baḥrānī, *al-Burhān*, vol. 2, p. 363; al-Fayḍ al-Kāshānī, *al-Ṣāfī*, vol. 1, p. 920; al-Majlisī, *Biḥār*, vol. 9, p. 102 and vol. 36, p. 104.

10. Al-'Ayyāshī, *Tafsīr*, vol. 2, p. 317; al-Baḥrānī, *al-Burhān*, vol. 2, p. 445; al-Fayḍ al-Kāshānī, *al-Ṣāfī*, vol. 1, p. 989; al-Majlisī, *Biḥār*, vol. 9, p. 102 and vol. 36, p. 105; cf. al-Sayyārī, *Kitāb al-Qirā'āt* in *Revelation and Falsification*, p. 79, no. 302 (arabic text) and pp. 161–162 (notes); On 'the majority' (*akthar al-nās*), in its technical sense denoting non-Shi'is, if not uninitiated Shi'is as opposed to 'the minority' (*aqall al-nās*), i.e. initiated Shi'is, see *Guide divin*, index under '*shī'a*'; Chapter 8 here, and now esp. E. Kohlberg, 'In Praise of the Few', in G. R. Hawting, J. A. Mojaddedi and A. Samely (eds), *Studies in Islamic and Middle Eastern Texts and Traditions, In Memory of Norman Calder*, *JSS*, suppl. 12 (2000), pp. 149–162.

11. Al-Sayyārī, *Kitāb al-Qirā'āt* in *Revelation and Falsification*, p. 111, no. 428 (arabic text) and p. 202 (notes); al-Qummī, *Tafsīr*, vol. 2, p. 198; al-Kulaynī, *al-Uṣūl*, vol. 2, p. 279, no. 8; al-Baḥrānī, *al-Burhān*, vol. 3, p. 340; al-Fayḍ al-Kāshānī, *al-Ṣāfī*, vol. 2, p. 369.

12. Al-Sayyārī, *Kitāb al-Qirā'āt* in *Revelation and Falsification*, p. 125, no. 478 (Arabic text) and p. 216 (notes); al-Kulaynī, *al-Uṣūl*, vol. 2, p. 291, no. 46.

13. Al-Sayyārī, *Kitāb al-Qirā'āt* in *Revelation and Falsification*, p. 129, no. 489 (Arabic text) and p. 219 (notes); al-Kulaynī, *al-Uṣūl*, ibid., no. 45.

and Jesus: 'Establish the religion *of the Family of Muḥammad*, and scatter not regarding it *and be united*.' Very hateful is that for the associationists, *those that associate with the walāya of ʿAlī* [i.e. other *walāyas*] thou callest them to *concerning the walāya of ʿAlī*. *Surely* God guides, *O Muḥammad* towards this religion he who repents, *he who accepts your call to the walāya of ʿAlī* [instead of God chooses unto Himself whomsoever He will, and He guides to Himself whosoever turns, penitent].[14]

Q 67:29: . . . and thou shalt certainly know, them, *O denying people; whereas I brought you a message from my Lord concerning the walāya of ʿAlī and of the imams after him, which of us finds himself in manifest error.*[15]

Q 70:1–3: A questioner asked of a chastisement about to fall / for the unbelievers *in the walāya of ʿAlī*, which none may avert, / from God, the Lord of the Stairways.[16]

One can continue expanding this list much further.[17] Other than the 'Qurʾān of the imams' one may simply point out that according to Shiʿi scribes the manuscript of the Qurʾān discovered by St Clair Tisdall (see note 3 above) contains an entire sura of seven verses precisely entitled the Sura of *walāya*, totally deleted from the original Revelation by the imam's adversaries:

14. Furāt al-Kūfī, *Tafsīr*, p. 387; al-Kulaynī, *al-Rawḍa min al-Kāfī*, ed. and Persian tr. by H. Rasūlī Maḥallātī (Tehran 1389/1969), vol. 2, p. 163, no. 502; al-Kulaynī, *al-Uṣūl*, vol. 2, p. 285, no. 32 (shorter version); al-Fayḍ al-Kāshānī, *al-Ṣāfī*, vol. 2, p. 509; cf. al-Sayyārī, *Kitāb al-Qirāʾāt* in *Revelation and Falsification*, p. 131, nos 491 and 492 (Arabic text) and pp. 220–221 (notes).

15. Al-Sayyārī, *Kitāb al-Qirāʾāt* in *Revelation and Falsification*, p. 163, no. 594 (arabic text) and p. 249 (notes); al-Kulaynī, *al-Uṣūl*, vol. 2, p. 291, no. 45.

16. Al-Sayyārī, *Kitāb al-Qirāʾāt* in *Revelation and Falsification*, p. 165, no. 601 (arabic text) and p. 251 (notes); al-Kulaynī, *al-Rawḍa*, vol. 1, p. 83, no. 18; al-Kulaynī, *al-Uṣūl*, vol. 2, p. 291, no. 47; al-Baḥrānī, *al-Burhān*, vol. 4, p. 381; al-Fayḍ al-Kāshānī, *al-Ṣāfī*, vol. 2, p. 742.

17. Apart from the references in works already cited (note 2 and esp. note 3), see also e.g. al-Majlisī, *Biḥār*, vol. 23, p. 374, no. 55; vol. 24, p. 336, no. 59; vol. 27, p. 159, no. 7; vol. 36, p. 100, no. 44 and vol. 51, p. 59, no. 57.

> In the Name of God the Compassionate the Merciful/ You who believed, believe in the Prophet and the *wālī* that We have sent in order that they may guide you upon the right path / A Prophet and a *wālī* one from the other and I am the Omniscient He who knows all/ Those that remain loyal to the Pact of God, for them a Garden of delights / Whereas those that deny Our verses after hearing them/ They will be ushered into the Gehenna until the Day of Resurrection when they shall be asked to account for the oppressors and negators of the messengers./ [God] created them as the messengers [*sic*] especially for [the cause of] the truth and he shall soon manifest them/ Praise the Glory of your Lord and [know that] ʿAlī is among the witnesses.[18]

This insistance on the original Revelation disclosed to Muḥammad concerning the *walāya* of the imams is, among other things, supposed to provide a literal Qur'ānic basis for the political and theological doctrines of the imamate. However, although not containing any literal indication of the *walāya* of the imams, and with reason, since all indications of this kind were systematically deleted by their adversaries, the official vulgate seems to abound in allusions to this notion. Exegetic annotations traced to the imams often refer to this.

According to several exegetic *ḥadīth*s attributed to the sixth imam, Jaʿfar al-Ṣadiq, in verse 2:257: 'He brings them forth from the shadows into the light', 'shadows' refers to the adversaries of the imams and 'light' to the imams and/or their *walāya*.[19]

Practically all the Imami and indeed Shiʿi sources in general unanimously affirm that the reason for the 'descent' of the famous verse 5:3 ('Today I have perfected your religion for you, and I have completed My blessing upon you') is the proclamation of

18. St Clair Tisdall, 'Shi'ah additions', the Arabic text of 'the sura' p. 226; English, p. 234; for a discussion on this 'sura' see *Guide divin*, pp. 224–228 (*Divine Guide*, pp. 87–91); also Brunner, *Die Schia und die Koranfälschung*, pp. 16, 95–96.

19. Al-ʿAyyāshī, *Tafsīr*, vol. 1, pp. 138–139; al-Majlisī, *Biḥār*, vol. 15/1, pp. 17, 129; al-Baḥrānī, *al-Burhān*, vol. 1, p. 244; Bar-Asher, *Scripture and Exegesis*, p. 197.

the *walāya* of ʿAlī by Muḥammad; hence the regular association of this verse with the events at Ghadīr Khumm. There are countless *ḥadīths* that refer to this matter.[20] One therefore often finds in Shiʿi works expressions such as 'Religion is perfected by *walāya*',/ 'The cause of *walāya* (or imamate) completes the faith' and 'It is by *walāya* (or imamate) that religion and the (divine) blessing is perfected'.[21]

Sources unanimously consider verse 67 of this same Sura 5 to be an allusion to the *walāya* of the imams; in effect God commands Muḥammad to openly reveal the truth regarding the *walāya* of ʿAlī and his descendants (see above); this verse would have been revealed prior to Ghadīr Khumm, whereas verse 5:3, which we have just examined, is said to have 'descended' shortly thereafter:

---

20. See e.g. al-ʿAyyāshī, *Tafsīr*, vol 1, p. 293; al-Qummī, *Tafsīr*, vol. 1, p. 190; Furāt al-Kūfī, *Tafsīr*, pp. 117–120; Abū Jaʿfar al-Ṭūsī, *Tafsīr al-tibyān*, 10 vols (Najaf, 1957), vol. 3, pp. 435ff.; Abū ʿAlī al-Faḍl al-Ṭabrisī, *Majmaʿ al-bayān fī tafsīr al-Qurʾān* (Tehran, 1395/1975), vol. 3, p. 159; al-Majlisī, *Biḥār*, vol. 9, p. 306; al-Baḥrānī, *al-Burhān*, vol. 1, p. 444; al-Fayḍ al-Kāshānī, *al-Ṣāfī*, vol. 1, p. 421; Sharaf al-Dīn al-Najafī al-Astarābādī, *Taʾwīl al-āyāt al-ẓāhira*, (Qumm, 1417/1997), pp. 151–152; Bar-Asher, *Scripture*, p. 197. For the especially important role of this verse among Ismailis see e.g. al-Qāḍī al-Nuʿmān, *Daʿāʾim al-Islām*, ed. A. A. A. Fyzee (Cairo, 1370/1951), vol. 1, p. 16 et passim; Abū Ḥātim al-Rāzī, *Kitāb al-zīna*, ed. ʿA. S. Sāmarrāʾī in his *al-Ghuluww wa'l-firaq al-ghāliya fi'l-ḥaḍārat al-islāmiyya* (Baghdad, 1972), pp. 256ff. See also the sources indicated by E. Kohlberg, 'The Attitude of the Imāmi-Shīʿīs to the Companions of the Prophet' (University of Oxford, 1971), p. 81, n. 5, as well as in general, ʿA. H. Amīnī, *al-Ghadīr fi'l-kitāb wa'l-sunna wa'l-adab* (Tehran, 1372/1952; rpr. 1986). On Ghadīr Khumm, see the article by L. Veccia Vaglieri in *EI2*, also *EIr*.

21. *Kamāl al-dīn bi'l-walāya; amr al-walāya/al-imāma min tamām al-dīn; bi'l-walāya/al-imāma kumila'l-dīn wa tummat al-niʿma*; see e.g. al-Faḍl b. Shādhān, *Kitāb al-īḍāḥ* (Beirut, 1402/1982), p. 185; al-Kulaynī, *al-Uṣūl*, vol. 1, p. 278; Ibn Bābūya, *Kamāl al-dīn wa tamām al-niʿma* (even the title refers to it), ed. ʿA. A. Ghaffārī (rpr. Qumm, 1405/1985), vol. 2, p. 658. See also the index in al-Majlisī's *Biḥār* and Bayhom-Daou, 'The Imam's Knowledge and the Quran' (see note 1 above), p. 195, n. 55 (the interpretation of the third expression mentioned above in which the verbs are put into the active form seems problematic).

5:67: 'O Messenger, deliver that which has been sent down to you from your Lord; for if you do not, you will not have delivered his Message. '[22]

Imam al-Bāqir is said to have stated that 'the way that is straightest' (*aqwam*) mentioned in verse 17:9: 'Surely, this Qur'ān guides to the way that is straightest', refers to the *walāya* of the imams.[23] In a commentary on Q 27:91, which tradition attributed to 'Alī:

Whosover comes with a good deed (*al-ḥasana*), he shall have better than it; and they shall be secure from terror that day. And whosover comes with an evil deed (*sayyi'a*), their faces shall be thrust into the Fire: 'Are you recompensed but for what you did?' It is said: 'The good deed is recognition of our *walāya* and love (*ḥubb*) for us, the *ahl al-bayt*. The evil deed is denial of our *walāya* and hatred (*bughḍ*) for us.[24]

According to a tradition going back to the Prophet regarding the same verse:

---

22. Al-'Ayyāshī, *Tafsīr*, vol. 1, pp. 331–332; al-Qummī, *Tafsīr*, vol. 1, pp. 199–202; Furāt al-Kūfī, *Tafsīr*, pp. 129–131; Ibn Bābūye, *Amālī (= al-Majālis)*, ed and Persian tr. M. B. Kamare'ī (Tehran, 1404/1984), 'majlis' 56, no. 10; al-Ṭūsī, *al-Tibyān*, vol. 1, pp. 574ff.; al-Baḥrānī, *al-Burhān*, vol. 1, p. 489; al-Majlisī, *Biḥār*, vol. 9, p. 207; al-Astarābādī, *Ta'wīl*, pp. 161–165. On commentaries by imam Muḥammad al-Bāqir on these and other verses, see A. R. Lalani, *Early Shi'a Thought: The Teachings of Imam Muḥammad al-Bāqir* (London, 2000), pp. 61ff. See note 7 above and the relevant text (remarking that an allusion to the *walāya* of 'Alī appeared in the original text of the Qur'an).

23. Al-'Ayyāshī, *Tafsīr*, vol. 2, p. 283; al-Baḥrānī, *al-Burhān*, vol. 2, p. 409; al-Fayḍ al-Kāshānī, *al-Ṣāfī*, vol. 1, p. 960; al-Majlisī, *Biḥār*, vol. 7, p. 120; al-Astarābādī, *Ta'wīl*, p. 273 (according to al-Kulaynī's *Kāfī*, this work reports a tradition going back to imam Ja'far that says 'imam' instead of '*walāya*').

24. Al-Kulaynī, *al-Uṣūl*, 'Kitāb al-ḥujja', 'Bāb ma'rifat al-imām', vol. 1, p. 262, no. 14. See also *al-Uṣūl al-sittat 'ashar* (Qumm, 1405/1984), p. 117; Furāt al-Kūfī, *Tafsīr*, pp. 311–312; al-Qummī, *Tafsīr*, vol. 2, p. 132 (where other instances of the term *ḥasana* are also commented upon as meaning the *walāya* of the imams); al-Majlisī, *Biḥār*, vol. 7, p. 117, no. 54; al-Astarābādī, *Ta'wīl al-āyāt al-ẓāhira*, pp. 403–405. Regarding the translation of *ahl al-bayt* see M. A. Amir-Moezzi, 'Considerations sur l'expression *dīn 'Alī*, Aux origines de la foi shi'ite', *ZDMG*, 150/1 (2000), pp. 48ff.; Chapter 1, this volume.

> The *walāya* of ʿAlī is a good deed that cannot give rise to an error. … Just as the *walāya* of his adversaries (*aḍdād*) is a misdeed that nothing can efface.[25]

According to *ḥadīths* going back to several of the imams, the exegesis of Q 39:56 ('Lest any soul should say, "Alas for me, in that I neglected God's side and was a scoffer. . . "') establishes a synonymous relationship between 'the side of God' and the figure of the imam and/or his *walāya.*[26]

Here again one can cite many more examples. Very often while speaking of the unbelievers when the Qur'ānic text employs the root *KFR* (to negate, deny, disbelieve, be impious etc.), exegetic traditions attributed to the imams add *bi-nubuwwat Muḥammad wa walāyat ʿAlī* ('to deny' the prophetic mission of Muḥammad and the *walāya* of ʿAlī). As has been seen, certain Qur'ānic terms are associated with *walāya*, namely *nūr* (light), *aqwam* (the most direct path), *ḥasana* (good deed), *janb Allāh* (God's side).

Other terms are likewise associated, in some cases even more frequently, in doctrinal literature: *al-ḥaqq* (the truth, real, right), *ḥikma* (wisdom), *sabīl* (path), *ṣirāṭ mustaqīm* (straight path), *naʿīm* (benefit, delight), *raḥma* (mercy), *ʿahd* (pact), *dhikr* (remembrance) and of course *īmān* (faith) and *amr* (cause, the *res religiosa*).[27] One need only refer to the exegetic glosses that deal with these instances in the Qur'ān; by just turning for example to pre-Buyid *tafsīrs*, one becomes convinced that, according to the Shiʿis, numerous passages in the 'Uthmānic vulgate are devoted to different aspects of the *walāya* of the imam and this in spite of

---

25. Al-Majlisī, *Biḥār*, vol. 8, p. 300, no. 50, also vol. 8, pp. 352ff.

26. Al-Ṣaffār al-Qummī, *Baṣā'ir al-darajāt*, ed. Mīrzā Kūchebāghī (Tabriz, n.d. [ca. 1960]), section 2, ch. 3, pp. 61–63; Furāt al-Kūfī, *Tafsīr*, pp. 366ff.; al-Majlisī, *Biḥār*, vol. 4, p. 9, no. 18 and vol. 7, p. 200, no. 78; al-Astarābādī, *Ta'wīl al-āyāt al-ẓāhira*, pp. 508–509.

27. See Bar-Asher, *Scripture and Exegesis*, p. 202.

censorship. Hence the following *ḥadīth* attributed to imam Jaʿfar: 'God has made of our *walāya*, we the *ahl al-bayt*, the axis (*quṭb*) around which the Qurʾān gravitates.'[28]

The Pillars of Islam

In the economy of the sacred, *walāya* is essential and of such fundamental importance that it is considered one of the Pillars (*daʿāʾim*) if not *the* Pillar of Islam.[29] M. M. Bar-Asher's observation that for Shiʿis the *walāya* of the imams is the most important of the canonical obligations and a precondition for all the rest is very pertinent. The many traditions describing *walāya* as one of the Pillars as well as a number of differences among these traditions lead him (just as J. Eliash before him) to wonder whether one must count *walāya* among the five Pillars or rather as a sixth one in itself.[30] Indeed, to cite al-Kulaynī (d. 329/940–941) as only one example, in a chapter of his *Uṣūl min al-Kāfī* dealing with the subject of the Pillars of Islam he reports fifteen traditions all going back to the fifth and sixth imams in which *walāya* is included separately as one of the five Pillars:[31]

28. Al-ʿAyyāshī, *Tafsīr*, vol. 1, p. 5; al-Baḥrānī, *al-Burhān*, vol. 1, p. 10; al-Fayḍ al-Kāshānī, *al-Ṣāfī*, vol. 1, p. 12; al-Majlisī, *Biḥār*, vol. 19, p. 8.

29. To designate the Pillars of Islam, Shiʿi literature tends to use the term *daʿāʾim* than *arkān*, which is employed more often by Sunni authors, see E. Kohlberg, 'The Attitude of the Imāmī-Shīʿīs to the Companions of the Prophet', p. 81, note 4.

30. Bar-Asher, *Scripture and Exegesis*, part 3.3 devoted to the necessity of *walāya*, pp. 196-198; J. Eliash, 'On the Genesis and Development of the Twelver-Shīʿī Three-tenet *Shahāda*', *Der Islam*, 47 (1971), pp. 265–272. On the same subject now see L. A. Takim, 'From *bidʿa* to *sunna*, the *wilāya* of ʿAlī in the Shīʿī *adhān*', *JAOS*, 120 (2000), pp. 166–177 (curiously the author appears to ignore Eliash's poineering article). See also Lalani, *Early Shīʿī Thought*, pp. 69f.

31. Al-Kulaynī, *al-Uṣūl*, 'Kitāb al-īmān wa'l-kufr', 'Bāb daʿāʾim al-islām', vol. 3, pp. 29–38.

> Islam is built upon five elements: canonical prayers, alms, the fast, pilgrimage to Mecca and *walāya*. More than the others, it is to the latter that people are called.[32]

> The components of the faith (*ḥudūd al-īmān*) are: the *shahāda* that there is no god but God and Muḥammad is the envoy of God; belief in what the prophet brought on behalf of God; the five canonical prayers, alms, fasting during the month of Ramaḍān, the pilgrimage to Mecca, *walāya* with regard to the *walī* among us (the imams); hostility to our enemy (*'adāwat 'aduwwinā*) and finally frequenting the truthful (*al-dukhūl ma'a'l-ṣādiqīn*).[33]

> Islam rests upon a tripod (*athāfī*): prayer, alms and *walāya*. Neither one of the three may have priority over the others.

---

32. Al-Kulaynī, *al-Uṣūl*, vol. 3, p. 29, no. 1 (tradition attributed to al-Bāqir); also vol. 3, pp. 29–30, no. 3 (al-Bāqir), the same text with an additional sentence, 'and the people accepted the (first) four and abandoned the last'. In another tradition also attributed to al-Bāqir (vol. 3, pp. 30–32, no. 5), it is said that among the five Pillars, *walāya* is the supreme Pillar for it is 'the key' (*miftāḥ*) to all the others; then follow in sequence: prayers, alms, the pilgrimage and fast. The imam's *walāya* is the highest degree of religion to the extent that 'if a man were to spend the entire night praying and all day fasting, offer all his possesions as alms and all the time he has to making the pilgrimage, but not recognise *walāya* of the *walī* of God, in order to undertake all his actions as guided by the latter, well then God would not reward him at all and he is not considered among people of the faith (*ahl al-īmān*)'. See nos 7 and 8 (al-Bāqir), vol. 3, p. 33. See also al-'Ayyāshī, *Tafsīr*, vol. 1, p. 259; Ibn Bābūya, *Amālī/al-Majālis*, 'majlis' 45, no. 14, p. 268.

33. Al-Kulaynī, *al-Uṣūl*, vol. 3, p. 29, no. 2 (Ja'far); also no. 11 (Ja'far, vol. 3, p. 35); Muḥammad b. Aḥmad Khwājagī Shīrāzī, *al-Niẓāmiyya fī madhhab al-imāmiyya* (Tehran, 1375 Sh./1996), pp. 153–155. I will return to the idea of hostility towards enemies of the imams. The latter expression, *al-dukhūl ma'a'l-ṣādiqīn*, is still a mystery to me; is it a question of associating with Shi'is, specifically the initiated among them, as a number of traditions recommend? (See e.g. several chapters by al-Kulaynī, *al-Uṣūl*, 'kitāb al-īmān wa'l-kufr' and 'kitāb al-'ishra' and esp. Ibn Bābūya, *Muṣādaqat al-ikhwān* Tehran, n.d. [ca. 1325 Sh./1946]). Regarding this list of 'terms of the faith' see also nos 6 and 9 (Ja'far, *al-Uṣūl*, vol. 3, pp. 32–33 and vol. 3, p. 34) where prayers, the fast and pilgrimage are not counted; nos 10 and 13 (al-Bāqir, vol. 3, pp. 34–35 and vol. 3, p. 36) where the list is extended by duties such as awaiting the Qā'im, piety, the struggle, humility, submission to the imams etc., see also al-Nu'mānī, *Kitāb al-ghayba*, ed. 'A. A. Ghaffārī and the Persian translation by M. J. Ghaffārī (Tehran, 1363 Sh./1985), ch. 11, no. 16.

One must bear in mind that when canonical duties such as canonical prayers, the fast or pilgrimage to Mecca do not appear on a list, it does not mean that they are not one of the Pillars, rather that they are integrated into *walāya* since the latter is 'the Key' to all the rest.[34]

As it is unthinkable for it not to be among the Pillars of Islam, the most telling example is the *shahāda*. When missing from a list it is included in *walāya*, since for a Shi'i, the *shahāda* implicitly contains a triple profession of faith: the unicity of God, Prophet Muḥammad's mission, the *walāya* of 'Alī and the imams in his lineage.[35] Without the imam, the *wālī* of God and his *walāya*, there would be no religion at all. God does not accept any of the religious duties without *walāya*.[36] In *al-Maḥāsin*, Abū Ja'far al-Barqī (d. 274/887 or 280/893) devotes three chapters of his 'kitāb 'iqāb al-a'māl' to the consequences of not recognising the imams and their *walāya*.[37] To cite a few typical examples of traditions from these chapters:

---

34. Al-Kulaynī, *al-Uṣūl*, vol. 3, p. 30, no. 4 (Ja'far). Tradition no. 15 (Ja'far, vol. 3, p. 38) refers only to prayers, alms and the holy war. It is true that the last is not one the Pillars of Islam and seems out of place in this chapter. Also Abū Ja'far al-Ṭabarī, *Bishārat al-Muṣṭafā li-shī'at al-Murtaḍā* (Najaf, 1963), p. 81; 'Imād al-Dīn al-Ṭabarī, *Tuḥfat al-abrār fī manāqib a'immat al-aṭhār* (Tehran, 1376 Sh./1997), pp. 155ff.

35. See e.g. al-Ṣaffār al-Qummī, *Baṣā'ir al-darajāt*, section 2, ch. 10, p. 78, no. 7; al-Qummī, *Tafsīr*, vol. 2, p. 208; Ibn Bābūya, *Kamāl al-dīn*, vol. 1, p. 258; Ibn Bābūya, *Amālī/al-Majālis*, 'majlis' 63, no. 13, p. 409 ('the attestation of Unicity – *al-tawḥīd* – is only accepted due to 'Alī and his *walāya*'); al-Majlisī, *Biḥār*, vol. 3, p. 14, no. 39; vol. 37, p. 141, no. 35; vol. 38, p. 118, no. 60. For other sources see Eliash, 'On the Genesis … of Three-tenet Shahāda', esp. pp. 266ff.; cf. Bar-Asher, *Scripture and Exegesis*, p. 198, who believes that differences in various lists of the Pillars would seem to reflect internal debates within the Imami community.

36. See above n. 32; Amir-Moezzi, *Guide divin*, pp. 304–305 (*Divine Guide*, p. 125).

37. Al-Barqī, *Kitāb al-maḥāsin*, ed. J. Muḥaddith Urmawī (Tehran, 1370/1950), 'kitāb 'iqāb al-a'māl', ch. 15 ('iqāb man shakka fī amīr al-mu'minīn), ch. 16 ('iqāb man ankara āl Muḥammad ḥaqqahum wa jahala amrahum' – we have seen that often *ḥaqq* and *amr* are synonymous with *walāya*) and ch. 17 ('iqāb man lam ya'rif imāmahu), vol. 1, pp. 89–93.

> God established ʿAlī as a point of reference (*ʿalam*) between Himself and His creation and there is none other. He who follows ʿAlī is a believer, he who rejects him is an unbeliever and he who doubts him, an associationist.[38]
>
> [God says to the Prophet]: 'I created the seven heavens and what they contain; I created the seven earths and what they contain. If one of My followers invoked Me from the beginning of creation [to the Resurrection] or if I were to encounter him while he rejects the *walāya* of ʿAlī, I would swiftly send him to hell.'[39]
>
> If at Mecca a servant worshipped God for a hundred years [lit. between al-Rukn and al-Maqām, two sacred sites considered places of worship in the holy city]; if he devoted his days to fasting and nights to prayer until old age but all the while remained unaware of our truth [or 'rights', *ḥaqq* i.e. *walāya*] he would receive no reward [from God].[40]
>
> He who dies without having known his imam dies a pagan's death as in the Age of Ignorance [i.e. pre-Islamic times – *al-jāhiliyya*].[41]

Other early Imami compilers of *ḥadīth*s report many other traditions of the same sort:

> The man who fasts the entire day and prays all night long, but encounters God (upon the Day of Resurrection) without (having professed) our *walāya*, will find God dissatisfied and even angry with him.[42]

---

38. Al-Barqī, *al-Maḥāsin*, vol. 1, ch. 15, p. 89, no. 34 (a tradition going back to al-Bāqir). The accusation of *shirk* is probably levelled at those who make association with *walāya*s other than that of ʿAlī. See above verse 42:13 according to 'the Qur'an of the imams' (note 14 and the related text; also note 86 below).

39. Al-Barqī, *al-Maḥāsin*, vol. 1, p. 90, no. 38 (Jaʿfar).

40. Al-Barqī, *al-Maḥāsin*, vol. 1, ch. 16, p. 90, no. 40, (Jaʿfar).

41. Al-Barqī, *al-Maḥāsin*, vol. 1, ch. 17, p. 92, no. 46 (Jaʿfar). Regarding this very famous tradition, *mīta jāhiliyya* and the early sources that report it see Amir-Moezzi, *Guide divin*, p. 301 (*Divine Guide*, p. 123) and n. 671. For similar traditions see also Ibn Bābūya, *Kitāb thawāb al-aʿmāl wa ʿiqāb al-aʿmāl*, ed. ʿA. A. Ghaffārī (Tehran, 1391/1971), pp. 242–244.

42. Al-ʿAyyāshī, *Tafsīr*, vol. 2, p. 89; Bar-Asher, *Scripture and Exegesis*, p. 196.

> Are you not satisfied (you who are faithful to the imams) that due to your *walāya* towards us your prayer is accepted, whereas theirs [i.e. of the adversaries of the imams] is not; that your alms are accepted whereas theirs are not; that your pilgrimage is valid whereas theirs is not.[43]

> The Prophet: 'The imams that will follow are twelve in number; the first is 'Alī b. Abī Ṭālib and the last is the Qā'im. In my community, after me they are my caliphs, legatees, my *awliyā'* and the Proofs of God. He who recognises them is a believer and he who does not is an infidel.'[44]

---

43. Al-Kulaynī, *al-Rawḍa min al-Kāfī*, vol. 2, p. 43, no. 316 (a tradition going back to Ja'far); a tradition also reported by al-Majlisī, *Biḥār*, vol. 8, pp. 300 and 352, as well as a similar tradition that ends with the sentence, 'Those who excuse themselves from fulfilling their canonical duties will in this world benefit from comfort, health or influence (*al-ni'am wa'l-ṣiḥḥa aw al-si'a*), but in the Hereafter they will experience only eternal punishment.' See also al-Kulaynī, *al-Rawḍa*, vol. 1, p. 154, no. 80 (Ja'far) or vol. 2, p. 89, no. 399 (Ja'far), 'God made five elements obligatory for Muḥammad's community: prayer, alms, fasting, the pilgrimage to Mecca and our *walāya*. Now for the first four, He allowed exemptions in special circumstances (*rukhṣa*, in cases such as illness, menstruation and financial difficulties these duties may be abandoned) whereas our *walāya* must never be abandoned.'

44. Ibn Bābūya, *Kamāl al-dīn*, vol. 1, p. 259 (a tradition going back to Ja'far which he received from his father and paternal forebears); also vol. 1, p. 261 (a tradition attributed to al-Riḍā). See also Ibn Bābūya, *Amālī/al-Majālis*, 'majlis' 73, no. 12, pp. 484–485 and 'majlis' 85, no. 28, pp. 583–584. Among the Ismailis, it is quite telling that a great thinker such as al-Qāḍī al-Nu'mān (d. 363/974), begins his monumental profession of faith, the *Da'ā'im al-islām* with 'kitāb al-walāya', ed. Fyzee, vol. 1, pp. 1–120. He reports a number of the traditions that we have just mentioned. It is true that a great majority of traditions from the corpus going back to the imams Muḥammad al-Bāqir and Ja'far al-Ṣādiq are common to both the Imamis and Ismailis. English translation: 'The Book of Walāya' in *The Pillars of Islam: Da'ā'im al-islām* of al-Qāḍī al-Nu'mān, by A. A. A. Fyzee, completed, revised and annotated by I. K. Poonawala, vol. 1 (New York and Oxford, 2002); see the important article by A. Nanji, 'An Ismaili Theory of *Walāya*, in the *Da'ā'im al-islām* of al-Qāḍī al-Nu'mān', in D. P. Little (ed.), *Essays on Islamic Civilization Presented to Niyazi Berkes* (Leiden, 1976), pp. 260–273. See also, Sulaym b. Qays (Ps.), *Kitāb Sulaym b. Qays al-Hilālī*, ed. Anṣārī, vol. 2, pp. 858–860 and pp. 928–929, nos 46 and 70 respectively.

The semantic levels and the theological and eschatological implications

A central issue and motivating factor for the revelation of the Qurʾān, both in its original complete version and in the so-called censored *textus receptus*, as the supreme Pillar of Islam and a canonical duty of the greatest priority, which determines the validity of all the others, for the Shiʿis *walāya* constitutes the core of the faith without which the religion loses its substance. Where does the sacred significance attached to it derive from?

What does it mean exactly for the Shiʿi religious consciousness? H. Corbin devoted studies of some consequence to this very issue.[45] The following brief summary is a modest attempt to supplement the renowned French scholar's work, mainly by drawing on the earliest sources for Imami *ḥadīth*s, which Corbin explored somewhat less than others.[46]

In a note in *The Divine Guide,* I proposed a cursory definition of *walāya*:

> In contrast to the semantic complexity of the term *walāya* in the administrative, social, and religious language of the beginnings of Islam and later in the technical terminology of sufism, *walāya*, in the context of early Shiʿism, has a quite simple translation with two interdependent and complementary meanings: applied to the imams of different prophets, it refers to their ontological status or their sacred initiatory mission; several nuances of the root *WLY*

45. See particularly H. Corbin, *En Islam iranien: Aspects spirituels et philosophiques*, vol. 1, 'Le shīʾisme duodécimain' (Paris, 1971–1972), chs 6 and 7, pp. 219–329; also *Histoire de la philosophie islamique* (Paris, 1986), sections II. A. 4. and II. A. 5, pp. 78–98.

46. Al-Kulaynī, *al-Uṣūl min al-Kāfī* is practically his only early source. In his studies, H. Corbin bases his argument mainly on philosophical and mystical texts of a much later period. May I reiterate that *Le Guide divin* is also a monograph devoted entirely to the imamate and the figure of the imam in early Shiʿism. See also the excellent summary by H. Landolt, 'Walāyah', *Encyclopedia of Religion*, vol. 15, pp. 316–323 (on Shiʿi *walāya*, pp. 319–320), as well as P. Walker, 'Wilāya', 'Shīʿism', *EI2*.

> are found in the meaning: the *walī*-imam is the 'friend' and the closest 'helper' of God and His prophet; he immediately 'follows' the latter in his mission; he is the 'chief', the 'master' of believers par excellence. In this understanding, *walī* is a synonym of *waṣī* (the inheritor, the heir [of the sacred cause of the prophets]) or *mawlā* (applied to the imam, the term means the master, the guide, the protector, the *patronus*). Applied to the faithful of the imams, *walāya* denotes the unfailing love, faith and submission that the initiated owe to their holy initiating guide; in this understanding, the term becomes the equivalent of *tawallī* (being the faithful friend or the obedient protegé of someone); 'true Shi'i' are called the *mutawallī* of the imams.[47]

Let us consider these two semantic levels more closely.

1. *Walāya* in relation to the imam

Walāya as a sacred mission of the imams is equivalent to the imamate, that is, briefly stated, the spiritual and temporal direction of the faithful. In this case, one may translate it as 'power', even 'sacred power', since it is granted to the imams by divine election. If the imam is called upon to direct the faithful after the Prophet's death, it is because the imamate/*walāya* is the indispensable complement to prophethood (*nubuwwa*) in accordance with the Shi'i pair *ẓāhir/bāṭin* that operates at every level of reality.[48]

According to this understanding, the prophet (*nabī*) is the messenger of the letter of the Revelation (*tanzīl*) for the masses (*'āmma/'awāmm*) that constitute the majority (*akthar*) of a given community. In the same way the imam (*wālī*), complementing the prophet's mission, teaches the hidden spiritual meaning (*ta'wīl*) of the Revelation to a minority (*aqall*) which constitutes the elite

47. *Guide divin*, p. 74 (*Divine Guide*, p. 29), n. 151.

48. See M. A. Amir-Moezzi, 'Du droit à la théologie, Les niveaux de réalité dans le shi'isme duodécimain', *L'Esprit et la Nature* (Actes du colloque tenu à Paris les 11 et 12 mai 1996), *Cahiers du groupe d'études spirituelles comparées*, 5 (1997), pp. 37–63.

(*khāṣṣa/khawāṣṣ*) of this community.[49] Without the initiatory teaching of the imam, the profound meaning of the Revelation would remain unfathomed, just as a text interpreted in letter but not in spirit would remain forever poorly understood.

This is why the Qur'ān is called the mute, Silent Book or Guide (*imām ṣāmit*), whereas the Imam is said to be the speaking Qur'ān (*qur'ān nāṭiq*).[50] 'Among you there is someone', the Prophet is said to have stated, 'who fights for a spiritual interpretation (*ta'wīl*) of the Qur'ān as I fought for the revelation in the word (*tanzīl*), and this person is 'Alī b. Abī Ṭālib.'[51]

As we know, in early Shi'i *ḥadīth*s, Muḥammad as the archetype of *nubuwwa* and the legislating prophets may symbolise prophethood and all the prophets as a whole; just as 'Alī, imam par excellence, archetype of *walāya*, may be the supreme symbol of imamate or of all the imams as a whole.[52] For according to Imami prophetology, all the prophets as messengers of various divine revelations in the letter (the *ẓāhir*) were accompanied in

49. See E. Kohlberg, 'In Praise of the Few', in G. Hawting et al., *Studies in Islamic and Middle Eastern Texts and Traditions* (Oxford, 2000), pp. 149–162. And Chapter 8, this volume.

50. M. Ayoub, 'The Speaking Qur'ān and the Silent Qur'ān: A Study of the Principles and Development of Imāmī Tafsīr', in A. Rippin (ed.), *Approaches to the History of the Interpretation of the Qur'ān* (Oxford, 1988), pp. 177–198; Bar-Asher, *Scripture and Exegesis*, pp. 88ff.

51. Al-'Ayyāshī, *Tafsīr*, vol. 1, pp. 15–16 (tradition no. 6 going back to Ja'far which he received from his paternal ancestors. See also tradition no. 13, going back to the same imam, 'God taught the prophet the letter of the Revelation; as for the interpretation of its hidden meaning, the Prophet of God taught it to 'Alī'); al-Khazzāz al-Rāzī, *Kifāyat al-athar* (Qumm, 1401/1980), pp. 76, 88, 117, 135 (on p. 66, it is the Qā'im who is said to be the warrior of *ta'wīl*); al-Shahrastānī, *al-Milal wa'l-niḥal* (Beirut, n.d.), p. 189; al-Baḥrānī, *al-Burhān*, vol. 1, p. 17; al-Majlisī, *Biḥār*, vol. 19, pp. 25–26; for other sources, see Bar-Asher, *Scripture*, p. 88, n. 1; also ch. 9, n. 30 and the related text.

52. See Chapter 5, this volume, *in fine*.

their mission by one or more imams whose task was to unveil the hidden meaning (the *bāṭin*) of the Word of God.[53]

This dimension and meaning of *walāya*/imamate are sufficiently well known and so there is no need to elaborate much further. However, there is more to the term. *Walāya* also denotes the essential nature of the figure of the imam, his ontological status. Now, the imam/*wālī* in the ultimate reality of his being, is the locus for the manifestation of God (*maẓhar, majlā*), the vehicle of the divine Names and Attributes (*al-asmā' wa'l-ṣifāt*). 'By God', Imam Ja'far is said to have declared, 'we (the imams) are the Most Beautiful Names (of God).'[54]

The imam reveals God, he provides access to what may be known of Him, the *Deus Revelatus*, the *ẓāhir* of God. The *bāṭin* of God, His Face, the unknowable and hidden dimension, is the level of the Essence (*al-dhāt*), the *Deus absconditus*.[55] One can never emphasise enough this fundamental conception of *walāya* in Shi'i esoterism. Whether, as I believe, it is the matter of an early doctrine professed by the imams themselves,[56] at least – according to

53. See e.g. the entire first part of the important early work, *Ithbāt al-waṣiyya li'l-imām 'Alī b. Abī Ṭālib* attributed to al-Mas'ūdī (d. 345/956) (in one of the most recent editions, Qumm, 1417/1996), pp. 20–90. See also U. Rubin, 'Prophets and Progenitors in the Early Shī'a Tradition', *Jerusalem Studies in Arabic and Islam*, 1 (1979), pp. 41–65.

54. Al-'Ayyāshī, *Tafsīr*, vol. 2, p. 42; al-Kulaynī, *al-Uṣūl*, 'Kitāb al-tawḥīd', 'Bāb al-nawādir', vol. 1, p. 296, no. 4.

55. Chapter 3 above; also 'Du droit à la théologie', pp. 47–48 and 62–63.

56. In several publications, apart from *Le Guide divin*, and 'Du droit à la théologie' mentioned already, see also 'Al-Ṣaffār al-Qummī (d. 290/902–903) et son *Kitāb Baṣā'ir al-Darajāt*', *JA*, 280/3–4 (1992), pp. 221–250. Briefly stated, in my opinion, taking into consideration the fluctuating descriptions that the heresiographers and other authors provided of the *ghulāt*, and considering traditions related to theories attributed to the *ghulāt* as reported by the earliest compilations of Imami *ḥadīth*s, added to our lack of knowledge regarding the nature of relations between different Shi'i branches in the earliest centuries, the distinction between 'moderate' and 'extremist' Shi'is during these early times seems artificial and not based on textual evidence.

M. G. S. Hodgson[57] – since the time of Jaʿfar al-Ṣādiq (d. 148/765) or of beliefs emanating from 'extremist' Shiʿi circles which later influenced so-called 'moderate' imamism, as H. Modaressi maintains,[58] it is nonetheless true that this conception of the divine nature of the imam has been reported since the second half of the third/ninth century[59] in the earliest Imami compilations of *ḥadīth*s and has thus formed an integral part of the Imami religious consciousness for at least a thousand years. This is often forgotten by scholars, surely because the Shiʿis themselves hardly speak of it, or if so allusively only, no doubt due to the discipline of the arcanum.

This explains certain sayings traced back to the imams that are inevitably associated with the *shaṭaḥāt* ('ecstatic utterances') of the mystics:[60]

> 'I am the Rewarder (*dayyān*) of men on the day of Retribution', 'Alī is supposed to have said; 'I am he who allocates between

---

57. 'How did the Early Shiʿa Become Sectarian', *JAOS* (1955), pp. 1–13, esp. pp. 8ff., and 'Djaʿfar al-Ṣādik' and 'Ghulāt', *EI2*.

58. H. Modarressi, *Crisis and Consolidation in the Formative Period of Shīʿite Islam: Abū Jaʿfar ibn Qiba al-Rāzī and His Contribution to Imāmite Shīʿite Thought* (Princeton, 1993), Part One, esp. pp. 19–53.

59. On the most important and earliest of these compilations, namely those by al-Barqī (d. 274/887 or 280/893), al-Ṣaffār (d. 290/902–903) and al-Kulaynī (d. 329/940–941) now see A. J. Newman, *The Formative Period of Twelver Shīʿism: Hadith as Discourse Between Qum and Baghdad* (Richmond, 2000).

60. These are sayings in which 'God speaks in the first person through the lips of the mystic'; see e.g. L. Massignon, *Essai sur les origines du lexique technique de la mystique musulmane* (Paris, 1922), see index under '*shaṭaḥāt*', and *La passion de Hallâj, martyr mystique de l'Islam*, 4 vols (2nd edn, Paris, 1975), see index under '*shaṭaḥāt*'; the introduction by H. Corbin to Rūzbihān Baqlī Shīrāzī, *Sharḥ-i shaṭḥiyyāt*, ed. H. Corbin and M. Moʿīn (Paris and Tehran, 1966; 2nd edn, Tehran, 2004); C. Ernst, *Words of Ecstasy in Sufism* (New York, 1985); P. Ballanfat, 'Réflexions sur la nature du paradoxe, La définition de Rūzbehān Baqlī Shīrāzī', *Kār Nāmeh* (Paris, 1995), pp. 2–3 and 25–40. It is important, however, to clarify the point that the bases, as well as the theological and anthropological implications, of the Sufi 'words of ecstasy' and the paradoxical sayings of the imams are different.

> Garden and Fire, none is to enter without my allocation. I am the Supreme Judge (*al-fārūq al-akbar*). . . I possess the decisive word (*faṣl al-khiṭāb*); I hold the penetrating view of the path of the book . . . I have knowledge of the fortunes and misfortunes as well as of the judgements. I am the perfection of religion. I am God's blessing for His creatures.'[61]

And:

> I am the Queen Bee (*ya'sūb*) of the initiates; I am the first among the ancients; I am the successor to the messenger of the lord of the worlds; I am the judge of Garden and Fire.[62]

In a tradition going back to the Prophet, regarding 'Alī Muḥammad declared:

> Here is the most radiant imam, the tallest lance of God, the most ample Threshold of God; let he who seeks God enter by this Threshold . . . Without 'Alī, the truth shall not be distinguished from the false, nor the faithful from the unfaithful; without 'Alī, God would not have been worshipped... Neither shield (*sitr*) nor veil (*ḥijāb*) between God and him . . . No! . . . 'Alī himself is the shield and the veil.[63]

A tradition has al-Ḥasan b. 'Alī saying:

> We (the imams) are the First and the Last; we are the commanders; we are the Light. The Light of spiritual beings comes from us.

---

61. Furāt al-Kūfī, *Tafsīr*, p. 178; the last two sentences are clearly allusions to Qur'ān 5:3 on the 'perfection of religion and blessing' as we have examined above.

62. Al-'Ayyāshī, *Tafsīr*, vol. 2, pp. 17–18; al-Majlisī, *Biḥār*, vol. 3, p. 389; al-Baḥrānī, *al-Burhān*, vol. 2, p. 20. Regarding the Shi'is symbolised as bees or about 'Alī as the 'Commander of Bees' (*amīr al-naḥl*), see I. Goldziher, 'Schi'itisches', *ZDMG*, 64 (1910), pp. 532–533, now in *Gesammelte Schriften*, ed. J. de Somogyi (Hildesheim, 1967–1970), vol. 5, pp. 213–214.

63. Furāt al-Kūfī, *Tafsīr*, p. 371. This kind of declaration already prefigures what I have called 'theo-imamosophic exhortations' of 'Alī, reported by later sources; see Chapter 3.

> We illuminate by the Light of God. We render joyful by His Joy [or we spiritualise by His spirit — *nurawwiḥu bi rawḥih/rūḥih* — the possessive adjective, here as well as below, may refer to the Light as well as to God; the ambiguity is undoubtedly intended]; within us His abode; towards us His source. Our first is identical to our last and our last identical to our first.[64]

According to a traditon reported by a number of sources, imam ʿAlī b. al-Ḥusayn Zayn al-ʿĀbidīn once transformed himself into a winged being and to the amazement of his disciples disappeared into the heavens. Upon his return, he declared that he had travelled to the loftiest of heavens (*aʿlā ʿilliyyin*) and is said to have responded to an adept thus:

> We [the imams] are the ones who built the most elevated heaven; why then would we not be able to scale its heights? We are the bearers of the [divine] Throne (*ʿarsh*) and we are seated upon the Throne. The Throne and Pedestal (*kursī*) belong to us.[65]

According to a *ḥadīth* attributed to imam Jaʿfar:

> We manifest Light in darkness. We are the Oft-Frequented Abode (*al-bayt al-maʿmūr*; Q 52:4) where the one who enters, enters in safety. We are the magnificence and grandeur of God . . . We are beyond all description; due to us eyes are brightened, ears listen; hearts are filled with faith.[66]

The sixth imam is also said to have declared:

---

64. Al-Ṭabarī al-Ṣaghīr, *Nawādir al-muʿjizāt* (Qumm, 1410/1990), p. 103, and *Dalāʾil al-imāma* (Qumm, 1413/1994), pp. 168–169; al-Ḥurr al-ʿĀmilī, *Ithbāt al-hudāt*, vol. 5, p. 157; al-Baḥrānī, *Madīnat al-maʿājiz* (Tehran, n.d. [ca. 1960]), pp. 204–205.

65. Al-Ṭabarī al-Ṣaghīr, *Nawādir al-muʿizāt*, p. 116, and *Dalāʾil al-imāma*, p. 201; al-ʿĀmilī, *Ithbāt al-hudāt*, vol. 5, p. 256; al-Baḥrānī, *Madīnat al-maʿājiz*, p. 294.

66. Al-Ṭabarī al-Ṣaghīr, *Dalāʾil al-imāma*, pp. 270–271; al-Baḥrānī, *Madīnat al-maʿājiz*, pp. 394–395.

God has made of us His Eyes among His worshippers, His eloquent tongue among His creatures, His benevolent and merciful hand extended over His servants, His face by which one is led to Him, His threshold which leads one to Him, His treasure in the heavens and on the earth . . . It is by our act of worship that God is worshipped; without us God would not be worshipped.

The last sentence (*bi ʿibādatinā ʿubida'llāh law lā naḥnu mā ʿubida'llāh*) may also be read: 'It is by virtue of the fact that we [the imams] are worshipped that God is worshipped; without us God would not be worshipped.' Here too the rather audacious ambiguity seems deliberate.[67]

To end this hardly exhaustive list, here is a dialogue between Jaʿfar al-Ṣādiq and one of his disciples who asks him if on the Day of Resurrection, the initiated believers (*al-mu'minūn*) will be able to see God. The imam replies:

'Yes, but they will have already seen him long before the advent of this Day.' 'When was this?' 'When God asked them: "Am I not your Lord?" and they replied "Yes, most certainly" (Q 7:172).' The disciple reports that his master then remained silent for a long time before declaring: 'The initiates see Him already in this world before the Day of Resurrection. Do you not see Him at this very moment, even before you now? [i.e. in my very being].' 'If I were to serve as ransom, may I with your permission report these words?' 'No, for a negator unaware of their true meaning, will use them to accuse us of assimilationism and unbelief.'[68]

67. Ibn Bābūya, *Kitāb al-Tawḥīd*, ed. H. al-Ḥusaynī al-Ṭihrānī (Tehran, 1398/1978), ch. 12, pp. 151–152, no. 8. According to another tradition, someone asks imam Jaʿfar, 'What would happen on earth if a physical living sage (*ʿālim ḥayy ẓāhir*; i.e., the imam) to whom people have recourse for what is licit and illicit were not present?' Jaʿfar answers: 'God could not be worshipped (in such a world)'; al-Fayḍ al-Kāshānī, *Nawādir al-akhbār*, ed. M. al-Anṣārī al-Qummī (Tehran, 1375 Sh./1996), 'kitāb al-nubuwwa wa'l-imāma', p. 129, no. 2 (based on Ibn Bābūya, *ʿIlal al-sharāʾiʿ*, vol. 1, ch. 153, p. 195, no. 3).

68. Ibn Bābūya, *Tawḥīd*, ch. 8, p. 117, no. 20; Amir-Moezzi, *Guide divin*, p. 141 (*Divine Guide*, p. 54), n. 277 (with other *ḥadīth*s similar in content). It is symptomatic that W. Chittick who provides an English translation of this

This aspect of *walāya* characterises the Imam (with an upper case 'I') in the cosmic, archetypical, metaphysical sense: the divine Perfect Man, if not Man-God, that is to say *walāya* as the locus of manifestation for the Attributes of God. The last part of the dialogue between Jaʿfar al-Ṣādiq and his disciple demonstrates clearly that this concept constitutes a secret that must be kept from the unworthy. It is even *the* ultimate Secret teaching of the imams.[69]

> All things have a secret, the secret of Islam is Shiʿism (literally: the Shiʿis, *al-shīʿa*) and the secret of Shiʿism is the *walāya* of ʿAlī.[70]

If we were to apply the technical meaning to these terms we would understand that a secret veiled behind the letter of a religion is the esoteric teaching of its initiated, and the key secret of this teaching is the divinity of the Imam, the divine Guide.

> 'Something in you resembles Jesus the son of Mary', the Prophet is supposed to have said to ʿAlī, 'and had I not feared that some groups

---

tradition in *A Shi'ite Anthology* (New York, 1981), p. 42, does not point out the '*shaṭḥ*' that it contains and which constitutes its focal point.

69. Amir-Moezzi, 'Du droit à la théologie', pp. 47–48, 55, 62–63.

70. Ibn ʿAyyāsh al-Jawharī, *Muqtaḍab al-athar* (Tehran, 1346/1927), p. 23 (a tradition attributed to Jaʿfar); see also a shorter version in al-Kulaynī, *al-Rawḍa*, vol. 2, p. 14. Although each imam in every cycle during mankind's sacred History has been the locus of manifestation for this cosmic Imam, ʿAlī remains His supreme vehicle and symbol. Which is why in a number of traditions – apart from the obvious meaning – ʿAlī also signifies the cosmic Imam or *walāya*/imamate in general; just as Muḥammad, beyond the obvious meaning may also signify the archetypal Messenger-Prophet or prophethood (*nubuwwa*) in general; see Chapter 5, this volume, *in fine* and note 52 above as well as the relevant text. One may make a similar comment regarding the terms *islām* (strictly referring to the Muslim religion and in a wider sense, the exoteric dimension, the 'letter' of each religion) and *shīʿa* (referring to the Shiʿis of Islam; and in a wider sense: the initiatic, esoteric dimension 'the spirit' of each religion), see note 95 below. Thus the *ḥadīth* attributed to Jaʿfar may also be understood as follows: 'All things have a secret; the hidden secret behind the "letter" of every religion is its initiatic, esoteric dimension and the secret of the latter is the *walāya* of the cosmic Man.'

> in my community would say what is said of Jesus by the Christians, I would have revealed something about you that would have made people gather the dust beneath your feet to seek blessings.'[71]

This secret dimension of *walāya* may be considered the esoteric of the esoteric (*bāṭin al-bāṭin*) of the imams' teachings. Thus *ḥadīth*s such as:

> Our teaching is the truth; truth of the truth; it is the exoteric, esoteric and esoteric of the esoteric; it is the secret and secret of a secret, a well-guarded secret, hidden by a secret.[72]
>
> Our doctrine [*amr*: cause, order, affair, teaching . . . as we have seen, the term is often identified with *walāya*] is a secret contained within a secret, a well-guarded secret, a secret whose only benefit is a secret, a secret veiled by a secret.[73]
>
> Our doctrine is hidden, sealed by the original Pact [*al-mīthāq* – I shall return to this matter regarding the pre-existence of *walāya*], God will render he who reveals it contemptible.[74]

One may say that the historical imam/*wālī*, physical, initiating master par excellence is the guardian of a Secret whose content is the metaphysical Imam, throne of the cosmic *walāya*: 'We are the treasure (*khazāna*) and the treasurers (*khuzzān/khazana*)

71. Al-Kulaynī, *al-Rawḍa*, vol. 1, p. 81. See also Sulaym b. Qays (Ps.), *Kitāb Sulaym b. Qays al-Hilālī*, ed. Anṣārī, vol. 2, p. 891, no. 58 and vol. 2, p. 910, no. 62; al-Baḥrānī Hāshim b. Sulaymān, *al-Lawāmiʿ al-nūrāniyya* (Isfahan, 1404/1983), pp. 373, 376.

72. Al-Ṣaffār al-Qummī, *Baṣāʾir al-darajāt*, section 1, ch. 12, p. 28, no. 4 (Jaʿfar).

73. *Baṣāʾir*, p. 28, no. 1 (Jaʿfar).

74. *Baṣāʾir*, p. 28, no. 2 (al-Bāqir). On the duty of preserving a secret (*taqiyya, kitmān, khabʾ*), now see E. Kohlberg, 'Taqiyya in Shīʿī Theology and Religion', in H. G. Kippenberg and G. G. Stroumsa (eds), *Secrecy and Concealment. Studies in the History of Mediterranean and Near Eastern Religions* (Leiden, 1995), pp. 345–380; supplementing a previous study by the same author, 'Some Imāmī-Shīʿī Views on *taqiyya*', *JAOS*, 95 (1975), pp. 395–402 (now in *Belief and Law in Imāmī Shīʿism* [Aldershot, 1991], article III).

of God's Secret.'[75] Both meanings of *walāya* vis à vis the imam are therefore inseparable: first, the historical imam is the locus of manifestation for the cosmic Imam, just as the latter, the absolute theophany is the locus of manifestation for God. Secondly, the ultimate content, the very 'marrow' of the historic imams' teachings is therefore the secret substance of different Revelations, the veritable spirit hidden behind the letter of these revelations, the mystery of the ontological Imam.

At this level, *walāya* may be translated as 'Friendship' (with God), 'Alliance' (with God), Proximity (of God) – all qualities implying the profound meaning of 'Saintliness' (the convential translation of *walāya*) – yet, although obviously corresponding to some of the meanings that the root WLY harbours, none of these terms is equal to the theological content of this very special dimension of the concept at hand. It is in this sense that *walāya* constitutes the esoteric dimension of the prophet's message and mission: *al-walāya bāṭin al-nubuwwa* as Shiʿis authors have tirelessly emphasised. It is the central term of an entire series of 'complementary pairs' that characterise the dialectic of manifest and hidden in Shiʿism.

Manifest	Hidden
ẓāhir	*bāṭin*
nubuwwa	*walāya*
Muḥammad	ʿAlī
tanzīl	*ta'wīl*
islām	*īmān*
muslim	*mu'min*
akthar/ʿāmma	*aqall/khāṣṣa* [76]

75. Al-Ṣaffār, *Baṣā'ir al-darajāt*, section 2, ch. 3; al-Kulaynī, *al-Uṣūl*, 'kitāb al-ḥujja', chs 13 and 14; al-Kulaynī, *al-Rawḍa*, vol. 1, pp. 101f.; Ibn Bābūya, *'Uyūn akhbār al-Riḍā*, ed. M. H. Lājevardī (Tehran, 1398/1978), vol. 1, chs 19 and 20; Ibn Bābūya, *Maʿānī'l-akhbār*, ed. 'A. A. Ghaffārī (Tehran, 1379/1959), p. 132; Ibn Bābūya, *Ṣifāt al-shīʿa* (+ *Faḍā'il al-shīʿa*), ed. Ḥ. Fashāhī (Tehran, 1342 Sh./1963–1964), pp. 60f.; Ibn 'Ayyāsh al-Jawharī, *Muqtaḍab al-athar*, p. 39.

76. See *Guide divin*, p. 308 (*Divine Guide*, p. 127); for the pair *islām/īmān* technically referring to 'Islam of the Majority/the religion of the Initiated i.e. Shiʿism' and 'submission exclusively to the letter of the Exoteric religion/initiation

Whether it relates to the imam's mission or his ontological status, in other words to the historical or metaphysical sense of imamate, the imam's *walāya* is said to be as ancient as creation.

> 'When God the Most High created the Heavens and the Earth', the Prophet is supposed to have said, 'He summoned them and they replied. Then He introduced my *nubuwwa* and the *walāya* of 'Alī b. Abī Ṭālib and they accepted. Then God created all beings and entrusted us the matter of (their) religion (*amr al-dīn*). So it came to be that the fortunate are fortunate by us and the unfortunate, unfortunate by us. We render what is licit for them licit and what is illicit for them illicit.'[77]

Walāya permeates the entire history of mankind and constitutes its spiritual substance since it is at the heart of all Revelations and prophetic missions. Al-Ṣaffār al-Qummī (d. 290/902–903) devoted several chapters in the second part of his book *Baṣā'ir al-darajāt* to these issues.[78] According to a number of traditions going back mainly to the fifth and sixth imams, Muḥammad al-Bāqir and Ja'far al-Ṣādiq, the pre-temporal Pact (*al-mīthāq*) – concluded between God and his creatures at the dawn of creation and to which the Qur'ānic verse 7:172 supposedly alludes – mainly concerns *walāya*.[79]

Other *ḥadīth*s specify that only the 'elite' of creation pledged an oath of allegiance with regard to the *walāya* of 'Alī (i.e. the cosmic Imam) namely, the Closest (*al-muqarrabūn*) among angels, the Messengers (*al-mursalūn*) among prophets and the tested ones

---

into the Esoteric religion', as well as *muslim/mu'min* signifying 'common' Muslim/initiated Shi'i, see *Guide divin*, index under these terms and note 95 below.

77. Ibn Shādhān, *Mi'a manqaba* (Qumm, 1413/1993), 'manqaba' 7, p. 48; al-Irbilī, *Kashf al-ghumma*, ed. H. Rasūlī Maḥallātī (Tabriz; rpr. Qumm, 1381/1962), vol. 1, p. 291; al-Khwārazmī, *Maqtal al-Ḥusayn* (Qumm, n.d.), vol. 1, p. 46.

78. Al-Ṣaffār, *Baṣā'ir al-darajāt*, section 2, chs 6–16, pp. 67–90. See also al-Majlisī, *Biḥār*, vol. 26, pp. 280ff.

79. *Baṣā'ir*, chs 7–12; see also notes 8 and 74 above as well as the relevant texts.

(*al-mumtaḥanūn*) among believers.[80] According to a tradition attributed to the Prophet, in the pre-existential world of Shadows (*'ālam al-aẓilla*), the status of prophets only attained its final stage once they recognised the *walāya* of the Impeccable Ones.[81] Similarly, the Pact accorded Adam, as referred to in Q 20:115, concerns *walāya* [82] – the essential purpose of every prophetic mission.

> Neither prophet nor any messenger was ever commissioned save by (or 'for') our *walāya (bi-wilāyatinā).*[83]
>
> Our *walāya* is the *walāya* of God. Every prophet was only ever sent [by God] for / by it.[84]
>
> The *walāya* of 'Alī is inscribed in all books of the prophets; a messenger was only ever sent to proclaim the prophethood of Muḥammad and the *walāya* of 'Alī. [85]

80. *Baṣā'ir*, ch. 6, pp. 67–68. For the technical term 'Tested' derived from the expression *al-mu'min imtaḥana 'llāhu qalbahu li'l-īmān* (the believer – or initiate whose heart is tested by God for faith; see *Le Guide divin*, index under *'imtiḥān (al-qalb)'* and esp. Chapter 10 in this volume.

81. *Baṣā'ir*, ch. 8. On 'the Worlds before this world', see *Guide divin*, section II. 1, p. 75ff (*Divine Guide*, ch. 2, section 1, pp. 29–37; see also Chapter 4, this volume).

82. *Baṣā'ir*, ch. 7, pp. 70–71; al-Qummī, *Tafsīr*, vol. 2, pp. 64–65; al-Astarābādī, *Ta'wīl al-āyāt al-ẓāhira*, pp. 313–314. According to some traditions, the allusion to *walāya* in this verse featured textually in the original revelation made to Muḥammad and was subsequently censured. 'We have entrusted Adam with Words concerning *Muḥammad, 'Alī, Fāṭima, al-Ḥasan, al-Ḥusayn and the imams in their lineage* but he forgot them'; al-Ṣaffār, *Baṣā'ir*, p. 71; al-Kulaynī, *al-Uṣūl*, 'Kitāb al-ḥujja', 'Bāb fīhi nukat wa nutaf min al-tanzīl fi'l-walāya', vol. 2, p. 283, no. 23; al-Baḥrānī, *al-Burhān*, vol. 3, p. 45; al-Fayḍ al-Kāshānī, *al-Ṣāfī*, vol. 2, p. 80; *Guide divin*, p. 212 (*Divine Guide*, pp. 84–85); Bar-Asher, 'Variant Readings', p. 64.

83. Al-Ṣaffār, *Baṣā'ir al-darajāt*, ch. 9, pp. 74–75 (Ja'far).

84. *Baṣā'ir*, p. 75 (al-Bāqir).

85. *Baṣā'ir*, ch. 8, p. 72 (al-Riḍā). See also al-Qundūzī, *Yanābī' al-mawadda* (n.p. [Iraq], 1385/1965), p. 82; al-Baḥrānī, *Ghāyat al-marām* (Qumm, n.d.), p. 207.

As we have already seen, the Qur'ān in its 'original complete version' would have clearly mentioned the fact that:

> He has laid down for you *O Family of Muḥammad* as religion that He charged Noah with, and that We have revealed to thee, *O Muḥammad*, and that We charged Abraham with, Moses and Jesus: 'Establish the religion *of the Family of Muḥammad*, and scatter not regarding it *and be united*.' Very hateful is that for the associationists, *those that associate to the walāya of 'Alī* [i.e. other *walāyas*] that thou callest them to *concerning the walāya of 'Alī. Surely* God guides, *O Muḥammad* towards this religion he who repents, *he who accepts your call to the walāya of 'Alī* [instead of 'God chooses unto Himself whomsoever He will, and He guides to Himself whosoever turns, penitent'].(Q 42:13)[86]

Adam was banished from paradise because he had forgotten the *walāya*.[87] The prophet Jonah was enclosed in the stomach of a whale because he had momentarily denied loyalty to *walāya*.[88] Certain Israelites were transformed into fish or lizards because they had neglected *walāya*.[89]

Without *walāya*, there is no religion. Without its spirit, the letter is barren, an empty shell, lifeless. It is therefore not surprising that Islam, ultimate religion of the most perfect of prophets, should – more than the others – be centred on the concept of *walāya*; what is more, if Muḥammad is Muḥammad it is so because – even more than the other prophets – during his celestial ascensions he was initiated into the mysteries of the *walāya* of the Imam, the Man-God symbolised by the cosmic 'Alī: "'Alī is a Sign of God [*āya* – just as a verse from the Qur'ān] for Muḥammad.

86. See notes 14 and 38 above.

87. In addition to references provided in n. 79, Ibn Bābūya, *Ma'ānī'l-akhbār*, pp. 107–109, and *al-Khiṣāl* (Najaf, 1391/1971), p. 246; Ibn Shahrāshūb, *Manāqib āl Abī Ṭālib*, 3 vols (Najaf, 1375–1376/1956), vol. 1, p. 214.

88. Furāt al-Kūfī, *Tafsīr*, p. 94; al-Majlisī, *Biḥār*, vol. 14, p. 401 and vol. 26, pp. 333ff. See also Bar-Asher, *Scripture and Exegesis*, p. 200.

89. Al-'Ayyāshī, *Tafsīr*, vol. 2, p. 35; al-Majlisī, *Biḥār*, vol. 5, p. 345 and vol. 14, p. 55; al-Baḥrānī, *al-Burhān*, vol. 2, p. 44; Bar-Asher, *Scripture*, pp. 200–201.

The latter did no more than summon [people] to the *walāya* of ʿAlī.'[90]

Commenting on Q 91:1, on Muḥammad's destiny as a prophet, imam Jaʿfar is said to have proclaimed: 'God opened his chest [heart] to the *walāya* of ʿAlī.'[91]

> 'The Angel Gabriel came to me', the Prophet supposedly reported, 'and said: "Muḥammad! Your Lord prescribes for you the love (*ḥubb*) and *walāya* of ʿAlī".'[92]
>
> The Prophet was elevated to the heavens twenty times; not once did God not entrust the *walāya* of ʿAlī – and the imams [that come] after him – even more so than what He recommended regarding canonical duties.[93]

This is why 'the *walāya* of ʿAlī beside the Prophet has nothing earthly about it; it descends from heaven, even from the Lips of God (*mushāfahatan*; i.e. a message transmitted orally to Muḥammad during his celestial ascensions)'.[94]

Walāya therefore constitutes the central message of Islam and of all religions before it:

> God made [of our] *walāya*, we the *ahl al-bayt*, the axis (*quṭb*) around which the Qur'ān gravitates; as well as the axis of all [sacred] Books. It is around the *walāya* that the clear verses of the Qur'ān turn; it is with the *walāya* that the sacred Writings are filled; by *walāya* that one clearly recognises the faith.[95]

---

90. Al-Ṣaffār, *Baṣā'ir*, ch. 7, pp. 71–72, nos 5 and 8 (al-Bāqir) and ch. 9, p. 77, no. 5 (Jaʿfar).

91. *Baṣā'ir*, ch. 8, p. 73.

92. *Baṣā'ir*, ch. 8, p. 74.

93. *Baṣā'ir*, ch. 10, p. 79 (Jaʿfar). See Chapter 5, this volume.

94. Al-Majlisī, *Biḥār*, vol. 28, p. 306, no. 13 (Jaʿfar). See Ibn al-Biṭrīq, *Khaṣā'iṣ*, ed. M. B. al-Maḥmūdī (Tehran, 1406/1986), p. 98 and Ibn Ṭāwūs, *al-Ṭarā'if fī maʿrifa madhāhib al-ṭawā'if* (Qumm, 1400/1979), p. 101.

95. A tradition going back to Jaʿfar, al-ʿAyyāshī, *Tafsīr*, vol. 1, p. 5; al-Baḥrānī, *al-Burhān*, vol. 1, p. 10; al-Fayḍ al-Kāshānī, *al-Ṣāfī*, vol. 1, p. 12; al-Majlisī, *Biḥār*, vol. 19, p. 78; *al-Uṣūl al-sittat ʿashar*, p. 60; see also note 28

Thus denying the imam's *walāya* amounts to denying all heavenly revelations. And justifiably so: the *walāya* of the Impeccable Ones, of the theophanic Guides, living examples of divinisation potential in man, is the ultimate aim of creation:

> The *walāya* of Muḥammad and his descendants is the ultimate aim and most noble goal (*al-gharaḍ al-aqṣā wa'l-murād al-afḍal*). God created his beings and commissioned his messengers especially to summon to the *walāya* of Muḥammad, 'Alī and the successors of the latter.[96]

---

above and the relevant text. Let us recall that in the technical lexicon of Shi'ism, the word 'faith' (*īmān*) means 'the teaching of the imams, esoteric dimension of religion, Shi'ism'. In response to the question, 'what is the difference between Islam and faith', imam Ja'far al-Ṣādiq is said to have answered, 'Islam is the exoteric dimension [of religion] to which people adhere [*al-islām huwa'l-ẓāhir alladhī 'alayhi'l-nās* – the latter term is one of the names by which Shi'is refer to non-Shi'is], the twofold profession of faith regarding the Oneness of God and Muḥammad's mission as Prophet, canonical prayers, alms, the pilgrimage to Mecca and fasting during the month of Ramaḍān. Now, in addition to this, Faith is knowledge of our teachings. He who professes and practices the former without knowing the latter though he may be a Muslim has gone astray [because, as we have seen, he neglects the principal canonical obligation, *walāya*],' al-Kulaynī, *al-Uṣūl*, 'Kitāb al-īmān wa'l-kufr', 'Bāb anna'l-islām yuḥqanu bihi'l-dam wa anna'l-thawāb 'alā'l-īmān', vol. 3, p. 39, no. 4. The same sixth imam is supposed to have further stated: 'Islam is the profession of divine Oneness and the acceptance of our Prophet's mission; it is by Islam that the price of blood is exacted, the conditions of marriage and rules of heritage established. There are a whole series of exoteric laws that the majority of people obey [*akthar al-nās*; another technical term for non-Shi'is, exoterist Muslims]. As for faith, it is guidance manifested in the heart. Exoterically, faith is linked to Islam whereas esoterically Islam is not linked to faith [*inna'l-īmān yushāriku'l-islām fi'l-ẓāhir wa'l-islām lā yushāriku'l-īmān fi'l-bāṭin*]. Faith is therefore superior to Islam', *al-Uṣūl*, vol. 3, pp. 41–42. For the equal value accorded to 'faith' and the teachings of the imams see also al-Nu'mānī, *al-Ghayba*, pp. 131, 188; Ibn Bābūya, *Amālī/al-Majālis*, 'majlis' 93, pp. 639ff.

96. (Pseudo?) al-imam al-Ḥasan al-'Askarī, *Tafsīr* (Qumm, 1409/1988), p. 379, no. 264. Regarding this source now see M. M. Bar-Asher, 'The Qur'ān Commentary Ascribed to Imam Ḥasan al-'Askarī', *Jerusalem Studies in Arabic and Islam*, 24 (2000), pp. 358–379. A section of this study is devoted to the doctrine of *walāya* in this work (pp. 377–378). The tradition just cited is referred to on p. 375.

An omnipresent message, whether explicit or implicit in the early Imami corpus, *walāya* constitutes the central meaning and purpose of *nubuwwa* just as the *bāṭin* is the *ẓāhir*'s raison d'être.[97]

2. *Walāya* in relation to the followers of the imams

The second semantic level of *walāya* relates to the followers of the imams, sometimes referred to as *ahl al-walāya*. It denotes love, faithfulness, devotion, loyalty and the submission that an adept owes to his master initiator – all qualities inherent in the root WLY. In this case, it is synonymous with other *maṣdar*s stemming from the same root, such as *tawallī/tawallā* (fifth form) and *muwālāt* (third form). In this sense one may say that Shiʿism is the religion of love for the Divine Guide: as the lapidary phrase attributed to Jaʿfar declares, '*walāya* is love (*al-walāya al-maḥabba*)'.[98]

By God the sixth imam allegedly remarked, if a stone were to love us, God would revive it with us; is religion anything other than love?[99]

---

97. However, the superiority of *walāya* over *nubuwwa* or *bāṭin* over *ẓāhir* does not imply (at least for the Imamis) superiority of the *wālī* over the *nabī* (more specifically the legislating prophet), since in his person, the latter at once acumulates *walāya* as well as *nubuwwa* and constitutes a source of wisdom for his imams. On the other hand, the wālī/cosmic Imam is superior to both; as the revealed Face of God, he is the ultimate aim of teachings proffered by all *nabī*s and *wālī*s. On this point, see M. A. Amir-Moezzi, 'Notes sur deux traditions hétérodoxes imamites', *Arabica*, 41 (1994), pp. 127–130; and esp. Chapter 5 above *in fine*.

98. Ibn 'Ayyāsh, *Muqtaḍab al-athar*, p. 45. 'Al-Matāwila', a term designating certain Shiʿis from Lebanon and Syria, seems to be the irregular plural of the active participle in the 5th form (*mutawallī*; 'métouali' in French). However, this etymology is not entirely certain. (see W. Ende, 'Mutawālī', *EI2*). It would thus denote 'people practising the *walāya* of the imams'.

99. Al-ʿAyyāshī, *Tafsīr*, vol. 1, p. 167; Ibn Bābūya, *al-Khiṣāl*, ed. 'A. A. Ghaffārī, (2nd edn, Qumm, 1403/1983), p. 21, no. 74; al-Baḥrānī, *al-Burhān*, vol. 1, p. 277; al-Fayḍ al-Kāshānī, *al-Ṣāfī*, vol. 1, p. 254; al-Majlisī, *Biḥār*, vol. 7, p. 377.

In addition, 'All things have a foundation (*asās*); the foundation of Islam is love for us, the *ahl al-bayt* (of the Prophet).'[100]

This is certainly how one must understand these kinds of expressions that recur very frequently in the *Ḥadīth*: *inna walāyat 'Alī* (and/or *al-a'imma*) *walāyat rasūl Allāh wa walāyat rasūl Allāh walāyat Allāh*, 'love of 'Alī (and/or the imams) is love for the Messenger of God (Muḥammad) and love of the Messenger of God is love for God'.[101]

However, in a doctrine strongly marked by a dualist conception of the world and its history, love for the imam is inevitably accompanied by hatred for his enemy. According to this conception, the faithful cannot only ally himself to the forces of Light, he must at the same time detach himself from the forces of Darkness. Given the fundamental role of knowledge in the Shi'i vision of the world,[102] to fervently adhere or belong to the forces of the initiation is inextricably linked to hostility towards those who are 'anti-initiation', for the latter use their power and violent means to repress even eliminate people of salutary gnosis. In this case therefore, *walāya/tawallī* is inseparable from its opposite namely *barā'a/tabarrī-tabarrā*.[103]

---

100. Al-Barqī, *al-Maḥāsin*, 'kitāb al-ṣafwa wa'l-nūr wa'l-raḥma', vol. 1, ch. 20, p. 150, no. 66; al-Khazzāz al-Rāzī, *Kifāyat al-athar*, p. 71; Ibn Bābūya, *al-Mawā'iẓ* (Qumm, n.d.), p. 29, and *Amālī*, p. 221; see Bar-Asher, *Scripture and Exegesis*, p. 194 (the distinction made between 'the duty to love the imam', pp. 192–195 and 'the duty of *walāya* to the imam', pp. 195–202, does not seem pertinent as these two notions are inseparable if not, depending on the context, identical).

101. See e.g. *al-Uṣūl al-sittat 'ashar*, p. 60; al-Majlisī, *Biḥār*, vol. 37, pp. 41ff.; vol. 38, pp. 118ff. All chapter 87 of the *Biḥār* is devoted to the *walāya*/love for 'Alī ('Love for him [i.e. 'Alī] is *walāya* and faith, whereas hatred of him is unfaithfulness and hypocrisy; from his *walāya* is *walāya* to God and His messenger and hostility to him is hostility to God and His messenger').

102. See *Guide divin*, section III–2, pp. 174–200 (*Divine Guide*, pp. 69–79); Chapters 5 and 8, this volume.

103. On this fundamental notion see the monograph by E. Kohlberg, '*Barā'a* in Shī'ī Doctrine', *Jerusalem Studies in Arabic and Islam*, 7 (1986), pp. 139–175. Many other works by the same scholar provide invaluable information on the

> The firmest handle of faith (. . . more so than prayer, alms, fasting, the pilgrimage to Mecca and the holy war . . .) is love (*ḥubb*) for God and hatred (*bughḍ*) for God, friendship (*tawallī*) of the friends of God and enmity (*tabarrī*) towards the enemies of God.[104]

> Friendship (*walāya*) with 'Alī is a good deed (*ḥasana*) that cannot give rise to any misdeed (*sayyi'a*) . . . and friendship with 'Alī's adversaries (*aḍdād*) is a misdeed that no good deed may redeem.[105]

> Love (*walāya*) of God is only won by love for His friends (*awliyā'*) and hostility (*mu'ādāt*) to His enemies.[106]

According to many traditions that are traced back to the Prophet himself, love for the imams can only be accepted when accompanied by dissociation from their enemies:

'dualist conception' that the Shi'is have of history and spirituality, 'The Term "Rāfiḍa" in Imāmī Shī'ī Usage', *JAOS* (1979), pp. 677–679 (rpr. in *Belief and Law in Imāmī Shī'ism*, article IV); 'Some Imāmī Shī'ī Views on the *ṣaḥāba*', *Jerusalem Studies in Arabic and Islam*, 5 (1984), pp. 143–175 (rpr. in *Belief and Law*, article IX); 'Non-Imāmī Muslims in Imāmī *fiqh*', *Jerusalem Studies in Arabic and Islam*, 6 (1985), pp. 99–105 (rpr. in *Belief and Law*, article X); 'In Praise of the Few' already cited; 'Evil', *EIr*, vol. 9, pp. 182–185. See also A. Arazi, '*Ilqām al-ḥajar li-man zakkā sābb Abī Bakr wa 'Umar* d'al-Suyuīṭī ou Le témoignage de l'insulteur des Compagnons', *Jerusalem Studies in Arabic and Islam*, 10 (1987), pp. 211–287; for much later periods, see J. Calmard, 'Les rituels shi'ites et le pouvoir. L'imposition du shi'isme safavide, eulogies et malédictions canoniques', in *Etudes Safavides*, ed. J. Calmard (Tehran, 1993), pp. 109–150 and Chapter 14, this volume.

104. Ibn Bābūya, *Ma'ānī'l-akhbār*, pp. 398–399, and *al-Mawā'iẓ*, p. 25 (a tradition attributed to the Prophet reported by Ja'far through his father and his paternal ancestors). Also al-Qundūzī, *Yanābī' al-mawadda*, p. 121; al-Daylamī, *Irshād al-qulūb* (Qumm, n.d.), vol. 2, p. 209; al-Irbilī, *Kashf al-ghumma*, vol. 1, p. 112; al-Baḥrānī, *Ghāyat al-marām*, p. 293.

105. Al-Majlisī, *Biḥār*, vol. 8, p. 300, nos 55 and pp. 352ff. (a tradition going back to the Prophet).

106. *Biḥār*, vol. 24, p. 348, no. 60 (al-Bāqir). On the pair *muwālāt/mu'ādāt* see the extensive tradition going back to the eleventh imam in (Pseudo?) al-imam al-Ḥasan al-'Askarī, *Tafsīr*, pp. 76–79, no. 39. See also al-Khwārazmī, *al-Manāqib* (Qumm, 1411/1990), ch. 6, pp. 64–79; Abū Ja'far al-Ṭabarī, *Bishārat al-Muṣṭafā li-shī'at al-Murtaḍā*, pp. 20ff.

> ʿAlī! *walāya* towards you and the imams in your lineage is only accepted due to *barāʾa* towards your enemies and those of the imams in your lineage. Angel Gabriel told me this in person.[107]

> By He who chose me from all His creatures and sent me as a messenger, if one were to worship God for a thousand years, this would not be accepted by God were one not to profess your *walāya* O ʿAlī and that of the imams in your lineage; and your *walāya* is only accepted if it is accompanied by *barāʾa* towards your enemies and those of the imams in your lineage.[108]

In spiritual life and sacred economy, *barāʾa* is thus as fundamental as *walāya*, which is why we may translate these terms as sacred Hatred and sacred Love respectively.[109] In some traditions, *barāʾa* is considered – not unlike *walāya* – as one of the Pillars of Islam.[110] According to a *ḥadīth* going back to al-Bāqir: 'God sent his prophets especially for sacred Love for us (the imams) and sacred Hatred towards our enemies.'[111]

A concise statement attributed to Jaʿfar al-Ṣadiq asks whether 'is faith anything other than love and hate?' (*hal al-īmān illā al-ḥubb wa al-bughḍ*). If one accords these terms their technical meaning, we may read the statement as: is the esoteric teaching within a religion anything other than love for the imams as well as for wise initiators of this faith and hatred towards the adversaries of the latter?[112]

---

107. Al-Majlisī, *Biḥār*, vol. 27, p. 60, no. 16.

108. Ibn Shādhān, *Miʾa manqaba*, 'manqaba' 9, p. 51; al-Karājakī, *Kanz al-fawāʾid* (Beirut, n.d.; rpr. Qumm, 1369/1949–1950), p. 185; al-Majlisī, *Biḥār*, vol. 27, p. 199, no. 66. To be compared with Ibn Ṭāwūs, *al-Yaqīn fī imrat amīr al-muʾminīn* (Najaf, 1369/1950), pp. 56–57.

109. *Guide divin*, index under '*walāya*' and '*barāʾa*'.

110. Al-ʿAyyāshī, *Tafsīr*, vol. 2, p. 117; al-Majlisī, *Biḥār*, vol. 25/1, pp. 214f.

111. Al-ʿAyyāshī, *Tafsīr*, vol. 2, p. 258; al-Baḥrānī, *al-Burhān*, vol. 2, p. 368; al-Fayḍ al-Kāshānī, *al-Ṣāfī*, vol. 1, p. 923.

112. For the *ḥadīth* see Shaykh ʿAbbās Qummī, *Safīnat al-Biḥār* (Tehran, 1370 Sh./1991), see under *ḥubb*, vol. 1, p. 199; for the technical meaning of *īmān*, see note 95 above.

The struggle between Good and Evil, Knowledge and Ignorance, Light and Darkness is woven into the fabric of existence. According to cosmogonic traditions, what marks creation from its origin is the battle between the armies of cosmic Intelligence (*al-ʿaql*) and those of cosmic Ignorance (*al-jahl*), respective symbols and archetypes of the Imam and his adepts on the one hand and Enemy of the Imam and his partisans on the other.[113]

This battle has repercussions in every period during all the cycles of history, opposing prophets and imams of each religion, People of the Right (*aṣḥāb al-yamīn*), against forces of ignorance, People of the Left (*aṣḥāb al-shimāl*). According to *Ithbāt al-waṣiyya*, since the creation of Adam, the world has known two kinds of 'government' (*dawla*): that of God in which the prophets and imams, the Guides of Light and Justice (*aʾimmat al-nūr, aʾimmat al-ʿadl*) are able to teach the religion of *walāya* openly, and that of Iblīs in which this faith can only be practised secretly since the world is under the influence of the Guides of Darkness and Injustice (*aʾimmat al-ẓalām, aʾimmat al-ẓulm*).

Since Iblīs was Adam's adversary (*ḍidd*), the history of Adamic humanity has been marked by adversity and violence on the part of demonic forces of ignorance that will always be predominant and in the majority during the current cycle; thus they will isolate and marginalise the persecuted initiates.[114]

---

113. M. A. Amir-Moezzi, 'Cosmogony and Cosmology (in Twelver Shiʿism)', *EIr*, vol. 6, pp. 317–322; E. Kohlberg, 'Evil (in Shiʿism)', *EIr*, vol. 9, pp. 182–185. On the tradition regarding Armies of Intelligence and Ignorance see Chapter 12 in this volume.; also D. K. Crow, 'The Role of *al-ʿAql* in Early Islamic Wisdom, with Reference to Imam Jaʿfar al-Ṣādiq' (PhD thesis, McGill University, 1996), ch. 13.

114. (Pseudo?) al-Masʿūdī, *Ithbāt al-waṣiyya*, pp. 17ff.; on *dawlat Allāh* and *dawlat Iblīs* see also al-ʿAyyāshī, *Tafsīr*, vol. 1, p. 199. Cf. the analysis by M. Molé, 'Entre le Mazdéisme et l'Islam, La bonne et la mauvaise religion', in *Mélanges Henri Massé* (Tehran, 1963), pp. 303–316 and esp. E. Kohlberg, 'Some Shīʿī Views on the Antediluvian World', *SI* (rpr. in *Belief and Law*, article XVI), pp. 45ff. and note 3, where other sources belonging to the Nuṣayriyya or Ismailis are cited. It is in reference to the power of the 'Guides of Darkness' and their loyal 'ignorant ones' that Shiʿi *ḥadīth*s employ expressions such as *walāyat al-ṭawāghīt* or *walāyat al-shayāṭīn*.

The adversaries of *walāya*, whom the faithful Shiʿi is urged not to frequent, are not necessarily pagans and unbelievers. The Israelites who betrayed Moses by pledging faith in the Golden Calf, and Muḥammad's Companions who rejected ʿAlī are not 'non-Jews' and non-Muslims but people who reject the esoteric dimension of their respective religions, emptying the latter from what is most profound, thus becoming what the *ḥadīth* call, 'the Muslim gone astray', that is to say those subject exclusively to the letter of Revelation and astray because they reject *walāya*.[115]

Barāʾa, like its inseparable opposite, *walāya*, is also as ancient as the world. This pair of opposing concepts is at the heart of the Shiʿi dualist vision of the world, a vision that may be illustrated by an entire series of contrasting terms typifying the dialectic of Good/Knowledge and Evil/Ignorance:

Good/Knowledge	Evil/Ignorance
imām	*ʿaduww al-imām*
aʾimmat al-nūr/al-ʿadl	*aʾimmat al-ẓalām/al-ẓulm*
ʿaql	*jahl*
aṣḥāb al-yamīn	*aṣḥāb al-shimāl*
walāya/tawallī/muwālāt	*barāʾa/tabarrī/muʿādāt*

Brought into being ever since the Origin of the universe, sacred Love/sacred Hatred also determines eschatology:

> He who enters into the *walāya* of Muḥammad's descendants has entered paradise; he who enters into the *walāya* of their enemies has entered hell.[116]

This tradition, variously formatted or expressed in approximately the same manner is repeated literally hundreds of times in *Ḥadīth* literature. Salvation due to love of the imams begins at the moment of death (*iḥtiḍār*) and the interrogation of the tomb (*al-musāʾala fiʾl-qabr*) conducted by Nakīr and Munkar. In

115. See notes 76 and 95 above as well as the relevant texts.

116. Al-Majlisī, *Biḥār*, vol. 8, p. 347, no. 7 (Jaʿfar).

a very long *ḥadīth* going back to the sixth imam, it is explained how upon the deathbed of one who has loved the imams, ʿAlī, Muḥammad and the angel Gabriel appeared before the Angel of Death to request him to be loving and kind to the dying person and ease his death.[117]

> Not a single death, from dawn to dusk, on land or sea, without Munkar and Nakīr questioning [him] regarding *walāya* of ʿAlī, his Lord, religion, prophet and imam.[118]

We have already seen that reward (*thawāb*) in the hereafter is only obtained by the grace of *walāya*. The most radical versions implying as much were reported in a systematic manner, perhaps for the first time by al-Barqī in his *Maḥāsin*:

> For one who loves us, the *ahl al-bayt,* and for whom this love is heartfelt (*ḥuqqiqa* (?) *ḥubbunā fī qalbih*), for him the sources of wisdom will flow from his tongue and faith will be strengthened in his heart. He will merit the reward of seventy prophets, seventy sincere believers, seventy martyrs and seventy worshippers having worshipped God for seventy years.[119]
>
> Cherish love and affection (*mawadda*) for the *ahl al-bayt*, for he who encounters God having loved us, will enter paradise by our intercession (*shafāʿa*). By He who has my life in His hands, no action will benefit man if not taken by knowledge of our truth (*ḥaqq*; as we have seen, one of the terms used to denote *walāya*).[120]

117. *Biḥār*, vol. 6, p. 197, no. 51.

118. *Biḥār*, vol. 6, p. 316, no. 6 (the Prophet). On the interrogation of the tomb and love of the imams see also vol. 6, pp. 236ff.; vol. 7, pp. 128, 186ff., 275ff., 331ff.; vol. 8, pp. 67ff.

119. Al-Barqī, *al-Maḥāsin*, 'kitāb thawāb al-aʿmāl', ch. 80, p. 61, vol. 1, no. 103, (Jaʿfar); al-Majlisī, *Biḥār*, vol. 27, p. 90.

120. *Maḥāsin*, ch. 81, p. 61, vol. 1, no. 105 (the Prophet through al-Ḥasan b. ʿAlī). On the notion of *shafāʿa*, see A. J. Wensink, *A Muslim Creed, Its Genesis and Historical Development* (Cambridge, 1932), pp. 61–64, 180–183; T. Huitema, *De Voorsprak* (shafāʿa) *in den Islam* (Leiden, 1936), and concerning Shiʿism now consult Bar-Asher, *Scripture and Exegesis*, ch. 4, section 2.5, pp. 180–189.

> He who longs to see God unveiled and wishes God to look upon him unveiled, let him love the descendants of the Prophet and dissociate himself from their enemies; let him have as imam one among them [i.e. the imams] in order that on the Day of Resurrection God looks upon him unveiled and that he sees God unveiled.[121]

At this level of meaning, *walāya* – synonymous with *maḥabba/ḥubb* (love), *mawadda* (affection) and *taslīm* (submission, undying loyalty, obedience)[122] – is directed either towards the historic imam or through him towards the metaphysical Imam, the manifestation of God. The first form, which is found especially in popular Shi'ism, is the foundation for the origin and development of the generally known adoration of the imams. The second is more often found among philosophers, theosophers and mystics.

Thus we may better appreciate how the Shi'i religious consciousness, in its various components, perceives the many levels of meaning attached to the famous phrase that Muḥammad is said to have uttered during his speech at Ghadīr Khumm and that the Imamis call the '*ḥadīth* of *walāya*', since according to them the Prophet there proclaimed the investiture of 'Alī to both the temporal and spiritual caliphate:

---

121. Al-Barqī, *Maḥāsin*, vol. 1, ch. 78, p. 60, no. 101 (al-Riḍā); it is interesting to note that some years later, Ibn Bābūya (d. 381/991) in his *Thawāb al-a'māl* reports a much more toned down version regarding the reward linked to *walāya* and *barā'a* (*Thawāb al-a'māl + 'Iqāb al-a'māl*, ed. 'A. A. Ghaffārī [Qumm, 1391/1971], vol. 30, p. 204). On this account of the 'rationalist' trend within early Imamism, see *Guide divin*, pp. 15–48 (*Divine Guide*, pp. 6–19).

122. On this important notion, signifying submission to the esoteric dimension of religion as it differs from *islām* understood to mean submission to the exoteric religion, see e.g. al-Ṣaffār, *Baṣā'ir al-darajāt*, section 10, ch. 20 ('Bāb fi'l-taslīm li āl Muḥammad'), pp. 520ff.; al-Kulaynī, *al-Uṣūl*, 'Kitāb al-ḥujja', 'Bāb al-taslīm wa faḍl al-musallimīn', vol. 2, pp. 234ff.; the term is also defined as obedience to the imam's directives as an anditode to the polemics surrounding matters of faith, see Ibn Bābūya, *al-Tawḥīd*, 'Bāb al-nahy 'ani'l-kalām', pp. 458f., and *Kamāl al-dīn*, ch. 31, no. 9 (*taslīm* as opposed to reasoning by analogy – *qiyās* – and personal opinion – *ra'y*).

Let he who considers me to be his *mawlā*, take ʿAlī to be his *mawlā*. O my God, love the one who loves him [i.e. ʿAlī] and be the enemy of whosover is hostile towards him.[123]

Conclusion

Walāya in its technical Shiʿi sense thus has three principal meanings that are at once complementary and interdependent: the imamate, love of the imam and theology of the metaphysical Imam[124] – complementary and interdependent meanings indeed.

---

123. *Man kuntu* mawlā-*hu fa-ʿAliyyun* mawlā-*hu Allāhuma* wāli *man* wālā-*hu wa ʿādi man ʿādāhu* ; on this '*ḥadīth al-walāya*' and its countless transmitters and sources, now see *Ṣaḥīfat al-imām al-Riḍā* (Qumm, 1408/1987), pp. 172–224, no. 109. See also ʿA. Ḥ. Amīnī, *al-Ghadīr fi'l-kitāb wa'l-sunna wa'l-adab* (Tehran, 1372/1952; rpr. 1986), index of *ḥadīth*s. Words belonging to the root WLY are pointed out in the text of the *ḥadīth*: the *mawlā* is the patron, the protector; it often has this meaning when describing God in the Qur'ān. It obviously also denotes that which is the object of *walāya*, i.e. love, devotion and loyalty. In the Shiʿi context, the term *mawlā* is applied either to God or more frequently to ʿAlī and the other imams; this moreover is symptomatic. Although highly informative the article 'Mawlā' by P. Crone in the *Encyclopedia of Islam* does not sufficiently take into account matters relating to Shiʿism (*EI2*, vol. 7, pp. 865–874).

124. It would be tempting to read into this text the famous phrase pronounced by Jaʿfar al-Ṣādiq, 'Our matter [*amr*; a very commonly used term for *walāya*] contains an exoteric (*ẓāhir*), an esoteric [dimension] (*bāṭin*) and an esoteric of the esoteric (*bāṭin al-bāṭin*)', al-Ṣaffār, *Baṣā'ir al-darajāt*, MS Mashhad, Āstān-i Quds I, Akhbār 62/169, fol. 18r.; MS Āstān-i Quds V/36, Akhbār 407/1933, fol. 20; MS India Office 932, fol. 22r.; the Kūtchebāghī edition used hitherto (section 1, ch. 12, p.29, no. 4) drops the term *bāṭin* and contains just *ẓāhir* and *bāṭin al-bāṭin*, which is clearly a mistake. Al-Majlisī, *Biḥār*, vol. 2, p. 71, no. 33 contains *ẓāhir, bāṭin al-ẓāhir* and *bāṭin al-bāṭin*. It seems to me that *bāṭin* and *bāṭin al-ẓāhir* are equal. A laconic statement by the mystic master Khāksār, Mudarris-i ʿĀlam (d. ca. 1950?), appears to concur: *walāyat sirr-i islām ast va maẓhariyyat sirr-i walāyat* (*walāya* is the secret of Islam and [the fact that imam is] the locus of manifestation for God is the secret of *walāya*), *Tuḥfa-yi darwīsh* (Tehran, 1337 Sh./1959), p. 40 (cf. note 72 above and the related text). It should be added that *walāya* in its most basic meaning of temporal authority does not connote any particularly Shiʿi notion; thus *ḥadīth*s may speak of *walāyat al-ṭawāghīt al-thalātha* (the authority of the three rebels verses God, i.e.

Let us recall a self-evident matter: if the historic or metaphysical imamate or theology of the divine Face of the Imam and love for the imam/Imam are all denoted by one and the same term, *walāya*, it is so because in the Shiʿi religious consciousness there is an organic link between these three principal meanings: the historic imamate is fundamentally the religion of love for the Face of God, which is none other than the cosmic Imam.[125]

It is especially interesting to re-read passages containing or concerning *walāya* in 'the Qur'ān of the imam', the vulgate and in

---

the first three caliphs), *walāyat fulān wa fulān* (the authority of such and such, i.e. Abū Bakr and 'Umar), *walāyat Banī Umayya, Bani'l-ʿAbbās*, etc.

125. Ḥaydar Āmulī, *Jāmiʿ al-asrār wa manbaʿ al-anwār*, ed. H. Corbin and O. Yahia (Tehran, 1969), 'al-aṣl al-thālith, al-qāʿida al-thāniya, fī asrār al-nubuwwa wa'l-risāla wa'l-walāya', pp. 379–394; Sulṭān Muḥammad Gunābādī Sulṭān 'Alī Shāh, *Walāyat-Nāmah* (Tehran, 1344 Sh./1966), section 1, ch. 6, pp. 20–21; section 2, chs 1–3, pp. 22–32; section 5, chs 1 and 2, pp. 61–71; section 9, ch. 1, pp. 157–170 and ch. 8, pp. 214–221; throughout section 10, pp. 226–243. One must point out the problem faced when dealing with esoteric teachings, namely that the authors' language is typically allusive. This richness in meaning better shows to what extent the notion of *wilāyat al-faqīh* – a theory that is central to Khomeynist ideology – plays upon ambiguity in order to assure, in the opinion of the Imami masses, the politico-religious charisma of the jurist-theologian and thus replace the figure of the imam with that of the former (see M. A. Amir-Moezzi, 'Réflexions sur une évolution du shi'isme duodécimain, tradition et idéologisation', in *Les retours aux Ecritures, Fondamentalismes présents et passés*, ed. E. Patlagean and A. Le Boulluec [Paris, 1993], pp. 63–82). That the term is vocalised and pronounced *wilāya* clearly makes no difference because the term maintains the same meaning (see M. Chodkiewicz, *Le Sceau des saints*, pp. 34ff.). But in the Sufism, the two terms may have different meanings, see V. Cornell, *The Realm of the Saint: Power and Authority in Moroccan Sufism* (Austin, 1998), mainly the introduction and pp. 216ff., 227ff., 272. Similarly, the mass of faithful have difficulty in grasping the distinction made between '*wilāya* pertaining to' the jurists (*wilāyat iʿtibāriyya*) and the 'creative *wilāya*' of the imams (*wilāyat takwīniyya*). Although this attempt by a politico-religious leader is understandable, one is perplexed by researchers who seem to measure *walāya* in religious texts by the yardstick of the doctrine of *wilāyat al-faqīh* (see e.g. A. A. Sachedina, *The Just-Ruler* (al-sulṭān al-ʿādil) *in Shi'ite Islam* (New York, 1988); Bayhom-Daou, 'The Imam's Knowledge', see n. 1 above, in which *walāya*, vocalised *wilāya*, is translated as 'the legislative authority of the imam' (p. 195); admittedly *dīn* is also without any explanation at all translated as 'the law' (p. 204).

traditions on the Pillars of Islam in the light of one or another or even all of these meanings.

According to the Shiʿi conception, the ultimate aim of knowing God and His Message transmitted by the revelations made to the prophets is knowledge of the imam and love for him. At this point, 'the journey of return' begins: knowledge and love of the imam directs the faithful towards knowledge of the latter's secret reality that is none other than the revealed Face of God. This twofold movement, descending and ascending, from God to one imam after another and from the imams to God – typifying the believer's gnostic spirituality – can be illustrated by the following *ḥadīth*s:

> My Lord, make yourself known to me, for if you do not make yourself known to me, I will not come to know your prophet. My Lord, make your prophet known to me, for if you do not make your prophet known to me, I will not come to know your Proof [*ḥujja*, i.e. the imam]. My Lord, make your Proof known to me, for if you if you do not make your Proof known to me, I shall be led astray, far from my religion.[126]
>
> The imam al-Ḥusayn: 'God created all beings especially to know and worship Him.'
>
> A disciple: 'What is the knowledge of God?'
>
> The imam: 'Knowledge, during each era, of the imam of this era.'[127]

This is why, in Shiʿism, a faith is either based on *walāya* with the esoteric dimension of every prophetic message, or it simply does not exist, that is to say in this case it is but a 'pseudo-faith', whether in this regard we have in mind the Pillars of Islam or the triple profession of the *shahāda* (the third of which concerns the *walāya* of ʿAlī) and the recitation of these formulaic declarations

126. A tradition going back to Jaʿfar reported by al-Kulaynī, *al-Uṣūl*, 'Kitāb al-hujja', 'Bāb fi'l-ghayba', vol. 2, pp. 135 and 144, nos 5 and 29; it constitutes the beginning of the prayer known as the prayer of Deliverance (*duʿā' al-faraj*), meant to be read during the Occulation to ease the pain of waiting for the Qā'im; see Ibn Bābūya, *Kamāl al-dīn*, vol. 2, ch. 45, pp. 512ff., no. 43.

127. Ibn Bābūya, *'Ilal al-sharā'iʿ* (Najaf, 1385/1966), ch. 9, p. 9, no. 1.

during the call to prayer (*adhān*) thus introducing *walāya* into the ritual.[128]

To conclude, a word about the 'organic' aspect of *walāya* bearing upon the subtle spiritual anatomy. It is *walāya* that carries out the transmutation of faith into an intensely felt religious and spiritual experience, first, for the common folk among Shi'is, obviously by means of the cult of the imams with all the naiveté, excesses and deviations which are common in popular religions; secondly, especially for the spiritual 'elite' engaged in a quest for the realisation of the light of *walāya (nūr al-walāya).* Far from being an abstract notion, the latter seems to designate a spiritual faculty, an internal 'organic' disposition since it can also be transmitted physically and is called the single and double Light of Muḥammad and 'Alī or more commonly, the Light of *walāya.*

As if in a continuation of certain works by U. Rubin,[129] I have devoted extensive studies to different aspects of this issue that constitutes one of the main foundations of Imami spiritual practices.[130] Let us therefore confine ourselves to a very brief summary of matters: several thousand years before the creation of the world, the luminous entities of the Impeccable Ones (Muḥammad, Fāṭima and the imams) are made to proceed forth by God from His own Light. He initiates them to the arcanum of the divine sciences. These archetypical Guides of Light in turn teach the sciences to the pre-existing entities of the initiates that have been created as particles.

---

128. See L. A. Takim, 'From *Bid'a* to *Sunna*: the *Wilāya* of 'Alī in the Shī'ī *Adhān*', *JAOS*, 120 (2000), pp. 166–177.

129. U. Rubin, 'Pre-existence and Light. Aspects of the Concept of Nūr Muḥammad', *Israel Oriental Studies*, 5 (1975), pp. 62–112, and 'Prophets and Progenitors in the Early Shī'a Tradition', *Jerusalem Studies in Arabic and Islam*, 1 (1979), pp. 41–65.

130. *Guide divin*, section II, pp. 73–154 (*Divine Guide*, pp. 29–60) (an abridged but updated version of the excursus on 'vision by the heart' pp. 112–145 [*Divine Guide*, pp. 44–55], was published in a special issue of *Connaissance des Religions*, 57–59 [1999], *Lumières sur la Voie du Coeur*, pp. 146–169); see also 'Cosmogony and Cosmology (in Twelver Shi'ism)', *EIr*, the second section; and Chapters 4 and 10, this volume.

Upon the creation of the world and the first man, the initiatic Light of *walāya* is deposited in Adam. Thus commences the long journey of the Light through the long chain of divine initiates to reach the historic Muḥammad and ʿAlī. The transmission takes place by two means: by natural physical geneology with the grace of 'blessed and purified loins', the seminal substance; and by initiatory spiritual genealogy whence prophets, imams and saints succeed each other. Having reached Muḥammad, Fāṭima, ʿAlī and the imams – earthly manifestations of these original Vehicles – the Light reaches its most intense level. It is transmitted by the latter to their physical descendants[131] and then to the faithful initiates who perpetuate its transmission. This is why, in Imami mysticism, one of the greatest spiritual aims is to realise in oneself – by diverse means, whether initiation, ascetism, rituals or practice – the Light of *walāya* in the heart whose essential 'components' are the transformatory knowledge and the abilility to perform miracles.

One who reaches this level does not become an imam (who has his own theological and ontological status) but attains the rank of saint comparable to the imam, and linked to him becomes a *wālī*, an Ally or Friend of God, a practical and living example of *walāya*. For Imami spirituality, such a *wālī* then ipso facto belongs to the Holy Family of the Prophet; for example, Salmān al-Fārisī, 'the stranger' about whom Muḥammad is said to have declared: 'Salman is one of us, the *ahl al-bayt*'[132] and al-Fuḍayl b. Yasār

131. One reason why in Shiʿi lands the real and supposed descendants of the imams (*sayyid*s and *ashrāf*) are treated with great respect. The virtues flowing from the Light of *walāya* are found in them in a potential state. However, according to mystics, these virtues are prone to be realised more easily among the imams' spiritual descendants. Regarding *sayyid*s now see the special issue, *Oriente Moderno*, 18 (77.2–1999), *Il Ruolo dei* Sādāt/Ashrāf *nella Storia e Civiltà Islamiche*, ed. B. Scarcia Amoretti and L. Bottini. Unfortunately, the spiritual dimension of capital importance is largely missing from this collection of articles.

132. For example al-Ṣaffār, *Baṣāʾir*, section 1, ch. 11, p. 25, no. 21.

al-Nahdī, a disciple about whom imam al-Bāqir reportedly said the same thing.[133]

The Shiʿi faith in general and the Imami expression of it in particular revolves around the double vision of the world that we recalled above: the dual conception of the world illustrated by the 'complementary pairs' (manifest/hidden; exoteric/esoteric; prophet/imam; *nubuwwa/walāya*; letter/spirit of the Revelation etc.) and the dualist conception illustrated by the 'opposing pairs' (Good/Evil; imam/enemy of the imam; Knowledge/Ignorance; People of the Right/People of the Left; *walāya/barāʾa* etc.).

The first may be symbolised by a 'vertical axis' since passing from the manifest to the hidden approaches the divine and the understanding of secrets of Being. This vertical axis of Initiation determines mankind's spirituality. Similarly, to the second vision of the world, one might apply the symbol of a 'horizontal axis', for this axis of the battle determines the history of creation, a history traversed by the leitmotif of the perpetual struggle between the forces of knowledge and ignorance.[134] With its various meanings *walāya* is the only notion that one can find on both axes. It holds an eminent place of fundamental importance both in its dual and dualist vision of the world. It thus constitutes the very substance of the religion of the Shiʿi faithful, both commoner and elite, called upon to constantly maintain himself where both 'axes' intersect.[135]

133. Al-Kashshī, *Ikhtiyār maʿrifat al-rijāl* (Mashhad, 1348 Sh./1969), p. 213.

134. *Guide divin*, pp. 308–310 (*Divine Guide*, pp. 127–128).

135. I wish to express my gratitude to M. M. Bar-Asher, R. Brunner and E. Kohlberg for their attentive reading of the first version of this text and for their instructive comments.

8

Only the Man of God is Human: Theology and Mystical Anthropology According to Early Imami Exegesis

At the heart of the Twelver corpus of sayings attributed to the imams[1] there is a series of traditions that divide humans into three categories: the Impeccable Ones (i.e. the Prophet, his daughter Fāṭima and the twelve imams, particularly the latter), their faithful supporters (that is to say, those who have joined the cause of the imams), and finally the others. The most ancient layer of the series might be the one that establishes this division in terms appropriate to a tribal lexicon. 'We are the descendants of Hāshim', Ja'far al-Ṣādiq (d. 148/765) is reported to have declared, 'Our faithful supporters [literally "our Shi'is"] are Arabs of noble stock and the others are Bedouins of low descent.'[2] Responding to a Qurashī

1. Concerning this corpus see, e.g., H. Löschner, *Die dogmatischen Grundlagen des shī'itischen Rechts* (Cologne, 1971), esp. the introduction; E. Kohlberg, 'Shī'ī *Ḥadīth*', *The Cambridge History of Arabic Literature*, vol. I: *Arabic Literature to the End of the Umayyad Period* (Cambridge, 1983), pp. 299–307. For a discussion of the older sources, see *Guide divin*, pp. 51–56; also my article, 'Remarques sur les critères d'authenticité du hadîth et l'autorité du juriste dans le shi'isme imâmite', *SI*, 85 (1997), pp. 5–39.

2. '*Naḥnu banū Hāshim wa shī'atunā al-'arab wa sā'ir al-nās al-a'rāb*', al-Kulaynī, *al-Rawḍa min al-Kāfī*, ed. H. Rasūlī Maḥallātī (Tehran, 1389/1969), vol. 1, p. 244, no. 183.

who spoke about his tribe and the nobility of the Arabs, imam Mūsā al-Kāẓim (d. 183/799) is reported to have declared:

> Leave all that be! There are three types of men: the noble of pure descent, the protected ally and the vile man of base descent. We are the nobles, our faithful supporters are the protected allies and those who do not share our doctrine are the vile.[3]

An analogous tradition, attributed to the same imam, provides even more precise information:

> There are three types of men: the noble of pure descent, the protected ally and the vile man of base descent. We are the nobles of pure descent; the protected ally is the one who faithfully loves us; the base man is one who dissociates himself from us and openly declares himself to be our enemy.[4]

---

3. *'Daʿ hādhā al-nās thalātha ʿarabī wa-mawlā wa-ʿilj fa-naḥnu al-ʿarab wa-shīʿatunā al-mawālī wa man lam yakun ʿalā mithli mā naḥnu ʿalayhi fa-huwa al-ʿilj'*, al-Kulaynī, *al-Rawḍa*, vol. 2, p. 30, no. 287. *ʿArab*, *mawlā* and *ʿilj* are part of the tribal vocabulary and indicate literally and respectively: 'a free Arab of noble stock, lord', 'protected ally, freedman, "client", whether or not of Arab race', and 'the non-Arab savage without religion, a barbarian'.

4. *'Fa-ammā al-ʿarab fa-naḥnu wa ammā al-mawlā man wālānā wa ammā al-ʿilj man tabarra'a minnā wa nāṣabanā'*, Ibn Bābūya al-Ṣadūq, *al-Khiṣāl*, ed. ʿA. A. Ghaffārī (rpr. Qumm, 1403/1983), p. 123, no. 116. The tradition brings together the different technical meanings of the root *w-l-y* 'protection' and 'alliance' in *mawlā*, 'love-proximity-fidelity' through the third form *wālā*. This last sense is in contrast to one of the meanings contained in the root *b-r-'*, whose fifth form *tabarra'a* is used in this tradition. The reference is of course to the pair of opposites *walāya/barā'a* or *tawallī/tabarru'* that is omnipresent in Imami, particularly early Imami, doctrine. I will return to this point. Concerning these technical terms and this pair, see U. Rubin, 'Barā'a: a Study of Some Qur'ānic Passages', *JSAI*, 5 (1984), pp. 71–91; E. Kohlberg, 'Barā'a in Shīʿī Doctrine', *JSAI*, 7 (1986), pp. 139–175; H. Landolt, 'Walāya', in M. Eliade (ed.), *Encyclopedia of Religion*, vol. 15; M. A. Amir-Moezzi, *Guide divin*, under '*walāya*' (*Divine Guide*, ibid.); J. Calmard, 'Les rituals shiʿites et le pouvoir. L'imposition du shiʿisme safavide: eulogies et malédictions canoniques', in J. Calmard (ed.), *Etudes Safavides* (Paris and Tehran, 1994), pp. 117–121 and Chapter 7, this volume. Finally, *nāṣabanā*, which I translate as 'openly declares himself to be our enemy', is evidently an allusion to the notion of *naṣb* and to the one who applies it, that

At first glance, it is clear that the tribal anthropological criteria have been abandoned in favour of those of a doctrinal nature where these criteria are understood as metaphors for the three categories that make up mankind: the spiritual guides, their supporters and their adversaries.

It is necessary at this juncture to recall two points that serve to clarify the implication of these traditions and at the same time to facilitate an understanding of what is to follow. Twelver Shiʿism, of the type that emerged from the doctrines that can be traced back to the historical imams, has a dualist vision of history that might be characterised as one determined by a perpetual combat between the two antagonistic forces of good and evil. These forces are represented, respectively, by the imam and his adepts on the one hand and the 'enemies' of the imam and their partisans on the other. This combat had already begun before the creation of the material world, with the conflict between the armies of cosmic knowledge (*ʿaql*, the cosmogonic Imam of the forces of good and the archetype of the terrestrial imam) and those of cosmic ignorance (*jahl*, the leader of the forces of evil and the archetype of the enemy of the imam).[5] This struggle has continued throughout time in a conflict that has pitted the imams of the various legislative prophets and their adepts against their adversaries, led by leaders who rejected the mission of the prophets and/or of the

---

is to say the *nāṣibī*, pl. *nawāṣib/nuṣṣāb*. In the technical Shiʿi lexicon, this latter is designated the adversary of ʿAlī (or someone who does not recognise ʿAlī's superiority over the other Companions), the enemy of all the *ahl al-bayt*, or, in a more general fashion, the adversary of the Shiʿis.

5. Concerning the cosmogonic account of the combat between *ʿaql* and *jahl*, see al-Barqī, *al-Maḥāsin*, ed. J. al-Ḥusaynī al-Muḥaddith (Tehran, 1370/1950), vol. 1, pp. 196–198; al-Kulaynī, *al-Uṣūl min al-Kāfī*, ed. J. Muṣṭafawī (Tehran, n.d.), vol. 1, pp. 24–27; (Pseudo-?) al-Masʿūdī, *Ithbāt al-waṣiyya* (rpr. Qumm, 1417/1996), pp. 15–17; Ibn Shuʿba, *Tuḥaf al-ʿuqūl*, ed. ʿA. A. Ghaffārī (Tehran, 1366 Sh./1986), pp. 423–425. For an overview, see my article 'Cosmogony and Cosmology in Twelver Shiʿism', *EIr*, vol. 4, pp. 317–322 and also Chapter 12, this volume.

imams.[6] This combat will only end with the definitive victory of the Mahdī/Qā'im over the forces of ignorance at the end of time (*ākhir al-zamān*).[7] This dualism lies at the basis of the doctrinal 'theory of opposites' (*ḍidd*, pl. *aḍdād*), which was characterised by speculations concerning fundamental 'pairs' such as imam/enemy of the imam (*imam/ʿaduww al-imām*), intelligence/ignorance, people of the right/people of the left (*aṣḥāb al-yamīn/aṣḥāb al-shimāl*), guides of light/guides of darkness (*a'immat al-nūr/a'immat al-ẓalām*), imams of guidance/imams of error (*a'immat al-hudā/a'immat al-ḍalāl*), sacred love (for the imam)/hatred (for the imam, but also that which was sworn by the imam's followers against their adversaries: *walāya/barā'a*) and so on.[8] During the Islamic period, the adversaries and the enemies are those who have rejected the *walāya* of ʿAlī and the imams who descended

---

6. According to the Shiʿi conception, divine truth (*ḥaqq*) manifests itself under two aspects: the exoteric aspect (*ẓāhir*) of truth is revealed by the legislator prophet, while the esoteric aspect (*bāṭin*) is revealed by the imam(s) who always accompanies the prophet in his mission. I will return to this point at greater length. On this subject see e.g. H. Corbin, *En Islam iranien: aspects spirituels et philosophiques* (Paris, 1971–1972), vol. 1, Book one, passim, and *Histoire de la philosophie islamique* (3rd edn, Paris, 1986), pp. 69–85. The initiatory mission of the imam (*imāma/walāya*) always meets with the hostility of the leaders of unbelief and those who follow them – that is to say, those who do not believe in the truthfulness of either the prophetic message or the mission of the imam, which for the Shiʿis is one and the same. This vision of the history of mankind is the main subject of the *Ithbāt al-waṣiyya* attributed to al-Masʿūdī (see the preceding note). Cf. also E. Kohlberg, 'Some Shīʿī Views on the Antediluvian World', *SI*, 52 (1980), pp. 41–66 (rpr. in *Belief and Law*, article XVI); and my *Guide divin*, pp. 106ff. (*Divine Guide*, p. 41ff.).

7. See e.g. A. A. Sachedina, *Islamic Messianism: the Idea of the Mahdi in Twelver Shiʿism* (Albany, NY, 1981); Amir-Moezzi, *Guide divin*, pp. 279–301 (*Divine Guide*, pp. 115–123); and my article 'Eschatology in Twelver Shiʿism', *EIr*.

8. As far as I know, no comprehensive critical study of the Imami 'theory of opposites' has yet been undertaken. Nevertheless, one can find elements of this issue in Kohlberg, 'Some Shīʿī Views on the Antediluvian World', esp. pp. 45–46, as well as in his other article, 'The Term "Rāfiḍa" in Imāmī Shīʿī Usage', *JAOS*, 99 (1979), (rpr. in *Belief and Law*, article IV); see also the important data discussed by M. Molé in 'Entre le mazdéisme et l'Islam: la bonne et la mauvaise religion', in *Mélanges Henri Massé* (Tehran, 1963), esp. pp. 314–315.

from him. In this case the reference is to almost all of the Companions, in particular the first three caliphs, to the Umayyads, to the ʿAbbasids, and more generally to all of those whom the Shiʿis call 'the majority' (*al-akthar*) or 'the masses' (*al-ʿāmma*), that is to say, those who would eventually come to be called 'the Sunnis'.[9]

The second point concerns another aspect of the Imami world view, an aspect that one might describe as 'dual'. In effect, Shiʿism perceives reality in all its aspects as consisting of two levels: an apparent, manifest, exoteric level (*al-ẓāhir*), and a second level, hidden by the first, that is secret and esoteric (*al-bāṭin*). This second level, in turn, could contain many other increasingly secret levels (*bāṭin al-bāṭin*). The teaching attributed to the imams establishes a correspondence between the levels and attempts to maintain an equilibrium between them, although the superiority of *bāṭin* over *ẓāhir* is detectable between the lines almost everywhere. This process is, fundamentally, hermeneutical. If the *bāṭin* gives direction and meaning to the *ẓāhir*, the latter constitutes in turn the basis and indispensable support for the *bāṭin*. Without esotericism, exotericism loses its meaning and without exotericism, esotericism finds itself stripped of its foundation.[10] This dialectic constitutes the fundamental correspondence between prophetology and imamology. The legislator prophet (*nabī/rasūl/nabī mursal*) brings to the mass of humanity (*al-ʿāmma*) a sacred Book

9. The attitude of the Shiʿis towards their adversaries is epitomised in the notion of *sabb al-ṣaḥāba*. On this subject, see I. Goldziher, 'Spottnamen der ersten Chalifen bei den Schīʿiten', *WZKM*, 15 (1901), pp. 320–332 (rpr. in *Gesammelte Schriften*, vol. 4, pp. 291–305); A. S. Tritton, *Muslim Theology* (London, 1947), pp. 27ff.; E. Kohlberg, 'Some Imāmī Shīʿī Views on the *Ṣaḥāba*', *JSAI*, 5 (1984), pp. 143–175 (rpr. in *Belief and Law*, article IX); A. Arazi, '*Ilqām al-ḥajar li-man zakkā sābb Abī Bakr wa-ʿUmar* d'al-Suyūṭī ou le témoignage de l'insulteur des Compagnons', *JSAI*, 10 (1987), pp. 211–287.

10. On the importance and omnipresence of this concept in Imamism, see my article 'Du droit à la théologie: les niveaux de réalité dans le shiʿisme duodécimain', *L'esprit et la nature, Cahiers du Groupe d'Etudes Spirituelles Comparés*, 5 (1997), pp. 37–63, where I study the role of the pair *ẓāhir/bāṭin* in various doctrinal fields (law, exegesis, theology, eschatology etc.), in the different semantic layers of certain technical terms, and in the different dimensions of the figure of the imam.

which has 'descended' from heaven (*tanzīl*). The imam/*wālī*, for his part, initiates a small elite (*al-aqall/al-khāṣṣa*) into the esoteric aspect of the sacred Book, thus 'returning [it] to its origin' (*taʾwīl*, see also n. 6 above). We can see here a recurrence of the 'pairs' of 'complementary terms': prophet/imam-*wālī*, *nubuwwa/walāya*, *tanzīl/taʾwīl*, *al-akthar/al-aqall*, *al-ʿāmma/al-khāṣṣa*, as well as many others that were also abundantly used, such as Muḥammad/ʿAlī (the first evidently representing legislative prophecy, that is the letter of the revealed message, and the second, the imam par excellence, representing the initiatory mission of the imams, the esoteric hermeneutics of revelation), *islām/īmān* (literally 'Islam/faith' in the technical sense of 'submission to the letter of the exoteric religion' and 'initiation into the esoteric religion of the imams').[11] All these 'pairs' can be understood as a continuation of the fundamental pair of *ẓāhir/bāṭin*. Yet the centre of gravity of the *bāṭin*, of *walāya* as the esoteric aspect of *nubuwwa*, is the notion of *ʿilm*, literally 'knowledge', which, however, in the context of the doctrinal traditions attributed to the imams, can only be translated as 'initiatory and secret knowledge'.[12] Apart from its ontological status, to which I will return, one could say that an imam is what he is by dint of his possession of *ʿilm* and his position as spiritual initiator. Alongside perpetual combat, continuous initiation forms the other constant element of the Imami world view. It too begins before the creation of the physical world with the primordial initiation of the pre-existing entities of the impeccable beings into the secret divine knowledge and, subsequently, the initiation by these impeccable beings of the shades/

11. See my 'Du droit à la théologie', and *Guide divin*, pp. 308–309 (*Divine Guide*, pp. 127–128).

12. See my monograph in *Guide divin*, III-2, 'la science sacrée', pp. 174–199 (*Divine Guide*, pp. 69–79). See also my 'Réflexions sur une évolution du shiʿisme duodécimain: tradition et idéologisation', in E. Patlagean and A. Le Boulluec (eds), *Les retours aux Ecritures: fondamentalismes présents et passés* (Louvain and Paris, 1993), esp. pp. 64–69. See also E. Kohlberg, 'Imam and Community in the Pre-Ghayba Period', in S. A. Arjomand (ed.), *Authority and Political Culture in Shiʿism* (Albany, NY, 1988), esp. pp. 25–28 (rpr. in *Belief and Law*, article XIII).

particles (*dharr/aẓilla*) of the pure beings (angels, prophets and faithful supporters from all the ages) into this same knowledge.[13] The initiation of the disciples by the imam or imams of each religion is a constant feature of all periods of history.[14] The end of time is marked by the universal initiation into the esotericism of all religions as set forth by the Qā'im, the eschatological saviour.[15] Just as perpetual combat determines human history, so continual initiation assures its spirituality. From this point of view, the supporters of the imams, the 'Shiʿis' of our texts, are not only the Shiʿis of the Islamic period, but also those who are initiated into the divine secret knowledge in all periods. At the same time their 'enemies', the people of ignorance, are generally the forces set in opposition to initiation in every period of history. They might be those who denied of the prophetic message (for example, Nimrod or Pharaoh denying the message of Abraham or Moses). They might be the supporters of exoteric religion who, failing to accept the initiatory teaching of the imam, cut off their religion from its hidden depths and thereby condemn themselves to ignorance, to oppression and finally to impiety (for example, the majority of the Jews and the Christians rejected the teaching of the imam or imams of their religions and thereby betrayed their prophets. The same goes for the majority Muslims who rejected the *walāya* of ʿAlī and the other imams who were of his progeny).[16]

13. Cf. my *Guide divin*, II-1, 'Les mondes d'avant le monde. Le Guide-Lumière', pp. 75–95 (*Divine Guide*, pp. 29–37), 'Cosmogony and Cosmology in Twelver Shiʿism', pp. 319–320; also Chapter 4, this volume.

14. *Guide divin*, 'L'humanité adamique: le "voyage" de la Lumière', pp. 96–112 (*Divine Guide*, pp. 38–43, 133–134); and 'cosmogony and Cosmology', p. 320; see also Chapter 4, this volume.

15. *Guide divin*, pp. 290–292 (*Divine Guide*, pp. 119–120); 'Eschatology in Imami Shiʿism', *EIr*, vol. 8, pp. 578–581.

16. See e.g. G. Vajda, 'Deux "Histoires des Prophètes" selon la tradition de shiʿites duodécimains', *Revue des Etudes juives*, 106 (1945–1946), pp. 124–133, and 'De quelques emprunts d'origine juive dans le *ḥadīth* shiʿite', in S. Morag et al. (eds), *Studies in Judaism and Islam Presented to S. D. Goitein* (Jerusalem, 1981), esp. pp. 242–244; M. M. Ayoub, 'Towards an Islamic Christology: an Image of Jesus in Early Shīʿī Muslim Literature', *MW*, 66 (1976); E. Kohlberg,

One is thus able better to understand the tripartite division of humanity, particularly the variants, which are probably later and which are much more significant. Many *ḥadīths*, ascribed to Jaʿfar al-Ṣādiq, introduce the notion of initiation into this division: 'People are divided into three categories: the spiritual initiator, the initiated disciple and the scum carried off by the waves. We [the imams] are the spiritual initiators, our supporters are the initiated disciples, and the others are the scum on the waves.'[17] In another place: 'The [true] men are of two types: the spiritual initiator and the initiated disciple. The others are vile beings, and vile beings are in the Fire [of hell].'[18] It is easy to see that the third category, which does not even include true human beings, designates the 'enemies' of the initiated. Elsewhere, this imam repeats the division in another form:

'The Term "Rāfiḍa" in Imāmī Shīʿī Usage', 'Some Shīʿī Views on the Antediluvian World', and 'Some Imāmī Shīʿī Views on the *Ṣaḥāba*' (see above).

17. *'Yaghdū al-nās ʿalā thalātha ṣunūf ʿālim wa mutaʿallim wa ghuthāʾ fa-naḥnu al-ʿulamāʾ wa shīʿatunā al-mutaʿallimūn wa sāʾir al-nās al-ghuthā"*, al-Ṣaffār al-Qummī, *Baṣāʾir al-darajāt*, ed. M. Kūchebāghī (2nd edn, Tabriz, n.d.), section 1, ch. 5, pp. 8–9; Ibn Bābūya, *Khiṣāl*, vol. 1, p. 123, no. 115.

18. *'Al-nās ithnān ʿālim wa mutaʿallim wa sāʾir al-nās hamaj wa'l-hamaj fi'l-nār'*, Ibn Bābūya, *Khiṣāl*, vol. 1, p. 39, no. 22. The term *hamaj*, which I have translated as 'vile beings', actually has three meanings: an individual of the lowest category, an old or lean sheep or ewe, or a small fly that pesters domestic cattle. We should note the expression 'in the Fire' and not 'towards the Fire' (*ilā'l-nār*, that is destined for or headed towards the Fire of Hell), as one might normally expect (aside from the edited text, the two manuscripts of the *Khiṣāl* that I have been able to consult also have *'fi'l-nār'*, MS Āstān-e Qods, Mashhad, 5/82, *akhbār* 516, fol. 11, and *akhbār* 517, fol. 18). This seems to signify that the vile beings are in hell already in this life. The same tradition is also attributed to the Prophet with the slight difference that *lā khayra fīhim* ('without anything of good in them') replaces *wa al-hamaj fi'l-nār*; see al-Dārimī, *al-Sunan* (Medina, 1986–1966), vol. 1, ch. 32, p. 80, no. 329; al-Shahrastānī, *Mafātīḥ al-asrār wa maṣābīḥ al-abrār*, facsimile publication of the unicum (Tehran, 1409/1986), fols 39a and 335b, cited by G. Monnot in 'Opposition and hiérachie dans la pensée d'al-Shahrastānī', in Amir-Moezzi, Jambet and Lory (eds), *Henry Corbin: philosophies et sagesses des religions du Livre* (Turnhout, 2005), p. 96, n. 16.

> Human beings are divided into three sections: the first consists of those found in the shadow of the [divine] Throne on the day when there is no other shadow (that is, on the Day of Resurrection). The second consists of those who are consigned to an accounting [of their acts] and to chastisement. The third group finally consists of those who have human faces, but whose hearts are those of demons.[19]

The first are the imams and their initiated supporters of all times. The second are their adversaries. The third, in all probability, are the leaders of the second group, that is, the 'guides of ignorance and darkness', the misguided *shayāṭīn* and seducers who draw 'the majority' along the road to perdition.

This anthropological conception appears to be supported by other elements of an anthropogonic order. As one might expect, these latter are not always coherent. In fact, they are rather confused, since they have been elaborated progressively down the ages and are made up of many strata. The authors of the most ancient compilations of traditions include Abū Jaʿfar al-Barqī (d. 274 or 280/887 or 893) and Muḥammad b. Yaʿqūb al-Kulaynī (d. 329/940–941), who record traditions that appear to be fragmentary, unbalanced in structure.[20] Their contemporary, al-Ṣaffār al-Qummī (d. 290/902–903), in this case as in many others, reports traditions that contain more information and have a more rigorous

19. *'Al-nās 'alā thalātha ajzā' fa-juz' taḥta ẓill al-'arsh yawma lā ẓilla illā ẓilluhu wa juz' 'alayhim al-ḥisāb wa'l-'adhāb wa juz' wujūhuhum wujūh al-ādamiyyīn wa qulūbuhum qulūb al-shayāṭīn*', Ibn Bābūya, *Khiṣāl*, vol. 1, p. 154, no. 192 (Jaʿfar al-Ṣādiq begins his words by enumerating the three categories of *jinn*: those who are in the company of the angels, those who fly through the air, and those who take the form of dogs and serpents. One can recognise here the two good categories and the one bad category, corresponding to the tripartite division of human beings).

20. Al-Barqī, *Maḥāsin*, vol. 1, pp. 131ff., 'Kitāb al-ṣafwa wa'l-nūr wa'l-raḥma', 'Bāb khalq al-mu'min'; al-Kulaynī, *al-Uṣūl*, vol. 2, pp. 232–234, 'Kitāb al-ḥujja', 'Bāb khalq abdān al-a'imma'; vol. 3, pp. 2–16 'Kitāb al-īmān wa'l-kufr', 'Bāb ṭīnat al-mu'min wa'l-kāfir'.

construction.[21] The anthropogonic episodes under discussion here are said to have occurred after the formation of the physical world at the moment of the creation of the souls (*arwāḥ*), hearts (*qulūb*, the seats of the souls) and bodies (*abdān*) of human beings. Here too we can see the omnipresent and radical division of creatures into two opposing groups: the guides of initiation and their adepts on the one side, the enemies and their supporters on the other. According to a tradition ascribed to al-Bāqir (d. 119/737):

> God created the [the body of] Muḥammad and [those of] his family from the clay (*ṭīna*) of *'Illiyyin* and created their souls and hearts from a clay found above the *'Illiyyin*. He created [the bodies of] our faithful supporters and of the prophets from a clay found below the *'Illiyyin*, just as he created their souls and hearts from the clay of *'Illiyyin*. *It is thus that the hearts of our faithful supporters came from the bodies of the Family of Muḥammad.* [This is an important phrase to which I will return.] In the same manner, God created the enemy of the family of Muḥammad [that is, his soul, his heart and his body] as well as the souls and hearts of his partisans from the clay of *Sijjīn*, and [the bodies of] the latter from a clay found below the *Sijjīn*. *It is in this manner that the hearts of these latter* [the partisans] *issued from the former* [their chiefs, the enemies of the imams].[22]

The terms *'Illiyyūn* (*'Illiyyin* in the accusative) and *Sijjīn* are both Qur'ānic and appear, respectively, in verses 18–21 and 7–9 of Sura 83:

> No indeed; the Book of the pious is in *'Illiyyin*
> And what shall teach you what is *'Illiyyūn*?
> It is a book inscribed

---

21. Al-Ṣaffār, *Baṣā'ir al-darajāt*, section 1, ch. 9, pp. 14–19. Concerning this compiler and the use of his major work for a better understanding of what I have called the 'esoteric, non-rational, original' Imami tradition, see my article 'Al-Ṣaffār al-Qummī (m. 290/902–903) et son *Kitāb baṣā'ir al-darajāt*', *JA*, 280 (1992), pp. 221–250. Concerning these three scholars see Newman, *The Formation Period of the Twelver Shī'ism.*

22. Al-Ṣaffār, *Baṣā'ir al-darajāt*, p. 14, no. 2; also Ibn Bābūya, *'Ilal al-sharā'i' wa'l-aḥkām* (Najaf, 1385/1966), ch. 96, pp. 117–118, nos 12–15.

Witnessed by those brought nigh.[23]
No indeed; the Book of the libertines is in *Sijjīn*;
And what shall teach you what is *Sijjīn?*
It is a book inscribed.[24]

Classical exegesis identifies *'Illiyyin* and *Sijjīn* respectively as one of the highest levels of Paradise and one of the lowest abodes of Hell, or as divine books that each list respectively the 'names' of the chosen and the damned. Although another tradition ascribed to Muḥammad al-Bāqir refers to *'Illiyyin* and *Sijjīn* as 'the seventh heaven [of paradise] and the seventh level [of hell?]',[25] discussions of these two terms in the early Imami corpus are almost always exegetical glosses on these verses quoted above and address the anthropogonic episodes under consideration here.

It is clear that here *'Illiyyin* and *Sijjīn* are, respectively, 'celestial' and 'infernal' 'places' that provide the primary matter of good and evil creatures. Moreover, in certain traditions, *'Illiyyin* appears to have been replaced by '*'arsh*' (the divine throne). This occurs, for example, in an important *ḥadīth* ascribed to Ja'far al-Ṣādiq, where the tripartite division of humanity reappears:

> God created us [our souls] from the light of His majesty, then he gave form to our creation [i.e. our body] from a well-guarded and secret clay taken from below the Throne, and placed this light in it. We are thus luminescent human creatures, favoured by God

23. *'Kallā inna kitāb al-abrār la-fī 'illiyyin / wa-mā adrāka mā 'illiyyūn / kitābun marqūm / yashhaduhu'l-muqarrabūn.'*

24. *'Kallā inna kitāb al-fujjār la-fī sijjīn / wa mā adrāka mā sijjīn / kitābun marqūm'.*

25. 'Alī ibn Ibrāhīm al-Qummī, *Tafsīr*, ed. Ṭ. al-Mūsawī al-Jazā'irī (rpr. Beirut, 1991), vol. 2, p. 437. Somewhat later, a *ḥadīth* attributed to Ja'far identifies 'the libertines' of the verse as Abū Bakr and 'Umar, and 'the pious' as the fourteen impeccable ones (ibid., vol. 2, p. 438). Another tradition, also attributed to the sixth imam, glosses the verses, '"*Sijjīn*, is a Book inscribed" on the hatred (*bughḍ*) towards Muḥammad and his descendants. "*'Illiyyin*, it is a Book inscribed" on the love (*ḥubb*) for Muḥammad and his descendants.' Cf. Furāt al-Kufī, *Tafsīr*, ed. M. al-Kāẓim (Tehran, 1410/1990), p. 543, no. 697.

> in a manner shared by no other. And he created the souls of our supporters from our clay and their bodies from another clay that is well guarded and secret [but] lower than ours…. It is for this reason that we and they have become human while the others have become only vile beings [*hamaj*, see note 18 above] [made] for the Fire and [facing/going towards] the Fire.[26]

The beings of good and evil are thus ontologically different. They are made of different substances, only the former merit being called human. The latter are only sub-humans, damned demonic beings that have nothing of humanity except their shape. According to a tradition ascribed to the third imam, al-Ḥusayn ibn ʿAlī (d. 61/680), people are of three types: human beings (*al-nās*), those who resemble human beings (*ashbāh al-nās*) and monsters with a human shape (*nasnās* or *nisnās*).[27] The tradition adds:

> We [the Impeccable Ones] are the human beings: those who resemble human beings are our supporters who are our friendly allies (*mawālī*) and come from us [this probably means 'they are formed of the same substance as us']; the monsters with a human

26. *'Inna llāha khalaqanā min nūr ʿaẓamatih thumma ṣawwara khalqanā min ṭīna makhzūna maknūna min taḥt al-ʿarsh fa-askana dhālika al-nūr fīhi fa-kunnā naḥnu khalqan wa-basharan nūrāniyyin lam yujʿal li aḥad fī mithl alladhī khalaqanā minhu naṣīb wa khalaqa arwāḥ shīʿatinā min ṭīnatinā wa abdānahum min ṭīna makhzūna maknūna asfal min dhālika al-ṭīna wa li dhālika ṣirnā naḥnu wa hum al-nās wa ṣāra sā'ir al-nās hamajan li'l-nār wa ilā'l-nār'*, al-Kulaynī, *al-Uṣūl*, vol. 2, pp. 232–233, no. 2. See also al-Ṣaffār, *Baṣā'ir al-darajāt*, section 1, ch. 9, p. 17, no. 12, *ʿarsh* in place of *ʿilliyyin*; see also *Guide divin*, pp. 96–100 (*Divine Guide*, pp. 38–39), see also Chapter 4, this volume.

27. *Nasnās/nisnās* is a fictitious malevolent being, often described as a kind of 'monkey' with a human face, covered with bushy hair. See, e.g., al-Jāḥiẓ, *Kitāb al-ḥayawān* (Cairo, n.d.), vol. 1, p. 189; vol. 7, p. 178; Zakariyā al-Qazwīnī, *ʿAjā'ib al-makhlūqāt*, in the margins of al-Damīrī, *Ḥayāt al-ḥayawān al-kubrā* (Cairo, 1356/1937), vol. 1, pp. 190ff.; al-Masʿūdī, *Murūj al-dhahab*, ed. and tr. Barbier de Meynard and C. Pavet de Courteille (Paris, 1861–1877), vol. 4, pp. 10–17. See also F. Viré, 'Ḳird', *EI2*.

appearance are the great majority', and he [imam al-Ḥusayn] pointed to the mass of the people.[28]

The following are supplementary details concerning the identity of these three types of people. The first group consists clearly of the long initiatory chain of prophets and their imams: Adam and Seth/Abel/Hibat Allāh (according to the different lists of imams of each prophet), Noah and Shem, Solomon and Āṣaf b. Barakhiyā, Abraham and Ishmael/Isaac, Moses and Aaron/ Joshua, Jesus and Simon/John/the apostles, Muḥammad and ʿAlī/ the other eleven imams, to cite only the most celebrated. Thus, each pair of prophet/imam(s) is connected to the following pair along chain of divinely initiated sages. Thus Imami Shiʿism, in the strict sense of the term, appears as the last link in a long chain of initiation, the beginning of which is traced back to Adam, 'the father of humanity', and the continuity of which until the end of time is assured by the twelfth imam, the hidden imam, the Lord of Time (*ṣāḥib al-zamān*) and the eschatological Saviour.[29]

The second group consists of the 'loyal followers' of the imams of the different prophets, that is the *shīʿa* of all times. But does this group also include all of the Shiʿis of Islam? Should one take

28. '*Fa-naḥnu al-nās... ashbāh al-nās fa-hum shīʿatunā wa hum mawālīnā wa hum minnā... al-nasnās/ nisnās fa hum al-sawād al-aʿẓam wa ashāra bi yadihi ilā jamāʿat al-nās*', Furāt al-Kūfī, *Tafsīr*, p. 64, no. 30; al-Kulaynī, *al-Rawḍa min al-Kāfī*, vol. 2, p. 54, no. 339.

29. On the initiatory chain of prophets and imams, see ʿAlī b. al-Ḥusayn b. Bābūya (the father of al-Ṣadūq), *al-Imāma wa'l-tabṣira min al-ḥayra* (Qumm, 1404/1985), pp. 21–23; (Pseudo?) al-Masʿūdī, *Ithbāt al-waṣiyya*, pp. 20–93; Ibn Bābūya al-Ṣadūq, *Kitāb man lā yaḥḍuruhu al-faqīh*, ed. al-Mūsawī al-Kharsān (5th edn, Tehran, 1390/1970), vol. 4, pp. 129–130, ch. 72, and *Kamāl al-dīn wa tamām al-niʿma*, ed. ʿA. A. Ghaffārī (Qumm, 1405/1985), vol. 1, pp. 211–213, ch. 22, no. 1; vol. 2, p. 664, ch. 58, nos 4–5; Ibn ʿAyyāsh al-Jawharī, *Muqtaḍab al-athar* (Tehran, 1346/1927), pp. 51–52. Also see C. Pellat, 'Masʿûdî et l'imâmisme', in *Le shîʿisme imâmite* (Paris, 1970), esp. pp. 80–81; U. Rubin, 'Prophets and Progenitors in the Early Shīʿa Tradition', *JSAI*, 1 (1979), pp. 41–65; Amir-Moezzi, *Guide divin*, pp. 106–108 (*Divine Guide*, pp. 41–42). The lists and the names of which they are comprised vary, sometimes considerably, from one source to another and certain names remain unidentified.

it that all those who call themselves Shiʿis were created from the heavenly substance of the Imam and have henceforth won their salvation through their doctrinal affiliation? If one consulted only the rich literature of the *faḍāʾil al-shīʿa*, which from a very early date became virtually a literary genre among the Shiʿis, one might tend to respond in the affirmative.[30] But other traditions provide a more nuanced picture. An initial group of texts, still anthropogonic in nature, aim at attenuating the radicalism of the anthropogonic traditions we have already considered and the certain kind of determinism that they convey. We are dealing here with traditions concerning 'the mixture of the two clays' (*ikhtilāṭ al-ṭīnatayn*): after the creation of good from the clay of *ʿIlliyyin* and evil from the clay of *Sijjīn*, God mixed the two clays. This, according to the traditions, is why a believer can beget an unbeliever and an unbeliever can beget a believer. Furthermore, this is why a believer can commit evil and an unbeliever can do good.[31] According to other accounts, which are often presented as exegetical glosses on Q 7:172 concerning the primordial pact (*mīthāq*), God took a handful of earth from which He created Adam and then poured on it sweet and pleasing water, and He let it rest for forty days. Then He poured salty and briny water over it and let it rest for another forty days. Once this clay had become muddy, God rubbed it vigorously and Adam's descendants came forth in the form of particles (*dharr*, literally 'ants'), on the right and left

30. Practically all compilations of Imami traditions, if not all the doctrinal works, include one or more chapters concerning 'the virtues of the Shiʿis' or 'the virtue of being a Shiʿi'. See, e.g., for the early period, al-Barqī, *al-Maḥāsin*, pp. 60–63, nos 78–87 'kitāb thawāb al-aʿmāl'; al-Kulaynī, *al-Uṣūl*, vol. 4, pp. 447ff. 'kitāb al-ʿishra', and *al-Rawḍa*, vol. 1, pp. 49ff., 115ff.; vol. 2, pp. 13ff., 43ff., 215ff. Ibn Bābūya has numerous quasi-monographic works on this subject: *Thawāb al-aʿmāl* (Tehran, n.d.); *Muṣādaqat al-ikhwān* (Tehran, n.d.; the introduction by S. Nafīsī dates from 1325 Sh./1946); and esp. *Ṣifāt al-Shīʿa + Faḍāʾil al-Shīʿa*, ed. with Persian tr. by Ḥ. Fashāhī (Tehran, 1342 Sh./1963–1964).

31. Al-Barqī, *al-Maḥāsin*, pp. 136–137, ch. 7, kitāb al-ṣafwa wa'l-nūr,'; al-Ṣaffār, *Baṣāʾir al-darajāt*, pp. 15–17, section 1, ch. 9, nos 5, 7, 8, 10; al-Kulaynī, *al-Uṣūl*, vol. 3, pp. 2–8 'Kitāb al-īmān wa'l-kufr', 'Bāb ṭīnat al-muʾmin wa'l-kāfir'.

of the clay, thereby giving birth to the 'people of the right' and the 'people of the left'.[32] As a consequence, none of the believers are free from evil or error, and therefore from chastisement. The '*Sijjīnī*' element in each person can become active at any moment through lack of awareness. On the other hand, an unbeliever has the ability to actualise the good in his basic nature in order to change his destiny. Thanks to the element of '*Illiyyin* within him, the veil that covers his conscience may be removed, thus allowing him to join the other side. This is perhaps one of the reasons why Imamism opts for an intermediate position between determinism and free will, a position designated by the expression 'a state between two states' (*amr bayn al-amrayn*).[33]

In certain other traditions, moreover, a clear distinction is drawn between two categories of Shi'is. Muḥammad al-Bāqir is reported to have said:

> You, faithful followers of the descendants of Muḥammad, you will be cleansed and washed clean just as kohl is washed off eyelids. Certainly one knows when one applies kohl to the eyes, but one does not know when it will be washed off. In the same manner, a man will wake up as a follower of our cause (*amr*) and lie down whilst abandoning it, or he will lie down as a follower and will wake up as a denier.[34]

---

32. Al-Ṣaffār, *Baṣā'ir al-darajāt*, pp. 70–71, section 2, ch. 7, nos 2 and 6; Muḥammad b. Mas'ūd al-'Ayyāshī, *Tafsīr*, ed. H. Rasūlī Maḥallātī (Tehran, 1380/1960), vol. 2, pp. 39–40; al-Kulaynī, *al-Uṣūl*, vol. 3, p. 10.

33. Cf., e.g., al-Kulaynī, *al-Uṣūl*, vol. 1, pp. 215–228 'Kitāb al-tawḥīd', 'Bāb al-jabr wa'l-qadar wa'l-amr bayn al-amrayn'; Ibn Bābūya, *Kitāb al-tawḥīd*, ed. H. al-Ḥusaynī al-Ṭihrānī (Tehran, 1398/1978), pp. 359–364, ch. 59, 'Bāb nafy al-jabr wa'l-tafwīḍ', pp. 364–390, ch. 60, 'Bāb al-qaḍā' wa'l-qadar'; and for speculations concerning the tradition '*lā jabr wa lā tafwīḍ bal amr bayn al-amrayn*', pp. 47, 69, 96, 143, 337–340, 344, 381–383, 407, 413; against the Jabriyya and the Tafwīḍiyya, see pp. 181 and 382.

34. Muḥammad b. Humān/Hammām al-Iskāfī, *Kitāb al-tamḥīṣ* (Qumm, n.d. [ca. 1995]), p. 37; al-Nu'mānī, *Kitāb al-ghayba*, ed. 'A. A. Ghaffārī with a Persian trans. by M. J. Ghaffārī (Tehran, 1363 Sh./1985), p. 301, ch. 12, no. 12.

The sixth imam is reported to have addressed his supporters in these terms:

> By God, you will be broken like glass (*al-zujāj*), but glass, having been treated, will return to what it was. By God, you will be smashed like dry clay (*al-fakhkhār*) and clay, once broken, will never return to what it was. By God, you will be severely sifted, tested and clearly distinguished from each other. By God, you will be purified completely until only a few of you remain.[35]

This notion of sifting, of purification, of being put to a test from which only a few of Shiʿis will emerge, appears in a substantial number of traditions.[36] This is a long way from the laudatory tone of the *faḍāʾil al-shīʿa*, at least when one considers that the term *shīʿa* only refers to a small number of 'true' Shiʿis.[37] Certain *ḥadīth*s

---

35. Al-Iskāfī, *Tamḥīṣ*, p. 43; al-Nuʿmānī, *Ghayba*, pp. 301–302, no. 13. 'Glass' (*al-zujāj*), a transparent and noble material, designates of course the 'true faithful'; 'dry clay' (*al-fakhkhār*), a dark and vile material, symbolises the 'nominal' Shiʿis who are weak in their faith. The tradition may also conceal a play on words: the root *z-j-j* evokes the idea of effort and perseverance while the root *f-kh-r* evokes the idea of pride and vanity.

36. Cf., e.g., al-Kulaynī, *al-Uṣūl*, vol. 2, pp. 194–199, 'Kitāb al-ḥujja', 'Bāb al-tamḥīṣ wa'l-imtiḥān'; al-Nuʿmānī, *Ghayba*, pp. 294–310; ch. 12, Amir-Moezzi, *Guide divin*, pp. 285–286 (*Divine Guide*, pp. 117–118). See in general the monograph compiled by al-Iskāfī, *Tamḥīs* (already cited).

37. It is true that the doctrinal, and certainly the historical, contexts of the *faḍāʾil al-shīʿa*, appear to be different from those of the traditions dealing with the testing of the Imamis. The former seem older to me. One can detect in them a 'proselytising' tone that usually characterises the beginnings of a religious movement. The latter often have an eschatological context: the 'true followers' are those who remain firm in their faith in the hidden imam and his return. The test is in fact the occultation of the imam; this when the true Shiʿis are distinguished from the false ones. But even in this particular context, a distinction is drawn between two categories of Shiʿis. Moreover, in other traditions, which do not seem to have any eschatological elements, note also the existence of these two distinct categories. The 'true' are only a small minority: 'a [true] believing woman (*muʾmina*) is rarer than a [true] believing man (*muʾmin*), and the latter is rarer than red sulphur (*al-kibrīt al-aḥmar*)'; 'all men are animals (*bahāʾim*) except for a handful of followers (*illā qalīl min al-muʾminīn*) and the [true] follower is a stranger (*gharīb*)'; 'a simple profession of love for us (*walāya*) does not

even refer to hostility between the two groups. The sixth imam is reported to have said: 'Some of you will spit in the faces of others, some of you will curse others, some of you will treat others as liars.'[38] Those who fail the test are the Shiʿis who do not have faith in all of the teachings of the imams, those who keep some elements and reject others. The 'sifted' follower, he who emerges victorious from the test, is certainly the one to whom Shiʿi *ḥadīths* frequently refers by the expression 'the follower whose heart has been tested by God for the faith' (*muʾmin imtaḥana llāh qalbahu liʾl-īmān*). A tradition repeated by many of the imams states clearly:

> Our teaching (*ḥadīthunā*) is difficult (*ṣaʿb*), extremely arduous (*mustaṣʿab*); it cannot be undertaken except by a messenger prophet (*nabī mursal*), an angel of proximity (*malak muqarrab*), or a believing follower whose heart has been tested by God for the faith.[39]

Certain particularly arduous or difficult aspects of the teaching are emphasised by words such as 'redoubtable' (*hayūb*), 'terrifying' (*dhaʿūr*), 'grievous' (*thaqīl*), 'exasperating' (*khashin*), 'distressing' (*makhshūsh*), 'veiled' (*mastūr/muqannaʿ*).[40] 'Our doctrine [*amrunā*, lit. "our cause"] is a secret (*sirr*), a secret contained in a secret, a secret that has been rendered secret (*mustasirr*), a secret on the subject of a secret.'[41] Muḥammad al-Bāqir is reported to have said:

---

turn a person into a follower, rather those who profess love simply diminish the solitude of our followers'. In another tradition, the imam Jaʿfar says allusively that the number of true Shiʿis is not above two dozen. See al-Kulaynī, *al-Uṣūl*, vol. 3, pp. 339–342, 'Kitāb al-īmān waʾl-kufr', 'Bāb qilla ʿadad al-muʾminīn'. On this point see E. Kohlberg, 'In Praise of the Few', in G. R. Hawting, J. A. Mojaddedi and A. Samely (eds), *Studies in Islamic and Middle Eastern Texts and Traditions, In Memory of Norman Calder, JSS*, Supplement 12 (2000), pp. 149–162.

38. Al-Iskāfī, *Tamḥīṣ*, p. 54; al-Nuʿmānī, *Ghayba*, p. 300, no. 10, ch. 12.

39. Cf., e.g., al-Ṣaffār, *Baṣāʾir al-darajāt*, pp. 20–28, section 1, chs 11 and 12 ; al-Kulaynī, *al-Uṣūl*, vol. 2, pp. 253–257, 'Kitāb al-ḥujja', 'Bāb fī-mā jāʾa anna ḥadīthahum ṣaʿb mustaṣʿab'.

40. Al-Ṣaffār, *Baṣaʾir al-darajāt*, pp. 21–25.

41. Ibid., pp. 28–29.

> Our teaching shrivels the hearts of men (*tashmaʾizzu minhu qulūbuʾl-rijāl*). Tell more to him who acknowledges it and leave him who denies it, because the coming of the ordeal (*fitna*) is inevitable when friend and ally alike (*biṭāna wa-walīja*)[42] will fall until no one remains but we [the imams] and our supporters (*shīʿatuna*).[43]

The imam ʿAlī is said to have declared:

> Our teaching is difficult, particularly arduous, exasperating, distressing. Offer it to people in small quantities (*faʾnbadhū ilāʾl-nās nubdhan*). To those who acknowledge it, tell more, but avoid telling more to him who denies it, because those who can bear this teaching are only an angel of proximity, a messenger prophet, or a faithful believer whose heart has been tested by God for the faith. [44]

This 'faithful believer whose heart has been tested' indicates he who has been initiated into the secret teaching of the imam. This point is made explicit in a *ḥadīth* going back to the fourth imam ʿAlī b al-Ḥusayn (d. 92/711 or 95/714), which concerns the relationship between Salmān al-Fārisī and Abū Dharr al-Ghifārī, two of the 'pillars' (*arkān*) of Shiʿism. The first is the archetype of the initiated follower having access to the arcane matters of the secret teaching. The second is the archetype of the ascetic and pious follower who has knowledge only of the exoteric elements of the teaching:

> Once a discussion regarding the duty of keeping the secret (*al-taqiyya*), was held in the presence of the [imam] ʿAlī b. al-Ḥusayn.[45] The imam said: 'By God, if Abū Dharr had known

42. *Biṭāna* and *walīja* are also part of the tribal vocabulary. A *biṭāna* is a member of the tribe (the term also signifies a 'close friend' and 'heart/the interior of a thing'), while a *walīja* is a stranger attached to a tribe through an alliance.

43. Al-Ṣaffār, *Baṣāʾir al-darajāt*, p. 23, no. 14.

44. Ibid., p. 21, no. 5.

45. Concerning *taqiyya*, see I. Goldhizer, 'Das Prinzip der Takija im Islam', *ZDMG*, 60 (1906); (rpr. in *Gesammelte Schriften*, vol. 5, pp. 59–72); K. M. al-Shaybī, 'al-Taqīya uṣūluhā wa-taṭawwuruhā', *Revue de la Faculté des Lettres d'Université d'Alexandrie*, 16 (1962), pp. 14–40; E. Meyer, 'Anlass und Anwend-

what was in the heart of Salmān, he would have killed him despite the fact that the Prophet had established a pact of brotherhood between these two. How much more so does this hold for others! Know that the secret knowledge of the spiritual initiator is difficult, particularly arduous, and cannot be undertaken by anyone except a messenger prophet, an angel of proximity, or a believing follower whose heart has been tested by God for the faith. Salmān became an initiate (*ṣāra Salmān min al-ʿulamāʾ*), which is why he formed part of us, the *ahl al-bayt* [of the Prophet] and why his origin is traced back to us.'[46]

---

ungsbereich der *taqiyya*', *Der Islam*, 57 (1980); E. Kohlberg, 'Taqiyya in Shīʿī Theology and Religion', in H. G. Kippenberg and G. G. Stroumsa (eds), *Secrecy and Concealment: Studies in the History of Mediterranean and Near Eastern Religions* (Leiden, 1995) (a study which magisterially complements an earlier article by the same scholar: 'Some Imāmī Shīʿī Views on *taqiyya*', *JAOS*, 95 [1975], pp. 395–402, also rpr. in *Belief and Law*, article 3); Amir-Moezzi, *Guide divin*, index under '*taqiyya*'.

46. Al-Ṣaffār, *Baṣāʾir al-darajāt*, p. 25, no. 21. On the level of practical spirituality, the expression 'testing of the heart for the faith' would seem to designate 'techniques' of vision by (or 'in') in the heart (*al-ruʾya biʾl-qalb*), which consisted of visualising the reality of the imam as a form of light in the subtle centre of the heart, cf. Amir-Moezzi, *Guide divin*, pp. 112–145 (*Divine Guide*, pp. 44–55); R. Gramlich, *Die schiitischen Derwishorden Persiens*, vol. 2: *Glaube und Lehre* (Wiesbaden, 1976), p. 207 and n. 1073, pp. 247–250. In certain traditions, 'the follower whose heart has been tested' (placed alongside the 'messenger prophet' and 'the angel of proximity') is replaced by expressions such as 'illuminated breasts' (*ṣudūr munīra*), 'healthy hearts' (*qulūb salīma*) or even 'fortified city' (*madīna ḥaṣīna*), defined as a metaphor for the 'concentrated heart' (*qalb mujtamaʿ*); cf. al-Ṣaffār, *Baṣāʾir al-darajāt*, p. 25, no. 20 and p. 21, no. 3. For the definition of *madīna ḥaṣīna*, see Ibn Bābūya, *al-Amālī* (*Majālis*), ed. with a Persian trans. by M. B. Kamareʾī (Tehran, 1404/1984), p. 4, 'majlis' 1, no. 6, and *Maʿānī al-akhbār*, ed. ʿA. A. Ghaffārī (Tehran, 1379/1959), p. 189. Other traditions stress the equality in soteriological rank between the tested follower and the prophets and imams: 'The spiritual initiator [i.e. the imam] and the initiated disciple will receive the same reward. On the Day of Resurrection, they will advance together tight against each other like two race horses' (*anna al-ʿālim waʾl-mutaʿallim fiʾl-ajr sawāʾ yaʾtiyān yawm al-qiyāma ka-farasay rihān yazdaḥimān*); al-Ṣaffār, *Baṣāʾir al-darajāt*, p. 3, section 1, ch. 2, no. 1. The long tradition of the 75 armies of *ʿaql* ends as follows: 'And the totality of these [75] qualities which form the armies of hiero-intelligence are only brought together in a prophet, a legatee [*waṣī*, i.e. the imam], or a follower whose heart has been tested by God for the faith … who does not cease to perfect himself and to purify himself of the armies

The 'true' Shiʿis thus appear to have been the initiated Shiʿis. They were those who, in contrast to the non-initiated Shiʿis, came from the imams and formed part of them. The notion of the 'mixing of the clays' enables one to say that a non-Shiʿi who discovers the *walāya* and is initiated into the divine knowledge thereby gains the status of a 'true Shiʿi'. In this case, his celestial nature will have succeeded in overcoming his infernal nature. The Imami 'matter between two matters' (*amr bayn al-amrayn*) mentioned above, between determinism and free will, implies in this context that it is not the origin of an individual that determines his destiny, but rather his destiny that, a posteriori, gives proof of his origin. Therefore, it is the 'true Shiʿis' who constitute the second category in our tripartite division.

Finally, a few remarks on the subject of the third category. As we have seen, this refers to the 'enemies', the forces arrayed against initiation, the sub-human creatures or the satanic monsters in human form. Within this context, the Imami views on the subject of 'metamorphosis' (*maskh*) appear in a new light. In the early corpus of Twelver traditions there are numerous attestations of *maskh*, namely a degrading reincarnation in animal form.[47] The beings who undergo metamorphosis of this type

---

of ignorance until he attains the highest state (*al-daraja al-ʿulyā*) occupied by the prophets and legatees' (see the sources above in note 5).

47. For example, al-Ṣaffār, *Baṣāʾir al-darajāt*, pp. 353–354, section 7, ch. 16; al-Kulaynī, *al-Rawḍa*, vol. 1, p. 285, vol. 2, pp. 37–38; Ibn Bābūya, *ʿUyūn akhbār al-Riḍā*, ed. M. Ḥ. Lājevardī (Tehran, 1378/1958), p. 271, vol. 1, ch. 27; al-Nuʿmānī, *Ghayba*, p. 387. This theme is more fully developed in the literature of the Shiʿis called Bāṭinīs. For example, in the corpus attributed to Jābir ibn Ḥayyān one finds a whole series of terms that designate many different types of reincarnation (often degrading): *naskh* (reincarnation in another human form), *maskh* (reincarnation in an animal form), *faskh* (reincarnation in a vegetable form), *raskh* (reincarnation in a mineral form). Cf. *The Arabic Work of Jābir b. Ḥayyān*, ed. E. J. Holmyard (Paris, 1928), 'Kitāb al-bayān', p. 11; *Mukhtār rasāʾil Jābir ibn Ḥayyān*, ed. P. Kraus (Paris and Cairo, 1935), 'Kitāb al-ishtimāl', pp. 549–550; *Zeitschrift für Geschichte der arabisch-islamischen Wissenschaften*, Arabic texts, ed. M. ʿA. Abū Rīda (1984), 'Kitāb al-maʿrifa', p. 57. The theme of *maskh* likewise occupies numerous chapters of *Kitāb al-haft* (one of the sacred writings of the Nuṣayrīs and certain Ismailis), ed. M. Ghālib (under the title *al-Haft al-sharīf*)

are called *musūkh*. In many cases, these are historical adversaries of the Shiʿis designated by name: a lizard (*wazagh*) defends ʿUthmān, the third caliph; it is most likely he is a reincarnation of the caliph.[48] The Umayyad ʿAbd al-Malik b. Marwān is also transformed into a lizard after his death.[49] Jaʿfar al-Ṣādiq touches the eyes of his close disciple Abū Baṣīr and thus enables him to see the true nature of the great majority (i.e. the non-Shiʿis) among the pilgrims to Mecca: they are monkeys (*qirada*) and pigs (*khanāzīr*).[50] The *musūkh*, and more generally the third category of people, are the 'adversaries', namely, according to the Shiʿi theory of the *ḍidd*s, the descendants of Cain who oppose the descendants of Abel.[51] Seen from this angle, one might conclude

(3rd edn, Beirut, 1980), and ed. ʿA. Tamer and A. Khalifé (under the title *al-Haft wa'l-aẓilla*) (2nd edn, Beirut, 1970). See also al-Shahrastānī, *Livres des religions et des sectes*, vol. 1, tr. D. Gimaret and G. Monnot (Louvain, 1986), p. 512, and note 40 by Gimaret, who points to the discussion of this subject in al-Bīrūnī, al-ʿĪjī and in Ibn al-Khaṭīb. For a general overview, see G. Monnot, 'La transmigration et l'immortalité', in his *Islam et religions* (Paris, 1986), article XII; U. Rubin, 'Apes, Pigs and the Islamic Identity', *IOS*, 17 (1997), pp. 89–105; S. Schmidtke, 'The Doctrine of the Transmigration of the Soul According to Shihāb al-Dīn al-Suhrawardī (killed 587/1191)', *Studia Iranica*, 28/2 (1999), pp. 237–254.

48. Al-Ṣaffār, *Baṣā'ir al-darajāt*, pp. 353–354, section 7, ch. 16, nos 1–2; al-Kulaynī, *al-Rawḍa*, vol. 2, p. 37.

49. Al-Kulaynī, *al-Rawḍa*, vol. 2, p. 38.

50. Al-Ṣaffār, *Baṣā'ir al-darajāt*, pp. 270–271, section 6, ch. 3, no. 4. On the disciples of Jaʿfar al-Ṣādiq carrying the *kunya* 'Abū Baṣīr' see *Guide divin*, pp. 86–87 (*Divine Guide*, p. 34), n. 182. On the Sunnī reaction to the Shiʿi doctrine of *maskh* see e.g. Ibn al-Jawzī, *Tadhkira ūlī'l-baṣā'ir fī maʿrifa al-kabā'ir*, MS. Garrett 1896, Princeton, fols 176ff. (cited by Kohlberg, 'Some Imāmī Shīʿī Views on the *Ṣaḥāba*', p. 171) or Ibn ʿArabī, *al-Futūḥāt al-makkiyya* (Bulāq, 1329/1911), vol. 2, p. 8, and *Muḥāḍarat al-abrār* (Beirut, 1968), vol. 1, p. 418.

51. According to Ḥaydar al-Āmulī, *al-Kashkūl fī mā jarā ʿalā āl al-rasūl* (Najaf, 1372/1953), p. 30 (according to H. Corbin, this author should be distinguished from his contemporary and namesake, who wrote the *Jāmiʿ al-asrār*; cf. his introduction to the edition of this latter work, produced with O. Yahia [Tehran and Paris 1969], p. 46). For other examples of the *ḍidd* according to the Shiʿis, see also al-Ashʿarī, *Maqālāt al-Islāmiyyin*, ed. H. Ritter (2nd edn, Wiesbaden, 1963), pp. 11ff.; Abū Jaʿfar al-Ṭūsī, *Kitāb al-ghayba* (Najaf, 1385/1965), pp. 250ff.; Ibn Kathīr, *al-Bidāya wa'l-nihāya* (Cairo, 1932–1939), vol. 8, p. 49;

that the reference is to demonic monsters, who assume a human shape during their lives and return to their true nature after death.

When considered alongside traditions dealing with the ontological connection between God and the Imam, the tripartite anthropological division also takes on a theological dimension. I have analysed these traditions, which clearly establish what specifically concerns or derives from the imams in the foundations of Imami theology, elsewhere.[52] Here I will only offer a brief overview in order to clarify the connection with mystical anthropology.

The divine being comprises two ontological planes: the Essence (*dhāt*), which is unknowable, unimaginable and unintelligible, to be comprehended only through a negative, apophatic theology;[53] and the Names and Attributes (*al-asmāʾ wa'l-ṣifāt*) thanks to which creatures in general and human beings in particular are able to approach that which is knowable of God. This is the domain of theophanic theology because, in effect, the names and attributes, which are revealed through God's Most Beautiful Names (*al-asmāʾ al-ḥusnā*), possess the places of manifestation (*maẓhar/majlā*) that, like the organs, permit a relationship between God and his creatures.[54] God's organs are nothing other than the different aspects of the cosmic Imam, the archetypal Perfect Man. The terrestrial imams, for their part, are manifestations of him on the physical plane. There are numerous traditions in which the imams repeat continuously: 'We are the eye (*ʿayn*) of God, we are the hand (*yad*) of God, we are the face (*wajh*) of God,

---

al-Jurjānī, *Kitāb al-taʿrīfāt* (*Livre des definitions*), tr. M. Gloton (Tehran, 1994), p. 412, no. 1692.

52. Cf. Amir-Moezzi, *Guide divin*, pp. 75ff., 114ff. (*Divine Guide*, pp. 29ff., 44ff.); see also Chapter 3, this volume.

53. See e.g. al-Kulaynī, *al-Uṣūl*, vol. 1, pp. 109ff., 140ff., 169ff.; Ibn Bābūya, *Tawḥīd*, chs 2, 6 and 7, *ʿUyūn akhbār al-Riḍā*, ch. 11, and *Khiṣāl*, p. 2ff; Amir-Moezzi, *Guide divin*, pp. 114–115 (*Divine Guide*, pp. 44–45); and Chapter 3, this volume.

54. Al-Kulaynī, *al-Uṣūl*, vol. 1, p. 143; Ibn Bābūya, *Tawḥīd*, ch. 11, pp. 139ff.; see also H. Corbin, *Le paradoxe du monothéisme* (Paris, 1981), esp. the first part; likewise his *En Islam iranien*, index, 'tanzīh' and 'théophanies': Amir-Moezzi, *Guide divin*, pp. 115–116 (*Divine Guide*, pp. 45–46).

we are His flank (*janb*), His heart (*qalb*), His tongue (*lisān*), His ear (*udhn*).'[55] The plane of essence constitutes the *Deus absconditus* (Hidden God), while the plane of names-attributes-organs constitutes the *Deus revelatus* (Revealed God), that is to say, the Imam. Commenting on Q 7:180: 'God possesses the Most Beautiful Names, invoke Him by these names', the sixth imam, Jaʿfar al-Ṣādiq, is reported to have declared: 'By God, we are the Most Beautiful Names; no act of the servants is accepted unless it is accompanied by recognition of us.'[56] In this division of essence/names-organs, one can clearly detect a transposition to the divine level of the omnipresent pair of *bāṭin/ẓāhir*. The esoteric, hidden and non-manifest aspect of God becomes His essence, which is forever inaccessible. His organs, which are the theophanic vehicles of His names, become His exoteric, revealed aspect. The Imam, who is the true revealed God, is therefore the exoteric aspect of God, and recognition of his reality is the equivalent of a recognition of what can be known of God. There are numerous traditions attributed to many imams where it is stated: 'He who knows us knows God, and he who fails to know us fails to know God.'[57] 'It is thanks to us that God is known, and it is thanks to us that He is adored.'[58] 'Without God we would not be known, and without us God would not be known.'[59]

---

55. We are dealing here with the ontological Imam, the cosmic man, of whom the terrestrial imam is the locus of manifestation on the physical plane. On the 'organs' of God and the theology of theophany (*tajallī*) as the 'antidote' to 'assimilationist' theology (*tashbīh*) and 'agnostic' theology (*taʿṭīl*) see e.g. al-Ṣaffār, *Baṣāʾir al-darajāt*, pp. 61–66, section 2, chs 3–4; al-Kulaynī, *al-Uṣūl*, vol. 1, pp. 196ff., 283ff.; Ibn Bābūya, *Tawḥīd*, chs 12–22 and 24, *ʿUyūn akhbār al-Riḍā*, pp. 114–116, 149–153, and *Kamāl al-dīn*, vol. 1, pp. 231ff, ch. 22; Amir-Moezzi, *Guide divin*, pp. 116–117 (*Divine Guide*, p. 45).

56. Al-ʿAyyāshī, *Tafsīr*, vol. 2, p. 42, no. 119; al-Kulaynī, *al-Uṣūl*, vol. 1, p. 196.

57. Al-Ṣaffār, *Baṣāʾir al-darajāt*, p. 6, section 1, ch. 3, Ibn Bābūya, *Kamāl al-dīn*, p. 261, ch. 24, no. 7; *Nahj al-balāgha* (the speech of ʿAlī b. Abī Ṭālib compiled by al-Sharīf al-Raḍī), ed. with a Persian trans. ʿA. N. Fayḍ al-Islām (4th edn, Tehran, 1351 Sh./1972), p. 470.

58. Ibn Bābūya, *Tawḥīd*, p. 152, ch. 12, no. 9.

59. Ibid., p. 290, ch. 41, no. 10.

Moreover, the cosmo-anthropogonic accounts state explicitly that the Imam, or the Impeccable Ones in general, issue from the light of God. Even before the creation of the physical world, God had a ray of light spring forth from His own light, from which proceeded a second shaft of light. The first was the light of Muḥammad, that of prophecy (*nubuwwa*) and of the exoteric aspect. The second was the light of ʿAlī, that of the imamate, or the *walāya*, and of the esoteric aspect:

> Two thousand years before the creation, Muḥammad and ʿAlī were a light before God, a light formed from the principal trunk from which a resplendent ray went forth. God said: 'Here is a light [taken] from my own light; its trunk is prophecy and its branch is the imamate. Prophecy comes from Muḥammad, my servant and messenger, and the imamate comes from ʿAlī, my proof and my friend. Without them I would not have created any of my creation.' … This is why ʿAlī always repeated: 'I come from Muḥammad as one light comes from another.'[60]

For his part, Muḥammad never ceased to reiterate that he had been created with ʿAlī thousands of years before the creation of the world from the same unique light.[61] Other accounts relate that this primordial light, taken from God's light, was the light of the *ahl al-bayt*, the *ahl al-kisāʾ* (the five 'People of the Mantle', that is, Muḥammad, ʿAlī, Fāṭima, al-Ḥasan and al-Ḥusayn; in this case we are told how their names are taken from the names of God), or rather the light of the fourteen Impeccable Ones.[62] Here again the

---

60. Ibn Bābūya, *ʿIlal al-sharāʾiʿ*, p. 174, ch. 139, also pp. 131ff, ch. 111.

61. Ibn Bābūya, *Amālī*, 'majlis' 41, no. 10, p. 236; Yaḥyā b. al-Biṭrīq, *al-ʿUmda fī ʿuyūn ṣiḥāḥ al-akhbār* (n.p., n.d.), pp. 44–45, and *Khaṣāʾiṣ waḥy al-mubīn fī manāqib amīr al-muʾminīn* (n.p., n.d.), pp. 37–38, 109–110; Amir-Moezzi, *Guide divin*, p. 76 (*Divine Guide*, p. 30).

62. Ibn Bābūya, *ʿIlal al-sharāʾiʿ*, pp. 135ff., ch. 116, and *Kamāl al-dīn*, p. 319, ch. 31; al-Khazzāz al-Rāzī, *Kifāyat al-athar* (Tehran, 1305/1888), pp. 110–111; Ibn al-Biṭrīq, *ʿUmda*, p. 120, and *Khaṣāʾiṣ*, p. 145; al-Ḥurr al-ʿĀmilī, *al-Jawāhir al-saniyya fiʾl-aḥādīth al-qudsiyya* (Baghdad, 1964), pp. 233, 278, 304ff.; Amir-Moezzi, *Guide divin*, pp. 77–78 (*Divine Guide*, p. 30). On the light

Impeccable Ones, who together symbolise the cosmic archetypal Imam, form an integral part of God and manifest through their light the ineffable light of God.

We have seen at the same time that the true believer-follower forms part of the imam. The soul and heart (the seat of the soul) of the imam come from the clay that is found above the *ʿIlliyyin*; the body of follower comes from another clay found below the *ʿIlliyyin*; but the body of the imam and the soul-heart of the follower are consubstantial since they are formed of the same clay of *ʿIlliyyin*.[63] Thus, the imam is always ontologically superior to his follower but is present, one might say 'organically', in the heart of the latter, and constitutes its true *bāṭin*. The imam *is* the heart and soul of his initiated followers. He is the hidden content of the inner life and spiritual quest of his true follower. At the same time, he is the exoteric aspect of God, of that which can be revealed of God, the *Deus revelatus*. The imam thus enables his followers to participate in the divine being. In recognising his heart, that is to say his true self, the true follower accedes to a knowledge of the reality of the imam that, as we have seen, is the equivalent of knowledge of the revealed God. Thus, he becomes fully aware of his own divine element. The heart of the true follower of the *walāya* is indeed the Face of God, which is the Imam. No Shiʿi mystic or theosoph has ever failed to interpret in this manner the celebrated *ḥadīth*: 'He who knows himself knows his Lord.'[64]

---

of Muḥammad in early Shiʿism, see U. Rubin, 'Pre-Existence and Light. Aspects of the Concept of *Nūr Muḥammad*', *IOS*, 5 (1975), pp. 62–119; Amir-Moezzi, *Guide divin*, pp. 75–112 (*Divine Guide*, pp. 29–43).

63. Just as the body of the enemy and the soul/heart of his partisans are made of the same substance of *Sijjīn*. Cf. above.

64. There are innumerable examples. We will confine ourselves to only a few particularly representative ones: Ḥaydar Āmulī, *Jāmiʿ al-asrār*, pp. 270, 307ff., 315, 464, and (in the same volume), *Risāla naqd al-nuqūd fī maʿrifat al-wujūd*, p. 675; Abu'l-Ḥasan Sharīf al-Iṣfahānī, *Tafsīr mir'āt al-anwār* (lithograph, n.p. [Iran], n.d.), the introductory section; Mullā Ṣadrā Shīrāzī, *Kitāb al-mashāʿir*, ed. H. Corbin (Tehran and Paris, 1964), pp. 186ff.; *Sharḥ al-Uṣūl min al-Kāfī* (lithograph, Tehran, 1283/1865), pp. 475ff.; Muḥammad Karīm

The participation of the imam and his initiated follower in the divine being is equally illustrated by the symbol that one might call the 'tree of the *walāya*'. In commenting on Q 14:24–25: 'A good tree whose root is firm and whose bough is in heaven; it gives its produce every season by leave of its Lord', a tradition ascribed to the fifth imam states: 'The root of the tree is Muḥammad, its bough is ʿAlī, its branches are the imams, its produce is initiated knowledge, its leaves are the followers.'[65] Other traditions, ascribed to the sixth imam, appear to be more audacious in that they suppress Muḥammad and replace him with God: 'God is the root of the tree, ʿAlī is its bough, the imams of his progeny are its branches, their knowledge is its produce, the followers are its leaves.'[66] The first two categories of people in our tripartite division are thus divine beings. They obey God's order and realise God's work on earth because they participate in the divine being

---

Khān Kermānī, *Ṭarīq al-najāt* (Kermān, 1344 Sh./1966), pp. 103 ff.; Sulṭān ʿAlī Shāh Gonābādī, *Bishārat al-muʾminīn* (Tehran, 1337 Sh./1959), ch. 6, and *Walāyat-nāmah* (2nd edn, Tehran, 1385/1965), pp. 11 ff., 18 ff., 171 ff., 258 ff. See also Corbin, *En Islam iranien*, index, under 'soi', and *Face de Dieu, face de l'homme* (Paris, 1983), pp. 237–310. On the development of this concept among Ismaili authors, see also Corbin's 'Epiphanie divine et naissance spirituelle dans la gnose ismaélienne', *Eranos Jahrbuch*, 23 (1955), esp. pp. 213 ff., 241–242, and his *Trilogie ismaélienne* (Tehran and Paris, 1961), index under 'connaissance de soi'. All our authors insist that knowledge or contemplation of oneself, which provides access to the knowledge and contemplation of the Face of God, which is the Imam, is based on love of the imam (*walāya/maḥabba/ḥubb*). For many of them, putting this concept into practice is explained by the 'technique' of 'vision by the heart' (see note 46 above).

65. Al-Ṣaffār, *Baṣāʾir al-darajāt*, pp. 58–59, section 2, ch. 2, – numerous traditions with variants. In certain traditions, Fāṭima is added as the 'seed' (*ʿunṣur*) of the tree. In other traditions, knowledge is suppressed in favour of the imams who are at the same time both the branches and the produce of the tree etc.

66. Ibid., pp. 59–60. Here again there are variants: the roots are the imams and the boughs are the *walāya* of all of those who seek refuge there; God is the root, ʿAlī is the seed – or even the top (*dharw*), Fāṭima is the bough, the imams are the branches, and the followers are the leaves etc. Cf. also ʿAlī b. Ibrāhīm al-Qummī, *Tafsīr*, vol. 1, pp. 398–399; Furāt al-Kūfī, *Tafsīr*, pp. 219–220; al-ʿAyyāshī, *Tafsīr*, vol. 2, p. 224; Hāshim b. Sulaymān al-Baḥrānī, *al-Burhān fī tafsīr al-Qurʾān* (Tehran, n.d.), vol. 2, p. 311.

thanks to love (*walāya*) and initiated knowledge (*ʿilm*). This is indeed what makes them human. Only the men of God deserve to be called human. The others, the enemies, the forces of violence and ignorance, are nothing but monsters in human form.

It seems useful to end my study with a *ḥadīth* attributed to ʿAlī, a *ḥadīth* that, it seems to me, recapitulates and summarises a good many of the points discussed here. The tradition is presented as a conversation between the first imam and his close disciple Kumayl b. Ziyād al-Nakhaʿī:[67]

> Kumayl! Remember well what I tell you. There are three types of people: the divine spiritual initiator (*ʿālim rabbānī*), the initiated disciple [proceeding] along the way of deliverance (*mutaʿallim ʿalā sabīl najāt*), and the stupid vile beings (*hamaj raʿāʿ*) who obey any appeal and are carried off by every wind. These latter are not illuminated by the light of knowledge (*ʿilm*) and do not lean on any firm pillar. Kumayl! Knowledge has greater value than material things (*māl*). It is knowledge that watches over you just as you watch over your material possessions. Wealth diminishes as it is spent, but knowledge increases as it is spent... The treasure of material goods perishes while the sages live lives that will last as long time shall endure (*hum aḥyāʾ waʾl-ʿulamāʾ bāqūn mā baqiyaʾl-dahr*). Their physical bodies disappear, but others, who resemble them in their hearts, take their place (*aʿyānuhum mafqūda wa amthāluhum fiʾl-qulūb mawjūda*).

And the imam, gesturing with his hand towards his chest, continued:

> There is superabundant knowledge here. If only I found men [strong enough] to carry it! Certainly, on occasion I meet someone who is perceptive enough, but I cannot confide in him because he

67. I rely here on the excellent translation by H. Corbin (*En Islam iranien*, vol. 1, pp. 113–114), which I have modified in places in order to remain closer to the original text and to the technical lexicon of early Shiʿism. Other differences from Corbin's text arise from the fact that he based his translation on the version in the *Nahj al-balāgha* (compiled by al-Sharīf al-Raḍī, d. 406/1016), while I relied on the version transmitted by Ibn Bābūya (d. 381/991–992), which seems to be older by at least several decades (for the sources, see the following note).

turns religion into a means of serving worldly interests, utilising the proofs of God [*ḥujaj Allāh*, that is the imams] and the favours of God to dominate the weak. On occasion I meet someone who obeys the sages but who, lacking an interior vision (*baṣīra*), cannot perceive the immensity of the knowledge and falls into doubt at the first difficulty that presents itself. Thus, neither the one nor the other [are worthy either of my trust or my knowledge] .... Must initiated knowledge thus die with the death of its carriers? No! The world will never lack a Qāʾim who, speaking for God, guarantees the safeguarding of His testimony, whether he is manifest and unveiled, or hidden. It is thanks to men such as these that the divine testimony and [the understanding of] its meaning have not been destroyed. How many are they? Where are they? Their number is small, but their rank is lofty. It is through them that God safeguards His witnesses until they transmit it to their peers and implant the seed in the heart of those who resemble them. For them, knowledge appears all at once (*hajama bihim al-ʿilm*) to show them the true nature of things. They set in motion the joy of certitude and find easy what the indulgent consider to be arduous. They are familiar with matters that frighten the ignorant. They go through this world in bodies of which the souls [that animate them] are suspended in the highest abode (*muʿallaqa biʾl-maḥall al-aʿlā*). Kumayl! They are the vicegerents of God, those who summon to His religion. Oh! How I yearn to see them![68]

---

68. Cf. Ibn Bābūya, *Kamāl al-dīn*, p. 290, ch. 26, no. 2, and *Khiṣāl*, pp. 186–187; cf. also al-Yaʿqūbī, *Taʾrīkh*, ed. M. T. Houtsma (Leiden, 1883; rpr. Qumm, 1414/1994), vol. 2, pp. 205–206; *Nahj al-balāgha*, pp. 1155–1158; also al-Majlisī, *Biḥār al-anwār* (Tehran and Qumm, 1376–1392/1956–1972), vol. 1, p. 186. The tripartite division of humanity is also found in *The Arabic Works of Jābir b. Ḥayyan*, ed. Holmyard, '*Kitāb al-bayān*', pp. 7 ff.; Kraus (ed.), *Mukhtār rasāʾil Jābir ibn Ḥayyān*, '*Kitāb al-baḥth*', pp. 502–503 (a slightly different version of the conversation between ʿAlī and Kumayl). See also P. Lory, *Alchimie et mystique en terre d'islam* (Paris and Lagrasse, 1989), pp. 51, 107. For other sources on this '*ḥadīth* Kumayl' see H. Modarressi, *Tradition and Survival: A Bibliographical Survey of Early Shiʿite Literature* (Oxford, 2003), pp. 77–78.

Part III: Hermeneutic and Spiritual Practice

9

'The Warrior of *Ta'wīl*': A Poem about 'Alī by Mollā Ṣadrā*

Of the works written by Mollā Ṣadrā (b. 979/1571 or 980/1572 in Shiraz, d. 1050/1640 in Basra), those in Persian, in particular his poetry, have attracted little scholarly attention. In 1961, having published the renowned philosopher's treatise, *Seh aṣl*, Seyyed Hossein Nasr published *Montakhab-e mathnavī* and, for the first time, eight *robā'īs*.[1] More recently, in 1997, Moḥammad Khājavī, the indefatigable editor and Persian translator of Mollā Ṣadrā's work, edited his *Dīvān*, containing, apart from the texts already published by S. H. Nasr, some forty other poems.[2] A few

* Given the Iranian context of this chapter as well as the language of the text analysed herein, the transliteration is, generally speaking, given in the Persian pronounciation.

1. Ṣadr al-Dīn Shīrāzī (Mullā Ṣadrā), *Seh aṣl*, ed. S. Ḥ. Naṣr (Tehran, 1340 Sh./1380/1961); *Montakhab-e mathnavī*, pp. 131–153 (based on two manuscripts: MS 849 from the Meshkāt collection of the Central Library, Tehran University, and the personal manuscript belonging to Mr Lājevardī of Qomm); *robā'īyāt*, pp. 159–160 (based on the manuscript signed by Mollā Ṣadrā, *Sharḥ al-hidāya*, Meshkāt collection, MS 254, as well as his *Rasā'il*, and *Riyāḍ al-'ārifīn* of Hedāyat, *Shams al-tawārīkh* of Golpāyagānī and *al-Dharī'a* of Āghā Bozorg Ṭihrānī.

2. Mollā Ṣadrā, *Majmū'e-ye ash'ār*, ed. M. Khājavī (Tehran, 1376 Sh./1418/1997); *Montakhab-e mathnavī*, pp. 79–100, *robā'īyāt*, p. 78; the other poems, pp. 3–78, are edited based on two manuscripts: MS 2992 of the Majles in Tehran and MS 322-D held by the Faculty of Theology at the Central Library, Tehran University. Author of *Lawāmi' al-'ārifīn fī aḥwāl Ṣadr al-muta'allihīn* (Tehran, 1366 Sh./1987), M. Khājavī, during the last two decades in Tehran,

months before the appearance of Khājavī's edition, the Library of Ayatollah Marʿashī Najafī published yet another collection of the philosopher's poetry, edited by the religious scholar Moṣṭafā Fayḍī.[3] This edition, prepared from a single manuscript, often gives a different 'reading' from the other two and contains a number of additional verses, unknown to the editions by Nasr and Khājavī. However, given that almost nothing is said about the manuscript used, the authenticity of these variants remains to be proved.[4] Nevertheless, with these three editions, we now undoubtedly have at our disposal almost all of the poetry by Mollā Ṣadrā, to which one ought to consider adding the verses scattered throughout his major philosophical texts.[5]

Mollā Ṣadrā's poetry often illustrates some of his theological and philosophical preoccupations and, perhaps even more so, his eschatological thought.[6] Though of uneven literary qual-

---

edited and translated into Persian some major works by Mollā Ṣadrā such as *Mafātīḥ al-ghayb, Asrār al-āyāt,* numerous *Tafsīr*s and *Sharḥ al-Uṣūl min al-Kāfī.*

3. *Mathnavī-ye Mollā Ṣadrā*, ed. Moṣṭafā Fayḍī (Qumm, 1376 Sh./1417/1997), *Mathnavī*, pp. 102–205.

4. In his (far too) brief preface, Dr Sayyid Maḥmūd Marʿashī, currently Director of the Marʿashī Library, briefly states that the manuscript comes from what has survived of the private collection of Muḥsin Fayḍ Kāshānī (d. 1091/1680), Mollā Ṣadrā's disciple and son-in-law, adding that it is undoubtedly a signed manuscript (ibid., pp. 3–4). In addition to a rather poor reproduction of an unnumbered folio (ibid., p. 5), this is the most that we learn about the manuscript. In the editor's introduction of almost one hundred pages regarding the philosopher, his milieu and his work, not a word is said about this manuscript either (ibid., pp. 7–102).

5. This, for example, is what M. Khājavī (*Majmūʿe-ye ashʿār*, pp. 77–78) does with the seven verses in Persian commenting on the Verse of Light; Mollā Ṣadrā, *Tafsīr āyat al-nūr*, ed. M. Khājavī (Tehran, 1362 Sh./1403/1993), p. 182 (Arabic text), p. 99 (Persian trans.); there are other passages as well, for example following his commentary on Q 32:4 (Mollā Ṣadrā, *Tafsīr* [lithograph, Tehran, n.d.], p. 531) and throughout his *Seh aṣl.*

6. On his eschatological beliefs, now consult C. Jambet, *Se rendre immortel*, also containing *Traité de la résurrection* (French translation of *Risālat al-ḥashr*) by *Mollā Ṣadrā Shīrāzī* (Paris, 2000); and C. Jambet, *L'acte d'être. La philosophie de la révélation chez Mollâ Sadrâ* (Paris, 2002).

ity, the poetry is nonetheless infused from beginning to end in a mystical spirit that creates a heightened effect. Although none of the poems is dated, the editors agree that, like any Iranian literary figure worthy to be so called, Mollā Ṣadrā would have composed these poems during the course of his adult life, all the while revising his earlier versions to modify or complete them in accordance with his intellectual and spiritual development.[7]

The relationship between *Montakhab-e mathnavī* (literary 'extracts', 'fragments' or 'selected pieces' from the *mathnavī*) and poems from the *majmūʿe* (collection), which also constitute a *mathnavī*, pose certain problems that at present remain unresolved. Both are presented in the manuscripts as independent collections;[8] however, many verses from the *Montakhab* reappear in the *majmūʿe*, but at times with considerable variation, whereas other verses do not appear at all. Do these collections stem from two entirely different sources hitherto unknown? If the poem is an independent work composed later than the *majmūʿe*, as M. Khājavī believes,[9] could the term *montakhab* have been a scribal addition? Does it consist of one and the same *mathnavī* or a collection of more or less independent poems dedicated to various themes but set to the same *ramal musaddas maḥdhūf* metre?[10]

The poem about ʿAlī is the fourth in the *majmūʿe*, and is entitled (by the author or the scribe?) 'In praise of the Prince of Believers

---

7. *Seh aṣl*, pp. xxxiii–xxxiv; *Majmūʿe-ye ashʿār*, pp. xii–xv. One might have concluded that the additional verses in the Fayḍī edition, *Mathnavī-ye Mollā Ṣadrā* were inserted later by the philosopher, but as we will further see below, the sheer mediocrity of some of these verses seems to disqualify this hypothesis.

8. *Majmūʿe-ye ashʿār*, p. xii. Only the manuscript used by M. Fayḍī seems to present them as one whole collection.

9. Ibid., p. xiii.

10. All the poems in the *majmūʿe* are in the *ramal musaddas maḥdhūf* metre (*fāʿilātun fāʿilātun fāʿilun*), the standard metre for Persian mystical *mathnavīs*. Some poems unfold in a logical progression and clearly form a coherent whole (for example, the last ten or eleven poems in the Collection are devoted to eschatology); others, touching upon religious, philosophical, mystical themes etc., often appear as independent pieces, separate from each other.

and the *ahl al-bayt* (of the Prophet) (*dar manqabat-e haḍrat-e amīr al-moʾmenīn va ahl-e beyt*)':[11]

1) *Shahsavār-e lā fatā shīr-e vaghā / az khodā vo moṣṭafā bar vey thanā*
Horseman of *lā fatā*, Lion of the battle / He whom God and the Pure Chosen One [Muḥammad] have praised

Lā fatā: this is an allusion to the tradition *lā sayfa illā Dhu'l-faqār wa lā fatā illā ʿAlī*, 'No sword save Dhu'l-Faqār, no chivalrous hero save ʿAlī.'[12] According to Twelver Shiʿi exegesis, God's praise of ʿAlī features in the very text of the Qurʾān. Mollā Ṣadrā returns to this in a later section of the poem.

2) *Sāqī-ye Kowthar valī-ye kardegār / dāde tīghash dīn-e Aḥmad rā qarār*
Cupbearer of Kowthar [a river in paradise], friend of God / He whose sword perfected the religion of Aḥmad [i.e. Muḥammad].

11. *Majmūʿe-ya ashʿār*, pp. 7–11; *Mathnavī-ye Mollā Ṣadrā*, pp. 107–110 (title: 'In praise of the Prince of Believers'; as we will see later, in this edition, the last thirteen verses of the poem are presented separately under the title, 'In praise of the *ahl-e beyt*'). For a discussion of the translation of *ahl al-bayt* (*ahl-e beyt* in Persian) see Chapter 1, this volume, notes 36 and 55 as well as the relevant texts.

12. Or *Lā fatā illā ʿAlī lā sayfa illā Dhu'l-faqār*; see for example Furāt al-Kūfī, *Tafsīr*, ed. M. al-Kāẓim (Tehran, 1410/1990), p. 95; Ibn Bābūya al-Ṣadūq, *Maʿānī'l-akhbār*, ed. ʿA. A. Ghaffārī (Tehran, 1379/1959), pp. 63 and 119; Furāt al-Kūfī, *al-Khiṣāl*, ed. ʿA. A. Ghaffārī (Qumm, 1403/1983), pp. 550 and 557 and *ʿIlal al-sharāʾiʿ* (Najaf, 1385/1966), pp. 7 and 160. On Dhu'l-faqār, literally 'double-edged', according to tradition a sword borne by the Angel Gabriel and given to Muḥammad, then handed by the latter to ʿAlī, see for example, al-Ṣaffār al-Qummī, *Baṣāʾir al-darajāt*, ed. M. Kūchebāghī (2nd edn, Tabriz, n.d. [ca. 1960]), section 4, ch. 4; al-Kulaynī, *al-Uṣūl min al-Kāfī*, ed. J. Muṣṭafāwī, 4 vols (Tehran, n.d.), 'Kitāb al-ḥujja', 'Bāb mā ʿinda'l-aʾimma min silāḥ rasūlī'llāh', vol. 1, pp. 337ff.; Ibn Bābūya al-Ṣadūq, *Amālī (al-Majālis)*, ed. Ṭabāṭabāʾī Yazdī (rpr. Tehran, 1404/1984), 'majlis' 17, p. 71 and 'majlis' 48, p. 289. About the pronounciation *faqār* and not the more conventional *fiqār*, see Abū ʿUbayd al-Bakrī, *Muʿjam mā staʿjam*, ed. M. al-Saqqā (Cairo, 1364–1371/1945–1951), vol. 1, p. 156 and vol. 3, p. 1026.

From the beginning of the poem, two of 'Alī's qualities are strongly emphasised: the fact that he is the friend of God, the *wālī*, and the warrior for the faith par excellence. As we shall see in what follows, for Mollā Ṣadrā these two qualities seem inseparable and together constitute the basis for a spiritual interpretation (*ta'wīl*) that he provides for the figure of 'Alī.[13]

3) *Az zabān-e tīgh zang-e kofr o jowr / ḥak namūd az ṣafḥe-ye 'ālam be-fowr*
With the language of his sword, the rust of infidelity and oppression / were instantly wiped off the face of the earth.

(See verse 16 below.)[14]

4) *Az vojūdash 'aql īmān yāfte / az jabīnash nūr reḍvān yāfte*
Through his existence reason discovered faith / Due to his forehead paradise acquired light. [15]

Further on, in the twenty-second poem of the *majmū'e* in Khājavī's edition, Mollā Ṣadrā makes a distinction between angelic reason (*'aql-e malakī*), illuminated by faith, and worldly reason, severed from On High, dark, sly and bestial, that of the misguided ones

13. Regarding 'Alī as he who serves the believers (i.e. the Shi'is) on the Day of Resurrection – *sāqī'l-mu'minīn fi'l-qiyāma* – or who serves the inhabitants of paradise with water from the river of Kawthar – *sāqī min nahr al-kawthar* – see al-Majlisī, *Biḥār al-anwār*, ed. based on the edition by Kumpānī (Tehran and Qumm, 1376–1392/1956–1972), 90 tomes in 110 vols, vol. 17, p. 324, vol. 26, p. 264, vol. 39, p. 61. For the enigmatic Qur'ānic term *kawthar*, see Q 108:1.

14. *Mathnavī-ye Mollā Ṣadrā* here gives *az zabān o tīgh* (by his language *and* his sword), which does not fit the context. Moreover, this Fayḍī edition includes a fourth verse which does not appear in the edition by Khājavī:

ennamā vo hal atā dar sha'n-e ū / qā'ed-e īmān-e mā īmān-e ū

'*Innamā* and *hal atā* are (revealed) regarding him / the commander of our faith is his faith.' Regarding *innamā* and *hal atā*, two Qur'ānic expressions, see here below verses 29 and 30 respectively as well as the explanations and relevant notes.

15. This fourth verse in the Khājavī edition is the eleventh in the edition by Fayḍī.

(*ʿaql-e gomgashtegān*).[16] ʿAlī, or the divine Allegiance (*walāya*) and the imamate which he represents, are here identified as the light of the faith that transforms human reason into angelic reason.[17]

5) *ʿAql-e peyghambar cho qorʾān āmadī / nafs-e vey mānand-e forqān āmadī*[18]
Like the Qurʾān, he (ʿAlī) manifests the intelligence of the Prophet / His individuality serves to distinguish between good and evil.

Furqān (pronounced *forqān* in Persian) stands for that which distinguishes good from evil, the licit and illicit, whence the code or collection of the Sacred law, more precisely the Qurʾān. This verse, as well as the six subsequent verses, sets up the relationship between imamology and prophetology, between the *wālī*, messenger of the esoteric dimension of religion and the *nabī*, messenger of the exoteric dimension (yet in a concealed fashion both *walāya* and *nubuwwa* culminate in the same figure of the *nabī*). *Walāya/imāma* is the locus of the secret of *nubuwwa*, revealing its essence.[19] Clearly, both these functions are symbolised respectively by ʿAlī al-Murtaḍā and Muḥammad al-Muṣṭafā.

---

16. *Majmūʿe-ye ashʿār*, pp. 47–48.

17. Regarding *ʿaql* and its different meanings (reason, intelligence, hiero-intelligence etc.) in early Imami literature, see M. A. Amir-Moezzi, *Guide divin*, pp. 15–33 (*Divine Guide*, pp. 6–13); see also D. S. Crow, 'The Role of *al-ʿAql* in Early Islamic Wisdom, with Reference to Imam Jaʿfar al-Ṣādiq' (PhD Thesis, McGill University, 1996).

18. In the Fayḍī edition, the second hemistiche reads: *vīn khalīfe hamcho forqān āmadī*; 'and this Caliph's (i.e. ʿAlī's) purpose to distinguish good from evil.'

19 H. Corbin, *En Islam iranien* (Paris, 1971–1972), vol. 1, Book 1, especially ch. 6; H. Corbin, *Histoire de la philosophie islamique* (Paris, 1986), section II-A, esp. pp. 69–85; see also Chapter 5 *in fine* and esp. Chapter 7, this volume. For Mollā Ṣadrā's position on the relationship between prophethood and *walāya*, the reader should consult his *Mafātīḥ al-ghayb*, ed. M. Khājavī (Tehran, 1363 Sh./1994), 'Miftāḥ' 14, '*Inna li'l-nubuwwa bāṭinan wa huwa'l-walāya*', pp. 483–495; Persian trans. M. Khājavī (Tehran, 1363 Sh./ 1994), pp. 810–825.

6) *Farq joz ejmāl o joz tafṣīl nīst / īn do hamrah qābel-e tabdīl nīst*
The difference is only between the concise and the explained / these two associates are not reducible

7) *Har che dar ejmāl bod bā moṣṭafā / gasht ẓāher az vojūd-e mortaḍā*
Whatever was implicit in Muṣṭafā/became manifest by the existence of Murtaḍā.[20]

The imam's teaching essentially consists of rendering the prophet's message explicit; this message is distilled in the Revelation. We are reminded of this by a number of traditions according to which the *ḥadīths*, that is mainly the imam's teachings, explain in detail (*tafṣīl*) that which the Qur'ān presents in a condensed form (*mujmal*).[21]

8) *Maʿnī-ye al-yawma akmalt īn bovad / gar to hastī mard-e dīn ey moʿtamad*
This is the deeper meaning of '*al-yawma akmaltu*' / (Know) O trusted friend, if you are a man of faith.

'*Al-yawma akmaltu lakum dīnakum wa atmamtu ʿalaykum niʿmatī*'
'This day have I perfected your religion for you, fulfilled My favour upon you'
According to the most classical and most frequently reiterated Imami exegesis, this part of the third verse of Sura 5, *al-mā'ida*, concerns the divine revelation of ʿAlī's *walāya* to Muḥammad.

---

20. The Fayḍī edition here includes an additional verse, poetically rather mediocre and philosophically quite confusing: '*ānchenān ke ʿaql-e kol bā nafs-e kol* (are we meant to read *kel* in order to rhyme with *monfaṣel*?] /*hast ān yek mojmal o īn monfaṣel* (should this be read *monfaṣol* to rhyme with *kol*?); 'Just like the Universal Intellect vis-à-vis the Universal Soul/ the first is condensed, the second is differentiated.'

21 E.g. al-Ṣaffār, *Baṣā'ir al-darajāt*, pp. 11–12; al-Kulaynī, *al-Uṣūl min al-Kāfī*, vol. 1, pp. 77ff. M. M. Bar-Asher is correct in presenting this notion as one of the methodological bases for Imami exegesis; see his *Scripture and Exegesis in Early Imāmī Shiism* (Leiden and Jerusalem, 1999), pp. 92–93.

This verse establishes *walāya*, loyal friendship towards the imams, as a religious duty (*farīḍa*) of the same order as canonical prayer and the pilgrimage to Mecca.[22] For Mollā Ṣadrā, the imam's teachings, in this instance those of ʿAlī consisting of the explanation of the prophet's message, constitute the essential content of *walāya*. It is by this teaching that God has perfected the religion.[23]

---

22. Furāt al-Kūfī, *Tafsīr*, pp. 117–120; ʿAlī b. Ibrāhīm al-Qummī, *Tafsīr*, ed. Ṭ. al-Mūsawī al-Jazāʾirī (rpr. Beirut, 1411/1991), vol. 1, p. 190; Abu'l-Naḍr al-ʿAyyāshī, *Tafsīr*, ed. H. Rasūlī Maḥallātī (Qumm, 1380/1960), vol. 1, pp. 292–293 (according to *ḥadīth* no. 21 reported by al-ʿAyyāshī, the revelation of the Qurʾān by the Angel Gabriel on a Friday and the day of ʿArafāt, originally contained the expression, 'by the divine Friendship of ʿAlī son of Abū Ṭālib': '*al-yawma akmaltu lakum dīnakum* bi-walāyat ʿAlī b. Abī Ṭālib *wa atmamtu ʿalaykum niʿmatī* ...' This obviously has a bearing upon early Shiʿi belief, according to which the ʿUthmānic recension is a censured and falsified version of the original revelation; on this, see E. Kohlberg, 'Some Notes on the Imamite Attitude to the Qurʾān', in S. M. Stern et al. (eds), *Islamic Philosophy and the Classical Tradition: Essays Presented to Richard Walzer* (Oxford, 1972), pp. 209–224; T. Lawson, 'Notes for the Study of the Shīʿī Qurʾān', *Journal of Semitic Studies*, 36 (1991), pp. 279–295; M. A. Amir-Moezzi, *Guide divin*, pp. 200–227 (*Divine Guide*, pp. 79–91); beginning of Chapter 7, this volume; M. M. Bar-Asher, 'Variant Readings and Additions of the Imāmī-Shīʿa to the Qurʾān', *IOS*, 13 (1993), pp. 39–74; R. Brunner, *Die Schia und die Korʾanfälschung* (Würzburg, 2001). For another interpretation of matters, see H. Modarressi, 'Early Debates on the Integrity of the Qurʾān', *Studia Islamica*, 77 (1993), pp. 5–39. On the different Shiʿi meanings of the term *walāya*, see esp. Chapter 7 in this volume.

23. The Fayḍī edition here contains fifteen additional verses:
Sāqī-ye Kowthar shah-e rūz-e jazā / ebn-e ʿamm-e Moṣṭafā serr-e khodā; 'The cupbearer of Kawthar [see verse 2 above], Lord of the Day of Retribution [allusion to ʿAlī's eschatological role, he is often called *qasīm al-janna wa'l-nār* – he who assigns (people) either to the Garden (of paradise) or to the Fire (of hell)]'; see e.g. Furāt, *Tafsīr*, p. 178; al-ʿAyyāshī, *Tafsīr*, vol. 2, pp. 17–18) / the first cousin of Moṣṭafā, God'. While eleventh in the Fayḍī edition, the following verse is fourth in the Khājavī edition.

Man gedāyam āmade dar kū-ye to / mīzanam shay'un lelāhi az [*sic* – the metre is uneven] *rū-ye to*; 'I am a beggar that wandered into your alley [O ʿAlī] / beseeching you to grant me the vision of your face [lit.: saying *shay'un li llāh* — something to (please) God (the beggar's prayer) – regarding your face]'.

Gar to khānī ommat-e khīsham yekī [sic; very clumsily expressed] / *jān daham bar yād-e rūyat bī shakī*; 'If you call me one of your faithful [lit. community] I will offer my life without hesitation simply at the thought of your face.'

9) *Ūst bābā-ye nofūs-e owliyā / hamchonān ke moṣṭafā bā anbiyā*
He ('Alī) is Father of the Friends (of God) / As (Muḥammad) Muṣṭafā is for the prophets;

10) *Owliyā yek yek cho farzandān-e ū / jīre khārān-e navāl-e khān-e ū*
The Friends his children are one by one/ Nourished by portions placed upon his tablecloth.

Āftābī var bekhānī dharre-am / tāj-e raf'at bogzarad az sedre-am: 'You are the sun, if you call me your atom / the crown of my glory will surpass the celestial Tree [allusion to *Sidrat al-muntahā* in Q 53:14–16].'

Man kī am gomgashte-yī dar rāh-e to / khāk būs o bande-ye dargāh-e to; 'Who am I? One astray on your path (O 'Alī) / kissing the dust and a servant at your threshold.'

Gar to khānī ommat-e'āsī-ye khad [= *khod] / man fedā sāzam del o jān tā abad*; 'If you call [me] a companion [lit. community] though a sinner / I would eternally sacrifice heart and soul.'

Ommat-e 'āṣī ṭalab kār-e to ast / gar bad ast ar nīk dar kār-e to ast; 'Your sinning companion thirsts for you / good or evil, he is in search of you.'

Ān bas-am kaz bandegān bāsham torā / bande che kāsh az sagān bāsham torā; 'I am content to be among your servants / what am I saying? I am more than happy to be your dog.'

Har ke rā chon to shahanshāhī bovad / farq-e ū az haft gardūn bogzarad: 'He who recognises you as a great king / will hold his head higher than the seven heavens.'

Gīsovānat hast ān ḥablo'l-matīn / ke forū hesht-ast az charkh-e barīn; 'Your locks are that secure rope [Q 3:103 and 112] / which fell from the most high heavens.'

Tā biyāvīzand dar vey ommatān / az belā-ye īn jahān yāband amān; 'In order that the companions hold on to them / to be saved from the trials of this world.'

Ey shafi' al-modhnibīn ey shāh-e dīn / chand bāsham īn chonīn zār o ḥazīn; 'O thou, intercessor for sinners [on *shafā'a* of the imams, now consult M. M. Bar-Asher, *Scripture and Exegesis*, pp. 180ff.], Sovereign of faith / how long must I remain so sad and forsaken?'

Rū-ye to hast āyatī az kardegār / mū-ye to bahr-e najāt-e jormkār; 'Your face is a sign of God / tresses of your hair, salvation for the blameworthy [regarding the pair 'face and hair', see verse 35 below].

Rū-ye to bāshad behesht o mū-ye to / gashte āvīzān be mā az rū-ye to; 'Your face is paradise and tresses of your hair / tumble over your face to reach us.'

Hamcho lafẓ o ma'nī-ye qor'ān be mā / gashte nāzel bahr-e ḥājat az samā; just as the Qur'ān, in letter and content / fell from heaven to fulfill our needs.'

Muḥammad, in his essential reality called 'the Light of Muḥammad', constitutes the origin and substance of prophethood (*nubuwwa*); just as the Light of ʿAlī is the very origin and substance of Divine friendship (*walāya*).[24]

11) *Ānke pāyash dūsh-e peyghambar bodī / ḥabbadhā shākhī ke īnash bar bodī*
He who placed his foot upon the Prophet's shoulder / How wonderful a tree that bears such fruit.[25]

12) *Ānke nafsash būd dast-e kardegār / īn yadollā rā ke dānad kard khār?*
He who was the hand of God in person / this Hand, who is able to lower it?

As the locus of manifestation and instrument for the will of God, the imam is often described as 'an organ' of God: eye, tongue, hand, ear, face, heart, and so on.[26] The last hemistich alluding to ʿAlī's adversaries serves as an introduction to the next fifteen verses where Mollā Ṣadrā allows himself a true spiritual interpretation of the warrior aspect of the first imam:

---

24. On Muḥammad's metaphysical relationship with the earlier prophets and ʿAlī's with the previous imams/*awliyā* respectively, see U. Rubin, 'Pre-existence and Light. Aspects of the Concept of Nūr Muḥammad', *IOS*, 5 (1975), pp. 62–112 and 'Prophets and Progenitors in the Early Shīʿa Tradition', *Jerusalem Studies in Arabic and Islam*, 1 (1979), pp. 41–65; M. A. Amir-Moezzi, *Guide divin*, sections II-1 and II-2, pp. 73–112 (*Divine Guide,* ch. 2, parts 1 and 2, pp. 29–79, see also Chapter 4, this volume); M. A. Amir-Moezzi, 'Cosmology and Cosmogony in Twelver Shīʿism', *EIr*, vol. 6, pp. 317–322, esp. pp. 319–321.

25. An allusion either to the event of Ghadīr Khumm or to when, according to some versions, Muḥammad bore ʿAlī on his shoulders, see L. Veccia Vaglieri, 'Ghadīr Khumm', *EI2*, M. Dakake and A. Kazemi Moussavi in *EIr*, or even perhaps to the episode in which, in order to remove the idols from the roof of the Kaʿba, Muḥammad lifted ʿAlī on to his shoulders (this episode is known as *isʿādu'l-nabī ʿAliyyan ʿalā saṭḥi'l-Kaʿba*); see al-Muwaffaq b. Aḥmad al-Khwārazmī, *al-Manāqib*, ed. M. B. al-Maḥmūdī (Qumm, 1411/1991), ch. 11; al-Majlisī, *Biḥār al-anwār*, vol. 35, p. 49 and vol. 38, p. 82. For Mollā Ṣadrā, this scene evokes the image of a tree (Muḥammad), bearing fruit (ʿAlī) on its branch (*shākh* meaning both 'tree' and 'branch').

26. Chapter 3, this volume, esp. note 27 for earliest sources.

13) *Gar kasī rā būdī az qadrash khabar / key chonān bā vey namū dandī ḍarar?*
He who had known his true value / How could he have done him harm?

14) *Kofr-hā-ye mokhtafī dar jāneshān / būd dā'em rahzan-e īmān-e shān*
Infidelity hidden in their depths [i.e. 'Alī's adversaries] / constantly ravaged their faith

15) *Dhāt-e ū chon būd tanzīl-e kalām / kard az shamshīr ta'vīl-e kalām*[27]
Just as his ['Alī's] essential reality formed the letter of revelation / So he made of his sword its spiritual interpretation

16) *Az zabān-e tīgh tafsīr-e sokhan / mīnamūd az bahr-e aṣḥāb-badan*[28]
Commentary on the Word by the language of the sword / He made it thus for the people of exteriority

Dhāt (lit. the essence of 'Alī, which I translate as 'essential reality') is the *walāya* that is presented by many traditions as the ultimate goal of the Revelation, the message hidden beneath the letter of the Qur'ān.[29] Those who oppose 'Alī are thus against what the Qur'ān contains as its most profound message. They are the adversaries of *walāya*, the esoteric dimension of *nubuwwa*. It is thus up to 'Alī to fight them in order that the Revelation does not become letter without spirit; which of course evokes the famous tradition attributed to the Prophet:

27. The Fayḍī edition here reads *ta'bīr* and *tafsīr* instead of *tanzīl* and *ta'vīl* as in the Khājavī edition.

28. Fayḍī edition: *az zabān-e tīgh tafsīr-e kalām / mīnamūd o dād dīn rā enteẓām*: translation of the second hemistich: 'He made and thus consolidated the faith.'

29. On this notion and early sources regarding it, refer to Chapters 5 and esp. 7, this volume.

> Among you there is someone who fights for the spiritual interpretation of the Qur'ān, just as I myself fought for its Revelation, and this person is ʿAlī b. Abī Ṭālib.[30]

ʿAlī's sword is thus depicted as the instrument of the inner expression or meaning of the Qur'ān, a symbol of sacred, as opposed to profane, violence that consists of emptying Islam of its essential content. It is interesting to note that the expression *aṣḥāb-e badan* (lit. 'people of the body', which I translate as 'people of the exterior') is employed in *Seh aṣl* as such, or in the form of *tan parast* (lit. 'body worshipper') to designate the official religious authorities of the period whom the philosopher justifiably denounces as

---

30. *'Inna fīkum man yuqātilu 'alā ta'wīli'l-Qur'ān kamā qātaltu 'alā tanzīlihi wa huwa 'Alī ibn Abī Ṭālib'*, in al-ʿAyyāshī, *Tafsīr*, vol. 1, p. 15; al-Khazzāz al-Rāzī, *Kifāyat al-athar* (Qumm, 1401/1980), pp. 76, 88, 117, 135 (on p. 66, in a Prophetic tradition, it is the Qā'im who is portrayed as 'the warrior of spiritual hermeneutics'); al-Majlisī, *Biḥār*, vol. 19, pp. 25–26; Hāshim b. Sulaymān al-Baḥrānī, *al-Burhān fī tafsīr al-Qur'ān*, 5 vols (Tehran, n.d.), vol. 1, p. 17. Cf. also the Prophetic tradition: 'I am the Lord of the revealed letter (of the Qur'ān) and ʿAlī is the Lord of spiritual hermeneutics (of the Qur'ān) – *'anā ṣāḥib al-tanzīl wa 'Alī ṣāḥib al-ta'wīl'* – see e.g. the Ismaili author Ḥamīd al-Dīn al-Kirmānī, *Majmūʿat al-rasā'il*, ed. M. Ghālib (Beirut, 1983), p. 156. See also Jaʿfar b. Manṣūr al-Yaman, *Kitāb al-Kashf*, ed. R. Strothmann (Bombay et al., 1952), pp. 54f., 66ff., 119f., 157ff.; al-Mu'ayyad fi'l-Dīn al-Shīrāzī, *al-Majālis al-Mu'ayyadiyya*, ed. M. Ghālib (Beirut, 1974–1984), vol. 1, pp. 219ff. D. Gimaret translates *ta'wīl* as 'spirit' and *tanzīl* as 'letter', of the Qur'ān; see Shahrastānī, *Livre des religions et des sectes*, Fr. trans. by D. Gimaret and G. Monnot (Paris and Louvain, 1986), vol. 1, p. 543. For other sources, see M. M. Bar-Asher, *Scripture and Exegesis*, p. 88, n. 1. See also the words attributed to ʿAmmār b. Yāsir, an old Companion of ʿAlī, spoken during the Battle of Ṣiffīn: 'By He who holds my life in His hand, just as before we fought our enemies for [the letter of] the Revelation, today we are fighting them for its spirit' (al-Masʿūdī, *Murūj al-dhahab*, ed. Pellat [Beirut, 1965–1979, § 1676]). See also Sulaym b. Qays (Ps.), *Kitāb*, ed. Anṣārī, vol. 2, p. 602, no. 6 and vol. 2, p. 770, no. 25; al-Ṭabrisī, Abū Manṣūr Aḥmad b. ʿAlī, *al-Iḥtijāj*, ed. M. B. al-Mūsawī al-Kharsān (Najaf, 1386/1966), vol. 1, p. 229; Shādhān b. Jabra'īl, *al-Faḍā'il*, p. 145; al-Rāzī, Muḥammad b. al-Ḥusayn, *Nuzhat al-karām*, ed. M. Shīrwānī (Tehran, 1402/1981), p. 556. The idea conveyed in these traditions constitutes the centre of gravity in Mollā Ṣadrā's poem.

'people of appearances' or 'of the exoteric' (*ahl-e ẓāher*), those that seek only to satisfy their bodies and personal ambitions.[31]

17) *Qāriyān būdand ahl-e Nahravān / līk kajrow dar nahān o dar ʿayān*
The people of Nahrawān were readers of the Qur'ān / Yet misguided secretly and openly.

18) *Dar darūn-shān naqsh hā-ye por ghalaṭ / maʿnī-ye Qor'ān nabāshad zīn namaṭ*
Within them mistaken impressions / That had no bearing upon the meaning of the Qur'ān.

19) *Ān ghalaṭ-hā ḥak namūd az tīgh-e tīz / kard az ta'vīl-e Qor'ān rastkhīz*
He (ʿAlī) wiped away these errors by the blade of his sword / From the hermeneutics of the Qur'ān he makes a resurrection.

The 'people of Nahrawān' obviously represent ʿAlī's adversaries, just as 'readers of the Qur'ān' stand for the 'misguided' religious figures with false ideas about the true 'meaning of the Qur'ān'. ʿAlī, symbol of *walāya*, is himself the true meaning; his adversaries are adversaries of meaning and therefore, according to the poet, those who are only aware of the letter and its reading, hence the expression, 'readers of the Qur'ān' (*qāriyān*).

Returning to the theme recalled above, and in an even more audacious manner, Mollā Ṣadrā repeats that ʿAlī's sword is not only an instrument for the *ta'wīl* (spiritual hermeneutics) of the Qur'ān, but it is also by doing away with people of exteriority, and by extension the letter they represent, that this *ta'wīl* in turn becomes an instrument for resurrecting meaning.

31. *Seh aṣl*, e.g. pp. 10 and 66. Generally speaking, this text by Mollā Ṣadrā is written against a certain type of *fuqahā'*, those that gravitated towards the circles of power at the Safawid court and/or those who denied the spiritual hermeneutics of the Scriptures; the same is true for another one of his books, *Kasr aṣnām al-jāhiliyya*, ed. M. T. Dānesh-Pažūh (Tehran, 1340 Sh./1962), mainly directed against the Sufis but also the literalist jurists. I shall return to this.

20) *Ṣeḥḥat-e Qor'ān chonīn bāyad namūd* [32]*/ eqtedā bā shāh-e dīn bāyad namūd*
It is thus that one must show the truthfulness of the Qur'ān / One must thus follow the example of the King of Religion ('Alī).

21) *Zang-e kofr az rūy-e dīn bestorde ast / 'khāṣef on-na'l' īn ḥedāthat būde ast* [33]
In this way he scraped away the rust concealing religion / This is why he was called 'repairer of the sandals'.

22) *Ḥarb bar ta'vīl karde murtaḍā / hamcho bar tanzīl* [34] *ṣadr-e anbiyā*
Murtaḍā ('Alī) fought for the spirit (of the Qur'ān) / Just as the leader of prophets (Muḥammad) fought for its letter.[35]

'Repairer of the sandals', *khāṣif al-na'l*: in some versions of the *ḥadīth* of the 'Warrior of *Ta'wīl*' (see verse 15 below and the relevant note), the Prophet refers to 'Alī by this nickname because it is said that whilst he was speaking, 'Alī was repairing a sandal.[36] The root *kh-ṣ-f* literally means to join two detached pieces or to sew what is torn. It seems that Mollā Ṣadrā wishes to suggest that

32. The Fayḍī edition reads *ṣoḥbat* instead of *ṣeḥḥat*; which is unintelligible.

33. In the Fayḍī edition, instead of *ḥedāthat* there is *chonīn farmūde*, 'Which is why he [i.e. the Prophet] said "repairer of sandals".'

34. Clearly a reference to the *ḥadīth* cited above in note 30, one must correct this error: instead of *tanzīl* the edited texts read *tafsīr*. What is more, in the second hemistich, the Fayḍī edition reads *shāh-e anbiyā* (King of the Prophets) and not *ṣadr-e anbiyā*.

35. Translations of *ta'wīl* and *tanzīl* rendered following those by D. Gimaret, referred to above in note 30.

36. Either his own, Ibn al-Athīr, *al-Nihāya fī gharīb al-ḥadīth wa'l-āthār*, ed. al-Zāwī and al-Tināḥī (Cairo, 1963–1966), vol. 2, p. 38; al-Qundūzī, *Yanābī' al-mawadda* (Bombay, n.d.), p. 59; al-Baḥrānī, *al-Burhān*, vol. 1, p. 17, or that belonging to the Prophet (Ibn Ḥanbal, *Musnad*, vol. 3, pp. 31 and 33); al-Muḥibb (*sic*, i.e. Muḥibb al-Dīn) al-Ṭabarī, *al-Riyāḍ al-naḍira* (rpr. Tehran, ca. 1985), vol. 2, pp. 52–53. In Talmudic literature, it is the prophet Enoch (Ukhnūkh/Idrīs) who is called then 'repairer of sandals' (in Hebrew: *tofer min 'alim*). The parallel deserves further consideration in a separate study. I owe this information to my friend and colleague M. M. Bar-Asher at the Hebrew University of Jerusalem, whom I cordially thank.

in his battle for *taʾwīl* ʿAlī, the messenger of the esoteric dimension of the Qurʾān, corrected errors caused by the rampant literalism that had crept into Muḥammad's religion; hence my translation of *khāṣif* as 'repairer'. Similarly, in the expression *ṣeḥḥat-e Qorʾān* that I have translated as 'truthfulness of the Qurʾān' (verse 20), the term *ṣeḥḥat* (*ṣiḥḥa* in Arabic) literally means 'health, state of something that is faultless', but also in Persian 'correction, rectification' (meaning of the second causative form of the root in Arabic). The wars conducted by ʿAlī are thus inseparable from his vocation of imam, of *wālī*, Friend of God and interpreter of the esoteric meaning of the Revelation.

The next five verses seem to emphasise this double dimension of the imam, namely the apparent as symbolised by 'the day' of the joyful and intrepid warrior of *taʾwīl*, and the hidden as symbolised by 'the night' of the sad Friend and Ally of God:

23) *Rūz-e hayjā chun be-peydā āmadī / chūn khor az ṣobḥ-e dovom khande zadī*
When he emerged on the day of the battle / He smiled as if a second sun.

24) *Shab cho dar meḥrāb-e ṭāʿat mīshodī / khūn ze gerye bar moṣallā mīzadī*
At night, when he went to the *miḥrāb* / He drowned the place of worship with his bitter tears.

25) *Rūz tīghash āb-e ātash bār būd / ashk-e chashmash shab dar-e raḥmat goshūd*
By day, his sword destroyed like a sea of fire / By night, his tears opened the doors of mercy.

26) *Dar waghā ḍaḥḥāk o shab bakkā bodī / bā khodā shab rūz bā aʿdā bodī*
In the clamour of battle, he laughed, and at night he wept / By night he was with God, by day with his enemies.

27) *Rūz kār-e doshmanān rā sākhtī / shab be kār-e dūstān pardākhtī*
By day he settled accounts with his adversaries / By night he cared for his friends.

The next seven verses form a series of allusions to Qurʾānic verses and *ḥadīths* that the Twelver tradition associates with the figure of the first imam:

28) *Alladhīna yonfiqūn dar sha'n-e ū / qaddemū bayna yaday eḥsān e ū*
'*Alladhīna yunfiqūn*' (is revealed) for his case / '*Qaddimū bayna yaday*' (refers to) his bounty.

Alladhīna yunfiqūn: Q 3:134: '*Alladhīna yunfiqūna fi'l-sarrā' wa'l-ḍarrā' wa'l-kāẓimīna'l-ghayẓ wa'l-ʿāfīn ʿani al-nās wa'llāhu yuḥibbu'l-muḥsinīn*': 'Those who spend (freely), whether in prosperity, or in adversity; who restrain anger and pardon (all) men – for God loves those who do good.'[37]
Qaddimū bayna yaday: Q 58:12: '*Yā ayyuhā lladhīna āmanū idhā nājaytumu'l-rasūli fa-qaddimū bayna yaday najwākum ṣadaqatan*'; 'O you who believe! When you consult the Messenger in private, expend something on charity beforehand.' [38]

29) *Khalʿat-e ennā hadaynā dar barash / mighfarī az lā fatā andar sarash*
The robe of honour, '*innā hadaynā*', draped around him / The headdress of '*lā fatā*' gracing his head.

Innā hadaynā: Q 76:3: '*Innā hadaynāhu al-sabīl*': 'We showed him the way';[39]

37. For how this verse is linked to ʿAlī, see for example, al-Baḥrānī, *al-Burhān*, vol. 1, p. 315; al-Fayḍ al-Kāshānī, *al-Ṣāfī fī tafsīr al-Qur'ān*, 3 vols (n.p. [Tehran?], n.d.), vol. 1, p. 152.

38. On the connection of this verse with ʿAlī, see Furāt al-Kūfī, *Tafsīr*, p. 469; al-Qummī, *Tafsīr*, vol. 2, p. 369; al-Ṭūsī, *Tafsīr al-Tibyān*, ed. A. Ḥ. al-ʿĀmilī, 10 vols (Najaf, 1380/1960–), vol. 9 (1389/1969), pp. 549–550; al-Faḍl b. al-Ḥasan al-Ṭabrisī/Ṭabarsī, *Majmaʿ al-bayān*, ed. H. al-Rasūlī al-Maḥallātī, 10 vols in 5 parts (Beirut, 1379/1959–1960), vol. 9, p. 253.

39. Al-Qummī, *Tafsīr*, vol. 2, p. 422; al-Ṭūsī, *al-Tibyān*, vol. 10, pp. 204ff.; al-Ṭabrisī, *Majmaʿ al-bayān*, vol. 10, pp. 402f. Generally, *Sūrat al-Dahr*, also known as '*al-Insān*' or '*Hal Atā*' (the first two words of the verse), is linked in

30) *Dar kafash az oʿṭiyanna rāyatī / dar delash az ennamā khosh āyatī*
In his hand, the standard of ‘*uʿṭiyanna*’/ In his heart, the beautiful sign (or verse) of ‘*innamā*’.

Uʿṭiyanna: an allusion to the *ḥadīth* which goes back to the Prophet, who during the battle of Khaybar is reported to have said: ‘*la-uʿṭiyanna al-rāya ghadan rajulan yuḥibbu'llāha wa rasūlahu wa yuḥibbuhu'llāhu wa rasūluhu yaftaḥu'llāhu ʿalā yadayhi laysa bi-farrār*’; ‘Tomorrow, I will pass the standard to a man [i.e. ʿAlī] who loves God and His Messenger and whom God and His Messenger love; thanks to him, God will grant victory and he will not flee.’[40] *Innamā*: Q 5:55: ‘*Innamā waliyyukumu'llāhu wa rasūluhu wa'lladhīna āmanū alladhīna yuqīmūna al-ṣalāt wa yu'tūna al-zakāt wa hum rākiʿūn*’: ‘Your friend is only God, and his Envoy, and the believers who perform the Prayer and give Alms and bow down.’[41]

31) *Anta mennī maʿnī-ye īmān-e ū / āyat-e taṭhīr andar sha'n-e ū*
‘*Anta minnī*’ is the meaning of his faith / the verse of ‘Purification’ concerns him.

Anta minnī: from the *ḥadīth* in which the Prophet reportedly spoke thus to ʿAlī: ‘*Anta minnī bi-manzila Hārūn min Mūsā illā*

Imami tradition to ʿAlī. For ‘*lā fatā*’ in the second hemistich, refer above to verse 1 and the relevant note.

40. See Ibn Ḥanbal, *Musnad*, vol. 3, p. 16; ʿAlī b. ʿĪsā al-Irbilī, *Kashf al-ghumma* (Qumm, 1381/1961), vol. 1, p. 212; al-Sayyid ʿAlī al-Hamadhānī, *al-Mawadda fi'l-qurbā*, in the margins of al-Qundūzī, *Yanābīʿ al-mawadda* (Bombay edition), p. 48; the last clause of the *ḥadīth* is an allusion to the *laqab* ‘al-Farrār’ which was bestowed on ʿUthmān by his adversaries who claimed he had fled from the battle of Uḥud; see I. Goldziher *Muhammedanische Studien* (Halle, 1888), vol. 2, pp. 122–124.

41. On the connection of this verse to ʿAlī, see e.g. Furāt al-Kūfī, *Tafsīr*, pp. 123–129; al-ʿAyyāshī, *Tafsīr*, vol. 1, pp. 327–329; al-Ṭūsī, *al-Tibyān*, vol. 3, pp. 549ff.; al-Ṭabrisī, *Majmaʿ al-bayān*, vol. 3, pp. 209ff.; al-Majlisī, *Biḥār*, vol. 9, pp. 34ff.; al-Ḥurr al-ʿĀmilī, *Ithbāt al-hudāt*, ed. H. Rasūlī Maḥallātī (Qumm, n.d.), vol. 3, pp. 542ff.; al-Baḥrānī, *al-Burhān*, vol. 1, pp. 482ff.

annahu lā nabiyya ba'dī'; 'You are to me as Aaron was to Moses, with one difference, after me there will be no other prophet', which for the Shi'is, proves that 'Alī was truly the imam and Muḥammad's successor.[42]

The verse of Purification (*āyat al-taṭhīr*): Q 33:33: '*Innamā yurīdu llāhu li-yudhhiba 'ankumu'l-rijsa ahl al-bayti wa yuṭahhirakum taṭhīrā. . .* ' ; 'And God only wishes to remove all abomination from you, you *ahl al-bayt* [of the Prophet], and to make you pure and spotless.'[43]

32) *Ū madīne-y 'elm rā bāb āmade / jān fedā dar jāme-ye khāb āmade*
He is the gate to 'the city of knowledge' / Offering himself for sacrifice, he slept in his [Muḥammad's] bed.

'City of knowledge': from the *ḥadīth* attributed to the Prophet: '*Anā madīnatu'l-'ilm* (another version: *madīnatu'l-ḥikma*) *wa 'Alī bābuhā*'; 'I am the city of knowledge [or wisdom] and 'Alī is its gate.'[44] The second hemistich alludes to the famous epi-

42. E.g. Ibn Bābūya, *'Ilal al-sharā'i'*, p. 222, *Kamāl al-dīn*, p. 278 and *'Uyūn akhbār al-Riḍā* (Tehran, n.d. [ca. 1980]), vol. 1, p. 232 and vol. 2, pp. 10, 59, 194; Ibn Shādhān al-Qummī, *Mi'a manqaba*, ed. N. R. 'Ulwān (Qumm, 1413/1994), 'manqaba' 57, p. 112; al-Sharīf al-Murtaḍā, *al-Shāfī fi'l-imāma* (lithograph, Tehran, 1301/1884), pp. 148ff.; Ibn Shahrāshūb, *Manāqib āl Abī Ṭālib* (Najaf, 1956), vol. 2, pp. 219ff. and vol. 3, p. 46. See M. Bar-Asher, *Scripture and Exegesis*, p. 156, n. 122.

43. Obviously, for Imamis the Qur'ānic expression, '*ahl al-bayt*' refers to 'Alī, Fāṭima and their descendants; see e.g. Furāt al-Kūfī, *Tafsīr*, pp. 331–342; al-Qummī, *Tafsīr*, vol. 2, pp. 193–194; al-Ṭūsī, *al-Tibyān* (1388/1968), vol. 8, pp. 307–308; al-Ṭabrisī, *Majma' al-bayān*, vol. 7, p. 357. For discussions regarding the expression *ahl al-bayt*, see M. Sharon, '*Ahl al-Bayt*. People of the House', *Jerusalem Studies in Arabic and Islam*, 8 (1986) and his 'The Umayyads as *Ahl al-Bayt*', *Jerusalem Studies in Arabic and Islam*, 14 (1991); W. Madelung, 'The *Hāshimiyyāt* of al-Kumayt and Hāshimi Shi'ism', *SI*, 70 (1989) and *The Succession to Muḥammad* (Cambridge, 1997), index under '*ahl al-bayt*'; also Chapter 1, this volume.

44. See e.g. Furāt, *Tafsīr*, pp. 63–64; Ibn Bābūya, *Kamāl al-dīn*, p. 241, *Kitāb al-tawḥīd*, ed. al-Ḥusaynī al-Ṭihrānī (Tehran, 1398/1978), p. 307 and

sode known as the *laylat al-mabīt* ('the night of shelter'), when, according to the *Sīra* of the Prophet, threatened by his adversaries, Muḥammad fled in the night from Mecca to Medina, and 'Alī slept in his bed to trick those hunting his cousin, thus endangering his own life for the nascent religion and its prophet.

33) *Ennamā anta bar ū nāzel shode / az salūnī 'elm-e dīn ḥāṣel shode*
'*Innamā anta*' is revealed for him / Due to '*salūnī*' the science of religion is acquired.

Innamā anta: Q 13: 7: '*Innamā anta mundhirun wa li-kulli qawmin hādin*': 'But you are truly a warner, and to every people a guide.' The Imami exegetic tradition identifies 'the warner' with the Prophet and 'the guide' with 'Alī.[45] *Salūnī*: an allusion to the formulaic expression '*salūnī* (or *is'alūnī*) *qabla an tafqidūnī*', 'Ask me before you lose me', a formula with which several of 'Alī's *khuṭbas* open,[46] and a direct allusion to the fact that the first imam is the Initiated Sage and therefore the source of all knowledge.

34) *Būde nafsash 'endaho 'elmo'l-ketāb / qol kafa be'llāh govāh-e īn kheṭāb*
''*Indahu 'ilmu'l-kitāb*' relates to his being / '*Qul kafā bi'llāh*' bears witness to this.

---

al-Khiṣāl, p. 574; generally, for an extensive bibliography on this *ḥadīth*, see *Ṣaḥīfat al-imām al-Riḍā* (Qumm, 1408/1366 Sh./1987), pp. 123–133.

45. Furāt, *Tafsīr*, p. 206; al-'Ayyāshī, *Tafsīr*, vol. 2, pp. 203–204; 'Alī b. al-Ḥusayn b. Bābūya, *al-Imāma wa al-tabṣira min al-ḥayra* (Qumm, 1404/1984), p. 132; Ibn Shādhān, *Mi'a manqaba*, 'manqaba' 4, p. 44; al-Ṭūsī, *al-Tibyān*, vol. 6, p. 223; al-Ṭabrisī, *Majma' al-bayān*, vol. 6, pp. 278–279; al-Ḥurr al-'Āmilī, *Ithbāt al-hudāt*, vol. 3, pp. 548ff.; al-Baḥrānī, *al-Burhān*, vol. 2, pp. 277ff.

46. One need only leaf through selections from the *Nahj al-balāgha* to note this. See Chapter 3, this volume.

ʿindahu ʿilmu'l-kitāb and *Qul kafā bi'llāh*: Q 13:43: '*Wa yaqūlu'lladhīna kafarū lasta mursalan qul kafā bi'llāhi shahīdan baynī wa baynakum wa man ʿindahu ʿilmu'l-kitāb*': 'The Unbelievers say: "No Messenger are you." Say: "Sufficient as a witness between me and you is God, and such as have knowledge of the Book".'

For Imami exegesis, God and ʿAlī, 'who have knowledge of the Book', suffice as witnesses to prove the truthfulness of Muḥammad's prophetic mission.[47]

35) *Moṣḥaf-e āyāt-e īzad rūy-e ū / selsele-y ahl-e valāyat mūy-e ū*
His face is the Book of the signs of God / The curls in his hair, the chain for people of the (divine) Friendship.

Mollā Ṣadrā here employs two terms from the technical vocabulary of erotic symbolism in Persian mystical poetry to allude to theological and hagiological functions of the imam; ʿAlī's 'face' or 'visage' (*rū*) is the locus for the manifestation of Divine signs. In many traditions, the person of the imam is said to be the Face of God.[48] Moreover, '*moṣḥaf-e āyāt-e īzad*', which I have translated as 'the Book of the signs of God', can be translated as 'the Book of verses from God', that is, the celestial revealed Book. The Figure of ʿAlī, the imam par excellence, thus constitutes the veritable revealed Word or conversely, the reality of Revelation is the Face of the imam. The tresses of his hair (*mū*), or locks or curls, link the 'people of the Divine Friendship' *ahl-e valāyat*. This expression obviously refers to the *awliyā' Allāh*, the friends or allies of God, the saints simply put. ʿAlī's *walāya* forms the substance of saintliness, assuring the proper succession of the men of God.[49]

---

47. See al-ʿAyyāshī, *Tafsīr*, vol. 2, pp. 220–221; al-Ṭūsī, *al-Tibyān*, vol. 6, pp. 267–268; al-Ṭabrisī, *Majmaʿ al-bayān*, vol. 6, p. 301; al-Majlisī, *Biḥār*, vol. 9, pp. 82–83; al-Baḥrānī, *al-Burhān*, vol. 2, p. 303; al-Kāshānī, *al-Ṣāfī*, vol. 1, p. 880.

48. See *Guide divin/ Divine Guide*, index under '*wajh*'. Cf. also above, verse 12.

49. In the Fayḍī edition, the poem on ʿAlī seems to end with this verse. This seems somewhat abrupt. The verses that follow are said to belong to an ode

36) *Goft peyghambar ke ey yārān-e man / dūstān o peyrovān-e moʾtaman* [50]
The Prophet declared: ʻO Companions / Friends and trusted comrades,

37) *Mīgozāram baʿd-e khod nazd-e shomā / bahr-e peydā kardan-e rāh-e khodā*
After me, I leave with you / So that you may follow the path of God,

38) *Do gerān qeymat cho māh o āftāb / ahl-e beyt o īn ketāb-e mostaṭāb*
Two precious (objects) like the sun and moon / My Family and this sublime Book.'

There is obviously a reference here to the tradition of the ʻtwo precious objects' (*ḥadīth al-thaqalayn*): ʻI leave behind two precious objects, the Book of God and My Family.'[51]

39) *ʿālemān-e ahl-e beyt-e Moṣṭafā* [52]*/ hamcho Qorʾān būde har yek bar shomā*
The wise initiators [i.e. the imams] among the *ahl al-bayt* of Muṣṭafā / Are for you, each identical to the Qurʾān.

ʿĀlim, in Persian *ʿālem*, here in the plural form *ʿālemān* (lit. ʻlearned one') is one of the most frequently used titles for the imams and refers, more specifically in the early Imami corpus and

---

to the *ahl al-bayt* and the Qurʾān (*dar madḥ-e ahl al-bayt ʿalayhim al-salām va Qorʾān kalām-e elāhī*); *Mathnavī-ye Mollā Ṣadrā*, p. 110.

50. The Fayḍī edition: *peyrovān o dūstān-e moʾtaman.*

51. *Innī tāriku fīkum al-thaqalayn kitāb Allāh wa ʿitratī*; on this tradition and its different versions, now consult M. M. Bar-Asher, *Scripture and Exegesis*, pp. 93–98. For supplementary sources, see *Guide divin*, p. 215, note 440 (*Divine Guide*, p. 86) and especially the extensive bibliography noted by the editor(s) of *Ṣaḥīfat al-imām al-Riḍā*, pp. 135–150.

52. Re. questions regarding its meaning, which we shall examine below, I prefer the interpretation *ʿālemān-e ahl-e beyt*, to the edited version, i.e. *ʿālemān o ahl-e beyt*. As for the Fayḍī edition, it reads *ʿāmelān-e ahl-e beyt* (ʻthe practising among the *ahl-e beyt*'), and in the second hemistich *ʻdāʾem rahnomā'* (ʻforever guiding') instead of *har yak bar shomā*.

in the 'esoteric non-rational tradition', to the master or sage who initiates a disciple into the secret teaching.[53]

It would seem, according to the second hemistich, that Mollā Ṣadrā opted for the equality between these Two Precious Objects, the Qur'ān and the Prophet's Family, However, in some versions of the *ḥadīth al-thaqalayn*, reported both in Shi'i and Sunni sources, it is explicitly stated that one of the Two Objects, which the majority of interpreters identify as the Qur'ān, is superior to the other (*al-thaqalayn aḥaduhumā akbar min al-ākhar*).[54]

However, a typically Shi'i version of the *ḥadīth* reads: 'I leave behind, after me, two precious objects: the Book of God and 'Alī b. Abī Ṭālib; know that for you 'Alī is greater than the Book of God, since for you, he is its interpreter',[55] that is to say, without the imam's interpretation the Qur'ān remains incomprehensible; which of course speaks to the Shi'i notion of the figure of the imam as the ultimate interpreter of the Qur'ān, the imam as the tongue of the Qur'ān or as the 'Speaking Book' (*kitāb Allāh al-nāṭiq, Qur'ān nāṭiq*), indeed what the following verses refer to:

---

53. Cf. *Guide divin*, section III.2, 'la Science sacrée', pp. 174–199 (*Divine Guide*, pp. 69–79); for the semantic shift of this term see M. A. Amir-Moezzi, 'Réflexions sur une évolution du shi'isme duodécimain: tradition et idéologisation', in E. Patlagean and A. Le Boulluec (eds), *Les retours aux Ecritures. Fondamentalismes présents et passés*, Bibliothèque de l'Ecole des Hautes Etudes, vol. 99 (Louvain and Paris, 1993), pp. 63–82. On the 'non-rational esoteric tradition', see *Guide divin*, pp. 33–48 (*Divine Guide*, pp. 13–19).

54. *Ṣaḥīfat al-imām al-Riḍā*, p. 135 and notes.

55. *Kitābu'llāh wa 'Alī b. Abī Ṭālib wa a'lamū anna 'aliyyan lakum afḍal min kitābi'llāh li-annahu yutarjimu lakum kitāba'llāhi ta'ālā*; see for example Ibn Shādhān al-Qummī, *Mi'a manqaba*, 'manqaba' 86, p. 140; al-Muwaffaq b. Aḥmad al-Khwārazmī, *Maqtal al-Ḥusayn* (Najaf, 1367/1948), vol. 1, p. 114; al-Ḥasan b. Muḥammad al-Daylamī, *Irshād al-qulūb ilā'l-ṣawāb* (Najaf, 1342/1923), p. 378.

40) *Har yekī zīshān kalām-e nāṭeqī / rāh-e ḥaqq rā nūr-e īshān sā'eqī*
Each of them [i.e. the imams] an eloquent word / Their light is a guide upon the path of the Real.[56]

41) *Gar nadādī nūr-e shān dīn rā neẓām / montasher gashtī dayājīr-e ẓalām*
If their [the imams] light did not lend order to religion / The dust of darkness [or 'of injustice'] would have spread everywhere.

42) *Gar nabūdī kashtī-ye anvār-e shān*[57]*/ dar jahālat gharqe gashtī ens o jān*[58]
If the Ark of their light did not exist / All creatures [lit. Humans and Jinns] would drown in ignorance.

43) *Ahl-e beyt-e anbiyā zīnsān bodand / ke najāt-e ommat az nīrān bodand*[59]
The Families of the Prophets have all been thus / Rescuing their communities from the Fire.

44) *Har ke bāshad 'ālem-e rāh-e khodā / īn safīne sāzad az bahr-e hodā*
Every wise person on the path of God / Holds fast to this Ark for guidance.

The Persian word *kashtī* (verse 42), just as the Arabic term *safīna* (verse 44), alludes to the famous *ḥadīth* about Noah's Ark: '*Ahl bayti* are akin to Noah's Ark; whoever enters there is saved and

56. On this notion see M. Ayoub, 'The Speaking Qur'ān and the Silent Qur'ān: A Study of the Principles and Development of Imāmī Tafsīr', in A. Rippin (ed.), *Approaches to the History of the Interpretation of the Qur'ān* (Oxford, 1988), pp. 177–198; M. M. Bar-Asher, *Scripture and Exegesis*, ch. 3, sections 1 and 2. It must be added that the term *kalām* in the first hemistich inevitably evokes the expression *kalām Allāh*, Speech or Word of God, i.e. the Qur'ān.

57. Instead of *anvār-e shān* the Fayḍī edition reads *a'lām-e shān* ('If the Ark of "their sign" or "the most famous among them" [?] did not exist').

58. Fayḍī Edition: *az jahālat gharqe gashtandī jahān* (sic; very awkward formulation); 'due to ignorance the world [singular form] would be [respecting the metre, the verb is given in the plural] drowned.'

59. Fayḍī Edition: *pīrān* ('the aged'?) instead of *nīrān*; which is meaningless.

whoever drifts is drowned.'[60] Thus Mollā Ṣadrā moves from 'Alī to other imams of the Prophet's Family. Like 'Alī, father to all of them, the imams are the instrument of the inner aspect of the Qur'ān, the messengers of the esoteric dimension of Muḥammad's religion. Which is why in his last four verses, the poet boldly returns to his accusation against 'the people of exteriority', those whom he had previously referred to as *aṣḥāb-e badan* (see verse 16 above), the false scholars who – unaware of the 'secrets and true intentions' (refer to verse 45) of religious precepts and seeking worldly pleasures – compromise their religion and faith.

These final verses seem to reflect Mollā Ṣadrā's position in *Seh aṣl* (written, as we know, in opposition to a certain category of literal-minded legalist-theologians) and are, more specifically, a summary of 'three basics' (hence the title of the work) that impede transformative gnosis: ignorance of reality and the ultimate goal of human existence which indeed must only be a step in preparation for the ultimate journey to the Hereafter (*ākherat*);[61] the love of power, wealth, baser instincts and worldly pleasures that together tarnish the heart and hinder self-knowledge;[62] finally, the snares and wiles of the ego as a result of which reality is perceived as its opposite, good appearing as evil and evil as good:[63]

45) *Kār-e jāhel nīst*[64] *gheyr az sokhriyat / nīst jān āgah ze*[65] *asrār o niyat*
The ignorant person only ridicules all / Surely, he knows neither the secrets nor true intentions.

---

60. *Mathalu ahli baytī mathalu safīnati nūḥin man rakibahā najā wa man takhallafa 'anhā ghariqa* (or *zukhkha fi'l-nār*, 'is pushed into the Fire', whence perhaps 'the fires/flames', *nīrān*, of verse 43). For the numerous sources regarding this *ḥadīth*, see *Ṣaḥīfat al-imām al-Riḍā*, pp. 116–120.

61. *Seh aṣl*, pp. 13ff.

62. Ibid., pp. 28f.

63. Ibid., pp. 32ff.

64. Fayḍī Edition: *chīst* instead of *nīst*: 'What else does the ignorant one do, if not ridicule everything?'

65. Instead of *jān āgah ze* the Fayḍī edition reads *chon vāqef bar*; which has the same meaning.

46) *Ṭabʿ-e jāhel hamcho ṭeflān tā abad / ʿākef āmad*[66] *sūy-e ladhdhāt-e jasad*
Like children, his nature remains forever / Captive to pleasures of the mortal body.

47) *Ṣanʿat-e donyā safīne sākhtan / kār-e nādān*[67] *dīn be donyā bākhtan*
The Great Work on earth is to prepare one's Ark / Whereas the ignorant only trades his faith for this world.

48) *Ān safīne sāzad az bahr-e najāt / ān hamī dar baḥr-e donyā gashte māt* [68]
One builds the Ark for salvation / The other remains adrift in the sea of the world.

It is interesting to note how, in the last two verses, and by virtue of images of the Ark (*safīna*) and the alchemical Great Work (*ṣanʿat*), Mollā Ṣadrā establishes a equivalent status between, on the one hand, the imams and their teachings, and, on the other, the resurrected body. It seems that according to this idea, which is related to his notion of 'substantial movement' (*al-ḥarakat al-jawhariyya*), the assimilation of the Imam's sacred teachings indicates the intensification of being (by internal alchemy) and the evolution of the resurrected body which traverses the physical world, as on an Ark, in order to attain salvation in the hereafter.[69] We shall return to this.

Let us conclude with a few words regarding the form and content of the poem. This work belongs to the genre of poetry

66. The Fayḍī edition reads *gashte ʿākef* instead of *ʿākef āmad*; same meaning.

67. Fayḍī edition: *jāhel* instead of *nādān*; which is obviously the same thing.

68. The Fayḍī edition provides a slightly different version of this verse: *īn hamī sāzad safīne dar najāt/ān yekī dar baḥr-e donyā gashte māt*. The phraseology is clumsy but the meaning remains the same.

69. See for example H. Corbin, *Corps spirituel et Terre céleste* (Paris, 1979), pp. 194–200 and *La philosophie iranienne islamique aux XVIIe et XVIIIe siècles* (Paris, 1981), pp. 69ff.; C. Jambet, *Se rendre immortel*, pp. 13ff. and 78ff.

termed *ghadīriyya*, a poem in celebration of the Figure and the *walāya* of ʿAlī, since the event at Ghadīr Khumm, according to Shiʿi tradition, is the ideal context for speaking of this. It appears that this genre, composed in Persian, was especially appreciated by philosophers and thinkers of the Safawid period. Those who wrote *ghadīriyya* include: Fayyāḍ Lāhījī (d. 1072/1661),[70] Lāmiʿ Darmiyānī (d. 1076/1665),[71] Fayḍ Kāshānī (d. 1091/1680)[72] and Ḥazīn Lāhījī (born in 1103/1691).[73]

Mollā Ṣadrā also has recourse to two complementary techniques in poetry: *talmīḥ*, a fleeting allusion to a character that the audience (or reader) is supposed to recognise, and *iḍmār*, literally, 'to introduce into the mind', from *ḍamīr*, which consists of stating only the beginning or part of a famous saying, obliging the audience (or reader) to mentally reconstruct the rest.[74] This process is unvarying in the Persian *ghadīriyya* since we encounter it in the fourth/tenth century in Kasāʾī Marwazī (d. 341/952)[75] and

70. The *qaṣīda* that begins thus: *Sezā-ye emāmat be ṣūrat be maʿnā/ ʿAliy-ye valī ān ke shāhast o mowlā; Dīvān-e Fayyāḍ-e Lāhījī*, ed. A. B. Karīmī (Tehran, 1372 Sh./1993), pp. 23–26.

71. *Maqbūl-e* anta minnī *o mamdūḥ-e* hal atā/*qāʾel be qowl-e* law kashaf *o dāfeʿ-e maḍārr; Dīvān-e Lāmeʿ*, ed. M. Rafīʿī and Z. Moṣaffā (Tehran, 1365 Sh./1986), p. 51.

72. *Āmadam bar sar-e thanā-ya ʿAlī/ey del o jān-e man fedā-ye ʿAlī*; Mullā Muḥammad Muḥsin Fayḍ Kāshānī, *Dīvān*, ed. M. F. Kāshānī (Tehran, 1371 Sh./1992), p. 423.

73. *Āmad saḥar ze kūy-e to dāman keshān ṣabā/ahdaʾl-salāma minka ʿalā tābiʿi hudā; Dīvān-e Ḥazīn-e Lāhījī*, ed. B. Taraqqī (Tehran, 1350 Sh./1971), p. 130.

74. Refer to the chapters devoted to these techniques (*talmīḥ* is also given as *tamlīḥ*) in works related to *badīʿ* such as Ṣāḥib b. ʿAbbād, *al-Iqnāʿ* (Qumm, n.d.); Taftāzānī, *Muṭawwal* (Tehran, 1333 Sh./1955) and *Mukhtaṣar al-maʿānī* (Qumm, 1386/1966); al-Qazwīnī al-Khaṭīb, *al-Talkhīṣ* (Cairo, n.d.). For the use of *talmīḥ* in Persian poetry, see S. Shamīsā, *Farhang-e talmīḥāt* (Tehran, 1366 Sh./1987); for *iḍmār*, see M. Dhākerī, 'Shegerd hā-ye nā maʾlūf dar sheʿr-e Saʿdī', *Nashr-i Dānish*, 16/2 (1378 Sh./1999), pp. 16–24, esp. pp. 21–23.

75. *Fahm kon gar moʾmenī faḍl-e amīr al-moʾmenīn/faḍl-e ḥeydar shīr-e yazdān Morteḍā-ye pākdīn* in M. A. Riyāḥi, *Kasāʾī-ye Marvazī* (Tehran, 1367 Sh./1988), p. 93. There is some doubt about the attribution of this poem.

Shāh Ni'mat Allāh Walī (d. 834/1430) in the eighth and ninth/fourteenth and fifteenth centuries.[76]

In purely formal terms, Mollā Ṣadrā's *mathnavī* is not especially original. The philosopher's personal contribution lies mainly in the nature of the content. First, the processes of *talmīḥ* and *iḍmār* are applied to relevant passages from the Qur'ān, *ḥadīths* and *sīra*. The poem thus draws exclusively from traditional disciplines (*naqlī*) and not from rational speculative sciences (*'aqlī*). Then, as we have seen, the poem on 'Alī is written in the same vein as the *Seh aṣl*. Resonating between the lines, one can hear echoes from long periods in exile and of suffering endured by the philosopher from Shiraz because of the actions of certain *fuqahā'*.[77] One knows, but often forgets, that Mollā Ṣadrā had himself been a jurist and theologian.[78] Yet, in addition to the *Seh aṣl*, a monographic epistle on the subject, in numerous places in his oeuvre he does not fail to attack the religious figures frequenting the circles of Safawid power and among them those who according to him, either through ignorance or hypocrisy, are unaware of the esoteric dimension (*'ilm al-bāṭin*) of Shi'ism,[79] the very same religious

76. *Ān amīr al-mo'menīn ya'nī 'Alī/vān emām al-mottaqīn ya'nī 'Alī; Dīvān-e Shāh Ne'matollāh-e Valī*, ed. J. Nūrbakhsh (Tehran, 1361 Sh./1982), p. 762; see also note 72 above: the poem by Lāmi' Darmiyānī in which both techniques are used. For *ghadīriyya* in Persian, see Ā. Sajjādī, 'Ghadīriyya hā ye fārsī', in S. J. Shahīdī and M. R. Ḥakīmī, *Yād-nāmeh ye 'Allāma Amīnī*, vol. 1 (Tehran, 1973), pp. 413–430. See also 'al-Qaṣīdat al-ghadīriyya' attributed to the Nuṣayri thinker al-Khaṣībī, in *Majmū' al-a'yād*, ed. R. Strothmann, *Der Islam*, 27 (1946), cited by M. M. Bar-Asher and A. Kofsky, *The Nuṣayrī-'Alawī Religion* (Leiden, 2002), pp. 122ff.

77. On this matter, and Mollā Ṣadrā's enforced retirement (self-imposed exile ?) for many years in Kahak, a small village near Qumm, see for example S. Ḥ. Naṣr, introduction to *Seh aṣl*, p. v; H. Corbin, *En Islam iranien*, vol. 4, pp. 60–61; A. Shafī'īhā's introduction to his edition of Mollā Ṣadrā, *al-Wāridāt al-qalbiyya fī ma'rifat al-rubūbiyya* (Tehran, 1358 Sh./1979), pp. 4–5; M. Khājavī, *Lawāmi' al-'ārifīn*, pp. 23ff.

78. See S. Ḥ. Naṣr's introduction to *Seh aṣl*, pp. xi–xii.

79. See e.g. *al-Asfār al-arba'a* (lithograph, Tehran, 1282/1865), p. 876; *Sharḥ al-Uṣūl min al-Kāfī*, p. 11; *Tafsīr sūrat al-baqara* (lithograph, Tehran, n.d.), pp. 183 and 450; *Kasr aṣnām al-jāhiliyya*, pp. 32ff.

scholars that his famous disciple and son-in-law Fayḍ Kāshānī ironically calls 'the possessors of turbans' (*arbāb-e ʿamā'em*) and 'the turbaned ones, worldly-wise and scholars from the masses' (*ahl-e ʿamāme va dastār ke dāneshmandān-e donyā va ʿolamā-ye ʿavāmmand*).[80]

Conversely, in certain religious circles Mollā Ṣadrā has always been considered a notorious heretic. Curiously, it seems that he was vilified not so much for his practice of philosophy but because he was perceived and denounced as a skilful theoretician of Sufism.[81] On the part of his detractors, this is obviously a confusion (and possibly a deliberate one) between mystical gnosis (*ʿirfān*) – to which Mollā Ṣadrā adheres – and Sufism, against a certain form of which, in fact, Mollā Ṣadrā had written his *Kasr aṣnām al-jāhiliyya*.[82] Given

80. Mullā Muḥsin Fayḍ Kāshānī, *Sharḥ-e ṣadr* in his *Risālāt* (Tehran, 1321 Sh./1943), pp. 15–16.

81. Which is at least what we are led to believe in the critical text by Yūsuf al-Baḥrānī in *Lu'lu'at al-Baḥrayn* (Najaf, 1386/1966), see index under 'Fayḍ Kāshānī' (citing Sayyid Niʿmat Allāh al-Shūshtarī who denounced Mollā Ṣadrā's philosophy and his Sufism) or Mīrzā Ḥusayn al-Nūrī al-Ṭabrisī/Ṭabarsī in *Mustadrak al-wasā'il* (lithograph, Tehran, n.d.), vol. 3, pp. 422–424, who acknowledges the breadth of Mollā Ṣadrā's knowledge, but adds, in a critical tone, that he supports 'claims' by the Sufis, frequently criticises the *fuqahā'* and admires Ibn ʿArabī. Attacking Mollā Ṣadrā's commentary on *Uṣūl min al-Kāfī*, Nūrī says it is a Sufi text and as evidence cites a satirical verse composed by an author that he does not name: 'The commentaries on *al-Kāfī* are many and precious / The first to have commented upon it as an infidel was Ṣadrā' (*Shurūḥu'l-Kāfī kathīra jalīlatu qadrā/wa awwalu man sharaḥahu bi'l-kufri Ṣadrā*).

82. Still, some Sufis did not hesitate to link themselves to the *taṣawwuf* of Mollā Ṣadrā, for example, Muḥammad Karīm Sharīf Qummī in his *Tuḥfat al-ʿushshāq* written in 1097/1685, cited by M. T. Dānesh-Pažūh in his introduction to *Kasr aṣnām al-jāhiliyya*, p. 4, or Quṭb al-Dīn Muḥammad Nayrīzī Shīrāzī (d. 1173/1759) in his *Faṣl al-khiṭāb*, cited by M. Istakhrī, *Oṣūl-e taṣavvof* (Tehran, 1338 Sh./1960), p. 30. It is true that Mollā Ṣadrā seems to be against the institutional Sufism of mystical orders that he considered decadent in comparison to a more authentic, original Sufism. His criticisms have nothing in common with those for example of Muḥammad Ṭāhir al-Qummī (d. 1098/1686; *Tuḥfat al-akhyār* [Qumm, 1393/1973]) and well before him, those of the Imami double of the Ḥanbalī Ibn al-Jawzī, Murtaḍā b. Dāʿī al-Ḥasanī al-Rāzī, the seventh/thirteenth century author of *Tabṣirat al-ʿawāmm fī maʿrifat maqāmāt al-anām*, ed. ʿA. Eqbāl (2nd edn, Tehran, 1364 Sh./1985), according to Āghā

this historical context of a conflict of ideas, the traditionalist aspect of the poem takes on a special meaning, namely confronting the adversary on his own territory. And this all the more so since the actual core of the poem lies indisputably in its insistence on the portrayal of 'Alī and the other imams in his lineage as warriors of *ta'wīl* and consequently the depiction of their enemies as adversaries of *ta'wīl.* It is also noteworthy that more than half the verses of the poem, both in the edition by Khājavī and that by Fayḍī, deal with these subjects. Certain others are tangentially linked to them.

In basing his discourse on the most traditional Imami interpretations of the Qur'ān and *Ḥadīth*, and more specifically on the famous tradition of the 'Warrior of *Ta'wīl*', Mollā Ṣadrā has himself made of the Figure of 'Alī, of his battles and adversaries nothing less than a spiritual hermeneutic. Elsewhere, he explicitly states that the divine science above all, the knowledge that transforms human beings, since it is based on contemplation (*mushāhada*) and unveiling (*mukāshafa*), is none other than knowledge of the esoteric meaning of the Qur'ān and *Ḥadīth.*[83] In other words, *ta'wīl*, as a spiritual hermeneutic, the discernment of the hidden meaning beneath the letter of sacred texts, constitutes the key to transformative gnosis. No other science or body of knowledge has such a virtue:

> Well then, which is the noblest of sciences? Is it Law, Rhetoric or Speculative Theology? Philology, Grammar, Medicine, Astrology or Philosophy? Geometry, Arithmetic, Astronomy or Physics? No,

---

Bozorg al-Ṭihrānī the author's name is Jamāl al-Dīn Murtaḍā Muḥammad b. al-Ḥusayn al-Rāzī, see *al-Dharī'a ilā taṣānīf al-shī'a*, 25 vols (Tehran–Najaf, 1353–1398/1934–1978), vol. 24, p. 123, all Imami scholars who maintained that Sufism in itself constitutes a heretic deviation. On Mollā Ṣadrā's very favourable opinion of early Sufism, now consult N. Pourjavady, 'Ḥallāj va Bāyazīd Basṭāmī az naẓar-e Mollā Ṣadrā', *Nashr-i Dānish*, 16/3 (1378 Sh./1999), pp. 14–24. On the opposition to Sufism in Imamism, see Pourjavady, 'Opposition to Sufism in Twelver Shiism', in F. de Jong and B. Radtke (eds), *Islamic Mysticism Contested. Thirteen Centuries of Controversies and Polemics* (Leiden, 1999), pp. 614–623.

83. *Seh aṣl*, pp. 74–75 and 83–84.

> none of these sciences, considered in isolation (*hīch yek az afrād-e īn ʿulūm*), has such a sublime status. It is exclusively to be found in the science of the esoteric aspects of the Qur'ān and *Ḥadīth* and not in the letter [of these texts] to which anyone can gain access (*īn ʿelm monḥaṣer ast dar ʿelm-e boṭūn-e qor'ān va ḥadīth na ẓāher-e ānche fahm-e hame kas bedān mīrasad*).[84]

Likewise in his other works, more specifically in his various prologues (and/or epilogues) Mollā Ṣadrā insists, sometimes heavy-handedly, on the importance, in the process of self-perfection, of the coming together of piety, spiritual unveiling and the discovery of the hidden meaning in sacred texts of Shiʿism.[85] In this way, the other sciences, including philosophy, are only steps in preparation for *the* Science, that is, *ta'wīl.*

The last verses of the poem on ʿAlī seem to indicate that, according to our philosopher, this knowledge plays a key role in the Great Spiritual Work, the formation of the subtle body of the resurrection. Throughout his oeuvre, and most explicitly in *Seh aṣl*,[86] Mollā Ṣadrā describes what he calls the true Science, *ʿilm*, as an all-encompassing knowledge in which the inner experience, the spiritual unveiling (*mukāshafa*) sustained by divine inspiration (*ilhām*) and knowledge of the hidden aspects of reality, determine and complement each other, rendering the faithful devotee, a divinely wise person (*ḥakīm muta'allih*), a man of inner vision (*baṣīr*) among 'people of the heart' (*aṣḥāb al-qulūb*).[87] The late

---

84. Ibid., p. 84.

85. For example *al-Asfār*, p. 2; *al-Shawāhid al-rubūbiyya fi'l-manāhij al-sulūkiyya*, ed. S. J. Āshtiyānī (2nd edn, Tehran, 1360 Sh./1981), p. 4; *al-Ḥikmat al-ʿarshiyya* (lithograph, Tehran, 1315/1897), p. 1, Persian trans. Khājavī, *ʿArshiyya* (Tehran, 1341 Sh./1963), p. 2, English trans. J. W. Morris, *The Wisdom of the Throne* (Princeton, 1981), pp. 90–92; *Sharḥ al-Uṣūl min al-Kāfī*, the entire prologue; *Asrār al-āyāt*, ed. M. Khājavī, (Tehran, 1362 Sh./1983), the whole *muqaddima*, Persian trans. Gh. Ḥ. Āhanī (Tehran, 1363 Sh./1984), pp. 3–55; *al-Wāridāt al-qalbiyya*, pp. 120–121 (Arabic text), pp. 186–187 (Persian trans.).

86. In particular chs 8 and 9.

87. On the mystical dimension of Mollā Ṣadrā's thought, now also consult P. Ballanfat, 'Considérations sur la conception du cœur chez Mullā Ṣadrā', (1),

Moḥammad Taqī Dānesh-Pažūh was certainly not mistaken when he wrote that, in his insistence upon the importance of the *bāṭin* and the path leading towards it, namely, *ta'wīl*, Mollā Ṣadrā seems to go much further than such mystical theosophers as Ḥaydar Āmolī, Rajab Bursī and Ibn Abī Jumhūr Aḥsā'ī.[88] For Mollā Ṣadrā, the true Shi'i scholar, the authentic continuator of the imams' path – in this case himself – must, above all, be a warrior of *ta'wīl*.

Kār-Nāmeh, 5 (1999), pp. 33–46; (2) *Kār-Nāmeh*, 6 (2000), pp. 67–84; J. Eshots, '*al-Wāridāt al-qalbiyya fī ma'rifat al-rubūbiyya*, resāle-yī 'erfānī az yek ḥakīm', *Kherad-Nāmeh Ṣadrā*, 15 (1999), pp. 74–82, 'Ṣadr al-Dīn Shīrāzī mobtaker-e ḥekmat-e 'arshī', *Kherad-Nāmeh Ṣadrā*, 20 (2000), pp. 61–66 and 'Unification of Perceiver and Perceived and Unity of Being', *Transcendent Philosophy*, 1 (2000), pp. 1–7.

88 Introduction to *Kasr aṣnām al-jāhiliyya*, p. 13.

10

Visions of the Imams in Modern and Contemporary Twelver Mysticism

Introduction*

During the course of a previous study, devoted to the theological and practical aspects of *ru'ya bi'l-qalb* in early Imamism, I briefly referred to their subsequent treatment by certain modern authors who belong to various Imami mystical orders.[1] The present study may thus be considered a supplement to the first. It is nevertheless vital to reiterate some of the concepts analysed in the first study – and in some of my other publications – in order to clarify the fundamental doctrines that underpin the material to be examined below.

The supersensible vision that the believer may have of the imam obviously bears upon Imamology and is thus at the confluence of several doctrinal chapters, in this case theology, anthropogony, anthropology and eschatology. The pair *ẓāhir/bāṭin* is omnipresent in Imamism.[2] God himself includes two ontological levels:

*I wish to express my gratitude to my friends Sadigh-Yazdtchi, Bagheri, Aghakhani and Bahmanyar whose kind assistance with my research was invaluable.

1. Amir-Moezzi, *Guide divin*, pp. 112–145: 'Excursus: la vision par le cœur' (*Divine Guide*, pp. 44–55); on Imami mystics, pp. 132–136. See also Chapter 11 in this volume.

2. See my article, 'Du droit à la théologie: les niveaux de réalité dans le shi'isme duodécimain', *Cahiers du Groupe d'Etudes Spirituelles Comparées*, 5, 'L'Esprit et la Nature' (1997), pp. 37–63.

that of Essence that constitutes His *bāṭin*, His level, which is forever unknowable, inaccessible, hidden in his absolute unknowlableness and the level of Names and Attributes which corresponds to the revealed, manifested Face, the *ẓāhir* of God and possesses as its absolute Vehicle or Organ, the Imam in the archetypal and metaphysical sense.[3]

It is absolutely impossible for the level of Essence to be perceived; but the Names and Attributes, the only knowable level of God, can be 'seen' by the 'eye of the heart' through vision of the Imam's Reality.[4] This Reality of the Imam, the true Revealed God of early Imami theology, is among other things, his 'body of light' present in the heart of the initiated believer designated by the well-established expression, 'the faithul believer whose heart has been tested for faith by God' (*al-mu'min qad imtaḥana'llāhu qalbahu li'l-īmān*).[5]

If this 'body' of the Imam can be seen 'by' or 'in' the initiate's heart (both meanings of the particle *bi-* in the expression *al-ru'ya bi'l-qalb*), according to cosmoanthropogonic traditions this is because they are consubstantial, both made from the same celestial matter known as *'Illiyyūn*.[6] According to the Aristotelian theory of the vision that early Imami speculative theology rather clumsily advances, there can be no vision unless the subject viewing and the object viewed are of the same nature.[7] However, the

---

3. Refer to Chapter 3 in this volume.

4. *Guide divin*, pp. 112–127 (*Divine Guide*, pp. 44–49); also G. Vajda, 'Le problème de la vision de Dieu (*ru'ya*) d'après quelques auteurs shīʿites duodécimains', in *Le shîʿisme imamite* (Paris, 1970), pp. 31–53; although it includes a short description of 'vision by the heart' (pp. 44–45), this study focuses mainly on only one of the two aspects of the theological problem, namely the impossibility of the vision of the Essence of God; in brief, a distinction between the two ontological levels of God is not made here.

5. *Guide divin*, pp. 137–139 (*Divine Guide*, pp. 53–54).

6. *Guide divin*, pp. 96ff. (*Divine Guide*, p. 38); also M. A. Amir-Moezzi, 'Cosmogony and Cosmology in Twelver Shiʿism', *EIr*, vol. 6, pp. 317–322, in particular p. 320b.

7. *Guide divin*, pp. 120–121, esp. n. 236 (*Divine Guide*, pp. 46–47); also G. Vajda, 'Le problème de la vision de Dieu', pp. 35–36 and 50–51; J. van Ess,

vision of the imam may take other forms: dreams, in the awakened state or in the world of the soul, completely independent of the believer's will and practice, a meeting or encounter in the physical world with the hidden imam and so forth.

As the latter is identified with the Qā'im, some mystics have not hesitated to describe an encounter as the point of departure for an individual eschatology of a believer on whom has been bestowed this great honour.[8] In the following study, given the space alloted, it is only possible to take into account the category of 'vision'; indeed dreams of the imam or encounters with the hidden imam can be considered under several different categories, each having its own theoretical and practical ramifications. I must add that I have already dealt with the issue of encounters with the Imami Qā'im, during both the minor and major Occultation at some length.[9]

Non-institutional mysticism

The special relationship that a believer is called upon to maintain with the imams and the specific implications of this relationship are contained in the very nature of Shi'ism in general and Imamism in particular, and this means that once we deal with issues of faith the mystical dimension is always present. This explains why the mystic, oriented essentially towards the figure of the imam, has always been present in the Imami milieu, among all tendencies and with a greater or lesser degree of discretion depending on the various periods, locations and individuals, both before and after the development of various paths in mystical brotherhoods from the Safawid period onwards (tenth/sixteenth century). After

---

Theologie und Gesellschaft im 2. und 3. Jh. Hidschra, 6 vols (Berlin, 1991–1997), vol. 5, pp. 83ff.

8. Chapter 13 in this volume, as well as my article, 'Eschatology in Imami Shi'ism' (henceforth 'Eschatology'), in *EIr*, vol. 8, pp. 575–581, in particular pp. 578b–579b.

9. Refer to the studies indicated in the preceding note.

the 'original tradition', strongly marked by an esoteric and initiatory mysticism, that predominated until the mid-fourth/tenth century, one can cite the works of authors such as Quṭb al-Dīn al-Rāwandī, Ibn Shahrashūb or Yaḥyā Ibn al-Biṭrīq in the sixth/twelfth century, Raḍī al-Dīn Ibn Ṭāwūs and ʿAlī b. ʿĪsā al-Irbilī in the seventh/thirteenth century, Ḥaydar Āmulī and Rajab al-Bursī in the eighth/fourteenth century and Ibn Abī Jumhūr al-Aḥsāʾī in the ninth–tenth/fifteenth–sixteenth centuries. However, a kind of mysticism of the imam is also evident among thinkers belonging to the 'rationalist theological-juridical tradition' especially post Shaykh al-Mufīd (d. 413/1022) and Shaykh al-Ṭūsī (d. 460/1067).[10]

* * *

In the course of several visits to Iran between the 1970s and the present I was able to collect the testimony of some dozen individuals on their visionary experiences of one or more of the imams, not only in many dreams but also visions in an awakened state. Judging from certain observations consistently reported by the subjects, the latter always occurred in a particular state of consciousness, a certain state of rapture, transformation of the usual environment, contraction of time and/or space (the few minutes of an experience, depending on the subject, in fact lasted long hours even entire days in real terms, at times the subject found

10. On these different 'traditions' within Imamism, see *Guide divin*, pp. 15–48 (*Divine Guide*, pp. 6–19) and M. A. Amir-Moezzi, 'Remarques sur les critères d'authenticité du hadîth et l'autorité du juriste dans le shiʿisme imâmite', *SI*, 85 (1997), pp. 5–39. Naturally, one finds many thought-provoking observations in the numerous studies devoted to the relationship between Shiʿism and Sufism; of these, let us limit ourselves to citing a few monographs: H. Corbin, 'Sayyid Haydar Amolî, théologien shîʿite du soufisme', in *Mélanges Henri Massé* (Tehran, 1963) and *Histoire de la philosophie islamique* (Paris, 1964), vol. 1, section 1; M. Molé, *Les mystiques musulmans* (Paris, 1965), ch. 4; K. M. al-Shaybī, *al-Ṣila bayna al-taṣawwuf waʾl-tashayyuʿ* (Baghdad, 1966); J. B. Taylor, 'Jaʿfar al-Sādiq, Spiritual Forebear of the Sufis', *IC*, 40/2 (1966) and 'An Approach to the Emergence of Heterodoxy in Medieval Islam', *Religious Studies*, 2/2 (1967); S. H. Nasr, 'Le shîʿisme et le soufisme. Leurs relations principelles et historiques', in T. Fahd (ed.), *Le shîʿisme imâmite* (Paris, 1970).

himself at great distance from his home), immersion in light from an unknown source, the advent of a miracle (granting of a secret wish, presence of some article or anything serving as physical proof of the imam's actual presence, successful treatment of an otherwise incurable disease) and initiation into a certain teaching hitherto unknown to the subject.[11] These individuals, male or female, from either urban or rural backgrounds, were of mature age and shared a common feature: a reputation of exemplary piety, moral rectitude and especially great generosity. They did not belong to any brotherhood and most of them even expressed an antipathy towards the various mystical orders.

In any case, these anonymous individuals do not often attract the attention of textual sources, which tend to favour famous figures: religious clerics, philosophers, mystics, men of letters, men in power. In this regard, works by the Iranian Mīrzā Ḥusayn al-Nūrī al-Ṭabarsī/Ṭabrisī (d. 1320/1902) constitute a veritable treasure trove of information. Renowned religious scholar, author of a vast body of work, teacher of the great Āghā Bozorg al-Ṭihrānī, the author of the famous *al-Dharīʿa ilā taṣānīf al-shīʿa*, Nūrī Ṭabrisī was both of traditionalist tendancy (akhbārī) and a mystic.[12] In the last chapter of his *Jannat al-maʾwā*[13] and its almost complete Persian paraphrase *Kitāb al-najm al-thāqib*[14] Mīrzā Ḥusayn

11. One obviously finds many of these permanent features in accounts of encounters with the hidden imam; see Chapter 13 of this volume.

12. Regarding him see D. MacEoin, 'Ṭabrīsī', *EI2*, vol. 10, p. 42. Add to these references: the autobiographical account contained in the last of the twelve final 'lessons' (*fawāʾid*) in Ṭabrīsī's *Mustadrak al-wasāʾil* (latest edn, Qumm, 1407/1987); Mudarris Ṭabrīzī, *Rayḥānat al-adab* (Tabriz, n.d.), vol. 3, pp. 389–391, under *ṣāḥib mustadrak al-wasāʾil*; the introduction by A. B. al-Ṭihrānī to Nūrī Ṭabrisī, *Dār al-salām fī mā yataʿallaqu biʾl-ruʾyā waʾl-manām*, ed. H. Rasūlī Maḥallātī (Qumm, 1380/1960); M. al-ʿĀmilī, *Aʿyān al-shīʿa*, vols 1–56 (Damascus, 1935 –1961), vol. 9, pp. 97–98; R. Brunner, *Die Schia und die Koranfälschung* (Würzburg, 2001), pp. 39–69 and 'La question de la falsification du Coran dans l'exégèse chiite duodécimaine', *Arabica*, 52/1 (2005), pp. 1–41, especially pp. 22–29.

13. In Arabic, published at the end of vol. 53, pp. 199–336, of al-Majlisī, *Biḥār al-anwār*, 110 vols (Tehran and Qumm, 1376–1392/1965–1972).

14. Latest edn (Qumm and Jamkarān, 1412/1991).

Nūrī presents a masterful summary of practices required for the preparation for a vision of the imam. Although these two works are monographs devoted to the hidden imam and to accounts of those who have had the honour of meeting him, the last few chapters, as the author himself reiterates, relate to the eventual vision of the Impeccable Ones (*maʿṣūmūn*), in this case the Prophet Muḥammad and especially the twelve imams. Being very familiar with Imami sources, Nūrī justifies his assertions by constantly citing traditions reported in previous authorative works:[15]

> One can become a confidant of secrets [i.e. of the Impeccable Ones] and worthy of being introduced into the close circle of the elect (*khāṣṣān va khavāṣṣ*) thanks to learning and its application (*ʿelm va ʿamal*), through total piety, knowledge, beseeching, repentance and the purification of the soul from all impurities, doubts, uncertainties, errors and vices . . . However, the goal here is not to indicate an absolutely certain method [to attain the vision] since even if all the religious obligations, rules and principles are observed, and all that is unlawful or even ill-advised abandoned, there are other preliminary veiled and secret factors that they [the imams? their initiates?] do not reveal and only explain to those who are worthy (*sāʾer-e moqaddamāt-e ān mastūr va makhfī va joz bar ahl-ash makshūf wa mobayyan nadārand*). The aim here is to indicate a path that will perhaps enable the good sent accomplishment [*neʿmat*, i.e. the vision], be it in a dream.[16]

Next, Nūrī enumerates an entire series of practices beginning with a devotional period of forty days (*arbaʿīn*; in Persian *chelle* i.e. *chehele*) placing emphasis on good deeds, acts of worship, prayer, repentance and during these forty nights, regular attendance at mosques: on Wednesdays, the mosque of Sahla (in Najaf); on Fridays, the mosque of ʿAlī in Kūfa or the mausoleum of al-Ḥusayn in Karbalāʾ. There follows a lengthy series of traditions – gleaned

15. Based on Mīrzā Ḥusayn Nūrī Ṭabrisī, *al-Najm al-thāqib* (Qumm and Jamkarān, 1412/1991), ch. 12, pp. 655–666, which is here more complete than the original Arabic text from *Jannat al-maʾwā*, pp. 325–332.

16. *Najm*, pp. 655–656.

from various sources including books of *ḥadīths*, moral literature or books of prayer – which stress the sacred value of the number forty, ending with the famous tradition dating back to the Prophet: 'He who sincerely worships God, for forty mornings, God will have sources of knowledge rise up from his heart towards his tongue.'[17] The author then continues as follows:

> It is also posssible that each individual shall be obliged to accomplish a specific action chosen from the good pious deeds and conduct inherited from the Prophet (*aʿmāl-e ḥasane-ye sharʿiyye va ādāb-e sonan-e aḥmadiyye*), according to his personal situation, his time, place and capabilities. He may discover this practice [by himself] by sustained attention and contemplation or by seeking help from someone wise and intelligent who is capable of internal perception (*dānā-ye naqqād-e baṣīr*). It may be that a certain practice, of word or deed, might better suit an individual, and in this case, the rate of success for practices varies greatly. One person might have to offer alms, another to teach, a third [to focus on] the canonical prayer, fasting or the pilgrimage etc. However, there are certain conditions one must follow in all cases: fulfill the canonical duties; avoid unlawful things; respect ritual purity with regard to food, drink and clothing; have pure intentions – all this to an even greater extent than required by canonical Law (*ziyāde az ānche be ẓāher-e sharʿ mītavān kard*).[18]

Next follows a number of specific prayers, drawn from books of prayer (some very old), or the repetition of specific passages from the Qurʾān, at times accompanied by simple rituals: specific ablutions, body positions, in this instance, lying on one's right flank while sleeping, repetition of a varying number, at times or places appropriate for the prayer. Nūrī calls these actions 'special practices' (*aʿmāl-e makhṣūṣe*) in order to attain the objective mentioned (i.e. the vision) not only of the imam of the Time (i.e. the hidden imam, the Qāʾim) but also of other imams, indeed even the

17. *Najm*, pp. 656–661.

18. *Najm*, p. 662.

Prophet.'[19] Elsewhere in his *Dār al-salām fī mā yataʿallaqu bi'l-ru'yā wa'l-manām*, a considerable monograph on sleep, dreams and visions, Nūrī devotes a small chapter to the vision of imams by reporting and notably commenting upon a tradition dating back to the seventh Twelver imam, Mūsā b. Jaʿfar (d. 183/799), based on *Kitāb al-ikhtiṣāṣ* by al-Mufīd:

> He who has a request to make to God or seeks to see us [we, the imams] and to know his situation before God (*an yaʿrifa mawḍiʿahu min Allāh*), ought for three consecutive nights to perform full ablutions and pray secretly through us (*falyaghtasil thalātha layālin yunājī binā*); then, he will see us, he will be pardoned thanks to us and his situation (before God) will be revealed to him.

Commenting upon the enigmatic statement 'praying secretly through us', Nūrī writes: 'By this is probably meant, to pray secretly to God and implore him in our name in order that one may see us . . . however, also affirmed is (*wa qīla*) the sense that the person must concentrate on the desire for our vision (*yahtammu bi-ru'yatinā*), surrender himself to us, our vision and love (*yuḥaddithu nafsahu binā wa-ru'yatinā wa-maḥabbatinā*).'[20] It is interesting to note that our author, a loyal believer, convinced of the truth and legitimacy of Imami tradition exclusively, devotes a long chapter to a formal refutation of the opinions held by Sufis and philosophers about truthful dreams.[21]

---

19. *Najm*, pp. 662–666.

20. *Dār al-salām*, vol. 3, p. 9 (chapter entitled *ʿAmal li-man yurīd an yarā aḥad al-a'imma*), complete version of the tradition in al-Mufīd, *al-Ikhtiṣāṣ*, ed. ʿA. A. al-Ghaffārī (Tehran, 1379/1958–1959), pp. 90–91; see *Biḥār*, vol. 7, p. 336; Persian version in *Najm*, pp. 664–665.

21. *Dār al-salām*, vol. 4, pp. 240–267 (chs *Fi dhikr maqālāt al-ṣūfiyya wa'l-radd ʿalayhim* and *Fī dhikr maqālāt al-ḥukamā' wa'l-falāsifa wa'l-radd ʿalayhim*). On the role of dreams in Iranian culture see Kh. Kiyā, *Kh(w)āb va pendāreh. Dar jostojū-ye vīžegī-hā ye kh(w)āb-hā ye Īrānī* (Tehran, 1378/1999). On dreams in Islam, now consult P. Lory, *Le rêve et ses interprétations en Islam* (Paris, 2003).

Thus as for non-institutional mysticism, Twelver sources report a certain number of cases regarding visions of the imams experienced mainly by great religious scholars, philosophers and mystics.

Aḥmad b. Muḥammad al-Ardabīlī known as 'Muqaddas' (d. 993/1585), a great religious leader of Najaf with mystical and philosophical leanings, is said to have experienced a number of visions of ʿAlī b. Abī Ṭālib and the hidden imam: the first and last imams. It is related that as a result of supernatural communication with these two imams, he found solutions to theological and legal problems (*masāʾil ʿilmiyya*).[22]

The great philosopher of Safawid Isfahan, Muḥammad Bāqir Mīr Dāmād (d. 1041/1631), known as 'the third Master' (after Aristotle and al-Fārābī), has left us an account of an ecstatic vision that he had of the imams, a vision during which ʿAlī taught him a 'prayer for protection'.[23]

Mullā ʿAbd al-Raḥīm b. Yūnus Damāvandī (d. ca. 1150/1737 or 1170/1757), philosopher and mystic, according to his own remarks and hints by other writers, regularly had visions of the

22. Niʿmatallāh al-Jazāʾirī, *al-Anwār al-nuʿmāniyya* (Tehran, n.d.), vol. 2, pp. 36ff.; *Najm*, pp. 454–455; Mudarris Tabrīzī, *Rayḥānat al-adab*, vol. 5, pp. 366–370; 'A. Ḥ. Balāghī, *Maqālāt al-ḥunafāʾ* (Tehran, 1369/1949), pp. 137–138; ʿAqīqī Bakhshāyeshī, *Foqahā-ye nāmdār-e shīʿe* (Qumm, 1405/1985), pp. 203–207.

23. This account is recorded by his disciple Quṭb al-Dīn Ashkevarī in his *Maḥbūb al-qulūb*; see H. Corbin, *En Islam iranien. Aspects spirituels et philosophiques (*Paris, 1971–1972), vol. 4, pp. 36–38. The monumental work by Ashkevarī is still in manuscript form; for some years, I. al-Dībājī and Ḥ. Ṣidqī have been working on a critical edition but to date only the two first sections (approx. one quarter) has been published (Tehran, 1378 Sh./1999 and 1382 Sh./2008). For the text of the prayer, see also the prayer collection *Muntakhab al-daʿawāt* (lithograph, Tehran, 1304/1886 and 1382 Sh./2004), pp. 57–58 (see also Corbin, *Islam iranien*, vol. 4, p. 37, n. 44). On the ecstatic experiences of Mīr Dāmād, see also his *Taqwīm al-īmān* published with al-Sayyid Aḥmad al-ʿAlawī, *Sharḥ* and al-Mullā ʿAlī al-Nūrī, *Taʿlīqāt*, ed. ʿA. Awjabī (Tehran, 1376/1998), pp. 81–86 of the editor's introduction.

third imam, al-Ḥusayn b. ʿAlī, and less frequently of the hidden imam.[24]

Finally, the most numerous examples concern the famous Sayyid Muḥammad Mahdī b. Murtaḍā al-Burujirdī al-Ṭabāṭabā'ī known as 'Baḥr al-ʿUlūm' (d. 1212/1797), the great religious leader of Najaf. According to his bio-hagiographers, Sayyid Baḥr al-ʿUlūm had, on many occasions, the privilege of visions of several of the Impeccable Ones including the hidden imam. The vastness of his knowledge and many miracle-working powers were, according to these sources, in large measure due to his experiences and supersensible contacts with the imams.[25]

Although the accounts are at times lengthy and detailed, the actual descriptions of the visionary experiences themselves are brief and allusive, as though shrouded by a veil of discretion. We are simply told that one or another imam is seen and then, in some cases, the standard features that we have already recognised appear: a special state of consciousness; the transformation of the environment; a supernatural light; the transmission of a secret and so forth. The reader or listener is aware that these few lines are the essence of the account and the vision of the holy imams is the reward for an exemplary life of devotion, quest for knowledge, moral rectitude and above all, and with special emphasis, unconditional love (*walāya, maḥabba*) for the imams and their Cause. The subject thus becomes an *exemplum*, even for the most

---

24. See his *Sharḥ-e asrār-e asmā'-e ḥosnā = Meftāḥ-e asrār-e ḥoseynī* in S. J. Ashtiyānī (ed.), *Montakhabātī az āthār-e ḥokamā-ye elāhī-ye Īrān* (Tehran and Paris, 1976), vol. 3, pp. 577–790, in particular pp. 577–578 and 628; *Janna*, p. 306; *Najm*, p. 506. Regarding this author, see also H. Corbin, *La philosophie iranienne islamique au XVIIe et XVIIIe siècles.* (Paris, 1981), pp. 340–393. The assertion made by S. J. Ashtiyānī, *Montakhabātī az āthār*, vol. 3, p. 576, even cited by H. Corbin in *La philosophie iranienne islamique*, p. 340, on Damāvandī's affiliation to the Dhahabiyya order does not seem to be founded on any reliable source.

25. See e.g. *Janna*, pp. 236ff.; *Najm*, pp. 474ff.; *Dār al-salām*, vol. 4, pp. 411ff., Mudarris, *Rayḥāna*, vol. 3, pp. 274–275, under Mīrzā Muḥammad Mahdī Shahrastānī; ʿAqīqī Bakhshāyeshī, *Foqahā*, pp. 290–297.

humble of followers, opening up the possibility of a spiritual future, accessible and renewable. In this regard, a report concerning Muqaddas Ardabīlī (known among other things, as we have seen, for his visions of the imams), collected by Mudarris in his *Rayḥānat al-adab* seems especially significant. After the death of Muqaddas, a religious scholar (*yekī az mujtahidīn*) sees him in a dream. Handsomely dressed in fine garments, he emerges from ʿAlī's mausoleum. The scholar then asks him: 'By virtue of which particular deed have you attained this state?' Muqaddas replies: 'I now realise that deeds do not count for much. I only benefit from my love and loyal friendship (*maḥabbat va valāyat*) of he who rests in this mausoleum.'[26]

Mystical Brotherhoods

The principal Twelver mystical brotherhoods developed from the Safawid period (tenth/sixteenth century) onwards in Iran and spread outwards to other Imami lands, notably Iraq, the Caucasus and India.[27] There are four major orders, each containing several branches: Dhahabiyya, Niʿmatullāhiyya, Khāksār and Shaykhiyya.[28] Here too, the vision of the imam plays an important role on the spiritual path. Certainly, piety, scrupulous observance of acts of worship, moral rectitude and, in particular, unfailing love for the Impeccable Ones are once more prerequisites for experiencing visions of the imams. However, other speculative information and technical methods may be added to these indispensable

26. *Rayḥāna*, vol. 5, p. 369.

27. See the masterful and now classic study by R. Gramlich, *Die schiitischen Derwischorden Persiens*, 3 vols (Wiesbaden, 1965–1981).

28. The above-mentioned work by R. Gramlich deals with the first three orders; regarding the last, see e.g. Corbin, *Islam iranien*, vol. 4, pp. 203–300; D. M. Mac Eoin, 'From Shaykhism to Babism. A Study in Charismatic Renewal in Shīʿī Islam' (University of Cambridge, 1979); V. Rafati, 'The Development of Shaykhī Thought in Shīʿī Islam' (University of California, 1979). Further on, I provide other sources for these mystical orders. See also Chapter 14, this volume.

conditions. The 'vision by [or in] the heart' (*al-ru'ya bi'l-qalb*), transforming the simple believer into a 'faithful believer whose heart has been tested by God', is found to be, among the large majority of the mystics, the key issue.[29] As this is a secret and highly initiatory practice, texts regarding it are rare, allusive and at times enigmatic. Expressions such as 'the inner vision of the heart' (*baṣīrat-e qalbiyye*), 'contemplation of the Lights of the heart or of the Love for the imams' (*moshāhadāt-e anvār-e qalbiyye/anvār-e valāyat*) appear frequently but it is rare for concrete details about the vision to be given.

Among the masters of the Dhahabiyya, Mīrzā Abu'l-Qāsim Sharīfī Shīrāzī known as 'Rāz' (d. 1286/1869) is perhaps the author who provides the most significant details. For example, in the fourth of his twelve responses to his disciple, Rā'iḍ al-Dīn Zanjānī, we read the following (the eulogical and brotherhood-related expressions are not translated):

> The Disciple: Why do we call ʿAlī b. Mūsā al-Riḍā [the eighth imam] the seventh *Qibla*?[30]
>
> The Master: Know, dear and honorable son, that this serious question touches upon one of the greatest secrets of the heart that no simple curious mind can easily discover . . . Its understanding is only possible through the unveiling of the heart by the lord of the hearts (*kashf-e qalbī-ye arbāb-e qulūb*) for even the most sound and powerful intelligences are unable to apprehend secrets of the heart and perception of the mysteries of *walāya* and love of God . . . The reason for this honorable title, like other titles for the holy imam, such as 'the Confidant of Souls' (*anīs al-nufūs)* and 'the Sun of Suns' (*shams al-shumūs*), is the radiance of the Light of his *walāya* in the heart of the faithful (*nūr-e valāyat-e ān ḥaḍrat dar qalb-e mo'menān tābesh dārad*). This holy Light does not only belong to him but all the imams are in fact the Light descended from God for the sake of creation (*a'emme . . . hamegī nūr-e monzal*

29. Cf. above notes 4 to 7 and the corresponding texts.

30. The initiatic chain of the Dhahabiyya goes back to the eighth imam via Maʿrūf al-Karkhī; see *Die schiitischen Derwischorden*, vol. 1, pp. 5ff.

az ḥaqq taʿālā bar khalāʾeqand). But as the initiatic chain of [our] School begins with the eighth imam, it is the blessed form of the latter which manifests itself in [a subtle centre called] 'the blackish innermost [part] of the heart of his Friends (*serr-e sovaydāʾ-e qalb-e awliyāʾ*)'.[31] This centre is the Seventh Mountain (*ṭūr-e haftom*) of the heart that is manifested to the Friends ... Know that the Sevenfold Mountains in the heart of the holy Friends designate the manifestations of the variously coloured seven Lights (*tajaliyyāt-e anvār-e sabʿe-ye motelavvene be alvān-e mokhtalefe*) and the seventh manifestation, is the black Light that is the Light of the sacrosanct Essence of Unicity (*nūr-e siyāh ke nūr-e dhāt-e aqdas-e aḥadiyyat ast*).[32] It is this Light that is manifested for the

---

31. The identification of the Light of the heart with the ultimate spiritual master, namely the imam, is an idea already present in the earliest Twelver sources; cf. *Guide divin*, pp. 125–126 (*Divine Guide*, pp. 48–49). This belief is also firmly held by the Kubrāwiyya order with whom the Dhahabiyya are affiliated. As a Kubrāwī Imami, Rāz Shīrāzī identifies 'the form of light' viewed at the subtle centre of the heart with the 'invisible master' who for a Dhahabī, is the eighth imam. On the 'invisible master', *shaykh al-ghayb*, also called 'sun of the heart', *shams al-qalb*, in Najm al-Dīn Kubrā, see F. Meier, *Die Rawāʾiḥ al-jamāl wa fawātiḥ al-jalāl des Najm ad-Dīn al-Kubrā* (Wiesbaden, 1957), chs 7, 13, 66 and 79; French trans. by P. Ballanfat as *Les éclosions de la beauté et les parfums de la majesté* (Nîmes, 2001). See also, H. Corbin, *L'homme de Lumière dans le soufisme iranien* (Paris, 1971), ch. 4, English trans., *The Man of Light* (New York, 1971). On one group's conversion to Shiʿism among the Kubrāwiyya, see M. Molé, 'Les Kubrawiyya entre sunnisme et shiʿisme au huitième et neuvième s. de l'Hégire', *REI* (1961), pp. 61–142. On the Kubrāwī affiliation of the Dhahabiyya, see *Die schiitischen Derwischorden*, vol. 1, pp. 9ff.; see also A. Khāvarī, *Dhahabiyye* (Tehran, 1362/1983), vol. 1, ch. 3; L. Lewisohn, 'An Introduction to the History of Modern Persian Sufism. Part II: A Socio-cultural Profile of Sufism from the Dhahabi Revival to the Present Day', *BSOAS*, 62/1 (1999), pp. 36–59.

32. I have advanced a hypothesis on the allusion to epiphanic coloured light in the sayings of the imams reported since the earliest compilations of Imami traditions; cf. *Guide divin*, pp. 127–128 (*Divine Guide*, pp. 49–50). On this phenomenon in the Kubrāwī tradition, see e.g. Najm Dāye Rāzī, *Mirṣād al-ʿibād*, ed. M. A. Riyāḥī (Tehran, 1973), ch. 3, sections 17 and 18, pp. 299–315; 'Alāʾ al-Dawla al-Simnānī, *al-ʿUrwa li-ahl al-khalwa waʾl-jalwa*, ed. N. Māyel Heravī (Tehran, 1362/1985), index under *'laṭāʾif rūḥānī'*, *'laṭīfa'*; Shams al-Dīn Lāhījī, *Mafātīḥ al-iʿjāz fī sharḥ Golshan-e rāz*, ed. M. R. Barzegar Khāleqī and 'E. Karbāsī (Tehran, 1371/1992), pp. 67, 83–84, 130, 344, 523; *Homme de Lumière*, chs 4–6 and index under 'lumière' and 'photismes'. On the relationship between coloured light and the inner master in Iranian spirituality, refer to

> Friends [i.e. Dhahabiyya mystics] in the blessed form of the eighth imam. It is a transparent black Light, magnificent and radiant, of overwhelming intensity; it is the 'Confidant of souls' and the '*Qibla* of the Seventh Mountain of the heart'. The great [mystics] consider it to be a canonical duty (*vājib*) to direct one's sincere prayer in the direction of this veritable *qibla*.
>
> First discover your *qibla* and then offer your prayer
>
> The prayer of lovers is offered with sorrow and resignation
>
> . . . That is why we call this imam 'the seventh *qibla*' . . . My son, grasp the true value of secrets of the hearts of Friends being revealed in order that God may lead you there; and hide this from those who are not worthy [in Arabic in the text: *fa-ghtanim yā waladī kashf asrār qulūbi'l-awliyā' laka la'allaka tahtadī ilā'llāhi ta'ālā wa ktumhā min ghayri ahlihā*].[33]

Elsewhere, especially in letters addressed to his closest disciples, Rāz Shīrāzī seems to provide other indications on the exercises of concentration on the heart whose aim is the vision of the imam. In a letter addressed to Mullā Ḥusayn Rawḍa Khān, the master seems to indicate – the language is highly allusive – that the practice ought to be accompanied by the famous *dhikr* that every Imami mystic knows as *nādi 'Alī*, termed *dhikr* of *walāya* by the Dhahabiyya and which Rāz identifies with nothing less than the Supreme Name of God (*ism a'ẓam*):

> Invoke 'Alī, locus of manifestation of wonders/ In him you will find support in all trials/ All your worries and hardships will vanish/By the grace of your *walāya*, O 'Alī, O 'Alī, O 'Alī (*nādi 'Aliyyan maẓhar al-'ajā'ib/tajidhu 'awnan laka fi'l-nawā'ib/kullu*

T. Pūrnāmdāriyān, *Ramz va dāstān-hā-ye ramzī dar adab-e fārsī* (Tehran, 1346/1985), pp. 240–275.

33. *Resāle dar ḥall-e eshkāl-e davāzdah so'āl-e...Rā'iḍ al-Dīn Zanjānī... az Mīrzā Bābā Rāz Shīrāzī*, in Ḥ. Palāsī Shīrāzī, *Tadhkira Shaykh Muḥammad b. Ṣadīq al-Kujujī* (Tehran, 1367/1947), pp. 125–126 (the entire treatise: pp. 112–150); also *Guide divin*, p. 136 (*Divine Guide*, p. 52); Khāvarī, *Dhahabiyye*, vol. 1, pp. 141–145.

> *hammin wa ghammin sa-yanjalī/bi-walāyatika yā ʿAliyyun yā ʿAliyyun yā ʿAlī*).[34]

In another letter, presented as a doctrinal treatise, Rāz seems to write that concentration on the visage of the living master of the School – in this case, himself – constitutes the first step in the experience of vision by the heart, as if the master's face was the exoteric form (*ẓāhir*) of the imam's light which is its esoteric (*bāṭin*) aspect. Following a series of guidelines regarding the meetings of dervishes, led by an elder, delegated by the Master, Rāz writes:

> May they be united in the practice of *dhikr*s in order to attain spiritual states and contemplations of the heart (*ḥālāt-e maʿnaviyye va moshāhadāt-e qalbiyye*) and thus benefit from the grace and mercy of God. Thus, they must concentrate, in these precise moments and during the *dhikr* and [exercise] of the presence in the heart (*awqāt-e khāṣṣe dar awqāt-e dhikr va ḥuḍūr-e qalb*), upon the Face of the Perfect Man [i.e. the imam] . . . this spiritual Face deriving from the mystery of the Light of *walāya* that they have [already] seen, esoterically, in their inner perception by the eye of the heart (*ān ṣūrat-e ruḥāniyye ke az gheyb-e nūr-e valāyat bāṭenan be baṣīrat va dīde-ye qalb-e khod dīde-and*) and no longer upon this perceptible exoteric face as seen by them in this external world and belonging to this humble servant [i.e Rāz himself] (*na ṣūrat-e ḥessiyye-ye ẓāher ke dar khārej az faqīr dīde-and*). May they scrupulously observe the respect and veneration (*adab va ḥormat*) of this Face which is the Face of God the most Noble, and the most noble of all faces, in order that due to this spiritual veneration their innermost self may be educated and they gradually reach the station of 'effacement in the master' (*fanāʾ*

34. (Anonymous), *Mujallil al-anwār yā kashkūl silsilat al-dhahab*, ed. Sh. Parvīzī (Tabriz, 1336/1958), pp. 21–22, the whole letter: pp. 16–22. According to a Dhahabī friend, the ʿAlī of this *dhikr* designates both the first and the eighth imam, namely ʿAlī b. Abī Ṭālib and ʿAlī b. Mūsā al-Riḍā, 'since the reality of the Impeccables is one'.

> *fi'l-shaykh*) which is none other than 'effacement in God' (*fanā' fi'llāh*)'.[35]

Concentration on the spiritual image of the master's face appears to be an initial step that must be rapidly passed. Mīrzā Jalāl al-Dīn Muḥammad Majd al-Ashrāf (d. 1331/1913), successor to Rāz as leader of the Dhahabiyya Aḥmadiyya seems even to advise against this practice. In his *Mir'āt al-kāmilīn*, when considering the preparatory exercises for *dhikr* and *fikr* (literally contemplation, meditation, also known as *tafakkur*, ultimately a matter of contemplation of the Face of God, that is, the Imam), Majd al-Ashrāf writes:

> As for the spiritual Face [lit. the meditative Face, *ṣūrat-e fekriyye*] the followers of the errant Path direct their inner contemplation onto the face of their physical master [or 'exoteric', *pīr-e ẓāherī*]. Now, in the true Path which is ours, to contemplate the visage of the master is to worship him and is considered pure polytheism (*'eyn-e sherk*) for this depends on the personal will of the follower whereas the inner manifestation of the Face of God which is the most noble of Faces [i.e. the Imam] does not depend upon the will of the follower but upon the grace of the Lord (*vajh-e ḥaqq akram al-vujūh bī ekhtiyār-e sālek mībāyad dar bāṭen be 'enāyat-e rabbāniyye peydā shavad*).[36]

Further on, in a poem, the author lists the Seven Mountains of the heart and the coloured Lights of each among them leading up to the black Light of the Face of the imam.[37]

---

35. *Mujallil*, pp. 35–36, the entire letter: pp. 22–40. Passage cited and translated into German in *Die schiitischen Derwischorden*, vol. 2, p. 248. On the very common mystical practice in Sufism of concentrating on the spiritual image of the master's visage (*murāqaba/murābaṭa/rabṭ ... 'alā wajh/ṣūra al-shaykh/murshid*) and for sources on it consult *Die schiitischen Derwischorden*, vol. 2, pp. 245–251.

36. Majd al-Ashrāf, *Mir'āt al-kāmilīn* (Shiraz, n.d.), pp. 7–8.

37. *Mir'āt*, pp. 10–11.

However, this issue regarding the kind of visual aid for concentration seems to depend on the progress made by the follower. Some years ago in Shiraz, a Dhahabī dervish showed me a piece of wood, about 20 x 10 cm, upon which was drawn the portrait (known at least since the Qājār period) of Imam ʿAlī. He explained that this piece of wood, called *shamāʾil* (image, portrait of a saint), was one of the items a novice mystic ought to possess. It is for those who are forbidden to concentrate upon the face of their living master, for fear of 'idolatry', and who are at the same time, unable to visualise 'the Face of Light' of the Imam. One therefore provides them with these 'portraits of 'Alī', the Imam par excellence, in order that they may use them, at least for some time, as a visual aid until they are able to put it aside.[38]

The vision of the imam's spiritual Face is designated, apparently by generations of Dhahabīs masters, by the technical term *wijha*, literally 'Face of a body, of an object' (*vejhe* in Persian pronounciation). This is undoubtedly also an allusion to the Qur'ānic usage of the term that designates 'the direction to turn for prayer' in verse 2:148: *wa li-kulli wijhatun huwa muwallīhā* ('To each a direction towards which to turn in prayer'). In a recent internal document belonging to the brotherhood and apparently written by Dr Ganjaviyān, the current *pīr* of the Dhahabiyya Aḥmadiyya, various pieces of information old and new about this issue are admirably summarised. Numerous *ḥadīth*s drawn from ancient compilations, for instance by Ibn Bābūya al-Ṣadūq as well as the teachings of previous Dhahabiyya masters, are brought to bear in order to arrive at the following conclusions: the *vejhe* can only designate the Face of the imam; the Impeccable Proof (*ḥojjat-e maʿṣūm*, i.e. the imam) is identical to the Face of God;

38. Recently in Tehran, Mme Živa Vesel, a colleague and CNRS scholar of Iranian studies, acquired a collection of fourteen of these wooden objects of unknown origin for safekeeping. It is interesting to note that on one of them, clearly of Indian origin, 'the portrait of 'Alī' is surrounded by a kind of mandala – a geometric figure that, as we know, is used in several Indian religions as an aid for concentration.

the vision of this Face is possible, not by the naked eye but by the eye of the heart; what is seen is not the physical body of the imam but his spiritual form and the vision is achieved by effacement and rebirth in the *walāya* of the latter. The author ends this passage with a poem by Rāz Shīrāzī:

> Thanks to his love, I have attained a state/in which I see nothing other than the eternal Witness.The Universes and all they contain were effaced when I reached the eternal Face of God. In the vastness of spaces beyond space/Without wings I have flown for thousands of years, and there I have seen the Face of the Real/All that I have heard and said was through Him.[39]

The regular practice of this discipline of spiritual life seems to provide the mystic with the ability to have regular contact with the imams, even apart from the special moments during exercises of *dhikr* and *fikr*. According to a mystical expression, the follower's entire existence can become 'a constant remembrance and uninterrupted meditation' (*dhekr-e davām va fekr-e modām*), thus rendering him worthy of the privilege of visits from the saintly Impeccable Ones. This is what emerges from a number of autobiographical accounts by Majd al-Ashrāf entitled 'epiphanic visions and spiritual itineraries' published posthumously with the authorisation of his great grandson, Sayyid Muḥammad Ḥusayn Sharīfī, a previous master of this branch of the Dhahabiyya.

---

39. *Ze ʿeshq-e ū be-jāʾī man rasīdam. Ke gheyr az shāhed-e bāqī nadīdam/ Hame kawnayn o māfīhā fanā shod. Be vajh Allāh-e bāqī chon rasīdam/Dar ān vosʿat sarā-ye lā makānī. Hezārān sāl rah bī par parīdam/Nadīdam ghayr-e vajh-e ḥaqq dar ānjā. Be ū būdī hame goft o shanīdam.* (Anonymous), *Veǧhe chīst*? Thanks to the kindness of some Dhahabī friends, I was able to obtain a copy of this text (pp. 150–160) from a work unknown to me; citations, p. 155. It is interesting to note that the last section of the epistle (pp. 156ff.) is devoted to citations from *Dār al-salām* by Nūrī Ṭabrisī in which, drawing on early *ḥadīth*s, the latter demonstrates that visions of the Impeccable Ones are necessarily true since Satan is absolutely incapable of taking their form, cf. *Dār al-salām*, ch. 8, with traditions from *ʿUyūn akhbār al-Riḍā* and *Majālis/Amālī* by Ibn Bābūya al-Ṣadūq.

Throughout a handful of texts, a long sequence of visions, dialogues and dreams unfolds of one or another imam, retold with great simplicity as if they were accounts of anodine relationships. Often we finds statements such as 'This morning, I found myself before Imam 'Alī when he said to me etc.', 'At dawn, I was before Imam al-Riḍā; Imam al-Jawād was also present etc.', 'Then at that very moment the hidden imam addressed me thus etc.', 'I met *Amīr al-mu'minīn* 'Alī, not recognising him at first, he then said to me: "But it is I, 'Alī"; I fell to the ground etc.' The outcome of these visions is either an initiation into a secret teaching (in the first few texts this is the knowledge of alchemy) or an ecstatic state leading to mystical knowledge, or at times a solution to a specific problem.[40] Generally, in the most ancient texts, initiatory knowledge (*'ilm*) and supernatural powers are described as resulting from the vision of the imam's Reality.[41]

Emerging from the Dhabiyya in the early twentieth century, the Oveysī mystical order, which is led by the 'Anqā family, also accords an important place to vision by the heart in spiritual progress. Their motto and emblem is *'alayka bi-qalbika*, a lapidary statement attributed to Uways (in Persian, Oveys) al-Qaranī, the famous ascetic who was a contemporary of the Prophet and is the school's namesake. This is a formulaic statement approximately translated as 'it is your duty to be watchful of your heart'. While staying guarded about technical aspects, the order quite recently asked a follower to publish a book on references to visions by the heart in sacred texts from Judaism, Christianity and

---

40. *Ṣūrat-e namāyeshāt va seyr hā-ye bāṭenī-ye ḥaḍrat-e Jalāl al-Dīn Muḥammad* in *Mujallil*, pp. 364–369; in several accounts, the author relates that he was initiated by the imams into alchemy.

41. Cf. *Guide divin*, p. 142 passim (*Divine Guide*, p. 55); one will find other information alluding to Dhahabī *vejhe* in Palāsī, *Tadhkira*, pp. 14, 18, 25, 36, 68; Anon, *Qaṣā'ed va madā'eḥ dar sha'n-e... 'Alī* (Tabriz, n.d.), poems nos 10 and 11; Anon, *Yek qesmat az tārīkh-e ḥayāt va karāmāt-e Sayyed Qoṭb al-Dīn Muḥammad Shīrāzī* (Tabriz, 1309/1891), pp. 7ff. and 37; Sayyid Quṭb al-Dīn Muḥammad, *Faṣl al-khiṭāb* (Tabriz, n.d.), ch. 18; Rāz Shīrāzī, *Ṭabāshīr al-ḥikma* (Shiraz, 1319/1900), pp. 16–67 and *Mirṣād al-'ibād* (Tabriz, n.d.), pp. 4, 10–17, 21.

Islam, as well as in Sufi texts, notably those of the masters of his school, Jalāl al-Dīn ʿAlī Mīr Abu'l-Faḍl (d. 1323/1905), Mīr Quṭb al-Dīn Muḥammad (d. 1962) and Shāh Maqṣūd ʿAnqā (d. 1986). The Light of the heart is considered to be the inner imam of the mystic. The realisation and vision of this imam as well as obedience to him guarantees progress along the spiritual path.[42]

* * *

The Niʿmatullāhiyya order is comprised of several families and branches,[43] all of which seem to accord the greatest importance to visions of the imam. Some passages from travel journals by Zayn al-ʿĀbidīn Shīrvānī (d. 1253/1837–1838) and the *Ṭarāʾiq al-ḥaqāʾiq* by Maʿṣūm ʿAlī Shāh (d. 1344/1926) would indicate that the vision of the imam is achieved by visualising the face of the order's living master (*ṣūrat-e morshed/vajh-e shaykh*). At times, citing the Qādirī Sufis' statement, '*Ḥifẓ taṣawwur ṣūrat al-shaykh fi'l-fikr* (Hold in the mind the image of the master's

42. Shaykh Muḥammad Qādir Bāqirī Namīnī, *Dīn va del* (Tehran, 1356/1977–1978). The practice of concentrating on the sevenfold subtle centres of the heart also exists among the Oveysīs; however, the previous master of the order, Shāh Maqṣūd, appears to have also taught concentration on the yogic *Chakras*, cf. his *Zavāyā-ye makhfī-ye ḥayātī* (Tehran, 1354/1975), pp. 45ff. Alchemy is also one of the spiritual practices among the Oveysiyya. In his somewhat hermetic text on the Great Work, Shāh Maqṣūd seems to repeatedly indicate that one of the resulting benefits of the Philosopher's Stone is the epiphany of the imam; Shāh Maqṣūd ʿAnqā, *Sirr al-ḥajar* (Tehran, 1359/1980), pp. 48–50, 81, 92, 105, 122.

43. See Gramlich, *Die schiitischen Derwischorden*, vol. 1, pp. 27–69; M. Ṣ. Sohā, *Tārīkh-e ensheʿābāt-e motaʾakhkhere-ye selsele-ye Neʿmatollāhiyye* in *Do resāle dar tārikh-e jadīd-e taṣavvof-e Īrān* (Tehran, 1370/1991), pp. 5–121; see also N. Pourjavady and P. L. Wilson, *Kings of Love: The Poetry and History of the Niʿmatullahī Sufi Order* (Tehran, 1978), esp. the introduction; L. Lewisohn, 'An Introduction to the History of Modern Persian Sufism. Part I: Niʿmatullāhiyya', *BSOAS*, 61/3 (1998), pp. 437–464. On the namesake of this order and their gradual conversion to Imami Shiʿism, one can find valuable information in J. Aubin, *Matériaux pour la biographie de Shāh Niʿmatullāh Walī Kermānī* (Tehran and Paris, 1956). The religious affiliation of authors will not be given here; all the more so because some among them are claimed by several branches of the order.

face)',[44] these authors also identify this step with technical terms such as *ḥuḍūr-e ṣūrat* (the presence of the face), *ḥuḍūr-e ṣūrat-e shaykh* (the presence of the master's face) or quite simply *ḥuḍūr-e qalb* (the presence of the heart), leading to the vision of the Impeccable Ones.[45]

In the introduction to his *Red Sulphur*, Muẓaffar ʿAlī Shāh Kermānī (d. 1215/1801) writes:

> The reality of the heart is this locus of manifestation of the divine Light and the mirror for epiphanies of the Imams' presence. It is a subtle divine entity, a simple spiritual entity (*laṭīfe-īst rabbānī va mojarrad-īst rūḥānī*). The physical form of this spiritual heart is the pineal shaped carnal organ located on the left of the hollow of the chest which is like a window opening upon the subtle spiritual entity . . . Every non-material epiphany realised in the spiritual heart manifests itself in the form and concrete representation at the level of the physical heart. The most perfect form, representation of the perfect epiphany ... is the Human form (*ṣūrat-e ensānī*).[46]

---

44. See e.g. Ismāʿīl b. Muḥammad al-Qādirī, *al-Fuyūḍāt al-rabbāniyya* (Cairo, n.d.), pp. 28–29. On Qādiri practices focused on the heart, see also, A. Ventura, 'La presanza divina nel Cuore', *Quaderni di Studi Arabi*, 3 (1985), pp. 123–134 and 'L'invocazione del cuore', in *Yād Nāma...Alessandro Bausani* (Rome, 1991), pp. 475–485. On the importance accorded the 'heart' in Sunni mysticism generally, see G. Gobillot and P. Ballanfat, 'Le cœur et la vie spirituelle chez les mystiques musulmans', *Connaissance des religions*, 57–59 (1999), pp. 170–204.

45. Zayn al-ʿĀbidīn Shirvānī Mast ʿAlī Shāh, *Riyāḍ al-siyāḥa* (Tehran, 1339/1920), pp. 369–374, esp. 373 and *Bustān al-siyāḥa* (Tehran, 1378/1958), pp. 430–432; Maʿṣūm ʿAlī Shāh, *Ṭarāʾiq al-ḥaqāʾiq* (Tehran, 1318–1319/1900–1901), vol. 1, p. 217 and vol. 3, p. 83. Consider however the nuances introduced to the practice of concentrating on the master's visage by Majdhūb ʿAlī Shāh (d. 1238/1822, another Niʿmatullāhī master) in Muḥammad Jaʿfar Kabūdarāhangī Majdhūb ʿAlī Shāh, *Rasāʾel majdhūbiyye*, ed. H. Nājī Iṣfahānī (Isfahan, 1377/1998), '*Resāle-ye eʿteqādāt*', pp. 93–99.

46. Muẓaffar ʿAlī Shāh, *Kebrīt-e aḥmar* with *Baḥr al-asrār*, ed. J. Nūrbakhsh (Tehran, 1350/1971), p. 5; also *Guide divin*, pp. 132–133 (*Divine Guide*, pp. 51–52); in the *Rasāʾel majdhūbiyye*, the text of *Kebrīt-e aḥmar* is attributed to Majdhūb ʿAlī Shāh bearing the title *Kanz al-asmāʾ*, pp. 131–154 (see also the editor's introduction, p. xxxvii). The incorrectness of this attribution

In the next part of the treatise, in a rather abstruse and hermetic vocabulary, the mystical master describes the *dhikr*s and signs that must be visualised – especially at the level of the heart – during visualisation exercises for the Light of the imam.[47] In his versified work devoted to alchemy, *Nūr al-anwār*, Muẓaffar ʿAlī Shāh alludes to three of his visions, through which he acquired perfect knowledge of the secrets of alchemy. During the first experience, he had a vision of ʿAlī and the Prophet, and in the third, his true master in alchemy, the imam al-Riḍā.[48]

The most detailed theoretical explanations seem to have been provided by Mullā Sulṭan Muḥammad Sulṭān ʿAlī Shāh (d. 1327/1909). In fact he devotes the whole of chapter 18 of the fourth section of his *Majmaʿ al-saʿādāt* to 'an explanation of knowledge of the imam as Light' (*dar bayān-e maʿrefat-e emām be nūrāniyyat*):

> One who possesses the senses [literally 'the eye and ear'] pertaining to the sense-perceptible Kingdom (*mulk*) of God can know the imam as a human being (*bashariyyat-e emām*) … but one whose senses pertaining to the celestial Kingdom (*malakūt*) are acti-

---

is convincingly demonstrated in the article by S. M. Āzmāyesh, '*Kebrīt-e aḥmar* va *Kanz al-asmā*'', *'Erfān-e Īrān*, new series, 1 (Paris, 1378/1999), pp. 181–195.

47. Among the *dhikr*s, one finds *nādi ʿAlī* (already examined above, note 34, here called 'the extensive ʿAlawī speech', *kaleme-ye ʿalaviyye-ye tafṣīliyye*), as well as 'the condensed ʿAlawī speech', *kaleme-ye ʿalaviyye-ye ejmāliyye*, i.e. the *dhikr*: *ʿLā fatā illā ʿAlī lā sayfa illā Dhi'l-faqār/yā ʿAlī yā īliyā yā bā Ḥasan yā bā Ṭorāb* ('No chivalrous hero except ʿAlī, no sword but Dhu'l-Faqār [name of the sword of celestial origin that according to tradition ʿAlī inherited from the Prophet] / O ʿAlī, O Īliyā, O Bā Ḥasan [i.e. Abu'l-Ḥasan], O Bā Turāb [meaning Abū Turāb; in this second hemistich two names and two *kunya*s of ʿAlī are given]), see *Kebrīt-e aḥmar*, pp. 7–16.

48. Muẓaffar ʿAlī Shāh, *Nūr al-anwār*, ed. N. Sobbūḥī (Tehran, n.d.), ch. 3, section 1; cited by P. Lory, 'Alchimie et philosophie chiite. L'œuvre alchimique de Muẓaffar ʿAlī Shāh Kirmānī', in Ž. Vesel, M. Beygbaghban and Th. de Crussol des Epesse (ed.), *La science dans le monde iranien à l'époque islamique* (Tehran and Paris, 1999), p. 341; see also *Nūr al-anwār*, p. 15 where the author says that the Great Work of alchemy gives rise to the epiphanic manifestation of the Impeccable Ones.

vated, he can attain knowledge of the imam as Light (*nūrāniyyat-e emām*) . . . When someone takes an oath [*bay'at*; this term technically refers to the handshake between master and disciple during the latter's initiation] with the imam or a master authorised by the imam [*shaykh-e mojāz az jāneb-e emām* i.e. the spiritual master of the order], the celestial form [or the face] of the imam (*ṣūrat-e malakūtī-ye emām*) is introduced into his heart by virtue of this oath.

It is this Face that we call the *walāya* of the holder of (spiritual) authority (*valāyat-e valī-ye amr*) . . . and the Love of 'Alī (*maḥabbat-e 'Alī*) and it is well and truly 'faith entering the heart' (*īmān-e dākhel-e qalb*)[49] . . . It is because of this Face that a filial relationship is established between the imam and the believer and that, as a consequence, a fraternal relationship is established between the followers… However, the luminosity of the Face remains hidden if one who bears this Face in his heart remains captive to the obscuring veils of the ego; but once these veils are lifted, the Light becomes manifest. In the microcosm [*'ālam-e ṣaghīr*, i.e. the external physical world], this epiphany is called 'the final manifestation of the Resurrector' [*ẓohūr-e qā'em*, i.e. the eschatological Return of the hidden imam] and [in the internal spiritual world] it constitutes one of the degrees of the Light of the imam in the heart and is designated by expressions such as 'Presence', 'Serenity' or 'Contemplation' (*ḥoḍūr, sakīna, fekr*).[50] This is what illuminates the follower, enabling him to know the imam as Light . . . The manifestation of this celestial Face awakens the adept's capacity for celestial perception (*madārek-e monāseb-e malakūt*), making it possible for him to contemplate the inhabitants of the heavens, the

49. One should note that the term *īmān* is one of the technical designations for the doctrine of the imams, i.e. of Shi'ism denoting the esoteric dimension of Muḥammad's message, whose exoteric aspect is called *islām*, see *Guide divin*, index under *'īmān'*.

50. The hidden imam is thus presented as the external figure of an internal Imam of Light that is none other than the Face of God. cf. Chapter 13 in this volume and Amir-Moezzi, *Eschatology*, pp. 578b–580. Note here the convergences between hermeneutical doctrine and early Imami theology, cf. Chapter 3, this volume.

imaginal world, even the world of souls and universal intelligences (*ʿālam-e methāl balke ʿālam-e nofūs va ʿoqūl*) … He may thus be able to free himself from any attachment to time and place; walk upon water or in the air; travel miraculously from one place to another (*ṭayy al-arḍ*); enter fire, etc.[51]

The author then explains that while waiting to attain this level of spiritual awareness, the follower is advised to concentrate constantly on the spiritual image of his master's face. Here, there is some ambiguity with the term 'Face'. Is it the master's face or really that of the imam? The ambiguity is undoubtedly deliberate in order to subtly suggest a kind of identity between the two. The text continues as follows:

It is this adept, and he alone, who is called 'the tested faithful' [*mu'min mumtaḥan*; an allusion to the formulaic statement 'the believer whose heart has been tested by God for faith', cf. above]. . . and it is this Face which is called the Supreme Name'; then the author cites a *ḥadīth* of the imams listing the magical and miraculous powers of the Supreme Name of God.[52]

---

51. Sulṭān ʿAlī Shāh Gonābādī, *Majmaʿ al-saʿādāt* (2nd edn, n.p., 1394/1974), pp. 289–291. At the beginning of ch. 9 in section 3, p. 198, the author explains that, for the 'the ones of a middling state' (*mutavasseṭīn*) knowledge of the Imam of Light is equivalent to knowledge of God. For the 'incompleted ones' (*nāqeṣīn*), this knowledge is of the historical imams. Finally for the 'accomplished' (*muntahīn*), this knowledge is of the epiphany of the Real (*ẓohūr-e ḥaqq*), where subject and object have fused and where there is neither a subject who knows nor an object that is known.

52. *Majmaʿ*, pp. 291–293. The author repeatedly states that 'the celestial form of the imam' in the heart (also called 'the Greatest Name', or 'the seed of *walāya*' (*ḥabbat al-walāya*) is planted by the master in the disciple's heart during *bayʿa* (the oath of allegiance). Its existence is thus an assurance of legitimacy and a sign of regular transmission. Conversely, only legitimate transmission assures the existence of 'the form of the imam' in the master and the possibility of it being transferred to the disciple. Implicitly emphasised is the delicate issue of spiritual authority and legitimacy. The schismatic adept ipso facto loses 'the seed of *walāya*'. Thus he cannot transmit what he no longer possesses. According to the time-honoured expression, the branch to which he gave birth lacks vigour

In another work, the *Valāyat-nāmeh*, Sulṭān ʿAlī Shāh revisits (though only in a fragmentary manner) some of the elements just mentioned: in the chapter on *dhikr*, vision by the heart;[53] the figure of the hidden imam as the exoteric aspect of the inner imam;[54] and the critical role of initiatory *bayʿa* as the point of departure for illumination of the heart by the imam of Light.[55] The successor to Sulṭān ʿAlī Shāh in the Gonābādī branch, Nūr ʿAlī Shāh II (d. 1337/1918), summarises his master's sayings in his *Sāleḥiyye* (written for his son and successor, Ṣāliḥ ʿAlī Shāh, d. 1966): 'The Light which manifests itself in the heart is of the imam, a Light more radiant than that of the sun.' He goes on to cite the *ḥadīth* attributed to ʿAlī, especially valued by Shiʿi mystics:

> To know me as Light is to know God and to know God is to know me as Light. He who knows me as Light is a believer whose heart God has tested for faith (*maʿrifatī bi'l-nūrāniyya maʿrifatu'llāh wa maʿrifatu'llāh maʿrifatī bi'l-nūrāniyya man ʿarafanī bi'l-nūrāniyya kāna muʾminan imtaḥana'llāhu qalbahu li'l-īmān*).[56]

Elsewhere he adds:

> The Heart contains two faces (*rū*): its exoteric (*ẓāhir*) manifest face represents life, guarrunting the existence of the body and organic energies. This face is the foundation upon which is posed the Light (*īn vejhi qāʿide-ye nūr ast*).[57] Its esoteric (*bāṭin*) hidden face whose locus of manifestation is found in the chest (*ṣadr*) is the place for the reunion and epiphany of the divine Names and Attributes;

---

and is bound to dry up sooner or later (see for example, Shirvānī Mast ʿAlī Shāh, *Riyāḍ al-siyāḥa* [Tehran, 1339/1920], pp. 201 and 238–239).

53. Sulṭān ʿAlī Shāh, *Valāyat-nāmeh* (Tehran, 1385/1965), section 9, chs 2–6.

54. *Valāyat-nāmeh*, section 9, ch. 9 and section 10, chs 1–2.

55. *Valāyat-nāmeh*, section 12.

56. Nūr ʿAlī Shāh Thānī, *Ṣāleḥiyye* (Tehran, 1387/1967), *ḥaqīqa* 86, pp. 159–160.

57. According to the Imami notion that *bāṭin* can only be founded upon *ẓāhir*.

> which is why it is called the Throne (*ʿarsh*). Indeed, 'the heart of the sage is the supreme Throne of God' . . . ʿAlī [as the archetypal Imam] is verily the Throne of God since by his esoteric Face he is God, which is why he is the confluence of secrets (*li-hādhā ʿAlī ʿarsh ast ke be-rū-ye bāṭin Allāh ast ke majmaʿ-e asrār ast*).[58]

Also mentioned in various passages of the same work, are the five or seven subtle 'levels' of the heart (*qalb, fu'ād, sirr, khafī, akhfā* and *ṣadr, qalb, rūḥ, ʿaql, sirr, khafī, akhfā*), their respective colours, (green, blue-grey, combined colours, *alvān-e āmīkhte*, red, white, colourless, *bī lawn*, yellow, black) and the corresponding *dhikr*s and oraisons.[59]

* * *

The Khāksār dervishes are not given much to writing.[60] Spiritual descendants of the ancient Middle Eastern *fityān* and of the *Qalandar*s who wander throughout the Indian sub-continent, they emerged in Iran during the nineteenth century. They are usually to be found amongst the itinerant dervishes of Iran, wearing long hair and long beards and all the paraphernalia of members of rare guilds of old style professions or in the milieu of the *zūr-khāneh* – the traditional Persian martial arts – and among the 'mystic *aèdes*', bards and travelling reciters (*naqqāl*) of the *Shāh-nāma* of Firdawsī.[61] Loyal to the Qalandarī tradition,

58. *Ṣāleḥiyye*, *ḥaqīqa* 587, p. 330.

59. *Ṣāleḥiyye*, pp. 149–150, 156, 328ff.; cf. *Guide divin*, pp. 133–134 (*Divine Guide*, pp. 51–52).

60. Gramlich, *Die schiitischen Derwischorden*, vol. 1, pp. 70ff., esp. pp. 85–88; N. Modarresī Chahārdehī, *Khāksār va Ahl-e ḥaqq* (Tehran, 1368/1989); S. A. Mīr ʿĀbedīnī and M. Afshārī, *Ā'īn-e qalandarī* (Tehran, 1374/1995), editor intro.; C. Tortel, *Saints ou démons? Les Qalandar-s Jalālī et autres derviches errants en terre d'islam* (*Russie méridionale et Inde aux XIIIe-XVIIe s.*) (PhD EPHE, Religious Sciences, Paris, 1999), ch. 4, pp. 191–197.

61. Modarresī, *Khāksār*, section 1; also M. A. Amir-Moezzi, 'De quelques interprétations spirituelles du *Šāhnāme* de Ferdowsī', in C. Balay, C. Kappler and Ž. Vesel (eds), *Pand o sokhan. Mélanges offerts à Charles Henri de Fouchécour* (Tehran and Paris, 1995), pp. 22–23. I owe the expression 'mystic

the various branches of the Khāksār favour the oral transmission of their teachings. To my knowledge, unlike other orders, the Khāksāriyya possess neither a publishing house nor a printing press. The rare publications of the order, for example the standard reference works by Maʿṣūm ʿAlī Shāh ʿAbd al-Karīm 'Modarres-e ʿĀlam' (who died, I believe in the 1950s) do not provide any information regarding the subject at hand.[62]

In the current state of research, the only Khāksār text containing elements concerning the vision of the imam seems to be a text in verse by Sayyid Aḥmad Dehkordī (d. 1339/1920) entitled *Borhān-nāme-ye ḥaqīqat*. At a given moment, the poet begins to describe the Sevenfold Mountains of the heart (*aṭvār-e sabʿe-ye qalbiyye*) with the *dhikr* appropriate to each level: *ṣadr* with the word *al-ʿalī*, *qalb* with *al-ḥayy*, *shaghāf* with *huwa'l-ḥayy*, *fu'ād* with *ʿalī Allāh*, *ḥabbat al-qalb* with *ʿalī al-aʿlā*, *suwaydā'* with *ʿalī al-ḥaqq*, and *sirr al-sirr* apparently in silence. It is at this ultimate level that the Face of God manifests in the heart of the mystic in the radiant form of the imam, of whom ʿAlī is the archetype, whom the poet calls 'the Sun of Truth' (*khorshīd-e ḥaqīqat*); this section ends with the following verse:

> What good news, announces, reveals this secret / ʿAlī is well and truly the Lord, there is no one but he.
>
> ʿAlī is the universal Truth, the Illuminator of creatures / ʿAlī is the mercy of God, the secret of the mighty Aḥmad [i.e the prophet Muḥammad] (*beshāratī ke zabān bar goshā vo fāsh begū/ʿAlī-st*

aède' to I. Mélikoff who applies it to the Anatolian *ashiks*; see for example, her work *Les traces du soufisme turc. Recherches sur l'islam populaire en Anatolie* (Paris, 1992), index under '*ashik*'.

62. Modarres-e ʿĀlam, *Toḥfe-ye darvīsh* (Tehran, 1337/1959) and *Ganjīne-ye awliyā' yā ā'īne-ye ʿorafā'* (Tehran, 1338/1960); 'Modarres-e ʿālam', the *laqab* of the Khāksār master means 'teacher of the world'; R. Gramlich spells it incorrectly 'Modarrisī-i ʿĀlim', see *Die schiitischen Derwischorden*, vol. 1, pp. 85–86.

khodā laysa ghayrahu dayyār. 'Alī ḥaqīqat-e kol nūr bakhsh-e 'ālamiyān/'Alī -st raḥmat-e ḥaqq serr-e aḥmad-e mokhtār).[63]

* * *

The theologico-mystical School of the Shaykhiyya derives its name from Shaykh Aḥmad Zayn al-Dīn al-Aḥsā'ī, originally from Baḥrayn (d. 1241/1826). The Shaykhīs works, and in particular the masters of the school, at times refer to the visions of one or another imam, but never, to my knowledge, following a specific spiritual 'technique'. Much is said about the imam's World and his Light; the eye of the heart, illumination (*ishrāq, tanwīr* etc.) of the follower. It cannot be otherwise since a number of *ḥadīth*s dating back to the imams refer to this, and the Shaykhiyya accord the greatest doctrinal importance to reading, meditation and commentary on *ḥadīth*s.[64]

What appears to be customary here as preparatory exercises for vision of the imam is a life dedicated to devotion, the most scrupulous observance of religious Law, ever more penetrating meditation on Imami works, more specifically the *ḥadīth*s of the imams, and above all, unfailing spiritual love for the imams and their Cause. One becomes convinced of this simply by leafing through Shaykhīs texts. Is this due to the practice of 'dissimulation' (*taqiyya*)? Or is it perhaps quite simply the product of my insufficient reading? Consulting some dozen works did not provide me with any precise indication regarding a technical exercise leading to a vision, as is the case among other orders; but some dozen works are still too few from a vast corpus of several thou-

63. S. A. Dehkordī, *Borhān-nāme-ye ḥaqīqat* (Tehran, n.d.), pp. 81ff.; also Balāghī, *Maqālāt al-ḥunafā'* (Tehran, 1369/1949), pp. 129–132.

64. See their monumental compilations of traditions, e.g. Muḥammad Karīm Khān and Muḥammad Khān Kermānī, *Faṣl al-khiṭāb*, pp. 1,508 in folio (lithograph, Tehran, 1302/1885); Muḥammad Khān and Zayn al-'Ābidīn Khān Kermānī, *Kitāb al-mubīn*, 2 vols in folio, pp. 617 and 634 (lithograph, n.p., 1305–1324/1887–1906).

sand titles, some of which are in several large folio volumes.[65] The literature of the Shaykhiyya still remains largely unexplored by researchers and the few observations that follow, as with all previous studies on the doctrinal teachings of this brotherhood, can only be considered provisional.

In a letter addressed to a friend, Shaykh Aḥmad al-Aḥsāʾī mentions his spiritual states rich with extraordinary dreams, premonitions, visions of the imams and ecstatic revelations of secrets. Most notably, he writes:

> It is reported of Imam Muḥammad al-Bāqir: 'When a follower loves us [the imams], makes progress in his loyal friendship (*walāya*) for us and dedicates himself to know us, there is not a question that he poses for which we do not inspire an answer in his heart.' I then had visions of the imams during which matters were revealed to me that I would be hard pressed to describe to others.[66]

Elsewhere, dealing with the question of the authenticity of traditions, he cites the *ḥadīth*, 'The vision of the perfect faithful initiate is equivalent to direct visual perception' (*mushāhadatu'l-mu'mini'l-kāmil ka'l-muʿāyana*) and maintains that the super sense-perceptible encounter with the imams provides the believer

65. For an idea of the richness of Shaykhiyya literature, see A. Q. Ebrāhīmī Kermānī, *Fehrest-e kotob-e... Shaykh Aḥmad-e Aḥsāʾī va sāʾer-e mashāyekh-e ʿeẓām va kholāṣe-ye aḥvāl-e īshān* (Kerman, 1377/1957); H. Corbin, 'L'Ecole Shaykhie en théologie shîʿite', *Annuaire de l'EPHE* (1960–1961), pp. 3–59 (rpr. in *Islam iranien*, vol. 4); V. Rafati, 'The Development of Shaykhi Thought in Shii Islam'; M. Momen, *The Works of Shaykh Ahmad al-Ahsaʾi. A Bibliography* (Newcastle-upon-Tyne, 1991); D. McEoin, *The Sources for Early Bābī Doctrine and History* (Leiden, 1992); I. S. Hamid, 'The Metaphysics and Cosmology of Process According to Shaykh Aḥmad al-Aḥsāʾī' (State University of New York, 1998). See also M. A. Amir-Moezzi and S. Schmidtke, 'Twelver Shīʾite Resources in Europe', *JA*, 285/1 (1997), pp. 73–122, especially pp. 87–120 (description of the Shaykhī collection at EPHE [Religious Sciences] and the Department of Oriental Studies at the University of Cologne).

66. Āghā Sayyid Hādī Hindī, *Tanbīh al-ghāfilīn wa surūr al-nāẓirīn* (n.p. [Tabriz], n.d.), pp. 53–54; Ebrāhīmī Kermānī, *Fehrest-e kotob*, vol. 1, p. 180.

with a 'spiritual initiation' (lit.savour' *dhawq*) due to which he can immediately perceive the authencity or otherwise of a tradition.[67]

Muḥammad Karīm Khān Kermānī (d. 1288/1870), a master of the Shaykhiyya from Kermān, has also left us an account of a vision he had of the ninth imam, Muḥammad al-Jawād, and of its consequences:

> After my encounter with the imam al-Jawād, I was careful to pay more attention to hidden things. I had a vision of (other) imams and felt guided by them. Henceforth, for my understanding in matters of Qur'ān and *Ḥadīth*, I have recourse directly to them and rely upon no one else. I profess nothing that is not based on them and their teachings. I do not submit (*taslīm*) or emulate (*taqlīd*) anyone but them. All my knowledge is as a result of these inner visions.[68]

According to the masters of the Shaykhiyya, the vision of the imam occurs in a 'World' that, following the philosophical School of the *Ishrāq*, specifically Quṭb al-Dīn al-Shīrāzī, the commentor on Suhrawardī, they call the World of Hūrqalyā.[69] This has been masterfully studied by H. Corbin in his *Corps spirituel et terre celeste* and one can only refer the reader to this rich and detailed

67. Al-Shaykh Aḥmad al-Aḥsā'ī, *Sharḥ al-ziyāra al-jāmiʿa* (lithograph, Tabriz, n.d.), pp. 73–74; *Fehrest-e kotob*, vol. 1, p. 185; Corbin, *Islam iranien*, vol. 4, p. 218; Amir-Moezzi, 'Remarques sur les critères d'authenticité du hadîth et l'autorité du juriste dans le shiʿisme imâmite', p. 34.

68. Mīrzā Niʿmatullāh Riḍawī (a direct disciple of Muḥammad Karīm Khān), *Tadhkirat al-awliyā'* (lithograph, Bombay, 1313/1895), p. 14; *Fehrest-e kotob*, vol. 1, p. 83; Amir-Moezzi, 'Remarques', p. 35.

69. See for example, *Sharḥ al-ziyāra*, pp. 369ff.; Aḥmad al-Ahsā'ī, *al-Risāla al-qaṭīfiyya* and *Jawāb ʿalā Mullā Ḥusayn al-Anbarī al-Kirmānī* in *Jawāmiʿ al-kalim* (lithograph, Tabriz, 1273/1856), vol. 1, pp. 136 and 153–154 respectively; Sayyid Kāẓim b. Qāsim al-Ḥusaynī al-Rashtī, *Sharḥ al-khuṭba al-ṭaṭanjiyya* (lithograph, Tabriz, 1270/1853), intro.; Muḥammad Karīm Khān Kirmānī, *Irshād al-ʿawāmm* (Kerman, 1354/1935), vol. 2, pp. 274–275; Abu'l-Qāsim Khān Ebrāhīmī, *Tanzīh al-awliyā'* (Kerman, 1367/1948), pp. 702–726; and here, section 14, note 72.

work.[70] Based on the analysis of the philosopher Muḥsin al-Fayḍ al-Kāshānī (d. 1091/1680), this World, part of the Imaginal World (to cite Corbin's translation of *'ālam al-mithāl*), is a world where the spirits take corporeal form and bodies take spiritual form.[71] This universe which has its own ontological reality and where (still based on Corbin), 'all phenomenology of the spirit is effected' for the Shaykhīs is not only the world of vision of the imam but also, quite simply the World of the Imam. It is up to the initiate-follower to develop his 'organs of Hūrqalyā' (*a'ḍā'-e hūrqalyāviyye*); and more specifically, of these, his 'eye capable of recognising the imam' (*chashm-e emām shenās*) by means of sincere prayers and purifying acts of ascetism, in order to be able to gain access to this World and there discover the Light of the imam.[72] In his *Irshād al-'awāmm* Muḥammad Karīm Khān writes: 'When the world we are [sic] scales the heights and reaches the World of the Hūrqalyā, at that very point he sees the Light of the Imam. Truth is revealed. Darkness then dissipates.'[73]

Abu'l-Qāsim Khān Ebrāhīmī (d. 1969) writes:

> In *Hūrqalyā*, you will be elevated above the phenomenon of the sense-perceptible world; you will have perceived and contemplated the eternal Image (*methāl-e azalī*), the pure Form (*ṣūrat-e pāk*) and the Light of your Imam, as a primordial Image completely covering the horizon of this world . . . You will then understand why it is that none save he governs and decides; how all else only execute his orders. You will perceive all actions and operations as

70. *Corps spirituel*, index under 'Hûrqalyâ'. See also M. Mo'īn, 'Havarqalyā', *Revue Fac. Lettres de l'Univ. de Téhéran* (1333/1955), pp. 78–105; according to Mo'īn, the etymology for this term is an expression in Hebrew, *habal qarnaīm* (suggesting something like 'double path') whence its vocalisation 'Havarqalyā'; see also Rafati, *Development of Shaykhi Thought*, pp. 106ff.

71. *Kalimāt maknūna* (Tehran, 1316/1898), p. 70.

72. Ebrāhīmī, *Tanzīh*, p. 725.

73. Muḥammad Karīm Khān, *Irshād*, vol. 2, p. 275; trans. in Corbin, *Corps spirituel*, pp. 262–264.

dominated by this imaginal Form (*ṣūrat-e methālī*) and permanently depending on the Imam.[74]

At the same time, as I have written elsewhere,[75] accounts of encounters with the hidden imam serve as hemeneutic elements for Kāẓim Rashtī (d. 1259/1843), the second master and actual founder of the order, who describes the vision of the last imam in individual eschatological terms. Considering at one and the same time these accounts and what tradition presents as the last signed letter by the hidden imam, a letter according to which the latter could not be seen until the End of Time,[76] Sayyid Kāẓim essentially proposes the following syllogism: according to his own words in his last letter, the hidden imam can only be seen at the End of Time; now, according to reliable sources, some people have seen him; therefore these individuals have reached the End of Time.[77] The conclusion drawn by this syllogism obviously designates 'an initiatic death': an encounter with the Qā'im leads to the death of the ego and an inner rebirth of the faithful-initiate. The vision of the hidden imam here signifies the End of the era of the occultation in the individual and coincides with his spiritual birth (*al-wilāda al-rūḥāniyya*).[78]

74. *Tanzīh*, p. 726; trans. in *Corps spirituel*, p. 290. See also Chapter 14, this volume.

75. Chapter 13, this volume.

76. For the text of this letter, its implications and the studies concerning it, see *Guide divin*, pp. 276ff. (*Divine Guide*, pp. 113–114) and Chapter 13, this volume.

77. Al-Sayyid Kāẓim al-Rashtī, *al-Rasā'il wa'l-masā'il* (lithograph, Tabriz, n.d.), pp. 356–365.

78. See also section 14 *in fine*. The eschatological thought of Sayyid Kāẓim Rashtī deserves a separate study. To the sources already mentioned in Chapter 14, one should add his *Dalīl al-mutaḥayyirīn* (lithograph, Tabriz, n.d.) and *Sharḥ qaṣīda lāmiyya li-ʿAbd al-Bāqī Efendī* (lithograph, n.p. [Tabriz], n.d.); some excerpts of this latter work have been translated into French by A. L. M. Nicolas, *Essai sur le Cheïkhisme* (Paris, 1910–1914), vol. 2, pp. 37–44 and 52–55.

Conclusion

> Among us (the imams), he who dies is not dead;[79] the light of the imam in the hearts of the faithful is more radiant than the morning star;[80] our teachings are a secret, a secret hidden by a secret . . . it is arduous, especially difficult; only a prophet-envoy, an angel of Proximity or a believer whose heart is tested by God for faith can bear it.[81]

The issue of the visions of the imams in their different forms seems to be a fertile hermeneutic field for these kinds of traditions which have been reported in the most ancient compilations of Twelver *ḥadīth*s and subsequently. Indeed, for the believer, even after ending their terrestrial lives, the imams are not dead. They continue to live and help their true believers by being present in their hearts and, at times, by rendering themselves visible to them. How might this be? In modern Imami mysticism, the answers are as varied as the range of mystical orders.

In non-institutionalised mysticism largely represented, at least in the texts, by religious scholars, the points of view are more or less similar to what is encountered in popular beliefs. The imam manifests himself in the physical world and thus becomes visible to the naked eye. The imam's being is an absolute miracle. Due

79. *Yamūt man māta minnā wa laysa bi-mayyit*, tradition dating back to ʿAlī: Al-Ṣaffār al-Qummī, *Baṣāʾir al-darajāt*, ed. M. Kūchebāghī (Tabriz, n.d. [ca. 1380/1960]), p. 275. On beliefs about the post-mortem life of the imams 'in their bodies' among some Shiʿis, especially in Kūfa, see M. Ayoub, *Redempting Suffering in Islām: a Study of the Devotional Aspects of ʿĀshūrāʾ in Twelver Shīʿism* (The Hague, 1978), pp. 245ff.; H. Halm, *Die islamische Gnosis. Die Extreme Shia und die ʿAlawiten* (Zurich and Munich, 1982), pp. 240ff. and 284ff.

80. *La-nūr al-īmām fī qulūb al-muʾminīn anwar min al-shams al-muḍīʾa biʾl-nahār*, tradition dating back to al-Bāqir: al-Kulaynī, *al-Uṣūl min al-Kāfī*, ed. J. Muṣṭafawī, 4 vols (Tehran, n.d.), 'kitāb al-ḥujja', vol. 1, p. 276.

81. *Ḥadīthunā sirr wa sirr mustasirr…ḥadīthunā ṣaʿb mustaṣʿab lā yaḥmiluhu illā nabī mursal aw malak muqarrab aw muʾmin imtaḥanaʾllāhu qalbahu liʾl-īmān*, traditions dating back to several of the imams; *Baṣāʾir*, pp. 26–29.

to this fact, and since he is alive, he is able to show himself to whomsoever has made himself worthy through leading a life of devotion, moral rectitude and unfailing love for the *ahl al-bayt*. To my knowledge, the issue of the nature of the imam's body which lets itself be 'seen' is not discussed in these kinds of sources; is it a physical body or does it take a subtle spiritual form? Nūrī Ṭabrisī, to cite him once more, is a perfect representative of this trend.

In a chapter of *al-Najm al-thāqib*, devoted to 'the place' where the hidden imam is located, he extends the discussion to include all the Impeccable Ones and categorically denies the possibility of any spiritual hermeneutics (*ta'wīl*) being applied either to their 'place of residence' or to a vision concerning them. According to him, when the imam manifests himself, anyone can see him; the problem lies in the fact that not just anyone is capable of recognising him.[82] Obviously familiar with traditions regarding the 'vision by the heart', Nūrī maintains that the 'eye of the heart' is the organ for seeing the ultimate reality of the imam's being; this, as we have seen in the introduction of our study, according to Imami theology is identical to the Names and Attributes of the revealed God. However, the author carefully avoids saying so. And this accounts only for the great initiates who make up a very limited number.[83] The manifestation of the imam in the physical world momentarily transfigures it (only in the immediate environment of the witness?) by introducing a break in the time-space continuum and overwhelms forevermore the inner world of the believer.

The mystical schools that developed from traditional Sufism (Dhahabiyya, Oveysiyya, Niʿmatullāhiyya, Khāksāriyya) developed an internalised conception of the imam. Faithful to the Shiʿi structural pair of *ẓāhir* and *bāṭin*, they maintain in essence that the Imam – the Perfect Man and divine Being par excellence – is exoterically manifested in our times by the hidden imam (the living

82. *Najm*, pp. 410ff.

83. *Najm*, p. 412.

occulted Qā'im) and esoterically by the imam in the follower's heart. This 'imam of light' is visible to the 'eye of the heart' not only through devotion and purity, but also a series of spiritual exercises carried out within the order: basically these are the various forms of *dhikr* and *fikr*, concentrating on the spiritual image of the living master's visage, but also the thaumaturgic sciences, chiefly alchemy. As R. Gramlich observes, we can certainly speak of a 'Shiʿi-influenced Sufism' but we may also consider it to be a reasonable state of affairs to the extent that a number of the concepts, beliefs and practices in question seem to have originated in early Shiʿism and undergone a gradual process of adaptation in the Sufi milieu.[84]

In this spiritual landscape, however, the theologico-mystical School of the Shaykhiyya from Kirmān constitutes a slightly different case. Having never hidden their differences, and at times their hostility towards the purely theological strands (both Uṣūlī and Akhbārī) on the one hand and the Sufi orders on the other,[85] this mystical order draws upon the theosophical tradition of the *Ishrāq*, chiefly and freely commented on by their eponymous founder, so as to advance an actual topography for the vision of the imam. *Hūrqalyā*, the World of the imam, is a spiritual *and* physical world, in which the imam can be an object of vision in his 'corporeal spiritual' body. Supported by the holy imams, it is up to the believer to develop his '*hūrqalyāwī* organs', particularly this 'eye of the heart capable of recognising the imam' in order to be able to perceive the 'realities' of this world. Here, in a fashion, we again encounter the consubstantiality of the subject doing the viewing and the object viewed referred to at the beginning of this study.

---

84. See *Guide divin*, pp. 129ff. and 316–317 (*Divine Guide*, pp. 50 and 130–131).

85. Lastly, see Abu'l-Qāsim Khān Ebrāhīmī, *Ejtehād va taqlīd*, in *Rasā'el-e marḥūm-e āqā-ye ḥājj Abu'l-Qāsim Khān*, facsimile of an autograph manuscript, Fonds Shaykhī (collection) de l'EPHE (sc. religieuses), SHA. VI.5, fol. 245ff. Regarding this collection, see note 65 above *in fine*.

As we have just seen, speculative explanations and spiritual practices vary from one strand to another. However, all the strands agree on the fundamental importance of devotion, the observance of acts of worship, moral rectitude and above all, *walāya*: the love-friendship-loyalty-submission offered to the imams.[86] A sign of spiritual authority and the criterion of veracity for inner progress, the vision of the imam also shows to what extent the Figure of the imam, to this day, remains pivotal for Twelver spirituality in its myriad forms.

86. For the fundamental importance of *walāya*, which the Imamis consider the essential core and one of the 'pillars' (*da'ā'im*) of Islam, see J. Eliash, 'On the Genesis and Development of the Twelver-Shī'ī Three Tenet *Shahāda*', *Der Islam*, 47 (1971), pp. 265–272; *Guide divin*, pp. 303–304 (*Divine Guide*, p. 125); M. M. Bar-Asher, *Scripture and Exegesis in Early Imāmī Shiism* (Leiden and Jerusalem, 1999), pp. 195–202; and esp. Chapter 7, this volume.

11

Notes on Prayer in Imami Shiʿism*

1

This chapter does not presume to speak about Henry Corbin or his monumental work in general. Rather, it seeks to briefly deal with a subject that was especially dear to him, namely prayer. At the outset, let us also clarify that we will not be examining this fundamental practice from the perspective of Islam in general, or the daily canonical prayer (Ar. *ṣalāt*; P. *namāz*).[1] We are concerned more specifically with a few little-known elements about the literature and some aspects of the superogatory prayer (*duʿāʾ*) in Twelver Shiʿism, considered in its various forms (invocation, supplication, prayer, pilgrimage prayer, occasional etc.) and often addressed to the entire group or to one or other of the Fourteen Impeccable Ones, that is, the Prophet Muḥammad, his daughter Fāṭima and especially the twelve imams.

* This chapter was previously published in a volume devoted to Henry Corbin's works, M. A. Amir-Moezzi, C. Jambet and P. Lory (eds), *Henry Corbin: philosophies et sagesses des religions du Livre*, Bibliothèque de l'Ecole des Hautes Etudes (Turnhout, 2005), vol. 126, pp. 65–80; hence the frequent references to his work.

1. See e.g. L. Gardet, 'Duʿāʾ', *EI2*, vol. 2, pp. 632–634; G. Monnot, 'Ṣalāt', *EI2*, vol. 8, pp. 956–965 (G. Monnot devoted part of his seminars during 1987–1988, at the Ecole Pratique des Hautes Etudes to the examination of prayer in Shiʿism and Sufism). See also A. d'Alverny, 'La prière selon le Coran II. La prière rituelle', *Proche-Orient Chrétien*, 10 (1960), pp. 303–317; S. D. Goitein, *Studies in Islamic History and Institutions* (Leiden, 1966), ch. 3, pp. 73–89; G. Monnot, 'Prières privées en islam traditionnel: autour d'un texte de Rāzī', *RHR*, 206/1 (1989), pp. 41–54; E. de Vitray-Meyerovitch, *La prière en Islam* (Paris, 1998).

In the course of his great work *Creative Imagination in the Sufism of Ibn 'Arabī*, Corbin devotes a few magnificent pages to prayer. In the third chapter of the second section entitled 'Prayer of Man, Prayer of God' he writes mainly about the 'reciprocity' of prayer:

> This idea of a *sharing* of roles in the manifestation of being, in the eternal theophany, is fundamental to Ibn 'Arabī's notion of prayer; it inspires what we have termed his method of prayer and makes it a 'method of theophanic prayer'. The notion of sharing presupposes a dialogue between two beings, and this [is a] living experience of a '*dialogic situation*' . . . True, this reciprocity becomes incomprehensible if we isolate the *ens creatum* outside the *Ens increatum* . . . For prayer is not a request for something: it is the expression of a mode of being, a means of existing and of *causing to exist*, that is, a means of causing the God who reveals Himself to appear, of 'seeing' Him, in order not to be sure in His essence, but in the *form* which precisely He reveals by revealing Himself by and to that form.[2]

A few pages later, he cites a poem – as audacious as it is brief – by the great Andalusian mystic:

> *It is He who glorifies me at the moment when I glorify Him. It is He who worships me at the moment when I worship Him* [which means that the Prayer of man *is* the Prayer of God].[3]

---

2. H. Corbin, *L'imagination créatrice dans le soufisme d'Ibn 'Arabī* (Paris, 1958), p. 185, English trans. Ralph Manheim, *Alone with the Alone, Creative Imagination in the Sufism of Ibn 'Arabī* (Princeton, 1997), pp. 247ff. (Corbin's italics). J. L. Vieillard Baron has written a excellent philosophical analysis of this section of the work in 'Temps spirituel et hiéro-histoire selon Henry Corbin : une phénoménologie de la connaissance psycho-cosmique', *Cahiers du Groupe d'Etudes Spirituelles Comparées*, 8, 'Henry Corbin et le comparatisme spirituel' (2000), pp. 25–37.

3. *L'imagination créatrice* p. 190, *Alone with the Alone*, p. 254.

All this is presented as a hermeneutical interpretation of the Qurʾānic verse 2:152, *fa-dhkurūnī adhkurkum* (lit. 'remember Me, and I shall remember you') that Henry Corbin, as he was wont, renders with an exegetic annotation, 'Have me present to your heart, I shall have you present to myself.'[4]

'Reciprocity' perhaps constitutes the most fundamental dimension of prayer; indeed it transforms prayer from a monologue that often seems flat and mechanical into a vibrant devotion deeply felt as an intense dialogue with the Person addressed – what Corbin calls 'the dialogic situation'. How is this dimension present in Imami prayer? Relatively speaking, this issue has not held Corbin's interest to any great extent. Indeed, this interest in Twelver prayer was expressed in a very limited context. During the academic sessions of 1968–1969 and 1969–1970, he devoted half his seminars at the Ecole Pratique des Hautes Etudes to an examination of the commentary that Shaykh Aḥmad al-Aḥsāʾī (d. 1241/1826) contributed on prayer relating to the 'spiritual pilgrimage of the twelve imams', that is to say, a text known as *al-Ziyārat al-jāmiʿa*, attributed to the tenth imam, ʿAlī al-Naqī, at least since the *Kitāb man lā yaḥḍuruhu'l-faqīh* by Ibn Bābūya al-Ṣadūq (d. 381/991).[5] The substance of this study, as well as other allusions to prayer in Imamism are fragmentary and scattered in *En Islam iranien.*

4. Ibid., p. 187. On the heart as 'an organ of prayer' in Ibn ʿArabī, see ibid., Part 2, ch. 2, pp. 164ff., *Alone with the Alone*, p. 250.

5. Now consult summaries of seminars by H. Corbin at Ecole Pratique des Hautes Etudes in the collection *Itinéraire d'un enseignement*, Institut Français de Recherche en Iran (Tehran, 1993), pp. 107–110 and 118–124; the work by Shaykh Aḥmad, *Sharḥ al-Ziyārat al-jāmiʿa* (Tabriz, 1276/1859); Ibn Bābūya, *Kitāb man lā yaḥḍuruhu'l-faqīh*, ed. al-Mūsawī al-Kharsān (Tehran, 1390/1970), vol. 2, pp. 370–376, no. 1625.

2

Prayer in its different forms, is undoubtedly the most regular and widespread illustration of Shiʿi devotion. There are thousands of them and the relevant literature is vast. Qualitatively, some prayers are of undeniable literary beauty, and are at times profoundly philosophical or mystical. As for the nature of the works that report these prayers, it may be possible to establish a kind of typology:

- Collections of prayers categorised according to their themes or the time and circumstances appropriate for recitation (specific moments during the day, particular days of the week, month, year, natural events etc.).
- Works devoted to the liturgical or ritualistic aspects of prayer (*ādāb al-ṣalāt, ādāb al-duʿāʾ*).
- Books of salutations (*ṣalawāt*) addressed to the Impeccable Ones.
- Prayers of an 'thaumatugic' kind, to be used as an element in divination (*istikhāra*), a talisman (*ṭilism*) or an amulet (*taʿwīdh*) etc.
- Oraisons and/or pilgrimage prayers (*ziyārāt*) at the tombs of the Impeccables. These are perhaps the most common. It is interesting to note that the same term, *ziyāra*, denotes both the pilgrimage, literally 'the visit' to the tomb, as well as the prayer recited on this occasion.

The oldest texts would have been compiled during the time of the imams themselves. Although the authenticity for the entirety of works such as *Nahj al-balāgha* (attributed to the first imam, ʿAlī b. Abī Ṭālib) and *al-Ṣaḥīfat al-sajjādiyya* (attributed to the fourth imam, ʿAlī b. al-Ḥusayn) is subject to discussion, it is nevertheless almost certain that they were constituted from an early core which is most likely authentic. The first contains a number of oraisons and the second is a collection of prayers.[6] In addition, early compilations of *ḥadīth*s, such as those by al-Kulaynī (329/940–941), Ibn

6. See e.g. L. Veccia Vaglieri, 'Sul "*Nahj al-balāghah*" e sul suo compilatore ash-Sharīf ar-Raḍī', *AIUON*, special issue, 8 (1958); the introduction by

Bābūya (381/991) or Shaykh al-Ṭūsī (460/1067) contain chapters, even entire 'books' devoted to prayers attributed to the imams.[7]

From the fifth/eleventh century onwards, the bibliographical and prosographical 'dictionaries', in this case the *Rijāl* by al-Najāshī or the *Fihrist* by the same al-Ṭūsī,[8] list works devoted to different aspects and forms of prayer written by Shiʿi thinkers and other learned individuals, the eldest of whom were contemporaries of and acquainted with the imams. These books, huge in number, would have been compilations of *ḥadīth*s dating back to one or another of the imams. Almost all of them seem to have been lost, but as is the case for other religious subjects, one may reasonably conclude that the contents of many of them were rescued and reported by other authors much later. Let us limit ourselves to some examples of famous authors from the third/ninth to the fifth/eleventh centuries:

(a) Works bearing the title *kitāb al-duʿā'*: ʿAlī b. Mahziyār al-Ahwāzī (Najāshī 253), Saʿd b. ʿAbd Allāh al-Ashʿarī al-Qummī (Najāshī 178),[9] Muḥammad b. Masʿūd al-ʿAyyāshī al-Samarqandī (Najāshī 351), Aḥmad b. Muḥammad b. Khālid al-Barqī (Najāshī 77, Ṭūsī 21), Ḥumayd b. Ziyād b. Ḥammād al-Dihqān (Najāshī 132), Muḥammad b. Yaʿqūb al-Kulaynī (Najāshī 377, Ṭūsī 135),[10]

W. Chittick to his English translation of *al-Ṣaḥīfat al-sajjādiyya*: *The Psalms of Islam* (London, 1988).

7. For example in chapters devoted to canonical prayers or pilgrimages in legalist texts by these authors, al-Kulaynī, *al-Furūʿ min al-Kāfī*, ed. ʿA. A. Ghaffārī (Tehran, 1391/1971); Ibn Bābūya, *Kitāb man lā yaḥḍuruhu'l-faqīh*, ed. al-Mūsawī al-Kharsān (Tehran, 1390/1970); al-Shaykh al-Ṭūsī, *Tahdhīb al-aḥkām*, ed. M. J. Shams al-Dīn (Beirut, 1412/1992), and 'The Book of Invocations' (*K. al-duʿā'*) in al-Kulaynī, *Uṣūl min al-Kāfī*, ed. J. Muṣṭafawī (Tehran, n.d.); for earlier compilations see further below.

8. Abu'l-ʿAbbās al-Najāshī, *Rijāl*, ed. M. al-Shubayrī al-Zanjānī (Qumm, 1407/1987); Abū Jaʿfar al-Ṭūsī, *al-Fihrist* (Beirut, 1403/1983).

9. This text seems identical to *Kitāb faḍl al-duʿā'* by al-Ashʿarī, cited by Ibn Ṭāwūs in several of his works; see E. Kohlberg, *A Medieval Muslim Scholar at Work: Ibn Ṭāwūs and his Library* (henceforth KIṬ) (Leiden, 1992), pp. 158–159.

10. Is this work the same as the *Kitāb al-duʿā'* by the same author in his *Uṣūl min al-Kāfī*, vol. 4, pp. 210–393?

Muḥammad b. al-Ḥasan al-Ṣaffār al-Qummī (Najāshī 354),[11] Muḥammad b. Ūrama al-Qummī (Najāshī 330) and *Kitāb adʿiyat al-aʾimma* by ʿUbayd Allāh b. Abī Zayd al-Anbārī (Najāshī 233).

(b) Prayers meant for specific occasions and described as *ʿamal al-ayyām/al-shuhūr*, collected for example in *Kitāb ʿamal yawm al-jumuʿa* by Muḥammad b. ʿAlī Ibn Abī Qurra (Najāshī 398);[12] *Kitāb yawm wa layla* by Muʿāwiya b. ʿAmmār al-Duhnī (Najāshī 411); several texts by Ibn ʿAyyāsh al-Jawharī such as *Kitāb ʿamal rajab, Kitāb ʿamal ramaḍān* or *Kitāb ʿamal shaʿbān* (Najāshī 85, Ṭūsī 33); *Kitāb al-najāḥ fī ʿamal shahr ramaḍān* by Faḍl b. Shādhān al-Nīsābūrī (Najāshī 307) and *Kitāb ʿamal yawm al-jumuʿa* by Abu'l-Fatḥ al-Karājakī (KIṬ 109).

(c) Various prayers offered in different circumstances, reported in collections such as *Kitāb al-tahajjud* by Ibn Abī Qurra already cited (Najāshī 398),[13] *Dafʿ al-humūm wa'l-aḥzān* by Aḥmad b. Dāwūd al-Nuʿmānī (KIṬ 138), the anonymous works *Majmūʿa mawlānā Zayn al-ʿĀbidīn*, apparently different from *Ṣaḥīfat al-sajjādiyya*[14] and *Majmūʿa adʿiya al-mustajābāt ʿan al-nabī wa'l-aʾimma* (KIṬ 266) and *Zād al-musāfir* by Aḥmad b. ʿAlī b. al-Ḥasan b. Shādhān al-Qummī.[15]

In Imamism, Shaykh al-Ṭūsī (460/1067) and Ibn Ṭāwūs (664/1266) are considered the two main 'pillars' for prayer literature. Indeed the famous *Miṣbāḥ al-mutahajjid* by Abū Jaʿfar

11. In many of his works, Ibn Ṭāwūs cites a *Kitāb faḍl al-duʿāʾ* by al-Ṣaffār al-Qummī which must be the same text (KIṬ, p. 159).

12. *Kitāb ʿamal shahr ramaḍān* (Najāshī 398) and *Kitāb ʿamal al-shuhūr* (ibid.) are also attributed to the same author. The first, known and used by Ibn Ṭāwūs, was perhaps part of the second (KIṬ, pp. 108–109).

13. As for Ibn Ṭāwūs, he speaks of a *Kitāb al-mutahajjid* (KIṬ, pp. 292).

14. It seems that *Iqbāl al-aʿmāl* by Ibn Ṭāwūs is the only source that includes some excerpts of this text attributed to the fourth imam (KIṬ, pp. 150).

15. Āghā Bozorg al-Ṭihrānī, *al-Dharīʿa ilā taṣānīf al-Shīʿa* (Tehran–Najaf, 1353–1398/1934–1978), vol. 12, p. 7, no. 40.

al-Ṭūsī may be considered *the* fundamental book in this literary genre.[16] Extremely popular, this voluminous collection has been commented upon extensively and translated into Persian on more than one occasion.[17] As for Raḍī al-Dīn Ibn Ṭāwūs, he is without a doubt, the most methodical author of prayer books. In his excellent work on this major figure of Imamism, Etan Kohlberg has demonstrated how Ibn Ṭāwūs, having more than seventy works of prayer by earlier authors at his disposal, organised for his readers a veritable syllabus for the religious formation of the individual through this spiritual practice.[18]

An admirer of the *Miṣbāḥ al-mutahajjid* by Shaykh al-Ṭūsī, who was one of his maternal forebears, Ibn Ṭāwūs wrote a complement to the work (apparently lost today) entitled *Kitāb (al) muhimmāt (fī* [or *lī*] *ṣalāḥ al-mutaʿabbid) wa (ʾl-) tatimmāt (li miṣbāḥ al-mutahajjid)* in which he advocated a programme based on five of his works devoted to prayer, to be read in the following order: *Falāḥ al-sāʾil, Zahrat al-rabīʿ, al-Shurūʿ fī ziyārāt wa ziyādāt ṣalawāt..., al-Iqbāl* and *Asrār al-ṣalawāt.* Elsewhere, he offers an even richer programme based on ten volumes of his works: *Falāḥ al-sāʾil* (2 volumes), *Zahrat al-rabīʿ, Jamāl al-usbūʿ, al-Durūʿ al-wāqiya, Miḍmār al-sabaq, Masālik al-muḥtāj...*, *al-Iqbāl* (2 volumes) and finally, *al-Saʿādāt biʾl-ʿibādāt.*[19] Apart

---

16. Latest edition by A. Bīdār (Tehran, 1373 Sh./1994).

17. For example the very old Persian translation most likely dating back to the seventh/thirteenth century, known as *Tarjama-ye mukhtaṣar-e Miṣbāḥ* (*Fihrist-e nuskha-hā-ye khaṭṭī-ye Kitābkhāne-ye... Marʿashī* [new edn, Qumm, 1378 Sh./1998], nos 877, 5987, 8911). Of the commentaries, see *Minhāj al-ṣalāḥ fī ikhtiṣār al-Miṣbāḥ* by al-ʿAllāma al-Ḥillī (d. 726/1325), in ten chapters, with its famous eleventh theological chapter entitled ʻal-Bāb al-ḥādī ʻasharʼ (latest edn, Qumm, 1419/1998); and in the eighth/fourteenth century, *Īḍāḥ al-Miṣbāḥ li ahl al-ṣalāḥ* by Bahāʾ al-Dīn al-Najafī (*Fihrist-e Kitābkhāne-ye Marʿashī*, MS 4568) and the modern *Mukhtaṣar Miṣbāḥ al-mutahajjid* by Mullā Ḥaydar ʿAlī b. Muḥammad al-Shīrwānī (*Fihrist-e Kitābkhāne-ye Marʿashī*, MS 3948).

18. Kohlberg, *A Medieval Muslim Scholar at Work*, passim, esp. the introduction, pp. 49ff.

19. Some of his books have now been edited, even more than once. Here only one edition is cited: *Falāḥ al-sāʾil* (Najaf, 1385/1965); *al-Iqbāl* (Tehran,

from these texts, Ibn Ṭāwūs left other important works on the subject of prayer such as *Muhaj al-daʿawāt,*[20] *al-Mujtanā min al-duʿā' al-mujtabā* [21] and *Fatḥ al-abwāb.*[22]

3

Elsewhere, we have at length examined two traditions within Imamism, namely the early esoteric non-rational tendency reported by the traditionalists of the Schools of Rayy and Qumm, and the theologico-legal tendency of the Baghdad School, mainly during the Buyid period.[23] The points at which they diverge are numerous and at times insurmountable; one sometimes gets the impression that a vast gulf lies between teachings deeply marked by esoterism, initiatory mysticism, even the thaumaturgy, reported by compilers such as al-Barqī, al-Ṣaffār al-Qummī, Furāt al-Kūfī, ʿAlī b. Ibrāhīm al-Qummī, al-ʿAyyāshī, al-Kulaynī, Ibn Abī Zaynab al-Nuʿmānī or even Ibn Bābūya al-Ṣadūq[24] and the rationalist

1407/1987); *Jamāl al-usbūʿ* (Tehran, 1330 Sh./1952); *al-Durūʿ al-wāqiya* (Qumm, 1374 Sh./1992).

20. Tehran, 1323/1905; there are several Persian translations (*Fihrist-e Kitābkhāne-ye Marʿashī*, MSS 2626, 4050, 6741).

21. Incomplete text published in the same volume as *Muhaj al-daʿawāt.*

22. Ed. Ḥ. Al-Khaffāf (Beirut, 1409/1989).

23. See M. A. Amir-Moezzi, *Guide divin*, pp. 15–48 (*Divine Guide*, pp. 6–19), and 'Al-Ṣaffâr al-Qummî et son *Kitâb baṣâ'ir al-darajât*', *JA*, 280 (1992), pp. 221–250 and 'Réflexions sur une évolution du shiʿisme duodécimain : tradition et idéologisation', in E. Patlagean and A. Le Boulluec (eds), *Les retours aux Ecritures: fondamentalismes présents et passés*, Bibliothèque des Hautes Etudes (Paris and Louvain, 1993), pp. 63–82.

24. Regarding these authors, see M. A. Amir-Moezzi, *Guide divin*, pp. 48–58 (*Divine Guide*, pp. 19–22) and 'Al-Ṣaffâr al-Qummî et son *Kitâb baṣâ'ir al-darajât*'; M. M. Bar-Asher, *Scripture and Exegesis in Early Imami* Shiʿism (Leiden, 1999); A. J. Newman, *The Formative Period of Twelver Shiʿism: Ḥadīth as Discourse Between Qum and Bagdad* (Richmond, 2000).

writings tinged with the Muʿtazilism of jurist-theologians such as al-Shaykh al-Mufīd, al-Sharīf al-Raḍī or al-Sharīf al-Murtaḍā.[25]

Yet prayer is one area on which both camps agree without too many reservations. The most typical illustration of this entente is found in the examples of invocations and prayers addressed to the Impeccable Ones. For supporters of the original esoteric tradition, the countless eulogistical formulae, invocations and titles given the Impeccable Ones in these invocations, contain in a very densely written style the most hidden doctrines of initiatic imamology.[26] This same density of discourse, which effectively makes it extremely allusive, also satisfies the followers of the rationalist tradition who do not find explicit imamological beliefs of the first tradition, which had been previously judged deviant and extremist but simply the demonstration of a profound and sincere devotion. A telling example is found in the very long and popular 'Prayer of the twelve imams' attributed to the great philosopher and Avicennian scholar Naṣīr al-Dīn al-Ṭūsī (d. 672/1274), which has been partially translated by Henry Corbin.[27]

This prayer is comprised of a succession of long sentences, often in rhyming prose, divided into fourteen 'moments' (one for each of the Impeccables) each containing two parts: an invocation to

25. For more on these authors see e.g. M. MacDermott, *The Theology of Al-Shaikh Al-Mufīd (d. 413/1022)* (Beirut, 1978); the introduction by A. al-Ḥusaynī to al-Sharīf al-Murtaḍā, *al-Dhakhīra fī 'ilm al-kalām* (Qumm, 1411/1990) (for this important work, now consult S. Schmidtke, 'II.Firk.Arab III. A copy of al-Sharīf al-Murtaḍā's *Kitāb al-Dhakhīra* completed in 472/1079-80 in the Firkovitch-collection, St Petersburg (in Persian: Nuskha yi kuhan az *Kitāb al-Dhakhīra* yi Sharīf Murtaḍā (tārīkh-i kitābat 472)', *Maʿārif*, 20/2 (2003), pp. 68–84; M. M. Jaʿfarī, *Sayyid Raḍī* (Tehran, 1999).

26. On this imamology refer to Chapters 3, 5 and 8, this volume.

27. *En Islam iranien*, vol. 1, pp. 70–73. In spite of its title, the invocation is addressed to the Fourteen Impeccable Ones and not only the twelve imams. The text of the prayer is based on the eclogue by Muḥammad Bāqir al-Majlisī, *Zād al-maʿād* (lithograph, Tehran, 1352/1933), in the margins of pp. 207–227. This is the edition used by H. Corbin. There are many others, the latest being: Qumm, 2 vols, n.d. (ca. 1995). (In the original text of the book, the author uses Corbin's translation.)

God in the form of a variable litany and a response in unison. The work in its entirety constitutes a long spiritual pilgrimage to the sanctuaries of the Fourteen Impeccables. Each sentence touches upon an aspect of hagiography or imamology. To convey an idea of this typical text, we cite a few excerpts:

> O dear God! Honour and hail, serve and bless the Prophet . . . the Lamp that glows, the Star that glistens . . . The prince of Messengers, the Seal of prophets . . . Honour and salvation upon you . . . O Messenger of God, O Merciful Guide, O Intercessor of the community, O witness of God before his creatures . . .
>
> ....
>
> O dear God! Honour and hail, serve and bless the Prince most pure, ʿAlī the victorious imam . . . the epiphany of miracles and wonders . . . the dazzling Meteor . . . Centre of the circle of secrets . . . Lion of God the victorious . . . Guide of East and West . . . O Husband of the virgin [Fāṭima] . . . O our Lord and Prince . . . intercede for us before God.
>
> ....
>
> O dear God! Honour and greet, serve and bless Fāṭima the glorious Lady, the beautiful, the most pure, the oppressed, the generous, the noble . . . who endured so many afflictions in the course of such a brief life . . . the Queen of women, She of the huge black eyes, Mother of the imams . . . the immaculate Virgin . . .O Fāṭima the Radiant . . . O our Lady and Sovereign . . . intercede for us before God.
>
> ....
>
> O dear God! Honour and greet ... the ascetic prince, Ḥusayn son of ʿAlī [the third imam], imam of prayer . . . ornament of thrones and temples, Afflicted by misfortune and sorrow . . . O martyr, O Oppressed One! Son of the Messenger of God, son of the Master of Believers, son of Fāṭima the Radiant ... O Prince of the Youths of paradise . . . intercede for us before God.
>
> ....
>
> O dear God! Honour and greet . . . the loyal and most true Prince, the wise, the steadfast, the forbearing, the compassionate, guide upon the path, he who serves the Shiʿis a full and pure wine . . .

O Jaʿfar son of Muḥammad [the sixth imam] . . . intercede for us before God.

....

O dear God! Honour and greet . . . the oppressed imam, the martyr who succumbed to poison. . . the wise one who knows secret sciences, the full moon in a starry night . . . companion of souls, Sun of suns . . . O ʿAlī son of Mūsā al-Riḍā [the eighth imam] . . . Son of the Messenger of God . . . God's witness before his creatures . . . intercede for us before God.

....

O dear God! Honour and greet . . . he who in his being recapitulates the Prophet's vocation, the impetuousness of the Lion of God [i.e. ʿAlī], the absolute pureness of Fāṭima, the forbearance of Ḥasan, the bravery of Ḥusayn . . . the *incognito* of the divine occultation, in truth the Resurrector, the Word of God . . . the Triumphant by God's command . . . Imam in concealment and to be discovered, who dispels sadness and sorrow ... Muḥammad son of Ḥasan [the twelfth imam, hidden imam and eschatological Saviour] invisible lord of the age and steward of the Most Merciful . . . intercede for us before God.

Thus Abū Jaʿfar al-Ṭūsī, one of the founding fathers of the rationalist current and Raḍī al-Dīn Ibn Ṭāwūs, one of the most brilliant representatives of the traditionalist tendency, work in partnership to glorify the spiritual role of prayer in Shiʿi faith. The same could be said of the famous rationalists al-Karājakī (449/1057), in his work *Riyāḍ al-ʿābidīn* or Abū ʿAlī al-Ṭabrisī (548/1153), author of *Kitāb kunūz al-najāḥ*, and traditionalists such as Faḍl Allāh al-Rāwandī (573/1177–1178), in his *Adʿiyat sirr*, and his contemporary, the anonymous author of *Nuzhat al-zāhid*.[28]

Following Ibn Ṭāwūs, the development of prayer literature occurred as a result of the work of authors such as Ibn Fahd al-Ḥillī

28. The first work seems to have been lost. Al-Ṭabrisī, *Kunūz al-najāḥ* (n.p. [Iran], 1318/1900). For *Adʿiyat sirr* by al-Rāwandī refer to *Fihrist-e Kitābkhāne-ye Marʿashī*, MS 499 and *Fihrist-e nuskha-hāye khaṭṭī-ye majmūʿa-ye...Mishkāt... dāneshgāh-e Tehrān* (Tehran, 1960–1969), vol. 1, p. 130. As for *Nuzhat al-zāhid*, it has been edited by R. Jaʿfariyān (Tehran, 1376 Sh./1997).

(841/1437) and his *ʿUddat al-dāʿī wa najāḥ al-sāʿī*, often summarised and also translated into both ancient and modern Persian;[29] and especially Taqī al-Dīn Ibrāhīm b. ʿAlī al-Kafʿamī (905/1499), author of two very popular key works, *al-Balad al-amīn* and *Junnat al-amān al-wāqiya wa jannat al-īmān al-bāqiya*.[30] From the Safawid to the modern period, and even up to contemporary times, there are dozens of works – of varying importance – which bear witness to the vitality of prayer literature. At either end of this long period, of particular note are, on the one hand, in the eleventh and twelfth/seventeenth century, texts by famous members of the Majlisī family, first the father Muḥammad Taqī, then the sons, Muḥammad Jaʿfar and the renowned Muḥammad Bāqir;[31] and on the other, the highly popular eclogues currently in use such as *Mafātīḥ al-jinān* by Shaykh ʿAbbās al-Qummī or the *Miftāḥ al-jannāt* by Sayyid Muḥsin al-Amīn.[32]

It is noteworthy that ever since the Safawid period and with the origin and expansion of specifically Imami philosophy, increasing numbers of philosophers, of both Neoplatonic and Aristotelian tendencies (although the distinction is subtle

29. Most recent edition by F. Ḥassūn Fāris (Qumm, 1420/1999). First summary, prepared by the author himself, entitled *Nabdhat al-dāʿī* (*Fihrist-e Kitābkhāne-ye Marʿashī*, MSS 35, 2642 and 8977); now edited by F. Ḥassūn Fāris as *Mukhtaṣar ʿuddat al-dāʿī* in the review *Turāthunā*, 55–56 (1421/2000). Most recent Persian trans.: Ḥ. Fashāhī (Tehran, 1379/1959–1960).

30. *Al-Balad al-amīn* (Tehran, 1383/1963); *Junnat al-amān* (Tehran, 1349 Sh./1971) (many other editions of this work exist). Numerous summaries in Arabic and Persian as well as several Persian translations, especially of the second.

31. Muḥammad Taqī al-Majlisī, *Riyāḍ al-muʾminīn* (Marʿashī, MS 9850) and *Sharḥ al-ziyārat al-jāmiʿat al-kabīra*, in the margins of Shaykh Aḥmad al-Aḥsāʾī, *Sharḥ al-ziyārat al-jāmiʿa* (see note 5 above). Muḥammad Jaʿfar al-Majlisī, *Miftāḥ al-najāḥ* (Marʿashī, MS 5153). Muḥammad Bāqir al-Majlisī, *Miqbās al-maṣābīḥ* (Marʿashī, MSS 2911 and 4226), *Rabīʿ al-asābīʿ* (Marʿashī, MS 8955; Mishkāt, 1/118), *Zād al-maʿād* (see note 27 above).

32. Numerous editions of these two books published in various countries (Iraq, Iran, Lebanon). For the first, see e.g. Tehran, 1381 Sh./2001. For the second, Beirut, 1389/1969.

and not always evident), wrote works of prayer and published commentaries on previous books on prayer. This, once again, demonstrates the extent to which prayer texts (including the earliest examples) as a result of many devotional factors, frequently of a mystical and theosophical nature, but also because of their extremely dense allusive style, easily lend themselves to hermeneutical excercises. Unfortunately, almost all of these philosophical texts are unedited and still remain in manuscript form. Let us limit ourselves to citing just a few well-known examples:

> Al-Shaykh al-Bahāʾī (1030/1621), *Miftāḥ al-falāḥ* (Marʿashī, MS 8197; Mishkāt, 1/216). The disciple of the latter, Ṣadr al-Dīn Muḥammad al-Nayrīzī, *Ādāb-e ʿabbāsī,* Persian paraphrase of the already cited work by his master (Marʿashī, MSS 3953 and 8988). Other disciple of Shaykh al-Bahāʾī, Muḥammad b. Yūsuf al-ʿAskarī al-Baḥrānī, *Zubdat al-daʿawāt* (Marʿashī, MS 5971; Mishkāt, 1/126).
>
> Sayyid Aḥmad al-ʿAlawī (d. between 1054/1644 and 1060/1650), famous cousin and disciple of Mīr Dāmād, *al-Jawāhir al-manthūra fi'l-adʿiyat al-maʾthūra* (Marʿashī, MS 1146) and *Makhzan al-daʿawāt* (Marʿashī, MS 6029).
>
> Mullā Muḥsin al-Fayḍ al-Kāshānī (1091/1680), student and son-in-law of Mullā Ṣadrā, *Dharīʿat al-ḍarāʿa* (Marʿashī, MS 598; Mishkāt 1/117), *Khulāṣat al-adhkār* (Mishkāt 1/105), *Lubb al-ḥasanāt* (Marʿashī, MS 8236).
>
> ʿAlī Aṣghar b. Muḥammad al-Qazwīnī, student of Mullā Khalīl al-Qazwīnī (1089/1678), *Safīnat al-najāt* (Marʿashī, MS 6043; Mishkāt 1/128).
>
> Ḥasan b. ʿAbd al-Rasūl al-Zunūzī (twelfth/eighteenth century), *Wasīlat al-najāt* (Marʿashī, MS 8745).
>
> Shaykh Aḥmad al-Aḥsāʾʾī (d. 1241/1826), *Sharh al-ziyārat al-jāmiʿa* (see note 5 above).

What mainly attracts the philosophers and exegetes or interpreters of prayer are the different aspects of *walāya* doctrine as the theological approach to the figure of the imam;[33] a doctrine perfectly illustrated by the brief phrases containing invocations addressed to the Impeccable Ones, such as those we have examined in 'The Prayer of the Twelve Imams' attributed to Naṣīr al-Dīn al-Ṭūsī. To better appreciate what is to follow, let us briefly review the broader outlines of this doctrine.

4

The Essence of God is forevermore and absolutely unknowable. What can be knowable in God, the unknown wishing to be known, are His Names and Attributes. The Imam, in the metaphysical and ontological sense, is the locus of manifestation, the epiphanic place (as Henry Corbin liked to say), of the divine Names. As for the terrestrial imam, the *wālī,* he is the locus of manifestation of the cosmic Imam. Thus, through a theological exposition of successive theophanies, the imam is described as the veritable revealed God, a divine being whose recognition is equivalent to the ultimate mysteries of being.[34] This theological doctrine of *walāya* is encountered, in a more or less developed form though explained in a fragmentary manner, from the era of the *ḥadīth* compilations in the third and fourth/ninth and tenth centuries onwards. Briefly, the figure of the imam acquires a level of saintliness equal to, if not implicitly greater than that of the Prophet. At the same time as being the most qualified of religious scholars, the most gifted of wise thaumaturges and the Most High locus of divine epiphany, the imam is also both guardian and content of the Secret (*sirr, bāṭin*) of all

33. Chapter 7, this volume.

34. Corbin has explained this very clearly; see for example *En islam iranien* (Paris, 1971–1972), vol. 1, chs 6 and 7, pp. 219ff. and *Histoire de la philosophie islamique* (Paris, 1986), sections II.A.4 and II.A.5, pp. 78ff. See also Amir-Moezzi, *Guide divin* as well as the works cited above in notes 26 and 33.

religions.[35] According to *walāya* doctrine, this Secret is no less than divinisation of the man of God. With their audacious tone comparable to the 'ecstatic utterances' (*shaṭaḥāt*) of the mystics, some *ḥadīth*s dating back to the imams are especially explicit in this regard:

> 'We [i.e. the imams] manifest light in darkness', imam Jaʿfar al-Ṣādiq is reported to have said, 'We are the oft-frequented House [*al-bayt al-maʿmūr*; an allusion to Q 52:4] where he who enters is safe. We are the magnificence and grandeur of God . . . We are beyond all description. By us, eyes shine, ears listen and hearts overflow with faith.'[36]
>
> 'God has made of us', relates another tradition from the same imam, 'His eye among His worshippers. His eloquent tongue among His creatures, His hand of beneficence and mercy extended over all His servants, His face towards which one turns, His threshold that leads to him, His treasure in heaven and on earth. It is by our act of worship that God is worshipped; without us, God would not be worshipped.'[37]

Another tradition reports the words of imam al-Ḥasan:

> 'We are the First and the Last. We are the commanders, we are the Light. The Light of spiritual beings comes from us. We illuminate (all things) by the Light of God. We spiritualise (all things) by His spirit (or "we render joyful by His joy," *nurawwiḥu bi rūḥih/rawḥih* [the possessive adjective, here and subsequently, can refer both to God as well to the Light of God].) In us, His dwelling

35. See Chapter 7, this volume; also Amir-Moezzi, 'Du droit à la thélogie: les niveaux de réalité dans le Shiʿisme duodécimain', *Cahiers du Groupe d'Etudes Spirituelles Comparées*, 5, 'L'Esprit et la nature' (1997), pp. 37–63.

36. Al-Ṭabarī al-Ṣaghīr, *Dalāʾil al-imāma* (Qumm, 1413/1994), pp. 270–271; al-Baḥrānī, *Madīnat al-maʿājiz* (Tehran, n.d., ca. 1960), pp. 394–395.

37. Ibn Bābūya, *Kitāb al-tawḥīd*, ed. H. al-Ḥusaynī al-Ṭihrānī (Tehran, 1398/1978), pp. 151–152 (the ambiguity of the last sentence, *bi ʿibādatinā ʿubida'llāh law lā naḥnu mā ʿubida'llāh*, which may also mean 'due to the fact that we are worshipped, God is worshipped; without us God would not be worshipped' seems deliberate).

> place. Towards us, His source. Our first is the same as our last and our last the same as our first.'[38]

According to a tradition transmitted by several sources, the fourth imam, ʿAlī Zayn al-ʿĀbidīn on one occasion, before the eyes of his disciples, transformed himself into a winged creature and disappeared into the sky. Upon his return, he reported that he had reached the loftiest of the heavens and replied thus to an astounded disciple:

> We [the imams] are the ones who constructed the highest heaven, why then would we not be able to scale its heights? We are the bearers of the divine Throne and we are seated upon the Throne. The Throne and the Pedestal are ours.[39]

The famous 'theo-imamosophical' sermons attributed to ʿAlī, the first imam, are of the same tenor:[40]

> I am the queen-bee (*yaʿsūb*) of the initiates; I am the First among the Last; I am the successor to the Messenger of the Lord of the worlds; I am judge of the Garden and Fire[41] ... I am the Rewarder on the day of Rewards ... I am the supreme Judge ... I have the decisive Word; I possess penetrating insight into the Path of the Book. I hold the knowledge of fortunes and misfortunes and that of judgements; I am the completion of the religion. I am the good deed by God for His creatures.[42]

---

38. Al-Ṭabarī al-Ṣaghīr, *Dalāʾil al-imāma*, pp. 168–169 and *Nawādir al-muʿjizāt* (Qumm, 1410/1990), p. 103.

39. Al-Ṭabarī al-Ṣaghīr, *Nawādir al-muʿjizāt*, p. 116 and *Dalāʾil al-imāma*, p. 201; al-Ḥurr al-ʿĀmilī, *Ithbāt al-hudāt* (Tehran, 1364 Sh./1985), vol. 5, p. 256; al-Baḥrānī, *Madīnat al-maʿājiz*, p. 294.

40. Regarding these sermons, see Chapter 3, this volume.

41. Al-ʿAyyāshī, *Tafsīr* (Qumm, 1380/1960), vol. 2, pp. 17–18; al-Baḥrānī, *al-Burhān fī tafsīr al-Qurʾān*, 5 vols (Tehran, n.d.), vol. 2, p. 20.

42. Furāt al-Kūfī, *Tafsīr*, ed. M. al-Kāẓim (Tehran, 1410/1990), p. 178. The last two sentences certainly refer to Qurʾan 5:3. For sources that report these sermons as well as their mystical and/or philosophical exegesis see Chapter 3, this volume.

There is therefore nothing unusual about the imam being the main object of the believers' invocations, or that they are fervently devoted to him, that his sanctuary is a most sacred pilgrimage site. It is significant that ever since an early work such as *Kāmil al-ziyārāt* by Jaʿfar b. Muḥammad Ibn Qūlūya/Qūlawayh al-Qummī (368/978–979),[43] undoubtedly the oldest transmitted monograph regarding pilgrimage and prayers at tombs of the Impeccable Ones, visits to these tombs, especially those of ʿAlī at Najaf and al-Ḥusayn at Karbalāʾ, are described as being as important as the pilgrimage to Mecca or Medina.[44]

Moreover, while it is true that each imam possesses his own saintliness, his unique representation in the devotions of the believers, at the same time, one must always bear in mind that the entire group of the Impeccable Ones, the twelve imams more specifically, forms a unique sacred entity and that they are considered identical as theophanic beings, the acting 'organ' of God and locus of manifestation for divine Names. Many prayers are addressed to this group as a single entity, just as 'the collective spiritual pilgrimage' (*al-ziyārat al-jāmiʿa*) is undertaken mentally at all the tombs of all the imams as though at a single sanctuary.[45] According to a tradition dating back to the seventh imam, Mūsā al-Kaẓim:

> He who visits [*zāra* i.e. who makes a pilgrimage to a shrine] the first among us [the imams], also visits the last among us and he who visits the last among us, also visits the first among us. He who expresses love for the first of us, has also expressed it for the last and he who loves the last of us, also loves the first.[46]

43. Ed. B. Jaʿfarī (Tehran, 1375 Sh./1996).

44. Ibid., passim, and esp. chs 10, 11, 15, 38, 39, 43, 59, 83, 88.

45. Of the earliest compilers we limit ourselves to the following: Ibn Qūlūya and Ibn Bābūya have related some exquisite texts on 'collective pilgrimage'. See *Kāmil al-ziyārāt*, ch. 104, pp. 330ff.; Ibn Bābūya, *Kitāb man lā yaḥḍuruhu'l-faqīh* (Tehran, 1390/1970), vol. 2, pp. 370–376, no. 1625 (see note 5 above).

46. Ibn Qūlūya, *Kāmil al-ziyārāt*, p. 350, no. 13.

Some phrases concerning the 'collective pilgrimage', dating back to the tenth imam ʿAlī al-Naqī and reported by Ibn Bābūya in his *Kitāb man lā yaḥḍuruhu'l-faqīh*, go even further and present this unique theophanic being which is composed of the whole group of imams as a divine reality hidden in the depths of each person, cradled within each reality. Every prayer in reality is addressed to the imam, to the being that reveals God; every sincere pilgrimage is made to the theophanic entity that the Shiʿa call the imam:

> Your worship is in each worshipper, your names in all names, your body in all bodies, your spirit in all spirits, your soul in all souls, your sign in all signs and your tombs in all tombs.[47]

It is the presence of a transcendental reality, mediated by the figure of the imam, that transforms prayer into an intense spiritual experience. The mystics have gone so far as to endow this experience with 'organic' fundamentals.

5

Vehicle for the revealed God, the spiritualised and internalised figure of the imam thus becomes the object of invocation. This is possible for the most humble of believers as well as the mystic, since prayer lends itself to contemplative practices and a visionary experience. Let us review for a moment what Corbin said regarding the initiatory practice of prayer in Ibn ʿArabī: 'Prayer is not a request for something: it is the expression of a mode of being, a means of existing and of *causing to exist*, that is, a means of causing the God who reveals Himself to appear, of "seeing" Him, not to be sure in His essence, but in the *form* which He reveals precisely by revealing Himself by and to that form.'[48]

---

47. Ibn Bābūya, *Kitāb man lā yaḥḍuruhu'l-faqīh*, vol. 2, p. 374.

48. See H. Corbin, *L'imagination créatrice dans le soufisme d'Ibn ʿArabī* (Paris, 1958) in note 2 above.

In Imami mysticism, the initiatory practice of prayer seems linked to what from the earliest sources is called 'the vision by (or 'in') the heart (*al-ruʾya biʾl-qalb*)'. Elsewhere, we have examined at length the many allusions to this secret practice, going back to the compilations of the third and fourth/ninth and tenth centuries, both in terms of its theoretical foundations and historical development.[49] We will therefore describe this practice only briefly here. Two *ḥadīth*s going back to the first and sixth imams respectively, perfectly illustrate how it is perceived in Imami mysticism. Someone once asked ʿAlī if he could see the God to whom he prayed. He replied: 'I would not worship a God that I could not see' and then added: 'However, the naked eye cannot attain Him by its sight; it is the hearts that see Him by means of the realities of faith.'[50]

Replying to a disciple's question regarding the vision of God on the Day of Resurrection, Jaʿfar al-Ṣādiq is said to have declared: 'The initiated followers already see Him in this world before the Day of Resurrection. Do you not see him at this very moment before you [i.e. in myself as the locus of manifestation of God]?' And in response to the bewildered disciple who seeks permission to relate this answer to others, the imam says: 'No, because a negator unaware of the true meaning of these words will use them to accuse us of associationism. Now, the vision of the heart differs from ocular vision and God transcends descriptions by the assimilationists and the heretics.'[51]

The initiate can thus experience a vision of the imam as the sublime divine theophany in his heart. Other traditions allude to the modalities of this spiritual experience: contemplation of light,

---

49. On *al-ruʾya biʾl-qalb* in Imamism, see Amir-Moezzi, *Guide divin*, pp. 112–145 (*Divine Guide*, pp. 44–55) and 'La vision par le cœur dans l'Islam shi'ite', *Connaissance des Religions*, special issue, 'Lumières sur la voie du cœur', 57–59 (1999), pp. 146–169; also Chapter 10, this volume.

50. Al-Kulaynī, *al-Uṣūl min al-Kāfī*, 'kitāb al-tawḥīd', ch. 9, no. 6; Ibn Bābūya, *Kitāb al-tawḥīd*, ch. 8, p. 109, no. 6.

51. Ibn Bābūya, *Kitāb al-tawḥīd*, p. 117, no. 20. For the translation of *muʾminūn* as 'initiates' at the beginning of this *ḥadīth*, see Amir-Moezzi, *Guide divin*, index, and Chapter 8 here.

or more exactly of coloured glimpses at the level of the heart; the nature or form of the object seen; consequences and implication of the experience etc. In brief, one can say that due to the spiritual teachings and to ascetic and initiatory practices *walāya*, love of the imam, can be crystallised at the level of the heart in the form of a luminous 'energy' composed of glimpses of several colours, or lights, named, among other things 'the light of *walāya*'. By practising concentration upon the heart, this light gives access to a living entity, present in the centre of the heart. This is none other than each person's inner Guide, 'the imam present in the heart'; for each individual seeker of truth this is an internal reflection of the external imam's reality, a reflection of the cosmic Imam who in turn is none other than the revealed Face of God. By a practice of successive theophanies, the mystical teaching of the imams thus enables one to discover God in one's own heart.

These allusions to the initiatic 'exercise' of 'the vision by the heart', perhaps related to what was taught in the entourage of the imams, appear to be the earliest attestations to it in esoteric Islamic literature. The practice would thus have been introduced to Islam by the Shi'a, but is also widespread in Sunni Sufism.[52]

As for Imami Sufi Shi'is, arriving on the scene from the Safawid period onwards, in a few major mystical orders (mainly from the eleventh/seventeenth century), they present themselves as inheritors of two traditions, the Imami and the Sufi.[53] It is they especially

52. On the role of the heart in Sunni Sufism, now consult G. Gobillot and P. Ballanfat, 'Le cœur et la vie spirituelle chez les mystiques musulmans', *Connaissance des Religions*, special issue, 'Lumières sur la voie du cœur', 57–59 (1999), pp. 170–204; see also A. Ventura, 'La presanza divina nel cuore', *Quaderni di Studi Arabi*, 3 (1985), pp. 54–74 and 'L'invocazione del cuore' in *Yād Nāma...Alessandro Bausani* (Rome, 1991), pp. 475–485.

53. Regarding these orders, see R. Gramlich, *Die schiitischen Derwischorden Persiens*, 3 vols (Wiesbaden, 1965–1981); and now, L. Lewisohn, 'An Introduction to the History of Modern Persian Sufism. Part I: Ni'matullāhiyya', *BSOAS*, 61/3 (1998), pp. 437–464 and 'An Introduction to the History of Modern Persian Sufism. Part II: A Socio-cultural Profile of Sufism from the Dhahabī Revival to the Present Day', *BSOAS*, 62/1 (1999), pp. 36–59. There are four major Imami mystical orders: the first three, Dhahabiyya, Ni'matullāhiyya and Khāksār,

who relate the initiatory practice of prayer to the experience of 'vision by the heart'. The role of the imam, an internalised figure in terms of being the object of prayer, is obviously central here. Here too, given the secret nature of the practices, the texts are highly allusive and the vocabulary very technical. However, with a basic understanding of the history of the practice, certain sources appear less obscure. For example, Mullā Muḥammad Sulṭān ʿAlī Shāh, great Niʿmatullāhī master of the thirteenth/nineteenth century, writes in his important work in Persian, *Majmaʿ al-saʿādāt*:

> He who possesses senses pertaining only to the sense-perceptible realm of God is able to know the imam only in his physical human form (*bashariyya*). But he whose senses pertaining to the celestial realm have been activated is able to acquire knowledge of the imam as Light (*nūrāniyyat-e imām*). When the disciple pledges an oath of allegiance to a master authorised by the imam [i.e. the legitimate spiritual master of the mystical order] and when the master places his hand in the disciple's, the celestial luminous form of the imam is introduced into the heart of the disciple through the initiatory hand gesture. This luminous form is variously called the Face of the imam, *walāya* or finally, the love of ʿAlī.
>
> It is by virtue of this Visage of Light that a filial relationship is established between the imam and his followers and that the initiated become true brothers ... In the external physical world, this divine manifestation occurs through the figure of the hidden imam (as the living imam of our time) and his final manifestation as the Resurrector. In the internal spiritual world, it constitutes one of the theophanic degrees of the Light of the imam in the heart, a degree that one denotes by terms such as 'presence', 'serenity' or 'contemplation' (*ḥuḍūr, sakīna, fikr*). This is what illuminates the adept, enabling him to recognise the imam as the light of the heart. This is what the Prince of initiates [i.e. ʿAlī] means when he declares:
>
> 'To know me as Light (*maʿrifatī bi'l-nūrāniyya*) is to know God and to know God is to know me as Light. He who knows me as Light is an initiate whose heart has been tested for faith by God (*mu'min*

---

consider themselves Sufis. The fourth, the Shaykhiyya, refuses to consider itself a Sufi order and describes itself as a theologico-mystical brotherhood.

> *imtaḥana'llāh qalbahu li'l-īmān*) . . . This indeed is *walāya* and he who professes my *walāya*, this person may truly accomplish his prayer.'[54]

Whence the Shiʿi adage that mystical texts repeat frequently in many forms: he who knows himself knows his imam, and he who knows his imam knows his Lord. In Imami mysticism, the vision of the Face of the imam in the heart – contemplation of the esoteric form of the physical imam – appears to be one of the main aims of spiritual practices of concentration. Thus is born the believer's spiritual being. The above-cited Sulṭān ʿAlī Shāh continues:

> The manifestation of the luminous Face of the imam in the heart brings wisdom to the adept and awakens his capabilities for celestial perception, giving him access to the contemplation of the inhabitants of the heavens. He can thus free himself from the shackles of time and space, walk on water or upon the air, travel miraculously from one place to another.[55]

Among certain masters of the Dhahabiyya order, the information is even more specific and the links to prayer become explicit. An Imami Shiʿi branch of the long established and powerful Kubrawiyya order, are bearers of a long spiritual and literary tradition dating back to the order's namesake, Najm al-Dīn Kubrā himself (617/1220–1221), a tradition that includes visionary experiences of contemplation of the inner master and the accompanying coloured luminosity.[56]

---

54. Mullā Muḥammad Sulṭān ʿAlī Shāh, *Majmaʿ al-saʿādāt* (2nd edn, n.p., 1394/1974), pp. 289ff. The expression 'the initiate [lit. 'faithful believer'] whose heart God has tested for faith' is found in the earliest sources, very often in relation to the practice of concentration on the heart; see *Guide divin*, index under '*imtiḥān (al-qalb)*'.

55. Mullā Muḥammad Sulṭān ʿAlī Shāh, *Majmaʿ*, p. 291.

56. On this subject, see H. Corbin, *L'homme de lumière dans le soufisme iranien* (2nd edn, Paris, 1971), English trans. as *The Man of Light in Iranian Sufism*, tr. Nancy Pearson (New York, 1971); the fundamental work by Najm al-Dīn Kubrā, ed. F. Meier in *Die Rawā'iḥ al-jamāl wa fawātiḥ al-jalāl des Najm*

First, the contemplative practice of 'vision by the heart' is denoted by the term, *wijha* or *wajha* (*vejhe* in Persian), as rich as it is evocative. Not only does it mean, 'what is related to the face' but also 'the direction in which prayer is oriented', referring to the Qur'ānic verse 2:148: *wa li-kulli wijhatun huwa muwallīhā* ('To each a direction towards which to turn in prayer', as translated by Arberry). According to the Dhahabi texts, the aim of this practice is the contemplation of the Face of the imam, identical to the Face of God. Vision is possible, not by the naked eye but by the eye of the heart and it is achieved by initiation, self-effacement and spiritual rebirth in the love of the imam.[57] The Light of 'the imam of the heart' is in fact composed of many layers of coloured lights, each revealing an aspect of the inner Guide's reality on the one hand and the adept's degrees of progress on the other. The adept is thus able to perform his true prayer since he has found the true direction of prayer, in this way fulfilling the initiatory requirement of the order as formulated by the master Rāz Shīrāzī (1286/1869): 'To perform your prayer, first discover the direction of prayer.'[58] He seems to be the author who has provided the most important information regarding this practice. In response to his disciple who asks him to explain why the Dhahabi dervishes call 'Alī al-Riḍā the eighth imam, 'the seventh direction of prayer' (*qibla-ye haftom*), he states:

> Know, dear and honourable son, that this important question touches upon one of the greatest secrets of the heart . . . its true understanding is only possible by the unveiling of the heart by the Masters of the heart (*kashf-e qalbī-ye arbāb-e qulūb*) . . . The reason

---

ad-Dīn Kubrā (Wiesbaden, 1957), has now been translated into French by P. Ballanfat as *Les éclosions de la beauté et les parfums de la majesté* (Nîmes, 2001).

57. See the anonymous summary, *Vejhe chīst?*, a publication of the Dhahabiyya Aḥmadiyya (n.p., n.d.), (above, Chapter 10).

58. *Cho qibla yāftī āngah namāz ast*, see for example, Rāz Shīrāzī, *Mirṣād al-ʿibād* (Tabriz, n.d.), p. 14, and *Risāla-ye ḥall-e ishkāl-e davāzdah su'āl-e ... Rā'iḍ al-Dīn Zanjānī*, in Ḥasan Palāsī Shīrāzī, *Tadhkirat Shaykh Muḥammad b. Ṣadīq al-Kujujī* (Tehran 1367/1947), p. 126.

> for this noble title, just as for other titles given the holy imam, such as 'companion of souls' (*anīs al-nufūs*) and 'the Sun of suns' (*shams al-shumūs*)[59] is the radiance of the Light of his love (*walāya*) in the believer's heart. This holy light does not only belong to him since all the imams are in fact the Light descended from God for His creatures. . . But as the initiatic chain of [our] School begins with the eighth imam, it is thus the blessed form of the latter that manifests itself in a [subtle centre called] 'the blackish secret of the heart' belonging to his Friends (*sirr-e suwaydāʾ-e qalb-e awliyāʾ*) This centre is the seventh level of the heart that manifests itself to the Friends . . . Know that the Seven Levels [or 'Seven Mountains' *aṭwār-e sabʿa*] in the heart of the saintly Friends denote the places for manifestation of seven Lights varying in colour; the seventh among them is the black Light, that is of the sacrosant Essence of Unitude. It is well and truly this Light that appears to the Friends [belonging to our order] in the blessed form of the eighth imam. It is the luminous form of a bright, magnificent, transparent black of extreme intensity. This is 'the companion of souls', the 'Sun of suns' and 'direction of prayer' located within the seventh level of the heart. For the great [mystics], directing one's true prayers in this true direction (*qibla*) is a canonical duty.[60]

Let us return to this '*dialogic state*' of prayer that Henry Corbin spoke about; to this reciprocity that transforms a simple invocation into a tranformative experience. By prayer, the Shiʿi seeker offers his imam his inner focus, his efforts at concentration and

---

59. We have already encountered these titles of the eighth imam in 'the prayer of the twelve imams' attributed to Naṣīr al-Dīn al-Ṭūsī (cf. note 27 above). Far from being simply poetic or metaphoric images, the Dhahabī mystic explains that, invoked by the faithful during prayer, they designate spiritual realities likely to be experienced by the mystic in what one might call an 'organic' fashion.

60. Rāz Shīrāzī, *Risāla-ye ḥall-e ishkāl-e davāzdah suʾāl*, pp. 125–126. See also A. Khāvarī, *Dhahabiyya* (Tehran, 1362/1963), vol. 1, pp. 141ff. Regarding these practices see Chapter 10, this volume. On the heart as the veritable Kaʿba (direction of prayer) among Muslim mystics, see L. Massignon, *La passion de Hallâj, martyr mystique de l'Islam* (Paris, 1975), index under '*qalb (qulûb)*' and '*Kaʿba, Kaʿbât*'. See also Corbin, *L'imagination créatrice*, section 2, ch. 2; M. Gloton, 'Les secrets du cœur selon l'Islam', *Connaissance des Religions*, special issue 'Lumières sur la voie du cœur', 57–59 (1999), pp. 118–145.

contemplation, above all his entire presence imbued with love (*walāya*). The Imam, the object of his follower's devotion and prayer, his true 'lord', provides him with either *ʿilm*, the salvational knowledge, or *ʿamal*, the miraculous act, or still more love, a surfeit of *walāya* with regard to the imam and all divine beings.[61] By prayer, the theological exposition of successive theophanies, as we have already discussed on many occasions, undergoes a transmutation into a theological exposition of presence: the physical, external, terrestrial imam renders God present in the sense-perceptible world, whereas the spiritual, internal imam renders the terrestrial imam present in the heart of the believer. This is so for mystics, philosophers and theosophers but also for the most humble of believers in whom we can discern this reciprocity. In his prayer the latter offers his supplication, his love and suffering. In return, the imam grants his wishes, alleviates his sorrow and brings him peace and serenity, assuring him of the imam's intercession (*shafāʿa*) before God, whether in this life or in the hereafter.[62]

In conclusion, let us once more call upon Corbin and through him Ibn ʿArabī, in order to appreciate to what extent prayer constitutes a spiritual space where, as we have seen, not only traditionalist and rationalist Imamis are in agreement but so also are Sunni and Shiʿi mystics:

> We are now very close to the denouement that will crown the *monâjât*, 'confidential psalm', remembrance, meditation, recurrent presence . . . . One who meditates on his God 'in the present' maintains Himself in His company. And a tradition (*khabar ilâhî*) from a reliable source tells us: 'I myself keep company with him who meditates on me [maintains me present in himself].' But if the faithful believer's divine Lord keeps him company when the faithful remembers Him internally, he must, if he is endowed with

61. See for example, Majd al-Ashrāf (a Dhahabī master), *Mirʾāt al-kāmilīn* (Shiraz, n. d.), p. 34.

62. On *shafāʿa*, now consult Bar-Asher, *Scripture and Exegesis in Early Imami Shiʿism*, pp. 180–189.

> inner vision, *see* he who is thus present. This is called contemplation (*moshâhada*) and visualisation (*rû'ya*).[63] Of course, one who is without this sense of vision does not see Him. But this, says Ibn 'Arabī with gravity, is the criterion by which each worshipper (*mosallî*) can recognise his own level of spiritual progress. Either he *sees* his Lord who shows Himself to him (*tajallî*) in the subtle organ that is his heart or else he does yet see Him in this way; then let him worship Him through faith *as though he saw Him.* This injunction, which carries a profound savour of Shi'i Imamism [the imam being the theophanic form par excellence], is nothing other than a summons to set the power of the Active Imagination to work. 'Let the faithful represent Him by his Active Imagination, face to face in his *Qibla*, in the course of his intimate dialogue.'[64]

Thus, the worshipper will direct himself, continues Corbin in his introduction to the thought of the great Andalusian mystic, from presence towards audition and from audition to vision to eventually perceiving the prayer of God which is no less than the ultimate reality of his own prayer, that is, 'the action of the Lord placing his faithful in the presence of his own Presence'.[65] It is here that, according to Sulṭān 'Alī Shāh, the expert scholar on Ibn 'Arabī, vision becomes imageless, prayer becomes silence and all silence inner prayer.[66]

---

63. It would be more precise to translate *ru'ya* as 'vision'.

64. H. Corbin, *Imagination créatrice dans le soufisme d'Ibn Arabî*, pp. 195–196, *Alone with the Alone, Creative Imagination in the Sufism of Ibn 'Arabi*, p. 262 (we have respected the author's italics and system of transliteration).

65. Ibid., p. 196 (p. 262).

66. Mullā Muḥammad Sulṭān 'Alī Shāh, *Majma' al-sa'ādā*, pp. 198–199. The Ni'matullāhī master links this evolution of the worshipper towards 'effacement' (*fanā'*) to knowledge, particularly that of the imam; according to him, knowledge of the 'incompleted ones' (*nāqiṣīn*) is limited to knowledge of the historical imams. For the 'intermediaries' (*mutawassiṭīn*), knowing God comes through knowing the imam as Light. Finally for the 'accomplished' (*muntahīn*), the highest manifestation of the Real is accompanied neither by sound nor image, because at this level, there is neither subject knowing nor object known.

Part IV: Aspects of Individual and Collective Eschatology

12

The End of Time and the Return to the Origin

Nowadays, in Islamic lands, the term 'eschatology' is almost always translated as *ʿilm al-maʿād, maʿād shenāsī* or *ʿelm-e maʿād* to cite only from the Arabic and Persian, the two major languages of Islamic culture; which is to say that learned Muslims have always perceived the notion of *maʿād* as generally referring to the ultimate end of man and the world, incorporating other aspects of the *eskaton* such as *ʿāqiba, ḥashr, baʿth, qiyāma* or *ākhira*. Now, as we know, *maʿād* literally means the place of return or the very movement of returning towards the point of departure, whence the countless speculations by theologians, philosophers and mystics generally considering this eschatological notion either as a return to the source of being, namely God, or as a return to existence after death or resurrection.[1]

As for Imami eschatology, it has already inspired a large number of studies;[2] however, to my knowledge, no critical study

1. L. Gardet, *Dieu et la destinée de l'homme* (Paris, 1967), passim; R. Arnaldez, 'Maʿād', *EI2*, vol. 5, pp. 899–901; M. Smith and Y. Y. Haddad, *The Islamic Understanding of Death and Resurrection* (Albany, NY, 1981); J.-R. Michot, *La destinée de l'homme selon Avicenne. Le retour à Dieu (maʿâd) et l'imagination* (Louvain, 1986) (this work, devoted to Avicenna's philosophy, also contains much valuable information on other authors and doctrinal trends).

2. E. Moeller, *Beiträge zur Mahdilehre des Islams* (Heidelberg, 1901); H. Corbin, *En Islam iranien. Aspects spirituels et philosophiques* (Paris, 1971–1972), vol. 4, pp. 301–460; A. A. Sachedina, *Islamic Messianism: The*

has as yet been devoted to the relationship that exists between the two crucial concepts of the End of Time and the Return to the Origin as established in the earliest sources, texts dating mainly from the pre-Buyid and Buyid periods,[3] and developed subsequently by later thinkers. Notwithstanding, it seems to me that this relationship proves to be fundamental for not only a better understanding of the specific concepts regarding Imami eschatology and messianism but also a better appreciation of the key role played by the figure of the imam.

Established almost definitively in the early fourth/tenth century, Twelver messianism is entirely centred around the figure of the hidden imam, the twelfth and last, or the eschatological Saviour.[4] The figure of the latter, his Occultation, his soteriological mission, his manifestation at the End of Time and the situation of the world at the moment of his coming constitute the principal subjects of the vast corpus of messianic and eschatological Imami literature, to such an extent that the more classical material such

---

Idea of the Mahdī in Twelver Shiʿism (Albany, NY, 1981); J. M. Hussain, *The Occultation of the Twelfth Imam: A Historical Background* (London, 1982). To place the analysis provided by these monographs in a larger historical context, see e.g. J. Aguade, *Messianismus zur Zeit der frühen Abbassiden: Das Kitāb al-Fitan des Nuʿaim b. Ḥammād* (Tübingen, 1979) or J. O. Blichfeldt, *Early Mahdism: Politics and Religion in the Formative Period of Islam* (Leiden, 1986). For sources and other studies, now consult M. A. Amir-Moezzi, 'Eschatology in Imami Shiʿism', *EIr*, vol. 8, pp. 575–581.

3. Regarding these sources, see M. A. Amir-Moezzi, *Guide divin*, pp. 48–58 (*Divine Guide*, pp. 19–22).

4. E. Kohlberg, 'From Imāmiyya to Ithnāʿashariyya', *BSOAS*, 39 (1976), pp. 521–534 (rpr. in *Belief and Law in Imāmī Shīʿism*, article XIV); V. Klemm, 'Die vier *Sufarāʾ* des Zwölften Imām. Zur formativen Periode der Zwölferšīʿa', *Die Welt des Orients*, 15 (1984), pp. 126–143; M. A. Amir-Moezzi, 'Al-Ṣaffâr al-Qummî (d. 290/902–3) et son *Kitâb basâʾir al-darajât*', *JA*, 280/3–4 (1992), pp. 221–250, esp. pp. 236–242; H. Modarressi, *Crisis and Consolidation in the Formative Period of Shīʿite Islam* (Princeton, 1993) part 1; S. A. Arjomand, 'The Consolation of Theology: Absence of the Imam and Transition from Chiliasm to Law in Shiʿism', *The Journal of Religion*, 21 (1996), pp. 548–571 and 'The Crisis of the Imamate and the Institution of Occultation in Twelver Shiʿism', *IJMES*, 28 (1996), pp. 491–515. Also, Chapter 13, this volume.

as the description of the final Tribunal of the resurrection, the fate of the elected in paradise or that of the damned in hell seem comparatively meagre and secondary.[5] The first major source for this genre of literature would be *Kitāb al-ghayba* by Abū ʿAbd Allāh Muḥammad ʿIbn Abī Zaynabʾ al-Nuʿmānī (d. ca. 345/956), which is the earliest monograph regarding the hidden imam that has come down to us.[6] Widely and regularly used by later authors, in this section it will constitute our main source.

The End of Time and the manifestation of the Saviour consists of two dimensions, responding it seems to the pair, *ẓāhir/bāṭin*, omnipresent in Shiʿism: a collective, universal, external dimension supposed to occur in 'history' in order to disrupt or shatter it, and then another entirely individual internal dimension, shattering the being of the faithful.[7] For the sake of clarity, it is useful to examine our subject – the relationship between the notions of *ākhir al-zamān* and *maʿād* – in each of these two dimensions.

1

What characterises the End of Time, and in a manner renders the manifestation of the Hidden Imam indispensable, is the widespread invasion of the earth by Evil, the crushing of the forces of Light by forces of Darkness, the universal rule of violence, injustice and ignorance; whence the sacred formulaic statement: 'The Mahdī/Qāʾim will rise at the End of Time and will fill the earth with justice just as before it overflowed with oppression and injustice (or "darkness") (*sa-yaqūmu'l-mahdī/al-qāʾim fī ākhir al-zamān fa-yamlaʾu'l-arḍ ʿadlan kamā maliʾat jawran wa ẓulman/ẓuluman*).' The universal Deliverance (*faraj*) will be accomplished only by violent means, by a terrible war.[8] The

5. Amir-Moezzi, 'Eschatology in Imami Shiʿism', pp. 575–576a.

6. Al-Nuʿmānī, *Kitāb al-ghayba*, Arabic text ed. ʿA. A. Ghaffārī with Persian trans. M. J. Ghaffārī (Tehran, 1363 Sh./1985).

7. 'Eschatology in Imami Shiʿism', pp. 576bf.

8. *Guide divin*, pp. 283ff. (*Divine Guide*, pp. 116ff.).

Saviour will not only deliver the oppressed of the period but also avenge all the accumulated injustices over the ages.

> He [i.e. the Mahdī] will rise, emboldened by the spirit of revenge and anger, grief-stricken with the wrath of God striking the creatures. He will be dressed in the shirt worn by the Messenger of God on the day of [the battle of] Uḥud, as well as al-Saḥāb, his 'turban with a train' (*ʿimāmathu al-saḥāb*), his imposing armour and his sword, Dhu'l-faqār. For eight months, he will have his sword drawn, killing with no respite.[9]

Aided in his mission by God, the Mahdī – final successor to Muḥammad – is bound to be victorious:

> He will bear the Prophet's standard (*rāya*) whose pole is made from pillars of the Throne of God (*ʿumud al-ʿarsh*), and His Mercy (*raḥma*); the fabric from His triumphal Assistance (*naṣr*). All that is touched by this standard, will be annihilated by God.[10]

Apart from divine assistance, the Mahdī is helped by other companions of war. Who might they be, and generally speaking, who are the protagonists of the Battle? The forces of Good, those that fight on the imam's side, are composed of various kinds of 'support'. First, according to Imami doctrine of the 'return to life' (*al-rajʿa*),[11] some individuals, mostly great figures from sacred history, victims of injustice and impiety of their day, will be revived in order to help the Mahdī in his final battle and to avenge their oppressors and tyrants; these antagonists will also return to life in

9. Al-Nuʿmānī, *Kitāb al-ghayba*, ch. 19, pp. 437–438, no. 2 (tradition attributed to Jaʿfar al-Ṣādiq).

10. Ibid., p. 438, no. 3 (Muḥammad al-Bāqir), p. 441, no. 5 (Jaʿfar al-Ṣādiq); see also al-Kulaynī, *al-Uṣūl min al-Kāfī*, ed. J. Muṣṭafawī, 4 vols (Tehran, n.d.), 'Kitāb al-ḥujja', 'Bāb mā ʿinda'l-a'imma min ṣilāḥ rasūl Allāh', vol. 1, pp. 337–343.

11. R. Freitag, *Seelenwanderung in der islamischen Häresie* (Berlin, 1985), pp. 29–34; J. van Ess, *Theologie und Gesellschaft im 2. und 3. Jahrhundert Hidschra* (Berlin and New York, 1991), vol. 1, pp. 285–308; E. Kohlberg, 'Radjʿa', *EI2*, vol. 8, pp. 371–373.

order to be punished.[12] The traditions differ on the exact identity of the saintly individuals but some names recur more frequently than others: ʿAlī b. Abī Ṭālib,[13] al-Ḥusayn b. ʿAlī and generally the Impeccable Ones (the Prophet Muḥammad, his daughter Fāṭima and the first eleven imams), the mysterious prophet mentioned in Q 19:54–55, Ismāʿīl 'True to his promises' (*ṣādiq al-waʿd*) [14] and Jesus Christ who according to a well-known tradition, will participate in prayers led by the Qāʾim.[15]

Just as when the major prophets faced trials in their missions, in his battle, the imam will be assisted by angels, archangels and celestial beings: the angels who accompanied Noah in the Ark, Abraham when he was cast into fire, Moses when he parted the sea, Jesus when God raised him to be with himself;[16] the different troops of angels mentioned in the Qurʾān, the *murdifīn* (angels in procession i.e. coming one after another, Q 8:9), the *munzalīn* (angels descended from Above, Q 3:124), the *musawwimīn* (the swooping angels, Q 3:125), the Cherubim (*karrūbiyyīn*), Gabriel, Michael, Seraphiel and the Frightful One (*al-ruʿb*), a terrifying celestial being, bringing victory to the Mahdī's army by 'marching' alongside it.[17]

---

12. The notion of *rajʿa* in the sense just mentioned is also called *ḥashr khāṣṣ* ('particular resurrection') as distinct from return to universal life for the Last Judgement called *ḥashr ʿāmm* ('general resurrection').

13. In this context, surnamed *ṣāḥib al-karrāt*, 'Master of cylical Returns'; *karra*, pl. *karrāt* is here synonymous with *rajʿa* (see E. Kohlberg, 'Radjʿa').

14. According to Imami tradition, he was the son of the Prophet Ezekiel and was seized, dismembered and executed by his own ungrateful people.

15. Ibn Qūlūya al-Qummī, *Kāmil al-ziyārāt* (lithograph, Iran, n.d.), ch. 19, pp. 65ff.; al-Majlisī, *Biḥār al-anwār* (Tehran and Qumm, 1376–1392/1956–1972), vol. 51, pp. 77–78 and vol. 53, pp. 101–117; in general, see al-Ḥurr al-ʿĀmilī, *al-Īqāẓ min al-hajʿa fi'l-burhān ʿalā'l-rajʿa*, ed. H. Rasūlī Maḥallātī (Qumm, 1381/1962).

16. Al-Nuʿmānī, *Kitāb al-ghayba*, ch. 19, pp. 439–440.

17. Ibid., ch. 13, pp. 337f.; Ibn Bābūya, *Kamāl al-dīn wa tamām al-niʿma*, ed. ʿA. A. Ghaffārī (Qumm, 1405/1985), vol. 1, ch. 33, p. 331.

There is particular insistence on the 313 angels who accompanied the Prophet on the day of the Battle of Badr.[18] In this eschatological context, comparisons with this famous battle are constantly made. Badr is considered Muḥammad's first major victory against the disbelievers and in a way represents the beginning of the establishment of Islam. The battle of the Qā'im will signal the ultimate and definitive victory of initiatory religion of the imams against their 'enemies'. Badr universally established the exoteric dimension of religion; the manifestation (*ẓuhūr*) and rising (*qiyām, khurūj*) of the Mahdī will universally establish the esoteric religion. Moreover, the core of the Saviour's Army is composed of initiates. The Companions of the Qā'im (*aṣḥāb al-qā'im*), whom tradition also calls 'the militia' (*jaysh*), 'the militia of anger' (*jaysh al-ghaḍab*) or 'men of sincere devotion' (*ahl al-ikhlāṣ/al-khullaṣ*)[19] are also, like the soldiers of Badr, 313 in number.[20]

An entire series of traditions describe them as warriors initiated into the secret Science (*'ilm*):[21] each one of them bears a sword upon which is inscribed a 'thousand words, each leading to another thousand', a sacred statement denoting Imami initiation.[22] At the moment of the Rising, when the Qā'im launches his appeal from Mecca, they will come to join him by supra-natural means, by the

---

18. Al-Nu'mānī, *Kitāb al-ghayba*, ch. 19, pp. 440f.

19. Ibid., pp. 285, 378f., 443f.; Ibn Bābūya, *Kamāl al-dīn*, vol. 1, pp. 268 and 331, vol. 2, pp. 378, 654, 671f.

20. It should be noted in passing that the numeric value of the term *jaysh* is 313: *jīm* = 3, *yā'* = 10, *shīn* = 300. On the existence of the esoteric science of letters in early Imamism, and for relevant sources, see *Guide divin*, index, under '*'ilm al-ḥurūf*' and '*ḥisāb al-jummal*'.

21. For more on this concept see *Guide divin*, pp. 174–199 (*Divine Guide*, pp. 69–75).

22. Al-Nu'mānī, *Kitāb al-ghayba*, pp. 447ff.; Ibn Bābūya, *Kamāl al-dīn*, vol. 2, p. 671; for the sacred formula see al-Ṣaffār al-Qummī, *Baṣā'ir al-darajāt*, ed. Mīrzā Kūchebāghī (Tabriz, n.d. [ca. 1960]), part 6, ch. 18, pp. 309–312; part 7, ch. 1, pp. 313–315; Ibn Bābūya, *al-Khiṣāl*, ed. M. B. Kamare'ī (Tehran, 1361 Sh./1982), pp. 326f.

power of the Supreme Name of God and by supernatural aerial travel. Once gathered in Mecca, their swords will descend from heaven. Sent by the imam to places throughout the earth, they will dominate absolutely everything; even the birds and wild beasts will obey them. For difficult decisions, they will receive directives from the imam that will be written on the palms of their hands. Knowledge of the Supreme Name of God will provide them with miraculous powers such as walking on water and soaring through the heavens, etc.[23]

Poised against the divine forces of justice and knowledge are those of oppression and ignorance led by illustrious eschatological characters such as al-Dajjāl or al-Sufyānī. Based on what emerges from messianic Imami traditions, we come to realise that the Qā'im's adversaries in the final battle are not the disbelievers but rather ignorant Muslims.[24]

---

23. Al-Kulaynī, *al-Rawḍa min al-Kāfī*, ed. H. Rasūlī Maḥallātī (Tehran, 1389/1969), vol. 2, p. 145; al-Nuʿmānī, *Kitāb al-ghayba*, pp. 352f., 445f.; Ibn Bābūya, *Kamāl al-dīn*, vol. 2, pp. 672f.

24. For a better appreciation of what is to follow, it seems necessary to recall some fundamental concepts that underpin the Imami 'theory of opponents' (*ḍiddiyya*). The omnipresent pair *ẓāhir/bāṭin* is obviously also at work in the revelation. Divine Truth is manifested in two forms: the exoteric aspect of Truth is revealed by the legislating prophethood (*nubuwwa*) which brings to the masses (*ʿāmma*) a Sacred text 'descended from heaven' (*tanzīl*). The secret dimension of Truth, its esoteric aspect, enveloped by the letter, is revealed thanks to the initiatory mission of the imam (*imāma, walāya, amr*), accompanying each prophetic mission and bringing to an elite minority (*khāṣṣa*) the veritable hermeneutics of the sacred Book which 'returns [the Book] to its Origin (*ta'wīl*)'. Each religion has thus had its 'Shiʿis'. As Muḥammad is considered the 'Seal of Prophets', historical Shiʿism presents itself as the last link in the chain of the initiatory tradition of sacred History. Due to this, the imam is naturally presented as the leader of the forces of knowledge. At the same time, it is said that these, especially the imam at the helm, always endure adversity inflicted by the forces of ignorance. Indeed each revelation of the divine Word within the community of the Book gives rise to a certain number of 'adversaries' (*ḍidd*, pl. *aḍdād*) or 'enemies' (*ʿaduww*, pl. *aʿdā'*) who deny the very existence of a hidden meaning to revelation, and thus oppose the imam's mission and betray the prophet by cutting off religion from its most profound element, dragging the majority of the community, the People of the Exoteric (*ahl al-ẓāhir*), into

> On the occasion of his Rising, our Qāʾim will have to confront ignorance (*jahl*) even greater than that of the ignorant ones faced by the Messenger of God during the Age of Ignorance [before Islam] (*juhhāl al-jāhiliyya*) . . . For, at the time of the Prophet, the people worshipped stones, rocks, plants and wooden statues, but when our Qāʾim will summon the people [to his Cause], they will interpret the entire Book of God [i.e. the Qurʾān] against him and will argue against him and use the Book to fight him (*kulluhum yataʾawwalū ʿalayhi kitābiʾllāh yaḥtajjū ʿalayhi bihi wa yuqātilūnahu ʿalayhi*).[25]

The enemies of the Mahdī are naturally the descendants of the adversaries in the history of Shiʿism. In a prophetic tradition reported by Jaʿfar al-Ṣādiq, after telling ʿAlī that the Mahdī will be one of the descendants of al-Ḥusayn, the Prophet addresses al-ʿAbbās b. ʿAbd al-Muṭṭalib, the namesake of the Abbasids, thus:

> 'Uncle of the Prophet! Do you wish me tell you about what the Angel Gabriel revealed to me?' 'Yes, Messenger of God.' – 'Gabriel said to me: "Your descendants will have to bear suffering inflicted by the descendants of al-ʿAbbās."' – 'Messenger of God, must I avoid women [to avoid having descendants]?' – 'No, God has already decided from whom they will come.'[26]

In addition, a number of eschatological traditions have a pronounced anti-Arab flavour, no doubt because, from the Imami perspective, those truly responsible for the decadence of religion from overlooking ʿAlī to the persecution and assassination of the imams and their followers were Arab Muslims. 'Misfortune to the

---

ignorance, injustice and violence. In the Islamic period, the 'Enemies' are those that reject the *walāya* of ʿAlī and as a consequence, that of the other imams. In this case, this means almost all of the Companions, particularly the first three caliphs, the Umayyads, the ʿAbbasids and generally speaking, those whom the Shiʿis call 'the majority' (*al-akthar*) or 'the masses' (*al-ʿāmma*), those who eventually came to be known as 'the Sunnis'; refer to Chapter 8 in this volume.

25. Al-Nuʿmānī, *Kitāb al-ghayba*, pp. 423–424 (tradition attributed to Jaʿfar al-Ṣādiq).

26. Al-Nuʿmānī, *Kitāb al-ghayba*, pp. 356f.

Arabs', 'Misfortune to the Arabs for the Evil that forebodes', 'Our Qā'im will be merciless against the Arabs', 'Between the Qā'im and the Arabs shall be nothing but the sword', 'Between the Arabs and us, only massacres will be left' and so on.[27]

At the same time, it is said that almost all of the Companions of the Qā'im are 'non-Arabs' or Persians (*'ajam*). In response to the question: 'How many among those accompanying the Qā'im are Arabs?' imam Ja'far al-Ṣādiq is said to have answered: 'Very few,' 'But there are many Arabs who profess this Cause', 'The people will inevitably be tested, separated, riddled (*yumaḥḥaṣū wa yumayyazū wa yugharbalū*); many will fall from this riddle.'[28] According to a tradition dating back to imam al-Bāqir, the 313 Companions of the Qā'im are all sons of *'ajam*[29] and a saying attributed to Ja'far al-Ṣādiq seems to indicate that they profess a religion entirely different than exoteric Islam since: 'They resemble worshippers of the sun and moon (*shibh 'abadat al-shams wa'l-qamar*).'[30]

In this gloomy picture of the Islamic community, the Shi'is are not better provided for than the others:

> 'When the standard of Truth (*rāyat al-ḥaqq*) [of the Qā'im] becomes manifest', Ja'far al-Ṣādiq is supposed to have said, 'the inhabitants of the Rising and Setting will curse it . . . due to what the people will have endured from his family before the Rising [*ahl baytihi* or according to another version, "from the Banū Hāshim"].'[31]

---

27. Al-Kulaynī, *al-Uṣūl*, 'Kitāb al-ḥujja', 'Bāb al-tamḥīṣ wa'l-imtiḥān', vol. 2, pp. 194–197; al-Nu'mānī, *Kitāb al-ghayba*, pp. 337f.; al-Iskāfī, *Kitāb al-tamḥīṣ* (Qumm, n.d. [ca. 1995]), pp. 42f.

28. Al-Nu'mānī, *Kitāb al-ghayba*, pp. 298–299; al-Iskāfī, *Kitāb al-tamḥīṣ*, p. 53.

29. Al-Nu'mānī, *Kitāb al-ghayba*, p. 448; al-Ṭūsī, Abū Ja'far, *Kitāb al-ghayba* (Tehran, 1398/1979), p. 284.

30. Al-Nu'mānī, *Kitāb al-ghayba*, pp. 451–452.

31. Ibid., pp. 424–425.

In another tradition, going back to the same sixth imam, it is said: 'This event [i.e. the Rising of the hidden imam] will not take place until some among you [the Shiʿis] spit in the face of the others, until some of you curse the others and accuse them of lying.'[32] Only a small minority, 'the true Shiʿis', that is, those initiated into the complete teachings of the imams, will be spared from the clutches of Evil. This minority is composed of followers each of whose 'hearts has been tested by God for faith' (*al-mu'min imtaḥana'llāh qalbahu li'l-īmān*), those that are supported by the strength of their *walāya*, their certitude and knowledge.[33]

The Mahdī's army, swelling in numbers with the mass of oppressed and volunteers won over to the Cause, will triumph. The Hijaz, Iraq, the East, Egypt, Syria and then Constantinople, will be conquered before the whole world surrenders to the Saviour. The 'Enemies' and their supporters will once and for all be wiped off the face of the earth; the world will be restored with justice, humanity will be revived by the light of knowledge. And what shall happen thereafter? The Saviour will prepare the world for the final Resurrection. According to some traditions, he will rule over the world for several years (seven, nine, nineteen . . . years) to be followed by the death of all humanity before the appearance of the final Tribunal. Other traditions report that after the death of the Qā'im, the government of the world will remain, for a relatively long time before the Day of Resurrection in the hands of the initiated wise ones.[34]

* * *

Let us now consider accounts of the Origins, in cosmogonic traditions. These may be divided into two groups. The first concern

32. Ibid., p. 300; al-Iskāfī, *Kitāb al-tamḥīṣ*, p. 43.

33. Refer to Chapter 8, this volume.

34. Al-Nuʿmānī, *Kitāb al-ghayba*, pp. 473–475; Ibn Bābūya, *'Ilal al-sharā'iʿ wa'l-aḥkām* (Najaf, 1385/1966), pp. 6f., and *Kamāl al-dīn*, vol. 1, p. 256; also Amir-Moezzi, *Guide divin*, pp. 279–301 (*Divine Guide*, pp. 115–123) and 'Eschatology'.

what we might call exoteric cosmogony: the *ex nihilo* creation, the First Created Things, the cosmos of the seven heavens and the seven subterranean worlds, angelology and demonology, the Pillars of the universe, the regions, their inhabitants and the age of the universe etc. This information is generally found in one form or another in Muslim cosmographic works and is thus common to both Shiʿi and Sunni literature. The second group seems specifically Shiʿi and presents a cosmogony that one might define as esoteric since it contains material regarding the initiatory doctrine of the imams.[35] The tradition that interests us here (mainly because a comparison with eschatological elements proves to be significantly informative) belongs to the second group. This is the long and important *ḥadīth* of the 'Armies (*junūd*) of *ʿaql* and *jahl*'. Several of the earliest sources report this tradition[36] and it has attracted the attention of many major interpreters of *ḥadīth*.[37] Here are some excerpts:

> Samāʿa b. Mihrān [Abū Muḥammad al-Ḥadramī al-Kūfī, disciple of the sixth and seventh imams, died in the second/seventh century in Medina] says: 'I was in the house of Abū ʿAbd Allāh

35. M. A. Amir-Moezzi, 'Cosmogony and Cosmology in Twelver Shiʿism', *EIr*, vol. 6, pp. 317–22.

36. Al-Barqī, Abū Jaʿfar, *Kitāb al-maḥāsin*, ed. J. Muḥaddith Urmawī (Tehran, 1370/1950), vol. 1, pp. 96–98; Kulaynī, *al-Uṣūl*, 'kitāb al-ʿaql wa'l-jahl', vol. 1, pp. 23–26; (Pseudo?) al-Masʿūdī, *Ithbāt al-waṣiyya* (Najaf, n.d.), pp. 1–3; Ibn Shuʿba, *Tuḥaf al-ʿuqūl ʿan āl al-rasūl*, ed. ʿA. A. Ghaffārī (Tehran, 1366 Sh./1987), pp. 423–425.

37. Al-Majlisī, *Mirʾāt al-ʿuqūl* (Tehran, n.d.), vol. 1, p. 45; Mullā Ṣadrā, *Sharḥ al-Uṣūl min al-Kāfī* (lithograph, Tehran, 1283/1865), pp. 14ff.; al-Qazwīnī, Mullā Khalīl, *al-Shāfī fī sharḥ al-Kāfī* (lithograph, Lucknow, 1308/1890), pp. 21f. I have already devoted a study to the various meanings, technical or otherwise, of the term *ʿaql* in the Imami corpus and have suggested translating it – in its cosmogonic dimension – as 'hiero-intelligence' to distinguish this level from other semantic levels of the notion such as 'reason', 'intellect', 'discernment' etc. See *Guide divin*, pp. 15–33 (*Divine Guide*, pp. 6–13); on this tradition see also D. Crow, 'The Role of al-ʿAql in Early Islamic Wisdom, with Reference to Imam Jaʿfar al-Ṣādiq' (McGill University, Montreal, 1966), ch. 13; E. Kohlberg, 'Evil: in Shiʿism', *EIr*, vol. 9, pp. 182–185, esp. 182.

> [i.e. Jaʿfar al-Ṣādiq] along with a group of his disciples. We spoke of Hiero-Intelligence and Ignorance. He then said: "Recognise Hiero-Intelligence and its Armies, Ignorance and its Armies and you will be on the well-guided path." — Samāʿa: "May I serve you as ransom! We only know what you enable us to know."'
>
> 'Abū ʿAbd Allāh: "God, may He be glorified and exalted, created Hiero-Intelligence and it was the first of the spiritual beings (*rūḥāniyyīn*) to be created, drawn from the right-hand side of the Throne and from the Light of God.
>
> "Then He ordered it to retreat and it retreated, to advance and it advanced. God then proclaimed: 'I created you glorious and gave you pre-eminence over all My creatures.' *Then* God created Ignorance from a bitter Ocean; He made it dark and commanded it to retreat and it retreated, to advance but it did not advance at all. God therefore said: 'Surely you have become arrogant' and He cursed it.
>
> "God then created seventy-five Armies for Hiero-Intelligence. When Ignorance saw the divine generosity to Hiero-Intelligence, it felt a fierce hostility (*ʿadāwa*) against it and addressed God thus: 'Lord! Here is a creature similar to me [Ignorance is also a "non-material" entity, a cosmogonical, archetypal counterforce]; You favoured and rendered it powerful; now, I am its adversary [lit. its Opponent, *ḍidd*] and I have no power. Give me troops similar to his.' 'So be it', answered God, 'but if you prove to be rebellious once again, I shall banish you and your troops from My Mercy.' 'Let it be so', said Ignorance. *Then* God created seventy-five Armies for it as well. Here then are the seventy-five Armies that God provided [for Hiero-Intelligence and Ignorance]: Good, minister of Hiero-Intelligence and its adversary (*ḍidduhu*), Evil, minister of Ignorance; Faith and its adversary Infidelity . . . Justice and its adversary Injustice . . . Clemency and its adversary Wrath . . . Knowledge and its adversary Ignorance . . . the Preservation of secrets and its adversary, Divulging of secrets . . . Wisdom and its adversary Passion . . . Joy and its adversary Sadness, etc."'

We will set aside theological issues of divine justice or the origin of Evil that the *ḥadīth* includes and that have attracted and held the attention of commentators. In the context of the issue that interests us, the parallel with messianic-eschatological traditions is striking. One must first note that the correspondence, even the identification between *ʿaql* and the figure of the imam is constant in the early corpus of traditions attributed to the historical imams. *ʿAql* is said to be the 'interior proof' (*al-ḥujja'l-bāṭina*) of God whereas the imam is His 'exterior proof' (*al-ḥujja'l-ẓāhira*) (bear in mind that *ḥujja*, pl. *ḥujaj*, is one of the most recurring titles for the imams in general and the hidden imam in particular).[38] The imam is the exterior *ʿaql*, whereas *ʿaql* is the interior imam of the loyal-faithful.[39] According to a Prophetic tradition reported by imam ʿAlī: 'The *ʿaql* in the heart is like a lamp in the centre of a home.'[40] And Jaʿfar al-Ṣādiq is said to have declared: 'The status of the heart (seat of *ʿaql*) within the body is the same as the status of the imam in the midst of men who owe him obedience.'[41] Similarly, the adversaries of the imams are frequently called 'the guiding leaders of Ignorance (*a'immat al-jahl*) and their supporters', 'the ignorant ones (*juhhāl, jahala, ahl al-jahl*)'.[42]

In the sayings of Jaʿfar al-Ṣādiq, as reported by Samāʿa b. Mihrān, the usage of the term *jund*, pl. *junūd* (army, troops) is obviously not without significance. It relates to the archetypal Battle between two forces: Intelligence and Ignorance, in which their troops, the virtues and the vices, are elevated to the rank of cosmic forces and counterforces. It is the first battle of a universal war that defines the entire History of humanity by setting the imams, various prophets and their followers against their adversaries – the forces of counter-initiation and their leaders. In this context, the eschatological battle of the Mahdī is the last of this endless cosmic War which will seal the definitive victory of the Forces of Intelligence over those of Ignorance. This victory thus constitutes the *maʿād*, the Return to the Origin, since by overcoming Ignorance and its Armies, the Mahdī restores

38. Al-Kulaynī, *al-Uṣūl*, vol. 1, p. 19.
39. Ibid., vol. 1, pp. 28–29; Ibn Shuʿba, *Tuḥaf al-ʿuqūl*, pp. 404ff.
40. Ibn Bābūya, *ʿIlal*, p. 98.
41. Ibid., p. 109.
42. *Guide divin*, see index.

the world to its original state, when *jahl* and its troops had not yet come into existence. In my translation of the *ḥadīth*, I have emphasised the adverb 'then' used on two occasions. This is so because Hiero-Intelligence was created first and 'then' Ignorance. The Armies of *ʿaql* come into existence first and 'then' those of *jahl*. Moreover, in his commentary, Mullā Ṣadrā underlines the importance of the adverb (*ḥarf*, '*thumma*' and '*fa-*') to develop his philosophy on the Good Origin of creation.[43] By establishing his worldwide government over a population exclusively composed of faithful initiates (I shall return to this point later in this chapter), this Origin of creation is started again by the Saviour, when the universe was only peopled with the Hiero-Intelligence and its troops.

2

On the individual dimension of eschatology, information is much scarcer, more discreet, following the principle that almost always prevails in esoteric aspects of the teachings of the imams. Moreover, as we will see, the developments concerning this dimension are found especially in the works of later authors but, not surprisingly, the latter support their claims with information gathered from the early corpus.

Witnessing the manifestation of the Mahdī and being one of his Companions constitutes the most fortunate soteriological aspect of Imami piety. However, of course not everyone can witness the End of the World and it is undoubtedly for this reason that many traditions repeatedly state that to have faith in the invisible presence and eventual final advent of the Mahdī is equivalent to being a part of his Army. This hopeful note, perhaps originally meant for those disappointed and frustrated by an indefinite delay of the Saviour, at the same time introduced an individual soteriological dimension into Twelver eschatology. Believing in the hidden imam is an article of faith for all the faithful; for Shiʿis, it even

43. Mullā Ṣadrā, *Sharḥ al-Uṣūl min al-kāfī*, pp. 18–19.

constitutes part of putting them to the test (*imtiḥān, tamḥīṣ*); this in turn is one of the conditions of the period of Occultation that distinguishes 'true Shiʿis' from those simply in name (see above). However, as with all esoteric doctrines, teachings dating back to the imams contain many levels of understanding meant for different categories of disciples.[44] In fact, some *ḥadīth*s seem to go much further than a simple invitation to an unconditional faith and an indefinite waiting period before the manifestation of the Saviour; they suggest that some especially advanced believers are able to know 'the place where the hidden imam is located', or, in other words, to establish contact with him and eventually see him:

> The Qāʾim will enter two Occultations [allusions to the minor Occultation, *al-ghayba al-ṣughrā*, from 260/874 to 329/940–941 and the major Occultation, *al-ghayba al-kubrā*, which began in 329 and continues to this day], one term short and the other long. During the first, only the elect few of the Shiʿis (*khāṣṣa shīʿatihi*) know where the imam is located and during the second, only those elect of the faithful Friends (*khāṣṣa mawālīhi*).[45]

The expression 'the elect of the Shiʿis' no doubt refers to the four 'representatives' (*nāʾib/wakīl/safīr*) of the hidden imam during the minor Occultation; according to tradition, during this period they alone had the privilege of knowing the 'location' of the imam. 'The elect of the faithful Friends' refers to the faithful who have been especially initiated in order to be able to communicate with the imam during the major Occultation.

> The Lord of this Cause (*ṣāḥib hādhāʾl-amr*) will enter two Occultations, one of which will last so long that some among you [the Shiʿis] will say that he is dead, others that he was killed and still

44. M. A. Amir-Moezzi, 'Du droit à la théologie: les niveaux de réalité dans le shiʿisme duodécimain', in *L'Esprit et la Nature*, Groupe d'Etudes Spirituelles Comparées, 5 (1997), pp. 37–63.

45. Al-Kulaynī, *al-Uṣūl*, 'Bāb fiʾl-ghayba', vol. 2, pp. 141–142; al-Nuʿmānī, *Kitāb al-ghayba*, pp. 249–250.

> others that he has [definitively] disappeared. Only some of the faithful (*aṣḥāb*) will remain true to his Cause, but none of his allied Friends (*wālī*) or others will know where he is located, except the faithful friend who champions his Cause (*al-mawlā'l-ladhī yalī amrahu*).[46]

Hagiographical literature devoted to the Awaited imam (*al-muntaẓar*) indeed contains several reports of encounters with the hidden imam.[47] Now, according to Imami belief, the last signed letter from him, received by ʿAlī b. Muḥammad al-Simmarī, his fourth and last 'representative' during the minor Occultation, stipulates, among other things, that the hidden imam will henceforth no longer be seen by anyone until the End of Time. This is why this letter signals the beginning of the major Occultation.[48] One of the many attempts to reconcile these contradictory facts, derives from the mystical milieu of Shiʿism and develops the individual dimension of eschatology. To my knowledge, this interpretation is used for the first time by Sayyid Kāẓim al-Rashtī (d. 1259/1843), second great master and true founder of the theological mystical Shaykhiyya order. In response to a disciple, during a long exposition on the relationship between the believers and the hidden imam, al-Rashtī presents a rich and dense system of thought that may be summed up by the following syllogism: the hidden imam cannot be seen until the End of Time (according to his last letter); now some people have seen the hidden imam (according to numerous reports from reliable sources), therefore these individuals have reached the End of Time (i.e. the End of their 'time', the 'time' of their own egos). The conclusion reached in this syllogism is obviously meant in the sense of an initiatory death: the vision of the Resurrector imam (one of the meanings

---

46. Al-Nuʿmānī, *Kitāb al-ghayba*, pp. 250–251.

47. Chapter 13, this volume.

48. Ibn Bābūya, *Kamāl al-dīn*, vol. 2, p. 516; al-Ṭūsī, *Kitāb al-ghayba*, p. 257; al-Majlisī, *Biḥār*, vol. 52, p. 151; Chapter 13, note 51 in this volume and the relevant text.

given by tradition to the word *qā'im*) signals the death of the ego and the resurrection, the rebirth, of the initiate.

Having cited the Prophetic *ḥadīth* 'Die before dying' (*mūtū qabla an tamūtū*) that mystical literature regularly advanced, Sayyid al-Rashtī gives a hermeneutical reading of some of the reports of encounters with the Qā'im. He concludes:

> These accounts may be interpreted spiritually (*maḥmūl 'alā'l-ta'wīl*). These thirsty men, overburdened, sick, threatened and tortured, are symbols (*rumūz*) of suffering imposed by the perilous desert of spiritual quest (*tīh al-ṭalab*) and the oppression of the thirst for the vision of the Beloved (*liqā' al-maḥbūb*). These dead men are brought to life by the imam, meaning to say, they have had a spiritual birth (*wilāda rūḥāniyya*) due to a vision of the radiant face of the imam and the initiation (*ṭa'līm wa talqīn*) that this vision includes.[49]

This conception of some encounters with the Mahdī[50] was subsequently repeated in one form or another by other mystics belonging to Imami mystical orders, such as, for example, Mīrzā Abu'l-Qāsim Rāz Shīrāzī (1286/1869), master of the Dhahabiyya, or Sayyid Aḥmad Dehkordī (1339/1920), master of the Khāksāriyya.[51]

It is obvious that the subject is a delicate one and when it concerns visionary experience, just as their predecessors had, these later authors limited themselves to allusive comments. Humility

---

49. Al-Rashtī, Sayyid Kāẓim, *al-Rasā'il wa'l-masā'il* (lithograph, Tabriz, n.d.), pp. 356–365; Chapter 13 in this volume.

50. This initiatic context of eschatological bearing does not necessarily concern all those individuals, quite numerous in fact, to whom the hidden imam – mainly as a humanitarian gesture – appeared for specific reasons or by chance, and whose reports fill chapters, and even entire monographs, such as the works by Ṭabarsī/Ṭabrisī Nūrī, *Jannat al-ma'wā*, published at the end of vol. 53 of the *Biḥār al-anwār* by al-Majlisī, and *al-Najm al-thāqib* (Qumm and Jamkarān, 1412/1991). See also Chapter 13, this volume.

51. Rāz Shīrāzī, *Mirṣād al-'ibād* (lithograph, Tabriz, n.d.) (published in a collection of his works), pp. 97–115, esp. pp. 98ff.; Dehkordī, Sayyid Aḥmad, *Burhān-nāme-ye ḥaqīqat* (lithograph, Tehran, n.d.), pp. 123ff.

and the duty to maintain secret (*taqiyya, kitmān*) are certainly factors, but also the penultimate sentence of the letter from the hidden imam, according to which whosoever claims to have seen the Mahdī before the End of Time is but an imposter and liar.[52] Still, the analysis of such reports of encounters that are initiatory, soteriological and eschatological in nature, reveal some significant recurring motifs. The imam of the Time is always bathed in light or depicted in a luminous form. He initiates the witness into secret teachings that plunge him into a state of ecstasy and fill him with bliss. It is this state that some authors do not hesitate to describe as initiatory death and spiritual resurrection. Finally, the imam can be seen either 'externally', as a luminous physical person, or 'internally', as a luminous spiritual form in the subtle centre of the heart (*laṭīfa qalbiyya*). Some examples follow.

In his treatise *al-Muwāsaʿa wa'l-muḍāyaqa*, Raḍī al-Dīn Ibn Ṭāwūs (664/1266) narrates in a highly allusive style, in the guise of a description of his companion's dreams, that he encountered the hidden imam in a state of deep contemplation, that the latter revealed secret knowledge of a higher order that drove him into a profound and intensely beatific state.[53]

Shams al-Dīn Muḥammad Lāhījī (912/1506–1507) devotes a chapter to the Seals of prophethood and *walāya* in his monumental commentary on the *Golshan-e Rāz* by Maḥmūd Shabistarī (720/1317). In his long mystical account, in which his own encounter with the hidden imam is only hinted at, he explains that manifestation of the Mahdī is equivalent to the revelation of realities, of divine knowledge and secrets (*ḥaqā'iq, maʿārif,*

52. Ṭabrisī Nūrī, *Jannat al-ma'wā*, p. 236 and *al-Najm al-thāqib*, p. 474 (the account by Sayyid Muḥammad Mahdī 'Baḥr al-ʿulūm').

53. Ibn Ṭāwūs, *Risāla fi'l-muḍāyaqa fī fawāt al-ṣalāt* (known as *al-Muwāsaʿa wa'l-muḍāyaqa*) published in the margins of Muḥammad Amīn al-Astarābādī, *al-Fawā'id al-madaniyya* (lithograph, n.p. [Iran], 1321/1904), pp. 30–40, in particular pp. 36–37. It is interesting to note that this legalistic text by Ibn Ṭāwūs, on the rules concerning the forgetting of canonical prayers, is not *a priori* mystical in nature. Discreetly including a report of his encounter with the hidden imam in it seems to be a form of *taqiyya*.

asrār-e elāhī) and it is this that constitutes the reality of the Resurrection, transforming simple followers into 'Companions of the Qā'im' (*aṣḥāb-e qā'im*) and veritable men of knowledge (*'ārifān-e ḥaqīqī*).[54]

Mullā Muḥammad Taqī al-Majlisī, known as Majlisī the First (1070/1659–1660), father of the famous author of *Biḥār al-anwār*, is said to have allusively stated in his *Sharḥ al-ziyāra al-jāmi'a'l-kabīra* that he encountered the Mahdī on many occasions, both in dreams and in an awakened state. It is reported that regarding the following ecstatic experience, he wrote:

> It is as though I tasted death and returned to my Lord due to his overwhelming presence [i.e. the Mahdī] and his blessed light (*ka-annī dhā'iq al-mawt wa rāji' ilā rabbī min fayḍ huḍūrihi'l-mutaḍammin wa nūrihi'l-mutabarrik*).[55]

Shaykh Aḥmad al-Aḥsā'ī (1241/1826), namesake of the Shaykhiyya order as well as Muḥammad Karīm Khān (1288/1870) his second successor in the Kirmānī branch, allude to their visionary experiences, in which the imams appear in the form of luminous beings, and mention that they achieved contentment through their initiation.[56] Although neither mystic master specifically mentions

54. Lāhījī, Shams al-Dīn Muḥammad, *Mafātīḥ al-i'jāz fī sharḥ Golshan-e Rāz*, ed. M. R. Barzegar Khāleqī and 'E. Karbāsī (Tehran, 1371 Sh./1992), pp. 265–268.

55. Al-Aḥsā'ī, Shaykh Aḥmad, *Sharḥ al-Ziyāra al-jāmi'a* (lithograph, Tabriz, n.d.), p. 268; Bihbahānī, Aḥmad b. Muḥammad 'Alī, *Mir'āt al-aḥwāl-e jahān-namā*, ed. 'A. Davānī (Tehran, 1372 Sh./1993), p. 70. The sentence clearly draws from two Qur'ānic passages. First, 'Every soul [one day] tastes death' (*kullu nafs dhā'iqatu'l-mawt*) (Q 3:185; 21:35 and 29:57). Secondly, 'O soul at peace, return unto thy Lord, well-pleased, well-pleasing!' (*yā ayyatuhā al-nafsu'l-muṭma'inna/irji'ī ilā rabbiki rāḍiyyatan marḍiyya*) (Q 89:27–28). The saying attributed to al-Majlisī seems thus to suggest that the encounter with the Resurrector signals the death of the ego and the resurrection of spiritual individuality.

56. Al-Hindī, Āghā Sayyid Hādī, *Tanbīh al-ghāfilīn wa surūr al-nāẓirīn* (lithograph, n.p. [Tabriz], n.d.), pp. 53–54; al-Riḍawī, Mīrzā Ni'mat Allāh, *Tadhkirat al-awliyā'* (lithograph, Bombay, 1313/1895), p. 14.

the Mahdī among the imams encountered, given their mystical profession of faith which includes considering the latter 'the living imam of the Time' who certainly enters into contact with his 'Companions',[57] one can reasonably conclude that the vision of the Qā'im was also part of their spiritual experiences.

Later mystics, belonging to other Imami orders (Niʿmatullāhiyya, Dhahabiyya, Khāksāriyya, Uwaysiyya) mention the possibility of the vision of the imam, in the form of a luminous entity, in the subtle centre of the heart, and thus benefiting from this secret initiation. The assertion is almost always founded on the *ḥadīth* dating back to ʿAlī b. Abī Ṭālib, applied to all the imams and to the Qā'im in particular, as the 'imam of this Age':

> To know me as Light is to know God, and to know God is to know me as Light. He who knows me as Light is a believer whose heart God has tested for faith' (*maʿrifatī bi'l-nūrāniyya maʿrifatu'llāh wa maʿrifatu'llāh maʿrifatī bi'l-nūrāniyya man ʿarafanī bi'l-nūrāniyya kāna mu'minan imtaḥana'llāhu qalbahu li'l-īmān*).[58]

This is 'vision by (or "in") the heart' (*al-ru'ya bi'l-qalb*), a spiritual experience whose outcome is said to be salvatory knowledge and paranormal powers.[59] It should be recalled that the expression 'the believer whose heart God has tested for faith' designates, among others, the Companions of the Qā'im, the 'true Shiʿi' (cf. above). These later authors continually justify and corroborate their asser-

---

57. Al-Kirmānī, Muḥammad Karīm Khān, *Tawḥīd nubuwwa imāma shīʿa* (lithograph, Tabriz, 1310/1892), pp. 56–59.

58. Muẓaffar ʿAlī Shāh Kirmānī, *Kibrīt-e aḥmar (+ Baḥr al-asrār)*, ed. J. Nūrbakhsh (Tehran, 1350 Sh./1971), pp. 5f.; Nūr ʿAlī Shāh Gonābādī the Second, *Ṣāliḥiyya* (2nd edn, Tehran, 1387/1967), pp. 159f.; Palāsī Shīrāzī, Ḥasan b. Ḥamza, *Tadhkere-ye Muḥammad b. Ṣadīq al-Kujujī* (Shiraz, n.d.), pp. 14, 18–25, 38, 68.

59. R. Gramlich, *Die schiitischen Derwischorden Persiens*, Zweiter Teil, *Glaube und Lehre* (Wiesbaden, 1976), p. 207, n. 1073 and pp. 247–250; *Guide divin*, pp. 112–145 (for earlier sources) (*Divine Guide*, pp. 44–56) and refer especially to Chapter 10, this volume (where many other sources and studies are cited).

tions by traditions from the early corpus of sayings attributed to the imams. It is true that, ever since the early period, the influence of the hidden imam is constantly likened to an illumination or a luminous ray and it appears that for the followers, benefiting from this radiating effusion is only possible by mysterious or occult means, since on each occasion, each one adds that this is a sacred secret.[60] For example, in a tradition dating back to the Prophet and reported by Jābir al-Anṣārī, it is said that, during the Occultation, only those whose heart has been tested by God for faith will remain loyal to the hidden imam, that they shall be illuminated by his Light and will benefit from his friendship (*walāya*) just as one benefits from the sun while it is hidden by clouds; the saying ends with these words: 'This is God's sealed secret, a hidden treasure of divine knowledge. Jābir! Hide this secret from those who are not worthy of it.'[61]

In one section of the famous and extensive 'Prayer during the Qā'im's Occultation', it says: 'O Lord, show us eternally his Light [i.e. of the Mahdī] which has no shadow and by which dead hearts are revived . . . (*yā rabbi arinā nūrahu sarmadan lā ẓulma fīhi wa aḥyi bihi'l-qulūb al-mayyita*).'[62]

The initiate with 'a tested heart' can thus attain the luminous Reality of the imam, the ultimate aim of Imami teaching. As the Mahdī is the living imam of the Time, that is the Time of Occultation, he is naturally the focus of these elements and constitutes the principal aid for meditation and spiritual practice. His 'Encounter' and the initiation undertaken during it, entails salvation and is equivalent to individual resurrection. It is in this sense that our mystics understand the early traditions, attributed to many of the imams, such as: 'The advent or the delay of the End of Time bears no prejudice for one who knows the Qā'im', and 'He who knows

60. Ibn Bābūya, *Kamāl al-dīn*, vol. 1, pp. 253, 372 and vol. 2, pp. 485f.

61. Ibid., vol. 1, p. 253.

62. Ibid., vol. 2, p. 515.

his imam is just as if he had already found himself inside the tent of the Awaited imam.'[63]

This individual eschatology corresponds fundamentally with certain cosmic and anthropogonic traditions of an esoteric nature. These accounts of the Origin can be regarded as narratives of the Primordial Initiation. I have described and analysed them elsewhere in detail.[64] Here, I will only describe them briefly in order to show their connection with individual eschatology.

Creation begins with calling a series of 'Worlds' and their inhabitants into existence; these are all non-material, as they have been created thousands of years before the creation of the material world. The first of these Worlds is called 'the Mother of the Book (*umm al-kitāb*)' and its inhabitants, the first created beings, are the luminous formless entities of the Impeccable Ones (the Prophet, Fāṭima and the imams), drawn from the Light of God Himself. This pleroma is the Imam in the original, cosmic, archetypal dimension. Next is created the First World of Particles (*'ālam al-dharr*, lit. 'ants', *al-awwal*) also called the First World of the Shadows (*'ālam al-aẓilla al-awwal*) or the World of the Primordial Pact (*'ālam al-mīthāq*). There the luminous entities take human form. Designated by expressions such as 'silhouettes of light' (*ashbāḥ nūr*), 'spirits made of light' (*arwāḥ min nūr*) or 'shadows of light' (*aẓilla nūr*), they undertake an archetypal circumambulation around the divine Throne, attesting to the Unicity (*tawḥīd, tahlīl*) and praising the Glory (*taḥmīd, tamjīd, taqdīs, tasbīḥ*) of God. Then the Particles or Shadows, that is, the non-material, pre-existent entities of the 'pure beings', enter this world: angels and other celestial entities, prophets and believers (*mu'minūn*), the latter being faithful to the imams of all the ages, those initiated to the esoteric dimension of all religions, different from the simple practitioners who have submitted only to the

63. Al-Nu'mānī, *Kitāb al-ghayba*, pp. 470–473.

64. *Guide divin*, pp. 75–110 (*Divine Guide*, pp. 29–43); 'Cosmogony and Cosmology in Twelver Shi'ism', *EIr*, vol 6, pp. 317–322; Chapter 4 in this volume.

exoteric religion (*muslimūn*). After taking an oath of allegiance, the 'pure beings' are initiated by the Imam of Light into the secret knowledge of the Unicity and the Glory (*asrār 'ilm al-tawḥīd wa'l-taḥmīd*).[65] The subsequent phases in the cosmo-anthropogony, such as the creation of the Second World of Particles and Adam's descendants, that is, their non-material entities or the creation of the physical world, are not dealt with here as these points do not bear upon our current subject.

One can readily see that in these accounts of the Origin we find the essential elements of individual eschatology: the imam in his form of light, the elect of tested believers, the initiation into secrets. Everything occurs as if the Encounter and initiation of the hidden imam bathed in light provokes the *ma'ād* of the faithful 'with the tested heart', his Return to this Origin where his non-material, pre-existent being was initiated by the luminous entity of the Imam with divine, secret knowledge, and his individual resurrection was effected by the same.

The initiatory dimension of the *ma'ād* is also very present in collective, universal eschatology. The supporters of the Qā'im during his final battle are exactly the same as the 'pure beings' initiated in the First World of the Particles: angels, celestial entities, prophets and saints, faithful initiates (cf. above). After his victory, the Saviour brings wisdom for all human beings won over to his Cause:

> During the Manifestation [of the Qā'im], God will place the hand of our Qā'im upon the head of the faithful; due to this hand, they will have their wisdom (*'aql*) unified and their sagaciousness (*ḥilm*) completed.[66]

65. It seems that what is taught are the thaumaturgic powers of the formulae that every Muslim knows: *lā ilāha illā'llāh; Allāhu akbar; al-ḥamdu li'llāh; subḥāna'llāh; lā ḥawl wa lā quwwa illā bi'llāh*. It should be recalled that these formulae also constitute the standard mystical *dhikr*s.

66. Al-Kulaynī, *al-Uṣūl*, vol. 1, p. 29; Ibn Bābūya, *Kamāl al-dīn*, vol. 2, p. 675. The term *ḥilm* here denotes an intelligence applied to the profane sphere, as differentiated from *'aql*, intelligence, intuition or knowledge applied in the sacred sphere, see *Guide divin*, pp. 16–17 (*Divine Guide*, p. 7).

Islam, along with other religions, especially Judaism and Christianity, distorted and abandoned by their followers, will be re-established in their original truth and integrity.[67] Moreover, the re-established religions will no longer be only exoteric dogmas but also spiritual esoteric teachings, for the Mahdī will provide the believers of each religion with the hermeneutics of the hidden meaning of their sacred Scripture.[68]

> [At the time of the Qāʾim] men will have their eyes enlightened by the [authentic] text of the Revelation and their ears touched by the explanation of its hidden meaning. Morning and evening, they will constantly be drinking from cups of wisdom ([...] *tujlā biʾl-tanzīl abṣāruhum wa yurmā biʾl-tafsīr fī masāmiʿihim wa yughbiqūna kaʾs al-ḥikma baʿd al-ṣabūḥ*) [a tradition dating back to ʿAlī b. Abī Ṭālib].[69]

By universal initiation, lifting the veil that separates the exoteric from the esoteric, the Qāʾim re-actualises the Primordial Initiation and returns the world to this original 'moment' when only those filled with wisdom inhabited the universe. In these terms, the End of Time marks, in the words of Lāhījī, a new Beginning (*istiʾnāf*),[70] literally *Apokatastasis*, the restoration of the world to its primordial state of light and wisdom.

In messianic Twelver eschatology, although not mentioned *expressis verbis*,[71] the *maʿād* begins well before the final Tribunal of the universal *qiyāma* and the division of men between Heaven

67. Al-Nuʿmānī, *Kitāb al-ghayba*, pp. 333ff., 342–343; Ibn Bābūya, *ʿIlal*, pp. 161–163.

68. Al-Ḥasan al-ʿAskarī (attrib.), *Tafsīr* (lithograph, Lucknow, 1310/1893), p. 186; al-Nuʿmānī, *Kitāb al-ghayba*, p. 345.

69. Al-Sharīf al-Raḍī, *Nahj al-balāgha*, Arabic text and Persian trans. by ʿA. N. Fayḍ al-Islām (6th edn, Tehran, 1351 Sh./1972), p. 458.

70. Lāhījī, Shams al-Dīn Muḥammad, *Mafātīḥ al-iʿjāz fī sharḥ Golshan-e Rāz*, p. 267.

71. Perhaps because of *taqiyya*, since in this way the 'orthodox' meaning of *maʿād* is made to recede into the background.

and Hell. It is intimately linked to the different episodes of cosmo-anthropogony, in such a way that one might say that the End of Time and the Return to the Origin define each other in a mutual relationship. Whereas in the universal dimension of eschatology, it is the End of the World which sets off the process of the Return to the Origin, in the individual dimension, the inverse seems to be the case since it is the re-actualisation of the Origin that gives rise to spiritual Resurrection.

* * *

It has often been said and written that Imami eschatology is a reflection of the frustration and thwarted hopes of a much-oppressed minority at the mercy of the vicissitudes of history. It is true that, as it appears in its foundational texts, the specifically vengeful attitude of Imamism crystallised around the Figure of the Awaited imam and his eventual advent. The very term *qāʾim* (in the sense of 'standing imam'), applied to the eschatological Saviour, is in contrast to *qāʿid* ('seated imam') which characterises the other imams, who especially after the tragedy of Karbalāʾ, refused to let themselves be entangled in the vagaries of armed rebellion and, indeed, justified their quietist policy by reasoning that armed uprising against oppression was the prerogative of the Mahdī upon his final manifestation:

> Any banner raised before the uprising of the Qāʾim belongs to a rebel against God (*inna kulla rāyatin turfaʿu qabla qiyāmi'l-qāʾim fa-ṣāḥibuhā ṭāghūt*).[72]

However, critical analyses of both early and later texts that deal with messianic beliefs clearly show that the chapter on eschatology is much more complex and can hardly be reduced to this one 'political' dimension. Indeed, just like some preceding faiths,

72. Al-Kulaynī, *al-Rawḍa*, vol. 2, pp. 121–122; al-Nuʿmānī, *Kitāb al-ghayba*, pp. 161–168; on the Imami quietist political attitude see *Guide divin*, pp. 155–173 (*Divine Guide*, pp. 61–69).

for example the Iranian religions, or the 'heterodox' Jewish, Judeo-Christian or Christian sects of the first centuries of the common era, precedents from which it seems to have inherited many elements, doctrinal Imami Shiʿism can only be appreciated, in its particular features, as an initiatory esoteric teaching with a mythical discourse. Summarising the research of scholars of the esoteric tradition, Antoine Faivre has very ably shown that the mythical language of esoteric doctrines (which he calls 'theosophical') always rests on the all-encompassing triptych, namely the origin, the present state of things and the final happenings.[73] In other words, this constitutes a cosmogony (often linked to a theogony and/or an anthropogony) marked by the force of Good, a cosmology in which – enduring the counter-force of Evil – the 'real' will be a perpetual continuation of the confrontation of both forces simultaneous with preparation for the final happenings, and lastly an eschatology which is essentially soteriological because it is founded on a return to the sacred Origin.[74] This triptych, in which each term bears its full meaning only in relation to the other two, characterises the fundamental *Weltanschauung* of Neoplatonism or of gnosticism built upon the triad: the original unity of beings, the division or the fall and finally the return to unity. One can look further back in history and cite the concepts of *bundahishn* (Creation), *gumezishn* (Mixture) and *wizarishn* (Separation)/*frashegird* (Transfiguration) in Mazdaeism and Zoroastrianism.

In this sense, the collective dimension of Imami messianism, emphatically marked by violence and a battle against Evil, re-enacts the primordial Battle between the forces of Hiero-Intelligence and Ignorance. Waged ever since the dawn of creation, this Battle defines the History of humanity since it has repercussions, from age to age, in the conflict setting the imams of all times and their initiates against the forces of darkness and counter-initiation. The

73. A. Faivre, *Accès de l'ésotérisme occidental* (Paris, 1986), p. 24.

74. Ibid., pp. 24–25, 117 and 158f.

definitive annihilation of the forces of Ignorance by the Saviour, by means of a liberating battle and enlightening initiation brings the world to this original state in which it was only inhabited by the Armies of *ʿaql* before those of *jahl* were created. As for the individual dimension, it completes the cycle of Initiation which also began at the origin of creation and continues throughout the Spiritual life of humanity, since it is renewed over the ages by the teaching of the imams of all times. The believer who discovers the Light of the imam of the Time and the initiation that he grants also returns to the Origin since he reenacts the primordial Initiation when in the World of Particles his pre-existing entity was initiated into divine secrets by the luminous form of the archetypal Imam.

13

A Contribution on the Typology of Encounters with the Hidden Imam*

The figure of the hidden imam and the spiritual and philosophical implications of the Occultation form part of the recurring themes in Henry Corbin's work, preoccupying him for almost two decades.[1] Since the studies by this late orientalist philosopher, other scholars have dealt with the same subject from other angles, with different interests.[2] I myself have devoted some of my studies to

---

* This chapter is the written version of a lecture presented at the conference 'On the work of Henry Corbin' held in Tehran by the Institut Français de Recherche en Iran (IFRI) on 30 and 31 October 1995. I thank Rémy Boucharlat, then director of IFRI, for kindly inviting me to the conference.

1. See e.g. 'Sur le douzième Imam', *Table Ronde* (Feb. 1957), pp. 7–21, Persian trans., 'Dar bāb-e emām-e davāzdahom', by Ī. Sepahbodī, *Revue Iranienne d'Anthropologie*, 2 (1958); German trans., 'Über den zwölften Imam', by H. Landolt, *Antaios*, 2 (1960); 'L'Imam caché et la rénovation de l'homme en théologie shî'ite', *EJ*, 28, 1959 (Zurich, 1960), pp. 47–108; 'Le combat spirituel du shî'isme', *EJ*, 30, 1961 (Zurich, 1962), pp. 69–125; 'Au pays de l'Imam caché', *EJ*, 32, 1963 (1964), pp. 31–87; *Histoire de la philosophie islamique* (Paris, [1st edn 1964] 1986), pp. 107–114; 'Juvénilité et chevalerie (javânmardî) en Islam iranien', *EJ*, 40, 1971 (1973), pp. 311–356 (rpr. in *L'homme et son ange* [Paris, 1983], part 3); *En Islam iranien. Aspects spirituels et philosophiques* (Paris, 1972), vol. 4, book 7 (in which previous studies are reviewed and supplemented), pp. 303–460.

2. E.g. J. M. Hussain, *The Occultation of the Twelfth Imam: A Historical Background* (London, 1982). On the various implications of the Occultation, especially in social, economic and political terms, see e.g. J. Calmard, 'Le chiisme imamite en Iran à l'époque seldjoukide d'après le *Kitâb al-naqḍ*', *Le monde*

this theme and, having a more or less similar conception to that held by Corbin, I attempted, on the one hand, to adopt a critical approach to supplement the material that he has contributed and, on the other hand, to restore to what one might call his intuitions, the historical-doctrinal foundations supported by the texts.[3]

---

iranien et l'Islam, 1 (1971); E. Kohlberg, 'The Development of the Imāmī Shīʿī Doctrine of *jihād*', *ZDMG*, 126 (1976) (rpr. in *Belief and Law*, article 15); A. A. Sachedina, 'A Treatise on the Occultation of the Twelfth Imamite Imam', *SI*, 48 (1978); idem, 'Al-Khums: the Fifth in the Imāmī Shīʿī Legal System', *JNES*, 39 (1980); idem, *Islamic Messianism: the Idea of the Mahdī in Twelver Shiʿism* (Albany, NY, 1981) and *The Just Ruler (al-sulṭān al-ʿādil) in Shiʿite Islam: The Comprehensive Authority of the Jurist in Imamite Jurisprudence* (New York and Oxford, 1988); W. Madelung, 'Authority in Twelver Shiʿism in the Absence of the Imam', in *La notion d'autorité au Moyen Age: Islam, Byzance, Occident. Colloques Internationaux de la Napoule*, 1978 (Paris, 1982) (rpr. in *Religious Schools and Sects in Medieval Islam*, article X), and 'A Treatise of the Sharīf al-Murtaḍā on the Legality of Working for the Government (*Mas'ala fi'l-ʿamal maʿa'l-sulṭān*)', *BSOAS*, 43 (1980) (rpr. in *Religious Schools*, article IX), and 'Shiʿite Discussions on the Legality of the *Kharāj*', *Proceedings of the Ninth Congress of the Union Européenne des Arabisants et Islamisants*, ed. R. Peters (Leiden, 1981) (rpr. in *Religious Schools*, article XI); N. Calder, 'Zakāt in Imāmī Shīʿī Jurisprudence', *BSOAS*, 44 (1981) and 'Khums in Imāmī Shīʿī Jurisprudence', *BSOAS*, 45 (1982); S. A. Arjomand, *The Shadow of God and the Hidden Imam* (Chicago, 1984); A. J. Newman, 'The Development and Political Significance of the Rationalist (usuli) and Traditionalist (akhbari) School in Imami Shiʿi History from the Third/Ninth to the Tenth/Sixteenth Century' (PhD thesis, UCLA, Los Angeles, 1986). On the issue of the break with the original tradition due to the Occultation, see N. Calder, 'Accomodation and Revolution in Imāmī Shīʿī Jurisprudence: Khumayni and the Classical Tradition', *Middle East Studies*, 18 (1982); J. R. Cole, 'Imami Jurisprudence and the Role of the Ulama: Mortaza Ansari on Emulation the Supreme Exemplar', in N. R. Keddie (ed.), *Religion and Politics in Iran. Shiʿism from Quietism to Revolution* (New Haven and London, 1983), and idem, 'Shiʿi Clerics in Iraq and Iran, 1772–1780: The Akhbari-Usuli Conflict Reconsidered', *Iranian Studies*, 28 (1985); S. Schmidtke, 'Modern Modifications in the Shiʿi doctrine of the Expectation of the Mahdi (*Intiẓār al-Mahdī*): The Case of Khumaini', *Orient*, 28/3 (1987) and my studies cited in the following note.

3. See *Guide divin*, ch. 4 and Appendix; 'Réflexions sur une évolution du shīʿisme duodécimain: tradition et idéologisation', in E. Patlagean and A. Le Boulluec (eds), *Les retours aux Ecritures. Fondamentalismes présents et passés*, Bibliothèque de l'EPHE (Sciences Religieuses), vol. 99 (Louvain and Paris,

In the context of this issue, Corbin gives special attention to the theme of encounters with the hidden imam during the Occultation.[4] This chapter seeks to respond to one of his wishes concerning this subject, a wish he expressed during his important study on 'the twelfth imam and spiritual chivalry' that constitutes Book VII of his *En Islam iranien*:

> Until the hour of the parousia, the hidden imam is visible only in dreams or in certain individual manifestations that thus bear the qualities of visionary events; they do not interrupt the period of *ghaybat*, precisely because they occur in this 'in-between time' [i.e. the time of the *mundus imaginalis, imaginal* time]; nor do they materialise in the stream of historical, material facts that the first observer on the scene can record and attest to. The accounts of these theophanic visions are rather numerous in Shiʿi books. It will be neccesary to establish a typological classification.[5]

I will therefore attempt to establish a typology of accounts of encounters with the hidden imam during the Occultation;[6] I believe this will shed new light on the development and evolution of the Imami dogma of Occultation as well as the role of the hidden imam in the spiritual economy of Imamism, all the while

---

1993); 'Remarques sur les critères d'authenticité du hadith et l'autorité du juriste dans le shīʿisme imamite', *SI*, 85 (1997), pp. 5–39.

4. H. Corbin, *En Islam iranien: Aspects spirituels et philosophiques* (Paris, 1971–1972), vol. 4, Book 7, ch. 2, in which previous studies are reviewed and completed; see also in particular, the article 'Au pays de l'Imam caché' (refer to note 1 above).

5. Ibid., vol 4, p. 330, a wish already expressed with a less elaborate philosophical argument, in 'L'Imam caché et la rénovation de l'homme' (see note 1 above), p. 85.

6. 'Encounters, meetings' and not 'contact' in general; absent from my exposition therefore are oral and written messages supposed to have emanated from the hidden imam and received directly or indirectly by the faithful. In this regard, see the brief but evocative text by E. Kohlberg, 'Authoritative Scriptures in Early Imāmī Shīʿism', in E. Patlagean and A. Le Boulluec (eds), *Les retours aux Ecritures. Fondamentalismes présents et passés* (Louvain and Paris, 1993), pp. 307–309.

determining to what extent observations by Henry Corbin (as summarised in the passage cited above on the nature and context of these encounters) prove to be verifiable.

* * *

In general, hagiographical literature devoted to the twelfth imam accords a prominent place to reports of encounters with him. As we know, according to the most widely accepted traditional material, the Occultation took place in 260/874 and, according to Imami dogma, continues to this day since it will only come to an end at 'the End of Time'. The numerous sources containing these reports therefore cover a period of about a thousand years, ranging from a few decades after the Occultation with, for example, al-Kulaynī (329/940–941)[7] down almost to recent times with monographs by Ḥusayn al-Ṭabarsī/Ṭabrisī al-Nūrī (1320/1902)[8] after al-Nīlī (alive in 803/1401) and al-Majlisī II (1111/1699) of course.[9] As we shall see, the further we advance in time, the more these accounts increase, vary and gain in substance.

---

7. Al-Kulaynī, *al-Uṣūl min al-Kāfī*, ed. J. Muṣṭafawī with Persian trans., 4 vols (Tehran, n.d. [vol 4, tr. H. Rasūlī Maḥallātī, 1386/1966]).

8. Conventially rendered: 'Ṭabarsī', but this is the Arabicised form of the name of the Iranian city of Tafresh, not far from Qumm; the correct spelling is therefore 'Ṭabrisī'; cf. the learned note by A. Bahmanyār in his edition of *Tārīkh-e Bayhaq* by Ibn Funduq al-Bayhaqī (Tehran, n.d.), pp. 347–353 and Muḥsin al-ʿĀmilī, *Aʿyān al-shīʿa*, vols 1–56 (Damascus, 1935–1961), vol. 9, pp. 97–98; see, however, the arguments by E. Kohlberg, 'al-Ṭabrisī', *EI2*. Mīrzā Ḥusayn Ṭabrisī Nūrī, *Jannat al-maʾwā*, published at the end of vol. 53 of the *Biḥār al-anwār* by al-Majlisī (Tehran, 1385/1965) (see following note), and *al-Najm al-thāqib* (in Persian) (Qumm and Jamkarān, 1412/1991) and also, *Kalima ṭayyiba* (in Persian) (Tehran, n.d.) that contains some accounts of the encounter.

9. Al-Nīlī, *al-Sulṭān al-mufarrij ʿan ahl al-īmān*, ed. Q. al-ʿAṭṭār (Qumm, 1384 Sh./2006); Muḥammad Bāqir al-Majlisī, *Biḥār al-anwār,* 110 tomes in 90 vols (Tehran and Qumm, 1376–1392/1956–1972), vols 52 and 53.

Encounters during the minor occultation

The first testimonies of this kind are those reported by Muḥammad b. Yaʿqūb al-Kulaynī (d. 329/940–941) in his *Uṣūl min al-Kāfī*, no doubt written some decades after the beginning of the Occultation, during the period said to be one of 'confusion' (*ḥayra*) in the community.[10] The year of al-Kulaynī's death coincides with the date that the Twelver community recognised as marking the end of the minor Occultation. For the Twelvers, these reports therefore stem from this period; al-Kulaynī himself seems convinced that he is writing during the first Occultation since he reports some traditions on the notion of two successive *ghaybas* of which the second will be longer.[11] Unlike later accounts, those reported by the famous compiler present a rather meagre typological variety: a list of a dozen individuals – Imami faithful or others – who were able to see the twelfth imam in his childhood, adolescence or youth. In a large majority of cases, no noteworthy event marks the encounter.[12]

In three cases, the imam proves his true nature by performing miracles: the transformation of a handful of clay into gold;[13] having a knowledge of languages (in this instance of the Hindus, *kalām al-hind*) and of intimate secrets from the life of the witness;[14] and finally, having knowledge of the future.[15] The miraculous powers of the hidden imam, and in particular the

10. Al-Kulaynī, *al-Uṣūl*, 'Kitāb al-ḥujja', 'Bāb fī tasmiya man ra'āhu 'alayhi'l-salām', vol. 2, pp. 120–126 and 'Bāb mawlid al-ṣāḥib 'alayhi'l-salām', vol. 2, pp. 449–468.

11. Ibid., 'Bāb fi'l-ghayba', vol. 2, pp. 138 and 140–141, nos 12, 19 and 20.

12. Ibid., 'Bāb fī tasmiya man ra'āhu', vol. 2, pp. 120–125, nos 1, 2, 4–14.

13. Ibid., vol. 2, p. 125, no. 15 (report from the resident of al-Madā'in and his travelling companion; cf. *Guide divin*, p. 281 [*Divine Guide*, p. 115]).

14. Ibid., 'Bāb mawlid al-ṣāḥib', vol. 2, pp. 453–454, no. 3 (a report by Abū Saʿīd Ghānim al-Hindī).

15. Ibid., vol. 2, p. 455, no. 4 (here the witness finds himself in the presence of the twelfth imam, hidden behind a curtain and thus only hears his voice; a report by al-Ḥasan b. al-Naṣr).

precise knowledge of secrets known only to the reporter, as well as his perfect knowledge of religious matters and his benevelonce towards those believers who consider him the supreme authority of the community, are the recurring themes of the messages from the imam, written or oral, as transmitted by his 'representatives'.[16]

Some of these messages are reported by another famous author from this period, ʿAlī b. al-Ḥusayn Ibn Bābūya, the father of al-Ṣadūq (who also died in 329/940–941), in his book *al-Imāma wa'l-tabṣira min al-ḥayra.*[17] Quite remarkably, Ibn Bābūya, 'the Father' did not report any encounters with the hidden imam, at first glance, a curious lacuna in a work meant 'to dissipate confusion or perplexed reactions' (*al-tabṣira min al-ḥayra*) of believers succumbing to uncertainty as to the existence or identity of the twelfth imam after his disappearance.[18] The relative importance of these accounts of contacts (meetings or messages) with the hidden imam, the paucity of information and the meagre typological variety of enounters in our author's work, may be explained precisely by factors that characterise this period as one of *ḥayra.*

An examination of the sources that have come down to us from this period reflect the hesitation, uncertainties and lacunae in a number of doctrinal elements that later became articles of faith; first, regarding the definitive number of imams and the very

16. Ibid., vol. 2, pp. 449–468.

17. ʿAlī b. al-Ḥusayn b. Bābūya, *al-Imāma wa'l-tabṣira min al-ḥayra* (Qumm, 1404/1985), ch. 38, pp. 140–142.

18. On this period, see Sachedina, *Islamic Messianism* (note 2 above), under '*ḥayra*' and especially the work by H. Modarressi indicated here below, note 31; according to tradition, Ibn Bābūya 'the Father' was a friend of al-Ḥusayn b. Rawḥ al-Nawbakhtī, the third 'representative' of the hidden imam during the minor Occultation (see below); he had two sons, including the renowned Ibn Bābūya al-Ṣadūq, after submitting a written request to the hidden imam for intercession before God; the father received a signed letter from the imam announcing the imminent birth of his children; see e.g. al-Najāshī, *al-Rijāl* (Tehran, n.d.), pp. 198–199; al-Ṭūsī, *Kitāb al-ghayba* (Najaf, 1385/1965), pp. 187f.; Quṭb al Dīn al-Rāwandī, *al-Kharā'ij wa'l-jarā'iḥ* (Tehran, 1389/1969), vol. 1, p. 189; al-ʿAllāma al-Ḥillī, *Khulāṣat al-aqwāl (= Rijāl al-ʿAllāma)* (Najaf, 1961), p. 94.

notion of *ghayba*. Abū Jaʿfar al-Barqī (274/887 or 280/893) does not provide any information in his *Kitāb al-maḥāsin* regarding these subjects. In the first chapter, entitled 'al-Ashkāl wa'l-qarā'in', the author reports traditions concerning the significance of numbers; these consider the numbers three to ten and say nothing about the number twelve.[19]

In *Baṣā'ir al-darajāt*, his contemporary al-Ṣaffār al-Qummī (290/902–903) cites only five traditons (from a total of 1,881) regarding the fact that the imams are twelve in number but says absolutely nothing about the Occultation.[20] It is only from al-Kulaynī onwards that traditions regarding the definitive number of imams and the Occultation of the last of them increase. But even in this case, an examination of the chains of transmission (*isnād*) of these traditions, both in al-Kulaynī as well as in monographs by two of his famous successors, *Kitāb al-ghayba* by al-Nuʿmānī (about 345/956 or 360/971),[21] and *Kamāl al-dīn* by Ibn Bābūya al-Ṣadūq (381/991)[22] show that information from older books on the *ghayba*, written mainly by authors belonging to other Shiʿi movements, was appropriated for the needs of

19. Abū Jaʿfar al-Barqī, *Kitāb al-maḥāsin*, ed. J. Muḥaddith Urmawī (Tehran, 1370/1950), vol. 1, pp. 3–13.

20. Al-Ṣaffār al-Qummī, *Baṣā'ir al-darajāt*, ed. Mīrzā Kūchebāghī (2nd edn, Tabriz, n.d. [editor's introduction is dated 1380/1960]); regarding this author and his book, see M. A. Amir-Moezzi, 'Al-Ṣaffâr al-Qummî (d. 290/902–903) et son *Kitâb baṣâ'ir al-darajât*', *JA*, 280/3–4 (1992), pp. 221–250. On the problems relating to the number of imams and the Occultation in al-Barqī and al-Ṣaffār, see E. Kohlberg, 'From Imāmiyya to Ithnāʿashariyya', *BSOAS*, 39 (1976) (rpr. in *Belief and Law*, article XIV), pp. 521–534, esp. pp. 522–523; Amir-Moezzi, *Guide divin*, pp. 249–252 (*Divine Guide*, pp. 101–103) and, 'Al-Ṣaffâr al-Qummî', pp. 240–242. On al-Barqī, al-Ṣaffār, al-Kulaynī and their compilations, now consult A. J. Newman, *The Formative Period of Twelver Shīʿism: Ḥadīth as Discourse Between Qum and Baghdad* (Richmond, VA, 2000).

21. Ibn Abī Zaynab al-Nuʿmānī, *Kitāb al-ghayba*, ed. ʿA. A. Ghaffārī (Tehran, 1397/1977); Arabic text and Persian trans. by M. J. Ghaffārī (Tehran, 1363 Sh./1985).

22. Ibn Bābūya al-Ṣadūq, *Kamāl al-dīn wa tamām al-niʿma*, ed. ʿA. A. Ghaffārī (Qumm, 1405/1985).

the Twelver cause.[23] For example, in the transmission chains of our authors we encounter the following names: Ibrāhīm b. Ṣāliḥ al-Anmāṭī, the author of *Kitāb al-ghayba* and a supporter of the fifth imam al-Bāqir, who believed he would be the hidden Qā'im.[24] The *wāqifī*s of the seventh imam, Mūsā al-Kāẓim, such as ʿAlī b. al-Ḥasan al-Ṭaṭārī al-Ṭā'ī and al-Ḥasan b. Muḥammad b. Sumāʿa, were both authors of a *Kitāb al-ghayba*.[25] Another Sevener author (a *wāqifī* of Mūsā? An Ismaili?), Muḥammad b. al-Muthannā al-Ḥaḍramī (third/ninth century) produced a *kitāb* which is part of '400 original collections' (*al-uṣūl al-arabaʿumi'a*) of the Imamis in which he reports a tradition by Jaʿfar stating there will be seven imams, the last being the Mahdī.[26] Probably a *wāqifī* of the eighth imam al-Riḍā as was his father, al-Ḥasan b. ʿAlī al-Baṭā'inī al-Kūfī, was the author of a work also bearing the title *Kitāb al-ghayba*.[27] Abū Saʿīd al-ʿUṣfurī (250/864), was a contemporary of the tenth and eleventh imams, and author of another *kitāb*, part of the '400 original collections', in which he speaks of eleven imams that he avoids naming, the last being the Qā'im.[28] Even the collection

23. See *Guide divin*, pp. 249–253 (*Divine Guide*, pp. 101–104); on earlier books on the *ghayba*, see Hussain, *Occultation of the Twelfth Imam* (refer to note 2 above), Introduction, section 2.1.1 and 2.1.2., pp. 2–6.

24. Al-Najāshī, *Rijāl*, pp. 12 and 19; al-Ṭūsī, *Fihrist kutub al-shīʿa*, ed. Sprenger and ʿAbd al-Ḥaqq (rpr. Mashhad, 1972), p. 14; Ibn Dāwūd al-Ḥillī, *Kitāb al-rijāl* (Tehran, 1964), pp. 15 and 416.

25. Al-Najāshī, *Rijāl*, pp. 193 and 39 respectively; on the first see also al-Ṭūsī, *Fihrist kutub al-shīʿa*, pp. 216–217.

26. 'Kitāb Muḥammad b. al-Muthannā', *al-Uṣūl al-arabaʿumi'a*, Tehran University, MS 962, fol. 53b. On the '400 original collections' see E. Kohlberg, *'al-Uṣūl al-arabʿumi'a'*, *Jerusalem Studies in Arabic and Islam*, 10 (1987) (rpr. in *Belief and Law*, article VII), pp. 128–166.

27. Āghā Bozorg al-Ṭihrānī, *al-Dharīʿa ilā taṣānīf al-shīʿa*, 25 vols (Tehran and Najaf, 1353–1398/1934–1978), vol. 16, p. 76, no. 382; on al-Baṭā'inī 'the Father', see also al-Kashshī, *Rijāl* (Bombay, 1317/1899), pp. 288–289.

28. *Al-Uṣūl al-arabaʿumi'a*, fols 10af.; *Kitāb Abī Saʿīd al-ʿUṣfurī* (Tehran, 1371/1951), p. 34.

by the Twelver, al-Ṣaffār, already cited, contains two traditions that seem to indicate that the imams will be seven in number.[29]

We also encounter signs of hesitation and a groping for answers regarding the forms of the Occultation including the notion of two Occultations, the second being much longer. For discussions about the Occultation, let us cite the case of Abū Sahl al-Nawbakhtī (311/923), a very influential man to whom two conceptions have been attributed. According to the first, of a spiritual nature, the hidden imam is 'existant in the world in substance and subsistant in essence' (*mawjūd al-ʿayn fi'l-ʿālam wa thābit al-dhāt*).[30] According to the second, the twelfth imam passed away but left a son who was living in secret and who had succeeded him; the line of the imams would thus be perpetuated during the Occultation, passing from father to son until the last manifests himself publicly as the Qā'im.[31] We know that

29. Al-Ṣaffār, *Baṣā'ir al-darajāt*, section, ch. 12, 3, p. 146, no. 24 and ch. 13, p. 150, no. 17 in which in a tradition dating back to Jaʿfar al-Ṣādiq, the angel Gabriel brought the Prophet a sheet of paper (*ṣaḥīfa*) bearing seven sealed messages meant to be opened successively by each imam upon his investiture; cf. also my article 'Notes sur deux traditions 'hétérodoxes' imamites', *Arabica*, 41 (1994), p. 132, note 21. The first truly reliable text to have come down to us in which the complete list of the twelve imams is given appears to be the *Tafsīr* by ʿAlī b. Ibrāhīm al-Qummī (d. ca. 307/919), ed. al-Mūsawī al-Jazā'irī (Najaf, 1386–1387/1966–1968), vol. 2, p. 44, text written a few years after the beginning of the minor Occultation.

30. Cited by Ibn Bābūya, *Kamāl al-dīn*, vol. 1, p. 90 based on *Kitāb al-tanbīh fi'l-imāma* by Abū Sahl al-Nawbakhtī, a work that has apparently been lost.

31. Cited by Ibn al-Nadīm, *al-Fihrist*, ed. R. Tajaddod (Tehran, 1971), p. 225. Here we recognise the earliest attempts to rationalise the Occultation. During the same period, Abū Jaʿfar Ibn Qiba (d. before 319/931) writes treatises on the Occultation that tend to reach the same conclusions (cf. his first two treatises, namely *Mas'ala fi'l-imāma* and *al-Naqḍ ʿalā Abi'l-Ḥasan ʿAlī b. Aḥmad b. Bashshār fi'l-ghayba* edited based on the recension by Ibn Bābūya in his *Kamāl al-dīn*, by H. Modarressi, *Crisis and Consolidation in the Formative Period of Shīʿite Islam: Abū Jaʿfar ibn Qiba al-Rāzī and his Contribution to Imamite Shīʿite Thought* [Princeton, 1993]). The greatest theoreticians who rationalised the *ghayba* were Shaykh al-Mufīd (d. 413/1022) and his two disciples al-Sharīf al-Murtaḍā (436/1044) and Abū Jaʿfar al-Ṭūsī (460/1067) who explicitly had

neither of these ideas was accepted. As for the notion of 'double occultations', this too existed in different forms in various Shiʿi movements, at the very least expressed by the *wāqifī*s of the seventh imam onwards.[32] Among the Twelvers, in the already cited *Kitāb al-ghayba* by al-Nuʿmānī, written in the mid-fourth/tenth century, clearly after the proclamation of the major Occultation, a tradition has imam Jaʿfar saying that of these two occultations, the first will be the longer.[33] At such a late date, this is surely a sign of hesitation. As a corollary to the preceding concept, belief in the 'delegation' (*niyāba/sifāra/wikāla*) to four official representatives of the hidden imam during the minor Occultation seems to have coalesced long after the proclamation of the major Occultation, most likely in the second half of the fourth/tenth century. As we have seen, al-Barqī and al-Ṣaffār do not even deal with the subject of occultation. Two other writers from the end of the third/ninth

---

recourse to a rational demonstration (*dalīl ʿaqlī*) notably based on the old Muʿtazilī principles of God's Justice and man's responsibility. As the latter is fallible and in need of guidance, divine Grace (*luṭf*) must necessarily and forever accord humanity the fortune of true direction that can only be provided by an infallible imam (see Sachedina, *Islamic Messianism*, pp. 108ff.; on works by early rationalist writers relating to the Occultation, see *Guide divin*, p. 248, n. 536 [*Divine Guide*, p. 101]).

32. Indeed some *wāqifī*s of the seventh imam believed that, after his death, the master was revived and entered into occultation before manifesting as the Qā'im, then dying definitively, after having accomplished his true mission; this then is a double death (see al-Ḥasan b. Mūsā Abū Muḥammad al-Nawbakhtī, *Firaq al-Shīʿa*, ed. H. Ritter [Istanbul, 1931], p. 68; Saʿd b. ʿAbdallāh al-Ashʿarī al-Qummī, *al-Maqālāt wa'l-firaq*, ed. M. J. Mashkūr [Tehran, 1963], p. 90). The *wāqifī*s of the eleventh imam included those who professed that he would enter upon two occultations, between which he would be manifested to his believers (cf. al-Nawbakhtī, *Firaq*, pp. 79–80; al-Qummī, *al-Maqālāt*, pp. 106–108). Faḍl b. al-Ḥasan al-Ṭabrisī (d. 548/1154), citing *Kitāb al-mashyakha* by al-Ḥasan b. Maḥbūb al-Sarrād (d. 224/838) (see Āghā Bozorg al-Ṭihrānī, *al-Dharīʿa*, vol. 21, p. 69, no. 3995), reports a tradition dating back to imam al-Bāqir in which it is said that the Mahdī will enter into two occultations, one of which will be short and another long (al-Ṭabrisī, *Iʿlām al-warā fī aʿlām al-hudā*, ed. al-Kharsān, Najaf, 1390/1970, p. 443).

33. Al-Nuʿmānī, *Kitāb al-ghayba*, ch. 10, p. 170, no. 1 (Arabic text only); p. 249, no. 1 (text with Persian translation) (refer to note 21 above).

century, namely Abū Muḥammad al-Nawbakhtī in his *Firaq*[34] and Saʿd b. ʿAbdallāh al-Ashʿarī in his *Maqālāt*,[35] make no mention of any 'representative'. The same is true for al-Nuʿmānī, an author of the first half of the fourth/tenth century. During this period, al-Kulaynī and al-Kashshī (ca. 340/950) in his *Rijāl*[36] provide names of a number of 'representatives' but never speak of an instance that is well and truly institutionalised.[37]

In a thoroughly substantiated study, Verena Klemm demonstrates convincingly that al-Ḥusayn b. Rawḥ al-Nawbakhtī (326/938), the 'third' *nāʾib*, appears to have been the first to claim to be the only representative of the imam and consequently the supreme leader of the community. According to Klemm, the dogma of the representation of the hidden imam by a single 'delegate' seems to have been constructed and spread by the influential Nawbakhtī family in Baghdad; two other claimants, Ibn Rawḥ, the two ʿAmrī/ʿUmarī were no doubt posthumously elevated to the rank of 'representative' to prove the continuity of this institution since the Occultation.[38] This conception of the *niyāba* was far

34. Cf. note 32 above; for a French translation of this work by al-Nawbakhtī, see M. J. Mashkour (i.e. Mashkūr), *Les sectes shiites* (2nd edn, Tehran, 1980).

35. Note 32 above; Persian translation, based on the edition by Mashkūr, prepared by Y. Faḍāʾī, *Tārīkh-e ʿaqāʾed va madhāheb-e shīʿe* (Tehran, 1371 Sh./1993).

36. Cf. note 27 above.

37. The names of the 'official' representatives are the two ʿAmrī/ʿUmarī, Abū ʿAmr and Abū Jaʿfar, al-Ḥusayn b. Rawḥ al-Nawbakhtī and Abu'l-Ḥasan al-Simmarī - and not as conventionally given, al-Samarrī; on this reading/vocalisation for the name of the 'fourth' representative, see H. Halm, *Die Schia* (Darmstadt, 1988), see index, in which the German scholar refers to *Ansāb* by al-Samʿānī and *Lubb al-lubāb* by al-Suyūṭī and aptly notes that the adjective formed from the city of Sāmarrā is 'Sāmarrāʾī' and not 'Samarrī'. Also presented as *nāʾib* of the hidden imam are for example, Ibrāhīm b. Mahziyār, al-Marzubānī al-Ḥārithī, Ḥājiz b. Yazīd etc. (al-Kulaynī, *al-Uṣūl min al-Kāfī*, vol. 2, pp. 449f.; al-Kashshī, *Rijāl*, under these names). On the four 'representatives' in general, see Hussain, *Occultation of the Twelfth Imam*, chs 4–7.

38. V. Klemm, 'Die vier *sufarāʾ* des Zwölften Imams. Zur formativen Periode der Zwölferschia', *Die Welt des Orients*, 15 (1984), pp. 126–143; this work brilliantly revives previous studies on the subject, in particular those by Javad

from being accepted without hesitation and resistance; it was not until half a century later, with the appearance of *Kamāl al-dīn* by al-Ṣadūq, that the idea first took shape in its definitive canonical form.[39]

All this tends to show that during this period the Imami community experienced what may be considered a serious identity crisis. This was the age of 'perplexity' (*ḥayra*) and of groping for certainties, of research and development, and the relatively painful establishment of a doctrine relating to the twelfth imam. These doctrines had to confront and overcome a great deal of resistance before they were established as articles of faith. The transition from Imamism to Twelverism most certainly did not take place without difficulty.[40]

In the introduction of his *Kitāb al-ghayba*, al-Nuʿmānī complains that a large majority of his coreligionists are still not aware of the hidden imam's identity and even go so far as to contest his existence.[41] Al-Shaykh al-Ṣadūq makes similar observations when he states that he was overwhelmed by questions on the identity of the hidden imam by the Shiʿis of Khurāsān, which spurred him to write his *Kamāl al-dīn*.[42] During this period of confusion, a time

---

Ali, 'Die beiden ersten Safire des Zwölften Imams', *Der Islam*, 25 (1939) and Hussain as indicated in the note above. On the great and influential Nawbakhtī family, see the now classic monograph by 'A. Eqbāl, *Khāndān-e Nawbakhtī* (2nd edn, Tehran, 1966). See also W. M. Watt, 'Sidelights on Early Imāmite Doctrine', *SI*, 31 (1970), pp. 287–298.

39. Ibn Bābūya, *Kamāl al-dīn*, vol. 2, ch. 42, p. 432, no. 12; but elsewhere the author presents another list of 'representatives' of the hidden imam according to cities (cf. ibid., vol. 2, ch. 43, p. 442, no. 16).

40. See in particular, E. Kohlberg, 'From Imāmiyya to Ithnāʿashariyya' (refer to note 20 above) and now, 'Early attestations of the term *ithnāʿashariyya*', *JSAI*, 24 (2000); see also *Guide divin*, section IV.1, pp. 245–264 (*Divine Guide*, pp. 99–108).

41. Al-Nuʿmānī, *Kitāb al-ghayba*, pp. 18–32 (Arabic text only), pp. 26–53 (text with Persian translation).

42. Ibn Bābūya, *Kamāl al-dīn*, vol. 1, pp. 2f.; in the introduction to his work, his father complains about the same kind of confusion, see *al-Imāma wa'l-tabṣira min al-ḥayra*, pp. 9f.

when schisms multiplied,[43] when opposing movements, benefiting from this state of affairs, redoubled their propaganda and, as a result, the Twelver movement saw many of its followers (including some of the most prominent figures) deserting,[44] the foremost concern of Twelver thinkers was to demonstrate the actual existence of the eleventh imam's son and at the same time to prove his imamate.

This no doubt accounts for the meagre typoglogical variety in reports of encounters with the hidden imam in the work of so prominent a scholar as al-Kulaynī. It is most important to state that some individuals had actually seen the imam, that he being regularly invested possessed initiatory knowledge (*ʿilm*), namely sacred knowledge and supra-natural powers, and that he is most

---

43. Based on what emerges from writings on the *firaq*, the majority of Shiʿis had very little knowledge of the twelfth imam. After the death of the eleventh imam, between eleven and fifteen schisms occurred among his supporters. One can nevertheless group these sects into four main categories: 1) those that supported the cessation of the imamate; not believing in the existence of a *mahdī*, one group maintained that al-Ḥasan al-ʿAskarī died without leaving an heir. Another group also believed that the eleventh imam died without leaving a child but simultaneously held that at the End of Time one of the imams would be raised in this world and accomplish the mission of the awaited Saviour. 2) the Jaʿfariyya: supporters of the imamate of Jaʿfar, brother of the eleventh imam, whom the Twelvers were later to call 'Jaʿfar the liar'. For the Jaʿfariyya sect, the eleventh imam died without a son and so the imamate fell to his brother. 3) the Muḥammadiyya: supporters of another brother of the eleventh imam, Muḥammad b. ʿAlī; an elder brother, he predeceased his father but his supporters believed in his occultation and claimed he would return as *mahdī*. 4) the *wāqifī*s of al-ʿAskarī for whom he was the Saviour who had not left behind a son. cf. al-Nawbakhtī, *Firaq al-Shīʿa*, pp. 90f.; al-Ashʿarī al-Qummī, *al-Maqālāt wa'l-firaq*, pp. 102f.; al-Masʿūdī, *Murūj al-dhahab*, ed. and Fr.trans. by Barbier de Meynard (Paris, 1861–1877), vol. 8, pp. 50f.; al-Shahrastānī, *Livre des religions et des sectes*, vol. 1, Fr. trans. by D. Gimaret and G. Monnot (Louvain and Paris, 1986), pp. 500f.; for more details on these schisms, see Sachedina, *Islamic Messianism*, pp. 42f.; Hussain, *Occultation of the Twelfth Imam*, pp. 56f.; E. Kohlberg, 'Muḥammadiyya' and 'Radjʿa', *EI2*.

44. As an example of those that deserted, there is Ibn Ḥawshab who converted to Ismailism; see H. Halm, 'Die *Sīrat Ibn Ḥaushab*. Die ismailitische *daʿwa* im Jemen und die Fatimiden', *Die Welt des Orients*, 12 (1981).

generous to his faithful followers.[45] The complexity and portrayal of the accounts, as well as the variety in the nature of encounters – so many essential elements in the rich typological diversity – hardly concerned authors of this period. Even much later, in the second half of the fourth/tenth century, apart from al-Ṣadūq (to whom I shall return later in this chapter), the identity and cohesion of the community around the figure of the twelfth imam, the hidden resurrector-imam, remain the main concerns of these authors.

Ibn Qūlūya (369/979) in his *Kāmil al-ziyārāt*,[46] al-Khazzāz al-Rāzī (second half of fourth/tenth century) in his *Kifāyat al-athar*[47] and Ibn ʿAyyāsh al-Jawharī (401/1011) in *Muqtaḍab al-athar*[48] especially seek to demonstrate that the imams are twelve in number and that the last among them, the son of al-ʿAskarī, is well and truly the hidden Qāʾim. Reports of encounters with the hidden imam in these authors, just as in al-Kulaynī, are very rare and incidental in nature. One may say that in these instances the accounts have a doctrinal dimension that serves to consolidate the identity of the community; moreover, this is also the case with reports of encounters before the Occultation.[49] One should add,

45. On *ʿilm* as a 'Secret Initiatory Science' see E. Kohlberg, 'Imam and Community in the Pre-Ghayba Period', in S. A. Arjomand (ed.), *Authority and Political Culture in Shiʿism* (Albany, NY, 1988) (rpr. in *Belief and Law*, article XIII), pp. 25–27 and esp. Amir-Moezzi, *Guide divin*, section III.2, pp. 174–199 (*Divine Guide*, pp. 69–79) and 'Réflexions sur une évolution' (note 3 above), pp. 63–69.

46. Jaʿfar b. Muḥammad Ibn Qūlūya al-Qummī, *Kāmil al-ziyārāt*, ed. Najaf (lithograph, Iran, n.d.), ed. Najaf (1937–1938); most recent ed. B. Jaʿfarī (Tehran, 1375 Sh./1996).

47. ʿAlī b. Muḥammad al-Khazzāz al-Rāzī, *Kifāyat al-athar fiʾl-naṣṣ ʿalāʾl-aʾimmat al-ithnayʿashar*, ed. al-Ḥusaynī al-Kūhkamarī (Qumm, 1401/1981).

48. Aḥmad b. ʿUbayd Allāh Ibn ʿAyyāsh al-Jawharī, *Muqtaḍab al-athar fiʾl-naṣṣ ʿalā ʿadad al-aʾimmat al-ithnayʿashar*, ed. H. Rasūlī Maḥallātī (Qumm, 1379/1959).

49. These are especially intimate accounts by believers who were privileged to see the twelfth imam in his youth, at his father's house, before his Occultation. In *Guide divin* (pp. 269–270) (*Divine Guide*, pp. 110–111) I have translated a typical account of this kind given by Aḥmad b. Isḥāq al-Ashʿarī, a disciple of the ninth, tenth and eleventh imams and one of the influential leaders of the traditionalists in Qumm during the third/ninth century.

however, that, as we shall see, they nevertheless contain the seeds for various types of accounts developed in later narratives, occasionally of great consequence.

Encounters during the major Occultation

With his *Kamāl al-dīn wa tamām al-niʿma*, Ibn Bābūya al-Shaykh al-Ṣadūq (381/991–992) may be considered the main architect of the rendering canonical of material pertaining to the hidden imam, his Occultation and eschatological Return; material that we now recognise as articles of the Imami faith. The vast number of traditions and sayings reported, the judicious use of prior sources, the rigour and structure of the work, explain why *Kamāl al-dīn* is a critical factor in the definitive formulation of Twelver belief in this area. In a chapter devoted to reports of encounters with the hidden imam, Ibn Bābūya obviously reports the witness accounts found in al-Kulaynī, but also many other narratives, some of which are set during the major Occultation.[50] Henceforth a question is raised and a fair number of Twelver thinkers are obliged to propose answers: how to believe in the authenticity of encounters during the major Occultation while in the last letter to his final representative, the imam declares the impossibility of any such encounter until the End of Time? Here, according to the tradition, is the text of this signed letter received by al-Simmarī in 329/941:

> In the Name of God, the Compassionate, the Merciful. O ʿAlī b. Muḥammad al-Simmarī, thanks to you, may God increase the reward of your brothers in religion [i.e. the Imamis]; yes, your death is due in six days. Prepare yourself and do not designate anyone to succeed you [as *nāʾib*] after your death. The advent of the second Occultation [variant: 'the complete Occultation'] is upon

50. Ibn Bābūya, *Kamāl al-dīn*, ch. 43, pp. 434–479; these accounts reported by Ibn Bābūya were methodically taken up by later authors, beginning with al-Mufīd in his *Irshād*, Arabic text and Persian trans. H. Rasūlī Maḥallātī, Tehran (1346 Sh./1968), ch. 38 and al-Ṭūsī in his *Kitāb al-ghayba* (Tabriz, 1322/1905), pp. 148f.

> us. During this time there will no longer be a manifestation, unless permitted by God, and this shall only take place after a long period when hearts have been hardened and the earth filled with violence. Some of my supporters will claim to have seen me with their own eyes. Beware! He who claims to have seen me with his own eyes before the uprising of al-Sufyānī and [the sounding] of the Cry [two of the warning signals for the End of Time and Return of the Qāʾim], such a person is a liar and imposter. Grandeur and Might are due to God, the Most High, alone.[51]

Here again, Ibn Bābūya appears to be the first to have reproduced this letter. However, he supplied reports of encounters during the major Occultation, and his example was followed by many later authors. From the inception of the major Occultation, ocular vision of the hidden imam, as referred to in the letter, seems to have been compromised not in a general sense, but as a condition for being a representative of the imam. What is declared impossible during the major Occultation, and therefore until the End of Time, is not an encounter with the hidden imam per se, but the claim to *niyāba* (representation) of the imam on the basis that he had encountered him. The follower may be granted the privilege of seeing the imam with their own eyes. However, if because of this, he subsequently declares himself 'representative' of the imam, he can only be considered – according to contents of the letter – a liar and an imposter.[52]

---

51. For the text of this letter see e.g. Ibn Bābūya, *Kamāl al-dīn*, ch. 45, vol. 2, p. 516, no. 44; al-Ṭūsī, *Kitāb al-ghayba*, p. 257; al-Majlisī, *Biḥār al-anwār*, vol. 52, ch. 23, p. 151, no. 1; For translations see e.g. H. Corbin, 'L'Imam caché et la rénovation de l'homme', p. 84, and 'Au pays de l'Imam caché', p. 45 and *En Islam iranien*, vol. 4, p. 324; V. Klemm, 'Die vier *sufarā*', p. 135; J. Eliash, 'Misconceptions Regarding the Juridical Status of the Iranian 'Ulamā', *IJMES*, 10 (1979), pp. 23–24; Sachedina, *Islamic Messianism*, p. 96; Hussain, *Occultation of the Twelfth Imam*, pp. 134–135; M. Momen, *An Introduction to Shiʿi Islam: The History and Doctrine of Twelver Shiʿism* (New Haven and London, 1985), p. 164; *Guide divin*, p. 276 (*Divine Guide*, pp. 113–114).

52. Cf. e.g. al-Sharīf al-Murtaḍā (436/1044), *Tanzīh al-anbiyāʾ* (Qumm, n.d.), pp. 233f.; al-Ṭūsī (460/1068), *Kitāb al-ghayba*, pp. 6–7 and 66–67; Raḍī al-Dīn Ibn Ṭāwūs (664/1266), *Kashf al-maḥajja* (n.p. [Iran], 1350/1931), pp. 34,

From Ibn Bābūya onwards, the accounts progressively increase and become more varied. As a general rule, each author reworks prior sources, adds some new testimonials collected by himself or his contemporaries, and on some rare occasions, also includes his own visionary experience of the hidden imam. As the religious identity of the community becomes more securely constructed, other dimensions are superimposed, which, as we have seen, aim to prove the existence of the hidden twelfth imam and thus the veracity of Twelverism. Before examining what distinguishes these different kinds of accounts, it will be useful to describe their common characteristics and in so doing reconsider the opinions held by Corbin cited at the beginning of this chapter.

The encounter always depends on the will of the imam and never the believer. Faith in and love for the imams and their

---

48 and 73–75 (several times and especially in the letter to his son Muḥammad, Ibn Ṭāwūs alludes to his meeting the hidden imam); regarding this author, now consult the brilliant study by E. Kohlberg, *A Medieval Muslim Scholar at Work: Ibn Ṭāwūs and his Library* (Leiden, 1992); al-Majlisī (1111/1699), *Biḥār al-anwār*, vol. 52, p. 151 (where, after reproducing a signed letter from the twelfth imam, the author takes up the position of his predecessors in a pithy statement: 'This letter undoubtedly concerns someone who claims to have met [the imam], declares himself his representative and allows himself [the right] to bring information to the Shi'is [supposed to emanate] from the imam, as was the case with the [four] representatives. If not [this letter] would be in contradiction with what is written here and what shall be written in future about those who have seen the imam [during the major Occultation])'; al-Ṭabrisī al-Nūrī (1320/1902), *al-Najm al-thāqib* (cf. note 8 above), ch. 8, pp. 559–568 and *Jannat al-ma'wā*, pp. 318–325 (the author reports in six points the various arguments of previous scholars as well as his own to prove not only the possibility but also the necessity of vision of the hidden imam during the major Occultation; according to him, there is always a secret group of thirty individuals in direct contact with the hidden imam). However, the issue appears to have remained delicate since in recent times a person as influential as al-'Allāma Sayyid Muḥammad Mahdī Baḥr al-'Ulūm (d. 1355/1937; regarding him see e.g. M. 'A. Mudarris, *Rayḥānat al-adab,* 8 vols [Tabriz, n.d.], vol. 1, pp. 234–235) has remained very discreet about his encounters with the hidden imam, vehemently arguing that based on the last letter of the imam, he who claims to have seen the Qā'im during the major Occultation is a liar (see his moving testimonial in al-Ṭabrisī al-Nūrī, *Jannat al-ma'wā*, p. 236 and *al-Najm al-thāqib*, p. 474).

cause, moral rectitude and the sincerity of the individual follower's needs are often presented as the conditions required. But they do not suffice. Appearance of the vision ultimately depends on the imam himself; in turn his decision is obviously based on divine Will. Certain locations seem especially favourable for an encounter: Mecca, beside the sepulchres of the imams, the Cave (*sardāb*) of Sāmarrā, the Sahla mosque in Najaf, the mosque in Jamkarān, renowned for being a sanctuary for the hidden imam, in proximity to Qumm. However, in principle the Qāʾim is able to become manifest anywhere. The encounter is always marked, more or less emphatically, by the wondrous. As we shall see, some elements regularly intervene in the course of accounts to indicate a break from ordinary reality: the miraculous appearance and disappearance of the imam, unexpected locations (a palace, an oasis, an island, a city) unknown to geography and towards which the chosen traveller is mysteriously led to meet the imam; confinement of space which often implies the contraction of time; the unfurling of secret knowledge and deployment of the imam's supernatural powers of all kinds, for example. All this makes the witness aware, often after the fact, that he was indeed in the presence of the hidden Saviour. Some elements of symbolic significance recur frequently and also indicate a change in the level of reality: a desert, the night, sleep or a state between sleep and wakefulness (symbolising 'moments' in which the senses are almost free from what they usually perceive), the changing or removal of clothing or sandals (symbolising shifts in the level of consciousness and consequently of reality), the symbolism of light in different forms (indicating the intrusion of the imam's reality into sensory reality).[53]

---

53. On the imam as 'light', see U. Rubin, 'Pre-existence and Light. Aspects of the Concept of Nūr Muḥammad', *IOS*, 5 (1975) and 'Prophets and Progenitors in the Early Shīʿa Tradition', *JSAI*, 5 (1984); *Guide divin*, sections II-1 and II-2, pp. 75–112 (*Divine Guide*, pp. 29–43); on the hidden imam in particular as 'light', see M. A. Amir-Moezzi, 'Eschatology: in Twelver Shiʿism: Individual eschatology', *EIr*.

The repeated presence of such elements seems to corroborate Corbin's idea that the 'place' and 'time' of the hidden imam are in this 'inter-world' that he designates by the brilliant expression, the 'imaginal world' – often rendered in latin as *mundus imaginalis*.[54] Let us limit ourselves to a few brief excerpts:

> By saying that these visions, these epiphanies are the hagiography, *the history* of the 12th Imam, one is led to believe that this history, accomplished in a parallel world, is an anti-history vis à vis history in the ordinary sense of the word; it does not enter *into* this history, any more than the image is immanent in the mirror (...) The place where it occurs is a spiritual place; similarly its time is 'between time(s)'.[55]
>
> Everything occurs as if (. . .) the place which is not at all contained, identifiable with a place in the topography of the sensory world, suddenly and fleetingly bursts into our world (...) For it is a fact that its 'where', its *ubi* in relation to our 'where', our place and our *situs* in this world is an *ubique*.[56]
>
> Here the intervention of the *mundus imaginalis* is critical. To 'save the phenomenon' the phenomenologist will profess 'realism of the *imaginal*'. There is no hermeneutic of the Great Occultation, without the existence of this *world parallel to our own* (...). Failing to admit to this parallel world, one fears will be the ruin of every kind of explanation here.[57]

From a strictly philosophical perspective, we can agree with this interpretation. However, from a phenomenological point of view,

---

54. Practically all the major works by Henry Corbin contain more or less detailed information on this important contribution in his studies; see esp. 'Pour une charte de l'Imaginal', in H. Corbin, *Corps spirituel et Terre céleste. De l'Iran mazdéen à l'Iran shî'ite* (rpr., Paris, 1979), pp. 7–19; the best introduction to the concept remains D. Shayegan, *Henry Corbin. La topographie spirituelle de l'Islam iranien* (Paris, 1990), see index, and 'Corbin, Henry', *EIr*, vol. 6, pp. 268–272; for a critical perspective, see E. Meyer, 'Tendenz der Schiaforschung: Corbins Auffassung von der Schia', *ZDMG*, suppl. 3/1 (1977).

55. *En Islam iranien*, vol. 4, p. 337.

56. 'Au pays de l'Imam caché', pp. 76–77; *En Islam iranien*, vol. 4, p. 374.

57. *En Islam iranien*, vol. 4, p. 329.

as defined by Corbin himself[58] – that is, as regards a religious phenomenon as it appears to the believers – matters differ. To my knowledge, among Imami thinkers, only two masters of the Shaykhiyya theological-mystical school in Kerman, namely Muḥammad Karīm Khān Kirmānī (1288/1870)[59] and Abu'l-Qāsim Khān Ibrāhīmī (d. 1969)[60] have described the 'location' of the hidden imam as being the world of *hūrqalyā/huwarqalyā* that Corbin equates with the 'imaginal world'.[61]

All the others – and there are at the least hundreds of these – they maintain that for more than a thousand years, the hidden imam has been and is in this world with his physical body. The miraculous events that accompany his presence are simply due to his ontological reality, due to the fact that he is the imam, the veritable manifestation of the Names and Attributes of God.[62] This is why Ibn Bābūya devotes lengthy chapters of his *Kamāl al-dīn* to famously long-lived individuals, and here, too, his example was followed by many others seeking to prove that 'with divine permission' a human being is able to enjoy an exceptionally long life.[63] Al-Ṭabrisī al-Nūrī, the great expert with traditionalist and mystical tendencies, whose monographs are veritable encyclopedias

---

58. E.g. ibid., vol. 1, pp. xixff. and see index.

59. Muḥammad Karīm Khān Kermānī, *Irshād al-ʿawāmm* (Kerman, 1354/1935), vol. 2, p. 275.

60. Sarkār Āqā Abu'l-Qāsim Khān Ibrāhīmī, *Tanzīh al-awliyā'* (Kerman, 1367/1948), pp. 724–726.

61. Corbin, *Corps spirituel et Terre céleste*, pp. 262–264 and 287–290; even the Imami authors (Mullā Ṣadrā, ʿAbd al-Razzāq Lāhījī, Muḥsin Fayḍ Kāshānī, Shaykh Aḥmad Aḥsā'ī) translated in this work did not adhere to this notion of the 'country' of the hidden imam.

62. See Chapter 3, this volume.

63. Ibn Bābūya, *Kamāl al-dīn*, vol. 2, chs 46–54, pp. 523–638 (*mā jā'a fi'l-taʿmīr wa dhikr al-muʿammarīn*); also al-Ṭūsī, *Kitāb al-ghayba*, pp. 85–95 (*al-jawāb ʿani'l-iʿtirāḍ ʿalā ṭūl ʿumrihi wa ziyādatihi ʿani'l-ʿumr al-ṭabīʿī wa kawnihi khāriqan li'l-ʿāda wa dhikr al-muʿammarīn*) and Muḥammad b. ʿAlī al-Karājakī, *al-Burhān ʿalā ṣiḥḥat ṭūl ʿumr ṣāḥib al-zamān* in the margins of *Kanz al-fawā'id* by the same author (Tabriz, n.d.), pp. 24–26 (*fi'l-taʿmīr wa'l-muʿammarīn*).

of reports of encounters with the hidden imam,[64] denied the possibility of any spiritual interpretation (*ta'wīl*) applied to the 'location' of the hidden imam. Under these conditions, it is with a great deal of reservation that one is able to accept the unambiguous statement by Corbin according to which, 'admittedly, there was no lack of naïve souls for whom the imam had to exist as a man entirely similar to our contemporaries frequented by each one of us every day; there has even been serious discussion about certain "macrobites" envisaging the biological possibility of survival down the centuries'.[65]

Moreover, as we shall see and in contrast to Corbin's idea, some thinkers have had recourse to spiritual hermeneutics of the Occultation and the vision of the hidden imam without necessarily feeling the need for the existence of a *mundus imaginalis*. Let us return to our typology. In the profusion of accounts, some of which are models of narrative beauty and others of stupefying brevity, in keeping with the event they relate, one can distinguish three categories according to the principal dimension conveyed. Of course, in some accounts several dimensions are present at the same time.

1. The humanitarian dimension

The vast majority of accounts belong to this category in which the extreme generosity of the hidden imam to his believers, and his concern for their welfare is emphasised – whence the sacred expression defining the role of the imam during his Occultation 'to assist the afflicted and to grant the wishes of the needy' (*ighāthat al-malhūf wa ijābat al-muḍṭarr*). The hidden imam is presented in these accounts as a benevolent father, especially sensitive to the needs and suffering of those near and dear to him. One should note that these accounts are not always related by Imami followers; some depict individuals with other beliefs who convert to Imamism

64. Al-Ṭabrisī al-Nūrī, *al-Najm al-thāqib*, p. 410.

65. *En Islam iranien*, vol. 4, pp. 329–330.

after encountering the hidden imam and recognising the Saviour. Here are some typical examples:

Report of a man of the Banī Rāshid of Hamadān (fourth/tenth century). Abandoned by the caravan and lost in the desert not far from Mecca, the narrator comes to an enchanting landscape in the midst of which stands a paradisaical palace. There he encounters the Qā'im. While leaving the palace, he finds himself next to Hamadān, near Asadābādh. The palace has disappeared but the man still holds in his hand the purse presented to him by the Saviour.[66]

Report of an Imami follower lost in the desert (fourth/tenth century). Just as the narrator is on the point of dying of thirst, the hidden imam appears and makes him drink. The Qā'im then orders him to close his eyes. When he re-opens his eyes, the imam is no longer there and the narrator finds himself in the midst of his caravan.[67]

The report of Muḥammad b. Aḥmad b. Abi'l-Layth (sixth/twelfth century). Threatened by death, the narrator seeks refuge in a cemetery of the Qurashīs in Baghdad. He falls asleep there and in his dreams sees the hidden imam who teaches him a prayer which will bring him salvation.[68]

The report by Amīr Isḥāq al-Astarābādī (eleventh/seventeenth century). Another case of a man lost in the desert on the verge of dying: he encounters the imam who rescues him taking him away on horseback and then teaches him the true version of the prayer attributed to ʿAlī and known as '*al-ḥirz al-yamānī*'. When he has

66. Ibn Bābūya, *Kamāl al-dīn*, vol. 2, pp. 453–454; Persian version in ʿA. A. Burūjirdī, *Nūr al-anwār* (Tehran, 1347/1928), pp. 175–177; H. Corbin, 'Au pays de l'Imam caché', pp. 77–79 and *En Islam iranien*, vol. 4, pp. 374–376.

67. Sayyid Muḥammad al-Ḥusaynī, *Kifāyat al-muhtadī* (Tehran, 1320/1902), pp. 119–120, citing *K. al-ghayba* by al-Ḥasan b. Ḥamza al-ʿAlawī al-Ṭabarī (fourth/tenth century).

68. Al-Faḍl b. al-Ḥasan al-Ṭabrisī, *Kunūz al-najāḥ* (n.p. [Iran], 1318/1900), pp. 46–47.

finished reciting the prayer al-Astarābādī has arrived at his destination while the imam has disappeared.[69]

The report by Shams al-Dīn Muḥammad b. Qārūn (eleventh/seventeenth century). The story as told by the narrator concerns his friend Abū Rājiḥ, an elderly Imami who was atrociously tortured and mutilated by the governor of Ḥilla. The following night, Abū Rājiḥ begged for help from the Qā'im. Flooding the house with light, the latter appeared and with his hand caressed the elderly man's head. Not only were his wounds immediately healed, but henceforth and until his death, he had the appearance of a healthy young man.[70]

The report by al-Ḥurr al-ʿĀmilī (d. 1104/1693). The author, a child struck with an incurable illness, sees all the imams in his dreams and begs for their help. The twelfth imam proffers him a mysterious drink that cures him instantaneously.[71]

2. The initiatory dimension

Often set alongside the humanitarian dimension, many accounts contain an initiatory aspect. During the encounter, the imam teaches the believer one or more prayers (this is most often the case), provides him with a solution to a theological, legal or spiritual problem, reveals knowledge of a secret. What is emphasised here, is the figure of the imam as 'the initiated and initiating sage' (*ʿālim*).[72] These accounts illustrate a typically Shiʿi theme of love-loyalty-submission (*walāya*) to the imam leading to initiation. Let us cite a few typical accounts:

---

69. Al-Majlisī, *Biḥār al-anwār*, vol. 52, p. 170; al-Ṭabrisī al-Nūrī, *al-Najm al-thāqib*, p. 366.

70. Al-Nīlī, *al-Sulṭān al-mufarrij*, pp. 37–40; al-Majlisī, *Biḥār al-anwār*, vol. 52, pp. 162–163; al-Ṭabrisī al-Nūrī, *al-Najm al-thāqib*, pp. 418–420.

71. Al-Ḥurr al-ʿĀmilī, *Ithbāt al-hudāt bi'l-nuṣūṣ wa'l-muʿjizāt* (n.p. [Iran], 1341/1922), p. 81; see also the discussion and examples provided by E. Kohlberg, 'Authoritative Scriptures in Early Imāmī Shīʿism', pp. 308–309.

72. For this translation of *ʿālim*, refer to the references provided above in note 45.

The report by Ibrāhīm b. ʿAlī b. Mahziyār (fourth/tenth century). The narrator encounters the hidden imam in a tent pitched in the desert near Mecca. The imam speaks at length about ethical and spiritual matters.[73]

The report by Ibn Ṭāwūs (dating from 641/1243). In a highly allusive manner, the author refers to his companion's dream in which he finds the hidden imam deep in meditation; the latter reveals knowledge of a mystical nature that plunges the initiate into a state of ecstacy.[74]

The report by Muḥammad b. ʿAlī al-ʿAlawī al-Ḥusaynī (seventh/thirteenth century). His life threatened by the governor of Egypt, the narrator seeks refuge in Karbalāʾ. Near the tomb of al-Ḥusayn, for many successive nights in a state between sleep and wakefulness, he encounters the hidden imam; the latter teaches him a prayer and a specific ritual. A few days later, the narrator learns that the governor he feared has been assassinated.[75]

The report by Amīr (ou Mīr) ʿAllām (eleventh/seventeenth century). This concerns his famous master Muqaddas Ardabīlī who discovered the solutions to his theological and legal problems (*masāʾil ʿilmiyya*) by spending time in contemplation near the

---

73. Ibn Bābūya, *Kamāl al-dīn*, vol. 2, pp. 443–453.

74. Raḍī al-Dīn Ibn Ṭāwūs, *Risāla fiʾl-muḍāyaqa fī fawāt al-ṣalāt* (better known as *al-Muwāsaʿa waʾl-muḍāyaqa*) published in the margins of al-Astarābādī, *al-Fawāʾid al-madaniyya* (n.p. [Iran], 1321/1904), pp. 30–40, quotation pp. 36–37 (I have unfortunately not been able to consult the more recent, undoubtedly better, edition of this text by M. ʿA. al-Ṭabāṭabāʾī al-Marāghī in *Turāthunā* [1407/1986–1987], vol. 2, pp. 2–3, entitled *Risāla ʿadam muḍāyaqa al-fawāʾit* – an edition pointed out by Kohlberg, *A Medieval Muslim Scholar*, p. 409).

75. Ibn Ṭāwūs, *Muhaj al-daʿawāt* (n.p. [Iran], n.d.), pp. 182–184 (according to dating by Kohlberg, *A Medieval Muslim Scholar*, p. 231, n. 311, the source for Ibn Ṭāwūs dates from the fourth/tenth century, and the story dates back approximately to the beginning of the minor Occultation; in this case, the encounter would have occurred during or just before the first Occultation); al-Ṭabrisī al-Nūrī, *Jannat al-maʾwā*, pp. 227–229 (Persian version in his *al-Najm al-thāqib*, pp. 256–259); now quite famous, this prayer is known as 'The Prayer of al-ʿAlawī al-Miṣrī'.

tomb of ʿAlī b. Abī Ṭālib, eventually engaging in supernatural communication with the first imam. One 'particularly sombre' evening, the imam advises him to go to the mosque at Kūfa. There the scholar encounters the Qā'im who provides answers to all his questions.[76]

To these accounts one should add the numerous stories of encounters accompanied by the teaching of prayers. Among them the different versions of the famous 'Prayer of Deliverance' (*duʿā' al-faraj*),[77] or as translated by Corbin, accounts of truly initiatic journeys, for example that to the Jamkarān sanctuary;[78] the Green

76. Al-Ṭabrisī al-Nūrī, *al-Najm al-thāqib*, pp. 454–455, citing *al-Anwār al-nuʿmāniyya* by Niʿmatallāh al-Jazā'irī; A. Ḥ. Balāghī, *Maqālāt al-ḥunafā'* (Tehran, 1369/1949), pp. 137–138.

77. The oldest version of this prayer seems to be the one reported by Ibn Bābūya, *Kamāl al-dīn*, vol. 2, ch. 45, pp. 512–515, no. 43 (the very beginning is already reported by al-Kulaynī, *Uṣūl*, 'Kitāb al-ḥujja', 'Bāb fi'l-ghayba', vol. 2, pp. 135 and 144, nos 4 and 29); for other prayers taught by the hidden imam and other versions of the 'Prayer for Deliverance', see al-Ṭabrisī al-Nūrī, *Jannat al-ma'wā*, report nos 4 to 6, 33, 36, 40 and 55.

78. Al-Ṭabrisī al-Nūrī, *Jannat al-ma'wā*, pp. 230–234 (Persian version in *al-Najm al-thāqib*, pp. 294–300, and *Kalima ṭayyiba*, pp. 457–461 slightly different version). Al-Nūrī claims he cites from *Ta'rīkh Qumm* (written in 378/988) by al-Ḥasan b. Muḥammad al-Qummī who would have reported it from the work, now apparently lost, by Ibn Bābūya al-Ṣadūq entitled *Mu'nis al-ḥazīn fī maʿrifat al-ḥaqq wa'l-yaqīn*. The Arabic original of *Ta'rīkh Qumm*, also seems to have been lost; we possess an old partially preserved Persian translation by Ḥasan b. ʿAlī Qummī dated 805–806/1402–1403 (ed. S. J. Tehrānī, 3rd edn, 1361 Sh./1982). This latter text contains only five of the twenty sections from the original Arabic version; it provides some information on the pre-Islamic period of Jamkarān but the account regarding the establishment of the sanctuary is missing. Corbin provides a partial translation of this account (based on *Kalima ṭayyiba* by al-Nūrī) in 'Au pays de l'Imam caché', p. 79 (where it should read 'Ramaḍān 373' instead of '379') and especially in *En Islam iranien*, vol. 4, pp. 338–346. On Jamkarān, see also M. A. Amir-Moezzi, 'Jamkarân et Mâhân, deux pèlerinages insolites en Iran', in M. A. Amir-Moezzi (ed.), *Lieux d'islam. Cultes et cultures de l'Afrique à Java* (Paris, 1996; 2nd edn, 2005).

Island in the White Sea[79] and the five maritime cities where the sons of the hidden imam are to be found.[80]

3. The eschatological dimension

These are not strictly speaking narrative accounts but mystical in conception with an eschatological angle based on the spiritual hermeneutics of some accounts from the categories above. To my knowledge, the first to have introduced this concept was al-Sayyid Kāẓim al-Rashtī (1259/1843), the second master of the Shaykhiyya and successor to Shaykh Aḥmad al-Aḥsāʾī (1241/1826), namesake of the school. Having considered both the last letter of the twelfth

79. Nūrallāh Shūshtarī, *Majālis al-muʾminīn* (Tehran, 1365 Sh./1987), vol. 1, pp. 78–79 (to my knowledge, this book from the eleventh/seventeenth century is the earliest source that mentions this account); Hāshim b. Sulaymān al-Baḥrānī, *Tabṣirat al-walī fī man raʾaʾl-qāʾim al-mahdī* (Tehran, n.d.), pp. 243–251; al-Majlisī, *Biḥār al-anwār*, vol. 52, pp. 159–180; al-Ṭabrisī al-Nūrī, *Jannat al-maʾwā*, pp. 213–221 and *al-Najm al-thāqib*, pp. 387–415; partial trans. by Corbin in 'Au pays de l'Imam caché', pp. 48–68 and especially *En Islam iranien*, vol. 4, pp. 346–367. The authenticity of this account was doubted by the Imamis themselves, and this ever since al-Majlisī (*Biḥār al-anwār*, p. 159: 'I devote a separate chapter to this account because I have not been able to find it in any of the reliable sources'); for further discussion on this topic, see Sayyid Jaʿfar Murtaḍā ʿĀmilī, *Dirāsa fī ʿalāmāt al-ẓuhūr waʾl-jazīrat al-khaḍrāʾ* (Qumm, 1411/1990), pp. 226 f.; A. Ṭarīqeh-dār, *Jazīre-ye khaḍrāʾ* (Qumm, 1372 Sh./1994).

80. Al-Ṭabrisī al-Nūrī, *al-Najm al-thāqib*, pp. 300–309, citing *Kitāb al-taʿāzī* by al-ʿAlawī al-Ḥusaynī (sixth/twelfth century); al-Ḥāʾirī al-Yazdī, *Ilzām al-nāṣib fī ithbāt al-ḥujjat al-ghāʾib* (Tehran, 1351/1922), pp. 148–149; Persian version in ʿA. A. Burūjirdī, *Nūr al-anwār*, pp. 165–175; a partial trans. by Corbin, 'Au pays de l'Imam caché', pp. 68–76 and *En Islam iranien*, vol. 4, pp. 367–374. Like the previous account, this one is also considered inauthentic and is thus rejected by a number of Imami scholars (see the works by ʿĀmilī and Ṭarīqeh-dār indicated in the preceding note). Al-Nūrī defends the account all the while advancing arguments to prove the necessity for the existence of the hidden imam's sons (*al-Najm*, pp. 309–312). In my view, this reflects the Akhbārī/Uṣūlī (traditionalist/rationalist) conflict, the former opting for authenticity of these accounts, the latter rejecting them as forged (regarding this refer to important comments made by the scathing leader of the rationalists, al-Shaykh Jaʿfar 'Kāshif al-Ghiṭā'' [d. 1227/1812] in the margins of Niʿmatallāh al-Jazāʾirī, *al-Anwār al-nuʿmāniyya* [Tehran, n.d.], vol. 2, p. 64).

imam and the many reports of encounters with him, in the course of an elaborate argument Sayyid Kāẓim proposes the following syllogism: the hidden imam cannot be seen until the End of Time; some individuals have seen him, therefore these people have reached the End of Time.[81] The argument and especially the syllogism have been taken up almost word for word and translated into Persian by Mīrzā Abu'l-Qāsim Rāz Shīrāzī (1286/1869), the master of the Dhahabiyya order[82] and by Sayyid Aḥmad Dehkordī (1339/1920), the master of the Khāksāriyya order.[83] The conclusion of the syllogism is obviously understood as an initiatory death: vision of the Resurrector-imam signals the death of ego and the rebirth of the initiate. This is what may be called individual eschatology. The eminent scholar Sayyid Kāẓim is very familiar with hagiographical literature devoted to the twelfth imam and has recourse to a hermeneutical reading of encounters with the latter to support his idea. After citing several of these accounts as examples,[84] he writes:

> These accounts lend themselves to be a spiritual interpretation (*maḥmūl ʿalā'l-ta'wīl*); the parched, devasted, threatened and tortured men are symbols (*rumūz*) of the suffering that the perilous desert of spiritual quest (*tīh al-ṭalab*) exacts upon the individual and of the oppression he feels as he thirsts for the vision of the Beloved (*liqā' al-maḥbūb*). These dead men are brought back to life by the imam, which is to say they have experienced a spiritual rebirth (*wilāda rūḥāniyya*); how so? By the vision of the radiant face of the imam and by virtue of the initiation (*taʿlīm*) that this blessed vision includes.[85]

81. Al-Sayyid Kāẓim al-Rashtī, *al-Rasā'il wa'l-masā'il* (Tabriz, n.d.), pp. 356–365.

82. Abu'l-Qāsim Rāz Shīrāzī, *Mirṣād al-ʿibād* (Tabriz, n.d.), pp. 98f.

83. Aḥmad Dehkordī, *Borhān-nāme-ye ḥaqīqat* (Tehran, n.d.), pp. 123ff.

84. Al-Rashtī, *al-Rasā'il wa'l-masā'il*, pp. 360–362.

85. Ibid., p. 362.

Then, with only slight variations, our three authors offer their disciples a practical path to be followed in preparation for the vision of the imam, and through that, their individual resurrection. It is interesting to note that all three have recourse to the same series of early traditions attributed to the imams. Let us present the essential aspects of their observations:[86] some traditions suggest that the fortunate believers can, during the major Occultation, come to know the 'location of the hidden imam', in other words, they are able to meet him. 'The Qāʾim will enter on two Occultations', states a tradition by Jaʿfar al-Ṣādiq, 'one short and another longer in duration. During the first, only certain elect Shiʿis (*khāṣṣa shīʿatihi*) will know the location; and during the second [occultation], only the elect among his faithful friends (*khāṣṣa mawālīhi*) will know the location.'[87] The 'elect Shiʿis' designate the 'representatives' during the minor Occultation. 'The elect among his faithful friends' are those believers who have been initiated so that they can enter into contact with the imam during the major Occultation. 'The Lord of this Cause [i.e. the hidden imam]', Jaʿfar al-Ṣādiq is also supposed to have said, 'will enter upon two Occultations – one will last so long that some among them [i.e. the Imamis] will say that the imam is dead, others that he was killed, and others yet that he has [definitively] disappeared. Only some of his adepts (*aṣḥāb*) will remain loyal to his Cause but no one, his friends (*wālī*) or others, will know where he is to be found except for the faithful friend (*mawlā*) who champions his Cause.'[88]

---

86. Al-Rashtī, *al-Rasāʾil waʾl-masāʾil*, pp. 362–365; Shīrāzī, *Mirṣād al-ʿibād*, pp. 107–110; Dehkordī, *Borhān-nāme-ye ḥaqīqat*, pp. 129–134. It is interesting to compare these preparatory practices of an essentially mystical kind with those that are moral, ascetic and specifically religious, proposed by al-Nūrī, *Jannat al-maʾwā*, pp. 325–326 and *al-Najm al-thāqib*, pp. 655–657, which draws upon other traditions dating back to the imams; see also Chapter 10, this volume.

87. E.g. al-Kulaynī, *al-Uṣūl min al-Kāfī*, 'Kitāb al-ḥujja', 'Bāb fiʾl-ghayba', vol. 2, pp. 140–141, no. 19; al-Nuʿmānī, *Kitāb al-ghayba*, ch. 10, pp. 249–250 (bilingual edn) and p. 170 (Arabic).

88. Al-Nuʿmānī, *Kitāb al-ghayba*, pp. 250–251 and 171–172 respectively.

According to our authors, this faithful elected friend can only be a 'believer whose heart has been tested by God for faith' (*al-mu'min imtaḥana'llāh qalbahu li'l-īmān*). This recurring formula that the imams enunciate generally designates the true believer initiated into the spiritual practice of 'vision by (or "in") the heart' (*al-ru'ya bi'l-qalb*), a secret practice that consists of discovering the imam in his form of light in the subtle centre of the heart' and resulting in the acquisition of salvational knowledge and supernatural powers.[89] Preparing the path that leads to an enounter with the hidden imam thus entails acquiring this secret, initiatory 'technique'. Once again, in this case the authors provide a hermeneutical reading of encounter narratives, in which the 'light' of the hidden imam intervenes, adding other early traditions in which the Occulted presence of the hidden imam is compared to a flood of light or a luminous radiance.[90]

All three cite the tradition attributed to the Prophet and reported by the Companion Jābir al-Anṣārī in which it is said that during the Occultation only those whose heart has been tested for faith will remain loyal to the hidden imam's Cause, that they will be illuminated by the light of the imam and will benefit from his *walāya* just as one benefits from the sun when it is hidden by clouds. And the tradition ends with these words: 'This is a secret sealed by God, a hidden treasure of divine knowledge. Jābir, keep this secret from those who are not worthy of it.'[91]

By 'testing of the heart' the initiate is able to encounter the imam and attain his Reality, namely his form as light. This knowledge entails salvation and is equivalent to individual resurrection.

89. On *al-ru'ya bi'l-qalb* in the early tradition and its continuation in mystical schools, see my *Guide divin*, pp. 112–145 (*Divine Guide*, pp. 44–56); for the practice of this 'technique' in Shi'i mystical orders, see R. Gramlich, *Die schiitischen Derwischorden Persiens*, vol. 2: *Glaube und Lehre* (Wiesbaden, 1976), p. 207, n. 1, 073 and pp. 247–250. See also Chapter 10, this volume.

90. Cf. e.g. Ibn Bābūya, *Kamāl al-dīn*, vol. 1, ch. 23, p. 253, no. 3, vol. 2, ch. 35, pp. 371–372, no. 5 and ch. 45, p. 485, no. 4 *in fine*.

91. Ibid., vol. 1, ch. 23, p. 253, no. 3 *in fine*.

It is in this sense that one should understand the traditions dating back to the imams, according to which 'the remotness or imminence of the End of Time, brings no harm to he who knows his imam' and 'he who knows his imam, is like one who already finds himself in the tent of the awaited imam',[92] for such a believer is already revived through knowledge of the imam who is the veritable Revealed God.[93]

---

92. Al-Nuʿmānī, *Kitāb al-ghayba*, ch. 25, pp. 470–473 (bilingual edn) and pp. 329–331 (Arabic). In general, on the individual dimension of Imami eschatology, see my article, 'Eschatology: in Twelver Shiʿism: Individual eschatology', *EIr*.

93. Any one of the imams can manifest himself to a 'tested believer' who has faith in the fundamental unity of all the imams' Reality and their teaching (cf. the saying attributed to Jaʿfar al-Ṣādiq: 'Our creation [i.e. ours, the imams] is one, our science is one, our merit is one, we are all one', e.g. al-Nuʿmānī, *Kitāb al-ghayba*, ch. 4, p. 127, bilingual edn and p. 86 Arabic). I have already cited the case of Muqaddas Ardabīlī and his supernatural communications with the first imam (above, 'initiatory dimension', 4th report); see also the case of Mullā ʿAbd al-Raḥīm b. Yūnus al-Damāwandī (d. ca. 1150/1737 or 1170/1757) who relates being blessed with 'direct' teaching from the third imam, al-Ḥusayn b. ʿAlī, see his *Sharḥ-e asrār-e asmā'-e ḥosnā = Meftāḥ-e asrār-e ḥusaynī* in *Montakhabātī az āthār-e ḥokamā-ye elāhī-ye Īrān*, ed. S. J. Āshtiyānī, Bibliothèque Iranienne (Tehran–Paris, 1976), vol. 3, pp. 577–790 and esp. pp. 577–578 and 628. Mullā ʿAbd al-Raḥīm is also known having encountered the hidden imam, see al-Ṭabrisī al-Nūrī, *Jannat al-ma'wā*, p. 306 and *al-Najm al-thāqib*, p. 506; regarding him see also H. Corbin, *La philosophie iranienne islamique aux XVIIe et XVIIIe siècles* (Paris, 1981), pp. 340–393. One of the greatest spiritual aims of Sufis belonging to the Dhahabiyya order is to encounter the eighth imam, ʿAlī al-Riḍā, to whom the order's initiatory chain is traced; see *Resāle-ye ḥall-e eshkāl-e davāzdah so'āl-e...Zanjānī az...Rāz-e Shīrāzī* (Tehran, 1367/1947), pp. 125–126; *Guide divin*, pp. 135–136 (*Divine Guide*, pp. 52–53). In general, Imami mystical works cite numerous cases of these 'direct' disciples of one or another imam, graced by the vision of the imam; cf. e.g. N. Modarresī Chahārdehī, *Khāksār va ahl-e ḥaqq* (2nd edn, Tehran, n.d.), pp. 80–83 – a rather muddled work but a treasury of information; ʿAbd al-Riḍā Khān Ibrāhīmī (master of the Shaykhiyya of Kerman), *Dūstī-ye dūstān* (Kerman, 1400/1979). These reports of encounters with imams other than the hidden imam, although of initiatory significance, do not appear to include an individual eschatological dimension.

14

An Absence Filled with Presences: Shaykhiyya Hermeneutics of the Occultation*

In *Le conflit des interprétations*,[1] Paul Ricoeur wrote: 'I call hermeneutics any discipline that proceeds by means of interpretation, and I give the word "interpretation" its strongest meaning: the discernment of hidden meaning within apparent meaning.' I begin with this quotation from the French philosopher, itself based on certain classical definitions of the term, because it seems a fine introduction to the present chapter. Curiously, the definition has a certain Shiʿi resonance: the 'hidden'/'apparent' pair obviously recalls the *bāṭin/ẓāhir* pair, omnipresent at all levels of Shiʿi doctrine.[2] The notion of the discernment of what is hidden immediately evokes that of *kashf al-maḥjūb*, central to all Muslim mysticism. And Shiʿism combined with mysticism perfectly describes the nature of the order of the Shaykhiyya. This chapter examines certain hermeneutics – in Ricoeur's sense – of the Occultation of the Twelfth Imam within this order.

---

* This chapter was originally given as a paper at the colloquium 'Die Zwölferschia in der Neuzeit', organised by Werner Ende and Rainer Brunner, for which they are most cordially thanked, at Albert-Ludwigs-Universität de Freiburg-im-Breisgau (4–7 October 1999).

1. P. Ricoeur, *Le conflit des interprétations* (Paris, 1969), p. 260.

2. On this question see my 'Du droit à la théologie: les niveaux de réalité dans le shiʿisme duodécimain', *Cahiers du Groupe d'Etudes Spirituelles Comparées*, 5, 'L'Esprit et la Nature' (Actes du colloque tenu à Paris, 11–12 May 1996) (Milan and Paris, 1997), pp. 37–63.

The eschatological dimension in general and the Occultation and its implications in particular, constitute the central themes of the Shaykhī doctrine since its founding sources; namely, the works of Shaykh Aḥmad al-Aḥsāʾī (d. 1241/1826) and Sayyid Kāẓim al-Rashtī (d. 1259/1843).[3] On the matter of the Occultation, successive masters of the order consistently used two fundamental notions,[4] which may be understood as two methodological, hermeneutic foundations. First, the existence of at least two levels to all reality, an obvious, manifest, exoteric level (*ẓāhir*) and another, secret, esoteric level, hidden by the first (*bāṭin*). In some cases this notion is multiplied into *ẓāhir al-ẓāhir*, *al-ẓāhir*, *bāṭin al-ẓāhir*, *al-bāṭin* and *bāṭin al-bāṭin*. The notion is of course applied first and foremost to the Qurʾān, *ḥadīth*s and other religious texts, but it is also used for other matters, such as canonical duties, legal data and points of doctrine. It was used as a hermeneutic method in the writings of Shaykh Aḥmad[5] and Sayyid Kāẓim,[6] and in an even more developed way by the two sons and consecutive successors to Muḥammad Karīm Khān: Muḥammad Khān (d. 1324/1906)[7]

---

3. On Shaykhī eschatology see V. Rafati, 'The Development of Shaykhī Thought in Shīʿī Islam' (University of California, 1979), ch. 4, pp. 102–125; also Appendix A, pp. 218–219, for a list of monographic writings by Shaykh Aḥmad al-Aḥsāʾī and Sayyid Kāẓim Rashtī on the Qāʾim. See also I. Samawi Hamid, 'The Metaphysics and Cosmology of Process According to Shaykh Aḥmad al-Aḥsāʾī' (State University of New York, 1998), ch. II.2.

4. This study will only discuss the Kirmānī branch of the Shaykhiyya order that recognises Muḥammad Karīm Khān Kirmānī (d. 1288/1870) and his descendants as the successors of Sayyid Kāẓim Rashtī. Branches such as those of Tabriz and, more recently, Islamabad will not be taken into account.

5. Al-Shaykh Aḥmad al-Aḥsāʾī, *al-Risāla al-Tawbaliyya*, called *Lawāmiʿ al-wasāʾil* (responses to questions by Mullā ʿAlī Tawbalī) in *Jawāmiʿ al-kilam/kalim*, vol. 1, pp. 95–99, response no. 15, and *al-Risāla al-Qaṭīfiyya* (responses to 71 questions by Shaykh Ṣāliḥ Qaṭīfī), vol. 1, pp. 117–120, response no. 9.

6. Sayyid Kāẓim al-Ḥusaynī al-Rashtī, 'Risāla fī jawāb Mullā ʿAlī Baraghānī' in *al-Rasāʾil wa'l-masāʾil* (Tabriz, n.d.), pp. 335–336, response no. 7; al-Rashtī, *Risāla fī bayān maqāmāt al-ẓāhir wa'l-bāṭin* (lithograph, n.p., n.d.).

7. Muḥammad Khān Kirmānī, 'Sharḥ lā ḥawl wa lā quwwa illā bi'llāh' in *Majmaʿ al-rasāʾil* (Kirmān, 1348 Sh./1970), vol. 3, pp. 62–111; and 'Risāla

and Zayn al-ʿĀbidīn Khān Kirmānī (d. 1360/1942).[8] Second, there is the notion of the universe as macrocosm (*al-ʿālam al-kabīr*), man as microcosm (*al-ʿālam al-ṣaghīr*), and the correspondence between the two. An event in the external world may have its counterpart in the corresponding internal world of man, and thus constitute one of its hidden, esoteric meanings. Thus, concomitantly, as an event that has happened in the world the Occultation corresponds to something deep inside the individual. Sayyid Kāẓim Rashtī[9] and Muḥammad Khān Kirmānī[10] have produced pages of luminous, profound writing on this notion, employing it as a hermeneutic method.

With these two constants of Shaykhī thought in mind, and in the interests of clarity, I have chosen to present the following analysis in two parts, the hermeneutics (in the sense of revelation of hidden meaning) of the Occultation first as macrocosmic event and then as microcosmic event.

The Occultation in the world

In the course of a recent research expedition to Iran (July–August 1999), I heard Zayn al-ʿĀbidīn Khān Ibrāhīmī, current master of the order in Iran,[11] say that according to the Twelver Shiʿi profession of faith, the twelfth, hidden imam is not only alive but his being has never stopped exercising its active, effective influence on the world. This influence is not an abstraction or

dar jawāb-i baʿḍi ikhwān', response no 2, in *Majmaʿ al-rasāʾil* (Kirmān, 1350 Sh./1973), vol. 78, pp. 132–149.

8. Zayn al-ʿĀbidīn Khān Kirmānī, 'al-Risāla al-Ḥasaniyya' (responses to questions by Mīrzā Ḥasan Sardrūdī), response no 3, in *Majmaʿ al-rasāʾil* (Kirmān, 1350 Sh./1973), vol. 28, pp. 78–93.

9. *Risāla fī jawāb Mullā ʿAlī Baraghānī*, pp. 334–335.

10. *Wāridāt*, 'Wārida' in *Majmaʿ al-rasāʾil* (Kirman, 1349 Sh./1971), vol. 27, pp. 23–32, no. 4.

11. The function of great universal master of the Shaykhiyya of Kirmān is currently undertaken by Sayyid ʿAlī al-Mūsawī of Baṣra; see D. MacEoin, 'Shaykhiyya', *EI2* , p. 417b.

just metaphysical concept; on the contrary, it is and must be concrete. And it is so because it is exercised through a certain number of flesh-and-blood persons called the Friends of the Hidden Imam (*dūstān-i imām-i ghāʾib*). Without pronouncing the term, Sarkār Aghā Ibrāhīmī was here clearly evoking the doctrine of the Fourth Pillar (*rukn rābiʿ*). This doctrine can be considered a kind of hermeneutics of the hidden Imam's Occulted presence and influence in the world. The first two grand masters of the school, Shaykh Aḥmad and Sayyid Kāẓim, would seem to have made only furtive allusions to the *rukn rābiʿ*.[12] The doctrine was first significantly developed at length in the immense body of work by the third master, Muḥammad Karīm Khān Kirmānī (d. 1288/1870); he not only wrote monographs on the subject,[13] but devoted long chapters of his major works to it,[14] as well as numerous parts of his *responsa*.[15] Calling into question the exclusive legitimacy of

---

12. See Abu'l-Qāsim Khān Ibrāhīmī (d. 1389/1969), *Fihrist-i kutub*, pp. 75–78. The author, son and successor to Zayn al-ʿĀbidīn Khān Kirmānī, published here two letters by Sayyid Kāẓim that allude to the *rukn rābiʿ*. I have not found any text by either of these authors on the subject, but I am still far from having completed my reading of their monumental writings. However, the importance of the concept of the Fourth Pillar and its constituent parts in the work of the Bāb, himself a disciple of Sayyid Kāzim, gives one to think that the two initial masters of the Shaykhiyya, and above all the second, spoke of it greatly; cf. D. M. MacEoin, 'From Shaykhism to Babism: A Study in Charismatic Renewal in Shiʿi Islam' (PhD thesis, Cambridge University, 1979), pp. 170f. 201f. and 'Early Shaykhī Reactions to the Bāb and His Claims', in M. Momen (ed.), *Studies in Bābī and Bahāʾī history* (Los Angeles, 1982), vol. 1, pp. 1–47, esp. pp. 34–36; T. Lawson, 'The Qurʾān Commentary of the Bāb' (PhD thesis, McGill University, 1987), pp. 48f., 80–81, 150f., 165f., 181–182, 253f., 294, 363.

13. For example, *Rukn-i rābiʿ* and *Tawḥīd nubuwwa imāma Shīʿa*.

14. For example *Irshād al-ʿawāmm*, 4 parts in 2 vols, the whole of vol. 4; *Ṭarīq al-najāt*, 4 parts in 1 vol., the whole of part 2, ch. 3; *Izhāq al-bāṭil*, ch. 3; *Sī faṣl*, the first four *faṣl*; *al-Fiṭra al-salīma*, the whole of vol. 3; *Hidāyat al-ṭālibīn*, ch. 2.

15. For example 'Risāla dar rafʿ-i shubuhāt-i baʿḍ-i ahl-i Karbalāʾ', in *Majmaʿ al-rasāʾil*, vol. 15, response no. 5; 'Risāla dar jawāb-i Sayyid Jawād Karbalāʾī', in *Majmaʿ al-rasāʾil*, vol. 66, response no. 2; 'Risāla dar jawāb-i Mullā Ḥasan Yazdī', in *Majmaʿ al-rasāʾil*, vol. 66, response no. 6; 'Risāla dar Jawāb-i Mullā Muḥammad Jaʿfar Kāzarūnī', in *Majmaʿ al-rasāʾil*, vol. 68, response

the official religious authorities and being made use of in various versions in Bābism, which was an involuntary offshoot of Shaykhism according to Muḥammad Karīm Khān and his successors, the *rukn rābiʿ* was thus much written about and also the cause of a great deal of the violence perpetrated against the Shaykhiyya of Kermān.[16] It was at this time that the Shaykhiyya's adversaries began to call them (amongst other names) 'Rukniyya'. Though subsequent masters continued to expound the notion, they had to explain the doctrinal foundation of the Fourth Pillar, to demonstrate its perfect orthodoxy within Imāmism, and thereby calm those who had been stirred up against it by impassioned public sermons.[17]

---

no. 10; 'Risāla dar Jawāb-i nawwāb 'Abbās Mīrzā b. Muḥammad Shāh Qājār', in *Majmaʿ al-rasāʾil*, vol. 70, response no. 5.

16. See e.g. MacEoin, 'From Shaykhism to Babism'; A. Amanat, *Resurrection and Renewal: The Making of the Babi Movement in Iran, 1844–1850* (London, 1989), pp. 48ff. For a short but useful review of the doctrinal differences between Imami theologian-jurists and the Shaykhiyya, see esp. S. A. Arjomand, *The Shadow of God and the Hidden Imam* (Chicago, 1984), index under 'Shaykhiyya', and M. Momen, *An Introduction to Shīʿī Islam: The History and Doctrine of Twelver Shiʿism* (Oxford, 1985), pp. 226–228. The open conflict between the Shaykhīs and the Uṣūlī clerics seems to go back to the anathema (*takfīr*) hurled against Shaykh Aḥmad al-Aḥsāʾī by Mullā Muḥammad Taqī Baraghānī Qazwīnī around the year 1238/1822 (see also Āghā Buzurg al-Ṭirānī, *Ṭabaqāt aʿlām al-shīʿa* [Najaf, 1956], vol. 2, pp. 226–228; M. Sharīf Rāzī, *Ganjīna-yi dānishmandān* [Tehran, 1354 Sh./1976], vol. 6, p. 162).

17. This is quite clear from many Shaykhī writings; for example Muḥammad Khān Kirmānī, *Yanābīʿ al-ḥikma* (Kirmān, 1383/1964), vol. 1, 'maqāla' 4, *Burhān-i qāṭiʿ* (a monograph on the subject), *Wasīlat al-najāt*, 'maqṣad' 4; Zayn al-'Ābidīn Khān Kirmānī, 'Risāla dar jawāb-i Muḥammad Ṣādiq Khān Nāʾīnī', in *Majmaʿ al-rasāʾil*, vol. 8, response nos 6–9, 'Risāla dar jawāb-i Āqā Mīrzā Sayyid Muḥammad Riḍawī', in *Majmaʿ al-rasāʾil*, vol. 11; 'Risāla dar jawāb-i Shaykh Ḥusayn b. Shaykh 'Alī Ṣaḥḥāf dar rukn-i rābiʿ', in *Majmaʿ al-rasāʾil*, vol. 79; Abu'l-Qāsim Khān Ibrāhīmī, *Tanzīh al-awliyāʾ*, chs 35–38 and 49–50; Ibrāhīmī, *Ijtihād wa taqlīd*, 2nd edn, all of the 'Tatmīm' and 'Risāla falsafiyya dar jawāb-i Shaykh Muḥammad Taqī Falsafī', response nos 11 and 12, and *Fihrist*, pp. 74–111 (partial trans. and commentary by H. Corbin, *En Islam iranien: Aspects spirituels et philosophiques* [Paris, 1971–1972], vol. 4, pp. 274–286); 'Abd al-Riḍā Khān Ibrāhīmī, *Dūstī-ye dūstān* (a monograph on the subject). It should be noted that 'Abd al-Riḍā Khān, son and successor to

What is the *rukn rābiʿ*?[18] The first three pillars of the profession of Imami faith are God's unicity (*tawḥīd*), the mission of the prophets (*nubuwwa*), and that of the Imam (*imāma*). The fourth, just as essential as the other three, is what the Shaykhī masters designate with the terms 'the Shiʿis (*al-shīʿa*)' or 'the allied saints or friends of the Imam' (*awliyāʾ* in Arabic, *dūstān* in Persian); that is, the true Shiʿis, those initiated into the esoteric teachings of the imams, the most worthy of whom are in spiritual relation with the hidden Imam. We can examine this issue more closely by considering the three essential components of the doctrine of the Fourth Pillar.

1. The Men of the Mystery (*rijāl al-ghayb*)

Throughout his monumental work *Irshād al-ʿawāmm*, Muḥammad Karīm Khān explains that the universe only has meaning from a gnostic perspective. The purpose of creation is knowledge (*maʿrifa*), the living and lived knowledge of the mysteries of God, man and the laws that govern the world. The existence of the Four Pillars and the dialectical relation connecting them to each other are determined by this living knowledge.[19] The reality

---

Abu'l-Qāsim Khān and penultimate master of the order, was assassinated on 26 December 1979, a few months after the triumph of the Islamic revolution in Iran (see E. Franz, 'Minderheiten im Iran. Dokumentation zur Ethnographie und Politik', *Aktueller Informationdienst Moderner Orient*, Sondernummer 8 [Hamburg, 1981], p. 192). In general terms, on the persecution of mystics in Iran from the Safawid period to modern times, it is useful to consult L. Lewisohn, 'An Introduction to the History of Modern Persian Sufism', Part 1, *BSOAS*, 61/3 (1998), pp. 437–464 and Part II, *BSOAS*, 62/1 (1999), pp. 36–59.

18. Corbin provides a discussion of this question, which is in fact an annotated translation of Abu'l-Qāsim Khān's presentation in his *Fihrist*, in *En Islam iranien* (see n. 17). In it he incorporates and expands his previous discussion in 'L'École Shaykhie en théologie Shiʿite', *EPHE* (1960–1961), pp. 50–59. This chapter seeks to further develop Corbin's work, which is to my knowledge the first and only one of its kind. See also Lawson, 'The Qur'ān Commentary of the Bāb'.

19. This explains the very structure of the *Irshād al-ʿawāmm*: vols 1 and 2: 'Dar shinākhtan-i khudāwand wa maʿrifat-i payghambarān wa bayān-i haqīqat-i maʿād', vol. 3, 'Dar maʿrifat-i imāmān', vol. 4, 'Dar maʿrifat-i Shīʿa'.

of the divine Unicity is the mystery of mysteries. The essential raison d'être of the Prophet's mission was to guide men on the path to understanding this mystery. The Imam's mission consists in making the reality of the prophetic message known. Finally, because the Occultation is a realised fact and the knowledge must remain alive, the raison d'être of the initiated[20] is to make the reality of the teaching of the imams known and thereby keep it alive.[21] The existence of this corps of initiates is thus absolutely necessary in the economy of the sacred; without it, all humanity would lose the transcendental meaning of its being and sink into the darkness of impious ignorance.[22]

This group of sages, whom H. Corbin calls *ecclesia spiritualis*,[23] is a secret spiritual hierarchy designated in Shaykhī writings by the ancient term *rijāl al-ghayb*, 'the men of the mystery'.[24] This expression has several meanings. First, the men in this hierarchy are in relation with the divine, invisible world, the world of mystery, the *ghayb*. In different ways, according to their place in the hierarchy, they are in relation with the hidden Imam (*ghayb* is of course from the same root as *ghayba*, 'Occultation'). Finally, they are themselves 'invisible', in the sense that as companions of the hidden Imam, their spiritual rank and real activities are completely hidden. Abu'l-Qāsim Khān Ibrāhīmī explicitly writes that a tradesman or peasant can just as easily belong to the hierarchy as a great cleric, without anyone knowing it.[25] The

20. On the translation of 'Shī'a' as 'initiated ones' see Chapter 8 in this volume.

21. Muḥammad Karīm Khān, *Irshād al-'awāmm*, vol. 4, pp. 5–75 and *Tawḥīd nubuwwa imāma shī'a*, pp. 45–54.

22. Zayn al-'Ābidīn Khān, 'Risāla dar jawāb-i Muḥammad Qulī Khān sipihr', in *Majma' al-rasā'il*, vol. 80, response no. 5; 'Abd al-Riḍā Khān Ibrāhīmī, *Dūstī-ye dūstān*, pp. 187–190.

23. *En Islam iranien*, vol. 4, p. 276.

24. See for example Zayn al-'Ābidīn Khān, 'Risāla dar jawāb-i Muḥammad Ṣādiq Khān Nā'īnī', response no. 9, with references to both the ancient texts and earlier Shaykhī writings.

25. *Fihrist*, p. 108.

exact number of these men is not known. The sources specify only that they belong to two main categories: the chiefs (*naqīb*, pl. *nuqabāʾ*) and the nobles (*najīb*, pl. *nujabāʾ*). Commenting on certain ancient traditions presented in the *Baṣāʾir al-darajāt* of al-Ṣaffār al-Qummī (d. 290/902–903) and the *Kāfī* of al-Kulaynī (d. 329/940–941), Muḥammad Karīm Khān makes the supposition that there are twelve *nuqabāʾ* and seventy *nujabāʾ*, while adding that because his predecessors, Shaykh Aḥmad and Sayyid Kāẓim, gave no specifics on this matter, his supposition should be considered no more than a hypothesis.[26] The Chiefs are the holders of sacred Power; they intervene in a secret manner in the affairs of the world to prevent ignorance-bred injustice and violence from entirely invading the earth. The nobles, on the other hand, have no earthly power but are rather the holders of sacred knowledge, and their function is to safeguard and transmit initiatory science.[27] This hierarchy is secret because humanity is going through a long cycle of ignorance and violence. If the friends of the hidden Imam are incognito, this is because men have lost the 'organs' necessary to recognise them. And this itself is a sign of divine wisdom, because otherwise the friends would either be persecuted or confused with those external powers that organise each human community socially and politically. Still, nothing prevents the members of this hierarchy from revealing their true function to certain rare individuals worthy of such a revelation.[28] A poem by Muḥammad Karīm Khān sums up these ideas very well:

---

26. *Irshād al-ʿawāmm*, vol. 4, pp. 275–276. An allusion by Sayyid Kāẓim also seems to indicate that there are twelve *nuqabā* (*see infra*).

27. Ibid., vol. 4, pp. 252–273; Kirmānī, Muḥammad Karīm Khān, *Ṭarīq al-najāt*, vol. 2, ch. 3, pp. 123–138; Muḥammad Khān Kirmānī, 'Risāla dar jawāb-i Shaykh Ḥusayn Rashtī', response no. 5, facsimile of the autograph MS (Kirmān, n.d.); Abu'l-Qāsim Khān Ibrāhīmī, *Tanzīh al-awliyāʾ*, chs 32 and 50; 'Abd al-Riḍā Khān Ibrāhīmī, *Dūstī-ye dūstān*, passim.

28. Muḥammad Karīm Khān, *Irshād al-ʿawāmm*, vol. 4, pp. 310–315; Zayn al-ʿĀbidīn Khān, 'Risāla dar jawāb-i Muḥammad Qulī Khān Sipihr', response no. 5 and 'Risāla dar jawāb-i Muḥammad Ṣādiq Khān Nāʾīnī', response

If there is error, this is because of our ignorance / The ignorant one acts only out of ignorance

When God saw people's ignorance / He chose a group of sages.

He manifested them amidst the masses / And he initiated them into the science of the Imam,

So they would reveal (true) government / and thereby put an end to polemic and enmities.

Through charisma, some are chiefs / Through dignity, others are Nobles

Through its power, the group of chiefs / replaces the Imam like a delegate;

Their power is the Power of God / They make anyone they wish obey.

The reign of the sovereigns of being / is the sign of their reign in both worlds.

The group of Nobles are all Sages / Guides for the community and guardians of the faith.

Dispensers of science in this world / Arbiters of judgement in the other World.[29]

The *nuqabā'* and *nujabā'* secretly direct men towards knowledge of the reality of the hidden Imam. In the way of symbols, they both hide and reveal that which is symbolised, the Mahdī. Muḥammad Karīm Khān employs an elegant formula to describe this situation: 'the men of the mystery' constitute together the name (*ism*) of the hidden Imam: they identify him, call out to him and make him known. But everyone knows that in Imamism, the name of the Mahdī must not be uttered – hence the secret nature of this spiritual hierarchy.[30]

---

no. 9; Abu'l-Qāsim Khān Ibrāhīmī, *Fihrist*, pp. 90–91 (annotated translation by Corbin, *En Islam iranien*, vol. 4, p. 276).

29. Muḥammad Karīm Khān, *Risāla manẓūma Raḥīmiyya*, pp. 41–42.

30. *Irshād al-ʿawāmm*, vol. 4, pp. 302–303. On the interdiction to pronounce the name of the twelfth imam and the ancient sources on this subject, see my *Guide divin*, pp. 257–260 (*Divine Guide*, pp. 105–106).

In this way, by applying it to the Occultation, Shaykhism actualises an extremely ancient Shiʿi belief, known since at least the Kumayl *ḥadīth*, which was reported, among others, by al-Yaʿqūbī (d. 284/897), in which ʿAlī speaks of a group of rare holy men, who cannot be detected but who are so many signs and proofs of God's existence on earth.[31]

2. The unicity of the speaker (*waḥdat al-nāṭiq*)

A second component of the doctrine of the *rukn rābiʿ* is the unicity of the speaker, also called the unique speaker (*al-nāṭiq al-wāḥid*). As in any hierarchy, 'the men of the mystery' have at their head a supreme authority, the wisest and most powerful among them, who is in a direct relationship with the Imam and is called the 'perfect Shiʿi' (*akmal al-shīʿa; shīʿa-i kāmil* in Persian) or 'the gate' (*bāb*) of the hidden Imam.[32] This pole (*quṭb*) which is of the earthly world (the hidden Imam is the pole of both worlds), is called *nāṭiq*, literally 'the speaker', once again because of the primary importance of initiatory knowledge: in any initiatory relation, the master is the one who speaks while the disciple is the one who listens in silence (*ṣāmit*). This is a cosmic law applying from God all the way down to the humblest of initiates. The notion is expounded in a didactic text by Muḥammad Karīm Khān, and further developed by Abu'l-Qāsim Khān: the order of

---

31. Al-Yaʿqūbī, *Ta'rīkh*, vol. 2, pp. 205–206; Ibn Bābūya, *Kamāl al-dīn*, ch. 26, p. 290, no. 2 and *al-Khiṣāl*, pp. 186–187; al-Sharīf al-Raḍī, *Nahj al-Balāgha*, pp. 1,155–1,158; see also Chapter 8 *in fine*. The secret hierarchy of saints is a familiar concept in Sunni Sufism, but it is also discussed in interesting ways in Imami Sufism; see Sayyid Ḥaydar Āmulī, *Jāmiʿ al-asrār*, pp. 223ff.; Shams al-Dīn al-Lāhījī, *Mafātīḥ al-iʿjāz fī sharḥ Gulshan-i rāz*, pp. 265ff. (on al-Lāhījī's Imamism see p. xl of the editors' introduction).

32. Muḥammad Karīm Khān, *Izhāq al-bāṭil*, ch. 3, pp. 91–92; Muḥammad Khān, 'Risāla dar jawāb-i Shaykh Ḥusayn Mazīdī', in *Majmaʿ al-rasā'il*, vol. 73, response no. 1; Zayn al-ʿĀbidīn Khān, 'Risāla dar jawāb-i Muḥammad Ṣādiq Khān Nā'īnī', response nos 6 and 7; Abu'l-Qāsim Khān Ibrāhīmī, *Tanzīh al-awliyā'*, ch. 50; Ibrāhīmī, 'Tatmīm' in *Ijtihād wa taqlid* and 'Risāla sharīfiyya dar jawāb-i Shaykh ʿAlī Akbar Sharīf al-Wāʿiẓīn', response no. 19.

the world is governed by teaching, initiation (*ta'līm*); God is the first master; He 'speaks' and the Angel Gabriel, the Angel of Revelation, listens while remaining 'silent', just as when Gabriel speaks the Prophet remains silent, and so on with the Prophet and the Imam, the Imam and his gate, and the Imam's *bāb* or gate and the rest of the initiates ('Shi'is').[33] The master has only one *bāb*: 'Alī was Muḥammad's *bāb* according to the ancient Prophetic *ḥadīth*: 'I am the city of knowledge and 'Alī is its gate' (*anā madīnat al-'ilm wa 'Alī bābuhā*); Salmān the Persian was 'Alī's gate, as Abū Khālid al-Kābulī was the fourth imam's gate, Jābir al-Ju'fī the fifth imam's and Mufaḍḍal al-Ju'fī the sixth's, etc.[34] Like all the other imams, the hidden Imam also has a 'gate', but since the Occultation lasts so long, the hidden Imam has been represented over time by a series of unique 'gates'. The hidden Imam is *nāṭiq* in relation to his 'gate', who is *ṣāmit* in relation to the Imam but *nāṭiq* in relation to other members of the secret hierarchy; whence the well-known saying 'Each period has its own Salmān' (*li-kulli 'asr salmān*).[35] According to the '*ḥadīth* of Mufaḍḍal', continually cited by our authors, 'The gate of the Twelfth [imam] is hidden by the very fact of the Occultation of the Twelfth [imam]' (*bāb-i thānī 'ashar bā ghaybat-i thāni 'ashar ghā'ib mīshawad*). That the spiritual hierarchy, with the unique speaker at its head, is secret results from the Occultation of the last Imam and thereby constitutes the secret meaning of the Occultation. In this our own era

33. Muḥammad Karīm Khān, *Irshād al-'awāmm*, vol. 4, pp. 383–384; Abu'l-Qāsim Khān, *Tanzīh al-awliyā'*, chs 25–32 and *Fihrist*, pp. 86ff. (partial trans. and commentary by H. Corbin, *En Islam Iranien*, vol. 4, pp. 281–282); 'Abd al-Riḍā Khān Ibrāhīmī, *Dūstī-ye dūstān*, pp. 102–103.

34. *Fihrist*, pp. 85–86. Another way of understanding this is that an imam is 'silent' during his predecessor's imamate, then accedes to the rank of 'speaker' upon his predecessor's death; see ibid., p. 86.

35. Muḥammad Khān Kirmānī, *Burhān-i qāṭi'*, pp. 76ff.; 'Risāla dar jawāb-i Shaykh Ḥusayn Mazīdī', response no. 1; Zayn al-'Ābidīn Khān, 'Risāla dar jawāb-i Muḥammad Ṣādiq Khān Nā'īnī', response no. 6; 'Abd al-Riḍā Khān Ibrāhīmī, 'Risāla dar jawāb-i āqā-ye muhandis Mūsā Žām', in *Majma' al-rasā'il-i fārsī*, vol. 17, response no. 2.

of ignorance, true science and true power can only be operative if they are exercised in secret, independent of all earthly power.[36]

> The [Shaykhī] idea of the *occultation* of the Imam forbids all socialisation of the spiritual, all materialisation of forms and hierarchies that could be identified with the 'instituted organisations' of visible external history.... The *ḥadīth* of Mofazzal (*Mufaḍḍal*) thus has serious, decisive consequences. Whosoever publicly proclaims himself the Imam's Bāb puts himself *eo ipso* outside Shiʿism, for he has profaned its fundamental secrecy.[37]

These lines by Corbin, based only on a text by Abu'l-Qāsim Khān, are corroborated by certain earlier Shaykhī writings, beginning with those of Muḥammad Karīm Khān. In effect, the notion of the 'unicity of the speaker' that is part of the doctrine of the Fourth Pillar is the source of the main charge against the Shaykhiyya of Kirmān, for two reasons. First, it radically calls into question the legitimacy of the theocratic corps of Uṣūlī jurist-theologians understood to be the official representatives of the hidden Imam, especially since, according to their adversaries, each of the Shaykhiyya masters declared *themselves* to be 'the unique speaker'.

Second, it launched Bābism (which later developed into Bahā'ism) as a new religion.[38] Starting with Muḥammad Karīm Khān Kirmānī, the Shaykhiyya masters were forced to defend the doctrine of the *rukn rābiʿ* on two fronts. They had to demonstrate first of all that when ʿAlī Muḥammad Bāb proclaimed himself to be the gate of the hidden Imam, the break between Shaykhism and Bābism had become irreversible: according to Shiʿi and Shaykhī

36. Muḥammad Khān, *Burhān-i qāṭiʿ*, p. 82; Abu'l-Qāsim Khān, *Fihrist*, pp. 88ff.

37. H. Corbin, *En Islam Iranien*, vol. 4, pp. 276 and 283 (analysis of above mentioned passages from the *Fihrist* of Abu'l-Qāsim Khān Ibrāhīmī).

38. Aḥmad Kasrawī's violently polemical works have at least the advantage of giving us a view, as broad as it is significant, of the anti-Shaykhī attacks; e.g. *Shīʿīgarī; Bikhānīd wa dāwarī konīd; Bahā'īgarī.*

dogmas, Bābism could only be a false religion.[39] Then, Muḥammad Karīm Khān and his successors insisted that no Shaykhī master had ever proclaimed himself 'the unique speaker' or even said he belonged to 'the men of the mystery'. Such a declaration would be in flagrant contradiction with the Shaykhī dogma of the necessarily hidden nature of everything that had any direct relation to the Occultation. The purpose of all the general information about the Fourth Pillar was only to prove the effective existence of the secret spiritual hierarchy and its supreme chief, but no Shaykhī in charge had ever given the slightest piece of specific information about particular individuals. To cite the well-known formula:

39. This explains the many Shaykhī writings against the Bāb and his doctrine: Muḥammad Karīm Khān, *Izhāq al-bāṭil* (Kirmān, 1351 Sh./1973) and *Rujūm al-shayāṭīn* with *Risāla dar radd-i Bāb-i khusrān ma'āb* (Tabriz, n.d. [ca. 1283/1866]), *Risāla-ye radd-i Bāb dar jawāb-i Nāṣir al-Dīn Shāh Qājār* (Kirmān, 1383/1963); 'Tīr-i shihāb dar radd-i Bāb-i khusrān ma'āb', in *Majma' al-rasā'il* (Kirmān, 1386/1967), vol. 1; *al-Shihāb al-thāqib* (Kirmān, 1353 Sh./1975). Muḥammad Karīm Khan's vigorous and systematic attacks, which go as far as anathematising the Bāb (*takfīr*) no doubt played a role in the transformation of Bābism, from a branch of Shaykhism into an independent religion. See MacEoin, 'From Shaykhism to Bābism', pp. 196ff., where he also presents other anti-Bābī Shaykhiyya writings. MacEoin further developed this study in 'Early Shaykhī Reactions to the Bāb and his Claims', in M. Momen (ed.), *Studies in Bābī and Bahā'ī history* (Los Angeles, 1982), vol. 1, pp. 1–47; see now his *The Sources for Early Bābī Doctrine and History* (Leiden, 1992), index under 'Shaykhism'; Muḥammad Khān Kirmānī, *Taqwīm al-'awaj* (lithograph, Bombay, 1311/1893); *Risāla dar radd-i Bāb-i murtāb* (Kirmān, n.d.); 'Risāla dar radd-i ba'ḍī ta'wīlāt-i bābiyya', in *Rasā'il* (Kirmān, 1398/1977), pp. 10–152; *al-Shams al-muḍī'a* (lithograph, Tabriz, 1322/1904); 'Risāla dar jawāb-i Sayyid Ḥusayn Karbalā'ī', in *Majma' al-rasā'il*, vol. 4, response no. 8; 'Risāla dar jawāb-i ba'ḍ-i ikhwān-i Shīrāz', in *Majma' al-rasā'il*, response no. 3; Zayn al-'Ābidīn Khān, 'Ṣā'iqa' in *Majma' al-rasā'il*, vol. 9 and *Mi'rāj al-sa'āda* (rpr., Kirmān, 1352 Sh./1974). For the reactions of the Bāb and the Bābiyya, see MacEoin, 'From Shaykhism to Babism', pp. 216ff.; M. Bayat, *Mysticism and Dissent: Socioreligious Thought in Qajar Iran* (New York, 1982), ch. 4; T. Lawson, 'Interpretation as Revelation: The Qur'ān Commentary of Sayyid 'Alī Muḥammad Shīrāzī the Bāb (1819–1850)', in A. Rippin (ed.), *Approaches to the History of the Interpretation of the Qur'ān* (Oxford, 1988), pp. 223–253; also M. Mudarris Chahārdihī, *Shaykhīgarī Bābīgarī* (Tehran, 2nd edn, 1351 Sh./1972)) (this muddled work is nonetheless a mine of information).

'the Fourth Pillar is generic, not specific' (*rukn-i rābiʿ nawʿī-st na taʿyīnī*).[40] According to Shaykhiyya sources, the Fourth Pillar as the hidden, esoteric meaning of Occultation prohibits all socialisation and collectivisation of religious spirituality.

Occultation means that the Imami doctrine is an individualistic type of spirituality, in which not only many collective canonical duties cannot be carried out because of the Imam's absence, but any claim to religious power in the world can only be heresy. In this connection, the sixth chapter of the *Sī faṣl* by Muḥammad Karīm Khān, on the problem of declaring *jihād* during the Occultation, is highly significant:

> How can we be accused of seeking power in this world [through the doctrines of the Fourth Pillar and the unicity of the speaker], of loving power and inciting people to rebel, when during the Occultation *jihād* is not legitimate (*dar zamān-i ghaybat jihādī nīst*)? To declare *jihād*, the presence of the Imam is necessary (*wājib*). ... According to the doctrine of our masters, [during the Occultation] not only can there not be *jihād*, but it is also forbidden to enact legal punishments (*ḥudūd*) such as killing, stoning, or flagellation; even the enjoining of good and preventing of evil (*amr-i bi maʿrūf wa nahy az munkar*) are forbidden in most cases. ...This is to be done only by the hidden Imam upon his Return (*ḥadd zadan wa jārī kardan makhṣūṣ-i imām ast dar waqt-i ẓuhūr-i amrash*). ... At this time [i.e. at time of the Occultation], the distinctive sign of the pious learned man and ascetic (*ʿālim-i mutadayyin-i zāhid*) is solitude and retreat. He transmits the light of the imams through science; otherwise, he avoids people (*az khalq iʿrāḍ kardan*).[41]

---

40. The most explicit texts on this matter are Muḥammad Karīm Khān, *Irshād al-ʿawāmm*, vol. 4, pp. 303–310; *Rujūm al-shayāṭīn*, pp. 81–91; *Sī faṣl*, pp. 26–33 and 102–103; *Chahār faṣl*, pp. 18–20; Muḥammad Khān Kirmānī, *Burhān-i qāṭiʿ*, pp. 17–23, 89–100, 120–127; *Wasīlat al-najāt*, 'maqṣad' 4; 'Risāla dar jawāb-i su'āl-i baʿḍī', in *Majmaʿ al-rasāʾil*, vol. 3; Abu'l-Qāsim Khān Ibrāhīmī, *Fihrist*, pp. 102–110; *Tarjama Rujūm al-shayāṭīn* (Persian trans. of Muḥammad Karīm Khān's work), intro., p. 13.

41. Muḥammad Karīm Khān, *Sī faṣl*, pp. 37–39; for the author's thinking on *jihād*, see also his *al-Risāla al-jihādiyya*. On the history of the Occultation's implications in the doctrinal and legal fields, see my *Guide divin*, appendix, pp. 319–335 (*Divine Guide*, pp. 133–139) and my article 'Remarques sur les critères

3. Alliance and dissociation (*tawallī* and *tabarrī/tabarru'* in Arabic; *tawallā* and *tabarrā* in Persian)

The *tawallī/tabarrā* pair constitutes the third important element of the *rukn rābiʿ*. It involves applying the very old Shiʿi notion of *walāya* and *barāʾa* to the time of the Occultation. Literally, these terms signify, respectively, 'proximity, alliance, association' and 'dissociation, renunciation'. The typically Shiʿi technical meaning of *walāya* is love of, obedience to, alliance with or loyalty to the imams and their cause; the opposite, *barāʾa*, means dissociation from, disobedience to, renunciation and abandonment of the adversaries of the imams.[42]

The fundamental importance of initiation, together with the radically dualist Shiʿi vision, which presents world history as a perpetual battle between the forces of Good and Evil, mean that *walāya/tawallā* and *barāʾa/tabarrā* are inseparable from each other: in a context of cosmic combat between the forces of knowledge and ignorance, to love and vow loyalty to the Imam, the master-initiator, must involve dissociation from and hostility to those who deliberately try to do damage to him and his teaching. This is why I have elsewhere translated the Shiʿi terms *walāya* and *barāʾa* as 'sacred love' and 'sacred hatred'.[43] For the Shaykhiyya masters, during the Occultation and because of it, *tawallā* for the

d'authenticité du ḥadīth et l'autorité du juriste dans le shiʿisme imamite', *SI*, 85 (1997), pp. 5ff. On the evolution of the Imami doctrine of holy war see E. Kohlberg, 'The Development of the Imāmī Shīʿī Doctrine of *jihād*', *ZDMG*, 126 (1976).

42. On *walāya/tawallā* see H. Corbin, *En Islam Iranien*, index, and *Histoire de la philosophie islamique* (Paris, 1986), pp. 66–98; H. Landolt, 'Walāya', in M. Eliade (ed.), *Encyclopaedia of Religion* (New York, 1987), vol. 15; M. M. Bar-Asher, *Scripture and Exegesis in Eary Imāmī Shiism* (Leiden and Jerusalem, 1999), pp. 195–201. On *barāʾa/tabarrā* see E. Kohlberg, '*Barāʾa* in Shīʿī Doctrine', pp. 139–175; J. Calmard, 'Les rituels shiʿites et le pouvoir. L'imposition du shiisme safavide: eulogies et malédictions canoniques', in idem (ed.), *Etudes Safavides*. Publications de l'Institut Français de Recherche en Iran (Tehran, 1993), pp. 117–120; and esp. Chapter 7 in this volume.

43. See *Guide divin*, index. On Imami dualism see ibid., pp. 308–310; Amir-Moezzi and Jambet, *Qu'est-ce que le shiʿisme?* (Paris, 2004), pp. 36f.

hidden Imam also and above all includes *tawallā* for the Imam's friends; that is, 'the men of the mystery' and their head, the 'gate' or 'unique speaker'. Likewise, *tabarrā* for the adversaries and deniers of the hidden Imam includes *tabarrā* for the adversaries and deniers of the secret spiritual hierarchy that renders the hidden Imam's influence on humanity effective.[44] Citing and synthesising the writings of earlier masters of the order on this subject, Abu'l-Qāsim Khān explicitly concluded in his *Fihrist* that, given the fact that 'the men of the mystery' are not known, our only possibility of being honoured by their influence and perhaps of becoming worthy to enter into contact with them is to believe in their existence and vow to love them with a pure, unwavering, disinterested love.[45] Because of the Occultation and its implications, Imamism became an essentially individual religion of pure mystic love for the hidden Imam and his friends and radical dissociation from their adversaries. To give a foundation to his ideas in this domain, Muḥammad Khān Kirmānī, in his *Hidāyat al-mustarshid*,[46] made use of certain ancient traditions: 'Is religion anything else but love?'[47] 'The most solid handle on faith [more solid than prayer, alms-giving, fasting, the pilgrimage to Mecca

44. Muḥammad Karīm Khān, *Irshād al-ʿawāmm*, vol. 4, pp. 274ff., 316ff., 378ff., *Izhāq al-bāṭil*, ch. 3; *Rukn-i rābiʿ*, pp. 34ff.; *Ilzām al-nawāṣib*, pp. 86–87 and 123ff.; *Hidāyat al-ṣibyān*, ch. 4; 'Risāla dar jawāb-i Mullā Muḥammad Jaʿfar Kāzarūnī', in *Majmaʿ al-rasāʾil*, vol. 69, response no. 10; Muḥammad Khān Kirmānī, *Burhān-i qāṭiʿ*, pp. 45–47, 167ff.; *Wasīlat al-najāt*, 'maqṣad' 4, ch. 2; *Hidāyat al-mustarshid*, ch. 5; Zayn al-ʿĀbidīn Khān Kirmānī, 'Risāla dar jawāb-i Mīrzā Sayyid Muḥammad Riḍawī', in *Majmaʿ al-rasāʾil*, vol. 11' 'Risāla dar jawāb-i Shaykh Muḥammad ʿAlī Bahrānī Āl-i ʿUṣfūr', in *Majmaʿ al-rasāʾil*, vol. 82, response no. 2; Abu'l-Qāsim Khān Ibrāhīmī, *Falsafiyya*, response nos 12–16, *Fihrist*, pp. 81–83 (partial trans. and commented on by H. Corbin, *En Islam iranien*, vol. 4, p. 277); ʿAbd al-Riḍā Khān Ibrāhīmī, *Dūstī-ye dūstān* (title may be translated into Arabic thus: *walāya/tawallī al-awliyā*; the entire work is devoted to the subject).

45. *Fihrist*, pp. 109–111.

46. Ch. 5, pp. 187–188.

47. *Hal al-dīn illa'l-ḥubb*, a *ḥadīth* going back to Jaʿfar al-Ṣādiq; see al-ʿAyyāshī, *Tafsīr*, vol. 1, p. 167; Ibn Bābūya, *al-Khiṣāl*, p. 21.

and holy war] is love God and hatred on God's behalf, friendship for the friends of God and enmity for God's enemies';[48] 'Each thing has a foundation; the foundation of Islam is love for us, the *ahl al-bayt* [of the Prophet]'.[49] Unable to personally know the Friends of the hidden Imam, the faithful were invited to believe in their existence and to love them, to make themselves worthy of them, and to prepare themselves spiritually for a possible encounter with them, by leading a life of devotion and purity and studying in depth the doctrine of the imams, for instance with the help of Shaykhī writings.[50]

Who were these adversaries of the hidden Imam, the secret spiritual hierarchy and the unique speaker? Shaykhī polemical writings, of which there are many, are aimed either generally at 'the people of ignorance' (*ahl/aṣḥāb-i jahl*) or, more specifically, at Bābism;[51] the Sufi orders, especially the Imami ones;[52] and above all a certain category of clerics from among the official jurist-the-

48. *Awthaqu ʿura'l-īmān al-ḥubb fi'llāh wa'l-bughḍ fi'llāh wa tawallī awliyā'i'llāh wa'l-tabarrī min aʿdā'i'llāh*, a *ḥadīth* going back to the Prophet; see Ibn Bābūya, *Maʿānī al-akhbār*, pp. 398–399 and *al-Mawāʿiẓ*, p. 25.

49. *Li-kulli shay' asās wa asās al-Islām ḥubbunā ahl al-bayt*, a *ḥadīth* going back to Jaʿfar al-Ṣādiq; see al-Barqī, *al-Maḥāsin*, vol. 1, p. 150; Ibn Bābūya, *al-Mawāʿiẓ*, p. 29 and *al-Amālī*, p. 221.

50. ʿAbd al-Riḍā Khān Ibrāhīmī, *Dūstī-ye dūstān*, pp. 102–104 et passim.

51. See *supra*; and more recently against Bahā'ism; see Abu'l-Qāsim Khān Ibrāhīmī, *Fikrat dar jawāb-i Aqā ʿAlī Darakī*, response nos 4 to 6. The term 'Bālāsarī' is sometimes applied to the non-Shaykhī Shiʿis and not necessarily to the adversaries of the Shaykhīs; see D. M. MacEoin, 'Bālāsarī', *EIr*. On the bloody conflict between Shaykhīs and Bālāsarīs in Kirmān in 1905 see G. Scarcia, 'Kerman 1905: la Guerra tra Sheikhī e Bālāsarī', *AIUON*, new series 13 (1963), pp. 195–238; H. Algar, *Religion and State in Iran 1785–1906* (Berkeley and Los Angeles, 1969), pp. 243–244; Bayat, *Mysticism and Dissent*, pp. 181f.

52. The main criticism here is against the Sufi masters, who usurp the imam's rank and recommend 'heterodox' practices; see Muḥammad Karīm Khān, *Irshād al-ʿawāmm*, vol. 4, pp. 235ff., 241, 294ff.; Muḥammad Khān, *Risāla dar jawāb-i Mullā Muḥammad ʿAlī Salmāsī*, in *Majmaʿ al-rasā'il*, vol. 27, response no. 1; Zayn al-ʿĀbidīn Khān, *Durūs* (vol. 1?), pp. 76–79 and 'Risāla dar jawāb-i Muḥammad Ibrāhīm Khān b. Amīr Aṣlān Khān', in *Majmaʿ al-rasā'il*, vol. 8.

ologians, the Uṣūlī *mujtahids*. More criticism is directed against the Uṣūlī *mujtahids* than any other group, but this criticism is also the most discreet. They are often designated pejoratively in Shaykhī writings as *ʿamala-i jahl* ('agents of ignorance'), *mullā* (*mollah*, as distinct from the true religious learned man, *ʿālim*), *ahl-i ẓāhir* ('people of the exclusively exoteric doctrines') and the like. It is true that the Shaykhiyya, who had themselves been attacked by numerous clerics ever since their order was founded, have always had to be on the defensive; still, in identifying certain *ʿulamāʾ* as enemies of the hidden Imam and inviting the faithful to practice *tabarrā* against them, they were adopting a position that could be called offensive. It was for obvious reasons of tactical dissimulation that, despite the incalculable number of passages criticising this type of figure, criticism that may be found in almost every great Shaykhī work, there is, to my knowledge, no specific chapter or monograph devoted entirely to the subject.[53] What this type of religious man is reproached for is using faith to attain power, glory or wealth; and worse yet, having betrayed Shiʿism, a fundamentally esoteric and theosophic doctrine, by reducing it to little more than the single domain of canon law. It was in speaking of this category of Imami jurist-theologians that Zayn al-ʿĀbidīn Khān declared, 'The enemy is now within the walls of the house' (*imrūz dushman khāna nashīn ast*).[54] When consulting Shaykhī sources, one has the clear impression that for the authors, the main adversaries and deniers of the friends of the hidden Imam were neither non-Muslims, or non-Shiʿis, or even

53. One has only to leaf through the main Shaykhiyya works, especially starting with those of Muḥammad Karīm Khān, to see this. Muḥammad Khān Kirmānī's work, *Risāla Bihbahāniyya*, sums up in a conciliatory tone the Shaykhiyya position toward the Uṣūlī clerics; see also Abu'l-Qāsim Khān Ibrāhīmī's clarifications in *Fihrist*, pp. 83, 89, 95–96, 102–104 and 109. On the tensions between the Shaykhīs and the Uṣūlī clerics see also Bayat, *Mysticism and Dissent*, chs 2 and 3; Amanat, *Resurrection and Renewal*, first part of ch. 1; D. M. MacEoin, 'Orthodoxy and Heterodoxy in Nineteenth-century Shiʿism', *JAOS*, 110/2 (1990), pp. 323–324.

54. Zayn al-ʿĀbidīn Khān Kirmānī, *Durūs*, p. 124.

non-Imamis; rather, they were to be found within the Twelver community itself. They are those who, refusing all hermeneutics of the Occultation, refuse even to believe in the existence of the secret spiritual hierarchy. Responding to religious detractors of the doctrine of the Fourth Pillar, who sarcastically ask how it is that 'the men of the mystery' and 'the unique speaker' never show themselves to defenders of the doctrine of the imams, Muḥammad Karīm Khān used a delightful allegory drawn from popular tales of the Kirmān region:

> One dark night, a monstrously ugly servant was carrying a child on his shoulders. The child [here the symbol of the men of the mystery, the Unique Speaker, or even the hidden Imam] wept the whole time and kept his eyes closed. The servant [here the symbol of certain 'official' Imami clerics] said, 'Why are you afraid? I won't leave you alone.' 'That's just the problem? It's not the dark night [symbol of the surrounding world, the non-Shiʿi world, or perhaps the Shiʿi community as a whole] that frightens me; it's you – you terrify me,' replied the child.[55]

The Occultation within man

As mentioned above, there is a correspondence between the world as macrocosm and man as microcosm.[56] To my knowledge, there are only a few instances of a hermeneutics of the Occultation as an internal event in Shaykhī literature. Following the logic of the Shaykhī authors, we could say that if the doctrine of the *rukn rābiʿ* represents the esoteric aspect (*bāṭin*) of the Occultation, then microcosmic hermeneutics applied to the individual are the esoteric aspect of the esoteric (*bāṭin al-bāṭin*),[57] since traditionally

55. Muḥammad Karīm Khān, *Irshād al-ʿawāmm*, vol. 4, pp. 306–307.
56. See above notes 9 and 10 and the texts cited there.
57. See above notes 5 and 8 and the texts cited there.

the more esoteric the doctrinal material is, the rarer, more allusive and more fragmentary our information about it becomes.[58] Sayyid Kāẓim al-Rashtī seems to have been the first author to clearly expound this type of hermeneutics of the Occultation. In his *Risāla fī jawāb Mullā ʿAlī Baraghānī*, he wrote:

> As for the hidden Qā'im, his example in you is your intelligence (*ʿaql*), which is manifest in the Primordial World (*al-ʿālam al-awwal*);[59] then you [that is, your mind] began the descent, and at that point cold, wet and all kinds of dense elements (*kathāfāt*) dominated you, which caused the occultation of intelligence and its dissimulation. However, intelligence never stops directing and organising the vital forces (*al-bunya*), the body, the mind and other functions, while remaining hidden and non-manifest. At the age of fourteen, intelligence begins to manifest itself, and at that time the vital forces begin to increase. Intelligence manifests itself and fills the body with equity and justice, just as earlier it overflowed with oppression and injustice [or 'darkness'],[60] due to the different dominations of the authoritarian soul (*al-nafs al-ammāra*), which is the [real] unjust sovereign (*sulṭān al-jawr*) [Thanks to the intelligence] the body becomes filled with faculties, such as apperception (*idrāk*), understanding (*fahm*), serenity (*ṭuma'nīna*), and calm (*sukūn*). In this way, the continuous growth of intelligence and its sovereignty are fortified until the age of forty, when its manifestation and balance reach their peak. As for the places of residence [literally, the 'cities', *madā'in*] of the hidden Imam, the Green Isle (*al-jazīra al-khaḍrā'*)[61] corresponds to the breast and the soul

58. See my 'Du droit à la théologie', esp. pp. 41ff.

59. This is no doubt an allusion to the cosmogonic dimension of *ʿaql*; See *Guide divin*, pp. 18–21 (*Divine Guide*, pp. 7–8) and my 'Cosmogony and Cosmology in Twelver Shiʿism', *EIr*, vol. 6, esp. p. 320.

60. This is a citation of the hallowed description of the hidden Imam's triumphant return at the end of time: 'the Mahdī will manifest himself [or "raise himself up"] at the End of Time and fill the earth with equity and justice just as before it overflowed with oppression and injustice [or "darkness"]' (*sa yaẓhuru'l-mahdī fī ākhir al-zamān fa yamla'u'l-arḍ qisṭan wa ʿadlan kamā mali'at jawran wa ẓulman [ẓuluman]*).

61. Allusion to the Green Isle in the White Sea, traditionally understood as the hidden Imam's place of residence during the Occultation; see Corbin,

> (*al-ṣadr wa'l-nafs*) and the White Sea corresponds to the lights of intelligence (*al-anwār al-ʿaqliyya*) thanks to which all cities and countries – that is, all the human faculties – reach their perfection in the light. These cities will be full of greenery and waterways if irrigated by science and action. (…) It is reported that the oath of fidelity (*bayʿa*) to the hidden Imam will be concluded in the fourth climate [i.e. in the median climate of the seven climates, at the centre of the world]; this corresponds to Jesus, who lives in the fourth Heaven, who is the Spirit of God and His Word (…) and who corresponds to man's heart, which is the first [organ] to which the orders and graces of intelligence come.[62] The Chiefs [*al-nuqabā'*; i.e. the chosen companions of the hidden Imam] correspond to the ten purified senses (the five external and five internal senses), plus the breast (i.e. the seat of the mind) and the body of light [*al-jism al-nūrānī*; i.e. the subtle spiritual body],[63] for their gaze is directed toward the supreme face [an enigmatic expression: *min ḥayth naẓaruhā ila'l-wajh al-aʿlā*]; whereas those who flee and cannot bear [the Return of the hidden Imam] correspond to the other faculties and organs, whose gaze is directed toward the lowest face (*naẓaruhā ila'l-wajh al-asfal*).[64]

In his *Fihrist*, Abu'l-Qāsim Khān mentioned two other writings by Sayyid Kāẓim which, according to his cursory description of them, could also involve an 'interiorist' hermeneutics of the Occultation.

The first, on the hidden Qā'im's *taṣarruf* – a technical term that could be translated as 'the esoteric government of world affairs' – and the support he brings to those who serve him, seems to have been lost. Of the second, on the profound reason (*ḥikma*, lit.

En Islam iranien, vol. 4, pp. 346ff. For the sources of this late tradition and discussions of it see Chapter 13, n. 79, this volume.

62. In Muslim eschatology, Jesus is generally considered one of the Mahdī-Qā'im's primary companions.

63. Sayyid Kāẓim seems to be indicating here that the *nuqabā'* form a group of twelve persons (see *supra* note 26 and the corresponding text); he says nothing, however, of the *nujabā'*.

64. Al-Sayyid Kāẓim al-Rashtī, *al-Rasā'il wa'l-masā'il*, pp. 334–335. The parallel and correspondence between *ʿaql* and the Imam are to be found very early in Shiʿism; see *Guide divin*, index under "*aql*' and here the opening of chapter 12.

wisdom) of the Occultation, there seems to be only an old lithographed version extant, which unfortunately I was not able to find.[65]

In addition to this symbolic hermeneutic, the Shaykhī authors propose a theological hermeneutic of the Occultation within man that is even more veiled and allusive. It is developed through a commentary on the famous *ḥadīth* attributed to ʿAlī: 'He who knows himself knows his Lord' (*man ʿarafa nafsahu fa-qad ʿarafa rabbah*). It seems that this hermeneutic, which dates back to al-Rashtī's work, was given a typically Shiʿi interpretation originating in the former theological approach of a theophany, centred on Imamology. Because the Divine Essence is forever unknowable, God can only be known through His Names and Attributes. The latter manifest themselves in the cosmic Imam, the metaphysical Perfect Man, who, in turn, manifests himself in a way perceivable to the senses through the persons of the historical imams.[66] The hidden meaning (*bāṭin*) of this tradition is therefore summed up in the formula: 'He who knows his Imam knows his Lord' (*man ʿarafa imāmahu fa-qad ʿarafa rabbah*).[67] Juxtaposing these two statements produces the following conclusion: 'He who knows himself knows his Imam, who is his Lord.' For the individual, knowledge of the reality of the Imam, who is the true God revealed, is the equivalent of knowledge of the true Self (*al-nafs al-ḥaqīqiyya*), the divine particle (*juzʾ ilāhī*) present in each

65. Abu'l-Qāsim Khān Ibrāhīmī, *Fihrist*, p. 313 ('Risāla dar jawāb-i Shaykh Muhammad b. Shaykh ʿAbd ʿAlī ʿAbd al-Jabbār al-Qaṭīfī') and p. 353 ('Risāla dar jawab-i su'ālāt-i Isfahān', response no. 3).

66. On this aspect of theology and illustrations of it in the 'theo-Imamosophical' sermons attributed to ʿAlī, see Chapter 3 in this volume.

67. Sayyid Kāẓim al-Rashtī, *Sharḥ al-khuṭba al-ṭatanjiyya/ṭutunjiyya*, pp. 13–14; al-Rashtī, 'Risāla fī jawāb ʿAbd Allāh Beg', in *al-Rasāʾil wa'l-masāʾil*, pp. 221–224, response no. 17; Muḥammad Karīm Khān, 'Risāla dar jawāb-i Mullā Muḥammad ʿAlī Dawānī', in *Majmaʿ al-rasāʾil*, vol. 67, response no. 29; Muḥammad Khān Kirmānī, 'Risāla dar jawāb-i Ḥājj ʿAbbās Būshihrī', in *Majmāʿ al-rasāʾil*, vol. 26, response no. 1; Zayn al-ʿĀbidīn Khān, 'Risāla dar jawāb-i Muḥammad Ṣādiq Khān Nāʾīnī', in *Majmaʿ al-rasāʾil*, vol. 8, response no. 3.

person's heart.[68] In this way, the Shaykhiyya masters contributed to a tradition of exegesis of the *ḥadīth* in question, a tradition very present in Imami mysticism from Ḥaydar Āmulī to Mullā Ṣadrā, Abu'l-Ḥasan al-Iṣfahānī, and all the way up to Sulṭān ʿAlī Shāḥ Gunābādī.[69] Moreover, for the Shaykhiyya this hermeneutic, which could be called theo-imamological, is related to a spiritual topography of the Imam's 'World' and a mystical physiology of the believer. As many studies have shown, in the Shaykhiyya vision, the World of the Imam's reality, called *hūrqalyā* (*hawarqalyā* or *huwarqalyā*), is a metaphysical world halfway between the spiritual and the physical worlds and ontologically as real as the perceptible world.[70] The description by the traditionalist philosopher Muḥsin al-Fayḍ al-Kāshānī (d. 1091/1680) of the *ʿālam al-mithāl* applies perfectly here: 'a world in which spirits are embodied and bodies are spiritualised'.[71] This 'location' of the concrete reality of spiritual visions and experiences may be reached by the believer who has developed the 'organs of *hūrqalyā*' (*aʿḍāʾ hūrqalyāwiyya*) – most

68. Al-Sayyid Kāẓim al-Rashtī, 'Risāla fī jawāb 'Abd Allāh Beg', p. 224; Muḥammad Karīm Khān, *Ṭarīq al-najāt*, pp. 103–105; Muḥammad Khān, *Wāridāt*, 'Wārida' 3 and esp. 8; Zayn al-ʿĀbidīn Khān, 'Risāla dar jāwāb-i Muhammad Sādiq Khān Nāʾīnī'.

69. Cf. Ḥaydar Āmolī, *Jāmiʿ al-asrār*, pp. 270, 307–309, 315, 464, 'Risāla naqd al-nuqūd fī maʿrifat al-wujūd', in *Jāmiʿ al-asrār*, p. 675; Mullā Ṣadrā Shīrāzī, *Kitāb al-mashāʿir*, pp. 186–188 and *Sharḥ al-Uṣūl min al-Kāfī*, pp. 475–476; Abu'l-Ḥasan Sharīf al-Iṣfaḥānī, *Tafsīr mirʾāt al-anwār*, intro., esp. pp. 13–15; Sulṭān ʿAlī Shāh Gunābādī, *Bishārat al-muʾminīn*, ch. 6, and *Walāyat-nāmeh*, pp. 11–12, 18–21, 171–173, 258–261. In his commentaries on this same *ḥadīth* al-Shaykh Aḥmad al-Aḥsāʾī seems to be close to this exegetical tradition, see his *Sharḥ al-Ziyāra al-jāmiʿa*, p. 323; al-Aḥsāʾī, *Sharḥ al-Fawāʾid*, pp. 25ff. See also J. Cole, 'Casting Away the Self: the Mysticism of Shaykh Aḥmad al-Aḥsāʾī', in R. Brunner and W. Ende (eds), *The Twelver Shia in Modern Times: Religious Culture and Political History* (Leiden, 2001), pp. 25–37.

70. M. Moʿīn, '*Havarqalyā*', *Nashriyye-ye Dāneshkade-ye Adabiyyāt-e Dānesgāh-e Tehrān* (1333 Sh./1955), pp. 78–105; Corbin, *En Islam iranien*, index under 'Hūrqalyā', and *Corps spirituel et terre céleste: De l'Iran mazdéen à l'Iran shiʿite* (Paris, 1979), chs 9–11; Rafati, 'The Development of Shaykhī Thought', pp. 106ff.

71. Al-Fayḍ al-Kāshānī, *Kalimāt maknūna*, p. 70.

importantly, the 'eye capable of knowing the Imam' (*chashm-i imām shinās*) – thanks to his perpetual devotions and purifying asceticism.[72] It should be noted that Muḥammad Karīm Khān Kirmānī and Abu'l-Qāsim Khān Ibrāhīmī explicitly identify the World of *hūrqalyā* with the 'place' of the hidden Imam during the major Occultation.[73] To reach the reality of the hidden Imam, the living Imam of our times, in the *hūrqalyā*, one must acquire the subtle body particular to this World (*jism hūrqalyāwī*) and the necessary organ, 'the eye capable of knowing the Imam', also called 'the heart's eye' (*chashm-i dil*). Conversely, the esoteric role of the historical Imam – here, of course, the hidden Imam understood as the living Imam of our time – is to enable the discovery of the internal Imam, the Lord hidden in the believer's heart, and to actualise that Imam.[74] The heart's eye and the subtle *hūrqalyāwī* body constitute the true Self, knowledge of which is the equivalent of knowledge of the Imam who is the Lord within each person.

72. See e.g. Shaykh Aḥmad al-Aḥsā'ī, *Sharḥ al-Ziyāra*, vol. 1, pp. 369ff., 'al-Risāla al-Qaṭīfiyya', in *Jawāmiʿ al-kalim*, vol. 1, p. 136, 'Risāla fī jawāb Mullā Ḥusayn al-Anbārī al-Kirmānī', in *Jawāmiʿ al-kalim*, vol. 1, pp. 153–154, 'Risāla fī jawāb Ākhūnd Mullā Ḥusayn Anārī', in *Jawāmiʿ al-kalim*, vol. 1, p. 204, 'Risāla Rashtiyya fī jawāb Mullā 'Alī b. Mīrzā Jān Rashtī', in *Jawāmiʿ al-kalim*, vol. 1, p. 312, response no. 28; Sayyid Kāẓim al-Rashtī, *Sharḥ al-khuṭba al-ṭatanjiyya/ṭutunjiyya*, intro. Muḥammad Karīm Khān, *Irshād al-ʿawāmm*, vol. 2, pp. 274–275; 'Risāla dar jawāb-i Mullā Muḥammad 'Alī Dawānī', in *Majmaʿ al-rasā'il*, vol. 67, response no. 61; 'Risāla dar amr-i jinn', last section, in *Majmaʿ al-rasā'il*, vol. 67; Zayn al-'Ābidīn Khān, 'Risāla dar jawāb-i Shaykh Muḥammad Bihbahānī dar Jābalqā wa Jābarsā', in *Majmaʿ al-rasā'il*, vol. 29, 'Risāla dar jawāb-i Muḥammad Ṣādiq Khān Nā'īnī', response no. 10; Abu'l-Qāsim Khān Ibrāhīmī, *Tanzīh al-awliyā'*, pp. 702–726.

73. Muḥammad Karīm Khān, *Irshād al-ʿawāmm*, vol. 2, pp. 275–276; Abu'l-Qāsim Khān Ibrāhīmī, *Tanzīh al-awliyā'*, pp. 724–726; tr. Corbin, *Corps spirituel et terre céleste*, pp. 262–264 and 287–290.

74. Abu'l-Qāsim Khān, *Tanzīh al-awliyā'*, p. 725. On 'vision by (or "within") the heart' (*al-ru'ya bi'l-qalb*) and 'the heart's eye' (*'ayn al-qalb*) in ancient and modern Imamism, see respectively *Guide divin*, pp. 112–145 (*Divine Guide*, ch. 2, section 3, 'Excursus: "Vision with the Heart"') and R. Gramlich, *Die schiitischen Derwischorden Persiens*, 3 vols (Wiesbaden, 1979–1981), vol. 2: *Glaube und Lehre*, p. 207, n. 1073 and pp. 247–250. And Chapter 10, this volume.

According to this hermeneutic of the Occultation within man, each person's hidden Imam, his true hidden Guide, is his true Self, his divine Self, buried in the secrecy of his heart.

At the end of the third/ninth century, the mysterious fate of the putative son of imam al-Ḥasan al-ʿAskarī threw the Imami community into disarray. The absence of the Imam's authority in a religion governed completely by the figure of the Imam, plunged the faithful into what is traditionally called *al-ḥayra* – confusion, perplexity.[75] Yet even after the Occultation theology was established, the problem of the absence of legitimate authority – in temporal matters of course, but perhaps even more in spiritual ones – remained intact. This is why, for more than a millennium, the history of Imami doctrine consists essentially in the devising of different solutions to this problem, solutions which vary according to the different religious movements but which are all various ways of filling the void created by this absence. Viewed from this angle, the history of post-*ghayba* Imamism may be perceived as a great attempt, rich in options, of coping with the absence of a legitimate supreme authority. Rationalist scholars, traditionalist scholars, philosophers, Sufis and so on, each in their own way, filled this absence with all sorts of presences. In this plurality of approaches to the problem, the Shaykhī hermeneutics of the Occultation, seeking to fill both the world and man with 'the presence' of the hidden Imam, undoubtedly constitutes one of the most complex and highly structured of these solutions.

---

75. This is a much-studied phenomenon; I note here only the most recent and authoritative monographs: J. M. Hussain, *The Occultation of the Twelfth Imam: A Historical Background* (London, 1982); V. Klemm, 'Die vier *Sufarā'* des Zwölften Imams. Zur formativen Periode der Zwölferschia', *Die Welt des Orients*, 15 (1984), pp. 126–143; H. Modarressi, *Crisis and Consolidation in the Formative Period of Shiʿite Islam: Abū Jaʿfar ibn Qiba al-Rāzī and his Contribution to Imāmite Shīʿite Thought* (Princeton, 1993); S. A. Arjomand, 'The Consolation of Theology: Absence of the Imam and Transition from Chiliasm to Law in Shiʿism', *The Journal of Religion*, 21 (1996), pp. 548–571; idem, 'The Crisis of the Imamate and the Institution of Occultation', *IJMES*, 28 (1996), pp. 491–515; idem, '*Imam Absconditus* and the Beginnings of a Theology of Occultation: Imami Shiʿism *circa* 280–90/900 A.D.', *JAOS*, 117/1 (1997), pp. 1–12.

Bibliography

Primary sources

Abu'l-Aswad al-Du'alī. *Dīwān*, ed. M. Ḥ. Āl-Yāsīn. Beirut, 1974.

Abū Dāwūd. *Sunan*, ed. M. M. ʿAbd al-Ḥamīd. Cairo, n.d.

Abū Dulaf. *Safar-Nāma dar Īrān*, bā taʿlīqāt-e V. Minorsky, tr. A. F. Ṭabāṭabāʾī. Tehran, 1342 Sh./1964.

Abu'l-Faraj al-Iṣfahānī. *Kitāb al-aghānī*. Būlāq, Cairo, 1285/1868.

—— *Maqātil al-Ṭālibiyyīn*, ed. S. A. Ṣaqr. Cairo, 1949; rpr. Qumm, 1416/1995.

Abu'l-Ḥajjāj, Yūsuf b. Muḥammad. *K. Alif-bāʾ*. Cairo, 1287/1870.

Abū Ḥanīfa, al-imām. *al-Fiqh al-akbar*. 2nd edn, Hyderabad, 1399/1979.

Abū Yūsuf, Yaʿqūb b. Ibrāhīm. *Kitāb al-kharāj*, ed. Iḥsān ʿAbbās. Beirut and London, 1985.

Afshārī, M. see Mīr ʿĀbedīnī, S. A.

al-Aḥsāʾī, Shaykh Aḥmad. *Jawāmiʿ al-kilam/kalim*. Lithograph, Tabriz, 1273–1276/1856–1858.

—— 'Risāla fī jawāb ākhūnd Mullā Ḥusayn Anbārī', in *Jawāmiʿ al-kilam*, vol. 1, p. 204.

—— 'al-Risāla al-Qaṭīfiyya', in *Jawāmiʿ al-kilam*, vol. 1, pp. 117–120.

—— 'Risāla Rashtiyya fī jawāb Mullā ʿAlī ibn Mīrzā Jān Rashtī', in *Jawāmiʿ al-kilam*, vol. 1, pp. 312–315.

—— 'al-Risāla al-Tawbaliyya (= Lawāmiʿ al-wasāʾil)', in *Jawāmiʿ al-kilam*, vol. 1, pp. 95–99.

—— *Sharḥ al-Fawāʾid*. Lithograph n.p. [Tabriz], 1254/1838.

—— *Sharḥ al-Ziyāra al-jāmiʿa*. Lithograph, Tabriz, n.d. and Tabriz, 1276/1859.

Akhbār al-dawla al-ʿAbbāsiyya, ed. ʿA.ʿA. Dūrī and A. J. Muṭṭalibī. Beirut, 1971.

Āl Ḥaydar, Sayyid Muṣṭafā. *Bishārat al-Muṣṭafā*. Tehran, n.d.

Alqāb al-rasūl wa ʿitratihi, in *Majmūʿa nafīsa fī taʾrīkh al-aʾimma*. Qumm, 1396/1976.

al-Amīn al-ʿĀmilī, Sayyid Muḥsin. *Aʿyān al-Shīʿa*. Damascus and Beirut, 1354–1382/1935–1963.

—— *Miftāḥ al-jannāt*. Beirut, 1389/1969.

Āmolī, Sayyid Ḥaydar. *Jāmiʿ al-asrār wa manbaʿ al-anwār* and *Naqd al-nuqūd fī maʿrifat al-wujūd*, ed. H. Corbin and O. Yahia. Tehran and Paris, 1969.

ʿAnqā, Shāh Maqṣūd. *Zavāyā-ye makhfī-ye ḥayātī*. Tehran, 1354/1975.

—— *Sirr al-ḥajar*. Tehran, 1359/1980.

al-Ardabīlī. *Jāmiʿ al-ruwāt*. Qumm, 1331 Sh./1953.

Ardashīr b. (or Bon-) Shāhī. *Ganjīne-ye adab*. Bombay, 1373/1952.

al-Ashʿarī. *Maqālāt al-Islāmiyyin*, ed. H. Ritter. Revised edn, Wiesbaden, 1963.

Ashkevarī, Quṭb al-Dīn. *Maḥbūb al-qulūb* (Parts 1 and 2), ed. I. al-Dībājī and Ḥ. Ṣidqī. Tehran, 1378 Sh./1999 and 1382 Sh./2004.

ʿAṭṭār Nīshābūrī, Farīd al-Dīn. *Tadhkirat al-awliyāʾ*, ed. M. Esteʿlāmī. 2nd edn, Tehran, 1355 Sh./1977.

al-ʿAyyāshī. *Tafsīr*, ed. H. Rasūlī Maḥallātī. Tehran, n.d.; Qumm, 1380/1960.

al-Baghawī, Abū Muḥammad. *Tafsīr al-Baghawī al-musammā bi Maʿālim al-tanzīl*, ed. Ḥ. ʿA. al-ʿAkk and M. Sawār. Beirut, 1992.

al-Baghdādī. *al-Farq bayn al-firaq*, ed. M. Badr. Cairo, 1328/1910; ed. M. ʿAbd al-Ḥamīd. Cairo, n.d.

al-Baḥrānī, Hāshim b. Sulaymān, *al-Lawāmiʾ al-nūrāniyya*. Isfahan, 1404/1983.

—— *al-Burhān fī tafsīr al-Qurʾān*. 5 vols. Tehran, n.d.

—— *Madīnat al-maʿājiz fī dalāʾil al-aʾimmat al-aṭhār wa maʿājizihim*. Tehran, n.d. [ca. 1960].

—— *Ḥilyat al-abrār fī faḍā'il Muḥammad wa ālihi'l-aṭhār*. Qumm, 1397/1978.

—— *Tabṣirat al-walī fī man ra'a'l-qā'im al-mahdī*. Tehran, n.d.

al-Baḥrānī, Yūsuf. *Lu'lu'at al-Baḥrayn*. Najaf, 1386/1966.

al-Baḥrānī al-Iṣfahānī. *ʿAwālim al-ʿulūm*. Qumm, 1409/1988.

al-Bakrī, Abū ʿUbayd. *Muʿjam mā staʿjam*, ed. M. al-Saqqā. Cairo, 1364–1371/1945–1951.

al-Balādhurī. *Futūḥ al-buldān*, ed. M. J. de Goeje. Leiden, 1866; rpr. 1968.

—— *Ansāb al-ashrāf*, vols. 2 and 3, ed. M. B. al-Maḥmūdī. Beirut, 1974.

—— vol. 4/a, ed. M. Schloessinger and M. J. Kister. Jerusalem, 1972.

—— vol. 4/b, ed. M. Schloessinger. Jerusalem, 1961.

—— vol. 5, ed. S. Goitein. Jerusalem, 1936.

al-Balkhī, Abu'l-Maʿālī Muḥammad. *Bayān al-adyān*, ed. M. T. Dānesh-Pažūh. Tehran, 1376 Sh./1997.

Bāqirī Namīnī, Shaykh Muḥammad Qādir. *Dīn va del*. Tehran, 1356 Sh./1977–1978.

al-Barqī. *Kitāb al-maḥāsin*, ed. J. Muḥaddith (Urmawī). Tehran, 1370/1950.

al-Bayhaqī. *Dalā'il al-nubuwwa*, ed. M. ʿUthmān. Cairo, 1969.

Bihbahānī, Aḥmad b. Muḥammad ʿAlī. *Mir'āt al-aḥwāl-e jahān namā*, ed. ʿA. Davānī. Tehran, 1372 Sh./1993.

al-Bīrūnī. *al-Āthār al-bāqiya*, ed. C. E. Sachau. Leipzig, 1878; tr. C. E. Sachau as *The Chronology of Ancient Nations*. London, 1897; rpr. Frankfurt, 1969.

al-Bukhārī. *Ṣaḥīḥ*. Cairo 1378/1958; French tr. O. Houdas and W. Marçais as *Les traditions islamiques*. Paris, 1903–1914; rpr. 1977.

al-Bursī al-Ḥāfiẓ, Rajab. *Mashāriq anwār al-yaqīn*. 10th edn, Beirut, n.d.; partial French tr. H. Corbin (ed. and completed by P. Lory) as *Les Orients des Lumières*. Paris and Lagrasse, 1996.

al-Damāvandī, ʿAbd al-Raḥīm. *Sharḥ-e asrār-e asmā'-e ḥosnā = Meftāḥ-e asrār-e ḥoseyni*, S. J. Ashtiyānī (ed.), *Montakhabātī az āthār-e ḥokamā-ye elāhī-ye Īrān*. Tehran and Paris, 1976.

al-Damīrī. *Ḥayāt al-ḥayawān al-kubrā*. Cairo, 1306/1888.

Dārāb Hormazyār's Rivāyat, ed. M. R. Unvala. Bombay, 1922.
al-Dārimī. *al-Sunan*. Medina, 1386/1966.
al-Daylamī, Ḥasan b. Muḥammad. *Irshād al-qulūb ilāʾl-ṣawāb*. Najaf, 1342/1923; Qumm, n.d.
Dehkordī, Sayyid Aḥmad. *Borhān-nāme-ye ḥaqīqat*. Tehran, n.d.
al-Dīnawarī, Abū Ḥanīfa. *K. al-Akhbār al-ṭiwāl*, ed. V. Guirgass. Leiden, 1888; Persian tr. Ṣ. Nashʾat. Tehran, 1346 Sh./1968; Persian tr. M. Mahdavī Dāmghānī. Tehran, 1366 Sh./1988.
Fayyāḍ-e Lāhījī. *Dīvān*, ed. A. B. Karīmī. Tehran, 1372 Sh./1993.
Firdawsī, *Shāh-Nāma*, ed. Moscow; rpr. Tehran, 1350 Sh./1972.
Furāt b. Ibrāhīm al-Kūfī. *Tafsīr*, ed. Muḥammad al-Kāẓim. Tehran, 1410/1990.
al-Ghaffārī, Qāḍī Aḥmad b. Muḥammad. *Tārīkh-e jahān ārā*. Tehran, 1343 Sh./1965.
Gorgānī, Fakhr al-Dīn Asʿad. *Vīs o Rāmīn*, ed. M. Mīnovī and M. J. Maḥjūb. Tehran, 1337 Sh./1959.
al-Ḥāʾirī al-Yazdī, ʿAlī. *Ilzām al-nāṣib fī ithbāt al-ḥujjat al-ghāʾib*. Tehran, n.d.; rpr. Isfahan, 1351/1932.
al-Ḥalabī. *al-Sīraʾl-Ḥalabiyya*. Beirut, n.d.
al-Ḥalabī, Muḥammad b. Ṭalḥa. *al-Durr al-munaẓẓam fiʾl-sirr al-aʿẓam*. n.p., 1331/1912.
al-Hamadhānī, al-Sayyid ʿAlī. *al-Mawadda fiʾl-qurbā*, in the margins of al-Qundūzī's *Yanābīʿ al-mawadda*. Bombay, n.d.
al-Ḥasan al-ʿAskarī (attrib.), *Tafsīr*. Lithograph, Lucknow, 1310/1893.
Ḥassān b. Thābit. *Dīwān*, ed. W. N. Arafat. London, 1971.
Ḥazīn-e Lāhījī. *Dīvān*, ed. B. Taraqqī. Tehran, 1350 Sh./1971.
al-Ḥillī, al-ʿAllāma. *Khulāṣat al-aqwāl (= Rijāl al-ʿAllāma)*. Najaf, 1961.
—— *Minhāj al-ṣalāḥ fī ikhtiṣār al-Miṣbāḥ*. Qumm, 1419/1998.
al-Ḥillī, al-Ḥasan b. Sulaymān. *Mukhtaṣar baṣāʾir al-darajāt*. Qumm, n.d.
al-Ḥillī, Ibn Dāwūd. *K. al-Rijāl*. Tehran, 1964 and Najaf, 1972.
al-Ḥillī, Ibn Fahd. *ʿUddat al-dāʿī wa najāḥ al-sāʿī*, ed. F. Ḥassūn Fāris. Qumm, 1420/1999.
—— *Mukhtaṣar ʿUddat al-dāʿī*, ed. F. Ḥassūn Fāris in *Turāthunā* (1421/2000), pp. 55–56; latest Persian tr. Ḥ. Fashāhī. Tehran, 1379/1959–1960.

Hindī, Sayyid Hādī. *Tanbīh al-ghāfilīn wa surūr al-nāẓirīn*. n.p. [Tabriz], n.d.

Hūd b. Muḥkim/Muḥakkam. *Tafsīr*, ed. B. Sharīfī. Beirut, 1990.

Ḥudūd al-ʿālam, tr. V. Minorsky as *The Regions of the World*. Oxford and London, 1937.

al-Ḥurr al-ʿĀmilī. *al-Īqāẓ min al-hajʿa fi'l-burhān ʿalā'l-rajʿa*, ed. H. Rasūlī Maḥallātī. Qumm, 1381/1962.

—— *al-Jawāhir al-saniyya fī al-aḥādith al-qudsiyya*. Baghdad, 1964.

—— *Ithbāt al-hudāt bi'l-nuṣūṣ wa'l-muʿjizāt*. 3rd edn, Tehran, 1364 Sh./1985.

al-Ḥusayn b. ʿAbd al-Wahhāb. *ʿUyūn al-muʿjizāt*. Najaf, n.d.; Najaf, 1369/1950.

al-Ḥusaynī, Sayyid Muḥammad. *Kifāyat al-muhtadī*. Tehran, 1320/1902.

Ibn ʿAbd Rabbih. *al-ʿIqd al-farīd*. Cairo, 1316/1898.

Ibn Abi'l-Ḥadid. *Sharḥ Nahj al-balāgha*. Cairo, 1330/1911, 4 vols; ed. M. A. Ibrāhīm. Cairo, 1965.

Ibn Abī Shayba. *al-Muṣannaf*, ed. S. M. al-Laḥḥām. Beirut, 1409/1989, 9 vols.

Ibn Abi'l-Thalj al-Baghdādī. *Ta'rīkh al-a'imma*, in *Majmūʿa nafīsa fī ta'rīkh al-a'imma*. Qumm, 1396/1976.

Ibn Abī Yaʿlā al-Farrā'. *Ṭabaqāt al-ḥanābila*. Damascus, 1923; rpr. Beirut, ca. 1980.

Ibn al-ʿArabī. *al-Futūḥāt al-Makkiyya*, ed. Būlāq. Cairo, 1329/1911.

—— *Muḥāḍarat al-abrār*. Beirut, 1968.

Ibn Aʿtham al-Kūfī. *al-Futūḥ*, Persian tr. Muḥammad b. Aḥmad Harawī (6th/12th c.), ed. Gh. Ṭabāṭabā'ī Majd. Tehran, 1374 Sh./1995.

Ibn al-Athīr. *al-Kāmil fi'l-ta'rīkh*, ed. C. J. Tornberg. Leiden, 1851–1876; rpr. Beirut, 1385–1386/1965–1966; Persian tr. of the volume on the conquest of Iran, M. E. Bāstānī Pārīzī as *Akhbār-e Īrān az* al-Kāmil-*e Ibn Athīr*. Tehran, 1349 Sh./1971.

—— *al-Nihāya fī gharīb al-ḥadīth wa'l-athar*, ed. al-Zāwī and al-Tināḥī. Cairo, 1963–1966; rpr. Beirut, n.d.

—— *Usd al-ghāba*, ed. M. Fāyiḍ et al. Cairo, 1963–1972.
Ibn ʿAyyāsh al-Jawharī. *Muqtaḍab al-athar*, ed. H. Rasūlī Maḥallātī. Qumm, n.d.
Ibn Bābūya, ʿAlī b. al-Ḥusayn. *al-Imāma wa'l-tabṣira min al-ḥayra*. Qumm, 1404/1984.
Ibn Bābūya al-Ṣadūq. *Amālī/Majālis*, M. B. Kamareʾī; rpr. Tehran, 1404/1984; ed. Ṭabāṭabāʾī Yazdī; rpr. Tehran, 1404/1984.
—— *ʿIlal al-sharāʾiʿ*. Najaf, 1385/1966.
—— *Kamāl al-dīn wa tamām al-niʿma*, ed. ʿA. A. Ghaffārī; rpr. Qumm, 1405/1985.
—— *K. al-khiṣāl*, ed. ʿA. A. Ghaffārī. Qumm, 1403/1984.
—— *K. man lā yaḥḍuruhu'l-faqīh*, ed. al-Mūsawī al-Kharsān. 5th edn, n.p., 1390/1970.
—— *K. al-tawḥīd*, ed. al-Ḥusaynī al-Ṭihrānī. Tehran, 1398/1978; classical Persian tr. Muḥammad ʿAlī b. Muḥammad Ḥasan Ardakānī as *Asrār-e towḥīd*. Tehran, n.d.
—— *Maʿānī al-akhbār*, ed. ʿA. A. Ghaffārī. Tehran, 1379/1959.
—— *al-Mawāʿiẓ*. Qumm, n.d.
—— *Muṣādaqat al-ikhwān*. Tehran, n.d. [ca. 1325 Sh./1946].
—— *Risālat al-iʿtiqādāt al-imāmiyya*. Tehran, n.d.; English tr. A. A. A. Fyzee as *A Shiʿite Creed*. Oxford, 1942.
—— *Ṣifāt al-Shīʿa*, with *Faḍāʾil al-Shīʿa*, ed. Ḥ. Fashāhī. Tehran, 1342 Sh./1963–1964.
—— *Thawāb al-aʿmāl wa ʿiqāb al-aʿmāl*, ed. ʿA. A. Ghaffārī. Tehran, 1391/1971.
—— *ʿUyūn akhbār al-Riḍā*, ed. M. al-Ḥusaynī al-Lājevardī. Tehran, 1378/1958; Persian tr. Riḍāʾī and Ṣāʿidī [based on the edn by M. B. Bihbūdī]. Tehran, 1976.
Ibn al-Biṭrīq al-Ḥillī. *al-ʿUmda fī ʿuyūn ṣiḥāḥ al-akhbār*. n.p., n.d.
—— *Khaṣāʾiṣ waḥy al-mubīn fī manāqib amīr al-muʾminīn*. n.p., n.d.; ed. M. B. al-Maḥmūdī. Tehran, 1406/1986.
Ibn Durayd. *Kitāb al-ishtiqāq*, ed. ʿA. M. Hārūn. Baghdad, 1399/1979.
Ibn al-Faqīh. *K. al-Buldān*, ed. Y. al-Hādī. Beirut, 1416/1996.
Ibn Fūrak. *Mushkil al-ḥadīth*, ed. M. M. ʿAlī. Cairo, 1979; ed. D. Gimaret. Damascus, 2003.

Ibn Ḥabīb. *Kitāb al-muḥabbar*, ed. I. Lichtenstaedter. Hyderabad, 1942.

Ibn Ḥajar al-ʿAsqalānī. *Tahdhīb al-tahdhīb*. Hyderabad, 1907–1909; rpr. Beirut, 1968.

Ibn Ḥamza. *al-Thāqib fi'l-manāqib*, ed. N. R. ʿUlwān. Beirut, 1411/1992.

Ibn Ḥanbal. *Musnad*, ed. Muḥammad al-Zuhrī al-Ghamrāwī. Cairo, 1313/1896.

—— *Kitāb al-sunna*. Mecca, 1349/1930.

Ibn Ḥazm. *al-Fiṣal fi'l-milal*, 5 vols. Cairo, 1347/1928; ed. Baghdad, n.d.

Ibn Hishām, ʿAbd al-Malik. *al-Sīra al-nabawiyya*, ed. M. Saqqā, I. Abyārī and ʿA. Shalabī. 2nd edn, Cairo, 1955.

Ibn al-ʿIbrī (Bar Hebraeus). *Ta'rīkh mukhtaṣar al-duwal*. Tehran, n.d.

Ibn ʿInaba. *ʿUmdat al-ṭālib fī ansāb āl Abī Ṭālib*. Qumm, 1417/1996.

Ibn Isḥāq. *Sīra Ibn Isḥāq al-musammāt bi kitāb al-mubtada' wa'l-mabʿath wa'l-maghāzī*, ed. M. Ḥamidullāh. Rabat, 1976.

Ibn al-Jawzī. *al-Muntaẓam fi'l-ta'rīkh*. Hyderabad, 1357/1938.

—— *Naqd al-ʿilm wa'l-ʿulamā' aw Talbīs iblīs*. Cairo, 1340/1921.

—— *al-Wafā bī aḥwāl al-Muṣṭafā*, ed. Muṣṭafā ʿAbd al-Wāḥid. Cairo, 1966.

Ibn Kathīr. *al-Bidāya wa'l-nihāya*. Cairo, 1932–1939, 14 vols; rpr. Beirut, 1977.

—— *Tafsīr*. Beirut, 1966.

Ibn Khallikān. *Wafayāt al-aʿyān*. Lithograph, n.p., 1284/1867.

Ibn Khuzayma. *K. al-tawḥīd*, ed. M. Kh. Harrās. Cairo, 1388/1968.

Ibn Manẓūr. *Lisān al-ʿarab*; rpr. Beirut, 1404/1983 and 1414/1994.

Ibn al-Nadīm. *al-Fihrist*, ed. G. Flügel. Wiesbaden, 1871; ed. M. R. Tajaddod. Tehran, 1350 Sh./1971.

Ibn Qūlūya (Qūlawayh) al-Qummī. *Kāmil al-ziyārāt*. Lithograph, Iran, n.d.; Najaf edn, 1937–1938; latest edn, B. Jaʿfarī. Tehran, 1375 Sh./1996.

Ibn Qutayba. *K. al-ʿArab* in M. Kurd ʿAlī's *Rasā'il al-bulaghā'*. 2nd edn, Cairo, 1365/1946, pp. 344–377.

—— (Pseudo-). *al-Imāma wa'l-siyāsa*, ed. M. M. al-Rāfiʿī. Cairo, 1322/1904.

—— *al-Maʿārif*, ed. Tharwat ʿUkāsha. 4th edn, Cairo, 1975.
—— *ʿUyūn al-akhbār*. Cairo, 1383/1963.
Ibn Rustam al-Ṭabarī al-Ṣaghīr. *Dalāʾil al-imāma*. Qumm, 1413/1992.
—— *Nawādir al-muʿjizāt fī manāqib al-aʾimmat al-hudāt*. Qumm, 1410/1990.
Ibn Sabʿīn. *Rasāʾil*, ed. ʿA. R. Badawī. Miṣr, n.d.
Ibn Saʿd. *al-Ṭabaqāt al-kubrā*, ed. Iḥsān ʿAbbās. Beirut, 1377–1380/1957–1960.
Ibn Shabba. *Taʾrīkh al-madīna al-munawwara*, ed. M. F. Shaltūt. Qumm, 1410/1989–1990.
Ibn Shādhān al-Qummī. *Miʾa manqaba*, ed. N. R. ʿUlwān. Qumm, 1413/1994.
Ibn Shahrāshūb. *Manāqib āl Abī Ṭālib*, ed. M. Burūjerdi. Lithograph, Tehran, 1316–1317/1898–1899; 3 vols, Najaf, 1956.
Ibn Shuʿba. *Tuḥaf al-ʿuqūl ʿan āl al-Rasūl*, ed. ʿA. A. Ghaffārī with Persian tr. M. B. Kamareʾī; rpr. Qumm, 1404/1984.
Ibn Ṭāwūs. *al-Durūʿ al-wāqiya*. Qumm, 1374 Sh./1992.
—— *Falāḥ al-sāʾil*. Najaf, 1385/1965.
—— *Faraj al-mahmūm fī taʾrīkh ʿulamāʾ al-nujūm*. Qumm, 1363 Sh./1985.
—— *Fatḥ al-abwāb*, ed. Ḥ. al-Khaffāf. Beirut, 1409/1989.
—— *al-Iqbāl*. Tehran, 1407/1987.
—— *Jamāl al-usbūʿ*. Tehran, 1330 Sh./1952.
—— *Kashf al-maḥajja*. n.p. [Iran], 1350/1931.
—— *al-Luhūf fī qatlā al-ṭufūf*. Qumm, 1364 Sh./1985.
—— *al-Malāḥim waʾl-fitan* as *al-Malāḥim waʾl-fitan fī ẓuhūr al-ghāʾib al-muntaẓar*. Qumm, 1398/1989.
—— *Muhaj al-daʿawāt* with *al-Mujtanā min al-duʿāʾ al-mujtabā*. n.p. [Iran], n.d.; Tehran, 1323/1905.
—— *Risāla fiʾl-muḍāyaqa fī fawāt al-ṣalāt* (called *al-Muwāsaʿa waʾl-muḍāyaqa*) in the margins of Muḥammad Amīn al-Astarābādī's *al-Fawāʾid al-madaniyya*. Lithograph, n.p. [Iran], 1321/1904.
—— *al-Ṭarāʾif fī maʿrifa madhāhib al-ṭawāʾif*. Qumm, 1400/1979.

—— *al-Yaqīn fī imrat amīr al-mu'minīn*. Najaf, 1369/1950.

Ibrāhīmī, 'Abd al-Riḍā Khān. *Dūstī-ye dūstān*. Kirmān, 1400/1979.

—— *Risāla dar jawāb-i āqā-ye muhandis Mūsā Žām*, in *Majma' al-rasā'il-i fārsī*, vol. 17. Kirmān, n.d.

Ibrāhīmī Kermānī, Abu'l-Qāsim Khān. *Ejtehād va taqlīd*, in *Rasā'el-e marḥūm-e āqā-ye ḥājj Abu'l-Qāsim Khān*, facsimile of autograph MS, Fonds Shaykhī de l'EPHE (sc. religieuses), SHA. VI.5; 2nd edn, Kirmān, n.d.

—— *Tanzīh al-awliyā'*. Kirmān, 1367/1947–1948.

—— *Fehrest-e kotob-e... Shaykh Aḥmad-e Aḥsā'ī va sā'er-e mashāyekh-e 'eẓām va kholāṣe-ye aḥvāl-e īshān*. Kirmān, 1377/1957.

—— *Fikrat dar jawāb-i āqā 'Alī Darakī*. Kirmān, 1385/1965.

—— *Risāla Falsafiyya dar jawāb-i Shaykh Muḥammad Taqī Falsafī*. Kirmān, 1350 Sh./1972.

—— *Tarjama Rujūm al-shayāṭīn*. Kirmān, 1351 Sh./1973.

—— *Risāla Sharīfiyya dar jawāb-i Shaykh 'Alī Akbar Sharīf al-Wā'iẓīn*. Kirmān, 1354 Sh./1976.

al-Irbilī, 'Alī b. 'Īsā. *Kashf al-ghumma*, ed. H. Rasūlī Maḥallātī. Qumm, 1381/1961–1962.

al-Iṣfahānī, Abu'l-Faraj. *K. al-Aghānī*. Būlāq [Cairo], 1285/1868.

—— *Maqātil al-Ṭālibiyyīn*, ed. A. Ṣaqr. Cairo, 1949.

al-Iskāfī, Muḥammad b. Hammām/Humām. *Kitāb al-tamḥīṣ*. Qumm, n.d. [ca. 1995].

Jābir b. Ḥayyān. *Mukhtār rasā'il Jābir b. Ḥayyān*, ed. P. Kraus. Paris and Cairo, 1935.

al-Jahshiyārī. *Kitāb al-wuzarā' wa'l-kuttāb*, ed. 'A. I. al-Ṣāwī. Cairo, 1357/1938.

al-Jāḥiẓ. *al-Bayān wa'l-tabyīn*, ed. 'A. M. Hārūn; rpr. Cairo, n.d., 4 vols.

—— *K. Dhamm akhlāq al-kuttāb*, in *Rasā'il al-Jāḥiẓ*, ed. 'A. M. Hārūn. Cairo, 1965, vol. 2, pp. 185–199; ed. 'A. Muhannā, *Rasā'il al-Jāḥiẓ*. Beirut, 1988, vol. 2, pp. 119–134; in *Three essays of Abū 'Othmān ibn Baḥr al-Jāḥiẓ*, ed. J. Finkel. Cairo, 1926, pp. 40–52.

—— *K. al-Ḥayawān*, ed. 'A. M. Hārūn. Cairo, n.d., 7 vols.

al-Juwaynī, imām al-ḥaramayn. *K. al-Irshād*, ed. J. D. Luciani. Paris, 1938.

—— *al-Shāmil fī uṣūl al-dīn*, ed. A. S. al-Nashshār, F. B. 'Awn and S. M. Mukhtār. Alexandria, 1389/1969.

al-Juwaynī, Ibrāhīm b. Muḥammad. *Farā'id al-simṭayn*, ed. M. B. al-Maḥmūdī. Beirut, 1398/1979.

Kabūdarāhangī, Muḥammad Ja'far Majdhūb 'Alī Shāh. *Rasā'el majdhūbiyye*, ed. H. Nājī Iṣfahānī. Isfahan, 1377 Sh./1998.

al-Kaf'amī, Taqī al-Dīn. *al-Balad al-amīn*. Tehran, 1383/1963.

—— *Junnat al-amān al-wāqiya*. Tehran, 1349 Sh./1971.

al-Karājakī, Muḥammad b. 'Alī. *Kanz al-fawā'id*. Tabriz, n.d.; Beirut, n.d.; rpr. Qumm, 1369/1949–1950.

al-Kāshānī, Muḥsin al-Fayḍ. *Dīvān*, ed. M. F. Kāshānī. Tehran, 1371 Sh./1992.

—— *Kalimāt maknūna*. Tehran, 1316/1898; ed. 'A. 'Uṭāridī Qūchānī. Tehran, 1383/1963.

—— *Nawādir al-akhbār*, ed. M. al-Anṣārī al-Qummī. Tehran, 1375 Sh./1996.

—— *al-Ṣāfī fī tafsīr al-Qur'ān*. Tehran, n.d., 2 vols.

—— *Sharḥ-e ṣadr* in his *Risālāt*. Tehran, 1321 Sh./1943.

Kashfī, Ja'far. *Tuḥfat al-mulūk*. Lithograph, n.p. [Iran], n.d., 2 vols.

al-Kashshī. *Ma'rifa akhbār al-rijāl*. Bombay, 1317/1899.

al-Khaṣībī/Khuṣaybī. *Kitāb al-hidāyat al-kubrā*. Beirut, 1406/1986.

Khayrkhāh-i Harātī. *Kalām-i pīr, ed. and English tr. W. Ivanow as A Treatise on Ismaili Doctrine*. Bombay, 1935.

al-Khawārazmī, al-Muwaffaq b. Aḥmad. *Maqtal al-Ḥusayn*. Najaf, 1367/1948.

—— *al-Manāqib*. Najaf, 1965; Qumm, n.d. [ca. 1990].

al-Khazzāz al-Rāzī. *Kifāyat al-athar*, ed. A. Kūhkamare'ī. Qumm. 1401/1980.

Kh(w)ājagī Shīrāzī, Muḥammad b. Aḥmad. *al-Niẓāmiyya fī madhhab al-imāmiyya*. Tehran, 1375 Sh./1996.

al-Kh(w)ānsārī. *Rawḍāt al-jannāt*, ed. A. Ismā'īliyān. Qumm, 1390–1392/1970–1972.

al-Kirmānī, Ḥamīd al-Dīn. *Majmū'at al-rasā'il*, ed. M. Ghālib. Beirut, 1983.

Kirmānī, Muḥammad Karīm Khān. *Chahār faṣl*. Kirmān, n.d.
—— *al-Fiṭra al-salīma*. 2nd edn, Kirmān, 1378/1958.
—— *Hidāya al-ṣibyān*. Lithograph, Bombay, 1313/1895.
—— *Hidāya al-Ṭālibin*. Lithograph, Tabriz, n.d.
—— *Ilzām al-nawāṣib*. n.p. [Kirmān?], n.d.
—— *Irshād al-ʿawāmm*. Kirmān, 1354–1355/1935–1936.
—— *Izhāq al-bāṭil*. Kirmān, 1351 Sh./1973.
—— 'Risāla dar amr-i jinn', in *Majmaʿ al-rasāʾil*, vol. 67. Kirmān, 1355 Sh./1977.
—— 'Risala dar jawāb-i ākhūnd Mullā Muḥammad Jaʿfar Kāzarūnī', in *Majmaʿ al-rasāʾil*, vols 68 and 69. Kirmān, 1355 Sh./1977.
—— 'Risāla dar jawāb-i Mullā Ḥasan Yazdī', in *Majmaʿ al-rasāʾil*, vol. 66. Kirmān, 1355 Sh./1977.
—— 'Risāla dar jawāb-i Mullā Muḥammad ʿAlī Dawānī', in *Majmaʿ al-rasāʾil*, vol. 67. Kirmān, 1355 Sh./1977.
—— 'Risāla dar jawāb-i Nawwāb ʿAbbās Mīrzā ibn Muḥammad Shāh Qājār', in *Majmaʿ al-rasāʾil*, vol. 70. Kirmān, 1356 Sh./1978.
—— 'Risāla dar jawāb-i Sayyid Jawād Karbalāʾī', in *Majmaʿ al-rasāʾil*, vol. 66. Kirmān, 1355 Sh./1977.
—— 'Risāla dar rafʿ-i shubuhāt-i baʿḍ-ī ahl-i Karbalā'', in *Majmaʿ al-rasāʾil*, vol. 15. Kirmān, 1380/1960.
—— *al-Risāla al-jihādiyya*. MS 2534, Madrasa Sipahsālār, Tehran.
—— *Risāla manẓūma Raḥīmiyya*. Lithograph, Bombay, 1313/1895.
—— *Risāla-ye radd-i Bāb dar jawāb-i Nāṣir al-Dīn Shāh Qājār*. Kirmān, 1383/1963.
—— *Rujūm al-shayāṭīn* with *Risāla dar radd-i Bāb-i khusrān maʾāb*. Tabriz, n.d. [ca. 1283/1866].
—— *Rukn-i rābiʿ*. 2nd edn, Kirmān, 1368/1948.
—— *al-Shihāb al-thāqib*. Kirmān, 1353 Sh./1975.
—— *Sī faṣl*. Kirmān, 1368/1948.
—— *Ṭarīq al-najāt*. Tabriz, 1344/1925.
—— *Tawḥīd nubuwwa imāma shīʿa*. Lithograph, Tabriz, 1310/1892.

—— 'Tīr-i shihāb dar radd-i Bāb-i khusrān ma'āb', in *Majmaʿ al-rasā'il*, vol. 1. Kirmān, 1386/1967.
—— and Muḥammad Khān. *Faṣl al-khiṭāb*. Lithograph, Tehran, 1302/1885.
Kirmānī, Muḥammad Khān. *Burhān-i qāṭiʿ*. Kirmān, 1351 Sh./1973.
—— *Hidāya al-mustarshid*. Lithograph, Kirmān, 1312/1894.
—— *Risāla Bihbahāniyya*. Kirmān, 1351 Sh./1973.
—— 'Risāla dar jawāb-i baʿḍ ikhwān', in *Majmaʿ al-rasā'il*, vol. 78. Kirmān, 1351 Sh./1973.
—— 'Risāla dar jawāb-i baʿḍ ikhwān-i Shīrāz', in *Majmaʿ al-rasā'il*, vol. 6. Kirmān, 1352 Sh./1974.
—— 'Risāla dar jawāb-i Ḥājj ʿAbd al-Karīm ibn Ḥājj ʿAbbās Būshihrī', in *Majmaʿ al-rasā'il*, vol. 26. Kirmān, 1352 Sh./1974.
—— 'Risāla dar jawāb-i Mullā Muḥammad ʿAlī Salmāsī', in *Majmaʿ al-rasā'il*, vol. 27. Kirmān, n.d.
—— 'Risāla dar jawāb-i Sayyid Ḥusayn Karbalā'ī', in *Majmaʿ al-rasā'il*, vol. 6. Kirmān, 1352 Sh./1974.
—— 'Risāla dar jawāb-i Shaykh Ḥusayn Mazīdī', in *Majmaʿ al-rasā'il*, vol. 73. Kirmān, 1351 Sh./1973.
—— *Risāla dar jawāb-i Shaykh Ḥusayn Rashtī*. Kirmān, n.d.
—— 'Risāla dar jawāb-i su'āl-i baʿḍī', in *Majmaʿ al-rasā'il*, vol. 3. Kirmān, 1348 Sh./1960.
—— *Risāla dar radd-i Bāb-i murtāb*. Kirmān, n.d.
—— 'Risāla dar radd-i baʿḍī ta'wīlāt-i bābiyya', in *Rasā'il*. Kirmān, 1398/1977.
—— *al-Shams al-muḍī'a*. Lithograph, Tabriz, 1322/1904.
—— 'Sharḥ lā ḥawl wa lā quwwa illā bi'llāh', in *Majmaʿ al-rasā'il*, vol. 3. Kirmān, 1348 Sh./1970.
—— *Taqwīm al-ʿawaj*. Lithograph, Bombay, 1311/1893.
—— 'Wāridāt', in *Majmaʿ al-rasā'il*, vol. 27. Kirmān, 1349 Sh./1971.
—— *Wasīla al-najāt*. Kirmān, n.d.
—— *Yanābīʿ al-ḥikma*. Kirmān, 1383/1964.

—— and Zayn al-ʿĀbidīn Khān, *Kitāb al-mubīn*. Lithograph, n.p., 1305–1324/1887–1906.

Kirmānī, Zayn al-ʿĀbidīn Khān. *Durūs*. Kirmān, n.d.

—— *Miʿrāj al-saʿāda*; rpr. Kirmān, 1352 Sh./1974.

—— 'Risāla dar jawāb-i Āqā Mīrzā Sayyid Muḥammad Riḍawī', in *Majmaʿ al-rasāʾil*, vol. 11. Kirmān, 1352 Sh./1974.

—— 'Risāla dar jawāb-i Muḥammad Ibrāhīm Khān ibn Amīr Aṣlān Khān', in *Majmaʿ al-rasāʾil*, vol. 8. Kirmān, 1352 Sh./1974.

—— 'Risāla dar jawāb-i Muḥammad Qulī Khān Sipihr', in *Majmaʿ al-rasāʾil*, vol. 80. Kirmān, 1357 Sh./1978.

—— 'Risāla dar jawāb-i Muḥammad Ṣādiq Khān Nāʾīnī', in *Majmaʿ al-rasāʾil*, vol. 8. Kirmān, 1352 Sh./1974.

—— 'Risāla dar jawāb-i Shaykh Ḥusayn ibn Shaykh ʿAlī Ṣaḥḥāf dar rukn-i rābiʿ', in *Majmaʿ al-rasāʾil*, vol. 79. Kirmān, 1356 Sh./1978.

—— 'Risāla dar jawāb-i Shaykh Muḥammad ʿAlī Baḥrānī Āl-i ʿUṣfūr', in *Majmaʿ al-rasāʾil*, vol. 82. Kirmān, 1357 Sh./1978.

—— 'Risāla dar jawāb-i Shaykh Muḥammad Bihbahānī dar Jābalqā wa Jābarsā', in *Majmaʿ al-rasāʾil*, vol. 29. Kirmān, 1356 Sh./1978.

—— 'al-Risāla al-Ḥasaniyya', in *Majmaʿ al-rasāʾil*, vol. 28. Kirmān, 1350 Sh./1972.

—— *Sāʿiqa*, in *Majmaʿ al-rasāʾil*, vol. 9. Kirmān, 1352 Sh./1974.

Kitāb Abī Saʿīd al-ʿUṣfurī. Tehran, 1371/1951.

Kitāb al-haft, ed. M. Ghālib as *al-Haft al-sharīf*. 3rd edn, Beirut, 1980; ed. ʿA. Tamer et A. Khalifé as *al-Haft wa al-aẓilla*. 2nd edn, Beirut, 1970.

al-Kulaynī, *al-Uṣūl min al-Kāfī*, ed. with Persian tr. J. Muṣṭafawī. Tehran, n.d., 4 vols (vol. 4, tr. H. Rasūlī Maḥallātī, 1386/1966).

—— *al-Furūʿ min al-Kāfī*, ed. H. Rasūlī Maḥallātī. Tehran, 1334 Sh./1956, 4 vols.

—— *al-Rawḍa min al-Kāfī*, ed. and Persian tr. H. Rasūlī Maḥallātī. Tehran, 1386/1969.

al-Kumayt b. Zayd. *Hāshimiyyāt*, ed. J. Horovitz as *Die Hāšimijjāt des Kumait*. Leiden, 1904; Arabic text rpr. Qumm, n.d.

Lāhījī, Shams al-Dīn. *Mafātīḥ al-iʿjāz fī sharḥ Golshan-e rāz*, ed. M. R. Barzegar Khāleqī and ʿE. Karbāsī. Tehran, 1371 Sh./1992.
Lāmeʿ Darmiyānī. *Dīvān*, ed. M. Rafīʿī and Z. Moṣaffā. Tehran, 1365 Sh./1986.
al-Maʿarrī, Abu'l-ʿAlā. *al-Luzūmiyyāt*, Khānjī. Cairo, 1924.
Majd al-Ashrāf. *Mirʾāt al-kāmilīn*. Shiraz, n.d.
al-Majlisī. *Biḥār al-anwār*, ed. on the basis of the edn by Kumpānī. Tehran and Qumm, 1376–1392/1956–1972, 90 vols in 110 tomes.
—— *Irshād al-qulūb*. Tehran, 1334 Sh./1956.
—— *Mirʾāt al-ʿuqūl*. Tehran, 1404/1984.
—— *Zād al-maʿād*. Lithograph, Tehran, 1352/1933.
al-Māmaqānī. *Tanqīḥ al-maqāl*. Tehran, 1349/1930, 3 vols.
al-Maqdisī, Muṭahhar b. Ṭāhir. *Kitāb al-badʾ wa'l-taʾrīkh*, ed. and French tr. Cl. Huart as *Le Livre de la Création et de l'Histoire*. Paris, 1899–1919, 6 vols.
al-Maqrīzī, Aḥmad b. ʿAlī. *Kitāb al-mawāʿiẓ wa'l-iʿtibār fi dhikr al-khiṭaṭ wa'l-āthār*. Būlāq, 1256/1840.
—— *al-Nizāʿ wa'l-takhāṣum fī mā bayna Banī Umayya wa Banī Hāshim*, ed. Ḥ. Muʾnis. Cairo, 1984; English tr. C. E. Bosworth as *'Book of Contention and Strife' Concerning the Relations between the Banū Umayya and the Banū Hāshim*. Manchester, 1980.
al-Marzubānī. *Akhbār shuʿarāʾ al-shīʿa*, ed. M. Ḥ. al-Amīnī. Najaf, 1388/1968.
al-Masʿūdī (attrib.). *Ithbāt al-waṣiyya*. Najaf, n.d.; Qumm, 1417/1996.
—— *Murūj al-dhahab*, ed. and French tr. Barbier de Meynard. Paris, 1861–1877; rev. edn, C. Pellat. Beirut 1968–1979.
—— *al-Tanbīh wa'l-ishrāf*, ed. M. de Goeje. Leiden, 1893–1894.
Maʿṣūm ʿAlī Shāh, Muḥammad Maʿṣūm. *Ṭarāʾiq al-ḥaqāʾiq*. Tehran, 1318–1319/1900–1901.
al-Māzandarānī, Muḥammad Bāqir. *Jannat al-naʿīm*. Lithograph, n.p., 1296/1878.

al-Minqarī. *Waqʿat Ṣiffīn*, ed. ʿA. M. Hārūn. Cairo 1382/1962.

Mīr ʿĀbedīnī, S. A. and Afshārī, M. *Āʾīn-e qalandarī*. Tehran, 1374 Sh./1995.

Mīr Dāmād. *Taqwīm al-īmān* with al-Sayyid Aḥmad al-ʿAlawī's *Sharḥ* and al-Mullā ʿAlī al-Nūrī's *Taʿlīqāt*, ed. ʿA. Awjabī. Tehran, 1376 Sh./1998.

Miskawayh, Aḥmad b. Muḥammad. *Tajārib al-umam*, ed. and tr. H. F. Amedroz and D. S. Margoliouth as *The Eclipse of the Abbāsid Califate*. London, 1920–1921.

al-Mubarrad. *al-Kāmil fi'l-lugha*, ed. M. Z. Mubārak. Cairo, 1356/1937; ed. and tr. M. A. al-Dālī. 3rd edn, Beirut, 1418/1997.

Mudarris, Muḥammad ʿAlī. *Rayḥānat al-adab*. Tabriz, n.d.

Mudarris-i ʿĀlam. *Ganjīne-ye awliyāʾ yā āʾīne-ye ʿorafāʾ*. Tehran, 1338 Sh./1960.

—— *Tuḥfa-ye darwīsh*. Tehran, 1337 Sh./1959.

al-Mufīd, Muḥammad b. Muḥammad b. al-Nuʿmān. *Awāʾil al-maqālāt*, ed. F. Zanjānī. Tabriz, 1371/1951–1952; French tr. D. Sourdel as *L'imamisme vu par le cheikh al-Mufīd*. Paris, 1972.

—— *al-Ikhtiṣāṣ*, ed. ʿA. A. Ghaffārī. Qumm, n.d.

—— *al-Irshād*, Arabic text and Persian tr. H. Rasūlī Maḥallātī. Tehran, 1346 Sh./1968; English tr. I. K. A. Howard as *The Book of Guidance*. London, 1981.

—— *Kitāb al-Jamal aw al-nuṣra fī ḥarb al-Baṣra*. Najaf, 1963.

—— *Sharḥ ʿaqāʾid al-Ṣadūq aw taṣḥīḥ al-iʿtiqād*, ed. A. Charandābī. Tabriz, 1371/1951.

Mujallil al-anwār yā kashkūl silsilat al-dhahab, ed. Sh. Parvīzī. Tabriz, 1336/1958.

Mujmal al-tawārīkh wa'l-qiṣaṣ, ed. M. T. Bahār. Tehran, 1318 Sh./1940.

Mullā Ṣadrā Shīrāzī, *al-Asfār al-arbaʿa*. Lithograph, Tehran, 1282/1865–1866.

—— *Asrār al-āyāt*, ed. M. Khājavī. Tehran, 1362 Sh./1983; Persian tr. M Khājavī. Tehran, 1363 Sh./1984.

—— *al-Ḥikmat al-ʿarshiyya*. Lithograph, Tehran, 1315/1897; Persian tr. Gh. Ḥ. Āhanī as *ʿArshiyya*. Tehran, 1341 Sh./1963;

English tr. J. W. Morris as *The Wisdom of the Throne*. Princeton, 1981.

—— *Kasr aṣnām al-jāhiliyya*, ed. M. T. Dānesh-Pažūh. Tehran, 1340 Sh./1962.

—— *Kitāb al-mashāʿir*, ed. H. Corbin. Tehran and Paris, 1964.

—— *Mafātīḥ al-ghayb*, ed. M. Khājavī. Tehran, 1363 Sh./1994; Persian tr. M. Khājavī. Tehran, 1363 Sh./1404/1994.

—— *Majmūʿe-ya ashʿār*, ed. M. Khājavī. Tehran, 1376 Sh./1418/1997.

—— *Mathnavī-ya Mollā Ṣadrā*, ed. Moṣṭafā Fayḍī. Qumm, 1376 Sh./1417/1997.

—— *Seh aṣl*, ed. S. Ḥ. Naṣr. Tehran, 1340 Sh./1380/1961.

—— *Sharḥ al-Uṣūl min al-Kāfī*. Lithograph, Tehran, 1283/1865.

—— *al-Shawāhid al-rubūbiyya fi'l-manāhij al-sulūkiyya*, ed. S. J. Āshtiyānī. 2nd edn, Tehran, 1360 Sh./1981.

—— *Tafsīr*. Lithograph, Tehran, n.d.

—— *Tafsīr sūrat al-baqara*. Lithograph, Tehran, n.d.

—— *al-Wāridāt al-qalbiyya*, ed. A. Shafīʿīha. Tehran, 1358 Sh./1980.

Muntakhab al-daʿawāt. Lithograph, Tehran, 1304/1886.

al-Murtaḍā b. Dāʿī al-Ḥusaynī. *Tabṣirat al-ʿawāmm fī maqālāt al-anām*. Lithograph, Tehran, 1327/1909; ed. ʿA. Eqbāl. 2nd edn, Tehran, 1364 Sh./1985.

Muslim. *al-Jāmiʿ al-ṣaḥīḥ*; rpr. Istanbul, 1383/1963.

Muẓaffar ʿAlī Shāh. *Kebrīt-e aḥmar* with *Baḥr al-asrār*, ed. J. Nūrbakhsh. Tehran, 1350/1971.

—— *Nūr al-anwār*, ed. N. Sobbūḥī. n.p. [Tehran], n.d.

al-Najafī al-Astarābādī, Sharaf al-Dīn. *Ta'wīl al-āyāt al-ẓāhira*. Qumm, 1417/1997.

al-Najāshī, Aḥmad b. ʿAlī. *Rijāl*. Bombay, 1317/1899; rpr. Qumm, n.d.; ed. M. al-Shubayrī al-Zanjānī. Qumm, 1407/1987.

Najm al-Dīn Kubrā. *Die Rawā'iḥ al-jamāl wa fawātiḥ al-jalāl des Najm ad-Dīn al-Kubrā*, ed. F. Meier. Wiesbaden, 1957; French tr. P. Ballanfat as *Les éclosions de la beauté et les parfums de la majesté*. Nîmes, 2001.

al-Nāshi' al-Akbar. *Masā'il al-imāma*, ed. J. van Ess. Beirut, 1971.

—— (Pseudo-). *Uṣūl al-niḥal*, ed. J. van Ess as *Frühe mu'tazilische Häresiographie*. Beirut and Wiesbaden, 1971.

al-Nawbakhtī, Ḥasan b. Mūsā. *Firaq al-shī'a*, ed. H. Ritter. Istanbul, 1931; French tr. M. J. Mashkour. 2nd edn, Tehran, 1980.

al-Nīlī, Bahā' al-Dīn 'Alī al-Najafī. *al-Sulṭān al-mufarrij 'an ahl al-Īmān*, ed. Q. al-'Aṭṭār. Qumm, 1384 Sh./2006.

Ni'matallāh, al-Jazā'irī. *al-Anwār al-nu'māniyya*. Tehran, n.d.

Niẓām al-Mulk. *Siyāsat-nāmeh*, ed. J. Sha'ār. Tehran, 1364 Sh./1985.

al-Nubāṭī, Abū Muḥammad al-'Āmilī. *al-Ṣirāṭ al-mustaqīm ilā mustaḥaqqī'l-taqdīm*. Najaf, 1338/1919.

al-Nu'mānī. *Kitāb al-ghayba*, ed. 'A. A. Ghaffārī. Tehran, 1397/1977.

—— *al-Muḥkam wa'l-mutashābih* (published under al-Sharīf al-Murtaḍā'). Lithograph, Iran, n.d.

Nūr 'Alī Shāh Iṣfahānī. 'Manẓūm-e khuṭbat al-bayān', in *Dīvān-e Nūr 'Alī Shāh Iṣfahānī*. Tehran, 1349 Sh./1970; and in *Majmū'e-ye āthār-e N. 'A. Sh. Iṣfahānī*. Tehran, 1350 Sh./1971.

Nūr 'Alī Shāh Thānī. *Ṣāleḥiyye*. Tehran, 1387/1967.

Nūrbakhsh, Sayyid Muḥammad. *al-Risālat al-i'tiqādiyya*, ed. M. Molé in *Professions de foi de deux kubrâwîs: 'Alî-i Hamadânî et Muḥammad Nûrbakhsh*, taken from *Bulletin d'Etudes Orientales*, 17 (1961–1962).

al-Nūrī al-Ṭabarsī/Ṭabrisī, Mīrzā Ḥusayn. *Dār al-salām fī-mā yata'allaqu bi'l-ru'yā wa'l-manām*, ed. H. Rasūlī Maḥallātī. Qumm, 1380/1960.

—— *Jannat al-ma'wā*, in al-Majlisī's *Biḥār al-anwār*, vol. 53. Tehran, 1385/1965.

—— *Kalima ṭayyiba*. Tehran, n.d.

—— *Mustadrak al-wasā'il*. Tehran: lithograph, n.d.; Qumm, 1407/1986.

—— *Nafas al-Raḥmān fī faḍā'il Salmān*. Tehran, 1285/1868.

—— *al-Najm al-thāqib*. Qumm and Jamkarān, 1412/1991.

Nuzhat al-zāhid, ed. R. Jaʿfariyān. Tehran, 1376 Sh./1997.
The Persian Rivāyats of Hormazyar Framarz, ed. B. N. Dhabhar. Bombay, 1932.
al-Qāḍī al-Nuʿmān, Abū Ḥanīfa. *Daʿāʾim al-islām*, ed. A. A. A. Fyzee. Cairo, 1951–1956, 2 vols; English tr. A. A. A. Fyzee, rev. I. K. Poonawala as *The Pillars of Islam*. New Dehli, 2002–2004, 2 vols.
al-Qāḍī Saʿīd al-Qummī. *al-Arbaʿīniyyāt li-kashf anwār al-qudsiyyāt*, ed. N. Ḥabībī. Tehran, 1381 Sh./2003.
al-Qādirī, Ismāʿīl b. Muḥammad. *al-Fuyūḍāt al-rabbāniyya*. Cairo, n.d.
al-Qasṭallānī. *Irshād al-sārī li sharḥ Ṣaḥīḥ al-Bukhārī*. Beirut, 1323/1905.
Qaṣāʾed va madāʾeḥ dar shaʾn-e… ʿAlī. Tabriz, n.d.
al-Qazwīnī, ʿAbd al-Jalīl. *Kitāb al-Naqḍ*, ed. al-Muḥaddith al-Urmawī. Tehran, 1979.
al-Qazwīnī, al-Khaṭīb. *al-Talkhīṣ*. Cairo, n.d.
al-Qazwīnī, Mullā Khalīl. *al-Shāfī fī sharḥ al-Kāfī*. Lithograph, Lucknow, 1308/1890.
al-Qazwīnī, Zakariyā. *ʿAjāʾib al-makhlūqat*, in the margins of al-Damīrī, *Ḥayāt al-ḥayawān al-kubrā*. Cairo, 1356/1937.
al-Quhpāʾī. *Majmaʿ al-rijāl*, ed. al-ʿAllāma al-Iṣfahānī. Isfahan, 1384–1387/1964–1967.
al-Qummī, ʿAlī b. Ibrāhīm. *Tafsīr*, ed. Ṭ. al-Mūsawī al-Jazāʾirī. Najaf, 1386–1387/1966–1968; re-ed. Beirut, 1411/1991.
al-Qummī, al-Ḥasan b. Muḥammad. *Taʾrīkh Qumm*. Arabic original lost, Persian tr. Ḥasan b. ʿAlī Qomī, ed. S. J. Tehrānī. 3rd edn, 1361 Sh./1982.
al-Qummī, Jaʿfar b. Muḥammad. *Kāmil al-ziyārāt*, see Ibn Qūlūya (Qūlawayh).
Qummī, Shaykh ʿAbbās. *Mafātīḥ al-jinān*. Tehran, 1381 Sh./2001.
—— *Safīnat al-Biḥār*. Tehran, 1370 Sh./1991.
al-Qundūzī. *Yanābīʿ al-mawadda*. Najaf, 1384/1965; n.p. [Iraq], 1385/1966; Bombay, n.d.
al-Qushayrī. *al-Risāla (al-Qushayriyya)*, ed. Maḥmūd and al-Sharīf. Cairo, 1974.

Quṭb al-Dīn, Sayyid Muḥammad. *Faṣl al-khiṭāb*. Tabriz, n.d.

Rashtī, Sayyid Kāẓim. *Dalīl al-mutaḥayyirīn*. Lithograph, Tabriz, n.d.

—— *al-Rasāʾil wa-l-masāʾil*. Lithograph, Tabriz, n.d.

—— *Sharḥ al-khuṭbat al-taṭanjiyya*. Tabriz, 1270/1853.

—— *Sharḥ qaṣīda lāmiyya li-ʿAbd al-Bāqī Efendī*. Lithograph, n.p. [Tabriz], n.d.

al-Rāwandī. *al-Kharāʾij waʾl-jarāʾiḥ*. Qumm, 1409/1988–1989.

Rāz Shīrāzī. *Mirṣād al-ʿibād*. Tabriz, n.d.

—— *Resāle dar ḥall-e eshkāl-e davāzdah soʾāl-e...Rāʾiḍ al-Dīn Zanjānī...az Mīrzā Bābā Rāz Shīrāzī*, in Ḥ. Palāsī Shīrāzī's *Tadhkira Shaykh Muḥammad b. Ṣadīq al-Kujujī*. Tehran, 1367/1947.

—— *Sharḥ kitāb khuṭbat al-bayān* (*sic*, instead of *Kitāb sharḥ khuṭbat al-bayān*). Shiraz, n.d.

—— *Ṭabāshīr al-ḥikma*. Shiraz, 1319/1900.

al-Rāzī, Abū Ḥātim. *Kitāb al-zīna*, ed. ʿA. S. Sāmarrāʾī in *al-Ghuluww waʾl-firaq al-ghāliya fiʾl-ḥaḍāra al-islāmiyya*. Baghdad, 1972.

Rāzī, Fakhr al-Dīn Muḥammad b. ʿUmar, *Tafsīr al-Fakhr al-Rāzī, called al-Tafsīr al-Kabīr and Mafāṭīh al-ghayb* Beirut, 1981–1983, 32 vols.

Rāzī, Najm Dāye. *Mirṣād al-ʿibād*, ed. M. A. Riyāḥī. Tehran, 1973.

al-Rāzī, al-Ṣanʿānī. *Taʾrīkh Ṣanʿāʾ*, ed. Ḥ. b. ʿA. al-ʿAmrī. Beirut and Damascus, 1989.

Riḍawī, Mīrzā Niʿmatullāh. *Tadhkirat al-awliyāʾ*. Lithograph, Bombay, 1313/1895.

Rūzbehān Baqlī Shīrāzī. *Sharḥ-e shaṭḥiyyāt*, ed. H. Corbin and M. Moʿīn. Paris and Tehran, 1966; re-ed. 2004.

Saʿd b. ʿAbd Allāh al-Ashʿarī. *al-Maqālāt waʾl-firaq*, ed. M. J. Mashkūr. Tehran, 1963.

Saddar Nasr – Saddar Bundehesh, ed. B. N. Bhabhar. Bombay, 1909.

al-Ṣaffār al-Qummī. *Baṣāʾir al-darajāt*, ed. M. Kūchebāghī. 2nd edn, Tabrīz, n.d. [ca. 1960].

Ṣāḥib b. ʿAbbād. *al-Iqnāʿ*. Qumm, n.d.

Ṣaḥīfat al-imām al-Riḍā. Qumm, 1408/1987.

Ṣāliḥ b. Aḥmad b. Ḥanbal. *Sīrat al-imām Aḥmad b. Ḥanbal*, ed. F. ʿAbd al-Munʿim Aḥmad. Alexandria, 1981.

al-Samʿānī. *al-Ansāb*, facsimile of MS in the British Museum, ed. D. S. Margoliouth. London and Leiden, 1912.

al-Ṣanʿānī, ʿAbd al-Razzāq. *al-Muṣannaf*, ed. Ḥ. al-R. al-Aʿẓamī. Beirut, 1972.

al-Ṣanʿānī, Ḍiyāʾ al-Dīn. *Nasma al-saḥar bi dhikr man tashayyaʿa wa shaʿar*, ed. K. S. al-Jabbūrī. Beirut, 1420/1999.

Shādhān b. Jabraʾīl. *al-Faḍāʾil*. Najaf, 1381/1962.

Shāh Niʿmatullāh Walī. *Dīvān*, ed. J. Nūrbakhsh. Tehran, 1361 Sh./1982.

al-Shahrastānī, Muḥammad b. ʿAbd al-Karīm. *al-Milal waʾl-niḥal*, ed. Kaylānī. Cairo 1967; French trans by D. Gimaret and G. Monnot as *Livre des religions et des sectes*. Paris and Louvain, 1986–1993.

—— *Mafātīḥ al-asrār wa maṣābīḥ al-abrār*, facsimile edn of *unicum*. Tehran, 1409/1989.

al-Sharīf al-Murtaḍā. *al-Dhakhīra fī ʿilm al-kalām*, ed. A. al-Ḥusaynī. Qumm, 1411/1990.

—— *Dīwān*. Tehran, 1365 Sh./1986.

—— *al-Shāfī fiʾl-imāma*. Lithograph, Tehran, 1301/1884–1885.

—— *Tanzīh al-anbiyāʾ*. Najaf, 1380/1960.

al-Sharīf al-Raḍī. *Dīwān*. Qumm, n.d.

—— *Nahj al-balāgha*, ed. and Persian tr. ʿA. N. Fayḍ al-islām. 4th edn, Tehran, 1351 Sh./1972.

Sharīf al-Iṣfahānī, Abū al-Ḥasan. *Tafsīr mirʾāt al-anwār*. Lithograph, n.p. [Iran], n.d.

Shihāb al-Dīn b. Ḥajar. *al-Fatāwā al-ḥadīthiyya*. Cairo, 1325/1907.

al-Shīrāzī, al-Muʾayyad fiʾl-Dīn. *al-Majālis al-Muʾayyadiyya*, vols 1 and 3, ed. M. Ghālib. Beirut, 1974 and 1984.

Shirvānī, Zayn al-ʿĀbidīn Mast ʿAlī Shāh. *Bustān al-siyāḥa*. Tehran, 1378/1958.

—— *Riyāḍ al-siyāḥa*. Tehran, 1339/1920.

Shūshtarī, Nūrallāh. *Majālis al-muʾminīn*. Tehran, 1365 Sh./1987.

Sibṭ Ibn al-Jawzī. *Tadhkirat khawāṣṣ al-umma fī ma'rifat al-a'imma*; rpr. Tehran, n.d.

al-Simnānī, 'Alā al-Dawla. *al-'Urwa li-ahl al-khalwa wa'l-jalwa*, ed. N. Māyel Heravī. Tehran, 1362 Sh./1985.

Sorūshiyān, Jamshīd Sorūsh. *Farhang-e beh-dīnān*, ed. M. Sotūdeh. Tehran, 1334 Sh./1956.

Sulaym b. Qays (Pseudo). *Kitāb al-saqīfa*. Qumm, n.d; ed. M. B. al-Anṣārī. Qumm, 1416/1995, 3 vols.

Sulṭān 'Alī Shāh Gonābādī. *Bishārat al-mu'minīn*. Tehran, 1337 Sh./1959.

—— *Majma' al-sa'ādāt*. 2nd edn, n.p., 1394/1974.

—— *Walāyat-Nāmeh*. Tehran, 1344 Sh./1966.

al-Suyūṭī. *al-Khaṣā'iṣ al-kubrā*, ed. M. Kh. Harrās. Cairo, 1967.

al-Ṭabarī, Muḥammad b. Jarīr. *Jāmi' al-bayān*, ed. M. M. Shākir and A. M. Shākir. Cairo, 1373–1388/1955–1969.

—— *Ta'rīkh al-rusul wa'l-mulūk*, ed. M. J. de Goeje et al. Leiden, 1879–1901; ed. M. A. F. Ibrāhīm. Cairo, 1960; English tr. by various translators as *The History of al-Ṭabarī*; vol. 15: *The Conquest of Iran*, tr. and annot. G. Rex Smith. Albany, NY, 1994.

al-Ṭabarī, Abū Ja'far. *Bishārat al-Muṣṭafā li-shī'at al-Murtaḍā*. Najaf, 1963.

al-Ṭabarī, al-Muḥibb(sic). *al-Riyāḍ al-naḍira*; rpr. Tehran, n.d. [ca. 1985].

al-Ṭabarī 'al-Ṣaghīr', see Ibn Rustam.

al-Ṭabrisī, Abū 'Alī al-Faḍl b. al-Ḥasan. *Kunūz al-najāḥ*. n.p. [Iran], 1318/1900.

—— *Majma' al-bayān fī tafsīr al-Qur'ān*. Tehran, 1395/1975.

al-Ṭabrisī/Ṭabarsī, Abu'l-Faḍl. *I'lām al-warā bi a'lām al-hudā*, ed. al-Kharsān. Najaf, 1390/1970; 3rd edn, Qumm, 1970.

al-Taftāzānī. *Mukhtaṣar al-ma'ānī*. Qumm, 1386/1966.

—— *al-Muṭawwal*. Tehran, 1333 Sh./1955.

al-Ṭarsūsī, Abū Ṭāhir. *Abū Muslim-Nāmeh*, ed. H. Esmaïli. Tehran, 2004.

al-Thaqafī. *Kitāb al-ghārāt*, ed. J. al-Muḥaddith al-Urmawī. Tehran, 1395/1975.

al-Ṭihrānī. *al-Dharīʿa ilā taṣānīf al-shīʿa*. Tehran and Najaf, 1353–1398/1934–1978, 25 vols.

al-Tirmidhī. *al-Jāmiʿ al-ṣaḥīḥ/Sunan*, ed. A. M. Shākir. Cairo, 1356/1937.

al-Ṭurayḥī, Fakhr al-Dīn. *Majmaʿ al-baḥrayn wa maṭlaʿ al-nayyirayn*. Tehran, 1321/1903.

al-Ṭūsī, Abū Jaʿfar. *Fihrist kutub al-shīʿa*. Najaf, 1356/1937; ed. Sprenger and ʿAbd al-Ḥaqq; rpr. Mashhad, 1972 and Beirut, 1403/1983.

—— *K. al-Ghayba*. Tabrīz, 1322/1905.

—— *Miṣbāḥ al-mutahajjid*, ed. A. Bīdār. Tehran, 1373 Sh./1994.

—— *al-Rijāl*, ed. M. Ṣ. Āl Baḥr al-ʿUlūm. Najaf, 1380/1961.

—— *Tafsīr al-tibyān*. Najaf, 1957, 10 vols.

—— *Tahdhīb al-aḥkām*, ed. al-Mūsawī al-Kharsān. Najaf, 1958–1962; ed. M. J. Shams al-Dīn. Beirut, 1412/1992.

al-Tustarī, Muḥammad Taqī. *Qāmūs al-rijāl*. Tehran, 1379/1958.

ʿUnṣur al-Maʿālī, Kay Kāwūs b. Iskandar. *Qābūs-Nāmah*, ed. Gh. Ḥ. Yūsufī. 8th edn, Tehran, 1375 Sh./1996.

al-Uṣūl al-sittat ʿashar. Qumm, 1405/1984.

al-Yaʿqūbī. *Taʾrīkh*, ed. M. Th. Houtsma. Leiden, 1883; rpr. Qumm, 1414/1994.

Yāqūt al-Ḥamawī. *Muʿjam al-buldān*, ed. F. Wüstenfeld. Leipzig, 1866; rpr. Tehran, 1965; ed. Beirut, 1376/1957.

Yek qesmat az tārīkh-e ḥayāt wa karāmāt-e Sayyid Qoṭb al-Dīn Muḥammad Shīrāzī. Tabriz, 1309/1891.

al-Zabīdī. *Tāj al-ʿarūs*. Qumm, n.d. [ca. 1980].

Le Zend-Avesta, ed. J. Darmesteter. Paris, 1892–1893, 3 vols.

al-Zubayr b. Bakkār. *Jamhara nasab Quraysh wa akhbāruhā*, ed. M. M. Shākir. Cairo, 1381/1961.

al-Zurqānī. *Sharḥ ʿalāʾl-Mawāhib al-laduniyya liʾl-Qasṭallānī*. Cairo, 1329/1911.

Secondary Sources

Agaeff, A. B. 'Les croyances mazdéennes dans la religion chiite', *Transactions of the Ninth International Congress of Orientalists* (London, 1893), pp. 505–514.

Aguade, J. *Messianismus zur Zeit der frühen Abbassiden: Das Kitāb al-Fitan des Nuʿaim b. Ḥammād*. Tübingen, 1979.

Algar, H. *Religion and State in Iran 1785–1906*. Berkeley and Los Angeles, 1969.

Ali, J. 'Die beiden ersten Safire des Zwölften Imams', *Der Islam*, 25 (1939), pp. 197–227.

Altorki, S. 'Milk-Kinship in Arab Society, An Unexplored Problem in the Ethnography of Marriage', *Ethnology*, 19 (1980).

al-Alūsī. *Bulūgh al-arab fī maʿrifa aḥwāl al-ʿarab*. Cairo, 1928.

Alverny, A. d'. 'La prière selon le Coran II. La prière rituelle', *Proche-Orient Chrétien*, 10 (1960), pp. 303–317.

Amanat, A. *Resurrection and Renewal: The Making of the Babi Movement in Iran, 1844–1850*. London, 1989.

al-ʿĀmilī, Jaʿfar. *Dirāsa fī ʿalāmāt al-ẓuhūr*. Qumm, 1411/1990.

Amīn, A. *Ḍuḥā'l-Islām*. Cairo, 1933.

al-Amīnī, ʿAbd al-Ḥusayn al-Najafī. *al-Ghadīr fi'l-kitāb wa'l-sunna wa'l-adab*. Beirut, 1397/1977; Tehran, 1372/1952; rpr. 1986.

Amir-Moezzi, M. A. *Le Guide divin dans le shiʿisme originel. Aux sources de l'ésotérisme en Islam*. Paris and Lagrasse, 1992 and 2005 (2nd edn with same pagination); English tr. D. Straight as *The Divine Guide in Early Shi'ism*. New York, 1994.

—— and C. Jambet. *Qu'est-ce que le shi'isme?* Paris, 2004.

—— 'Al-Ṣaffâr al-Qummî (d. 290/902–3) et son *Kitâb baṣâ'ir al-darajât*', *JA*, 280/3–4 (1992), pp. 221–250.

—— 'Réflexions sur une évolution du shiʿisme duodécimain: tradition et idéologisation', in E. Patlagean and A. Le Boulluec (eds), *Les Retours aux Ecritures. Fondamentalismes présents et passés*. Louvain and Paris, 1993, pp. 63–82.

—— 'Notes sur deux traditions 'hétérodoxes' imāmites', *Arabica*, 41 (1994), pp. 127–133.

—— 'Etude du lexique technique de l'ésotérisme imāmite', in *Annuaire de l'EPHE, section des sciences religieuses*, 102 (1994–1995), pp. 350–355.

—— 'De quelques interprétations spirituelles du *Šāhnāme* de Ferdowsī', in C. Balay, C. Kappler and Ž. Vesel (eds), *Pand o sokhan. Mélanges offerts à Charles Henri de Fouchécour*. Tehran and Paris, 1995, pp. 17–36.
—— 'Aspects de l'imāmologie duodécimaine I. Remarques sur la divinité de l'Imām', *Studia Iranica*, 25/2 (1996), pp. 193–116.
—— 'Contribution à la typologie des rencontres avec l'imam caché (Aspects de l'imamologie duodécimaine II)', *JA*, 284/1 (1996), pp. 109–135.
—— 'Jamkarân et Mâhân, deux pèlerinages insolites en Iran', in M. A. Amir-Moezzi (ed.), *Lieux d'islam. Cultes et cultures de l'Afrique à Java*, Paris, 1996; 2nd edn, 2005, pp. 154–167.
—— 'Remarques sur les critères d'authenticité du hadîth et l'autorité du juriste dans le shīʿisme imāmite', *SI*, 85 (1997), pp. 5–39.
—— 'Du droit à la théologie: les niveaux de réalité dans le shiʿisme duodécimain', *Cahiers du Groupe d'Etudes Spirituelles Comparées*, 5, 'L'Esprit et la Nature', Actes du colloque tenu à Paris (11–12 May 1996). Milan and Paris, 1997, pp. 37–63.
—— and S. Schmidtke, 'Twelver Shī'ite Resources in Europe', *JA*, 285/1 (1997), pp. 73–122.
—— 'L'Imam dans le ciel. Ascension et initiation (Aspects de l'imamologie duodécimaine III)', in M. A. Amir-Moezzi (ed.), *Le voyage initiatique en terre d'islam. Ascensions célestes et itinéraires spirituels*. Bibliothèque de l'Ecole des Hautes Etudes, vol. 103. Louvain and Paris, 1997, pp. 99–116.
—— 'Seul l'homme de Dieu est humain. Théologie et anthropologie mystique à travers l'exégèse imamite ancienne (Aspects de l'imamologie duodécimaine IV)', *Arabica*, 45 (1998); English tr. in E. Kohlberg (ed.), *Shīʿism*. Aldershot, 2003, article II.
—— 'La vision par le cœur dans l'Islam shi'ite', *Connaissance des Religions*, special issue, 'Lumières sur la voie du cœur', 57–59 (1999), pp. 146–169.
—— 'Savoir c'est pouvoir. Exégèses et implications du miracle

dans l'imamisme ancien (Aspects de l'imamologie duodécimaine V)', in D. Aigle (ed.), *Les miracles des saints dans l'hagiographie chrétienne et islamique médiévale.* Bibliothèque de l'Ecole des Hautes Etudes, vol. 106. Turnhout, 2000, pp. 241–275.

—— 'Considerations sur l'expression *dīn ʿAlī*, Aux origines de la foi shi'ite', *ZDMG*, 150/1 (2000), pp. 29–68.

—— 'Fin du temps et retour à l'origine (Aspects de l'imamologie duodécimaine VI)', *Revue des Mondes Musulmans et de la Méditerranée*, special issue, 'Millénarisme et messianisme en Islam', ed. M. Garcia Arenal, 91–94 (2000), pp. 53–72.

—— 'Une absence remplie de présences: herméneutiques de l'Occultation chez les Shaykhiyya (Aspects de l'imamologie duodécimaine VII)', *BSOAS*, 64/1 (2001), pp. 1–18; English tr. in R. Brunner and W. Ende (eds), *The Twelver Shia in Modern Times: Religious Culture and Political History.* Leiden, 2001.

—— 'Notes à propos de la *walāya* imamite (Aspects de l'imamologie duodécimaine X)', *JAOS*, 122/4 (2002), pp. 722–741; also in G. Gobillot (ed.), *Mystique musulmane. Parcours en compagnie d'un chercheur: Roger Deladrière.* Paris, 2002.

—— 'Visions d'imams en mystique duodécimaine moderne et contemporaine (Aspects de l'imamologie duodécimaine VIII)', in E. Chaumont et al. (eds), *Autour du regard: Mélanges islamologiques offerts à Daniel Gimaret.* Louvain and Paris, 2003, pp. 97–124.

—— '"Le combattant du *ta'wīl*": un poème de Mollā Ṣadrā sur ʿAlī (Aspects de l'imamologie duodécimaine IX)', *JA*, 292/1–2 (2004), pp. 331–359; rpr in T. Lawson (ed.), *Reason and Inspiration in Islam: Essays in Honour of Hermann Landolt.* London, 2005.

—— 'Notes sur la prière dans le shīʿisme imamite', in M. A. Amir-Moezzi, C. Jambet and P. Lory (eds), *Henry Corbin: philosophies et sagesses des religions du Livre*, Bibliothèque de l'Ecole des Hautes Etudes, vol. 126. Turnhout, 2005. pp. 65–80.

—— ʻal-Ṭūsī, Abū Djaʻfar', *EI2*.
—— 'Cosmogony and Cosmology, v. In Twelver Shiʿism', *EIr*, vol. 4, pp. 317–322.
—— 'Ebn Shahrāshūb', *EIr*, vol. 8, pp. 53–54.
—— 'Imami Shiʿism iii. Eschatology', *EIr*, vol. 8, pp. 575–581.
—— and J. Calmard. 'Fāṭema bent Muḥammad', *EIr*, vol. 9, pp. 400–404.
—— see also under E. Kohlberg and M. A. Amir-Moezzi.
Anawati, G. C. 'Le nom suprême de Dieu (*Ism Allāh al-Aʿẓam*)', *Atti del Terzo Congresso di Studi Arabi e Islamici*. Naples, 1967.
Andrae, T. *Die Person Muhammads in Lehre und Glauben seiner Gemeinde*. Stockholm, 1918.
Antes, P. *Zur Theologie des Schiʿa. Eine Untersuchung des Jāmiʾ al-asrār wa Manbaʾ al-anwār von Sayyid Ḥaidar Āmolī*. Freiburg, 1971.
ʻAqīqī Bakhshāyeshī, A. *Foqahā-ye nāmdār-e shīʿe*. Qumm, 1405/1985.
Arazi, A. '*Ilqām al-ḥajar li-man zakkā sābb Abī Bakr wa ʻUmar* d'al-Suyuīṭī ou Le témoignage de l'insulteur des Compagnons', *JSAI*, 10 (1987), pp. 211–287.
Arendonk, C. von. *Les débuts de l'imamat zaydite du Yémen*. French tr. J. Ryckmans. Leiden, 1960.
Arjomand, S. Amir. *The Shadow of God and the Hidden Imam*. Chicago, 1984.
—— (ed.), *Authority and Political Culture in Shīʿism*. Albany, NY, 1988.
—— 'Shiʿism, Authority and Political Culture', in Amir-Arjomand (ed.), *Authority and Political Culture in Shīʿism*, pp. 1–24.
—— 'The Consolation of Theology: Absence of the Imam and Transition from Chiliasm to Law in Shiʿism', *The Journal of Religion*, 21 (1996), pp. 548–571.
—— 'The Crisis of the Imamate and the Institution of Occultation in Twelver Shiʿism', *IJMES*, 28 (1996), pp. 491–515; rpr. in E. Kohlberg (ed.), *Shīʿism*. Aldershot, 2003, article 5.
—— 'Imam *absconditus* and the Beginning of a Theology of

Occultation: Imami Shi'ism *circa* 280–90/900 A.D.', *JAOS*, 117/1 (1997), pp. 1–12.

Arnaldez, R. 'al-Insān al-Kāmil', *EI2*.

—— 'Lāhūt et Nāsūt', *EI2*.

—— 'Ma'ād', *EI2*.

Atallah, W. 'Ancien et nouveau langage dans la "Sîra" d'Ibn Hishâm', in *La vie du prophète Mahomet, Actes du colloque de Strasbourg (October 1980)*. Paris, 1983.

—— 'Les survivances préislamiques chez le Prophète et ses Compagnons', Arabica, 24/3 (1977).

Aubin, J. *Matériaux pour la biographie de Shāh Ni'matullāh Walī Kermānī*. Tehran and Paris, 1956.

Ayoub, M. *Redempting Suffering in Islām: a Study of the Devotional Aspects of 'Āshūrā' in Twelver Shī'ism*. The Hague, 1978.

—— 'Towards an Islamic Christology: An Image of Jesus in Early Shī'ī Muslim Literature', *MW*, 66 (1976).

—— 'The Speaking Qur'ān and the Silent Qur'ān: A Study of the Principles and Development of Imāmī Tafsīr', in A. Rippin (ed.), *Approaches to the History of the Interpretation of the Qur'ān*. Oxford, 1988, pp. 177–198.

Azami, Ch. A. 'Payghambarān Mountain Temple', *Journal of the K.R. Cama Oriental Institute*, 73 (1987), pp. 45–55.

—— 'Parmgar Fire Temple', *Journal of the K.R. Cama Oriental Institute*, 74 (1988), pp. 200–206.

A'ẓamī Sangesarī, C. A. 'Bāzmāndegān-e yazdgerd-e sevvom', *Īrān Shenākht*, 10 (1377 Sh./1998), pp. 183–191.

Āzmāyesh, S. M. '*Kebrīt-e aḥmar* va *Kanz al-asmā'*', *'Erfān-e Īrān*, new series, 1 (1378/1999), pp. 181–195.

Badawī, 'A. R. *al-Insān al-kāmil fi'l-islām*. Cairo, 1950.

—— *Shaṭaḥāt al-ṣūfiyya*. 3rd edn, Kuwait, 1978.

Bahār, M. T. *Sabk shenāsī: Tārīkh-e taṭavvor-e nathr-e fārsī*. 2nd edn, Tehran, 1337 Sh./1959.

Bailey, H. W. *Zoroastrian Problems in the Ninth Century Books*. Oxford, 1943.

Balāghī, 'A. Ḥ. *Maqālāt al-ḥunafā'*. Tehran, 1369/1949.

—— *Tārīkh-e Najaf-e ashraf va ḥīra*. Tehran, 1328 Sh./1949–1950.

Ballanfat, P. 'Réflexions sur la nature du paradoxe. La définition de Rûzbehân Baqlî Shîrâzî', *Kâr Nâmeh*, 2–3 (1995), pp. 25–40.

—— 'Considérations sur la conception du cœur chez Mullā Ṣadrā (1)', *Kār-Nāmeh*, 5 (1999), pp. 33–46; (2), *Kār-Nāmeh*, 6 (2000), pp. 67–84.

—— see also under Gobillot, Najm al-Dīn Kubrā.

Bar-Asher, M. M. *Scripture and Exegesis in Early Imāmī Shiism*. Leiden and Jerusalem, 1999.

—— and A. Kofsky, *The Nuṣayrī-ʿAlawī Religion: An Enquiry into its Theology and Liturgy*. Leiden, 2002.

—— 'Deux traditions hétérodoxes dans les anciens commentaires imamites du Coran', *Arabica*, 37 (1990), pp. 21–314.

—— 'Variant Readings and Additions of the Imāmī-Shīʿa to the Quran', *IOS*, 13 (1993), pp. 39–74.

—— 'The Qur'ān Commentary Ascribed to Imam Ḥasan al-ʿAskarī', *JSAI*, 24 (2000), pp. 358–379.

Barthold, W. *Mussulman Culture*, English tr. Sh. Suhrawardy. Calcutta, 1934; rpr. Philadelphia, 1977.

Bāstānī Pārīzī, M. E. *Khātūn-e haft qalʿe*. Tehran, 1344 Sh./1966; 3rd edn, 1363 Sh./1984.

—— 'Benā hā-ye dokhtar dar Īrān', *Majalle-ye bāstān shenāsī*, 1–2 (1338 Sh./1959), pp. 105–137.

Bayat, M. *Mysticism and Dissent. Socioreligious Thought in Qajar Iran*. New York, 1982.

Bayhom-Daou, T. 'The Imam's Knowledge and the Quran According to al-Faḍl b. Shādhān al-Nīsābūrī (d. 260 A.H./874 A.D.)', *BSOAS*, 64/2 (2001), pp. 188–207.

Beeston, A. F. L. 'The So-called Harlots of Ḥaḍramawt', *Oriens*, 5 (1952).

—— 'Kingship in Ancient South-Arabia', *JESHO*, 15 (1972).

Bianchi, U. (ed.) *La 'doppia' creazione dell'uomo negli Alessandrini, nei Cappadoci nella gnosis*. Rome, 1978.

Blichfeldt, J. O. *Early Mahdism: Politics and Religion in the Formative Period of Islam*. Leiden, 1986.

Blochet, E. 'Etudes sur l'histoire religieuse de l'Iran I. De l'influence de la religion mazdéenne sur les croyances des peuples turcs', *RHR*, 38 (1898), pp. 26–63.

Birkeland, H. *The Legend of Opening of Muhammad's Breast*. Oslo, 1955.

Bolūkbāshī, 'A. 'Tābūt gardānī, namāyeshī tamthīlī az qodrat-e qodsī-ye khodāvandī', *Nashr-e Dānesh*, 16/4 (1378 Sh./2000), pp. 32–38.

Bonte, P. 'Egalité et hiérarchie dans une tribu maure', in *Al-Ansāb. La quête des origines*. Paris, 1991.

—— Conte, E., Hames, C. and A. W. Ould Cheikh (eds), *Al-Ansāb. La quête des origines*. Paris, 1991.

Bosworth, C. E. 'The Persian Impact on Arabic literature', in E. Beeston et al. (eds), *The Cambridge History of Arabic Literature: Arabic Literature to the End of the Umayyad Period*. Cambridge, 1983, pp. 155–167.

—— 'The Persian Contribution to Islamic Historiography in the Pre-Mongol Period', in R. G. Hovannisian-G. Sabagh (ed.), *The Persian Presence in the Islamic World*. Cambridge, 1998, pp. 218–236.

—— and V. Minorsky. 'Rayy', *EI2*.

Boyce, M. 'Bībī Shahrbānū and the Lady of Pārs', *BSOAS*, 30/1 (1967), pp. 30–44.

—— *A History of Zoroastrianism*, vol. 2. Leiden, 1978.

—— 'Anāhīd, i. Ardwīsūr Anāhīd; ii. Anaitis', *EIr*, vol. 1, pp. 1003–1006.

Bravmann, M. M. *The Spiritual Background of Early Islam*. Leiden, 1972.

Browne, E. G. *A Literary History of Persia*; rpr. Cambridge, 1928, 4 vols.

Brunner, R. *Die Schia und die Koranfälschung*. Würzburg, 2001.

—— and W. Ende (eds), *The Twelver Shia in Modern Times: Religious Culture and Political History*. Leiden, 2001.

—— 'La question de la falsification du Coran dans l'exégèse chiite duodécimaine', *Arabica*, 52/1 (2005), pp. 1–42.

Budge, A. W. *The History of Alexander the Great being the Syrian Version of the Pseudo-Callisthenes*. Cambridge, 1889.

Busse, H. 'Jerusalem in the Story of Muḥammad's Night Journey and Ascension', *Jerusalem Studies in Arabic and Islam*, 14 (1991).

Caetani, L. *Annali del'Islam*. Milan, 1905–1925.

Calder, N. 'Zakāt in Imāmī Shīʿī Jurisprudence', *BSOAS*, 44 (1981).

—— 'Accomodation and Revolution in Imāmī Shīʿī Jurisprudence: Khumayni and the Classical Tradition', *Middle East Studies*, 18 (1982).

—— 'Khums in Imāmī Shīʿī Jurisprudence', *BSOAS*, 45 (1982).

Calmard, J. 'Le chiisme imamite en Iran à l'époque seldjoukide d'après le *Kitâb al-naqḍ*', *Le monde iranien et l'Islam*, 1 (1971).

—— 'Les rituels shi'ites et le pouvoir. L'imposition du shi'isme safavide, eulogies et malédictions canoniques', in J. Calmard (ed.), *Etudes Safavides*. Publications de l'Institut Français de Recherche en Iran, Tehran, 1993.

—— 'Moḥammad b. al-Ḥanafiyya dans la religion populaire, le folklore, les légendes dans le monde turco-persan et indo-persan', *Cahiers d'Asie Centrale*, 5–6 (1998), pp. 201–220.

—— see also Amir-Moezzi, 'Fāṭema bent Muḥammad'.

Capezzone, L. 'Abiura dalla Kaysāniyya e conversione all'Imāmiyya: il caso di Abū Khālid al-Kābulī', *RSO*, 66/1–2 (1992), pp. 1–14.

—— 'Un miracolo di ʿAlī ibn Abī Ṭālib: i versi attribuiti ad al-Sayyid al-Ḥimyarī e il modello storiografico delle fonti relative al *radd al-šams*', in *In memoria di Francesco Gabrieli (1904–1996)*, *RSO*, 71, supp. 2 (1997), pp. 99–112.

Carra de Vaux. 'Djirdjīs', *EI2*.

Carter, M. 'The Kātib in Fact and Fiction', *Abr Nahrain*, 11 (1971), pp. 42–55.

Chabbi, J. *Le Seigneur des tribus. L'Islam de Mahomet*. Paris, 1997.

—— 'La représentation du passé aux premiers âges de l'historiographie califale', in *Itinéraires d'Orient: Hommages à Claude Cahen*, Res Orientales VI. Paris, 1995, pp. 21–46.

Chaumont, M. L. 'Le culte d'Anâhitâ à Stakhr et les premiers Sassanides', *RHR*, 153 (1958), pp. 154–175.

—— 'Le culte de la déesse Anâhitâ (Anahit) dans la religion des monarques d'Iran et d'Arménie au 1er siècle de notre ère', *JA*, 253 (1965), pp. 167–181.

—— 'Anāhīd, iii. The Cult and its Diffusion', *EIr*, vol. 1, pp. 1,006–1,009.

Chavannes, E. *Documents sur les Tou-kiue (Turcs) occidentaux*. St Petersburg, 1903.

Chelhod, J. *Les structures du sacré chez les arabes*. Paris, 1986.

—— 'La *baraka* chez les Arabes', *RHR*, 148/1 (1955).

—— 'Du nouveau à propos du "matriarcat" arabe', *Arabica*, 28/1 (1981).

Chittick, W. *A Shiʿite Anthology*. New York, 1981.

—— *The Psalms of Islam*, English tr. of *al-Ṣaḥīfat al-sajjādiyya*. London, 1988.

Chodkiewicz, M. *Le Sceau des saints, Prophétie et sainteté dans la doctrine d'Ibn ʿArabī*. Paris, 1986.

Chokr, M. *Zandaqa et zindīqs en Islam au second siècle de l'hégire*. Damascus, 1993.

Choksy, J. K. *Conflict and Cooperation: Zoroastrian Subalterns and Muslim Elites in Medieval Muslim Society*. New York, 1997.

Christensen, A. *L'Iran sous les Sassanides*; rpr. Osnabrück, 1971.

Cole, J. R. 'Imami Jurisprudence and the Role of the Ulama: Mortaza Ansari on Emulation of the Supreme Exemplar', in N. R. Keddie (ed.), *Religion and Politics in Iran. Shiʿism from Quietism to Revolution*. New Haven and London, 1983.

—— 'Shiʿi Clerics in Iraq and Iran, 1772–1780: The Akhbari-Usuli Conflict Reconsidered', *Iranian Studies*, 28 (1985).

Colpe, C. 'Der "Iranische Hintergrund" der islamischen Lehre vom Vollkommenen Menschen', in Ph. Gignoux (ed.), *Recurrent Patterns in Iranian Religions. From Mazdaism to Sufism*, *Studia Iranica*, 11 (1992), pp. 9–12.

Conte, E. 'Entrer dans le sang. Perceptions arabes des origines', in

Conte, E. et al. (eds), *Al-Ansāb. La quête des origines*. Paris, 1991.

Corbin, H. *L'Imagination créatrice dans le soufisme d'Ibn ʿArabī*. Paris, 1958.

—— *Trilogie ismaélienne*. Tehran and Paris, 1961.

—— *L'Homme de Lumière dans le soufisme iranien*. Paris, 1971.

—— *En Islam iranien. Aspects spirituels et philosophiques*. Paris, 1971–1972.

—— *Temple et contemplation*. Paris, 1980.

—— *Corps spirituel et Terre céleste. De l'Iran mazdéen à l'Iran shiʿite*. Paris, 1979.

—— *Le paradoxe du monothéisme*. Paris, 1981.

—— *La philosophie iranienne islamique aux XVIIè et XVIIIè siècles*. Paris, 1981.

—— *Temps cyclique et gnose ismaélienne*. Paris, 1982.

—— *L'Homme et son ange*. Paris, 1983.

—— *Face de Dieu, Face de l'Homme*. Paris, 1983.

—— *Alchimie comme art hiératique*, ed. P. Lory. Paris, 1986.

—— *Histoire de la philosophie islamique*. Paris, 1986 (including the two parts published separately in 1964 and 1974).

—— *L'Iran et la philosophie*. Paris, 1990.

—— 'Epiphanie divine et naissance spirituelle dans la gnose ismaélienne', *Eranos Jahrbuch*, 23 (1955).

—— 'Sayyid Haydar Amolî, théologien shîʿite du soufisme', in *Mélanges Henri Massé*. Tehran, 1963.

—— 'Cosmogonie et herméneutique dans l'œuvre de Sayyed Jaʿfar Kashfī', in *Annuaire EPHE 1970–71*; (now in *Itinéraire d'un enseignement*, Institut Français de Recherche en Iran, Tehran, 1993).

—— 'La gnose islamique dans le recueil de traditions (*Mashâriq al-anwâr*) de Rajab Borsi', *Annuaire de l'EPHE, section des sciences religieuses*, 1968–1969 and 1969–1970 (now in *Itinéraire d'un enseignement*).

Cornell, V. *The Realm of the Saint: Power and Authority in Moroccan Sufism*. Austin, TX, 1998.

Crone, P. 'Mawlā', *EI2*.

—— and Cook, M. *Hagarism: The Making of the Islamic World*. Cambridge, 1977.

Crow, D. K. 'The Role of *al-ʿAql* in Early Islamic Wisdom, with Reference to Imam Jaʿfar al-Ṣādiq', PhD thesis, McGill University, 1996.

Cuisenier, J. and Miquel, A. 'La terminologie arabe de la parenté. Analyse sémantique et analyse componentielle', *L'Homme*, 5/3–4 (1965).

Cumont, F. *Textes et monuments relatifs aux mystères de Mithra*. Brussels, 1896–1899.

—— *Les mystères de Mithra*. (Rpr. of 3rd edn, Brussels, 1913) Paris, 1985.

Daftary, F., "Alī in Classical Ismaili Theology', in A. Y. Ocak (ed.), *From History to Theology: Ali in Islamic Beliefs*. Ankara, 2005, pp. 59–82.

Daniel, E. *The Political and Social History of Khurasan under Abbasid Rule (747–820)*. Minneapolis and Chicago, 1979.

—— 'Arabs, Persians and the Advent of the Abbasids Reconsidered', *JAOS*, 117/3 (1997), pp. 542–548.

Dean-Otting, M. *Heavenly Journeys: A Study of the Motif in Hellenistic Jewish Literature*. Frankfurt, Bern and New York, 1984.

Desparmet, J. *Le Mal magique*. Algiers and Paris, 1932.

Dhākerī, M. 'Shegerd hā-ye nā maʾlūf dar sheʿr-e Saʿdī', *Nashr-i Dānish*, 16/2 (1378 Sh./1999), pp. 31–35.

Djaït, H. *La Grande Discorde: Religion et politique dans l'Islam des origines*. Paris, 1989.

Duchesne-Guillemin, J. 'Le *xvarenah*', *AION*, s. linguistica, 5 (1963), pp. 19–31.

—— 'La royauté iranienne et le xvarenah', in Gh. Gnoli and A. V. Rossi (eds), *Iranica*. Naples, 1979, pp. 375–386.

—— 'Encore le *xvarenah*', *Studia Iranica*, 20 (1991), pp. 193–195.

Duppont-Sommer, A. and M. Philonenko (eds), *La Bible. Ecrits intertestamentaires*. Paris, 1987.

Dūrī, ʿA.ʿA. *al-Judhūr al-taʾrīkhiyya liʾl-shuʿūbiyya*. Beirut, 1963.

—— *Nashʾat ʿilm al-taʾrīkh ʿindaʾl-ʿarab*. Beirut, 1960.

Eftekhār-Zādeh, M. R. *Eslām dar Īran. Shuʿūbiyye nehḍat-e moqāvamat-e mellī-ye Īrān ʿalayh-e Omaviyān va ʿAbbāsiyān*. Tehran, 1371 Sh./1992.

Eliash, J. 'Misconceptions Regarding the Juridical Status of the Iranian 'Ulamā'', *IJMES*, 10 (1979).

—— 'On the Genesis and Development of the Twelver-Shīʿī Three-tenet *Shahāda*', *Der Islam*, 47 (1971), pp. 265–272.

—— 'The Shi'ite Qurʾān: Reconsideration of Goldziher's Interpretation', *Arabica*, 16 (1969), pp. 15–24.

Elmore, G. *Islamic Sainthood in the Fullness of Time, Ibn al-ʿArabī's Book of the Fabulous Gryphon*. Leiden, 1999.

Ende, W. 'Mutawālī', *EI2*.

—— *see also* under Brunner.

Enderwitz, S. *Gesellschaftlicher Rang und ethniche Legitimation. Der arabische Schriftseller Abū ʿUthmān al-Ǧāḥiẓ über die Afrikaner, Perser und Araber in der islamischen Gesellschaft*. Freiburg, 1979.

—— 'Shuʿūbiyya', *EI2*.

Eqbāl, ʿA. *Khāndān-e Nawbakhtī*. 1st edn, Tehran, 1311 Sh./1932.

Ernst, C. *Words of Ecstasy in Sufism*. New York, 1985.

Eshots, J. 'Ṣadr al-Dīn Shīrāzī mobtaker-e ḥekmat e ʿarshī', *Kherad-Nāmeh Ṣadrā*, 20 (2000), pp. 61–66.

—— 'Unification of Perceiver and Perceived and Unity of Being', *Transcendent Philosophy*, 1/3 (2000), pp. 1–7.

—— '*al-Wāridāt al-qalbiyya fī maʿrifat al-rubūbiyya*, resāle-yī 'erfānī az yek ḥakīm', *Kherad-Nāmeh Ṣadrā*, 15 (Tehran, 1999), pp. 74–82.

Ess, J. van. *Theologie und Gesellschaft im 2. und 3. Jahrhundert Hidschra. Eine Geschichte des religiösen Denkens im frühen Islam*, I–VI. Berlin and New York, 1991–1997.

—— 'Les Qadarites et les Gailānīya de Yazīd III', *SI*, 31 (1970).

—— 'Das *Kitāb al-irjā'* des Ḥasan b. Muḥammad b. al-Ḥanafiyya', *Arabica*, 21 (1974) and 22 (1975).
—— 'Ibn Kullāb et la *Miḥna*', *Arabica*, 37 (1990), pp. 173–233; French tr. C. Gilliot, of 'Ibn Kullāb und die Miḥna', *Oriens*, 18–19 (1967).
Fahd, T. *Le Panthéon de l'Arabie centrale à la veille de l'Hégire*. Paris, 1968.
—— *La Divination arabe*. Strasburg, 1971; rpr. Paris, 1987.
—— 'Ǧa'far al-Ṣādiq et la tradition scientifique arabe', in *Le shī'isme imāmite*, Actes du colloque de Strasbourg (6–9 May 1968). Paris, 1970.
—— 'Le monde du sorcier en Islam', *Le Monde du sorcier*, 'Sources Orientales'. Paris, 1966.
—— *see also (Le) shī'isme imāmite.*
Falaturi, A. 'Die Zwölfer-Schia aus der Sicht eines Schiiten, Problem ihrer Untersuchung', in *Festschrift Werner Caskel*. Leiden, 1968, pp. 2–25.
Faqīhī, A. A. *Āl-e Būye va owḍā'-e zamān-e īshān*. 2nd edn, Tehran, 1365 Sh./1986.
Fischer, M. *Iran: from Religious Dispute to Revolution*. Cambridge, 1980.
Fouchécour, Ch. H. de. *Moralia. Les notions morales dans la littérature persane du 3e/9e au 7e/13e siècle*. Paris, 1986.
Freitag, R. *Seelenwanderung in der islamischen Häresie*. Berlin, 1985.
Friedländer, I. ''Abdallāh b. Saba', der Begründer der Shī'a und sein Jüdischer Ursprung', *Zeitschrift für Assyriologie*, 23 (1909), pp. 32–63.
Friedmann, Y. 'Finality of Prophethood in Sunni Islam', *JSAI*, 7 (1986), pp. 177–215.
—— 'Classification of Unbelievers in Sunnī Muslim Law and Tradition', *JSAI*, 22 (1998), pp. 163–195.
Gabrieli, F. *Al-Ma'mūn e gli 'Alidi*. Leipzig, 1929.
—— 'Literary Tendencies', in G. E. von Grunebaum (ed.), *Unity and Variety in Muslim Civilization*. Chicago, 1955, pp. 87–106.

Gardet, L. *Dieu et la destinée de l'homme*. Paris, 1967.

—— 'Fins dernières selon la théologie musulmane', *Revue Thomiste*, 2 (1957).

—— 'Les Noms et les Statuts', *SI*, 5 (1956).

—— 'Duʿā'', *EI2*.

Gennep , A. van. *Les Rites de passage*. Paris, 1909.

Gershevitch, I. 'Margarites the Pearl', in Ch. H. de Fouchécour and Ph. Gignoux (ed.), *Etudes irano-aryennes offertes à Gilbert Lazard. Studia Iranica*, 7 (1989,) pp. 113–136.

Gesenius-Buhl, *Hebräisches und Aramäisches Handwörterbuch*. 17th edn, Leiden, 1951.

Ghirshman, R. *Iran, Parthes et Sassanides*. Paris, 1962.

—— *Bîchâpour*, vol. 1. Paris, 1971.

Gibb, H. A. R. 'The Social Significance of the Shuʿūbiyya', *Studia Orientalia Ioanni Pedersen Dicata*. Copenhagen, 1953, pp. 105–114; rpr. in Shaw and Polk (eds), *Studies on the Civilization of Islam*. Boston, 1962, pp. 62–73.

—— 'Abū'l-Sarāyā al-Shaybānī', *EI2*.

Gignoux, Ph. '*Imago Dei*: de la théologie nestorienne à Ibn al-ʿArabī', in Ph. Gignoux (ed.), *Recurrent Patterns in Iranian Religions. From Mazdaism to Sufism. Studia Iranica*, 11 (Paris, 1992).

Gimaret, D. *Les noms divins en Islam*. Paris, 1988.

Gil, M. *A History of Palestine 634–1099*. Cambridge, 1992.

—— 'The Exilarchate', in D. Frank (ed.), *The Jews of Medieval Islam: Community, Society and Identity. Proceedings of the International Conference held by the Institute of Jewish Studies (London 1992)*. Leiden 1995.

Giladi, A. 'Some Notes on *taḥnīk* in Medieval Islam', *JNES*, 3 (1988).

Gilliot, C. 'Le portrait 'mythique' d'Ibn ʿAbbās', *Arabica*, 32 (1985).

—— 'Muqātil, grand exégète, traditionniste et théologien maudit', *JA*, 279/1–2 (1991).

—— 'Les 'informateurs' juifs et chrétiens de Muḥammad', *JSAI*, 22 (1998).

Gloton, M. 'Les secrets du cœur selon l'Islam', *Connaissance des Religions*, special issue, 'Lumières sur la voie du cœur', 57–59 (1999), pp. 118–145.

Gnoli, Gh. 'Un particolare aspetto del simbolismo della luce nel Mazdeismo e nel Manicheismo', *AION*, new series 12 (1962), pp. 95–128.

—— '*Axvaretem Xvareno*', *AION*, 13 (1963), pp. 295–298.

—— 'Un cas possible de différenciation lexicale entre *dari* et *fârsi*', in C. H. de Fouchécour and Ph. Gignoux (eds), *Etudes irano-aryennes offertes à Gilbert Lazard*. Paris, 1989, pp. 151–164.

Gobillot, G. *La conception originelle (fiṭra), ses interprétations et fonctions chez les penseurs musulmans*, Cahiers des Annales Islamologiques. Cairo, 2000.

—— and Ballanfat, P. 'Le cœur et la vie spirituelle chez les mystiques musulmans', *Connaissance des religions*, 57–59 (1999), pp. 170–204.

Goitein, S. D. *Studies in Islamic History and Institutions*. Leiden, 1966.

Goldziher, I. *Muhammedanische Studien*. Halle, 1889–1890; tr. S. M. Stern and C. R. Barber as *Muslim Studies*. London, 1967–1971.

—— *Vorlesungen über den Islam*. Heidelberg, 1910.

—— *Gesammelte Schriften*, ed. J. de Somogyi. Hildesheim, 1967–1970.

—— 'Polyandry and Exogamy among the Arabs', *The Academy*, 13/26 (1880).

—— 'Islamisme et parsisme', *RHR*, 43 (1901), pp. 1–29.

—— 'Spottnamen der ersten Chalifen bei den Schī'iten', *WZMG*, 15 (1901), pp. 320–332; rpr. in *Gesammelte Schriften*, vol. 4, pp. 291–305.

—— 'Das Prinzip der *takijja* im Islam', *ZDMG*, 60 (1906), pp. 201–204; rpr. in *Gesammelte Schriften*, vol. 5, pp. 59–72.

—— 'Neuplatonische und gnostische Elemente im Ḥadīt', *ZA* (1908).

—— 'Schi'itisches', *ZDMG*, 44 (1910), pp. 532–533, rpr. in *Gesammelte Schriften*, vol. 5, pp. 213–214.

Goodenough, W. H. 'Comments on the Question of Incestuous Marriages in Old Iran', *American Anthropologist*, 51 (1949), pp. 326–328.

Gramlich, R. *Die schiitischen Derwischorden Persiens*. Wiesbaden, 1979–1981, 3 vols.

—— *Die Wunder der Freunde Gottes. Theologien und Erscheinungsformen des islamischen Heiligewunders*, Freiburger Islamstudien, 11. Wiesbaden, 1987.

—— 'Der Urvertrag in der Koranauslegung (zu Sura 7, 172–173)', *Der Islam*, 60 (1983), pp. 205–230.

Grenet, F. and B. Marshak. 'Le mythe de Nana dans l'art de la Sogdiane', *Arts Asiatiques*, 53 (1998), pp. 5–18.

—— 'Résumé des cours', *L'Annuaire de l'Ecole Pratique des Hautes Etudes, Sciences Religieuses*, 105 (1996–1997), pp. 213–217.

Grignaschi, M. 'Quelques spécimens de la littérature sassanide conservés dans les bibliothèques d'Istanbul', *JA*, 240 (1967), pp. 33–59.

—— 'La *Nihâyatu-l-arab fî akhbâri-l-Furs wa-l-'Arab* (première partie)', *BEO*, 22 (1969), pp. 15–67.

—— 'La *Nihâyatu-l-arab fî akhbâri-l-Furs wa-l-'Arab* et les *Siyaru Mulûki-l-'Ajam* du Ps. Ibn al-Muqaffa'', *BEO*, 26 (1973), pp. 83–184.

—— 'La *Siyâsatu-l-'âmmiyya* et l'influence iranienne sur la pensée politique islamique', *Hommage et Opera Minora Monumentum H.S. Nyberg*, vol. 3, *Acta Iranica*. Leiden, 1975, pp. 124–141.

Gril, D. 'Le miracle en islam, critère de la sainteté?', in D. Aigle (ed.), *Saints orientaux* (hagiographies médiévales comparées, 1). Paris, 1995, pp. 69–81.

Gruber, C. and F. Colby, eds, *The Prophet's Ascension: Cross Cultural Encounters with the Islamic Mi'rāj Tales*. Bloomington, IN, 2010.

Grunebaum, G. E. von. 'Firdausī's Concept of History', in his *Islam: Essays in the Nature and Growth of a Cultural Tradition*. London, 1955.

Haddad, Y. Y., see Smith, M.

Halm, H. *Die islamische Gnosis. Die Extreme Shia und die ʿAlawiten*. Zurich and Munich, 1982.

—— *Die Schia*. Darmstadt, 1988; French tr. as *Le chiisme*. Paris, 1994.

—— 'Die *Sīrat Ibn Ḥaushab*. Die ismailitische *daʿwa* im Jemen und die Fatimiden', *Die Welt des Orients*, 12 (1981), pp. 107–135.

Hamid, I. S. 'The Metaphysics and Cosmology of Process According to Shaykh Aḥmad al-Aḥsāʾī'. PhD thesis, State University of New York, 1998.

Ḥamīdī, S. J. *Nehḍat-e Abū Saʿīd Ganāvehī*. 3rd edn, Tehran, 1372 Sh./1993.

Harandī, M. J. *Fuqahāʾ wa ḥukūmat. Pažūheshī dar tārīkh-i fiqh-i siyāsī-yi shīʿa*. Tehran, 1379 Sh./2000.

Harmatta, J. 'The Middle Persian-Chinese Bilingual Inscription from Asian and the Chinese Sāsānian Relations', *La Persia nel Medioevo* (Accademia Nazionale dei Lincei). Rome, 1971, pp. 363–376.

Hassuri (Ḥaṣūrī), ʿA. *Ākherīn shāh*. Tehran, 1371 Sh./1992.

Hedāyat, Ṣ. *Neyrangestān*; rpr. Tehran, 1344 Sh./1966.

Henning, W. B. 'The Murder of the Magi', in *Selected Papers II, Acta Iranica*, 15, series 2, vol. 6. Leiden, Tehran and Liège, 1977, pp. 139–150.

—— 'A Sogdian God', in *Selected Papers II, Acta Iranica*, 15, series 2, vol. 6. Leiden, Tehran and Liège, 1977, pp. 617–630.

Henninger, J. *La société bédouine ancienne*. Rome, 1959.

Herrenschmidt, Cl. 'Note sur la parenté chez les Perses au début de l'empire Achéménide', in H. Sancisi-Weerdenburg et al. (eds), *Achaemenid History*, vol. 2, 'The Greek Sources'. Leiden, 1987, pp. 53–67.

—— 'Le *xwētōdas* ou mariage "incestueux" en Iran ancien', in P. Bonte (ed.), *Epouser au plus proche. Inceste, prohibitions et stratégies matrimoniales autour de la Méditerranée*. Paris, 1994, pp. 113–125.

Hinds, M. 'Miḥna', *EI2*.

Hodgson, M. G. S. *Venture of Islam: Conscience and History in a World Civilization*. Chicago 1961–1974, vol. 1, 'The Classical Age of Islam'.

—— 'How did the Early Shīʿa Become Sectarian?', *JAOS*, 75 (1955), pp. 1–13, rpr. in E. Kohlberg (ed.), *Shīʿism*. Aldershot, 2003, article 1.

—— "ʿAbdallāh b. Saba", *EI2*.

—— 'Bayān b. Samʿān', *EI2*.

—— 'Ghulāt', *EI2*.

Holmyard, E. J. *The Arabic Works of Jābir b. Ḥayyān*. Paris, 1928.

Horovitz, J. 'Muhammeds Himmelfahrt', *Der Islam*, 9 (1919).

Hoyland, R. G. *Seeing Islam as Others Saw It: A Survey and Evaluation of Christian, Jewish and Zoroastrian Writings on Early Islam*. Princeton, 1997.

Hrbek, I. 'Muḥammads Nachlass und die Aliden', *Archiv Orientální*, 18 (1950).

Huart, C. 'La poésie religieuse des nosaïris', *JA*, 14 (1879), pp. 241–248.

Huitema, T. *De Voorsprak* (shafāʿa) *in den Islam*. Leiden, 1936.

Hussain, J. M. *The Occultation of the Twelfth Imam: A Historical Background*. London, 1982.

Iqbāl see Eqbāl.

Istakhrī, M. *Oṣūl-e taṣavvof*. Tehran, 1338 Sh./1960.

Jaʿfarī, M. M. *Sayyid Raḍī*. Tehran, 1999.

Jaʿfariyān, R. *Tārīkh e tashayyuʿ dar Īrān: az āghāz tā qarn e dahom e hejrī*. Qumm, 1375 Sh./1996.

Jambet, C. *L'acte d'être. La philosophie de la révélation chez Mollâ Sadrâ*. Paris, 2002.

—— *Se rendre immortel*, suivi du *Traité de la résurrection* (French tr. of *Risālat al-ḥashr) de Mollā Ṣadrā Shīrāzī*. Paris, 2000.

—— see also Amir-Moezzi and Jambet.

James, E. O. *The Nature and Function of Priesthood*. London, 1955.

Juynboll, G. H. A. *The Authenticity of the Tradition Literature. Discussions in Modern Egypt*. Leiden, 1969.

—— 'Some New Ideas on the Developments of *Sunna* as a Technical Term in Early Islam', *JSAI*, 10 (1987); rpr. in *Studies on the Origins*, article V.

—— *Studies on the Origins and Uses of Islamic Ḥadīth*. London, 1996.

Karīmān, Ḥ. *Ray-e bāstān*. Tehran, 1345–1349 Sh./1966–1970.

Kasrawī, A. *Bahā'īgarī*; rpr. Tehran, n.d.

—— *Bekhānīd wa dāvarī konīd*; rpr. n.p., n.d.

—— *Shī'īgarī*; rpr. Tabriz, 1330 Sh./1951.

Kennedy, H. *The Early 'Abbāsid Caliphate*. London, 1986.

Khājavī, M. *Lawāmi' al-'ārifīn fī aḥwāl Ṣadr al-muta'allihīn*. Tehran, 1366 Sh./1987.

Khalidi, T. *Islamic Historiography: The Histories of Mas'ūdī*. Albany, NY, 1975.

Khāvarī, A. *Dhahabiyye*. Tehran, 1362/1983.

Kister, M. J. 'You Shall Only Set Out for Three Mosques', *Muséon*, 82 (1969).

—— 'Ḥaddithū 'an Banī Isrā'īl wa lā ḥaraja', *IOS*, 2 (1972).

Kiyā, Kh. *Kh(w)āb va pendāreh. Dar jostojū-ye vīžegī-hā ye kh(w)āb-hā ye Īrānī*. Tehran, 1378 Sh./1999.

Klemm, V. 'Die vier *Sufarā'* des Zwölften Imams. Zur formativen Periode der Zwölferschia', *Die Welt des Orients*, 15 (1984), pp. 126–143; English tr. in E. Kohlberg (ed.), *Shī'ism*. Aldershot, 2003, article 6.

Kohlberg, E. *A Medieval Muslim Scholar at Work. Ibn Ṭāwūs and his Library*. Leiden, 1992.

—— *Belief and Law in Imāmī-Shī'ism*. Variorum, Aldershot, 1991.

—— (ed.), *Shī'ism*. Aldershot, 2003.

—— and M. A. Amir-Moezzi, *Revelation and Falsification: The* Kitāb al-Qirā'āt *of Aḥmad b. Muḥammad al-Sayyārī*. Leiden, 2009.

—— 'Some Notes on the Imāmite Attitude to the Qur'ān', in S. M. Stern, A. Hourani and V. Brown (eds), *Islamic Philosophy and the Classical Tradition. Essays Presented by His Friends and Pupils to R. Walzer on His Seventieth Birthday*. Oxford, 1972, pp. 209–224.

—— 'An Unusual Shīʿī *isnād*', *IOS*, 5 (1975), pp. 142–149; rpr. in *Belief and Law*, article VIII.

—— 'Some Imāmi-Shīʿi Views on *taqiyya*', *JAOS*, 95 (1975), pp. 395–402; rpr. in *Belief and Law*, article III.

—— 'From Imāmiyya to Ithnā-ʿashariyya', *BSOAS*, 39 (1976), pp. 521–534; rpr. in *Belief and Law*, article 14.

—— 'The Development of the Imāmī Shīʿī Doctrine of *jihād*', *ZDMG*, 126 (1976); rpr. in *Belief and Law*, article XV.

—— 'Abū Turāb', *BSOAS*, 41 (1978), pp. 64–86; rpr. in *Belief and Law*, article VI.

—— 'The Term "Muḥaddath" in Twelver Shīʿism', in *Studia Orientalia memoriæ D.H. Baneth dedicate*. Jerusalem, 1979, pp. 39–47; rpr. in *Belief and Law*, article V.

—— 'The Term "Rāfiḍa" in Imāmī Shīʿī Usage', *JAOS*, 99 (1979), pp. 677–679; rpr. in *Belief and Law*, article IV.

—— 'Some Shīʿī Views on the Antediluvian World', *SI*, 52 (1980), pp. 41–66; rpr. in *Belief and Law*, article XVI.

—— 'Shīʿī Ḥadīth', in A. F. L. Beeston et al. (eds), *The Cambridge History of Arabic Literature*, vol. 1: *Arabic Literature to the End of Umayyad Period*. Cambridge, 1983, pp. 299–307.

—— 'Some Imāmī Shīʿī Views on the *ṣaḥāba*', *JSAI*, 5 (1984), pp. 64–86; rpr. in *Belief and Law*, article IX.

—— 'Non-Imāmī Muslims in Imāmī *fiqh*', *JSAI*, 6 (1985), pp. 99–105; rpr. in *Belief and Law*, article X.

—— '*Barā'a* in Shīʿī doctrine', *JSAI*, 7 (1986), pp. 139–175.

—— '*Al-uṣūl al-arabʿumi'a*', *JSAI*, 10 (1987), pp. 128–166; rpr. in *Belief and Law*, article VII.

—— 'Imam and Community in the Pre-Ghayba Period', in S. A. Arjomand (ed.), *Authority and Political Culture in Shi'ism*. New York, 1988, pp. 25–53; rpr. in *Belief and Law*, article XIII.

—— '"Alī b. Mūsā Ibn Ṭāwūs and his Polemic against Sunnism', Proceedings of the Symposium *Religionsgespräche im Mittelalter*. Berlin, 1992, pp. 325–350.

—— 'Authoritative Scriptures in Early Imāmī Shī'ism', in E. Patlagean and A. LeBoulluec (eds), *Les retours aux Ecritures. Fondamentalismes présents et passés*. Louvain and Paris, 1993, pp. 295–312.

—— 'Taqiyya in Shī'ī Theology and Religion', in H. G. Kippenberg and G. G. Stroumsma (eds), *Secrecy and Concealment. Studies in the History of Mediterranean and Near Eastern Religions*. Leiden, 1995, pp. 345–380.

—— 'Early Attestations of the Term *ithnā'ashariyya*', *JSAI*, 24 (2000), pp. 343–357.

—— 'In Praise of the Few', in *Studies in Islamic and Middle Eastern Texts and Traditions, In Memory of Norman Calder*, ed. G. R. Hawting, J. A. Mojaddedi and A. Samely, *JSS*, supp. 12 (2000), pp. 149–162.

—— 'Vision and the Imams', in E. Chaumont et al. (eds), *Autour du Regard: Mélanges Gimaret*. Louvain and Paris, 2003, pp. 125–157.

—— 'Radj'a', *EI2*.

—— 'Evil', *EIr*, vol. 9, pp. 182–185.

Kraus, P. *Jābir b. Ḥayyān. Contribution à l'histoire des idées scientifiques dans l'islam*. Cairo, 1942; rpr. Paris, 1986.

Lalani, A. R. *Early Shī'a Thought: The Teachings of Imam Muḥammad al-Bāqir*. London, 2000.

Lammens, H. *Etudes sur le règne du Calife Omaiyade Mu'āwia 1er*. Paris. 1908.

—— *Fātima et les filles de Mahomet*. Rome, 1912.

—— *Le berceau de l'Islam, l'Arabie occidentale à la veille de l'Hégire*. Rome, 1914.

—— 'Le culte des Bétyles et les processions religieuses chez les Arabes préislamites', *BIFAO*, 17 (1919–1920).

Landolt, H. 'Walāyah', *The Encyclopedia of Religion*, vol. 15, pp. 316–323.

Laoust, H. *Les schismes dans l'islam*. Paris, 1977.

—— 'Le rôle de ʿAlī dans la *Sīra* chiite', *REI*, 30/1 (1962), pp. 7–26.

Lassner, J. *The Shaping of ʿAbbāsid Rule*. Princeton, 1982.

Lawson, T. 'Interpretation as Revelation: The Qur'ān Commentary of Sayyid ʿAlī Muḥammad Shīrāzī, the Bāb (1819–1850)', in A. Rippin (ed.), *Approaches to the History of the Interpretation of the Qur'ān*. Oxford, 1988, pp. 223–253.

—— 'Notes for the Study of a "Shīʿī Qur'ān"', *Journal of Semitic Studies*, 36 (1991), pp. 279–295.

—— 'The Dawning Places of the Lights of Certainty in the Divine Secrets Connected with the Commander of the Faithful by Rajab Bursī', in L. Lewisohn (ed.), *The Legacy of Mediaeval Persian Sufism*. London and New York, 1992.

—— 'The Hidden Words of Fayḍ Kāshānī', in M. Szuppe (ed.), *Iran: Questions et connaissances*, vol. 2: *Périodes médiévale et moderne*. Paris, 2002, pp. 427–447.

—— 'The Qur'ān Commentary of the Bāb'. PhD thesis, McGill University, 1987.

Lazard, G. *La formation de la langue persane*. Paris, 1995.

—— '*Pahlavi, pârsi* et *dari*: les langues de l'Iran d'après Ibn al-Muqaffaʿ', in C. E. Bosworth (ed.), *Iran and Islam: In Memory of the Late Vladimir Minorsky*. Edinburgh, 1971, pp. 361–391; rpr. in *La formation*, part 3.

—— '*Pârsi* et *dari*: nouvelles remarques', in C. Altman et al. (eds), *Aspects of Iranian Culture: In Honour of Richard Nelson Frye*, N.S. *Bulletin of the Asia Institute*, n.s. 4 (1990), pp. 141–148; rpr. in *La formation*, part 9.

Lecker, M. 'Ḥudhayfa b. al-Yamān and ʿAmmār b. Yāsir. Jewish Converts to Islam', *Quaderni di Studi Arabi*, 11 (1993), pp. 149–162.

Lecomte, G. 'Aspects de la littérature du *ḥadīth* chez les imāmites', in *Le shīʿisme imāmite*, Colloque de Strasbourg, 6–9 Mai 1968. Paris, 1970, pp. 91–101.

Le Strange, G. *The Lands of the Eastern Califate*. 2nd edn, Cambridge, 1930; rpr. London, 1966.

Levy, R. 'Persia and the Arabs', in A. J. Arberry (ed.), *The Legacy of Persia*. Oxford, 1953, pp. 56–73.

Lewis, B. 'Abū al-Khaṭṭāb', *EI2*.

Lewisohn, L. 'An Introduction to the History of Modern Persian Sufism. Part I: Ni'matullāhiyya', *BSOAS*, 61/3 (1998), pp. 437–464.

—— 'An Introduction to the History of Modern Persian Sufism, Part II: A Socio-cultural Profile of Sufism, from the Dhahabī Revival to the Present Day', *BSOAS*, 62/1 (1999), pp. 36–59.

Loebenstein, J. 'Miracles in Šī'ī Thought. A Case Study of the Miracles Attributed to Imām Ğa'far al-Ṣādiq', *Arabica*, 50/2 (2003), pp. 199–244.

Lory, P. *Jābir b. Ḥayyān, Dix Traités d'alchimie. Les dix premiers Traités du Livre des Soixante-Dix*. Paris, 1983.

—— *Alchimie et mystique en terre d'islam*. Paris and Lagrasse, 1989.

—— *Le rêve et ses interprétations en Islam*. Paris, 2003.

—— 'Alchimie et philosophie chiite. L'œuvre alchimique de Muẓaffar 'Alī Shāh Kirmānī', in Ž. Vesel, M. Beygbaghban and Th. de Crussol des Epesse (eds), *La science dans le monde iranien à l'époque islamique*. Tehran and Paris, 1999, pp. 339–352.

—— 'Les paradoxes mystiques (shatahât) dans la tradition soufie des premiers siècles', *Annuaire de l'EPHE, Sciences Religieuses*, 102 (1994–1995), 103 (1995–1996).

Löschner, H. *Die dogmatischen Grundlagen des schi'itischen Rechts*. Erlangen and Cologne, 1971.

MacDermott, M. *The Theology of al-Shaikh al-Mufīd (d. 413/1022)*. Beirut, 1978.

MacDonald, D. B. 'Malāḥim', *EI2*.

Mac Eoin, D. M. *The Sources for Early Bābī Doctrine and History*. Leiden, 1992.

—— 'Early Shaykhī Reactions to the Bāb and His Claims', in M. Momen (ed.), *Studies in Bābī and Bahā'ī History*, vol. 1. Los Angeles, 1982, pp. 1–47.

—— 'Orthodoxy and Heterodoxy in Nineteenth-Century Shi'ism: The Cases of Shaykhism and Bābism', *JAOS*, 110/2 (1990), pp. 323–329.
—— 'From Shaykhism to Bābism. A Study in Charismatic Renewal in Shīʿī Islam', PhD thesis, Cambridge University, 1978.
—— 'Shaykhiyya', *EI2*, vol. 9, pp. 416–18.
—— 'Bālāsarī', *EIr*, vol. 3, pp. 583–585.
Madelung, W. *The Succession to Muḥammad*. Cambridge, 1997.
—— *Religious and Ethnic Movements in Medieval Islam*. London, 1992.
—— *Religious Schools and Sects in Medieval Islam*. London, 1985.
—— 'Bemerkungen zur imamitischen Firaq-Literatur', *Der Islam*, 43 (1967), pp. 37–52; rpr. in *Religious Schools*, article XV.
—— 'The Assumption of the Title Shāhanshāh by the Buyids and the Reign of the Daylam (*Dawlat al-Daylam*)', *JNES*, 28 (1969), pp. 84–108 and 168–183; rpr. in *Religious and Ethnic Movements*, article VIII.
—— 'Ibn Abī Jumhūr al-Aḥsā'ī's Synthesis of *Kalām*, Philosophy and Sufism', in *La signification du Bas Moyen Âge dans l'histoire et la culture du monde musulman*, (Actes du 8e Congrès de l'Union Européenne des Arabisants et Islamisants). Aix-en-Provence, 1978, pp. 147–156; rpr. in *Religious Schools*, article XIII.
—— 'A Treatise of the Sharīf al-Murtaḍā on the Legality of Working for the Government (*Mas'ala fi'l-ʿamal maʿa'l-sulṭān*)', *BSOAS*, 43 (1980); rpr. in *Religious Schools*, article IX.
—— 'Frühe muʿtazilische Häresiographie: das *Kitāb al-uṣūl* des Ǧaʿfar b. Ḥarb?', *Der Islam*, 57 (1980); rpr. in *Religious Schools*, article VI.
—— 'Shiʿite Discussions on the Legality of the *Kharāj*', in R. Peters (ed.), *Proceedings of the Ninth Congress of the Union Européenne des Arabisants et Islamisants*. Leiden, 1981; rpr. in *Religious Schools*, article XI.
—— 'New Documents Concerning al-Ma'mūn, al-Faḍl b. Sahl and ʿAlī al-Riḍā', in W. al-Qāḍī (ed.), *Studia Arabica et Islamica: Festschrift for Iḥsān ʿAbbās*. Beirut, 1981, pp. 333–346.

—— 'Authority in Twelver Shiism in the Absence of the Imam', in *La notion d'autorité au Moyen Age, Islam, Byzance, Occident*, Colloques internationaux de la Napoule, 1978 (Paris, 1982), pp. 163–173; rpr. in *Religious Schools*, article X.
—— 'Mazdakism and the Khurramiyya', in W. Madelung, *Religious Trends in Early Islamic Iran*. Albany, NY, 1988.
—— 'The Hāshimiyyāt of al-Kumayt and Hāshimi Shi'ism', *SI*, 70 (1990).
—— ''Abd Allāh b. 'Abbās and Shi'ite Law', in Vermeulen and van Reeth (eds), *Law, Christianity and Modernism in Islamic Society*. Louvain, 1998.
—— 'al-Khaṭṭābiyya', *EI2*.
—— 'Khurramiyya ou Khurramdīniyya', *EI2*.
—— 'Ḳarmaṭī', *EI2*.
—— 'Baḥrānī, Hāshem', *EIr*, vol. 3, pp. 528–529.
Mahdavī Rād M. 'A. 'Ābedī A. and Rafī'ī', A. 'Ḥadīth', in *Tashayyo'. Seyrī dar farhang va tārīkh-e tashayyo'*. Tehran, 1373 Sh./1994.
Marquart, J. *Īrānshahr nach der Geographie des Ps. Moses Xorenac'i*. Berlin, 1901.
Mashkūr, M. J. *Sāsāniyā*; rpr. Tehran, n.d. [ca. 1339 Sh./1960].
—— *Īrān dar 'ahd-e bāstān. Dar tārīkh-e aqvām va pādshāhān-e pīsh az eslām*. 2nd edn, Tehran, 1347 Sh./1968.
Massignon, L. *Essai sur les origines du lexique technique de la mystique musulmane*. Paris, 1922.
—— *La Passion de Hallâj*; rpr. in 4 vols., Paris, 1975.
—— 'Der Gnostische Kult der Fatima im Shiitischen Islam', in *Opera Minora*, vol. 1, ed. Y. Moubarac. Paris, 1969, pp. 514–522.
—— 'Salmân Pâk et les prémices spirituelles de l'Islam iranien', *Société d'Etudes Iraniennes*, 7, (1934); *Opera Minora*, vol. 1, pp. 443–483.
—— 'Esquisse d'une bibliographie nuṣayrie', in *Mélanges syriens offerts à Monsieur René Dussaud*. Paris, 1939, pp. 913–922; *Opera Minora*, vol. 1, pp. 640–649.

—— 'L'Homme Parfait en Islam et son originalité eschatologique', *Eranos Jahrbuch*, XV (1948), pp. 287–314; *Opera Minora*, vol. 1, pp. 107–125.
—— 'La Mubâhala de Médine et l'hyperdulie de Fatima', *Opera Minora*, vol. 1, pp. 550–572.
—— 'La notion du vœu et la dévotion musulmane à Fatima', *Opera Minora*, vol. 1, pp. 573–591.
—— 'Le Jour du Covenant', *Oriens*, 15 (1962).
Matar, Z. *The Faraj al-mahmūm of Ibn Ṭāwūs: a Thirteenth Century Work on Astrology and Astrologers*. New York, 1986.
—— 'Some Additions to the Bibliography of Mediaeval Islamic Astronomy from the *Faraj al-Mahmūm* of Ibn Ṭāwūs', *Archiv Orientalni*, 57 (1989), pp. 319–322.
—— 'The Chapter on Death-Prediction (*Qaṭʿ/Quṭūʿ*) from the *Kitāb Faraj al-Mahmūm* by Ibn Ṭāwūs', in A. Regourd and P. Lory (eds), *Sciences occultes et Islam*, *BEO*, 44 (1993), pp. 119–125.
Matīnī, J. 'ʿIlm va ʿulamāʾ dar zabān-e Qorʾān va aḥādīth', *Iran-Nameh*, 2/3 (1363 Sh./1984), pp. 147–162.
Māyel-Heravī, N. (ed.), *Meʿrāj-Nāmah-ye Abū ʿAlī Sīna be enḍemām-e taḥrīr-e ān az Shams al-Dīn Ebrāhīm Abarqūhī*. Mashhad, 1365 Sh./1986.
Mélikoff, I. *Les traces du soufisme turc. Recherches sur l'islam populaire en Anatolie*. Paris, 1992.
Meskūb, Sh. *Sūg-e Siyāvash*. Tehran, 1971.
Meyer, E. 'Anlass und Anwendungsbereich der *taqiyya*', *Der Islam*, 57 (1980), pp. 246–280.
—— 'Tendenz der Schiaforschung: Corbins Auffassung von der Schia', *ZDMG*, Supp. III, 1 (1977), pp. 42–63.
Mez, A. *Die Renaissance des Islams*. Heidelberg, 1922; rpr. Hildesheim, 1968.
Michot, J. R. *La destinée de l'homme selon Avicenne. Le retour à Dieu (maʿâd) et l'imagination*. Louvain, 1986.
Minorsky, V. [Bosworth, C. E.], 'Rayy', *EI2*.

Miquel, A. see Cuisenier.

Mīr Feṭrūs. ʿA. ʻJonbesh-e sorkh jāmegānʼ, *Iran Nameh*, 9/1 (1991), pp. 57–89.

Mishkāt Kermānī, A. *Tārīkh e tashayyuʿ dar Īrān*. Tehran, 1358 Sh./1980.

Modarressi, H. *Crisis and Consolidation in the Formative Period of Shīʿite Islam: Abū Jaʿfar ibn Qiba al-Rāzī and his Contribution to Imāmite Shīʿite Thought*. Princeton, 1993.

—— ʻEarly Debates on the Integrity of the Qur'ānʼ, *SI*, 77 (1993), pp. 5–39.

—— ʻThe Just Ruler or the Guardian Jurist, An Attempt to Link Two Different Shi'ite Conceptsʼ, *JAOS*, 111 (1991), pp. 549–562.

Modarresī Chahārdehī, N. *Khāksār va Ahl-e ḥaqq*. Tehran, 1368/1989.

Modīr Shānetchī, N. ʻ*Kotob-e arbaʿe-ya ḥadīth-e shīʿe*ʼ, *Nāmeh-ye Āstān-e Qods*, 1–2, new series, 18 (n.d. [ca. 1975]), pp. 22–71.

Moeller, E. *Beiträge zur Mahdilehre des Islams*. Heidelberg, 1901.

Mohājerānī, ʿA. *Barrasī-ye seyr-e zendegī va ḥekmat va ḥokumat-e Salmān-e Fārsī*. Tehran, 1378 Sh./1999.

Moḥammadī Malāyerī, M. *Tārīkh va farhang-e Īrān dar dowrān-e enteqāl az ʿaṣr-e sāsānī be ʿaṣr-e eslāmī*, vol. 1. Tehran, 1372 Sh./1993; vol. 2, *Del-e Īrān shahr*. Tehran, 1375 Sh./1996.

—— *Farhang-e Īrān-e pīsh az eslām va āthār-e ān dar tamaddon-e eslāmī va adabiyyāt-e ʿarabī*. Tehran, 1374 Sh./1995.

Moʿīn, M. *Mazdayasnā va ta'thīr-e ān dar adabiyyāt-e fārsī*. Tehran, 1326 Sh./1948.

—— ʻHavarqalyāʼ, *Nashriyye-ye Dāneshkade-ye Adabiyyāt-e Dānesgāh-e Tehrān* (1333/1955), pp. 78–105.

Molé, M. *Culte, mythe et cosmologie dans l'Iran ancien*. Paris, 1963.

—— *Les mystiques musulmans*. Paris, 1965.

—— *Professions de foi de deux kubrâwîs: ʿAlî-i Hamadânî et Muḥammad Nûrbakhsh*, extract from *Bulletin d'Etudes Orientales*, 17 (1961–1962).

—— ʻLes Kubrâwiyya entre sunnisme et shiʿisme aux 8e et 9e s. de l'hégireʼ, *REI* (1961).

—— 'Entre le Mazdéisme et l'Islam, La bonne et la mauvaise religion', in *Mélanges Henri Massé*. Tehran, 1963.

Momen, M. *An Introduction to Shiʿi Islam. The History and Doctrine of Twelver Shiʿism*. Oxford, 1985.

—— *The Works of Shaykh Ahmad al-Ahsaʾi: A Bibliography*. Newcastle-upon-Tyne, 1991.

Monnot, G. *Penseurs musulmans et religions iraniennes. ʿAbd al-Jabbār et ses devanciers*. Paris, 1974.

—— 'La transmigration et l'immortalité', in Monnot (ed.), *Islam et religions*. Paris, 1986.

—— 'Prières privées en islam traditionnel: autour d'un texte de Rāzī', *RHR*, 206/1 (1989), pp. 41–54.

—— 'Opposition et hiérarchie dans la pensée d'al-Shahrastānī', in M. A. Amir-Moezzi, C. Jambet and P. Lory (eds), *Henry Corbin: philosophies et sagesses des religions du Livre*, Bibliothèque de l'Ecole des Hautes Etudes, no. 126. Turnhout, 2005, p. 96, pp. 93–103.

—— 'Ṣalāt', *EI2*.

Moosa, M. *Extremist Shiites. The Ghulat Sects*. New York, 1987.

Moqaddam, M. *Jostār dar bāre-ye Mehr va Nāhīd*, vol. 1. Tehran, 1978.

Morony, M. G. *Iraq after the Muslim Conquest*. Princeton, 1984.

—— 'The Effects of the Muslim Conquest on the Persian Population of Iraq', *Iran*, 14 (1976), pp. 41–55.

—— 'Conquerors and Conquered: Iran', in G. H. A. Juynboll (ed.), *Studies on the First Century of Islamic Society*. Carbondale and Edwardsville, IL, 1982, pp. 73–87.

—— 'Kisrā', *EI2*.

Moscati, S. 'Per una storia dell'antica shiʿa', *RSO*, 30 (1955), pp. 56–70.

Moṣṭafavī, S. M. T. 'Boqʿe-ye Bībī Shahrbānū dar Rayy', *Gozāresh hā-ye bāstān shenāsī*, 3 (1334 Sh./1956), pp. 3–40.

Mottahedeh, R. 'The Shuʿūbīyah Controversy and the Social History of Early Islamic Iran', *IJMES*, 7 (1976), pp. 161–182.

Nagel, T. *Untersuchungen zur Entstehung des abbasidischen Kalifats*. Bonn, 1972.

—— *Studien zum Minderheitenproblem im Islam*, vol. 1. Bonn, 1973.

—— *Rechtleitung und Kalifat, Versuch über eine Grundfrage der islamischen Geschichte*. Bonn, 1975.

—— 'Ein früher Bericht über den Aufstand des Muḥammad b. ʿAbdallāh im Jahre 145 h.', *Der Islam*, 46 (1970), pp. 227–262.

Nafīsī, S. *Bābak-e Khurramdīn, delāvar-e Ādharbāyjān*; rpr. Tehran, 1342 Sh./1963.

—— *Tārīkh-e ejtemāʿī-ye īrān az enqerāḍ-e Sāsāniyān tā enqerāḍ-e Omaviyān*. Tehran, 1342 Sh./1964.

—— *Tārīkh-e naẓm va nathr dar zabān-e fārsī tā pāyān-e qarn-e dahom-e hejrī*. Tehran, 1344 Sh./1966.

al-Najafī, Ḥ. *al-Durra al-bahiyya fī faḍl Karbalāʾ wa turbatihā al-zakiyya*. Najaf, 1970.

Nanji, A. 'An Ismaili Theory of *Walāya* in the *Daʿāʾim al-Islām* of al-Qāḍī al-Nuʿmān', in D. P. Little (ed.), *Essays on Islamic Civilization Presented to Niyazi Berkes*. Leiden, 1976, pp. 260–273.

Nasr, S. H. 'Le shīʿisme et le soufisme. Leurs relations principielles et historiques', in T. Fahd (ed.), *Le shīʿisme imāmite,* Actes du Colloque de Strasbourg (6-9 Mai 1968). Paris, 1970, pp. 215–233.

Nātel Khānlarī, P. *Zabān shenāsī-ye fārsī*. 2nd edn, Tehran, 1344 Sh./1966.

Nawas, J. A. 'A Reexamination of Three Current Explanations for al-Maʾmūn's Introduction of the *miḥna*', *IJMES*, 26 (1994), pp. 615–629.

Newman, A. J. *The Formative Period of Twelver Shīʿism: Hadith as Discourse Between Qum and Baghdad*. Richmond, VA, 2000.

—— 'The Development and Political Significance of the Rationalist (usuli) and Traditionalist (akhbari) School in Imami Shiʿi History from the Third/Ninth to the Tenth/Sixteenth Century', PhD thesis, UCLA, Los Angeles, 1986.

Nicolas A. L. M. *Essai sur le Chéīkhisme*. Paris, 1910–1914.
Nöldeke, T. *Geschichte der Perser und Araber zu Zeit der Sasaniden aus der arabischen Chronik des Tabari*. Leiden, 1879; rpr. 1973.
—— *Das iranische Nationalepos*. 2nd edn, Berlin and Leipzig, 1920.
Nwiya, P. *Exégèse coranique et langage mystique*. Beirut, 1970.
Omar, F. *The ʿAbbāsid Califate 750/132 — 786/179*. Baghdad, 1969.
al-Oraibi, A. 'Shīʿī Renaissance. A Case Study of the Theosophical School of Bahrain in the 7th/13th Century', PhD thesis, McGill University, Montreal, 1992.
Paret, R. *Der Koran. Kommentar und Konkordanz*. Stuttgart, etc., rpr. 1978.
—— 'Der Plan einer neuen, leicht kommentierten Koranübersetzung', in Paret (ed.), *Orientalische Studien Enno Littmann zu seinem 60. Geburtstag*. Leiden, 1935.
—— 'Die Bedeutung des Wortes *baqīya* im Koran', in *Alttestamentliche Studien Friedrich Nötscher zum 60. Geburtstag*. Bonn, 1950.
Parpola, S. 'The Assyrian Tree of Life: Tracing the Origins of Jewish Monotheism and Greek Philosophy', *JNES*, 52/3 (1993), pp. 161–208.
Patton, W. M. *Aḥmad ibn Ḥanbal and the Miḥna*. Leiden, 1897.
Pellat, Ch. *Le milieu baṣrien et la formation de Ǧāḥiẓ*. Paris, 1953.
—— *The Life and works of Jahiz*. Translations of selected texts. London, 1969.
—— 'Ǧāḥiẓ à Bagdad et à Sāmarrā', *RSO*, 27 (1952), pp. 63–78; rpr. in his *Etudes sur l'histoire socio-culturelle de l'Islam (VIIe-XVe s.)*. London, Variorum, 1976, article I.
—— 'Une charge contre les secrétaires d'Etat attribué à Jāḥiẓ', *Hespéris*, 43 (1956), pp. 29–50.
—— 'Masʿûdî et l'imâmisme', in T. Fahd (ed.), *Le shîʿisme imâmite*, Actes du Colloque de Strasbourg (6–9 Mai 1968). Paris, 1970, pp. 69–90.
—— 'Ḥilm', *EI2*.
—— 'al-Jāḥiẓ', *EI2*.

Piemontese, A. M. 'Le voyage de Mahomet au Paradis et en Enfer: une version persane du *mi'rāj*', in C. Kappler (ed.), *Apocalypses et voyages dans l'au-delà*. Paris, 1987.

Pinault, D. 'Zaynab bint 'Alī and the Place of the Women of the Households of the First Imāms in Shī'ite Devotional Literature', in Gavin R. G. Hambly (ed.), *Women in the Medieval World*. New York, 1998, pp. 69–98.

Proksch, O. *Über die Blutrache bei den vorislamischen Arabern und Mohammeds Stellung zu ihr*. Leipzig, 1899.

Puech, H. C. *Le manichéisme, son fondateur, sa doctrine*. Paris, 1949.

—— 'le Manichéisme', in *l'Histoire des Religions, Encyclopédie de la Pléiade*, vol. 2, pp. 523–645.

Pūrjavādī (Pourjavady), N. and Wilson, P. L., *Kings of Love. The Poetry and History of the Ni'matullahī Sufi Order*. Tehran, 1978.

—— 'Ḥekmat-e dīnī va taqaddos-e zabān-e fārsī', in Pourjavady, *Būy-e jān*. Tehran, 1372 Sh./1993, pp. 1–37.

—— 'Ḥallāj va Bāyazīd Basṭāmī az naẓar-e Mollā Ṣadrā', *Nashr-i Dānish*, 16/3 (1378 Sh./1999), pp. 14–24.

—— 'Opposition to Sufism in Twelver Shiism', in F. de Jong and B. Radtke (eds), *Islamic Mysticism Contested. Thirteen Centuries of Controversies and Polemics*. Leiden, 1999, pp. 614–623.

—— '*Mā be majles-e mehtarān sokhan nagūyīm*. Fārsī gūyī ye 'Abdallāh-i Mubārak va adab-e īrānī', *Nashr-i Dânesh*, 16/4 (1378 Sh./2000), pp. 21–25.

Pūrnāmdāriyān, T. *Ramz va dāstān-hā-ye ramzī dar adab-e fārsī*. Tehran, 1346/1985.

Qāderī, T. 'Matn hā-ye akhlāqī-andarzī dar zabān hā-ye īrānī-ye miyāne — ye gharbī va Sharqī', in A. K. Bālā Zādeh (ed.), *Mehr o dād o bahār. Memorial Volume of Dr. Mehrdād Bahār*. Tehran, 1377 Sh./1998, pp. 221–232.

al-Qāḍī, W. 'The Development of the Term *Ghulāt* in Muslim Literature with Special Reference to the Kaysāniyya', in A. Dietrich (ed.), *Akten des VII. Kongresses für Arabistik und*

Islamwissenschaft. Göttingen, 1976, pp. 295–319; rpr. in E. Kohlberg (ed.), *Shīʿism*. Aldershot, 2003, article 8.

Radtke, B. and O'Kane, J. *The Concept of Sainthood in Early Islamic Mysticism*. London, 1996.

—— 'The Concept of *Wilāya* in Early Sufism', in L. Lewisohn (ed.), *Classical Persian Sufism: from its Origins to Rumi*. London and New York, 1993, pp. 483–496.

Rafati, V. 'The Development of Shaykhī Thought in Shīʿī Islam', PhD thesis, University of California, 1979.

Raphaël, F. et al. (eds), *L'apocalyptique*. Paris, 1987 (Actes du Colloque du Centre de Recherches d'Histoire des Religions de l'Université de Strasbourg, 1974).

Rekaya, M. 'al-Maʾmūn', *EI2*.

Richard, Y. *L'Islam Chi'ite. Croyances et idéologies*. Paris, 1991.

Riyāḥi, M. A. *Kasāʾī-ye Marvazī*. Tehran, 1367 Sh./1988.

Robertson Smith, W. *Kinship and Marriage in Early Arabia*. 2nd edn, Cambridge, 1903.

—— *Lectures on the Religion of the Semites*. 2nd edn, Edinburgh, 1914.

Rosenthal, F. *A History of Muslim Historiography*. Leiden, 1952.

—— *Knowledge Triumphant: The Concept of Knowledge in Medieval Islam*. Leiden, 1971.

Rubin, U. *The Eye of the Beholder: The Life of Muḥammad as Viewed by the Early Muslims*. Princeton, 1995.

—— 'Pre-existence and Light. Aspects of the Concept of Nūr Muḥammad', *IOS*, 5 (1975), pp. 62–119.

—— 'Prophets and Progenitors in Early Shīʿa Tradition', *JSAI*, 1 (1979), pp. 41–65.

—— 'The *īlāf* of Quraysh. A Study of Sūra CVI', *Arabica*, 31, 2 (1984), pp. 165–188.

—— '*Barāʾa*: A Study of Some Quranic Passages', *JSAI*, 5 (1984), pp. 71–91.

—— 'The Kaʿba, Aspects of Its Ritual Functions and Position in Pre-Islamic and Early Islamic Times', *JSAI*, 8 (1986), pp. 81–95.

—— 'Apes, Pigs and the Islamic Identity', *IOS*, 17 (1997), pp. 89–105.

Ruska, J. *Arabische Alchemisten. II. Ja'far al-Sādiq, der sechste Imām.* Heidelberg, 1924.

Sabri, T. 'L'hagiographie de Fâṭima d'après le Biḥâr al-Anwâr de Muḥammad Bâqir Majlisî (m. 1111/1699)', PhD thesis, Paris, III, June 1969.

Sachedina, A. A. *Islamic Messianism: The Idea of the Mahdī in Twelver Shi'ism.* Albany, NY, 1981.

—— *The Just-Ruler* (al-sulṭān al-'ādil) *in Shi'ite Islam.* New York, 1988.

—— 'A Treatise on the Occultation of the Twelfth Imamite Imam', *SI*, 48 (1978).

—— 'Al-Khums: the Fifth in the Imāmī Shī'ī Legal System', *JNES*, 39 (1980).

—— 'Abū al-Khaṭṭāb', *EIr*, vol. 1, p. 329.

Ṣādeqī, 'A. A., *Takvīn-e zabān-e fārsī.* Tehran, 1357 Sh./1978.

Ṣadīqī, Gh. Ḥ. *Jonbesh hā-ye dīnī-ye īrānī dar qarn hā-ye dovvom va sevvom-e hejrī.* Tehran, 1372 Sh./1993 (the finished version of his *Les mouvements religieux iraniens aux IIe et IIIe siècle de l'hégire.* Paris, 1938).

al-Ṣadr, M.*Ta'rīkh al-ghayba al-ṣughra.* Beirut, 1972.

St. Clair Tisdall, W. 'Shi'ah Additions to the Koran', *The Moslem World*, 3/3 (1913), pp. 227–241.

Sajjādī, Ḍ. '*Ghadīriyya* hā-ye fārsī', in S. J. Shahīdī and M. R. Ḥakīmī (eds), *Yād nāme-ye 'Allāma Amīnī*, vol. 1 Tehran, 1973, pp. 413–430.

al-Sāmarrā'ī, A. S. *al-Ghuluww wa'l-firaq al-ghāliya fī al-ḥaḍāra al-islāmiyya.* Baghdad, 1392/1972.

Samawi Hamid, I. 'The Metaphysics and Cosmology of Process According to Shaykh Aḥmad al-Aḥsā'ī', PhD thesis, State University of New York (Buffalo), 1998.

Sanders, P. 'Koran oder Imām? Die Auffassung von Koran im Rahmen der imāmitischen Glaubenslehren', *Arabica*, special issue, 'Les usages du Coran, Présupposés et méthodes', 47/3-4 (2000), pp. 420–440.

Santillana, D. *Istituzioni di diritto musulmano malichita con riguardo anche al sistema sciafiita.* Rome, 1938.

Sarkārātī, B. 'Morvārīd pīsh-e khūk afshāndan', in his *Sāye hā-ye shekār shodeh*. Tehran, 1378 Sh./1999, pp. 51–70.

Scarcia, G. 'Kerman 1905: la "guerra tra Sheikhī e Bālāsarī". Moderni indizi di una problematica antica', *AIUON*, new series, 13 (1963), pp. 195–238.

Scarcia Amoretti, B. and Bottini, L. (ed.) *Il Ruolo dei* Sādāt/Ashrāf *nella Storia e Civilità Islamiche, Oriente Moderno*, 18, special number, 77.2 (1999).

—— 'Ibn Ṭabāṭabā', *EI2*.

Schacht, J. *The Origins of Muhammadan Jurisprudence*. Oxford, 1950.

—— 'A Revaluation of Islamic Traditions', *JRAS*, 42 (1949).

Schaeder, H. H. 'Die islamische Lehre vom Volkommenen Menschen', *ZDMG*, 79 (1925), pp. 192–268.

Scheffczyk, L. ed. *Der Mensch als Bild Gottes*. Darmstadt, 1969.

Schmidtke, S. *Theologie, Philosophie und Mystik im zwölfershiʿitischen Islam des 9./14. Jahrhunderts. Die Gedankenwelten des Ibn Abī Jumhūr al-Aḥsāʾī (um 838/1434-35 nach 906/1501)*. Leiden, 2000.

—— 'Modern Modifications in the Shiʿi Doctrine of the Expectation of the Mahdi (*Intiẓār al-Mahdī*): the Case of Khumaini', *Orient*, 28/3 (1987).

—— 'The Influence of Shams al-Dīn Shahrazūrī (7th/13th century) on Ibn Abī Jumhūr al-Aḥsāʿī (d. after 904/1499). A Preliminary Note', in L. Edzard and C. Szyska (eds), *Encounters of Words and Texts: Intercultural Studies in Honor of Stefan Wild on the Occasion of his 60th Birthday. Presented by his Pupils in Bonn*. Hildesheim, 1997, pp. 223–232.

—— 'The Doctrine of the Transmigration of the Soul According to Shihāb al-Dīn al-Suhrawardī (killed 587/1191) and his Followers', *Studia Iranica*, 28/2 (1999), pp. 237–254.

—— 'II.Firk. Arab III. A Copy of al-Sharīf al-Murtaḍā's *Kitāb al-Dhakhīra* Completed in 472/1079-80 in the Firkovitch-Collection St Petersburg'; Persian tr. as 'Nuskha-yi kuhan az *Kitāb al-Dhakhīra*-yi Sharīf Murtaḍā (tārīkh i kitābat 472)', *Maʿārif*, 20/2 (2003), pp. 68–84.

—— see also Amir-Moezzi.

Schrieke, B. 'Die Himmelsreise Muhammeds', *Der Islam*, 6 (1916).

Schwartz, J. 'Le voyage au ciel dans la littérature apocalyptique', in F. Raphaël et al. (ed.), *L'apocalyptique*. Paris, 1987 (Actes du Colloque du Centre de Recherches d'Histoire des Religions de l'Université de Strasbourg, 1974), pp. 91–126.

Sellheim, R. 'Prophet, Chalif und Gescichte', *Oriens*, 18–19 (1965–1966).

—— 'Das Todesdatum des Ibn al-Nadīm', *IOS*, 2 (1972), pp. 428–432.

—— 'al-Mubarrad', *EI2*.

Serjeant, R. B. *Studies in Arabian History and Civilization*. London, 1981.

—— 'The Saiyids of Ḥaḍramawt', *An Inaugural Lecture at the School of Oriental and African Studies, 1956*. London, 1957; rpr. in *Studies*, article VIII.

—— '*Ḥaram* and *ḥawṭah*, the Sacred Enclave in Arabia', in A. R. Badawi (ed.), *Mélanges Taha Husain*. Cairo 1962; rpr. in *Studies*, article 3.

—— 'The 'Constitution' of Medina', *The Islamic Quarterly*, 8 (1964); rpr. in *Studies*, article 5.

—— 'The *Sunnah Jāmiʿah*, Pacts with the Yathrib Jews and the *taḥrīm* of Yathrib, Analysis and Translation of the Documents Comprised in the So-called "Constitution" of Medina', *BSOAS*, 41 (1978); rpr. in *Studies*, article 6.

Sezgin, F. *Geschichte des arabischen Schrifttums*. Leiden, 1967–1986.

Shahīdī, S. J. 'Baḥthī dar bāre-ye shahrbānū', in his *Cherāgh-e rowshan dar donyā-ye tārīk*. Tehran, 1333 Sh./1954–1955, pp. 171–189.

Shahmardān, R. *Parastesh gāh hā-ye zartoshtiyān*. Bombay, 1345 Sh./1967.

Shaked, Sh. *From Zoroastrian Iran to Islam*. Aldershot, 1995.

—— 'From Iran to Islam: on Some Symbols of Royalty', *JSAI*, 7 (1986), pp. 75–91; rpr. in *From Zoroastrian Iran*, article 7.

—— 'A Facetious Recipe and the Two Wisdoms: Iranian Themes in Muslim Garb', *JSAI*, 9 (1987), pp. 24–35; rpr. in *From Zoroastrian Iran*, article 9.

—— 'Andarz. In Pre-Islamic Persia', *EIr*, vol. 2, pp. 11–16.

Shamīsā, S. *Farhang-e talmīḥāt*. Tehran, 1366 Sh./1987.

Sharīf, M. B. *al-Ṣirāʿ bayn al-mawālī wa'l-ʿarab*. Cairo, 1954.

Sharīf Rāzī, M. *Ganjīna-ye dāneshmandān*. Tehran, 1354 Sh./1976.

Sharon, M. *Black Banners from the East: the Establishment of the 'Abbasid State – Incubation of a Revolt*. Leiden and Jerusalem, 1983.

—— 'The 'Abbasid Daʿwa Reexamined on the Basis of a New Source', *Arabic and Islamic Studies*, Bar-Ilan University (1973).

—— 'The Development of the Debate Around the Legitimacy of Authority in Early Islam', *JSAI*, 5 (1984), pp. 121–142.

—— '*Ahl al-Bayt* – People of the House', *JSAI*, 8 (1986).

—— 'The Umayyads as *ahl al-bayt*', *JSAI*, 14 (1991).

al-Shaybī, K. M. *al-Ṣila bayna al-taṣawwuf wa'l-tashayyuʿ*. Baghdad, 1966.

—— *al-Fikr al-shīʿī wa'l-nazaʿāt al-ṣūfiyya*. 2nd edn, Baghdad, 1395/1975.

——– 'al-Taqiyya uṣūluhā wa taṭawwuruhā', *Revue de la Faculté des Lettres de l'Université d'Alexandrie*, 16 (1962–1963), pp. 14–40.

Shayegan, D. *Henry Corbin. La topographie spirituelle de l'Islam iranien*. Paris, 1990.

—— 'Corbin, Henry', *EIr*, 6, pp. 268–272.

(*Le*) *shîʿisme imâmite*, Actes du Colloque de Strasbourg (6–9 Mai 1968), ed. T. Fahd. Paris, 1970.

Silvestre de Sacy, A. I. *Chrestomathie arabe*. Paris, 1806.

Skjaervø, P. O. '*Farnah*: mot mède en vieux-perse?', *BSL*, 78 (1983), pp. 241–259.

Slotkin, J. S. 'On a Possible Lack of Incest Regulations in Old Iran', *American Anthropologist*, 49 (1947), pp. 612–617.

Smith, M. and Haddad, Y. Y. *The Islamic Understanding of Death and Resurrection*. Albany, NY, 1981.

Soden, W. von. *Akkadisches Handwörterbuch* (AHW). Wiesbaden, 1965.
Sohā M. Ṣ. *Tārīkh-e enshe'ābāt-e mota'akhkhere-ye selsele-ye ne'matollāhiyye* in *Do resāle dar tārikh-e jadīd-e taṣavvof-e Īrān*. Tehran, 1370 Sh./1991.
Soucek, P. P. 'Farhād and Ṭāq-i Bustān: the Growth of a Legend', in P. Chelkowski (ed.), *Studies in Art and Literature of the Near East in Honor of Richard Ettinghausen*. Washington, 1974.
Sourdel, D. 'La politique religieuse du calife 'abbâsside al-Ma'mûn', *REI*, 30/1 (1962), pp. 26–48.
Southgate, M. S. 'Alexander in the Works of Persian and Arab Historians of the Islamic Area', in *Iskandarnamah: a Persian Medieval Alexander Romance*, English tr. M. S. Southgate. New York, 1978.
Spitaler, A. 'Was bedewtet *baqīja* im Koran?', in *Westöstlische Abhandlungen Rudolf Tschudi zum Siebzigsten Geburgtstag*. Wiesbaden, 1954.
Spooner, B. 'Iranian Kinship and Marriage', *Iran*, 4 (1966), pp. 51–59.
Spuler, B. *Iran in früh-islamischer Zeit*. Wiesbaden, 1952.
—— 'Iran: the Persistant Heritage', in G. E. von Grunebaum (ed.), *Unity and Variety in Muslim Civilization*. Chicago, 1955, pp. 167–182.
Strack, E. *Six Months in Persia*. London, 1882.
Straface, A. 'Il concetto di estremismo nell' eresiografia islamica', *AION*, 56 (1996), pp. 471–487.
—— '*Ḥulul* and *Tağassud*: Islamic Accounts of the Concept of Incarnation', in U. Vermeulen and J. M. F. Van Reeth (eds), *Law, Christianity and Modernism in Islamic Society*. Louvain, 1998, pp. 125–132.
Strothmann, R. *Das Staatsrecht der Zaiditen*. Strasbourg, 1912.
—— 'History of Islamic Heresiography', *Islamic Culture*, 17 (1938), pp. 95–110.
Stroumsa, S. *Freethinkers of Medieval Islam. Ibn al-Rāwandī, Abū Bakr al-Rāzī and Their Impact on Islamic Thought*. Leiden, 1999.

Tafazzoli (Tafaḍḍolī), A. *Tārīkh-e adabiyyāt-e Īrān-e pīsh az eslām*, ed. Ž Āmūzegār. Tehran, 1376 Sh./1997.

Takeshita, M. *Ibn Arabi's Theory of the Perfect Man and its Place in the History of Islamic Thought*. Tokyo, 1987.

Takim, L. A. 'From *Bidʿa* to *Sunna*: the *Wilāya* of ʿAlī in the Shīʿī *Adhān*', *JAOS*, 120 (2000), pp. 166–177.

Taqī-Zādeh, Ḥ. *Az Parvīz tā Changīz*. 2nd edn, Tehran, 1330 Sh./1952.

Ṭarīqeh-dār, A. *Jazīre-ye khaḍrā'*. Qumm, 1372 Sh./1994.

Taylor, J. B. 'Jaʿfar al-Ṣādiq, Spiritual Forebear of the Sufis', *Islamic Culture*, 40 (1966), pp. 97–113.

—— 'An Approach to the Emergence of Heterodoxy in Medieval Islam', *Religious Studies*, 2/2 (1967), pp. 65–82.

Tobin, T. H. *The Creation of Man: Philo and the History of Interpretation*. Washington DC, 1983.

Tor, D. G. 'An Historiographical Re-examination of the Appointment and Death of ʿAlī al-Riḍā', *Der Islam*, 78/1 (2001), pp. 103–128.

Tortel, C. 'Saints ou démons? Les Qalandar-s Jalālī et autres derviches errants en terre d'islam (Russie méridionale et Inde aux XIIIe-XVIIe s.)', PhD, EPHE (sc. religieuses), Paris, 1999.

Tritton, A. S. *Muslim Theology*. London, 1947.

Tucker, W. F. 'Rebels and Gnostics: al-Mughīra b. Saʿīd and the Mughīriyya', *Arabica*, 22 (1975), pp. 42–61.

—— 'Bayān b. Samʿān and the Bayāniyya: Shīʿite Extremists of Umayyad Iraq', *Muslim World*, 65 (1975), pp. 86–109.

—— 'Abū Manṣūr al-ʿIjlī and the Manṣūriyya: A Study in Medieval Terrorism', *Der Islam*, 54 (1977), pp. 39–57.

—— ''Abd Allāh b. Muʿāwiya and the Janāḥiyya: Rebels and Ideologues of the Late Umayyad period', *SI*, 51 (1980), pp. 39–57.

Tyan, E. *Institutions du droit public Musulman*. Paris, 1954–1956.

Vajda, G. 'Les zindīqs en pays d'Islam au début de la période abbasside', *RSO*, 17 (1937), pp. 173–229.

—— 'Deux "Histoires des Prophètes" selon la tradition des shi'ites duodécimains', *Revue des Etudes Juives*, 106 (1945–1946), pp. 124–133.

—— 'Le problème de la vision de Dieu (*ru'ya*) d'après quelques auteurs shī'ites duodécimains', in *Le shī'isme imâmite*. Paris, 1970.

—— 'De quelques emprunts d'origine juive dans le hadīth shi'ite', in S. Morag et al. (eds), *Studies in Judaism and Islam Presented to S.D. Goitein*. Jerusalem, 1981, pp. 242–244.

Vatikiotis, P. J. 'The Rise of Extremist Sects and the Dissolution of the Fatimid Empire in Egypt', *Islamic Culture*, 46 (1957), pp. 121–142.

Veccia Vaglieri, L. 'Sul *Nahj al-balāghah* e sul suo compilatore ash-Sharīf ar-Raḍī', *AIUON*, special no. (1958).

—— 'Ghadīr Khumm', *EI2*.

Ventura, A. 'La presanza divina nel Cuore', *Quaderni di Studi Arabi*, 3 (1985), pp. 123–134.

—— 'L'invocazione del cuore', in *Yād Nāma...Alessandro Bausani*. Rome, 1991, pp. 475–485.

Vermaseren, M. J. *Corpus Inscriptionum et Monumentorum Religionis Mithriacae*, I–II. The Hague, 1956–1960.

Vieillard Baron, J. L. 'Temps spirituel et hiéro-histoire selon Henry Corbin: une phénoménologie de la connaissance psycho-cosmique', *Cahiers du Groupe d'Etudes Spirituelles Comparées*, 8, 'Henry Corbin et le comparatisme spirituel' (2000), pp. 25–37.

Viré, F. 'Ḳird', *EI2*.

Vitray-Meyerovitch E., de. *La prière en Islam*. Paris, 1998.

Walbridge, J. 'A Persian Gulf in the Sea of Lights: the Chapter on Naw-Rūz in the *Biḥār al-Anwār*', *Iran*, 35 (1997), pp. 83–92.

Walker, P. 'Shī'ism: Wilāya', *EI2*.

Wasserstrom, S. M. 'The Moving Finger Writes: Mughīra b. Sa'īd's Islamic Gnosis and the Myths of its Rejection', in *History of Religions*, 25/1 (1985), pp. 62–90.

—— 'The Shīʿīs are the Jews of our Community: An Interreligious Comparison within Sunnī Thought', *IOS*, 14 (1994), pp. 297–324.

Watt, W. M. *Muhammad at Mecca*. Oxford, 1953.

—— *Muhammad, Prophet and Statesman*. Oxford, 1961.

—— *Islamic Political Thought*. Edinburgh, 1968.

—— *The Formative Period of Islamic Thought*. Edinburgh, 1973.

—— 'Created in His Image: A Study of Islamic Theology', *Transactions of Glasgow University Oriental Society*, 18 (1959–1960), pp. 36–49.

—— 'Shiʿism under the Umayyads', *JRAS* (1960), pp. 158–172.

—— 'Muʾākhāt', *EI2*.

Wellhausen, J. *Reste arabischen Heidentums*. Berlin and Leipzig, 1884.

—— 'Die Ehe bei den Arabern', *Nachrichten von der Königlichen Gesellschaft und der Georg-Augusts-Universität zu Göttingen*, 11 (1893).

Wensinck, A. J. *A Muslim Creed, Its Genesis and Historical Development*. Cambridge, 1932.

—— *Concordance et indices de la tradition musulmane*. Leiden, 1936.

—— 'Muhammad und die Propheten', *Acta Orientalia*, 2 (1924).

West, E. W. 'The Meaning of the *Khvêtûk-das* or *Khvêtûdâd*', in M. Müller (ed.), *The Sacred Books of the East*, vol. 18, Pahlavi Texts. Oxford, 1882.

Widengren, G. *Les religions de l'Iran*, Paris, 1968; French tr. of *Die Religionen Irans*. Stuttgart, 1965.

—— 'The Sacral Kingship of Iran', in *La regalità sacra*. Contribute al tema dell'VIII congresso internazionale di storia delle religioni (Rome, April 1955). Leiden, 1959, pp. 242–257.

Witton Davies, T. *Magic, Divination and Demonology* (London, 1933; rpr. Baghdad, n.d. [ca. 1960]).

Yarshater, E. 'Taʿzieh and Pre-Islamic Mourning Rituals in Iran', in P. Chelkowski (ed.), *Taʿzieh: Ritual and Drama in Iran*. New York, 1979, pp. 80–95.

—— 'Iranian National History', in *The Cambridge History of Iran*, vol. 3(1), *The Seleucid, Parthian and Sassanian Periods*, ed. E. Yarshater. Cambridge, 1983, pp. 359–477.

—— 'Mazdakism', in *The Cambridge History of Iran*, vol. 3(2), *The Seleucid, Parthian and Sassanian Periods*, ed. E. Yarshater. Cambridge, 1983, pp. 1,001–1,056.

—— 'The Persian Presence in the Islamic World', in R. G. Hovannisian and G. Sabagh (eds), *The Persian Presence in the Islamic World*. Cambridge, 1998, pp. 4–125.

Zaman, M. Q. *Religion and Politics under the Early 'Abbāsids: The Emergence of the Proto-Sunnī Elite*. Leiden, 1997.

Zarrīnkūb, 'A.Ḥ. *Arzesh-e mīrāth-e ṣūfiyye*. Tehran, 1343 Sh./1965.

Index